Irene C. Fountas & Gay Su Pinnell

The Writing Minilessons Book

Your Every Day Guide for Literacy Teaching

GRADE 3

HEINEMANN
Portsmouth, NH

Heinemann
145 Maplewood Avenue, Suite 300
Portsmouth, NH 03801
www.heinemann.com

Offices and agents throughout the world

©2023 by Irene C. Fountas and Gay Su Pinnell

All rights reserved. No part of this book may be reproduced in any form or by any electronic or mechanical means, including information storage and retrieval systems, without permission in writing from the publisher, except by a reviewer, who may quote brief passages in a review.

> *Heinemann's authors have devoted their entire careers to developing the unique content in their works, and their written expression is protected by copyright law. We respectfully ask that you do not adapt, reuse, or copy anything on third-party (whether for-profit or not-for-profit) lesson sharing websites.*
>
> **—Heinemann Publishers**

"Dedicated to Teachers" is a trademark of Greenwood Publishing Group, Inc.

The authors and publisher wish to thank those who have generously given permission to reprint borrowed material: Please see the Credits section beginning on page 631.

Photography: Photo of Albert Einstein on page 281 by ©Science History Images /Alamy

Library of Congress Cataloging-in-Publication Data

Names: Fountas, Irene C. author. | Pinnell, Gay Su, author.
Title: The writing minilessons book, grade three : your every day guide to
   literacy teaching / Irene C. Fountas & Gay Su Pinnell.
Description: Portsmouth, NH : Heinemann, 2023. | Includes bibliographical
   references. | Summary: "The Writing Minilessons Book for grade 3
   contains brief, focused, explicit lessons for whole-group instruction
   that help children understand and apply the characteristics of effective
   writing and nurture their ability to write with purpose, imagination,
   and voice."— Provided by publisher.
Identifiers: LCCN 2022010864 (print) | LCCN 2022010865 (ebook) | ISBN
   9780325118826 (paperback) | ISBN 9780325135311 (ebook)
Subjects: LCSH: Composition (Language arts)—Study and teaching
   (Elementary) | English language—Composition and exercises—Study and
   teaching (Elementary) | Third grade (Education)
Classification: LCC LB1576 .F6647 2023 (print) | LCC LB1576 (ebook) | DDC
   372.62/3044—dc23/eng/20220310
LC record available at https://lccn.loc.gov/2022010864
LC ebook record available at https://lccn.loc.gov/2022010865

Editors: Kerry L. Crosby and Sue Paro
Production: Cindy Strowman
Production Assistant: Anthony Riso
Cover and Interior Designs: Ellery Harvey and Kelsey Roy
Illustrators: Sarah Snow and Will Sweeney
Typesetter: Sharon Burkhardt
Manufacturing: Erin St. Hilaire and Jaime Spaulding

Printed in the United States of America on acid-free paper

1 2 3 4 5 6 7 8 9 10   LSB   27 26 25 24 23 22
May 2022 Printing / 34025

CONTENTS

Introductory Chapters

	Introduction: Welcome to *The Writing Minilessons Book, Grade 3*	1
CHAPTER 1	The Role of Writing in Literacy Learning	7
CHAPTER 2	What Is a Writing Minilesson?	27
CHAPTER 3	Minilessons for Building a Community: Management	47
CHAPTER 4	Minilessons for Studying Genres and Forms of Writing	57
CHAPTER 5	Minilessons for the Study of Craft, Conventions, and Writing Process	67
CHAPTER 6	Putting Minilessons into Action: Assessing and Planning	89

1 Management

UMBRELLA 1	Building Community Through Oral Storytelling	101
WML 1	Get to know your classmates.	102
WML 2	Tell a story about something from your Me Box.	104
WML 3	Tell a story about your name.	106
WML 4	Tell a story inspired by a book.	108
WML 5	Tell stories about people and places you don't want to forget.	110
UMBRELLA 2	Working Together in the Classroom	113
WML 1	Show respect to each other.	114
WML 2	Use an appropriate voice level.	116
WML 3	Find ways to solve problems when you need help.	118
WML 4	Return materials to where they belong.	120
WML 5	Turn and talk to share your thinking.	122

iii

UMBRELLA 3	Establishing Independent Writing	125
WML 1	Learn the guidelines for independent writing.	126
WML 2	Use writing tools to help with your writing.	128
WML 3	Choose the paper for your writing projects.	130
WML 4	Confer with your teacher or other writers about your writing.	132

UMBRELLA 4	Introducing the Writing Folder	135
WML 1	Keep a list of your finished writing projects.	136
WML 2	Write what you have learned how to do as a writer and illustrator.	138
WML 3	Write your goals as a writer.	140
WML 4	Use the word list to help with your writing.	142
WML 5	Use checklists to help with revising and editing.	144

2 Genres and Forms

Functional Writing

UMBRELLA 1	Writing Friendly Letters	149
WML 1	Write a letter to someone for a reason.	150
WML 2	Write the parts of a letter.	152
WML 3	Write the important information in your letter.	154

UMBRELLA 2	Writing Procedural Texts	157
WML 1	Notice the qualities of good procedural texts.	158
WML 2	Choose what you want to teach and how you will teach it.	160
WML 3	Write and/or draw the steps or instructions.	162

UMBRELLA 3	Writing to a Prompt: Getting Ready for Test Writing	165
WML 1	Read the directions carefully and make sure you understand what is being asked.	166
WML 2	Start your response with a main idea sentence.	168
WML 3	Write a short response.	170
WML 4	Write a long response.	172
WML 5	Write a response that compares and contrasts two things.	174
WML 6	Write an effective concluding sentence.	176

Narrative Writing

UMBRELLA 4		**Writing Memory Stories**	**179**
	WML 1	Notice the qualities of good memory stories.	180
	WML 2	Choose a small moment or memory that is important to you.	182
	WML 3	Write details about the most important moments in the story.	184
	WML 4	Share your thoughts and feelings about the memory or experience.	186
	WML 5	Tell why the story is important.	188
UMBRELLA 5		**Writing Realistic Fiction Stories**	**191**
	WML 1	Notice the qualities of good realistic fiction stories.	192
	WML 2	Think about your own experiences for ideas.	194
	WML 3	Use a storyboard to make a plan.	196
	WML 4	Make your characters believable.	198
	WML 5	Think about what the main character learns.	200

Informational Writing

UMBRELLA 6		**Making Informational Books**	**203**
	WML 1	Notice the qualities of good informational books.	204
	WML 2	Decide how to organize your book.	206
	WML 3	Write a strong introduction.	208
	WML 4	Support your ideas with examples.	210
	WML 5	Make your nonfiction writing interesting and informative.	212
	WML 6	Write a strong conclusion.	214

Persuasive Writing

UMBRELLA 7		**Exploring Opinion Writing**	**217**
	WML 1	Use your writer's notebook to get ideas for opinion writing.	218
	WML 2	Write an introduction that clearly states your opinion.	220
	WML 3	Provide reasons and examples for your opinion.	222
	WML 4	Write a strong conclusion.	224
UMBRELLA 8		**Introducing Persuasive Writing Through Powerful Messages**	**227**
	WML 1	Find your message.	228
	WML 2	Find a new way to share your message.	230
	WML 3	Make your message stand out.	232

Poetic Writing

Umbrella 9	**Making Poetry Anthologies**	**235**
WML 1	Make your own poetry anthology.	236
WML 2	Collect poems that show something about you.	238
WML 3	Respond to poems you collect.	240
WML 4	Write a poem in response to a poem.	242

Umbrella 10	**Writing Poetry**	**245**
WML 1	Poems look and sound different from other kinds of writing.	246
WML 2	Remove words to make your poem more powerful.	248
WML 3	Use repeating words or phrases to make your writing interesting.	250
WML 4	Use metaphors and similes to describe something.	252

Umbrella 11	**Writing Different Kinds of Poems**	**255**
WML 1	Write a poem to show a feeling or an image.	256
WML 2	Write a shape (concrete) poem.	258
WML 3	Write a lyrical poem.	260
WML 4	Write a poem for two voices.	262

Other Forms

Umbrella 12	**Making Picture Books**	**265**
WML 1	Notice the qualities of picture books you love.	266
WML 2	Plan what to put on each page.	268
WML 3	Make decisions about what you will say with words and show with pictures.	270
WML 4	Choose where to place the pictures and words.	272

Umbrella 13	**Making Biographical Multimedia Presentations**	**275**
WML 1	Choose and research a subject.	276
WML 2	Organize and write the words for your slides.	278
WML 3	Add pictures, sound, and video to make your presentation interesting.	280
WML 4	Practice and present your presentation.	282

UMBRELLA 14	**Making Photo Essays**	**285**
WML 1	Notice the qualities of photo essays.	286
WML 2	Choose photos to include and decide how to order and place them on the pages.	288
WML 3	Add text that explains the photos.	290
WML 4	Provide an introduction or conclusion to explain the photo essay.	292

UMBRELLA 15	**Experimenting with Writing in New Ways**	**295**
WML 1	Revisit an old topic in a new way.	296
WML 2	Write with a different set of eyes.	298
WML 3	Write a new version of an old tale.	300

3 Craft

UMBRELLA 1	**Reading Like a Writer and Illustrator**	**305**
WML 1	Notice the decisions writers make.	306
WML 2	Notice the decisions illustrators make.	308
WML 3	Learn from authors through writer talks.	310

UMBRELLA 2	**Describing Characters**	**313**
WML 1	Describe how characters look.	314
WML 2	Tell what characters do.	316
WML 3	Tell what characters think and say.	318

UMBRELLA 3	**Crafting a Setting**	**321**
WML 1	Use your senses to describe the setting.	322
WML 2	Make a sketch to show your thinking about the setting.	324
WML 3	Show how the setting is important to the character in a story.	326

UMBRELLA 4	**Adding Dialogue to Writing**	**329**
WML 1	Add dialogue to make your writing more interesting.	330
WML 2	Make it clear who is speaking when you use dialogue.	332
WML 3	Include action with dialogue in your writing.	334

UMBRELLA 5	Crafting a Lead	337
WML 1	Start your writing with action.	338
WML 2	Start your writing with talking.	340
WML 3	Start your writing with a description of the setting.	342
WML 4	Start your writing with an interesting fact.	344

UMBRELLA 6	Crafting an Ending	347
WML 1	End your writing with advice.	348
WML 2	End your writing with a feeling.	350
WML 3	End your writing with a call to action.	352
WML 4	End your writing with a question.	354

UMBRELLA 7	Making Powerful Word Choices	357
WML 1	Use words to show not tell.	358
WML 2	Choose interesting words to describe the way people say something.	360
WML 3	Choose interesting words to describe actions.	362

UMBRELLA 8	Making Your Sentences Clear and Interesting	365
WML 1	Start your sentences in different ways.	366
WML 2	Vary the length of your sentences.	368
WML 3	Use connecting words and phrases to help sentences flow.	370

UMBRELLA 9	Writing with Voice in Fiction and Nonfiction	373
WML 1	Speak directly to the reader.	374
WML 2	Show your voice with different styles of print.	376
WML 3	Show your voice with humor.	378
WML 4	Read your writing aloud to hear how it sounds.	380

UMBRELLA 10	Using Text Features in Nonfiction Writing	383
WML 1	Use headings to tell what a part is about.	384
WML 2	Make a table of contents for your book.	386
WML 3	Use sidebars to give extra information.	388
WML 4	Write captions under pictures.	390

UMBRELLA 11	**Expanding Nonfiction Writing**	**393**
WML 1	Use description to give the reader a picture.	394
WML 2	Tell how two things are the same or different.	396
WML 3	Tell about an experience from your life to teach more about a topic.	398
UMBRELLA 12	**Drawing People**	**401**
WML 1	Use shapes to draw people in different positions.	402
WML 2	Draw people in a setting.	404
WML 3	Use color to capture the way people really look.	406
WML 4	Add details that show how a person feels.	408
UMBRELLA 13	**Adding Meaning Through Illustrations**	**411**
WML 1	Use illustrations to show more than what the words say.	412
WML 2	Use colors to create a feeling.	414
WML 3	Draw motion or sound lines to show something moving or making noise.	416
WML 4	Draw your picture so the reader knows what is important.	418
WML 5	Use light to show the time of day and details to show the season.	420
UMBRELLA 14	**Illustrating and Using Graphics in Nonfiction Writing**	**423**
WML 1	Use photographs and detailed illustrations in your nonfiction book.	424
WML 2	Draw diagrams to give information.	426
WML 3	Use a close-up to show a detail of a bigger picture.	428
WML 4	Use maps and legends to give readers information.	430
WML 5	Use comparisons to help readers understand size.	432
UMBRELLA 15	**Exploring Design Features and Text Layout**	**435**
WML 1	Make your illustrations interesting in a variety of ways.	436
WML 2	Use scenes to show action and details.	438
WML 3	Use the size, color, and placement of words in interesting ways.	440

4 Conventions

UMBRELLA 1	Writing Words	**445**
WML 1	Write your letters clearly and make them the right size within a word.	446
WML 2	Break words into syllables to write them.	448
WML 3	Use what you know about words to write new words.	450

UMBRELLA 2	Learning About Punctuation and Capitalization	**453**
WML 1	Notice how authors use capitalization.	454
WML 2	Notice how authors use punctuation.	456
WML 3	Use quotation marks to show what someone said.	458
WML 4	Use commas to separate words in a list.	460
WML 5	Use an apostrophe to show something belongs to someone or to make a contraction.	462
WML 6	Use an ellipsis to show a pause or to build excitement.	464

UMBRELLA 3	Learning to Paragraph	**467**
WML 1	Make a new paragraph for a new idea.	468
WML 2	Use paragraphs to show when a new speaker is talking.	470
WML 3	Use good spacing to set off paragraphs.	472

5 Writing Process

Planning and Rehearsing

UMBRELLA 1	Introducing and Using a Writer's Notebook	**477**
WML 1	Make your writer's notebook your own.	478
WML 2	Write in your writer's notebook for at least ten minutes a day.	480
WML 3	Collect your thinking in your writer's notebook.	482
WML 4	Keep your writer's notebook organized.	484
WML 5	Keep building your writer's notebook.	486

UMBRELLA 2	Writer's Notebook: Getting Ideas from Your Life	**489**
WML 1	Make a heart map to discover what is important in your life.	490
WML 2	Use maps to get ideas.	492

WML 3	Make webs to get ideas from your memories and experiences.		494
WML 4	Think about special places to get ideas.		496
WML 5	Think about people to get ideas.		498
WML 6	Use lists to gather ideas from your life.		500
WML 7	Collect artifacts in your writer's notebook.		502
WML 8	Observe the world around you to get ideas for your writing.		504
UMBRELLA 3	**Writer's Notebook: Getting Inspiration from Writers and Artists**		**507**
WML 1	Collect memorable words and phrases from authors you love.		508
WML 2	Use poems to inspire writing ideas.		510
WML 3	Use books or parts of books to inspire writing ideas.		512
WML 4	Use song lyrics to inspire writing ideas.		514
WML 5	Use art to inspire writing ideas.		516
UMBRELLA 4	**Writer's Notebook: Becoming an Expert**		**519**
WML 1	Make lists of topics you know, are interested in, and care about.		520
WML 2	Use webs to focus a topic.		522
WML 3	Make a list of questions and wonderings you have about a topic.		524
WML 4	Take notes in your own words about your topic.		526
WML 5	Interview or watch an expert on your topic and take notes.		528
WML 6	Choose and sketch a few objects to represent the big ideas of your topic.		530
UMBRELLA 5	**Thinking About Purpose, Audience, and Genre/Form**		**533**
WML 1	Think about your purpose.		534
WML 2	Think about your audience.		536
WML 3	Think about the kind of writing you want to do.		538
UMBRELLA 6	**Observing and Writing Like a Scientist**		**541**
WML 1	Write your predictions.		542
WML 2	Sketch and take notes about your observations.		544
WML 3	Write a procedure.		546
WML 4	Explain why you think something happened.		548

Drafting and Revising

UMBRELLA 7	**Adding Information to Your Writing**		**551**
WML 1	Use different tools to add to your writing.		552
WML 2	Add describing words or phrases to help the reader picture the idea.		554

WML 3	Add details to slow down the exciting or important part of the story.	556
WML 4	Add information to support your ideas and help the reader understand your topic.	558
WML 5	Use connecting words to add more information to your writing.	560

UMBRELLA 8	**Revising to Focus and Organize Writing**	**563**
WML 1	Take out information that does not add to the important ideas or message.	564
WML 2	Organize your writing to make sure the order makes sense.	566
WML 3	Change words to make your writing more specific.	568
WML 4	Skip time to focus your story.	570
WML 5	Group similar ideas together in paragraphs.	572

Editing and Proofreading

UMBRELLA 9	**Editing and Proofreading Writing**	**575**
WML 1	Make sure your writing makes sense.	576
WML 2	Make sure you made your letters easy to read.	578
WML 3	Make sure you wrote the words you know correctly.	580
WML 4	Check your punctuation and capitalization.	582

Publishing

UMBRELLA 10	**Adding Book and Print Features**	**585**
WML 1	Choose a title for your book.	586
WML 2	Make an author page.	588
WML 3	Dedicate your book to someone and thank people who helped you.	590
WML 4	Make endpapers for your book.	592

UMBRELLA 11	**Publishing and Self-Assessing Your Writing**	**595**
WML 1	Choose a piece you want to publish.	596
WML 2	Publish your writing.	598
WML 3	Use a self-assessment rubric.	600
WML 4	Select a piece of writing that shows your growth as a writer.	602

Appendix: Suggested Sequence of Lessons	**605**
Glossary	**623**
Credits	**631**

Introduction

Welcome to *The Writing Minilessons Book, Grade 3*

For third graders, writing and drawing have become powerful ways to communicate their thoughts, ideas, and plans. For you, your students' writing and drawing provide a window into their understandings of written language. Through their writing, you can infer what your students understand about genre, craft, conventions, and the writing process. Through your teaching, your students will grow and deepen their understandings across these areas. And now, the journey begins.

Organization of Lessons

In this book, you will find 200 writing minilessons that help students develop as artists and writers. The minilessons are organized across five sections:

- Section 1: Management (MGT)
- Section 2: Genres and Forms (GEN)
- Section 3: Craft (CFT)
- Section 4: Conventions (CNV)
- Section 5: Writing Process (WPS)

The sections contain groups of minilessons, or "umbrellas." Within each umbrella, the minilessons are all related to the same big idea so you can work with each concept for several days. The umbrellas are numbered sequentially within each section, and the minilessons are numbered sequentially within each umbrella. Each writing minilesson is identified by section, umbrella, and minilesson. For example, MGT.U1.WML1 indicates the first minilesson in the first umbrella of the Management section.

Content of Lessons: *The Literacy Continuum*

Almost all lessons in this book are based on the behaviors and understandings presented in *The Fountas & Pinnell Literacy Continuum: A Tool for Assessment, Planning, and Teaching*. This volume presents detailed behaviors and understandings to notice, teach for, and support for prekindergarten through middle school, across eight instructional reading, writing, and language contexts. In sum, *The Fountas & Pinnell Literacy Continuum* describes proficiency in reading, writing, and language as it changes over grades and over levels. When you teach the lessons in this book, you are teaching for the behaviors and understandings that third graders need to become proficient readers and writers over time.

Organized for Your Students' Needs

We have provided a suggested sequence of lessons (see pp. 4–5) for you to try out and adjust based on your observations of your students. The sequence provides one path through the lessons. If this is your first time teaching minilessons, you may want to stick to it. However, with 200 lessons from which to choose, you will not have time to teach every minilesson in this book. Choose the lessons that make sense for your class and omit any lessons that would be too advanced or too easy. You will be able to locate the lessons easily because they are organized into sections. We organized the lessons into sections for these reasons:

- Students in any given third-grade class will vary greatly in their literacy experiences and development. Lessons organized by topic allow you to dip into the sections to select specific umbrellas or lessons that respond to your students' needs. You can find lessons easily by section and topic through the table of contents.

- Writing is a complex process and involves many levels of learning—from figuring out the idea to communicate, to putting the thinking into language, to thinking about what to draw and write, to the mechanics of getting it on paper. Having the lessons organized by section enables you to focus on the areas that might be most helpful to your students at a specific point in time.

Key Words Used in Minilessons

The following is a list of key terms that we will use as we describe minilessons in the next chapters. Keep them in mind so that together we can develop a common language to talk about the minilessons.

- **Umbrella** A group of minilessons, all of which are directed at different aspects of the same larger category of understanding.

- **Minilesson** A short, interactive lesson to invite students to think about one idea.

- **Principle** A concise statement of the concept students will learn and be invited to apply.

- **Writing** All the kinds of writing, including drawings, that third-grade students will do, whether they write a list of words, one sentence, or many pages.

- **Mentor Text** A fiction or nonfiction text in which the author or illustrator offers a clear example of the minilesson principle. Students will have heard the text read aloud and talked about it. Mentor texts can be books you have read to them as well as texts that you have written or ones that you and the students have written together. Occasionally, student writing can also serve as a mentor text.

- **Text Set** A group of either fiction or nonfiction books or a combination of both that, taken together, help students explore an idea, a topic, or a type of book (genre). You will have already read the books to them before a lesson. Students will have also made important connections between them.

- **Anchor Chart** A visual representation of the lesson concept using a combination of words and images. You create it as you talk with the students. It summarizes the learning and can be used by the students as a reference tool.

The chapters at the beginning of this book help you think about the role of talking, drawing, and writing in third grade, how the lessons are designed and structured, and the materials and resources you will need to teach the lessons.

Suggested Sequence of Lessons

If you are new to third-grade minilessons, you may want to use the Suggested Sequence of Lessons (Figure I-1) for teaching writing minilessons across the year. This sequence weaves in lessons from the different sections so that students receive instruction in all aspects of writing and drawing throughout the school year. Lessons are sequenced in a way we think will support most third-grade students, but you need first to observe what most of your students are doing as talkers, artists, and writers. Then choose the specific lessons that will lead them forward.

Every group of third graders is different, so it is impossible to prescribe an exact sequence of lessons. However, this sequence will give you a good starting place as you begin to teach the lessons in *The Writing Minilessons Book, Grade 3*. As you use the suggested sequence, consider the following:

- The number of days assigned to each umbrella suggests how many days you will likely need to spend on teaching the minilessons in an umbrella. On occasion, you may need to give students time in between lessons to apply the lesson during independent writing. You do not have to teach a writing minilesson every day, though it is a goal if it fits with your students' learning.

- You may want to spend more time on some concepts than on others by revisiting or repeating lessons according to your students' needs and interests.

If you use *Fountas & Pinnell Classroom™ Shared Reading Collection* (2022) or *Interactive Read-Aloud Collection* (2019), or *The Reading Minilessons Book, Grade 3* (2019), note that the Suggested Sequence of Lessons follows the sequences found in these resources to help organize reading and writing instruction across the year. If you do not have the texts suggested in the lessons as mentor texts, simply pick similar books and examples from your own classroom library or school library. Characteristics of the books used in the lessons are described on the opening page of the umbrellas for the writing minilessons. It is our intention that whenever

Suggested Sequence of Lessons

Months	Texts from *Fountas & Pinnell Classroom*™ Shared Reading Collection	Text Sets from *Fountas & Pinnell Classroom*™ Interactive Read-Aloud Collection	Reading Minilessons (RML) Umbrellas	Writing Minilessons (WML) Umbrellas	Teaching Suggestions for Extending Learning
Months 1 & 2	Cat Belly	The Importance of Kindness	MGT.U1: Working Together in the Classroom	**MGT.U1: Building Community Through Oral Storytelling (5 days)**	We recommend teaching this umbrella first because it serves several purposes. It allows children to orally rehearse stories, build community through listening to one another's stories, and get ideas for writing. It is helpful to provide time between the lessons in this umbrella for students to tell their stories. For example, instead of teaching a minilesson, provide a time each day for a few students to share their stories, or have students tell their stories in pairs or small groups. You could also have them tell stories to one another as they work on the lessons in MGT.U2. Alternating between lessons in MGT.U1 and MGT.U2 is a nice way to build community while establishing important routines.
	Marissa Margolis, Pet Sitter				
		Connecting Across Generations: Family			
			MGT U2: Exploring the Classroom Library	**MGT.U2: Working Together in the Classroom (5 days)**	If you are using *The Reading Minilessons Book, Grade 3*, you do not need to teach the lessons that repeat in MGT.U2. Both the RML and WML books establish the same basic routines. You may choose to teach these lessons while students are engaged in storytelling (MGT.U1) so
	The Rain Forest				

possible students will have already seen and heard the mentor texts by the time they are used in a lesson. To read more about using the Suggested Sequence of Lessons to plan your teaching, see Chapter 6.

Figure I-1: The complete Suggested Sequence of Lessons is on pages 605–622 in this book and in the online resources.

Introduction: Welcome to *The Writing Minilessons Book, Grade 3*

Chapter 1 | The Role of Writing in Literacy Learning

Writing can contribute to the building of almost every kind of inner control of literacy learning that is needed by the successful reader.

—Marie Clay

LOOK AROUND A THIRD-GRADE CLASSROOM, bustling with the energy of independent learners. Some students are busy observing, sketching, and writing notes in their writer's notebooks about the latest wonder in the science center. Other students are deep into their research about a topic they love and care about. Still others are off making books. They are writing how-to books, making poetry books, and writing about their favorite memories. They are composing multimedia presentations and narrating digital photo essays on computers. Partners read each other their writing and offer suggestions, and the teacher confers with individual writers who are eager to share the latest additions to their writing. The classroom is filled not only with the excitement of exploration but with the tools of literacy.

Students in your third-grade classroom are learning to be part of a community of talkers, scientists, mathematicians, artists, readers, and writers. The writing minilessons in this book play an important role in this process.

In the lessons, students will draw and write in many different ways for many different purposes and audiences across the curriculum (Figure 1-1).

The writing minilessons in this book will help students see the stories in their lives and will help you provide time and space for them to share their stories—orally as well as in written form. We recommend that third graders use a writer's notebook to collect ideas for writing. Several minilessons in the Writing Process section are dedicated to helping students build a writer's notebook and develop the habit of using quick writes to write in their notebooks for at least ten minutes a day outside of writers' workshop. They learn that a writer's notebook is a place to generate and try out ideas, play with craft moves, and learn about their identities and interests. Students begin to live their lives with a writer's eye—seeing ideas for writing in everyday occurrences. If they have daily opportunities to write and draw, they will learn to see themselves as writers and artists.

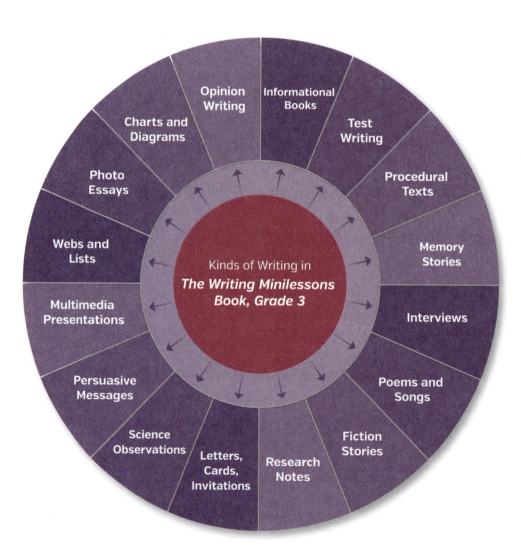

Figure 1-1: Students will have opportunities to write and draw in a variety of ways across the year.

Students' Writing Shows What They Know

Students learn differently from one another, but all make progress toward the kind of writing they see in the world, from books to digital media. Observing third graders write and looking at their writing will give you evidence of what they know. Notice whether they

- initiate writing quickly,
- have things to write about,
- choose topics and stories they care about,
- show enthusiasm for their writing,
- draw pictures with details,
- write words with standard and approximated spellings,
- talk about their pictures and messages,
- try out different kinds of writing (different genres and forms),
- write several sentences or paragraphs to communicate a continuous message,
- read what they have written,
- try out new learning in their writing,
- use capitalization and punctuation to clarify their writing, or
- revise, or change, their writing to make it more interesting, more detailed, or clearer.

When you notice what your students are doing with writing and drawing, you can build on their strengths and help them take the next steps as writers and illustrators. In Figure 1-2, notice all the things third-grader Tatiana is doing in her writing. Also notice areas in which she can grow based on her budding understandings. It is important to note that students take on new behaviors and understandings over time. Your goal in analyzing students' writing is not to "fix" or improve a particular piece of writing (though you might use one piece to teach one or two important new things) but to give students the tools to think in new ways. Analyzing your students' writing gives you direction for what you might teach to lead them forward. When you meet students where they are and build on their strengths, they are more engaged and interested in learning how to make their writing and art more like the texts they are reading.

Chapter 6 includes information about the tools provided in the online resources to assess your students' writing. *The Fountas & Pinnell Literacy Continuum* and the assessment sections in the writing minilessons will guide your observation of students' writing behaviors and your analysis of their writing pieces. When you take time to talk to students and read their writing, you learn what they have understood from your teaching, what they have yet to understand, and what you might teach them next.

Third Graders Connect Oral Language, Reading, and Writing

A child's journey to becoming literate begins at birth. Tatiana has developed the understandings she demonstrates in Figure 1-2 over many years. As caregivers engage a child in language interactions, the child learns to communicate, and this oral language foundation paves the way for learning about written language—reading and writing. All aspects of a child's oral and written language—listening, speaking, reading, and writing—develop together and support each other as the child's literacy understandings grow. Each literacy experience they have contributes to what they are able to show in their own writing.

Figure 1-2: Tatiana's memory story is evidence of what she understands about writing and provides a window into possible next steps.

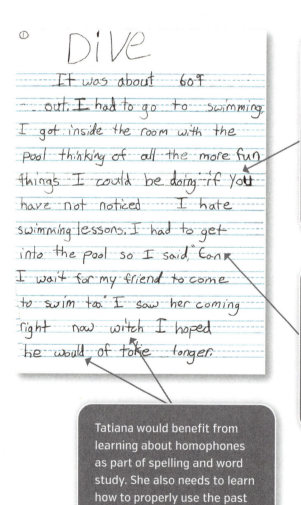

Tatiana understands that a lead is meant to hook the reader and hint at what the story is about. The reader instantly wonders why she hates swimming lessons and wants to read on. She also understands that writers share their thoughts and feelings in memory stories.

Tatiana shows that she understands how to use dialogue meaningfully in her story. She also knows how to punctuate it. A next step for her might be how to use paragraphs to show speaker changes in dialogue.

Tatiana would benefit from learning about homophones as part of spelling and word study. She also needs to learn how to properly use the past tense (e.g., *would have taken*).

> I walked down with my friend and my instruckter he was supper mean in my apoinyin. What I mean is that I dont like my instructer for swimming leassns. I sat down and dangled my legs in the water it was ice cold water I then put one leg then the other and pushed myself off in to the cold water. I went under

Tatiana will benefit from lessons on how to reveal a character's traits through actions or dialogue.

Tatiana experimented with talking directly to the reader to add voice to her writing.

Tatiana has learned to choose strong, descriptive verbs. Here, she used the word *dangled*. Later in the story, she used the words *angling* and *arching* to describe her body movements.

Tatiana shows strength in using punctuation and capitalization. However, she still needs support identifying when she has run two sentences together without punctuation.

Though Tatiana uses mostly conventional spelling and controls several high-frequency words, she would benefit from lessons on using what she knows about words to help her spell other words. For example, she knows how to spell *look* but she misspells *took*. She also would benefit from learning more about word patterns, particularly the VCe pattern.

Throughout this piece, Tatiana demonstrates that she can tell a detailed story sequentially, even using some transition words. A next step for her in revision might be to learn how to cut and summarize certain parts to stay focused on the big idea and move a story along.

> the water then swam to the other side of the pool and then toke a break waiting for the other person in my group to come to the other side. I swam back and she came back with me we got back back. Then it was time to do my favoite strock it was back strock I had got on my back streched my arms and went all the way to the

Chapter 1: The Role of Writing in Literacy Learning

[Student writing sample, page 4:]

other side. I came back we had 15 minutes! At 10 minutes we could to dives my all time faviorte But We still had 5 more minutes left So my instruter said to me and the person in my group "Can you do a flip in the water" "Um ya I can do a flip in the water" I said I got ready bent forwords and fliped in the water.

> Here is more evidence that Tatiana understands that she can make dialogue sound like real talking. Her voice comes through clearly as she writes *Um ya*. She would benefit from learning how to use punctuation to further show her voice.

> Tatiana understands that writers build suspense. She uses the time as a countdown to the big moment.

[Student writing sample, page 5:]

Right after I went my friend went she almost did it but not all the way around. The flips toke up the five minutes we had intill dives! Ten minutes left this was also my last swimming leossen! We got out of the pool ready to dive I stand up arched my back and pushed off. Deep down then I floated back up "can you do a back

> Tatiana will benefit from proofreading minilessons and rereading to make sure her thoughts are complete.

[Student writing sample, page 6:]

dive" my instruter asked me and my friend. "Um maybe." I said "Well let's try back jumps first ok" my instructer told us "ok" I said. I went first I anggled myself back I jumped that was easy I said to myself I todally could do that in a dive. The other person in my group went Now it was the dive I was so nevois

> Tatiana shows a beginning understanding that she can show how a character is feeling through dialogue by adding the word *Um* to show some reluctance.

> Tatiana again demonstrates that she understands that it is important to add feelings to a memory story. She will benefit from minilessons on *showing* feelings instead of telling. This behavior appears to be on the cutting edge of her learning.

The Writing Minilessons Book, Grade 3

> You can see further evidence that Tatiana will benefit from minilessons that help her recognize when sentences are not complete.

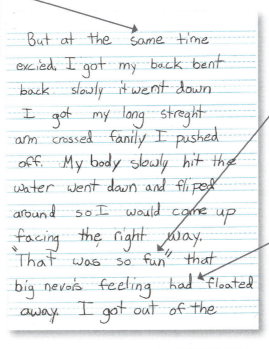

> Tatiana shows that she understands that writers select meaningful moments to write about.

> Tatiana again shows a strong choice of words. A next step for her might be to learn more about figurative language (e.g., how to use similes and metaphors).

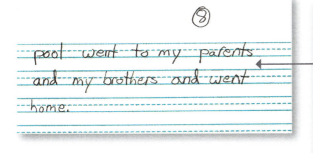

> Tatiana understands that she needs to conclude the story, but she will benefit from minilessons on how to write different endings. Another next step might be learning that memoirs often have a reflective element. She clearly chose a memory that is important to her, but would benefit from learning that writers of memory stories (or memoirs) often reflect on what they have learned from their experience or why the memory is important to them.

Third graders understand that their thoughts and ideas can be put into language, language can be put into writing, and the writing can be read (Figure 1-3).

The first umbrella in the Management section is dedicated to oral storytelling. This umbrella serves several purposes. It allows your students to get to know one another and to build community while also helping them generate ideas for future writing. We recommend capturing their oral stories on a chart titled *Stories We've Told* so students remember to add these ideas to their writer's notebooks once the notebook is introduced. Besides building a bank of story ideas, the lessons in this umbrella give students opportunities to orally rehearse stories before writing them down. For your students to be able to write their stories, they first need to be able to tell their stories.

> **The Contributions of Writing to Language, Literacy, and Learning**
>
> As students take on literacy, they grow in oral language, reading, and writing. As they write, they
>
> - Link spoken language to written language
> - Work on communicating meaningful messages
> - Say words slowly to hear the individual sounds in syllables and words
> - Experiment with more complex language structures
> - Read their writing
> - Use vocabulary they have heard or read
> - Begin to use punctuation to craft the way they want their audience to read their writing

Figure 1-3: Contributions of writing to literacy learning

By listening to stories read to them and by telling stories themselves (stories from their own lives or retellings of stories from books), third graders grow in their understanding of story structure. They develop the ability to use increasingly more sophisticated patterns of language and build strong vocabularies as they listen to and talk about books, ask questions about their classmates' writing, and clarify their own writing for an audience. As they write their oral stories, they have conversations about their writing that deepen their ability to explain their thinking. They learn to organize their thinking, to elaborate with story details, to develop vocabulary, and to more accurately describe what they want to say. Oral storytelling and rehearsal are not only useful for writing stories. Talking about what to write also helps with nonfiction writing. For example, it is helpful for students to say something in their own words before they jot down notes while doing research on a topic. Third graders can more easily move from research to writing when they have opportunities to talk about their learning before writing.

Students Have Opportunities to Write Across the Day

In the third-grade classroom, it is important to carve out a dedicated time for writing as well as to embed writing opportunities into a variety of daily classroom activities across the curriculum. From the time they enter the literacy-rich classroom, students are engaged in writing. They answer survey questions on charts, create writing pieces with their class members, write explanations for their math solutions, and make sketches of their scientific observations. They talk about the decisions authors make for their books, and they make their own books. Providing third graders with a predictable

Structure of Writers' Workshop		
Whole Class	Writing Minilesson	5–15 minutes
Individuals and Small Groups	Independent Writing Individual Conferences Guided Writing Groups	35–50 minutes (The time will expand as students build stamina across the year.)
Whole Class	Group Share	5–10 minutes

time to write each day allows them the opportunity to experiment with writing, to work on writing projects over several days, and to apply their new learning from writing minilessons. Consider setting aside the following times in your day for writing, and think about how you might build writing across content areas and into other established routines in your classroom.

Independent Writing Time During Writers' Workshop Independent writing time is typically bookended by a writing minilesson and a chance for students to share their writing (Figure 1-4). They learn about an aspect of writing during a writing minilesson and then have a chance to apply what they learned in that lesson as they write their own text independently for a period of time. The teacher has the opportunity to confer with individual writers or to work with small groups in guided writing (see pages 24–25 for information about guided writing). Students engage in both print and digital writing across a variety of genres and forms. They choose their own writing topics and often also select the genre and form that best fit with their purpose and audience. They spend time exploring and growing ideas in a writer's notebook (Figure 1-5) and engage in both print and online research. The writers' workshop ends with a whole-group meeting in which students share their writing and, if applicable, the ways they used their new understandings from the writing minilesson. Chapter 2 describes how the writing minilessons in this book follow and support this structure. Using the Management minilessons will help you establish a productive and engaging independent writing time with your third graders.

Ten-Minute Daily Quick Writes Students need regular, daily opportunities to write in their writer's notebooks in addition to the time they spend writing in their notebooks during independent writing time. Carving out ten minutes a day for students to engage in notebook writing helps them develop the habit of writing every day, increases stamina, and inspires creativity and engagement in

Figure 1-4: A writers' workshop structure allows for whole-class learning, individual and small-group instruction from the teacher, independent writing, and whole-class sharing.

Figure 1-5: Students use reader's notebooks and writer's notebooks as tools to collect their thinking and ideas. A reader's notebook is used primarily for writing about reading. The writer's notebook is used for collecting and experimenting with ideas for writing original pieces.

Chapter 1: The Role of Writing in Literacy Learning

writing. Some teachers invite students to write first thing in the morning when they are often brimming with things they want to talk about. Other teachers use small windows of time they have between specials or after lunch to give students the opportunity to settle back into the classroom. This time should feel relaxing and low-pressure for students. Whether you offer a generative prompt that is open-ended enough to allow for choice or you ask them to reread their notebooks and add to a notebook entry or write about something that piques their interest, you are teaching students that writing is valued in your classroom. Providing this time outside of writers' workshop frees them to experiment with writing in a different way from the way they work on a writing project or in their writers' notebooks during independent writing. They get to exercise their writing muscles in a different manner, which fuels the work they do in writers' workshop. These daily ten-minute quick writes not only generate ideas for future writing projects but also help keep the writer's notebook fresh and relevant for use during writers' workshop.

Writing About Reading During Readers' Workshop After engaging in an inquiry-based reading minilesson, students spend time independently reading and writing about their reading. For example, they might write a weekly letter to their teacher about their reading, record character traits on a web, summarize a story, or write an opinion about a book in a book review. During this time, teachers often confer with individual readers about applying what they learn from the reading minilesson to their independent reading, or they work with small groups in a guided reading lesson. Students also might write about guided reading books as part of a reading lesson.

We recommend that third graders collect their thinking and writing about books in a reader's notebook (Figure 1-5). The *Reader's Notebook, Intermediate* (Fountas and Pinnell 2011) provides sections for students to record their reading, take notes about reading minilessons, and write about their reading in a variety of ways. *The Reading Minilessons Book, Grade 3*, has an extensive section of reading minilessons dedicated to writing about reading to support students in using a reader's notebook and in writing about reading in different genres and forms.

Though writing about reading is a wonderful way for students to grow as both readers and writers, be cautious about how much time you have them spend engaged in writing during reading time. Third graders need time to gradually increase their reading stamina. Nevertheless, you can certainly use this time to make important reading and writing connections.

Shared/Interactive Writing Time During shared writing, students have an opportunity to collaborate on a piece of writing with you as the scribe. Though shared writing is often a part of writing minilessons, you might also find it helpful to dedicate a time to writing as a whole group a few times a week. The pieces you create as a class can be used as mentor texts during writing minilessons or writing conferences. Shared writing can be done with

> When you teach English learners, you can adjust your teaching—not more teaching, but different teaching—to assure effective learning throughout each lesson. Look for the symbol below to see ways to support English learners.

EL CONNECTION

either a whole class or a small group. Some of the students in your class, particularly English learners, might also benefit from interactive writing, which is the same as shared writing except that students share the pen with you to write letters, word parts, or words. Interactive writing is used mostly in small groups because fewer third graders need this high level of support in connecting letters and sounds.

Third Graders Make Literacy Connections Across Content Areas

Besides having dedicated times for writing in a writers' workshop, students need to be immersed in a variety of literacy experiences throughout the day so they can make important connections between reading, writing, and word study. In a literacy-building environment, students are immersed in talking, reading and writing. They hear books read aloud, read independently, write their own books, experience reading and phonics lessons, share poetry, and write and draw about their reading. They learn to observe and write like scientists and research like historians. They learn about language and word origins and grow in vocabulary across the content areas. They learn to try out new craft techniques as they begin to think like the authors and illustrators of the mentor texts they study. All of this supports students' writing development.

Interactive Read-Aloud and Shared Reading Reading aloud to third graders is essential. We call it "interactive" because it is so important for students to talk with each other about the books they hear. They also love shared reading with enlarged print books and charts, reading together from the same book, song, or poem (Figure 1-6). Books they read many times become "theirs." Interactive read-aloud and shared reading expose students to a variety of stories, informational books, songs, and poems. As third graders listen to and discuss these books and poems, they hear the way written language sounds and notice what other writers and illustrators do in their books. When you spend time teaching students to notice how the illustrator designed the cover,

Figure 1-6: Students develop an understanding of story structure, knowledge of how books work, and conventions of print through interactive read-aloud and shared reading (shown here).

Chapter 1: The Role of Writing in Literacy Learning

Figure 1-7: Students apply what they learn in a reading minilesson when they read independently.

the colors used in the illustrations, an interesting choice of words, or the rhythm of a repeating line, they become aware of the author's or illustrator's craft in a simple and authentic way.

Reading Minilessons, Guided Reading, and Independent Reading

Reading minilessons build on the literary understandings developed during interactive read-aloud and shared reading (Figure 1-7). Students learn more about what illustrators and writers do, how written language sounds, and how stories and information are organized. They learn about the author's message, how print and words work, and about different kinds of writing. They participate in shared writing as they work with you to create anchor charts for reading minilessons and learn how to write and draw about their reading. Third graders grow in all of these understandings as they participate in brief, small-group guided reading lessons in which they read books at their instructional level. Students are also given opportunities throughout the day to read independently. As they engage with a variety of texts independently, they not only apply what they have learned during reading minilessons and guided reading but also make their own discoveries about print, writer's and illustrator's craft moves, and other literary elements. We have written extensively about reading minilessons and guided reading in *The Reading Minilessons Book, Grade 3* and in *Guided Reading: Responsive Teaching Across the Grades* (Fountas and Pinnell 2017). Good teaching in reading is essential to the teaching of writing and vice versa. Writing minilessons help students transfer what they have learned in reading to their own writing. In turn, what they learn about writing will make them stronger readers. It is a deeply reciprocal process.

Writing Across the Curriculum Writing plays an important role in the content areas as well (Figure 1-8). Students draw and write as they solve math problems and explain their solutions. They record information during science experiments, they sketch and write their observations in the science center, and they write predictions and wonderings about scientific phenomena. Writing, along with talking and reading, is one of the vehicles for learning across the curriculum. Encourage your students to make books in science and social studies—for example, a how-to book for conducting a science experiment, an informational book about something in history or in your community, or a lab book of science observations. In the Genres and Forms section, you will find several umbrellas that introduce different kinds of writing that can be used across the curriculum. For

Figure 1-8: Examples of third graders' writing across the curriculum

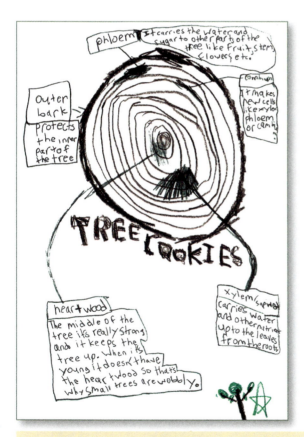

Anisa took notes in her writer's notebook about famous women in history as part of a unit combining social studies and biographies.

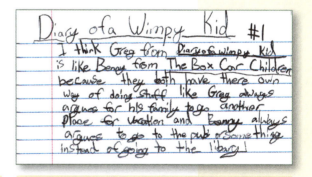

Cooper made a poster to describe what he learned in science about tree cookies. He chose to use a diagram and labels to show the information he learned.

During independent reading, Jamie wrote in his reader's notebook comparing two characters from two different books.

Chapter 1: The Role of Writing in Literacy Learning

example, GEN.U13: Making Biographical Multimedia Presentations provides a way for students to display their learning about current or historical figures. In the Writing Process section, as part of the planning process, there is an umbrella that demonstrates how to observe and write like a scientist. GEN.U14: Making Photo Essays offers students yet another creative way to tell about something they have learned.

As described earlier, third graders also have several opportunities throughout the day to write about their reading in a reader's notebook. You can teach them a variety of ways to respond to their reading through modeled or shared writing. The writing minilessons in this book focus on having students write their own original pieces, but writing about reading is still an important part of becoming a writer.

Phonics and Phonemic Awareness Through inquiry-based writing minilessons, students have opportunities to revisit important word-solving actions and be reminded of key principles about the way words work to support their use of conventional spelling. For example, in CNV.U1: Writing Words, they learn to break words into syllables and to use what they know about words to write new words. Writing provides the opportunity to apply what they have learned through phonics and word study lessons. It is important for third grade teachers to provide a specific time for daily phonics, spelling, and word study lessons (see *Fountas & Pinnell Phonics, Spelling, and Word Study System, Grade 3*, 2019). Additionally, third graders benefit from opportunities to learn the sounds in words through shared reading of songs, poems, and rhymes. The following list has a few simple ways to help them develop in these areas. Many of these activities can be done in the word work center, during morning meeting, or during circle time.

- Connect sounds and letters to known words and names.
- Demonstrate making words and word parts with magnetic letters.
- Use word webs (e.g., write a word in the middle of the web and brainstorm words with the same root or same word part for the spokes of the web).
- Use word ladders to change parts of words to make new words (e.g., *port, part, past, last, list*).
- Provide games that focus on a word study principle (e.g., lotto, bingo, concentration) and teach students how to play.

Students Engage in the Writing Process

All writers, regardless of age or experience, engage in the same aspects of the writing process every time they write. Although components of the writing process are usually listed in a sequence, writers can and will use any or all of the components at any point while writing (Figure 1-9). Throughout the

Figure 1-9: The writing process is not linear. Sometimes writers will go forward (the solid arrows) and sometimes they will go back (the dotted arrows) before they move forward again. Individual writers develop their own writing process. Not all writing projects go entirely through to publishing, but all projects provide an opportunity to apply what students are learning in writing minilessons.

process, writers and illustrators often use a writer's notebook to generate ideas, make plans, and try out new craft moves. The lessons in the Writing Process section will help you set up this tool if you want to use it with your students. You can read more about the writing process and the writer's notebook in Chapter 5.

- **Planning and Rehearsing** In this part of the writing process, students gather ideas and talk about them with others. Third graders learn to become more intentional planners. They think about their purpose and audience and choose the genre or form of writing that is most effective for their purpose and best communicates their message. During planning, students are often engaged in collecting ideas in their writer's notebooks or rereading entries to decide what they might want to develop into a more in-depth writing piece.

- **Drafting and Revising** This part of the process is focused on getting ideas down on paper and learning how to make changes to improve the writing. Through writing minilessons, students learn the craft moves

Chapter 1: The Role of Writing in Literacy Learning

authors and illustrators make. They use their writer's notebooks to experiment with ideas for writing and to try out the new craft moves.

- **Editing and Proofreading** For third graders, editing and proofreading mean applying what they have learned about the conventions of writing to make their writing clear for readers.
- **Publishing** This part of the process means sharing a finished piece with an audience. Third grade is a good time to think about broadening these audiences to give students authentic experiences for sharing their writing. There are a variety of ways to publish both formally and informally using different materials and tools.

Of course, drawing and reading are fundamental parts of this process, as well. The minilessons in the Writing Process section are designed to support students as they engage in each step of this process.

Third Graders Learn About Writing by Seeing and Doing

Students benefit from seeing examples and demonstrations of drawing and writing before they try drawing and writing on their own. Use modeled, shared, interactive, or guided writing so that students see writing happening.

Modeled Writing

Modeled writing, which includes drawing, has the highest amount of teacher support (Figure 1-10). Students see what it looks like to produce a piece of writing as you demonstrate creating a particular genre, or type of writing. As you draw and write, talk through the decisions you are making as an artist or writer. Sometimes, you will have prepared the writing before class, but you will still talk about your thought process. Modeled writing or drawing is often used within a writing minilesson to demonstrate what a particular kind of writing looks like and how it is produced.

Modeled writing is a powerful way to teach writing because it allows you to teach from experience. When you are a teacher who writes, you can talk about the mentor texts you might have consulted, explain why you chose a certain craft move, and share your struggles with the writing process. You will also discover what is helpful to a writer and what might actually be limiting. Write from your own experiences and interests. You don't have to oversimplify your writing to demonstrate important writing principles from it. You also don't have to share your entire writing piece. Excerpts of modeled writing work just fine during a minilesson. Your students will value the fact that the example comes from a real piece of writing that you care

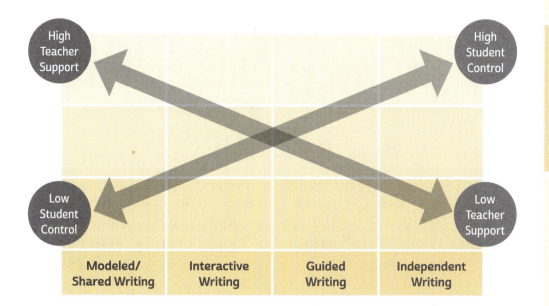

Figure 1-10: Each instructional context for writing has a different amount of teacher support and student control (from *The Literacy Quick Guide* by Irene C. Fountas and Gay Su Pinnell, 2018).

about. Students will connect with the authenticity of your writing and get even more excited about their own.

Shared Writing

In shared writing, use the students' experiences and language to create a collaborative text. English learners especially benefit from being able to read a text to which they have contributed. Shared writing is used for most of the charts in the writing minilessons, though you might decide to use modeled, or occasionally, interactive writing. Although you are the scribe who writes the text on chart paper displayed on an easel or whiteboard, students participate by contributing ideas. First, students talk about their experiences and ideas. Then, you and your students decide together what to say and how to say it (composing). Moving from thoughts or ideas to saying the words to putting the ideas in print (constructing), perhaps with a drawing, is a process third graders need to engage in over and over. The process begins with a plan you make together, and then you move to writing the message word by word as the students observe and talk about the process.

Shared writing provides the opportunity to occasionally pause and ask students to say multisyllable words slowly, breaking them into syllables to support their writing of more complex words. It is important for the students to say the word for themselves. Other times, you (with the students' input) will write the word, sentence, or phrase on the chart quickly to keep the lesson moving. Reread what you have written as you go along so that students can rehearse the language structure, anticipate the next word, and check what has been written. The chart then becomes a model, example, or reference for future reading, writing, and discussion (Figure 1-11).

 EL CONNECTION

Chapter 1: The Role of Writing in Literacy Learning

Shared writing is often integrated into writing minilessons, but you may want to occasionally carve out a time focused solely on creating a piece of writing with your students. This can be particularly helpful when introducing a new genre. For example, you might spend a day or two writing about a class memory before you embark on GEN.U4: Writing Memory Stories.

Interactive Writing

Interactive writing and shared writing are very similar. The only difference is that in interactive writing students "share the pen" by writing letters, word parts, or words. Occasionally, while making teaching points about various features of letters and words as well as punctuation, invite a student to the easel to contribute a letter, a word, a part of a word, or a type of punctuation. This process is especially helpful to English learners and students who need support with letter/sound relationships and spelling. Consider using interactive writing with small groups of these students during independent writing time.

Guided Writing

Guided writing allows for differentiated learning in order to address the common needs of a small, temporary group of students. By conducting conferences with students and examining their writing, you determine which students would benefit from small-group teaching. For example, you may have introduced a new kind of writing to the whole group but notice that there are a few students who need more support to take on the new learning. Or, you have noticed a few students experimenting with writing poetry and you want to support their new interest. In each case, you can pull a guided writing group together to deepen and expand students' understandings about genre, craft, conventions, and the writing process. When the new learning is accomplished, the group is disbanded. Whether you are reviewing or teaching something new that the whole class is not quite ready for, the small-group setting of guided writing allows you to closely observe your

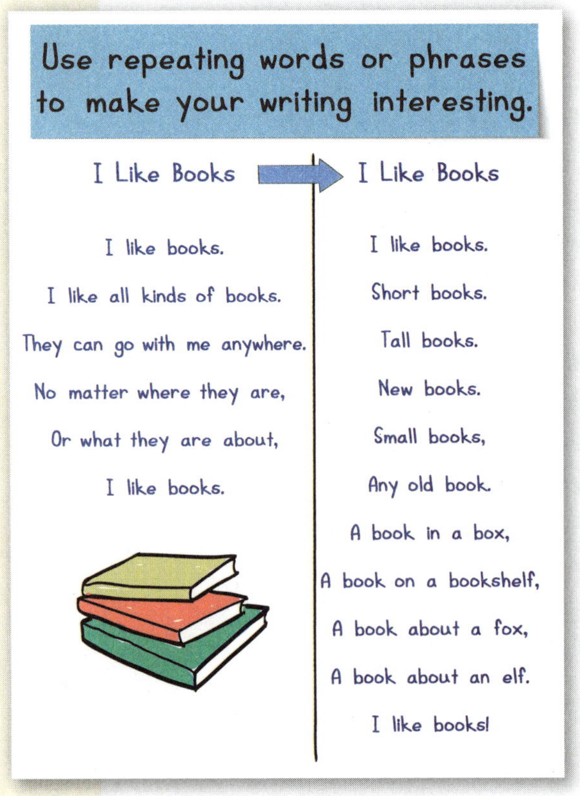

EL CONNECTION

Figure 1-11: In shared writing, the teacher and students come up with the ideas, but the teacher does all the writing. This shared writing piece was written during a minilesson about poetry.

Use repeating words or phrases to make your writing interesting.

I Like Books

I like books.
I like all kinds of books.
They can go with me anywhere.
No matter where they are,
Or what they are about,
I like books.

→

I Like Books

I like books.
Short books.
Tall books.
New books.
Small books,
Any old book.
A book in a box,
A book on a bookshelf,
A book about a fox,
A book about an elf.
I like books!

Structure of a Guided Writing Lesson	
Teach a Minilesson	Teach a single principle that is useful for a small group of writers at a particular point in time. Keep the lesson brief, and allow student inquiry to drive the learning.
Students Have a Try	Provide a piece of writing and invite students to apply the new thinking. Support students' learning with additional teaching, as needed. Point out effective applications of the principle by group members.
Students Apply the Principle to Their Own Writing	Invite students to try out the principle using an existing piece of writing or, as appropriate, by beginning a new piece of writing. Students continue to work at the small table as you observe and provide guidance that deepens individual students' understanding of the principle.
Students Share	Invite students to share what they noticed and learned during the lesson. Reinforce the principle, and encourage students to share the next steps they will take in their writing.

students' writing behaviors and provide specific guidance. Guided writing lessons are brief and focused. Typically a guided writing lesson lasts only ten to fifteen minutes and can take place while the rest of the class is engaged in independent writing (Figure 1-12).

Figure 1-12: Structure of a guided writing lesson from *The Literacy Quick Guide* (Fountas and Pinnell 2018)

Independent Writing

When students draw and write for themselves, all their understandings about drawing and writing—literacy concepts, word solving, purpose, audience—come together in a way that is visible. Sometimes they will write about their reading. Sometimes they will write in the content areas (e.g., science or social studies). Sometimes they will write from their personal experiences, and other times they will write about what they know or have learned about a topic through their observations and research. Through their participation in writing minilessons, students take on new understandings. Through independent writing, they try them out.

Figure 1-13 summarizes the features of modeled writing, shared writing, interactive writing, guided writing, and independent writing. In writing minilessons, you might use any one or more levels of support: modeled, shared, and interactive writing. The ultimate goal of writing minilessons is to support students in developing their own independent drawing and writing.

Levels of Support for Writing

Type of Writing	Characteristics
Modeled	• Whole class or small group • Teacher composes the text (creates and says the sentences) • Teacher writes the print and/or draws images • Used to demonstrate ideas and refer to • Used as a resource to read
Shared	• Whole class or small group • Teacher and students compose the text (create and say the sentences) • Teacher writes what the students decide together • Used to record ideas to read or refer to later • Often included in writing minilessons to show something about writing or drawing
Interactive	• Whole class or small group • Teacher and students plan what to write and/or draw • Teacher and students share the pen to write and illustrate the text • Slows down the writing/drawing and allows focus on specific drawing and writing concepts (e.g., saying words slowly to hear sounds, breaking words into syllables, techniques for drawing) • The writing/drawing can be used as a mentor text during writing minilessons and as a reference for independent writing • Often used as a shared reading text later
Guided	• Small group • Teacher provides a brief lesson on a single writing principle that students apply to their own writing • Allows for close observation and guidance • Used to differentiate instruction • Teaching might involve modeled, shared, or interactive writing • Similar to a writing minilesson but in a small-group setting
Independent	• Individuals • Students decide what to say or draw and then write or illustrate their own texts (in a variety of genres and forms) • Supported by writing conferences with the teacher • Engages students in all aspects of the drawing and writing processes

Figure 1-13: Choose the level of support that helps you reach your goals for your students. These supports apply to both writing and drawing.

Once you get to know the students in your class and understand what they can do on their own and what they can do with your support, you will be able to decide which level of support is most appropriate for a particular purpose. When the processes for each kind of writing are established, you can use them as needed throughout the day.

Chapter 2 | What Is a Writing Minilesson?

Every minilesson should end with students envisioning a new possibility for their work, and the key to successful minilessons is helping the group of students sitting in front of us to envision the difference this lesson might make in their work.

—Katie Wood Ray and Lisa Cleaveland

A WRITING MINILESSON IS BRIEF. It focuses on a single writing concept to help students write successfully. A writing minilesson uses inquiry, which leads students to discover an important understanding that they can try out immediately.

Writing minilessons provide ways to make the classroom a community of learners. They engage students in telling stories and drawing, both of which are foundations of writing. They engage them in making books, writing in a variety of genres, learning about writer's and illustrator's craft, exploring the conventions of writing, and navigating through the writing process. Writing minilessons help third graders emerge as readers and writers by allowing them to think about one small understanding at a time and apply it for themselves independently.

> In an **inquiry lesson**, students engage in the thinking and develop the thinking for themselves. They learn from the inside, instead of simply being told what to understand. *Telling* is not the same as teaching.

Five Types of Writing Minilessons

This book has 200 lessons in five color-coded sections (Figure 2-1):

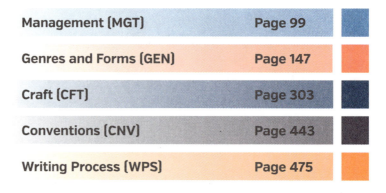

Figure 2-1: The writing minilessons are organized within five sections.

Management (MGT)	Page 99
Genres and Forms (GEN)	Page 147
Craft (CFT)	Page 303
Conventions (CNV)	Page 443
Writing Process (WPS)	Page 475

Minilessons in the Management section help students become a strong community of diverse learners who work and learn together peacefully and respectfully. Most of your minilessons at the beginning of the school year will focus on organizing the classroom and building a community in which students feel safe to share ideas and learn about one another. Repeat any of the lessons as needed across the year. A guiding principle: teach a minilesson on anything that prevents the classroom from running smoothly. In these lessons, students will learn

- routines that will help them work well with their classmates,
- ways they can participate,
- the importance of listening, taking turns, and other listening and speaking conventions when in a group, and
- how to work independently and manage materials, including their writer's notebooks and writing folders.

Minilessons in the Genres and Forms section support students by helping them see that they can write and draw like the authors of the books that they read. Through inquiry, students study the characteristics and qualities of different genres and forms. They learn how to

- teach others something they know how to do in procedural text,
- use ideas from their own lives to write memory stories and realistic fiction,
- tell what they know about a topic in informational books,
- write friendly letters,
- make multimedia presentations about a biographical subject,
- write about their opinions,

- plan and create photo essays, and
- write and craft different types of poems.

Each time students are exposed to a different genre or form, they expand their understanding of ways they can write. They learn more about the way illustrators and authors craft writing. The minilessons in this section address behaviors from across the grade 3 Writing continuum in *The Fountas & Pinnell Literacy Continuum*.

Minilessons in the Craft section help third graders learn about the decisions writers and illustrators make as they craft their pieces of writing. Through the umbrellas in this section, students explore the way authors use details in their writing to describe the characters and the setting. They look at the ways authors add dialogue to stories and text features to nonfiction writing. They experiment with different ways to start and end their writing and examine the ways authors choose words and craft sentences to make their writing interesting. The minilessons in this section address the behaviors and understandings in the Craft section of the grade 3 Writing continuum in *The Fountas & Pinnell Literacy Continuum*.

Minilessons in the Conventions section help students develop more sophisticated understandings of "how print works." They learn, for example, that

- proper formation, size, and spacing of letters is important,
- you can use what you know about words to write other words,
- words can be broken into syllables to help in spelling them,
- punctuation and capitalization play important roles in communicating a writer's message, and
- writers use paragraphing to organize their writing and signal new ideas.

The lessons in this section address the behaviors primarily in the Conventions section of the grade 3 Writing continuum in *The Fountas & Pinnell Literacy Continuum*.

Minilessons in the Writing Process section guide third graders through the phases of the writing process: planning and rehearsing, drafting and revising, editing and proofreading, and publishing. The minilessons in this section support your students in using a writer's notebook regularly, looking for writing ideas in their own lives, and getting inspired by other writers and artists. Other lessons teach third graders to think about why they are writing, whom they are writing for, and what kind of writing will serve their purpose. Finally, minilessons in this section help students learn how to add to their writing, how to cut and reorganize it, how to proofread it, and how to publish and assess it.

Writing Minilessons Are Grouped into Umbrella Concepts

Within each of the five major sections, lessons are grouped in what we call "umbrellas." Each umbrella is made up of several minilessons that are related to the larger idea of the umbrella. Lessons are placed together in an umbrella to show you how the lessons build the concept over time. When you teach several minilessons about the same idea, students deepen their understandings and develop shared vocabulary. These connections are especially helpful to English learners.

In most cases, it makes sense to teach the minilessons in an umbrella one right after another. But for some umbrellas, it makes sense to spread the minilessons over time so that students gain more experience with the first idea before moving on to the next.

Anchor Charts Support Writing Minilessons

Anchor charts are an essential part of each writing minilesson (Figure 2-2). They capture your students' thinking during the lesson and hold it for reflection at the end of the lesson. The chart is a visual reminder of the important ideas and the language used in the minilesson. Each writing minilesson features at least one sample chart, but use it only as a guideline. Your charts will be unique because they are built from ideas offered by the students in your class.

Each minilesson provides guidance for adding information to the chart. Read through lessons carefully to know whether any parts of the chart should be prepared ahead or whether the chart will be constructed during the lesson or left until the end. After the lesson, the charts become a resource for students to refer to throughout the day and on following days. They are a visual resource for students who need to not only hear but also see the information. Students can revisit these charts as they apply the minilesson principles to their writing or as they try out new routines in the classroom.

EL CONNECTION

Figure 2-2: Constructing anchor charts with and in front of your class provides verbal and visual support for all learners.

Guidelines for Writing Time

Get started quickly and quietly.

Get your writing folder and materials.

Work on a writing project or write in your writer's notebook.

Write for the entire writing time.

You can refer to them during guided writing lessons and when you confer with students about their independent writing. When you create charts with third graders, consider the following:

Make your charts simple, clear, and organized. Keep the charts simple without a lot of dense text. If the topic requires more information on the chart, make sure to print neatly in dark, easy-to-read colors.

Make your charts visually appealing and useful. All of the minilesson charts contain visual support, which will be helpful for all students, especially English learners. Students will benefit from the visuals to help them in understanding the concept and, in some cases, reading some of the words. The drawings are intentionally simple to give you a quick model to base your own drawings on. You might find it helpful to prepare them on separate pieces of paper or sticky notes ahead of the lesson and tape or glue them onto the chart as the students construct their understandings. This time-saving tip can also make the charts look more interesting and colorful because certain parts will stand out for the students.

Some of the art you see on the sample charts is available from the online resources to represent concepts that are likely to come up as you construct the charts with students. The downloadable chart art is provided for your convenience. Use it when it applies to your students' responses, but do not let it determine or limit their responses. Valuing the ideas of the class should be your primary concern.

Make your charts colorful. The sample minilesson charts are colorful for the purposes of engagement and organization. Color can be useful, but be careful about the amount and type you choose. Color can support English learners by providing a visual link to certain words or ideas. However, color can also be distracting if overused. Be thoughtful about when you choose to use color to highlight an idea or a word on a chart so that students are supported in reading continuous text. Text that is broken up by a lot of different colors can be very distracting for readers. You will notice that the minilesson principle is usually written in black or a dark color across the top of the chart so that it stands out and is easily recognized as the focus of the lesson. In most cases, the minilesson principle is added at the end of the lesson after students have constructed their own understanding of the concept.

Use the charts to support language growth. Anchor charts support language growth in all students, especially English learners. Conversation about the minilesson develops oral language and then connects oral language to print when you write words on the chart, possibly with picture support. By constructing an anchor chart with the students, you provide print that is immediately accessible to them because they helped create it and have ownership of the language. After a chart is finished, revisit it as often as needed to reinforce not only the ideas but also the printed words (Figure 2-3).

Figure 2-3: Characteristics of high-quality anchor charts

Umbrellas and Minilessons Have Predictable Structures

Understanding how the umbrellas are designed and how the minilessons fit together will help you keep your lessons focused and brief. Each umbrella is set up the same way, and each writing minilesson follows the same predictable structure (Figure 2-4). Use mentor texts that you have previously read and enjoyed with your students to streamline the lessons. You will not need to spend a lot of time rereading large sections of the text because the students will already know the texts well.

A Closer Look at the Umbrella Overview

All umbrellas are set up the same way. They begin with an overview and end with questions to guide your evaluation of students' understanding of the umbrella concepts plus several extension ideas. In between are the writing minilessons.

At the beginning of each umbrella (Figure 2-5 on page 35), the minilessons are listed and directions are provided to help you prepare to teach them. There are suggestions for books from *Fountas & Pinnell Classroom™ Interactive Read-Aloud Collection* and *Shared Reading Collection* to use as mentor texts. There are also suggestions for the kinds of books you might select if you do not have these books.

A Closer Look at the Writing Minilessons

The 200 writing minilessons in this book help you teach specific aspects of writing. An annotated writing minilesson is shown in Figure 2-6 on page 36. Each section is described in the text that follows.

Before the Lesson

Each writing minilesson begins with information to help you make the most of the lesson. There are four types of information:

The Writing Minilesson Principle describes the key idea the students will learn and be invited to apply. The idea for the minilesson principle is based on the behaviors in the grade 3 sections of *The Fountas & Pinnell Literacy Continuum*, but the language has been carefully crafted to be accessible and memorable for third graders.

The minilesson principle gives you a clear idea of the concept you will help students construct. The lessons are designed to be inquiry-based because the students need to do the thinking to understand the concept for themselves instead of hearing it stated at the beginning.

Structure of a Writing Minilesson

Minilesson	• Show examples/provide demonstration. • Invite students to talk about their noticings. • Make an anchor chart with clear examples.
Have a Try	• Have students try out what they are learning (usually with a partner).
Summarize and Apply	• Summarize the learning. • Write the minilesson principle on the chart. • Invite students to apply the principle during independent writing time.
Confer	• Move around the room to confer briefly with students.
Share	• Gather students together and invite them to talk about their writing.

Figure 2-4: Once you learn the structure of a writing minilesson, you can create your own minilessons with different examples.

Although we have crafted the language to make it appropriate for the age group, you can shape the language to fit the way your students talk. When you summarize the lesson, be sure to state the principle simply and clearly so that students are certain to understand what it means. State the minilesson principle the same way every time you refer to it.

The Goal of the minilesson is based on behaviors in *The Fountas & Pinnell Literacy Continuum*. Each minilesson is focused on one single goal that leads to a deeper understanding of the larger umbrella concept.

The Rationale is the reason the minilesson is important. It is a brief explanation of how this new learning leads students forward in their writing journey.

Assess Learning is a list of suggestions of specific behaviors and understandings to look for as evidence that students understand and can apply the minilesson concept. Keep this list in mind as you teach.

Minilesson

The **Minilesson** section provides an example of a lesson for teaching the writing minilesson principle. We suggest some precise language and open-ended questions that will keep students engaged and the lesson brief and focused. Effective minilessons, when possible, involve inquiry. That means students actively think about the idea and notice examples in a familiar piece of writing. They construct their understanding from concrete examples so that the learning is meaningful for them.

Create experiences that help students notice things and make their own discoveries. You might, for example, invite students to look at several nonfiction informational books carefully chosen to illustrate the minilesson principle. The students will know these books because they have heard them read aloud and have talked about them. Often, you can use the same books in several writing minilessons to make your teaching efficient. Invite students to talk about what they notice across all the books.

As third graders explore the mentor text examples using your questions and supportive comments as a guide, make the anchor chart with your students' input. From this exploration and the discussion, students come to the minilesson principle. Learning is more powerful and enjoyable for students when they actively search for the meaning, find patterns, talk about their understandings, and share in making the charts. Students need to form networks of understanding around the concepts related to literacy and to be constantly looking for connections for themselves.

A Closer Look at the Umbrella Overview

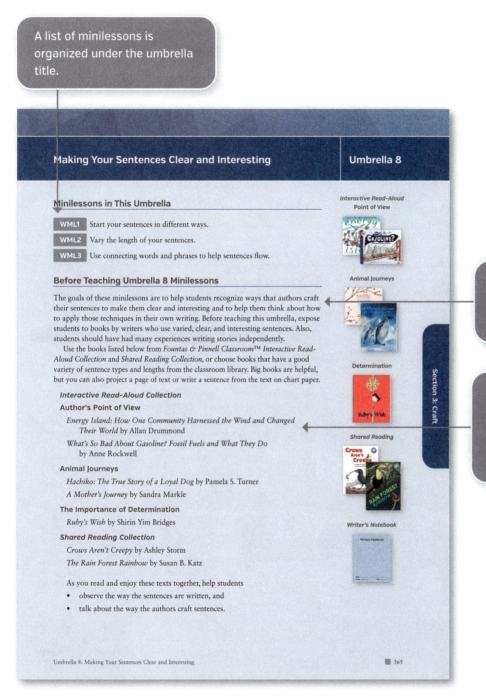

Figure 2-5: Each umbrella is introduced by a page that offers an overview of the umbrella.

A Closer Look at a Writing Minilesson

The Writing Minilesson Principle is a brief statement that describes what students will be invited to learn and apply.

This code identifies this lesson as the third writing minilesson in the eighth umbrella of the Craft section.

Look for these specific behaviors and understandings as you **assess** students' learning after presenting the lesson.

Important vocabulary used in the minilesson is listed.

Precise language is suggested for teaching the lesson.

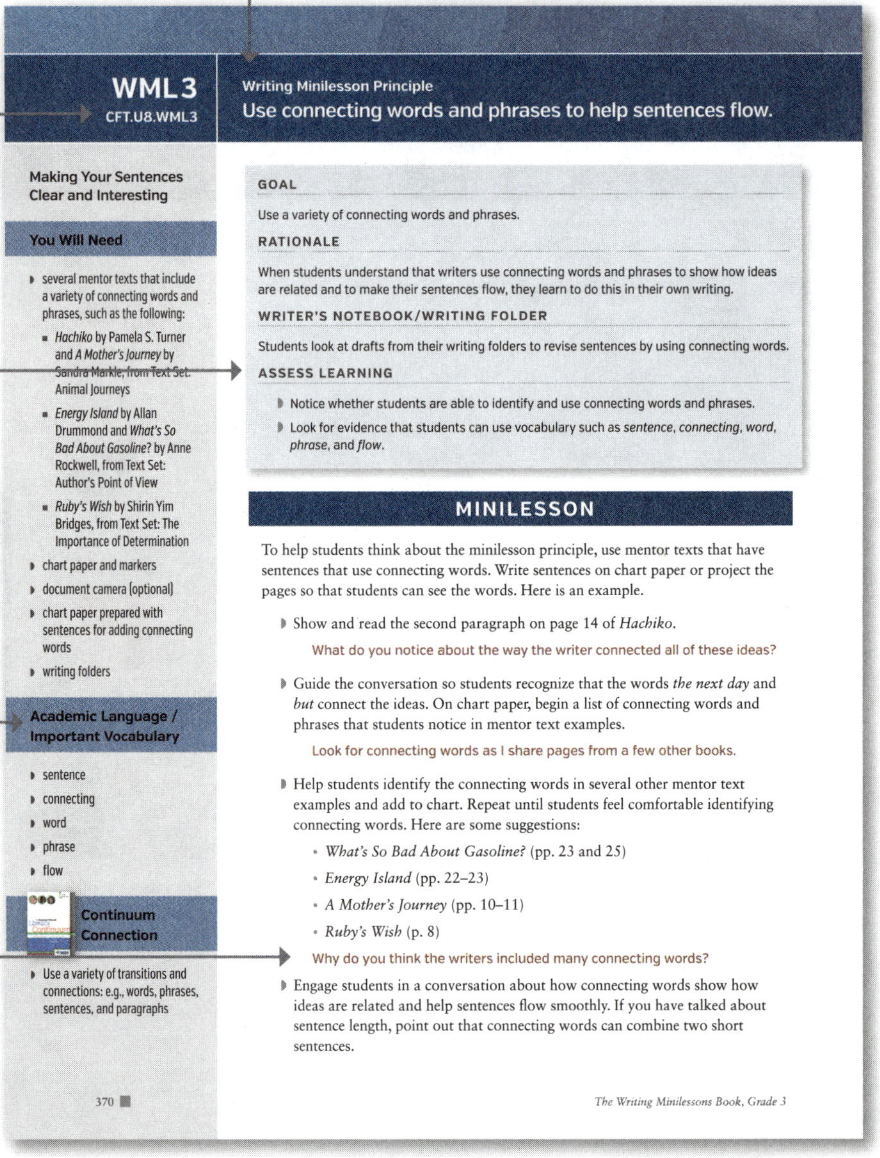

WML3
CFT.U8.WML3

Writing Minilesson Principle
Use connecting words and phrases to help sentences flow.

Making Your Sentences Clear and Interesting

You Will Need

- several mentor texts that include a variety of connecting words and phrases, such as the following:
  - *Hachiko* by Pamela S. Turner and *A Mother's Journey* by Sandra Markle, from Text Set: Animal Journeys
  - *Energy Island* by Allan Drummond and *What's So Bad About Gasoline?* by Anne Rockwell, from Text Set: Author's Point of View
  - *Ruby's Wish* by Shirin Yim Bridges, from Text Set: The Importance of Determination
- chart paper and markers
- document camera (optional)
- chart paper prepared with sentences for adding connecting words
- writing folders

Academic Language / Important Vocabulary

- sentence
- connecting
- word
- phrase
- flow

Continuum Connection

- Use a variety of transitions and connections: e.g., words, phrases, sentences, and paragraphs

GOAL
Use a variety of connecting words and phrases.

RATIONALE
When students understand that writers use connecting words and phrases to show how ideas are related and to make their sentences flow, they learn to do this in their own writing.

WRITER'S NOTEBOOK/WRITING FOLDER
Students look at drafts from their writing folders to revise sentences by using connecting words.

ASSESS LEARNING

- Notice whether students are able to identify and use connecting words and phrases.
- Look for evidence that students can use vocabulary such as *sentence*, *connecting*, *word*, *phrase*, and *flow*.

MINILESSON

To help students think about the minilesson principle, use mentor texts that have sentences that use connecting words. Write sentences on chart paper or project the pages so that students can see the words. Here is an example.

- Show and read the second paragraph on page 14 of *Hachiko*.
  What do you notice about the way the writer connected all of these ideas?
- Guide the conversation so students recognize that the words *the next day* and *but* connect the ideas. On chart paper, begin a list of connecting words and phrases that students notice in mentor text examples.
  Look for connecting words as I share pages from a few other books.
- Help students identify the connecting words in several other mentor text examples and add to chart. Repeat until students feel comfortable identifying connecting words. Here are some suggestions:
  - *What's So Bad About Gasoline?* (pp. 23 and 25)
  - *Energy Island* (pp. 22–23)
  - *A Mother's Journey* (pp. 10–11)
  - *Ruby's Wish* (p. 8)

  Why do you think the writers included many connecting words?
- Engage students in a conversation about how connecting words show how ideas are related and help sentences flow smoothly. If you have talked about sentence length, point out that connecting words can combine two short sentences.

370

The Writing Minilessons Book, Grade 3

Figure 2-6: All the parts of a single writing minilesson are contained on a two-page spread.

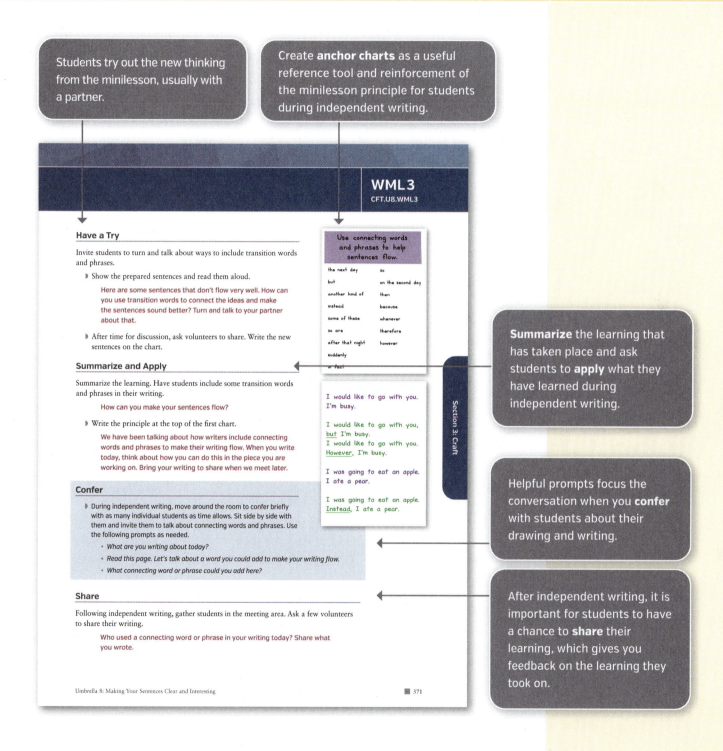

EL CONNECTION

Writing minilessons provide many opportunities for them to express their thoughts in language, both oral and written, and to communicate with others. Students learn more about language when they have opportunities to talk. The inquiry approach found in these lessons invites more student talk than teacher talk, and that can be both a challenge and an opportunity for you as you work with English learners. However, building talk routines, such as turn and talk, into your writing minilessons can be very helpful in providing opportunities for English learners to talk in a safe and supportive way.

When you ask students to think about the minilesson principle across several stories or informational books that they have previously heard read aloud and discussed, they are more engaged and able to participate because they know the stories and informational books and begin to notice important things about writing through them. Using familiar texts, including some writing that you and your students have created together, is particularly important for English learners. When you select examples for a writing minilesson, choose books and other examples that you know were particularly engaging for the English learners in your classroom. Besides choosing accessible, familiar texts, it is important to provide plenty of wait-and-think time. For example, you might say, "Let's think about that for a minute" before calling for responses.

When working with English learners, look for what the students know about the concept instead of focusing on faulty grammar or language errors. Model appropriate language use in your responses, but avoid correcting a child who is attempting to use language to learn it. You might also provide an oral sentence frame to get the student response started, for example, *The illustrator chose* _____ *because* _____. Accept variety in pronunciation and intonation, remembering that the more students speak, read, and write, the more they will take on the understanding of grammatical patterns and the complex intonation patterns that reflect meaning in English.

Keep the minilesson brief. If students show evidence of understanding the concept after one or two examples, move on. You do not have to use every example listed in the minilesson section.

Have a Try

Before students leave the whole group to apply the new thinking during independent writing, give them a chance to try it with a partner or a small group. **Have a Try** is designed to be brief, but it offers you an opportunity to gather information on how well students understand the minilesson goal. In Management lessons, students might quickly practice the new routine that they will be asked to do independently. In the other lessons, students might verbalize how they plan to apply the new understanding to their writing. Add further thinking to the chart after the students have had the chance to try out or talk about their new learning. Have a Try is an important step in reinforcing the minilesson principle and moving the students toward independence.

The Have a Try part of the writing minilesson is particularly important for English learners. Besides providing repetition, it gives English learners a safe place to try out the new idea before sharing it with the whole group. These are a few suggestions for how you might support students during this portion of the lesson:

- Pair students with partners that you know will take turns talking.
- Spend time teaching your students how to turn and talk (see MGT.U2: Working Together in the Classroom). Teach them how to provide wait time for one another, invite the other partner into the conversation, and take turns.
- Provide concrete examples to discuss so that students are clear about what they need to think and talk about. English learners will feel more confident if they are able to talk about a mentor text that they know very well.
- When necessary, provide the oral language structure or language stem for how you want the students to share their ideas. For example, ask them to start with the sentence frame *I noticed the writer* _____ and to rehearse the language structure a few times before turning and talking.
- Provide students with some examples of how something might sound if they were to try something out in their own writing. You might say something like this: "Marco, you are writing about when you fell off your bike. You could start with dialogue. For example, you could write, 'OW! Help me!'"
- Observe partnerships involving English learners and provide support as needed.

Summarize and Apply

This part of the lesson includes two parts: summarizing the learning and applying the learning to independent writing.

The **summary** is a brief but essential part of the lesson. It brings together the learning that has taken place through the inquiry and helps students think about its application and relevance to their own learning. Ask your students to think about the anchor chart and talk about what they have learned. Involve them in stating the minilesson principle. Then write it on the chart. Use simple, clear language to shape the suggestions. Sometimes, you may decide to summarize the new learning to keep the lesson short and allow enough time for the students to apply it independently. Whether you state the principle or share the construction with the students, summarize the learning in a way that they understand and can remember.

After the summary, students **apply** their new understandings to their independent writing. The invitation to try out the new idea must be clear enough for students but "light" enough to allow room for them to have their own ideas for their writing. The application of the minilesson principle should not be thought of as an exercise or task that needs to be forced to fit their writing but instead as an invitation for deeper, more meaningful writing. Certain craft techniques may apply only to particular genres. If students are not currently working on something to which they can apply their new learning, encourage them to revisit an old piece of writing or to experiment with the new idea in their writer's notebooks.

We know that when students first take on new learning, they often want to try out the new learning to the exclusion of some of the other things they have learned. When you teach dialogue, for example, expect to see long stretches of dialogue in their writing. Encourage them to try out new techniques while reminding them about the other things they have learned.

Before students begin independent writing, let them know that they will have an opportunity to share what they have done with the class after independent writing. Third graders love to share!

Confer

EL CONNECTION

While students are busy writing independently, move around the room to observe and **confer** briefly with individuals. Sit side by side with them and invite them to talk about what they are doing. In each minilesson, we offer prompts focused on the umbrella concept and worded in clear, direct language. Using direct language can be particularly supportive for English learners because it allows them to focus on the meaning without having to work through the extra talk that we often use in our everyday conversations. Occasionally you will see sentence frames to support English learners in both their talk and their writing.

If a student is working on something that does not fit with the minilesson principle, do not feel limited to the language in this section. Respond to the student in a sincere and enthusiastic way. Remember that the invitation to apply the new learning can be extended another time. This will not be the only opportunity.

General prompts, such as the following, are provided to get students talking so that you can listen carefully to the thinking behind the writing (in using the word *writing* we include drawing). Be sure to let students do most of the talking. The one who does the talking does the learning!

- *How is your writing going?*
- *How can I help you with your writing?*

- *What do you think about this piece of writing?*
- *What do you want to do next in your writing?*
- *What is the best part of your writing (book) so far?*
- *Is any part of your writing (book) still confusing for the reader?*
- *What would you like to do with this writing (book) when it is finished?*

Observational notes will help you understand how each writer is progressing and provide purposeful, customized instruction every time you talk with students about their writing (Figure 2-7). You can use your notes to plan the content of future minilessons. You can also take pictures of, scan, or make copies of key pieces to discuss with families.

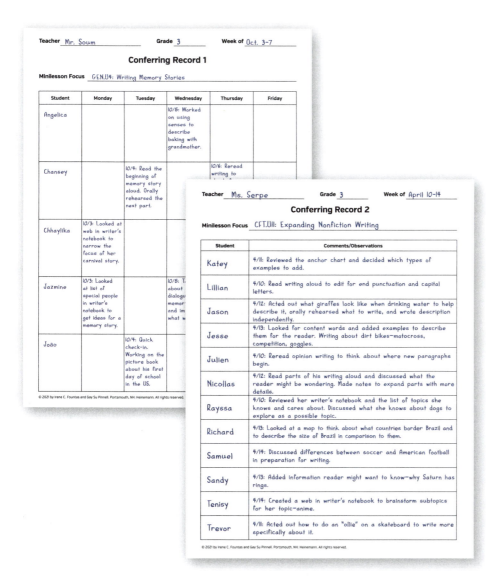

Figure 2-7: Choose one of these downloadable forms to record your observations of students' behaviors and understandings. Visit **fp.pub/resources** to download these and all other online resources.

Chapter 2: What Is a Writing Minilesson?

Share

At the end of independent writing, gather your students together for the opportunity to **share** their learning with the entire group. During group share, you can revisit, expand, and deepen understanding of the minilesson's goal as well as assess learning. Often, students are invited to bring their drawing and writing to share with the class and to explain how they tried out the minilesson principle. As you observe and talk to students during independent writing time, plan how to share by assessing how many students tried the new learning in their writing. If only a few students were able to apply the minilesson principle to their writing, you might ask those students to share with the whole group. However, if you observe most of the class applying the principle, you might have them share in pairs or small groups.

You might also consider inviting students to choose what to share about their writing instead of connecting back to the minilesson principle. For example, one student might share a detail added to make an illustration more interesting. Another might share a letter she is writing to the principal. Another might read his story to the class.

EL CONNECTION

Share time is a wonderful way to bring the community of learners back together to expand their understandings of writing and of each other as well as to celebrate their new attempts at writing. There are some particular accommodations to support English learners during the time for sharing:

- Have students share in pairs before sharing with the group.
- While conferring, help them rehearse the language structure they might use to share their drawing and writing with the class.

Teach the entire class respectful ways to listen to peers and model how to give their peers time to express their thoughts. Many of the minilessons in the Management section will be useful for developing a peaceful, safe, and supportive community of writers.

A Closer Look at the Umbrella Wrap-Up

Following the minilessons in each umbrella, you will see the final umbrella page, which includes a section for assessing what students have learned and a section for extending the learning.

Assessment

The last page of each umbrella, shown in Figure 2-8, provides questions to help you **assess** the learning that has taken place through the entire umbrella. The information you gain from observing what the students can already do, almost do, and not yet do will help inform the selection of the next umbrella

A Closer Look at the Umbrella Wrap-Up

Umbrella 8 — Making Your Sentences Clear and Interesting

Assessment

After you have taught the minilessons in this umbrella, observe students in a variety of classroom activities. Use *The Fountas & Pinnell Literacy Continuum* to notice, teach for, and support students' learning as you observe their attempts at writing.

- What evidence do you have of students' new understandings related to writing sentences?
  - Can students explain why writers start sentences in different ways, vary sentence lengths, and use connecting words?
  - Do they attempt to vary sentences in their own writing?
  - Are they using vocabulary such as *sentences*, *clear*, *interesting*, *start*, *different*, *vary*, *length*, *connecting*, *word*, *phrase*, and *flow*?
- In what ways, beyond the scope of this umbrella, are students' reading and writing behaviors showing an understanding of making writing clear and interesting?
  - Are students looking for ways to show voice in their writing?
  - Do they use varied word choice to make their writing more powerful?

Use your observations to determine the next umbrella you will teach. You may also consult Suggested Sequence of Lessons (pp. 605–622) for guidance.

EXTENSIONS FOR MAKING YOUR SENTENCES CLEAR AND INTERESTING

- Use shared writing to create a song or a chant that uses sentences with varying lengths. Engage in conversation about how the rhythm and beat are affected by sentence length.
- Work with students in small groups to share writing samples and talk about different ways the sentences could be written to make the writing more interesting.
- If you are using *The Reading Minilessons Book, Grade 3* (Fountas and Pinnell 2019) you may choose to teach LA.U9: Analyzing the Writer's Craft.

The Writing Minilessons Book, Grade 3 — 372

> Gain important information by **assessing** what students have learned as they apply and share their learning of the minilesson principles. Observe and then follow up with individuals in conferences or in small groups in guided writing.

> Optional suggestions are provided for **extending** the learning of the umbrella over time or in other contexts.

Figure 2-8: The final page of each umbrella offers suggestions for assessing the learning and ideas for extending the learning.

you teach (see Chapter 6 for more information about assessment and the selection of umbrellas).

Extensions for the Umbrella

Each umbrella ends with several suggestions for **extending** the learning of the umbrella. Sometimes the suggestion is to repeat a minilesson with different examples. Third graders will need to experience some of the concepts more than once before they are able to transfer actions to their independent writing. Other times, students will be able to extend the learning beyond the scope of the umbrella.

Effective Writing Minilessons

The goal of all writing minilessons is to help students think and act like writers and illustrators as they build their capacity for independent writing

Figure 2-9: Characteristics of effective minilessons

Effective Writing Minilessons . . .

- are based on a **writing principle** that is important to teach to third graders
- are based on a **goal** that makes the teaching meaningful
- are **relevant to the specific needs of students** so that your teaching connects with the learners
- are very **brief, concise, and to the point**
- use **clear and specific language** to avoid talk that clutters learning
- stay **focused on a single idea** so students can apply the learning and build on it day after day
- use an **inquiry approach** whenever possible to support active, constructive learning
- often include **shared, high-quality mentor texts** that can be used as examples
- are **well paced** to engage and hold students' interest
- are **grouped into umbrellas** to foster depth in thinking and coherence across lessons
- **usually build one understanding on another** across several days instead of single isolated lessons
- provide time for students to **"try out" the new concept** before they are invited to try it independently
- engage students in **summarizing the new learning and applying it to their own writing**
- build **important vocabulary** appropriate for third graders
- help students **become better artists and writers**
- **foster community** through the development of shared language
- **can be assessed** as you observe students engaged in authentic writing
- **help students understand what they are learning** how to do as artists and writers

The Writing Minilessons Book, Grade 3

and drawing across the year. Whether you are teaching lessons about routines, genre, craft, conventions, or the writing process, the characteristics of effective minilessons, listed in Figure 2-9, apply.

Writing minilessons can be used to teach anything from a new routine to a new genre to a new craft move and more. Teach a writing minilesson whenever you see an opportunity to nudge students forward as writers and illustrators.

Chapter 3 | Minilessons for Building a Community: Management

> *We need a caring classroom community in which multiple perspectives are developed and used to think critically and expand learning. We need a community in which children come to appreciate the value of different perspectives for their own development, in which they recognize changes in their own and others' thinking and that difference is the source for the change.*
>
> —Peter Johnston

INDIVIDUALS LEARN BETTER AND HAVE more fun when they have some routines for working safely and responsibly. The lessons in Section 1: Management establish these routines. Students learn how to

- listen,
- take turns,
- show kindness to one another,
- draw and write independently,
- share their writing,
- take care of classroom materials,

- use their writing folder resources, and
- use and return materials.

They become independent problem-solvers who can work and play as members of a community.

Building a Community of Writers

Writers need to feel valued and included in a community whose members have learned to trust one another with their stories. The minilessons in the Management section are designed to help students build this trust and learn to include one another in discussions and play. The first lesson in MGT.U1: Building Community Through Oral Storytelling (WML1: Get to know your classmates) sets the tone for building this community. As students share stories about who they are, where their families come from, what languages they speak, what foods they eat, and what activities they enjoy, they begin to explore their identities and learn about the identities of others. Self-identity influences the way an individual reads and writes; it impacts the perspective one brings to these literacy experiences. When we celebrate students' unique identities and perspectives, we teach students to value and include one another. This is one of the reasons the share time at the end of independent writing is so important. This time of sharing inspires writing ideas, but it does so much more. It provides a time to celebrate writing and carves out space to celebrate each writer in the classroom community.

Create a Peaceful Atmosphere

The minilessons in the Management section will help you establish a classroom environment in which students are confident, self-determined, and kind and in which every person's identity is valued. The lessons are designed to contribute to peaceful activity and shared responsibility. Through the minilessons in MGT.U2: Working Together in the Classroom, students learn how to use their words and actions to show respect to one another. They also learn to keep supplies in order, help others, use the appropriate voice level for an activity, and problem-solve independently (Figure 3-1).

All of these minilessons contribute to an overall tone of respect in every classroom activity. They are designed to help you establish the atmosphere you want. Everything in the classroom reflects the students who work there; it is their home for the year.

Teach the minilessons in MGT.U2 in the order that fits your class needs, or consult the Suggested Sequence of Lessons (pp. 605–622). You may need to reteach some of these lessons because as the year goes on you will be

Figure 3-1: Characteristics of a peaceful atmosphere for the community of readers and writers

working in a more complex way. A schedule change or other disruption in classroom operations might prompt a refresher minilesson. Any problem in your classroom should be addressed through minilessons that focus on building a community of learners.

Design the Physical Space

In addition to creating a peaceful atmosphere, prepare the physical space in a way to provide the best support for learning (Figure 3-2). Each umbrella in Section 1: Management will help your third graders become acquainted with the routines of the classroom and help them feel secure and at home. Make sure that the classroom has the following qualities.

> **Welcoming and Inviting.** Pleasing colors and a variety of furniture will help. There is no need for commercially published posters or slogans, except for standard references such as the Consonant Cluster Linking Chart (available in online resources) or colorful poetry posters. The room can be filled with the work that the students have produced beginning on day one, some of it in languages other than English. They should see signs of their learning everywhere—shared writing, charts, drawings of various kinds, and their names. Be sure that your students'

Figure 3-2: In this meeting area, the teacher has access to everything she needs for interactive read-aloud, shared reading, and minilessons, and the students have plenty of room to sit comfortably.

names are at various places in the room—on desks or tables, on a jobs chart, and on some of the charts that you will make in the minilessons. A wall of framed students' photographs and self-portraits sends the clear message that this classroom belongs to them and celebrates their unique identities. The classroom library should be as inviting as a bookstore or a library. Place books in baskets and tubs on shelves to make the front covers of books visible and accessible for easy browsing. Clearly label the supplies in the writing center so students can see the materials that are available and can access them and return them independently (Figure 3-3). Better yet, have students make labels independently or with you during shared or independent writing. Third graders also love to be involved in the naming of the different classroom areas so they truly feel like they have ownership of the classroom.

▶ **Organized for Easy Use.** The first thing you might want to do is to take out everything you do not need. Clutter increases stress and noise. Using scattered and hard-to-find materials increases the students' dependence on you. Consider keeping supplies for reading, writing, and word study in designated areas. The writing center might be used to store paper, highlighters, drawing materials, staplers, etc. Over the course of the year, introduce different kinds of media into this space so students can experiment with collage, 3D objects, and materials that have different textures.

Figure 3-3: All the materials in the writing center are organized. Each kind of material is kept in a separate, labeled container.

In the first few days of school, students learn how to get supplies and return supplies. Some teachers choose to have caddies at tables instead of keeping supplies on a shelf in the writing center so that students can spread out and get started right away.

Work areas are clearly organized with necessary, labeled materials and nothing else. Labels with pictures and words as well as an arrow pointing to where the items belong show students exactly what goes where (Figure 3-4).

▸ **Designed for Whole-Group, Small-Group, and Individual Instruction.** Writing minilessons are generally provided as whole-class instruction and typically take place at an easel in a meeting space. The space is comfortable and large enough for all students to sit as a group or in a circle. It will be helpful to have a colorful rug that helps students find an individual space to sit without crowding one another. Some teachers mark the rug with tape to help students space appropriately. You might also use a rug that delineates individual spaces with colors, lines, or shapes. The meeting space is next to the classroom library so that books are displayed and handy. The teacher usually has a larger chair or seat next to an easel or two so that he can display the mentor texts,

Figure 3-4: A label on the shelf helps students know where to return materials.

Chapter 3: Minilessons for Building a Community: Management

make anchor charts, do shared or interactive writing, or place big books for shared reading. This space is available for all whole-group instruction; for example, the students come back to it for group share. In addition to the group meeting space, assign tables and spaces in the classroom for small-group writing instruction. Use low shelving and furniture to define and separate learning areas and to create storage opportunities. Third graders need tables and spaces throughout the classroom where they can work independently and where you can easily set a chair next to a student for a brief writing conference.

- **Respectful of personal space.** Third-grade students need a place to keep a personal box, including items such as a writer's notebook, writing folder, independent reading book, and reader's notebook. Students can keep these boxes on their individual desks, or you can distribute them around the room to avoid traffic jams when students retrieve them. If students make their own poetry anthologies (see GEN.U9: Making Poetry Anthologies), they decorate them and place them face out on a rack for easy retrieval. Artifacts like these add considerably to the aesthetic quality of the classroom.

Establish Independent Writing

The final two umbrellas in the Management section will help you establish a productive and constructive independent writing time with your third graders. The minilessons will help them learn what to do and what tools to use during independent writing time.

At the beginning of the year, keep the writing time short (you may even start with just fifteen minutes of independent writing time) so they can feel successful right away. Add a few minutes every day until they are able to sustain writing for thirty to forty minutes. Involve students in setting goals for stretching their writing time and celebrate each time you reach them as a class. You will soon have them begging for more time to do this important work. Third graders also begin to see the value of working on a piece of writing over time. Through this umbrella, they also learn that writers receive feedback and guidance from other writers. They learn the routines for talking productively with a teacher and their classmates about their writing.

Independent Writing Time

Through the minilessons in MGT.U3: Establishing Independent Writing, students learn the guidelines for independent writing—the routines needed to be independent and productive. They learn to get started with their writing quickly and quietly, to increase their stamina, and to become efficient in storing their writing and materials at the end of writing time. They learn how to use various writing tools to support their writing, such as a writer's notebook, a writing folder, and various kinds of paper. Students also learn that writers are never finished. They learn that when they finish making a book or working on a piece of writing, they can start another, work in their writer's notebooks, or work on a different writing project in their writing folders.

Writing Tools

Students will use three main tools during independent writing: writer's notebook, writing folder, and hanging file. The writer's notebook and the writing folder are the primary tools.

- Writer's notebook—a place to collect ideas for writing and try out new learning about the craft of writing and drawing each day
- Writing folder—a two-pocket folder with brads in the middle for fastening resources; a place to store writing that is in progress
- Hanging file in a box or crate—a place to keep finished writing projects (Figure 3-5)

Writer's Notebook Lessons in the Management section establish the routines for when to use and how to manage writer's notebooks. Because the writer's notebook is used throughout the writing process, minilessons about introducing and using it are in Section 5: Writing Process. In-depth information about writer's notebooks as well as a description of the minilessons that support using writer's notebooks with third graders begin on page 84 of this book.

Figure 3-5: The main writing tools for students to use during independent writing time are a writer's notebook and a writing folder. A hanging file is used to store finished writing projects.

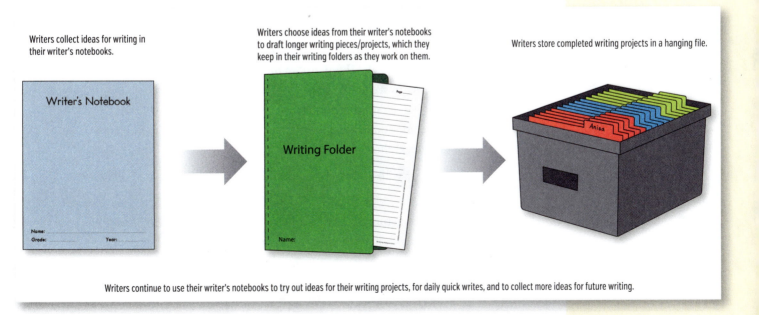

Writers collect ideas for writing in their writer's notebooks.

Writers choose ideas from their writer's notebooks to draft longer writing pieces/projects, which they keep in their writing folders as they work on them.

Writers store completed writing projects in a hanging file.

Writers continue to use their writer's notebooks to try out ideas for their writing projects, for daily quick writes, and to collect more ideas for future writing.

Chapter 3: Minilessons for Building a Community: Management

Writing Folder The writing folder is a place to keep writing projects—drafts of books and other writing pieces on which students are working outside of their writer's notebooks. When students learn about making picture books, for example, they will take an idea out of the writer's notebook, begin a draft of the book, and keep the draft in the writing folder. As they develop this writing piece, they use the writer's notebook to try out ideas and craft moves that they may or may not use in the draft.

We suggest using folders with a pocket on each side and fasteners in the middle so you can secure resources for students to use during independent writing. For efficiency, fasten all the writing folder resources inside students' writing folders, and then they will be ready for you to teach the minilesson for how to use each one. The writing folders can be stored in students' personal boxes along with other literacy resources, such as an independent reading book, a reader's notebook, a writer's notebook, and a word study folder.

Hanging File As students finish a writing project, have them move it to the hanging file kept in a filing cabinet or in crates placed in the four corners of the room to minimize traffic. Using files in four colors will help students locate their files more easily, as will making sure students' names are visible on file tabs. This allows students to have their finished writing in one place for periodic reflection on their growth as writers. Occasionally, you might want to ask them to write a reflection about their writing and staple the reflection to the piece of writing. The collection of finished writing will help you and your students see their growth over time and will help you communicate that growth during conferences with students and with their parents or caregivers.

Paper Choices

Having a choice of paper gives students a chance to envision how they want their writing to look. Third graders often use draft paper, which provides space for revising and editing, and then choose other types of paper when publishing. In MGT.U3.WML3 (Choose the paper for your writing projects), you teach students to see possibilities for how different sizes, colors, and shapes of paper can be used. We suggest offering a wide variety of paper, which might include some of the following choices (available as templates in the online resources) throughout the year.

- Draft paper with dots in the margin to encourage writing on every other line
- Paper with picture boxes and lines in varying formats (e.g., picture box on the top with lines on the bottom or picture box on the side with wrapping lines)

- Paper in landscape and portrait layouts that can be stapled into booklets
- Paper formatted for text features (e.g., sidebar, table of contents, and materials list)
- Author page
- Dedication page
- Letter format

When you give students the ability to choose from a variety of paper for their writing projects, you teach them to make important decisions as writers and illustrators.

Writing Folder Resources

Besides providing a place for students to keep ongoing writing projects, writing folders include important resources for revising and proofreading and for helping students view themselves as writers. MGT.U4: Introducing the Writing Folder addresses these resources. Available for downloading from the online resources, the writing folder resources are the following:

- Genres and Forms at a Glance (types of writing for third grade)
- My Writing Projects (a document to record writing projects)
- What I Have Learned How to Do as a Writer and Illustrator (a place for students to record what they have learned as writers)
- My Writing Goals (a place for students to write how they will stretch themselves as writers)
- Commonly Misspelled Words
- Revising Checklist
- Proofreading Checklist

The resources give students agency and promote their independence by giving them tools for sustaining their own writing. Introduce the resources over time so that students learn how to best use each one. For example, you might choose to introduce the revising and proofreading checklists after teaching minilessons in the Writing Process section about revising and editing.

The writing folder resource titled My Writing Projects (Figure 3-6) helps students reflect on their writing lives. The record of finished writing pieces gives individual writers a sense of accomplishment and provides a way for you and your students to notice patterns in their writing choices. Use this record to help your writers reflect during writing conferences: Are there different kinds of writing they would like to try? Are they choosing topics

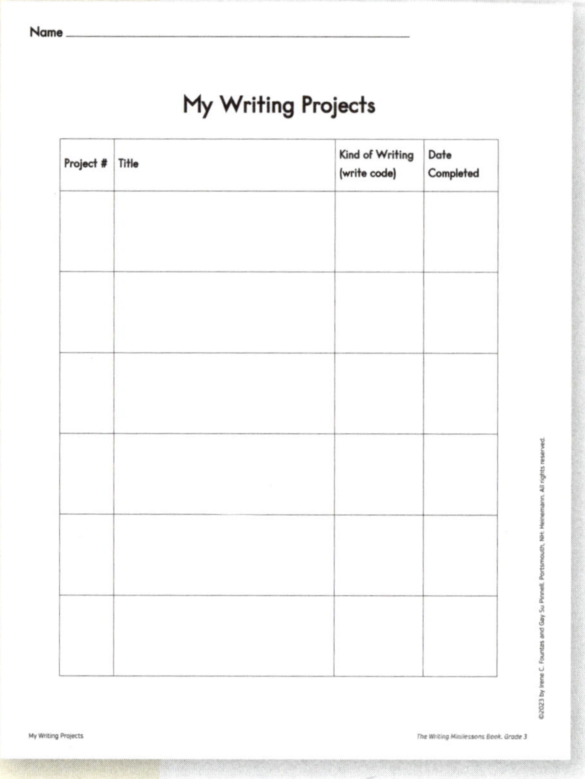
Name ____________________

My Writing Projects

Project #	Title	Kind of Writing (write code)	Date Completed

My Writing Projects   *The Writing Minilessons Book, Grade 3*

Figure 3-6: Students use this template to record the title, genre, and completion date of their writing projects. All writing folder resources are available from **fp.pub/resources**.

they care about? Is there a way to write about the same topic in a different way? It can help them think about what they have learned as writers and set goals for future writing.

Management minilessons help students navigate these resources, manage the tools of writing, and understand the routines that create a productive community of writers. Use the structure of these lessons to support any routine you think would benefit the writers in your classroom.

Chapter 4 : Minilessons for Studying Genres and Forms of Writing

Genre study is where we put all of our reading-like-a-writer skills together. When we read like writers for genre, we read across a set of mentor texts and notice many categories of writerly moves including ideas (what writers generally write about in that genre) and also craft and structure (how they write about it).

—Allison Marchetti and Rebekah O'Dell

EXPOSING STUDENTS TO DIFFERENT GENRES, forms, and modes of writing broadens their vision for what writing can be. The minilessons in the Genres and Forms section use inquiry and mentor texts to help students understand the characteristics of different genres and how to use that knowledge when they write. Through the umbrellas in this section, students are also exposed to various forms of writing and composition. Besides learning how to write in the genres of memory story, realistic fiction, opinion writing, informational text, and procedural text, students also learn how to write in various forms and modes. They learn to make picture books, write poems, design multimedia presentations, write letters, and think about different ways to communicate a persuasive message (e.g., making bumper stickers, designing posters, writing songs, making slogans for T-shirts or hats).

It is always helpful for students to read and study a genre either before or while writing in it. If you have *Fountas & Pinnell Classroom™ Interactive Read-Aloud Collection* and/or *The Reading Minilessons Book, Grade 3*, use the genre study text sets and the minilesson umbrellas that address genre study to immerse students within a genre and to help them define the genre in their own words. The genre study process, outlined in both the *Interactive Read-Aloud Collection* lessons and *The Reading Minilessons Book, Grade 3*, is designed to help students develop a deep understanding of the characteristics of genres as readers. We have written extensively about this topic and process in our book *Genre Study: Teaching with Fiction and Nonfiction Books* (Fountas and Pinnell 2012).

It is important for students to be exposed to a variety of genres as both readers and writers, and we hope the writing minilesson umbrellas in the Genres and Forms section will further extend their genre understandings. However, we caution you to avoid jumping directly from one genre study to another. Students need time to experiment with different forms of writing. They also need time to choose their own genres based on their purpose and audience. As Ralph Fletcher points out in his book *Joy Write: Cultivating High-Impact, Low-Stakes Writing* (2017), writers need time to play with writing. The lessons in the genre umbrellas are designed to expose students to different characteristics of a genre and offer ways for them to think about writing in them. They are not meant to take students through a rigid sequence of steps for writing in that genre. Writers each have their individual ways of working on writing. You will want to make sure you respect a student's own writing process and topic choices while helping them develop new genre understandings.

Third Graders Love to Make Books

Bookmaking is a powerful way for students to explore different genres and to bring together all their important literacy experiences. As students begin to write longer, more complex texts, it is important for them to continue to learn how to engage in forms of composition that include a visual element. Visual composition and the combination of graphics and print have become increasingly important over time as people engage in social media—reading memes, gaining information from infographics, and telling stories through pictures. Picture books, including comic books, are an excellent way for third graders to think deeply about how print and graphics work together because they are so familiar with them. Matt Glover (2009) said it well:

> The reason for making books is simple. Books are what children have the greatest vision for, and having a clear vision for what you are making is important in any act of composition. (13)

Invite your students to make their own books, just like the authors of the books they love (Figure 4-1). The act of making picture books benefits you and the students in lots of ways.

- Third graders see themselves as authors, illustrators, and readers.
- They develop feelings of independence and accomplishment at having created something that is uniquely theirs.
- They try out a larger range of craft techniques, such as adding meaning through illustrations, incorporating text features (e.g., sidebars and diagrams), and organizing their ideas across pages or sections.
- They build stamina by working on a book over several days.
- Writing and reading reinforce one another, so as students make their own books, they become more aware of the decisions that authors and illustrators make in their books.
- Students expand their understanding about print, illustrations, and text structure.

Figure 4-1: Mia shows her understanding of books with her own informational book about a favorite topic, dogs. In these excerpts from her book, she included features she has seen in nonfiction books: a cover, a table of contents, pictures with labels, and headings.

Cover

Table of Contents

Introduction
Dogs are really good pets. There are over 100 types of dogs you can choose from. Dogs are good pets because some can be playful and you can have a ton of fun with them. But, if you want a dog but you don't think you have time to play with them or don't want a dog that is playful, there are some that you can just pet, and they will sleep. I hope if you get a dog, you will love it, enjoy it and be happy you got a dog. I hope you learn about dogs in this book. So, let's get started.

How to Take Care of a Dog
When you take care of a dog, you need to walk a dog at least once or twice a week. You have to feed a dog two times a day. One at night, one in the morning. You can give them some treats too.

Chapter 4: Minilessons for Studying Genres and Forms of Writing

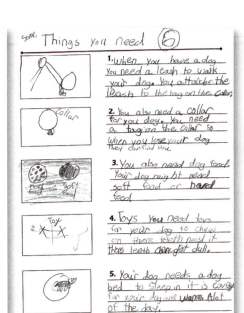

Some Types of Dogs
When you choose a dog, there are a ton of different choices. Some of them are: Westie, Wheaton Terriers, Golden Retrievers, Collie, Bernese Mountain Dog, and more. If you want a small dog, some good dogs for you would be: Westie, Chihuahua, Pug and more. If you want a dog that is medium, you might want: Wheaton Terrier, Bernese Mountain Dog, Golden Retriever, there are more too. There are also big dogs but I am not going to name them. You will be able to find a dog just right for you.

Some Things You Need
1. When you have a dog, you need a leash to walk your dog. You attach the leash to the tag on the collar.

2. You also need a collar for your dog. You need a tag on the collar so when you lose your dog, they can find you.

3. You also need dog food. Your dog might need soft food or hard food.

4. Toys. You need toys for your dog to chew on. Their teeth need it. Their teeth can get dull.

5. Your dog needs a dog bed to sleep in. It is comfy for your dog and warm a lot of the day.

Food
There are two types of food. Soft food is for puppies that don't have strong teeth or dogs that are too old. Hard food might hurt their teeth so they need soft food. Hard food is food that you put a little water in and your dog will eat it. The hard food would feel hard, not soft. It will be in a circle. You will choose a good type of food.

▸ The books they write show evidence of what they know about drawing and writing, and you can use that information to decide what they need to learn next.

▸ They learn to use book and print features such as about the author pages, dedications, and acknowledgments.

The minilessons in the Genres and Forms umbrella GEN.U12: Making Picture Books invites students to study the qualities of picture books before they make their own. Other umbrellas provide opportunities for them to try making specific kinds of books. In GEN.U6: Making Informational Books, students study the qualities of expository nonfiction picture books. When you teach GEN.U2: Writing Procedural Texts, GEN.U4: Writing Memory Stories, or GEN.U5: Writing Realistic Fiction Stories, offer students the choice to make these genres in the form of a picture book.

Third Graders Learn All About Writing Craft Through Poetry

When you teach students to read and write poetry, they learn craft moves that cross over all genres and forms. They learn how to be precise and efficient in their language, how to create sensory images, how to use figurative language, and how to evoke emotion in a reader. We have written previously that, in a way, everything writers need to know about reading and writing exists within a poem. Third graders benefit from learning to write poetry because they

- become aware of and appreciate the sound and imagery of language,
- reflect on themselves and the world in new ways,
- learn to use words, sounds, and rhythm in unique, creative ways,
- become able to capture the essence of a message or image with a sparse amount of language.

We recommend that you integrate poetry throughout the school year instead of teaching poetry for just a few weeks as part of a unit. Some teachers reserve one day a week or one week a month during writers' or readers' workshop time to hold a poetry workshop (Figure 4-2). During this time, students focus on reading poetry, responding to poetry in words or images, and writing and illustrating their own poetry.

We also recommend you help your students develop personal poetry books or anthologies. In them, they collect poems they love, respond to

Figure 4-2: Structure of poetry workshop

Structure of Poetry Workshop

Poet Talk	• Offer advice from a poet or tell about a poet's life.
Poetry Read-Aloud and Writing Minilesson	• Read a poem aloud and teach a minilesson that can be applied to poetry. • Besides the minilessons dedicated to poetry, there are several lessons in the Craft and Writing Process sections that can be taught or retaught with poetry as the focus.
Poetry Projects and Poetry Centers	• Confer with students as they participate in reading, writing, and responding to poems.
Poetry Share	• Allow time for students to share poems they have written or memorized.

Chapter 4: Minilessons for Studying Genres and Forms of Writing

poetry through drawing and writing, and write their own poetry. The first minilesson in GEN.U9: Making Poetry Anthologies introduces the idea to students and invites them to decorate the front covers and create tables of contents (Figure 4-3). Providing students with multiple ways to respond, including with art, makes the poetry experience more meaningful and joyful. Third graders love making watercolor paintings or collages in response to poems they have read or to ones they have written. Encourage them to perform poems using movement and their voices. When they have opportunities to respond to poetry authentically, they learn more about the characteristics of poetry and how to write it themselves.

Whether students work on poetry during poetry workshop or writers' workshop, they are involved in the same writing process they go through when writing prose (Figure 4-4):

- They look at mentor texts (poems).
- They apply what they learn in minilessons.
- They collect ideas for poetry topics in a writer's notebook.
- They draft, revise, and edit their poems.
- They create art to accompany their poems.

Figure 4-3: Students are invited to decorate the front cover of their poetry anthologies and to create a table of contents that lists both their own poems and the poems of published writers.

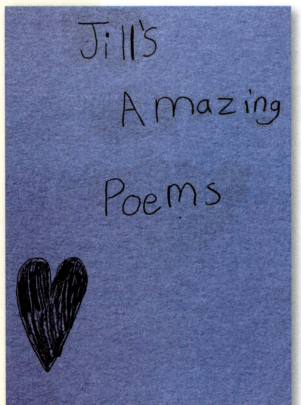

Some teachers choose to create poetry centers for their poetry workshop.

- Consider setting up a center to explore memorable words and phrases from books and poems. Encourage students to write their own poems using the words and phrases as inspiration. Invite them to cut out words from magazines or newspapers and make poems out of them by gluing them in a poetry book or writer's notebook.

- Set up a poetry window with clipboards, colored pencils, etc. Outline a portion of the window so students can look through and describe or sketch what they see. Invite them to write poems about the things they see through the poetry window.

- Create an illustration or art center where students have access to a variety of art media to illustrate poems they have read or written.

For more ideas, we highly recommend *Awakening the Heart: Exploring Poetry in Elementary and Middle School* (Heard 1999), *A Place for Wonder: Reading and Writing Nonfiction in the Primary Grades* (Heard and McDonough 2009), and *Poems Are Teachers: How Studying Poetry Strengthens Writing in All Genres* (VanDerwater 2018). Create a culture of poetry in your school: post poems meaningfully on the walls of the school (e.g., poems about food around the cafeteria doors or poems about water around sinks and water fountains), designate a poetry gallery where you

Figure 4-4: CK wrote different kinds of poems in his poetry anthology. He experimented with the use of metaphor in his poem "Awesome." He also loves to write shape, or concrete, poems.

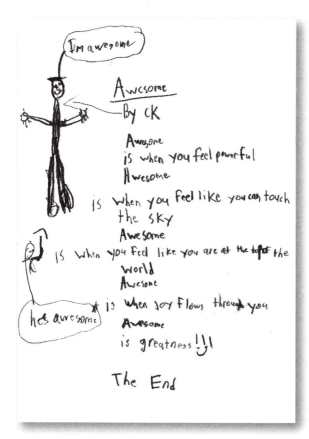
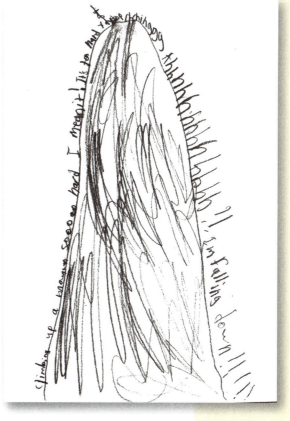

Chapter 4: Minilessons for Studying Genres and Forms of Writing

invite students to add mentor poems as well as their own poems, create schoolwide poetry readings, or share a poem of the day as part of morning announcements. When you immerse students in poetry, you will see the results in their writing across genres.

Third Graders Enjoy Sharing Their Opinions

Third graders have strong opinions about the books they read, their hobbies and interests, their school, and their world. The umbrellas dedicated to opinion and persuasive writing provide students with the tools to express these opinions in a variety of ways.

Opinion writing is embedded in writing across the curriculum. Writing about reading, in particular, is an accessible way for students to start writing about their opinions in the early grades. They share books they love and list reasons for why they love them. They write letters stating their opinions about characters, messages, illustrations, and writing styles. They create their own book talks, sharing why their audience might be interested in reading a certain book. Several minilessons in *The Reading Minilessons Books, Grade 3*, are designed to support students in writing their opinions about their reading.

Writing minilessons build on experiences students have had writing their opinions about books. In GEN.U7: Exploring Opinion Writing, students learn how to choose topics they have genuine opinions about, how to effectively introduce and state their opinions, how to provide supportive examples for their opinions, and how to conclude their opinion writing in meaningful ways.

Opinion writing sets the stage for persuasive writing but is slightly different. In opinion writing, the ultimate goal is not always to convince someone to agree with an opinion or to take action, as it is in persuasive writing. The purpose is simply to share a point of view and the reasons for it and leave it up to the audience to use this information any way they want. Think about movie or book reviews—critics write what they think about a piece, and the audience decides whether to watch the movie or read the book. Letters to the editor and online reviews are similar. The writers offer opinions to inform the audience about an issue or about something they have experienced or purchased but don't necessarily try to convince the reader to think the same way. In some cases, the purpose of an opinion piece is simply to start a conversation. That being said, we have all read reviews that shout, "Do not buy this product!" or letters to the editor that call for citizens to take action. It is important to note that while opinion writing does not have to have this persuasive quality, it sometimes does.

The lines between opinion writing and persuasive writing are often blurred, and it is our job to help students understand that people write about their opinions in many different ways. It is not productive to create strict boundaries between opinion and persuasive writing. There may be times that a writer includes some persuasive techniques in an opinion piece. What *is* important for third graders to understand is that they can share their opinions and provide reasons for their thinking to an audience. As they hone their purpose for writing their opinion, they may decide to use language and strong evidence to persuade their audience. Their writing might be anywhere along the continuum between opinion and persuasive writing. In grade four, students will learn specifically how to write persuasive texts by writing persuasive essays, learning techniques for how to convince or persuade their audience to embrace an opinion or to act in some way. Their experiences with opinion and persuasive writing establish a foundation for learning argumentative writing, which they begin exploring in grades five and six. In argumentative writing, students learn how to consider both sides of a debated topic, to address counterpoints, and to use craft techniques to persuade people on the opposing side of an issue using well-researched evidence. Figure 4-5 shows the delineation between these different forms of writing and the blurred lines between them.

These different forms of writing, particularly opinion writing, often appear on state exams. Learning to write about their own opinions will help students write opinions to satisfy certain test prompts. GEN.U3: Writing to a Prompt: Getting Ready for Test Writing helps students learn how to respond to a prompt but certainly overlaps with opinion writing in terms of teaching students to state a claim and provide evidence for their thinking. Giving students time and space to develop authentic opinions about topics they care about prepares them to not only share their opinions in writing but also to engage in thoughtful and meaningful discussion across the curriculum.

Opinion Writing	Persuasive Writing	Argumentative Writing
A writer states an opinion for the purpose of informing others of a particular perspective. The writer supports the opinion with reasons for a point of view and may include supporting details or facts. An opinion piece may serve the purpose of beginning a conversation.	A writer states an opinion for the purpose of convincing others to take a particular point of view. The writer attempts to provide compelling reasons for the point of view and includes details or facts to support it. The writer might also include an emotional appeal to persuade the reader.	A writer takes one side of a clearly debatable issue with the purpose of convincing others to join a side. The writer demonstrates a strong knowledge of a topic or issue and selects compelling points, based on evidence from research, to support the point of view. The writer also provides counterpoints to knock down reasons and points on the other side of the argument.

Test Writing: Writing to a Prompt

Students are often asked to state an opinion and provide reasons for that opinion to answer a prompt on state tests. Depending on the prompt, test-writing may include some of the characteristics of opinion, persuasive, and in rare cases, argumentative writing.

Figure 4-5: These three types of writing have both similarities and differences. There is no hard line between them.

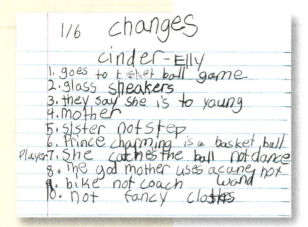

Figure 4-6: Gwyneth planned her own version of Cinderella in her writer's notebook.

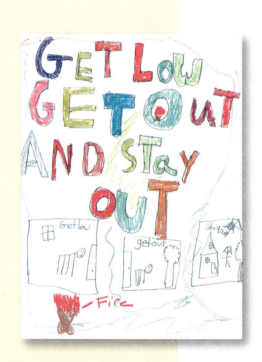

Figure 4-7: Isabella decided to make a public service announcement poster about what to do in the case of fire.

Third Graders Learn to Experiment with Writing in New Ways

Third graders get excited about trying writing that they see in the world. Engagement always increases with authenticity. When you give them multiple ways to compose and offer them new ways to play with their writing, they become more motivated to write, especially when you approach the writing with a spirit of inquiry. Use GEN.U15: Experimenting with Writing in New Ways to spark your own creativity. Approach the learning within this umbrella with your own sense of discovery and wonder. Writing involves composing, and there are so many ways to compose, whether through images, movements, or words. Allowing yourself and your students to dream up all the ways they might compose something new will reinvigorate the writing happening in your classroom. We recommend that you break up this umbrella across the year, repeat the lessons at different times, and add your own creative ideas.

This umbrella offers students ways to re-envision their writing. In the first minilesson, students learn that they can write about the same topic in different ways. For example, Mia has written an informational book about dogs (Figure 4-1), several poems about dogs, and a memory story about a time her dog got lost. In WML2, students learn how changing perspective in a piece of writing can give it a brand-new twist. They are introduced to the idea of personification and learn how writing from the point of view of an object or animal can be a playful way to gain inspiration for new writing. In WML3, students learn that familiar folktales can inspire new ways to write (Figure 4-6).

GEN.U8: Introducing Persuasive Writing Through Powerful Messages also invites writers to compose in new ways and builds on their experiences with opinion writing. In this umbrella, students think about a message that is important to them and then look at how people market their messages in the world. They brainstorm different ways to compose and share their messages (e.g., developing a logo for merchandise, writing a song, or making a public service announcement poster) for their intended audience (Figure 4-7).

Third graders need lots of opportunities to write in different ways so they can envision the importance of writing. Students want to write when they understand that it serves an authentic and meaningful purpose. As you work through the minilessons in the Genres and Forms section, you offer students a range of ways to write and open their eyes to the ways writing can serve a variety of purposes.

Chapter 5

Minilessons for the Study of Craft, Conventions, and Writing Process

One of our primary goals is for children to be self-directed writers who have the ability to follow their own intentions. We want children to be engaged for reasons beyond the fact that they are required to write. We want them to choose projects because they want to entertain their friends or share what they know about a topic or convince someone to do something. Without the ability and opportunity to find authentic writing projects, it will be more difficult for them to become truly self-directed.

— Matt Glover

FOR STUDENTS TO BECOME ENGAGED in the writing process, they have to care about their writing. Teachers of writing know that their students are more engaged when they are able to make choices about their writing. Choice comes in many forms. Writers choose the length of their writing, their topic, their purpose, their audience, the kind of writing they will do, and how they will craft it. They make choices about where to put things on the page, how to punctuate a sentence, what to revise and edit, and whether to ultimately publish a piece of writing. If we want to develop authentic writers in our classrooms, we have to provide time, space, and instruction for students to engage in these decisions. The umbrellas and minilessons in the last three sections of this book—Craft, Conventions, and Writing Process—set the stage for you to develop writers who make these decisions, have a sense of agency, and care deeply about their writing work.

Applying Craft, Conventions, and Writing Process Minilessons

The umbrellas in the Craft, Conventions, and Writing Process sections can be used in several ways. They are perfect for selecting when you notice that your students are ready for or in need of a certain lesson. Let's say you have noticed that several of your students are starting to organize similar information together in their nonfiction books, and you know they would benefit from learning about headings. So you decide to teach the Craft minilesson on headings or the entire Craft umbrella CFT.U10: Using Text Features in Nonfiction Writing.

Alternatively, you might choose to simply follow the Suggested Sequence of Lessons (pp. 605–622), which weaves the umbrellas from these three sections across the year. Students can apply their new learning about craft to writing in a single genre they are all working on (e.g., memory stories) or to writing in whatever genres individuals have chosen to work on. Whichever way you decide to use these lessons, be thoughtful about whether your students are writing something that will allow them to try out the minilessons. Some umbrellas in the Craft section are quite easy to apply to certain kinds of writing. For example, you might want to introduce CFT.U4: Adding Dialogue to Writing when students are writing memory stories because they can probably imagine what was said at the time of their stories. If they have difficulty applying new learning to their current writing, consider inviting them to revisit finished work in their writing files or folders. They also can apply the new learning to something they have started in their writer's notebooks. Sometimes, you might ask all students to finish or lay aside what they are currently writing in order to try out a principle or genre and return to their unfinished piece later. The writer's notebook is the perfect place to try out these new ideas. There are several umbrellas in the Craft, Conventions, and Writing Process sections that can be applied across all kinds of writing (e.g., CNV.U2: Learning About Punctuation and Capitalization and WPS.U7: Adding Information to Your Writing).

When deciding which minilessons from these three sections to teach, you will also want to consider where most students are in the writing process. If most students are just starting a new informational piece, you might teach WPS.U4: Writer's Notebook: Becoming an Expert, which helps them explore and research topics of interest. If many students are working on revising their work, you might teach a Craft lesson or a lesson from the drafting and revising part of the Writing Process section. If you want to engage students in editing their work, choose an umbrella from the Conventions section or one of the editing umbrellas in the Writing Process section. Whenever you decide to teach these minilessons, think of it as adding tools to your writers' toolboxes. For many students, you will hand them the right tool at exactly the right time. But others will tuck that tool away and use it when they are ready.

Studying the Craft of Writing

What do we mean when we talk about the craft of writing with third graders? Third graders appreciate writer's craft even before they know what it is. They comment on the details in Jerry Pinkney's illustrations, they are entertained by Patricia Polacco's beautiful word choices, or they know how to turn to the exact page they want in a Gail Gibbons book because they have figured out how the book is organized. Through the talk that surrounds interactive read-aloud and shared reading, third graders know a lot about the craft of writing. Craft minilessons take this budding knowledge and pull back the curtain on the decisions authors make to create books that are interesting and exciting to read.

The minilessons in the Craft section are based on the behaviors and understandings in the Craft section of the grade 3 Writing continuum in *The Fountas & Pinnell Literacy Continuum*. It is important to note that minilessons that teach these behaviors and understandings are not limited to the Craft section of this book. There are minilessons that address aspects of craft built into the Genres and Forms section because craft is part of writing in any genre (e.g., creating believable characters in realistic fiction or organizing an informational book). Even minilessons in the Conventions section have an aspect of craft to them. For example, capitalization and punctuation have to do with the conventions of writing, but writers also use punctuation and capitalization to communicate their ideas and voice (e.g., using multiple exclamation points to indicate excitement or using all caps to indicate yelling). Whenever writers make decisions about their writing, they are making craft moves. The first umbrella in the Craft section, U1: Reading Like a Writer and Illustrator, sets the stage for noticing the writer's and illustrator's craft decisions whenever a book is read. The minilessons in the Craft section allow you to focus specifically on the following aspects of craft, each of which can be applied across a variety of genres.

Organization

This aspect of craft includes the structure of the whole text—the beginning, the arrangement of ideas, and the ending. In CFT.U5: Crafting a Lead and CFT.U6: Crafting an Ending, you lead the students through an inquiry process using mentor texts to discover how they might try different beginnings and endings in their own writing. In CFT.U10: Using Text Features in Nonfiction Writing, they learn that they can use headings, sidebars, and tables of contents to organize information for their readers. All these minilessons help students learn how to organize and arrange their ideas as writers while also contributing to their understandings as readers.

Idea Development

Idea development is how writers present and support their ideas with examples and details. For third graders, this means thinking about the details they can add to describe what their characters are like and where their stories take place (e.g., CFT.U2: Describing Characters and CFT.U3: Crafting a Setting). They also learn to provide more specific and interesting examples to support their ideas in nonfiction writing. In CFT.U11: Expanding Nonfiction Writing, students learn how to use personal anecdotes and comparisons to further develop their ideas. Though they may have learned about some of these craft ideas in previous grades (e.g., crafting a setting or describing a character), the examples they encounter in mentor texts grow in complexity as they listen to and read more sophisticated texts. As they model their own writing off of these mentor texts, idea development in their own writing becomes more complex.

Language Use

This aspect of craft addresses the way writers use sentences, phrases, and expressions to describe events, actions, or information. As third graders grow as readers, their writing begins to reflect the language in books. For example, students learn to use dialogue in more sophisticated ways. Notice how Levy begins his story with dialogue to hook the reader (Figure 5-1). He follows the dialogue with description, making the reader wonder why the characters would be packing sleeping bags to go to a museum. CFT.U4: Adding Dialogue to Writing teaches students how to interweave action and dialogue to avoid long strings of continuous conversation. They may have learned to add dialogue to their writing previously, but in third grade, they learn to use it meaningfully and judiciously to move along the plot. Besides learning to vary action and dialogue, third graders also learn to use a variety of

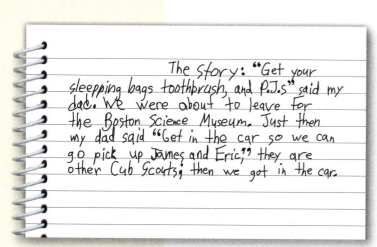

Figure 5-1: Levy has learned from the books he has read how to effectively use dialogue. The text reads "Get your sleeping bags, toothbrush and P.J.s," said my dad. We were about to leave for the Boston Science Museum. Just then, my dad said, "Get in the car so we can pick up James and Eric." They are other Cub Scouts; then we got in the car.

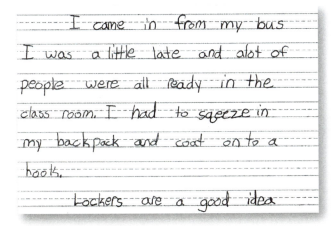

For her opinion piece, Kadee specifically chose the verb *squeeze* to help her reader understand that it is tight to hang all her stuff on a hook at school, setting up why lockers would be a good idea.

Using her senses to expand her descriptions helped Kadee think about her specific word choices. Her choice of the word *beating* to describe how the fire felt against the character's back brings a vivid picture to the reader.

sentence structures and lengths in their writing. In CFT.U8: Making Your Sentences Clear and Interesting, your writers learn not only how to vary their sentences but also how to use connecting words and phrases to increase sentence fluency and flow.

Word Choice

Word choice matters. A writer's choice of a specific word can change the whole meaning of a sentence. Consider the difference between writing *The woman strolled down the road* and *The woman sprinted down the road*. In the first sentence, we understand that the woman must have felt pretty relaxed to be strolling along. The latter conveys much more urgency; we wonder what caused her to hurry. Third graders quickly pick up on the importance of word choice once they are taught to pay attention to it. You can begin planting the seeds for this in your interactive read-aloud and shared reading lessons. As you read, linger on a few important words, think aloud about why the author chose them, repeat a word, and simply comment how much you love the author's choice of words. When you heighten your students' awareness of how carefully writers choose words, they begin to think about their own word choices (Figure 5-2). CFT.U7: Making Powerful Word Choices supports students in looking closely at their own choice of words, particularly how to select strong and specific verbs.

Figure 5-2: Kadee understands that word choice is important no matter what genre she is writing in. Notice the specific word choices in both her opinion and fiction pieces.

Chapter 5: Minilessons for the Study of Craft, Conventions, and Writing Process

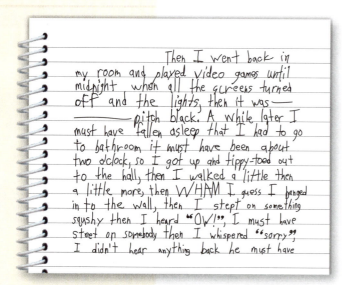

Figure 5-3: Levy used punctuation, capitalization, and humor to infuse his memory story with voice. Notice how he used an elongated dash before *pitch black* to create a little suspense. He capitalized the words WHAM and OW and wrote about "stepping on something squishy" to describe stepping on a person.

Voice

It is through the writer's voice that readers get a sense of the author's feelings and passion for a story or topic. Voice is a writer's unique style. The voices of third graders often naturally shine through their writing pieces. They have unique ways of seeing the world, and the way they use their words often conveys this perspective. When students are encouraged to share their feelings in a story or to write the way they talk, they learn important lessons about voice. Voice is also very closely linked to the conventions of writing. When students learn to punctuate their writing with exclamation points, question marks, and even more sophisticated punctuation, their voices become even stronger. In CFT.U9, students learn how to talk directly to the reader, use different styles of print, and integrate humor as other ways to infuse voice into a piece of writing (Figure 5-3).

Drawing

Drawing is important and is used at every stage of the writing process. There are several minilessons in the Craft section to help you and your students take a close look at illustrator's craft moves—the decisions illustrators make to communicate their ideas. Through these lessons, students' drawings become increasingly realistic and detailed. CFT.U12: Drawing People teaches students how to use shapes to draw people in different positions, how to show them in a setting, and how to add details to show feelings. Another minilesson addresses how to use color realistically, helping students notice details of skin tone and hair and eye color.

Drawing in third grade is used in multiple ways—as a tool for idea generation and planning, as a mode of composition (e.g., making pictures books and persuasive posters), and as a way to add meaning or information to a piece of writing. Through careful examination of mentor texts in the drawing minilessons, students learn how to look at the illustrations in books with an illustrator's eye. In CFT.U13: Adding Meaning Through Illustrations, minilessons focus on many of the craft moves illustrators make, such as using color to create a feeling or mood, drawing motion and sound lines, and using layout and perspective to draw attention to important information. Making picture books is a wonderful way for students to apply the minilessons in this umbrella. Students learn how to use illustrations to add meaning beyond what they write with words. The more students learn about drawing, the more they learn about the process of revising their writing. They get excited to add new details to their pictures after talking about their stories and learning new illustration techniques. This in turn impacts the details they add to their writing.

The minilessons in CFT.U14: Illustrating and Using Graphics in Nonfiction Writing help students expand their understanding of how to show factual information through detailed drawings, diagrams, maps and legends, close-ups, and photographs (Figures 5-4 and 5-5).

Through CFT.U15: Exploring Design Features and Text Layout, students learn that they can use scenes, borders, and text layouts to make their pictures interesting (Figure 5-6). When you teach students to draw and use media in interesting ways, they become inspired to use art in their own ways to communicate their messages and ideas.

Teaching the Conventions of Writing

Conventions and craft go hand in hand. They work together to communicate meaning. A writer can have great ideas, understand how to organize them, and even make interesting word choices. But the ideas can get lost if the writer doesn't form letters correctly, spell words in recognizable ways, or use conventional grammar and punctuation. For writing to be valued and understood, writers need to understand the conventions of writing. Sophisticated writers might play with these conventions and sometimes break the rules for their use, but they are aware that they are making an intentional decision to do so.

Teaching conventions to third graders can be tricky. Approach it with a spirit of inquiry and discovery. Students are more motivated to use conventions when they see the rewards of others being able to read and understand their writing. Avoid being so rigid in your teaching of conventions that students are afraid to take risks. Third graders should celebrate their efforts to spell a new word. How limited and boring their writing would be if they used only the

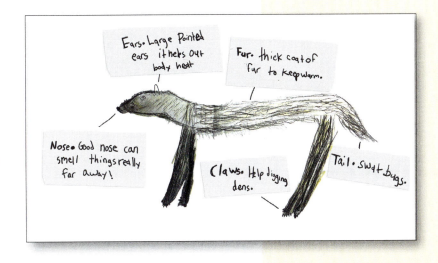

Figure 5-4: Farhan chose to use a two-page spread for his diagram of a wolf in his informational book *Wolves*. He also added interesting facts to his labels of the wolf's body parts.

Figure 5-5: Farhan used what he learned about making close-up illustrations to show the details of a wolf's mouth.

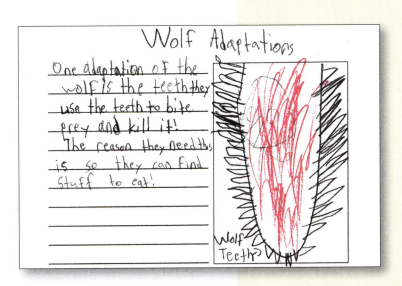

Figure 5-6: Dahlia combined art techniques to make this illustration for an informational book about sharks.

words they knew how to spell! The minilessons in the Conventions section are designed to strike a balance between teaching students to write clearly while making them comfortable to take risks with their new learning. The minilessons in this section are based on the behaviors and understandings in the Conventions section of the grade 3 Writing continuum in *The Fountas & Pinnell Literacy Continuum*; however, just like craft, the conventions of writing are not limited to this section. There are aspects of conventions woven into the writing minilessons in every section. The Conventions section, in conjunction with these other sections, addresses the following conventions of writing.

Text Layout

For third graders, text layout might mean making sure that there is proper space between their words and that their letters are proportionate to one another (see CNV.U1: Writing Words). Students also learn that when they use a computer, they can use different font styles and sizes to convey meaning. In addition, learning about text layout involves learning about where to place print and pictures on a page, including placement of headings and titles. Many of the conventions related to text layout are taught within the Craft section, particularly in CFT.U15: Exploring Design Features and Text Layout. This umbrella is a perfect example of the close relationship between craft and conventions in writing. When you introduce a variety of paper templates (available in the online resources) that show a variety of ways to lay out a page, you teach students that writers make important choices about where they place print and pictures.

Grammar and Usage

For third graders, grammar and usage are best taught in the context of writing. For example, students experience how to use past, present, and future tenses as they participate in shared writing. They learn how to use adjectives, adverbs, prepositions, and conjunctions in the act of writing. The more students engage in writing and translating their talk into writing, the more experience they will have in using grammar. Before students can name the parts of speech or identify a verb tense as past, present, or future, they have an internal sense of how the language works because they have used it to converse with and communicate to others. Oral storytelling, classroom conversation, interactive read-aloud, and shared reading experiences further immerse students in how the language sounds and works. These oral experiences are especially important for English learners. When students write their thoughts and ideas, their oral language experiences will influence what and how they write.

The lessons in *The Writing Minilessons Book, Grade 3*, prepare students to write in various genres and forms, to craft their writing in ways they have seen authors and illustrators do in their books, and to use the writing process. Students' writing that is produced from these minilessons presents opportunities for you to teach specifics of English grammar and usage through the curriculum and activities that are part of your classroom instruction.

Capitalization

Most third graders are at a stage in which they begin to solidify and expand their understanding of when to capitalize words. The first minilesson in CNV.U2: Learning About Punctuation and Capitalization uses inquiry to help students engage in a study of when writers use capitals. Minilessons reinforce the concepts of using capital letters at the beginning of names, for the first letter of the first word in a sentence, and for most of the words in a title. Students also learn to capitalize the first letter in the names of places, days, months, cities, and states. The minilessons in CFT.U4: Adding Dialogue to Writing support students in learning how to use properly capitalize and punctuate dialogue.

Punctuation

Third graders have a beginning understanding that punctuation makes their writing readable for others. CNV.U2: Learning About Punctuation and Capitalization helps students further develop their understanding that punctuation also communicates how the reader should read a sentence (e.g., an ellipsis signals the reader to pause). When students understand the role of punctuation in writing, they begin to see punctuation as a way to craft their messages. Writers communicate voice with punctuation. They communicate emotions—excitement, fear, sadness, confusion. Punctuation is inextricably linked with the craft of writing. When third graders learn the conventions of punctuation, they begin to notice how authors use and sometimes play with them in their books. The second minilesson in CNV.U2 engages students in an inquiry-based study of punctuation in which students have the opportunity to discover for themselves how writers use punctuation. You can continue this study over several days, adding their noticings about different kinds of punctuation to an anchor chart. Writing minilessons make students curious about what writers do and eager to imitate what they notice in their own writing.

Spelling

As third graders grow in their knowledge of the way words work, they move away from approximated spelling and begin to use conventional spelling more consistently in their writing. Encourage students to write the words they know quickly and accurately and to use a range of strategies to make their best attempts at words they do not know. In CNV.U1: Writing Words, students learn to break words into syllables to write them and to use what they know about words to help them spell other words. Because third graders encounter and use more sophisticated vocabulary in both their reading and writing, these lessons focus on writing multisyllable words. In MGT.U4: Introducing the Writing Folder, students are taught how to refer to a list of commonly misspelled words to support their use of conventional spelling. Consider using the format of these lessons to also teach students to check their spelling using digital tools like spell-check when writing on a computer.

These minilessons should accompany a strong phonics, spelling, and word study component in your classroom. The minilessons in the Conventions section are meant to *reinforce* and *supplement* what you are teaching in your phonics, spelling, and word study instruction and to help students transfer what they are learning to their writing.

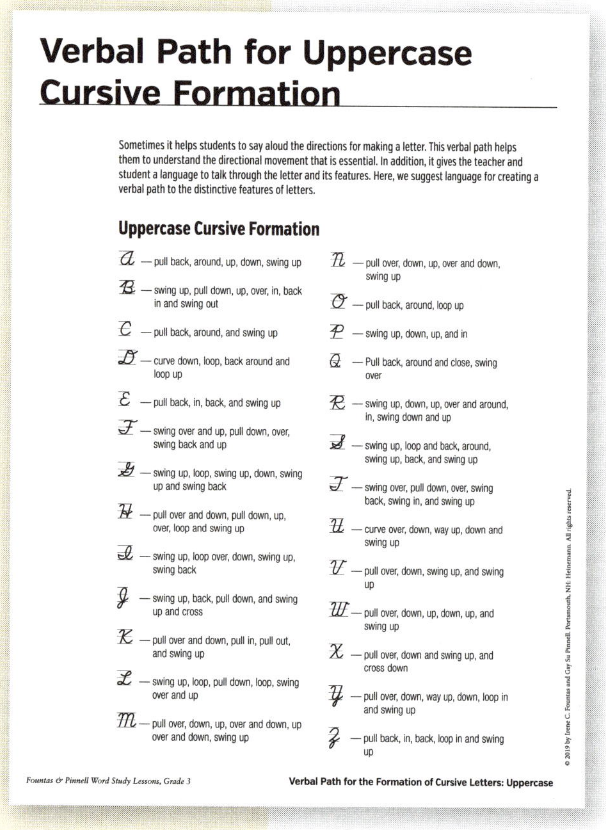

Verbal Path for Uppercase Cursive Formation

Sometimes it helps students to say aloud the directions for making a letter. This verbal path helps them to understand the directional movement that is essential. In addition, it gives the teacher and student a language to talk through the letter and its features. Here, we suggest language for creating a verbal path to the distinctive features of letters.

Uppercase Cursive Formation

A — pull back, around, up, down, swing up
B — swing up, pull down, up, over, in, back in and swing out
C — pull back, around, and swing up
D — curve down, loop, back around and loop up
E — pull back, in, back, and swing up
F — swing over and up, pull down, over, swing back and up
G — swing up, loop, swing up, down, swing up and swing back
H — pull over and down, pull down, up, over, loop and swing up
I — swing up, loop over, down, swing up, swing back
J — swing up, back, pull down, and swing up and cross
K — pull over and down, pull in, pull out, and swing up
L — swing up, loop, pull down, loop, swing over and up
M — pull over, down, up, over and down, up over and down, swing up
N — pull over, down, up, over and down, swing up
O — pull back, around, loop up
P — swing up, down, up, and in
Q — Pull back, around and close, swing over
R — swing up, down, up, over and around, in, swing down and up
S — swing up, loop and back, around, swing up, back, and swing up
T — swing over, pull down, over, swing back, swing in, and swing up
U — curve over, down, way up, down and swing up
V — pull over, down, swing up, and swing up
W — pull over, down, up, down, up, and swing up
X — pull over, down and swing up, and cross down
Y — pull over, down, way up, down, loop in and swing up
Z — pull back, in, back, loop in and swing up

Fountas & Pinnell Word Study Lessons, Grade 3 **Verbal Path for the Formation of Cursive Letters: Uppercase**

Figure 5-7: Use the language of the Verbal Path for Letter Formation for both print and cursive consistently to support students in making letters.

Handwriting and Word Processing

Besides being important for legibility, effective handwriting also increases writing fluency so the writer can give more attention to the message and less attention to the mechanics of writing. By third grade, students should be printing letters with automaticity and fluency. The first lesson in CNV.U1: Writing Words reinforces the idea that letters need to be formed legibly and proportionately. It is common for third graders to form letters correctly, but not proportionately. For example, some students will make a lowercase letter the same size as an uppercase letter. They also occasionally need reminders about using good spacing and writing on the line instead of making letters float between the lines. CNV.U1.WML1 can be applied to both print and cursive writing. If students need more support with letter formation, we have included the Verbal Path for Letter Formation for both print and cursive (Figure 5-7) as online resources. When you consistently use the same words for directing letter formation, you help students internalize the directions and support their fluency with handwriting. You can also find suggestions in online resources for the order in which to teach cursive letters (Figure 5-8).

The minilessons and resources related to handwriting are not intended to replace any handwriting curriculum you already have in place. Avoid confusing students with conflicting ways of directing the formation of letters. The paper choices available in the online resources provide lines with dashes for students who need this kind of support, but feel free to use the paper that is consistent with your school's handwriting program.

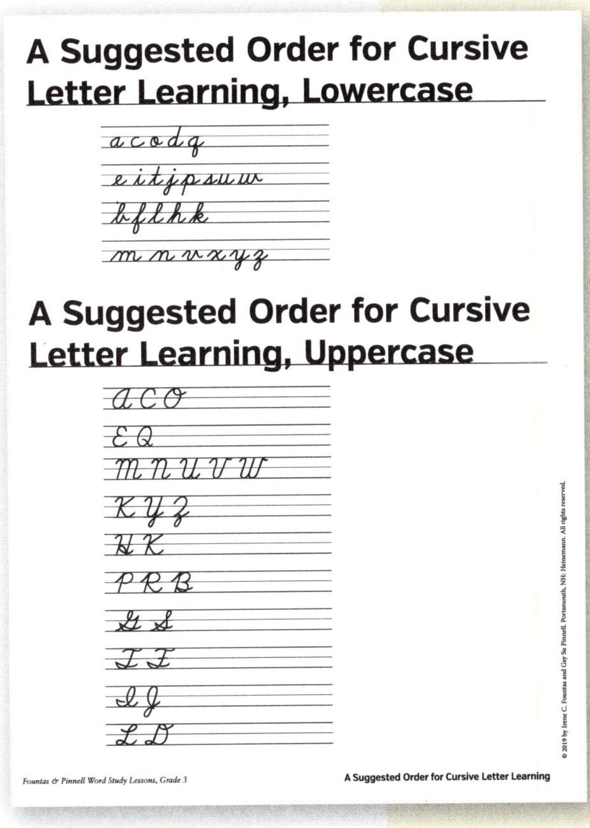
A Suggested Order for Cursive Letter Learning, Lowercase

a c o d q
e i t j p s u w
b f l h k
m n v x y z

A Suggested Order for Cursive Letter Learning, Uppercase

A C O
E Q
M N U V W
K Y Z
H K
P R B
G S
T F
I J
L D

Fountas & Pinnell Word Study Lessons, Grade 3 A Suggested Order for Cursive Letter Learning

Figure 5-8: Use the Suggested Order for Cursive Letter Learning to introduce upper- and lowercase cursive letters.

Third graders will also need to learn keyboarding skills to increase their writing fluency. One way to support your students' development of keyboarding skills is to on occasion offer the option of "publishing" a piece of writing on a computer. Figure 5-9 shows typed instructions for a game Riley created as part of a study of procedural texts. She decided to publish the game's instructions by typing them so they could be read easily by others. Notice that the teacher decided not to edit the student's work to perfect this final copy. The published piece reflects Habso's current understanding of how to edit and proofread her writing. A few times a year, Riley's teacher will work with students to polish a piece in the same way an editor would help the author of a published work. In most cases, third grade published pieces are edited by the student and are not necessarily perfect. In the next section on the writing process, we discuss other ways you might choose to publish a text.

Learning About the Writing Process

The umbrellas in the Writing Process section introduce and immerse students in the phases of the writing process from planning to publishing as addressed in Chapter 1 (Figure 1-9). They are based on the behaviors and understandings in the Writing Process section of the grade 3 Writing continuum in *The Fountas & Pinnell Literacy Continuum*. The umbrellas in the Writing Process section introduce students to the following phases of the writing process.

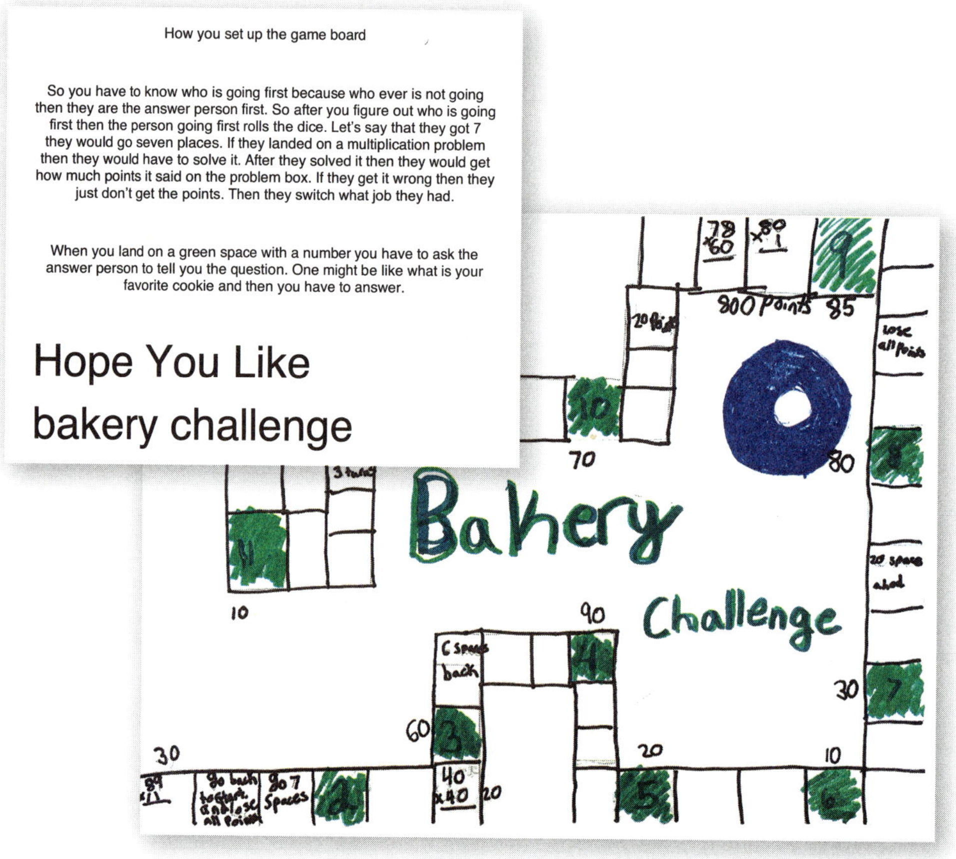

Figure 5-9: Occasionally, third graders can type their writing as one way to "publish" their pieces. Here, Riley has published directions for her game, Bakery Challenge, by typing them and posting them with her gameboard.

> How you set up the game board
>
> So you have to know who is going first because who ever is not going then they are the answer person first. So after you figure out who is going first then the person going first rolls the dice. Let's say that they got 7 they would go seven places. If they landed on a multiplication problem then they would have to solve it. After they solved it then they would get how much points it said on the problem box. If they get it wrong then they just don't get the points. Then they switch what job they had.
>
> When you land on a green space with a number you have to ask the answer person to tell you the question. One might be like what is your favorite cookie and then you have to answer.
>
> Hope You Like bakery challenge

Planning and Rehearsing

For third graders, talk is an important part of planning and rehearsing their writing. Some of the talk is about their ideas—*what* they are writing. Some of the talk is about *why* they are writing and for *whom*—the purpose and the audience. Knowing the purpose for writing often leads to discussions about what type of writing to do and what kind of paper is best for that purpose. For example, if writers want to

- say thank you, they might write a note or a letter,
- teach others how to do something, they might write a recipe, a set of directions, or how-to book,
- create a public service announcement, they might make a poster or a sign, or
- remember an experience or entertain their audience, they might write a story.

In all of these cases, the writer thinks about the purpose, determines what kind of writing will serve that purpose, and then begins to write a message. In Figure 5-10, Mia's letter to her teacher shows that she has already done a lot of planning. She has clearly thought about something she is interested in sharing with an audience and determined that an informational text with sections will best serve her purpose. You can see the completed piece in Figure 4-1. WPS.U5: Thinking About Purpose, Audience, and Genre/Form helps students think and talk about their purpose and audience and how they affect the choice of a genre and form. Revisit this umbrella several times a year so students have the opportunity to thoughtfully choose not only the topic they write about but also the genre they write in.

In addition to learning how to choose their own purpose, topic, and genre, students need explicit opportunities to generate and collect ideas for writing during the planning process. From discussions during interactive read-aloud, third graders understand that writers get their ideas from their own experiences and from what they have learned. Minilessons in the Writing Process section support students in further developing this understanding through the use of a writer's notebook. Students learn how to gather ideas from their own lives, from writers and artists, and from what they have learned about topics they are interested in. They discover stories by making webs of their favorite memories, drawing maps of special places, and sketching memories of spending time with people they care about. They learn that they can get ideas from making lists. You can read more about using writer's notebooks with third graders on pages 84–88.

Figure 5-10: Mia wrote a letter to her teacher explaining her plans to write an informational piece about dogs. She explained why she chose her topic and how she planned to organize the information into sections. She also identified her teacher as her potential audience.

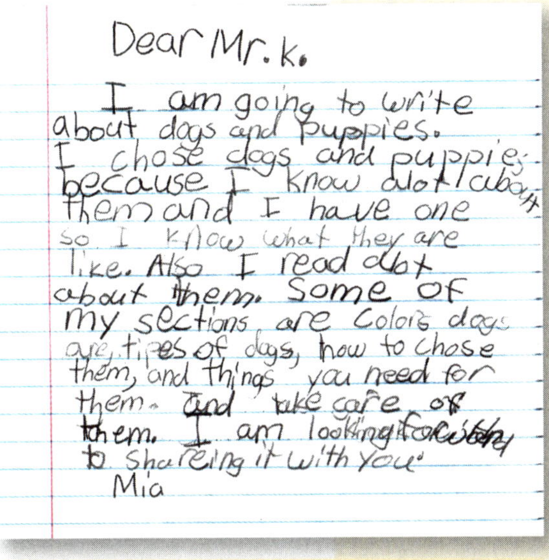

Dear Mr. K.,
I am going to write about dogs and puppies. I chose dogs and puppies because I know a lot about them and I have one so I know what they are like. Also I read a lot about them. Some of my sections are colors dogs are, types of dogs, how to choose them, and things you need for them and take care of them. I am looking forward to sharing it with you.
Mia

Drafting and Revising

Most third graders are enthusiastic about drafting ideas that excite them. When they choose their own topics and have a vision for the type of writing they want to do, they are often deeply engaged in getting their ideas down on paper. They also often revise while drafting, changing things as they go. However, these same students may be initially reluctant to revise their writing once it is drafted; it is indeed hard to change something you have written and care about. For other writers, the task of drafting sometimes feels daunting. It can be helpful for those students to know that they can revise and change their writing. Whether students are enthusiastic or reluctant to draft their ideas, there are several things you can put into place to make it an inviting process.

Chapter 5: Minilessons for the Study of Craft, Conventions, and Writing Process

- Invite them to tell their stories or talk about the information they are going to write about to a partner or small group.

- Introduce the idea of a discovery draft—a very quick draft to get ideas down on paper and "discover" what you really want to say. The discovery draft can be very freeing for some students who think their first draft has to be perfect.

- Share the advice of authors. When students understand that even published authors sometimes struggle to get their ideas down on paper, they become more open to the process.

- Allow students choice in what they are writing about and often what types of genres/forms they are writing in. When students are engaged in authentic writing, they are more open to revision work.

As students learn new crafting techniques from authors they love and are explicitly taught ways to revise their writing, they become invested in the revision process. Revising becomes contagious when students have opportunities to share and celebrate their changes with one another. Minilessons in WPS.U7: Adding Information to Your Writing and WPS.U8: Revising to Focus and Organize Writing offer different ways to revise. Students learn to reread their writing to make sure it makes sense and to add new information for more detail or clarification. In Figure 5-11, Devon rewrote a sentence three times in his writer's notebook using what he had learned about adding specific details to give his readers a picture. His revision work shows he understands that writers change their writing to make it more specific. Devon's teacher might strengthen his revision skills by teaching the minilessons in CFT.U7: Making Powerful Word Choices to help him learn to choose words that reflect his ideas rather than choosing words that sound interesting but do not really match the context of the sentence (e.g., *luxurious*). When students revise, you gain insight into what they understand about craft. They learn that writing is an ongoing process and that you can always change it and make it better.

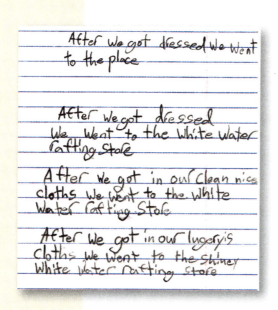

Figure 5-11: Devon used his writer's notebook to revise a sentence three times from his memory story about white-water rafting. He decided to apply the last revision to his writing piece: *After we got in our luxurious clothes, we went to the shiny white water rafting store.*

Proofreading and Editing

In third grade, your primary goal is guiding students to reread and revisit their work to help them notice what they can do to make their writing clearer for their readers. Third graders are learning more and more about writing conventions, print, and the way words work every day. You can teach them how to proofread to make sure the words they know are spelled correctly and have them check their writing for punctuation and capitalization. The minilessons in WPS.U9: Editing and Proofreading Writing teach students how to proofread and edit, beginning with rereading their writing pieces to make sure they make sense. Notice how Misha circled all capitals at the beginning of her sentences to make sure she capitalized the first word and punctuated the end of each sentence (Figure 5-12). She also used a caret to clarify something for the reader. When students do their own proofreading and editing, it gives you a window into what they understand about conventions and what they might need to learn next. For example, Misha will benefit from lessons on how to punctuate dialogue. When you teach your students how to edit their own work, they feel more ownership over the piece and develop a sense of agency.

Publishing

When we say *publish* in third grade, we really mean "share it with others." Students are invited to share their independent drawing and writing daily as they experiment with new ideas taught through the lessons in this book. However, publishing takes this sharing a step further by having students prepare their books for an audience to read. Publishing might mean having students type or bind their writing with cardboard or other materials to resemble a book. Published books can go into your classroom library for others to check out and read (Figure 5-13). Publishing can also take the form of framing a piece of writing or drawing, displaying it, posting it on a bulletin board, or holding informal writing celebrations. For example, you can have students share their books with another class or with a teacher or administrator, or you can invite families and guests to look at published books.

Third grade is a good time to continue thinking about broadening students' understanding of audience. The minilessons in WPS.U5: Thinking About Purpose, Audience, and Genre/Form help you and the students think about potential audiences both within the school and in the greater community. Consider asking local government officials, community organizations, or university professors and other experts in a field to listen to your students' writing and provide feedback. One third grade class invited

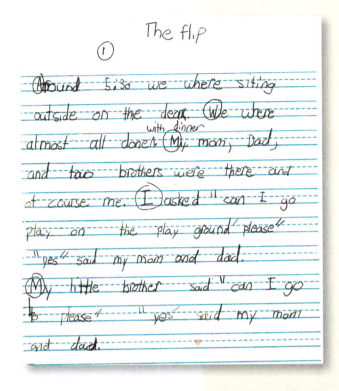

Figure 5-12: Misha used what she has learned about capitalization and punctuation to proofread her writing.

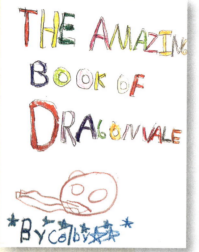

Figure 5-13: Students can publish books in a variety of ways. *My Tree Study* is bound with a dowel and a rubber band. *The Amazing Book of Dragonvale* is simply a large piece of construction paper folded and bound with staples. Spiral bindings, like for *Soccer*, are also durable options.

experts from a conservation and wildlife organization to listen to their research presentations about animals. The experts were invited during the writing process and gave them feedback on their work. The students revised their work based on this feedback and then published it for a poster session presented by the third grade. Parents and classes from other grades were invited to walk through the poster session over the course of a day. Students stood next to their presentations and explained their learning. The entire process resembled what research scientists do—engaging in peer review, in this case, with the wildlife organization—and presenting information in a poster session, a format common at scientific conferences.

Sharing their writing and celebrating risks taken and new techniques tried with a range of audiences present, students with the opportunity to see how different audiences react to their writing and how they might approach their writing differently in the future. When we give students the opportunity to share their writing with authentic audiences, their engagement and motivation for writing increase. The widespread use of virtual meetings helps make the world even smaller. Your students can connect with an audience from their local community or from across the world.

You can also teach your students how to add book and print features like covers, an author page, a dedication, and endpapers as part of the publishing process (WPS.U10: Adding Book and Print Features). In Figure 5-14, Levy wrote a summary and a teaser for the back of his memory book *Night at the Museum* after becoming aware of different book and print features through minilessons and mentor texts. He extended this learning by noticing epilogues and creating his own with a preview of the next book in his series.

Lastly, in WPS.U11: Publishing and Self-Assessing Your Writing students not only learn how to publish their writing but also learn how to reflect on their growth as a writer through self-assessment. In WML3, students learn how to use a rubric to self-assess their writing in particular genres. This lesson can be repeated to demonstrate how to use a rubric for any genre your students are writing in. WML4 asks students to look over their writing pieces and select ones that show their growth as a writer. Ask students to write about their growth on the sheet What I Have Learned How to Do as a

Well, I'm a Cub Scout and I'm going to be sleeping in the Boston Science Museum, and I have to go to the bathroom in the middle of the night and I get lost . . .

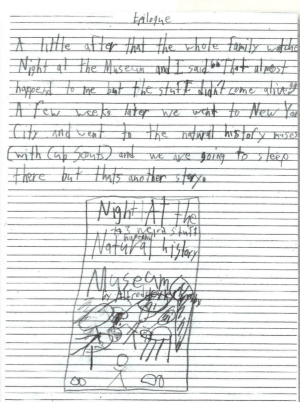

Epilogue
 A little after that, the whole family watched Night at the Museum, and I said, "That almost happened to me, but the stuff didn't come alive." A few weeks later, we went to New York City and went to the natural history museum (with Cub Scouts), and we are going to sleep there, but that's another story.

Writer and Illustrator, downloadable from the online resources and kept in the writing folder. Other teachers ask students to write on an index card or a piece of paper and attach it directly to the piece to be kept in a portfolio (Figure 5-15).

Figure 5-14: As part of the publishing process, Levy wrote a summary for the back of his book and an epilogue with a teaser for his next book.

> My favorite piece was "I saw a Snake in the Grand canyon" it was my best piece because it had a lot of detail and exsitement! I learned that I like to write memory storys.

Figure 5-15: Periodically asking students to reflect on and name what they have learned helps them realize their growth as a writer.

Chapter 5: Minilessons for the Study of Craft, Conventions, and Writing Process

Using a Writer's Notebook with Third Graders

Author Ralph Fletcher writes, "Keeping a writer's notebook can help you be more alive to the world. It can help you develop the habit of paying attention to the little pictures and images of the world you might otherwise ignore" (Fletcher 1996).

Writers notice, listen, and observe every day, all the time. They notice everything in their world—what they see, hear, and smell. They use writer's notebooks to collect these observations plus their thinking, their memories, lists, artifacts, and sketches so they can use them as sparks for writing. Writers read and reread their notebooks and add more and more ideas. It is a place for them to experiment with writing and try things out. It is a tool you can offer your students to help them expand and grow as writers.

We recommend introducing a writer's notebook to third graders at the very beginning of the year so they have a place to write daily and generate ideas from the start. A writer's notebook gives students a place to jot down ideas, explore different techniques, and experiment with quick writes. We provide a series of minilessons in the Writing Process section to help you introduce and use the writer's notebook. If you do not have access to the *Writer's Notebook, Intermediate* (Fountas and Pinnell 2023) for each of your students, use a simple composition book and glue in sections and insert tabs yourself to make it a neat, professional notebook that can be cherished.

WPS.U1: Introducing and Using a Writer's Notebook introduces the idea of a writer's notebook, invites students to personalize their notebooks, and establishes the routine of writing in the notebook for ten minutes a day, ideally outside of writers' workshop (see pages 15–16 for more information). The rest of the umbrellas addressing the writer's notebook provide specific ways to engage students in writing daily and generating ideas. The sections of the *Writer's Notebook, Intermediate* are organized to match the teaching in these umbrellas. If you are using your own writer's notebooks, create your own sections in a way that you think best meets your students' needs. However, we encourage you to leave a substantial amount of space in the writer's notebook for free writing and drawing where writers can repeat any of the different ways they have learned to generate ideas through quick writes, experiment with new craft techniques, try out ideas for a writing project, or even start a writing piece. Students can turn anything they write in the writer's notebook into a longer piece outside of the notebook, or they can use the notebook as a source of ideas for any of their writing.

Helping Your Third Graders Build Their Writer's Notebooks

Showing your students how to build their writer's notebooks can lead to a joyful, robust, and truly independent writing time in your classroom. When you establish the habit of daily quick writing in the writer's notebook, you help students develop ways to generate ideas that they can repeat independently across the school year. Through quick writes, students learn that they can get ideas from their lives, from writers and artists, and from researching topics they find interesting.

Getting Ideas from Your Life

In WPS.U2: Writer's Notebook: Getting Ideas from Your Life, students learn a variety of ways to mine their own lives for writing ideas. The first minilesson invites students to make their own heart maps as a way of discovering what is important in their lives (Heard 2016). This map can be used throughout the year for writing topics across genres. Students learn that maps of places can also be a resource for writing ideas (Figure 5-16). They are taught how to make their own maps of a place and to think about the stories that are hidden in the different spaces on that map. Besides thinking about places, students also learn that sketching and writing about special people can be a source of writing ideas. Through the rest of the umbrella, students learn they can use lists, artifacts, and their observations of the world around them to get ideas and write quickly in their writer's notebooks. If you are using *Writer's Notebook, Intermediate*, this umbrella can be used with Section 1: Ideas from My Life. The last lesson in WPS.U1 teaches students that they can continue to build their notebooks in Section 4: More Writing and Sketching by revisiting any of these ways of writing about their own lives.

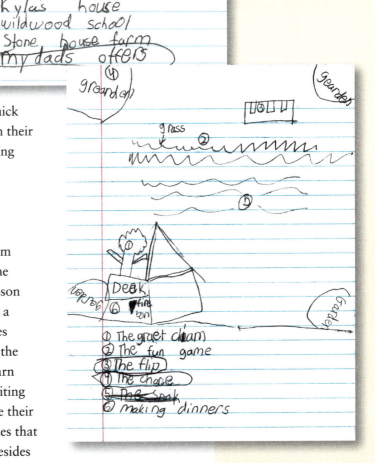

Figure 5-16: Misha used her writer's notebook to make a list of places that are important to her. She then made a map of her backyard and labeled it with numbers that correspond to stories that happened in those spots. She circled the ones that she plans to quickly write about in her notebook.

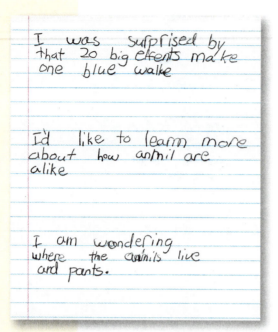

Figure 5-17: Carlos used his writer's notebook to write about some of the things he found surprising in his research about blue whales and some of the wonderings he has about animals in general.

Getting Ideas from Writers and Artists

WPS.U3: Getting Inspiration from Writers and Artists is designed to teach students that other people's work can be a source of inspiration for their own writing ideas. Through these minilessons, they respond in a variety of ways to books, poems, songs, and pieces of artwork. For example, in WML3, students learn that they can use books or parts of books to get writing ideas. They learn that they can write quickly about a memory triggered by a book, tell about a time that they felt like the character, or use the opening line of a book as a story starter. Other lessons invite them to make a sketch inspired by song lyrics or to write as if they were living inside of a painting. Through these minilessons, they learn that when they don't know what to write about, they can turn to the creations of others for inspiration. The writing inspired this way does not need to be connected in any way to the original piece of art; it is simply a jumping-off point for their own ideas. If you are using *Writer's Notebook, Intermediate*, this umbrella can be used with Section 2: Inspirations from Writers and Artists.

Using the Writer's Notebook to Become an Expert

Though nonfiction writing can come out of any of the ideas that writers collect in their writer's notebooks, you might find it helpful to dedicate a section of the notebook to the development of nonfiction writing. In WPS.U4: Writer's Notebook: Becoming an Expert, students learn to make lists to generate topic ideas, to use webs to focus their ideas, and to brainstorm their questions and wonderings about a topic (Figure 5-17). They also use the notebook to take notes on their topics and to prepare to interview experts on their topics (Figure 5-18). The minilessons in this umbrella can be used with Section 3: Becoming an Expert if you are using the *Writer's Notebook, Intermediate*.

The minilessons focused on the writer's notebook are meant to be generative. Once students learn how to use lists, webs, sketches, maps, research questions, etc., they can continue to build their notebooks using these ideas. They learn that a writer's notebook is a place to write quickly and exercise their writing muscles. They learn that it is a place to experiment with ideas, try things out, and have fun with writing.

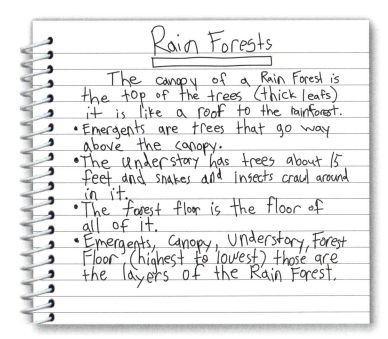

Figure 5-18: Students learn to use their writer's notebooks to take notes about their topics, including identifying and defining important topic-related vocabulary.

Using the Writer's Notebook Throughout the Writing Process

The writer's notebook is used throughout the writing process. Writers use it to collect ideas as they plan for writing, to begin a draft to see if an idea works, and to try out craft moves as they revise their writing (Figure 5-19). The writer's notebook can also be used as a tool to support editing. For example, you might encourage or invite students to try writing a word a few different ways in their notebooks to figure out the spelling. As students publish, they can use their notebooks to develop different book and print features, such as an author page, a dedication, or acknowledgments.

As shown in Figure 3-5, a writer's notebook is typically used alongside a writing folder, in which students keep ongoing writing projects. Students often begin a writing project, such as a story or an informational book, by rereading

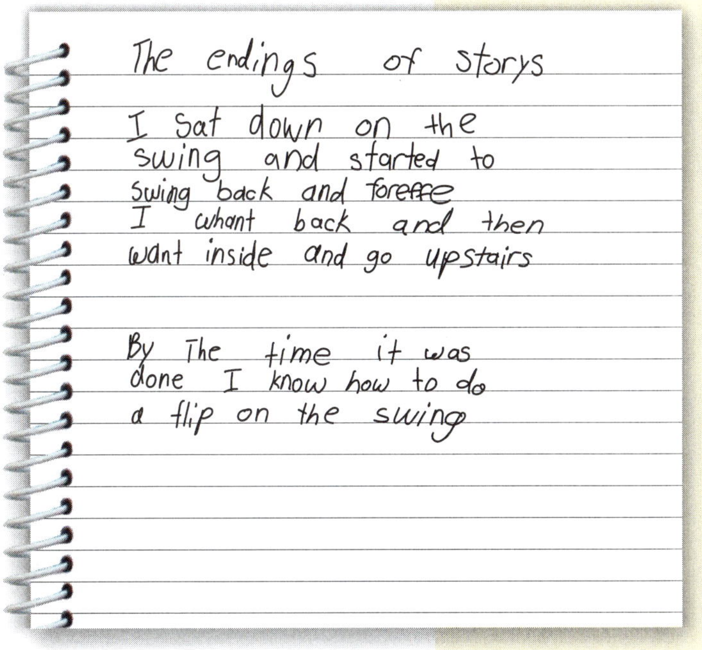

Figure 5-19: Misha used her writer's notebook to try different endings to her story.

Chapter 5: Minilessons for the Study of Craft, Conventions, and Writing Process

Figure 5-20: Students use their writer's notebooks to collect ideas for writing.

their writer's notebooks for topic ideas. Other times, students will start an idea in their writer's notebooks and discover that they want to expand it into a longer project. They take the idea out of the notebook and choose paper that makes sense for the type of writing they are doing. Students continually use their writer's notebooks as they work on their writing projects to try out different crafting techniques and to continue to collect ideas, especially as peers share their own writing project ideas. Ideas are contagious. Hearing one person's memory story often triggers a related memory for someone else. When students share their writing, encourage them to bring their writer's notebooks so they can capture ideas inspired by their classmates' writing on a writing ideas list (Figure 5-20).

Once the writer feels a writing project is complete, we recommend that the finished product (whether published or not) be moved to a storage file somewhere in your classroom. As described earlier, sometimes teachers ask students to write a reflection about what they learned from the writing project in their writing folder. After completing a writing project, they return to their writer's notebooks to continue gathering ideas or to find another idea they want to explore for a writing project.

So many things contribute to your students' development in writing. When you surround students with literacy activities, help them notice what other writers and illustrators do, provide them with time to write, encourage their efforts with enthusiasm, and gently guide them through writing minilessons, you create the right conditions for third graders to grow into confident, engaged writers.

With a choice of so many writing minilessons, how do you decide which lesson to teach when? Most of your decisions will be based on your close observations of your students as they write. What do you see them doing on their own? What might they be able to do with your help? What are they ready to learn? Chapter 6 offers guidance and support for making those decisions.

Chapter 6

Putting Minilessons into Action: Assessing and Planning

With assessment, you learn what students know; the literacy continuum will help you think about what they need to know next.

—Irene Fountas and Gay Su Pinnell

WRITING MINILESSONS ARE EXAMPLES OF explicit, systematic teaching that address the specific behaviors and understandings to notice, teach for, and support in *The Fountas & Pinnell Literacy Continuum*. Goals for each lesson are drawn from the sections on Writing; Writing About Reading; Phonics, Spelling, and Word Study; Oral and Visual Communication; and Digital Communication. Taken together, the goals provide a comprehensive vision of what students need to become aware of, understand, and apply to their own literacy and learning about writing. Each minilesson lists Continuum Connections, which are the exact behaviors from *The Fountas & Pinnell Literacy Continuum* that are addressed in the lesson.

Figure 6-1 provides an overview of the processes that take place when a proficient writer creates a text and represents what students will work toward across the years. Writers must decide the purpose of a text, their audience, and their message. They think about the kind of writing that will help them communicate the message. They make important craft decisions,

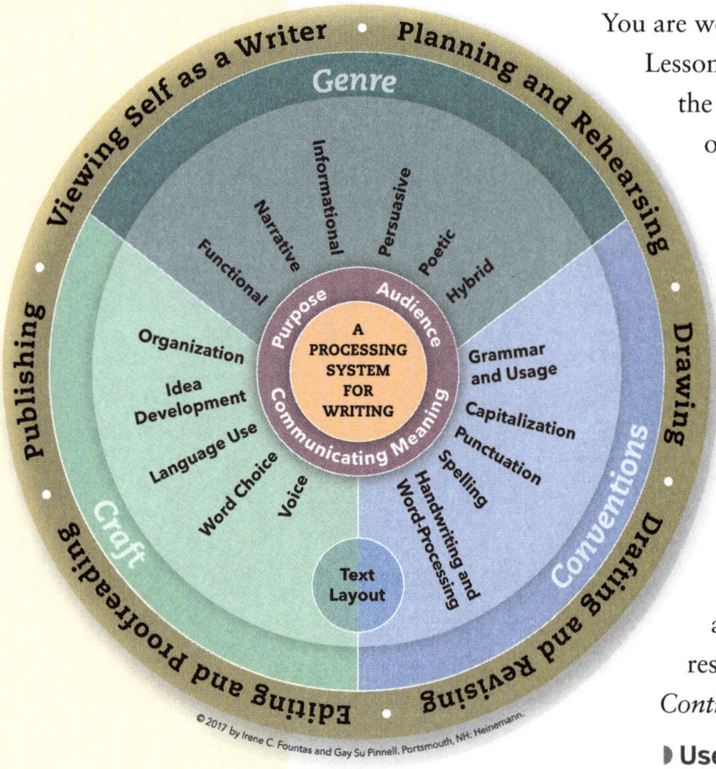

Figure 6-1: The writing wheel diagram, shown full size on the inside back cover, illustrates how the writing process encompasses all aspects of writing.

such as how to organize the piece, what words to use, and how they want the writing to sound. While keeping the message in their heads, writers must also consider the conventions of writing, such as letter formation, capitalization, punctuation, and grammar. They work through a writing process from planning and rehearsing to publishing. All lessons in this book are directed to helping writers expand their processing systems as they write increasingly complex texts.

Decide Which Writing Minilessons to Teach

You are welcome to follow the Suggested Sequence of Lessons discussed later in this chapter (located in the appendix and available as a downloadable online resource). However, first look at the students in front of you. Teach within what Vygotsky (1979) called the "zone of proximal development"—the zone between what they can do independently and what they can do with the support of a more expert other (Figure 6-2). Teach on the cutting edge of your students' present competencies.

Select minilessons based on what you notice the majority of your class needs to learn to develop writing behaviors. Here are some suggestions and tools to help you think about the students in your classroom, the main resource being *The Fountas & Pinnell Literacy Continuum*:

▶ **Use the Writing continuum** to help you observe how students are thinking, talking, and writing/drawing. Think about what they can already do, almost do, and not yet do to select the emphasis for your teaching. Think about the ways you have noticed students initiate and sustain writing. Observe students' contributions and participation during writing minilessons, writing conferences, and guided writing. Use the Writing Process section to assess how they are developing their own independent writing process.

- Are they volunteering ideas when you talk about what to write?
- Do they demonstrate confidence in trying to write words they don't yet know how to spell?
- How are students applying some of the things they are learning during writing minilessons to independent writing?

The Writing Minilessons Book, Grade 3

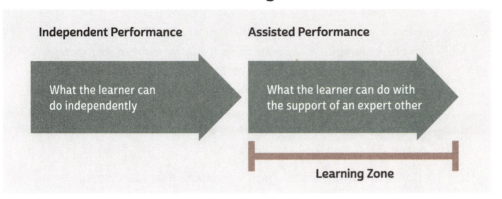

Figure 6-2: Learning zone from *Guided Reading: Responsive Teaching Across the Grades* (Fountas and Pinnell 2017)

- **Scan the Writing About Reading continuum** to analyze students' drawing and writing in response to the books you have read aloud. This analysis will help you determine next steps for having them respond to the books and poems you read together.

- **Review the Phonics, Spelling, and Word Study continuum** to evaluate students' phonological awareness, letter knowledge, and understanding of how to write words. These insights will help you make important choices about how to support students using writing minilessons as well as phonics, spelling, and word study lessons.

- **Consult the Oral and Visual Communication continuum** to help you think about some of the routines students might need for better communication between peers, especially as they share their writing with one another. You will find essential listening and speaking competencies to observe and teach for.

- **Review the Digital Communication continuum** to help you evaluate your students' understanding of digital literacy and citizenship. The behaviors in this section will help you integrate technology and make it an integral part of your students' writing work.

- **Record informal notes** about the interactions you have while conferring or the interactions you see between children as they write and share their writing. Look for patterns in these notes to notice trends in their drawing and writing. Use *The Fountas & Pinnell Literacy Continuum* to help you analyze your notes and determine strengths and areas for growth across the classroom. Your observations will reveal what students know and what they need to learn next as they build knowledge about writing over time. Each goal becomes a possible topic for a minilesson (see Conferring Record 1 and Conferring Record 2 in Figure 2-7).

- **Establish routines for reading your students' writing regularly.** It is helpful to create a system for reading through a few writing folders every day. Some teachers divide the number of writing folders across five days and read through one set each day. As you read your students' writing, make notes about the patterns you see across student writing. What writing principles would the whole group benefit from learning in a writing minilesson? Which principles might be better addressed in a small guided writing group? And, which goals might you want to address in individual conferences?
- **Consult district, state, and/or accreditation standards.** Analyze the suggested skills and areas of knowledge specified in your local and state standards. Align these standards with the minilessons suggested in this book to determine which might be applicable within your classroom.
- **Use the Assess Learning and Assessment sections** within each lesson and at the end of each umbrella. Take time to assess the students' learning after the completion of each lesson and umbrella. The guiding questions on the last page of each umbrella will help you to determine strengths and next steps for your third graders. Your notes on the online resources shown in the next two sections will also help you make a plan for your teaching.

Figure 6-3: Use the downloadable form to plan your own writing minilessons.

Teacher Mrs. Ha Grade 3 Year

Planning a Writing Minilesson

Umbrella: CFT.U7: Making Powerful Word Choices	
Minilesson Principle: WML1: Use words to show not tell.	
Continuum Goal(s): • Use language to show instead of tell • Use range of descriptive words to enhance meaning	
Minilesson Revisit In My Mosque (pp. 3 and 10). • Make a picture in your mind of what is happening in the story as I read aloud to you. Talk about the words that the author used to create a picture. • What do the words help you understand? Jot students' ideas on the chart.	**Examples:** In My Mosque by M. O. Yuksel **Chart:** Show don't tell. Writing: "In my mosque, we line our shoes in rows, like colorful beads, before stepping inside." "Butterflies flutter inside me as my friends and I race to see who can spread the most prayer mats and hand out the most tasbihs." What it shows: Write students' responses Use shared writing to provide an example of showing instead of telling.
Have a Try	Use shared writing to write a description to show that someone is embarrassed or disappointed.
Summarize and Apply	• Today we looked at how authors use words to show not tell. Today, think about how you might do that in your writing.
Confer	• What is another way you can say this to show rather than tell the reader? • What picture do you want the reader to see while reading?
Share	Have a few students read their examples aloud to the group. Ask the listeners to describe what they can see or understand from those words. Add student examples to the chart.

Use Online Resources for Planning and Teaching

The writing minilessons in this book are examples of how to engage third graders in developing the behaviors and understandings of competent writers as described in *The Fountas & Pinnell Literacy Continuum*. Use any of the planning forms in the online resources (**fp.pub/resources**) to help you plan your teaching.

The form shown in Figure 6-3 will help you plan each part of a new writing minilesson. You can design a lesson that uses a different set of example texts from the ones suggested in this book, or you can teach a concept in a way that fits the current needs of your students. The form shown in Figure 6-4 will help you plan which lessons to teach over a period of time to address the goals that are important for the students.

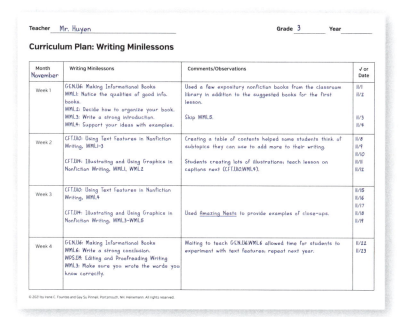

Figure 6-4: Use this downloadable form to make notes about specific writing minilessons for future planning.

The minilessons are here for you to teach according to the instructional needs of your class. You may not be able to use all 200 lessons in a year, so select lessons based on assessment of the needs of your students. Record or check off the lessons you have taught so that you can reflect on the work of the semester and year. You can do this with the Writing Minilessons Record (Figure 6-5).

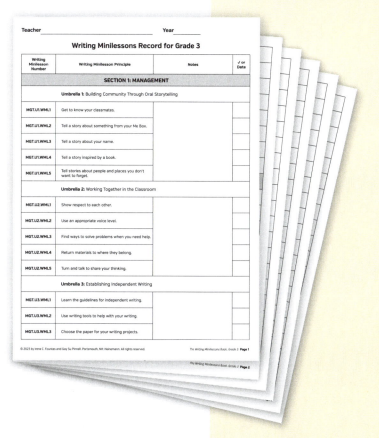

Figure 6-5: Writing Minilessons Record for Grade 3

Meet Students' Needs and Build on Their Strengths

If you are new to writing minilessons, you may want to adhere closely to the suggested sequence, but remember to use the lessons flexibly to meet the needs of the students you teach and to build upon their strengths. Base your decisions about when or whether to use certain lessons on what you notice that they can already do, almost do, and not yet do.

- Omit lessons that you think are not necessary.
- Repeat lessons that you think need more time and instructional attention. Or, repeat lessons using different examples for a particularly rich experience.

Chapter 6: Putting Minilessons into Action: Assessing and Planning

- Move lessons around to be consistent with the curriculum that is adopted in your school or district.

Consider using the analysis tool in Figure 6-6 along with *The Fountas & Pinnell Literacy Continuum* after you have taught the minilessons in a few umbrellas. We suggest using this tool, or one of the other assessment tools offered in the online resources, to focus on one or two pieces of a student's writing. Set aside time to analyze the writing of five students a day. By the end of the week, you will have a snapshot of what the students understand and what they do not yet understand. Use Guide to Observing and Noting Writing Behaviors (Figure 6-7) quarterly as an interim assessment. This observation form comes in two versions, one for individuals and one for the whole class.

Patterns and trends across students' writing will help you plan what to address through whole-group minilessons, small-group guided writing lessons, or individual conferences. Not only will this allow you to be responsive in your teaching, but it will also give you a sense of how to build upon each student's strengths. Consult the Suggested Sequence of Lessons

Figure 6-6: Use this form to analyze student writing to make a plan for future teaching.

Analyzing Student Writing for Planning

Use *The Literacy Continuum* and the Assessment section at the end of each umbrella you have taught to analyze a student's writing for evidence of writing behaviors and understandings.

Name: Tatiana Grade: 3 Genre: Memory Story Date: 10/17

Umbrellas Taught: GEN.U4: Writing Memory Stories, CFT.U4: Adding Dialogue to Writing, WPS.U8: Revising to Focus and Organize Writing

	Strengths	Next Steps	Plan (WML, GW, IC)
Genre	• Selects a meaningful topic. • Shares feelings about the memory. • Uses dialogue to add meaning to the story.	• Understand that memory stories include reflections from the writer about the memory. • Tell details about the most important parts.	• GW: Work with Tatiana, Katey, Jazmine, and Chansey on adding reflections. • WML: Teach WPS.U7: Adding Information to Your Writing.
Craft	• Writes a strong lead. • Writes in a way that speaks directly to the reader. • Uses descriptive verbs (dangling, angled). • Uses some transition words.	• Learn to show instead of tell. • Learn how to reveal characters by what they say and do.	• WML: Teach CFT.U7: Making Powerful Word Choices, WML1. • IC: Work on revealing characters through dialogue.
Conventions	• Uses correct punctuation of dialogue. • Writes many high-frequency words correctly.	• Learn how to use paragraphs to show speaker change. • Notice when two related sentences run together. • Use words with the same letter pattern to write other words (e.g., look, took).	• IC: Help her read parts of the writing aloud and think about where punctuation would go. • WML: Reteach CNV.U1: Writing Words, WML3.
Writing Process	• Uses writer's notebook to generate ideas. • Chooses a topic that she knows about and cares about.	• Reread writing and take out unimportant ideas to clarify the message.	• WML: Reteach WPS.U8: Revising to Focus and Organize Writing, WML1.

WML: Writing Minilesson GW: Guided Writir

Guide to Observing and Noting Writing Behaviors–Individual Student, Grade 3

Guide to Observing and Noting Writing Behaviors–Whole Class, Grade 3

Date: 2/1

Write students' names/initials and the date when each student consistently demonstrates this behavior. Use this form quarterly if possible to assess your entire class.

Behaviors and Understandings	Malik	Grace	Leo	Evan	Lucas	Rika	Mose	Max	Owen	Tani
Genre										
Make picture books that convey meaning through pictures and words.	10/8			10/8	10/8	10/8	10/8	10/8	10/8	
Write a variety of informational books (all-about, question-answer books).	12/8	12/8	12/8	12/8		12/8	12/8		12/8	12/8
Write a variety of procedural texts that include steps/instructions.	1/8	1/8	1/8	1/8	1/8	1/8	1/8	1/8	1/8	1/8
Write memory stories that include emotion and convey the significance of the story.	11/2	11/2	11/2	11/2	11/2	11/2	11/2	11/2	11/2	11/2
Write friendly letters that include date, salutation, closing, and signature.	9/21	9/21	9/21	9/21		9/21	9/21	9/21	9/21	9/21
Experiment with writing a variety of types of poems.		1/21		1/21		1/21	1/21	1/21	1/21	1/21
Write realistic fiction that includes a problem, a series of events, and a solution.	1/15		1/15		1/15	1/15	1/15	1/15	1/15	
Write opinion pieces with supportive reasons and examples.										
Craft										
Choose a title that fits the content of the piece.	9/21	9/21		9/21		9/21	9/21	9/21		9/21
Write stories in chronological order.	9/21	9/21	9/21	9/21	9/21	9/21	9/21	9/21	9/21	9/21
Write informational texts that are ordered by logic (e.g., related ideas, categories, sequence).	12/8	12/8	12/8		12/8	12/8	12/8		12/8	12/8
Write engaging beginnings and endings.	1/15			1/15		1/15	1/15	1/15	1/15	1/15
Introduce ideas followed by supportive details and examples.	12/8			12/8	12/8		12/8	12/8	12/8	12/8
Use some text features (e.g., headings, sidebars, table of contents).	12/8	12/8	12/8	12/8	12/8	12/8	12/8	12/8	12/8	12/8
Illustrate nonfiction with graphics (e.g., photographs, diagrams).	12/8	12/8	12/8	12/8	12/8	12/8	12/8	12/8	12/8	12/8
Communicate the main points to an audience.	12/8	12/8	12/8			12/8	12/8	12/8		
Develop a logical plot with a story problem, multiple events, and resolution.	1/15		1/15		1/15	1/15	1/15	1/15	1/15	1/15

 The Writing Minilessons Book, Grade 3 **Page 1**

Figure 6-7: Use the observation forms about every quarter. One form helps you focus on an individual child. The other form offers a snapshot of the whole class.

when necessary to decide if you want to wait to teach a particular umbrella, but don't be afraid to be responsive to your learners. You can always repeat or skip lessons if you have decided to teach them before they come up in the sequence.

Understand the Suggested Sequence of Lessons

The Suggested Sequence of Lessons (pp. 605–622 and also in online resources) is intended to establish a strong classroom community early in the year, work toward more sophisticated concepts across the year, and bring together the instructional pieces of your classroom. The learning that takes place during writing minilessons is applied in many situations in the classroom and so is reinforced daily across the curriculum and across the year.

Because many writing minilessons use mentor texts as a starting point, the lessons are sequenced so that they occur after students have had sufficient opportunities to build some clear understandings of aspects of writing through interactive read-aloud and shared reading. From these experiences, you and your students will have a rich set of mentor texts to pull into writing minilessons. If you are using shared and/or interactive writing regularly in your classroom to write together with the class, bring those texts into lessons as other mentor texts. They will be extremely meaningful since you will have developed them collaboratively. Your own modeled writing is another extremely powerful source for a mentor text.

The Suggested Sequence of Lessons follows the suggested sequence of text sets in *Fountas & Pinnell Classroom™ Interactive Read-Aloud Collection* (2019) and books in *Shared Reading Collection* (2022). If you are using either or both of these collections, you are invited to follow this sequence of texts. If you are not using them, the kinds of books students will need to have read are described on the first page of each umbrella in this book.

The text sets in the *Interactive Read-Aloud Collection* are grouped together by theme, topic, author, or genre, not by skill or concept. That's why in many minilessons, we use mentor texts from several different text sets and why the same books are used in more than one umbrella.

We have selected the most concrete and clear examples from the recommended books. In most cases, the minilessons draw on mentor texts that have been introduced within the same month. However, in some cases, minilessons taught later in the year might draw on books you read much earlier in the year. Most of the time, students will have no problem remembering these early books because you have read and talked about them. Sometimes students have responded through art, dramatic play, or writing. Once in a while, you might need to quickly reread a book or a portion of it before teaching the umbrella so it is fresh in the students' minds, but this is not usually necessary. Looking at some of the pictures and talking about the book is enough.

Use the Suggested Sequence to Connect the Pieces

To understand how the Suggested Sequence of Lessons can help you bring these instructional pieces together, let's look at a brief example from the suggested sequence. In month 2, we suggest reading the text sets Exploring Memory Stories and Author/Illustrator Study: Patricia Polacco from the *Interactive Read-Aloud Collection*. (You do not need any specific books in this text set; use any set of similar books available.) One of the suggestions for extending learning after the Exploring Memory Stories text set is to make a timeline of memories or use a graphic organizer to plan a memory story. These quick writes can be done in the students' writer's notebooks or with the whole class in shared writing. Later, the books from the *Interactive Read-Aloud Collection* become mentor texts in both reading and writing minilessons. In reading minilessons, students are engaged in understanding characters' feelings, motivations, and intentions—all important aspects of memory stories. The writing minilessons in GEN.U4: Writing Memory Stories introduce students to particular aspects of writing in this genre. You may also choose to write a memory story as a class using shared writing or in small groups using interactive writing for students who need extra support. A class-made memory story can also serve as one of the mentor texts. These mentor texts help students learn specific understandings about making a memory story, such as choosing a small moment, learning how to include thoughts and feelings, and telling why the memory is important (Figure 6-8). The first minilesson in GEN.U4 engages students in an immersive study of the genre. They spend time with a partner or small group studying memory stories and noticing the qualities of good memory story writing.

Studying the genre and engaging in shared writing experiences give students the background that helps them go deeper when they experience minilessons on specific topics. They are able to draw on their previous experiences with texts to fully understand the concepts in the minilessons. They can then apply this learning to their own independent writing. The Suggested Sequence of Lessons is one way to organize your teaching across the year to make these connections.

Connecting All the Pieces

Read aloud and enjoy memory stories with the class.

Use shared or interactive writing to write about a class memory.

Study mentor texts using writing minilessons.

Teach writing minilessons on specific aspects of memory stories.

Have students write their own memory stories.

Figure 6-8: The Suggested Sequence of Lessons helps you connect all the pieces of your classroom instruction and leads to students' own independent writing.

Add Writing Minilessons to the Day in Grade 3

After deciding what to teach and in what order to teach it, the next decision is when. In *Fountas & Pinnell Classroom™ System Guide, Grade 3* (2019), you will find frameworks for teaching and learning across a day. Using the schedules and the information in this book as guides, think about when you might incorporate writing minilessons as a regular part of the day in third grade. One suggestion is to provide a dedicated time each day (ideally 35–50 minutes) for independent writing, which is bookended by a writing minilesson and a time for sharing (Figure 1-4).

Third graders thrive on structure, organization, and predictability. When you set routines and a consistent time for writing minilessons and independent writing, you teach students what to expect. They find comfort in the reliability of the structure. Students write joyfully when they know they can count on time to experiment with and explore drawing and writing. They delight in knowing that what they have to say is valued. Writing minilessons build on the joy and enthusiasm students bring to all that they do in the classroom setting.

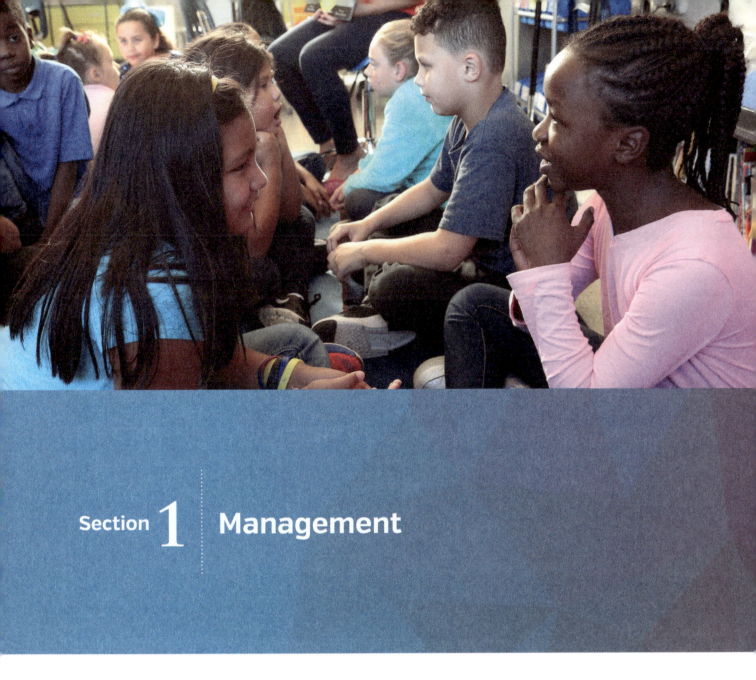

Section 1 | Management

MANAGEMENT MINILESSONS WILL help you set up routines for building a community of learners in the classroom. They allow you to teach effectively and efficiently and are directed toward the creation of an orderly, busy classroom in which students know what is expected and how to act responsibly and respectfully in a community of learners. A class that has a strong feeling of community is a safe place for all students to do their best work and enjoy learning. Most of the minilessons at the beginning of the school year will come from this section.

1 Management

UMBRELLA 1	Building Community Through Oral Storytelling	**101**
UMBRELLA 2	Working Together in the Classroom	**113**
UMBRELLA 3	Establishing Independent Writing	**125**
UMBRELLA 4	Introducing the Writing Folder	**135**

Building Community Through Oral Storytelling

Umbrella 1

Minilessons in This Umbrella

- **WML1** Get to know your classmates.
- **WML2** Tell a story about something from your Me Box.
- **WML3** Tell a story about your name.
- **WML4** Tell a story inspired by a book.
- **WML5** Tell stories about people and places you don't want to forget.

Before Teaching Umbrella 1 Minilessons

This umbrella is primarily about building a community in which all students feel included and honored for who they are. At the same time, the minilessons will help students prepare for writing by generating story ideas and by providing oral rehearsal for stories that can be written later. Through the stories, students will explore their own identities and get to know one another, thereby building the foundation for a community of writers. Oral storytelling yields multiple benefits:

- Students gain an understanding that people share what they are thinking through language, both oral and written.
- Students learn that one person's stories can inspire ideas for their own stories.
- Students can rehearse what they want to say and how to say it before writing.
- Students work well together in class because they get to know one another by hearing stories about each other's experiences and interests.

For mentor texts, use the books listed below from *Fountas & Pinnell Classroom*™ *Interactive Read-Aloud Collection*, or choose books from the classroom library that tell stories that are personal to the writers.

Interactive Read-Aloud Collection

The Importance of Kindness

Under the Lemon Moon by Edith Hope Fine

Last Day Blues by Julie Danneberg

The Can Man by Laura E. Williams

As you read and enjoy these or other texts together, help students
- discuss how the stories make them think about events in their own lives, and
- talk about what events from an author's own life may been used as the basis for the stories.

Interactive Read-Aloud
Kindness

WML1

MGT.U1.WML1

Writing Minilesson Principle
Get to know your classmates.

Building Community Through Oral Storytelling

You Will Need

- chart paper and markers
- sticky notes

Academic Language / Important Vocabulary

- community
- questions
- interview

Continuum Connection

- Reveal something important about self or about life
- Understand that the writer can look back or think about the memory or experience and share thoughts and feelings about it
- Use conventions of respectful conversation
- Express and reflect on their own feelings and recognize the feelings of others
- Refrain from speaking over others
- Demonstrate respectful listening behaviors
- Ask questions for clarification or to gain information

GOAL

Learn about classmates through interviewing.

RATIONALE

Students learn to value the special qualities of their classmates and feel valued for who they are when they get to know one another. Getting to know one another creates a positive classroom community in which students can freely express themselves. It is important to keep in mind that not all students come from a peaceful home setting, so adapt the lesson as needed to ensure that each student in the class is comfortable sharing.

ASSESS LEARNING

- Notice whether students show an interest in getting to know each other.
- Observe whether students recognize and value special qualities in themselves and others.
- Look for evidence that students can use vocabulary such as *community*, *questions*, and *interview*.

MINILESSON

Engage students in an interactive lesson about getting to know and appreciate one another by modeling how to ask questions. Here is an example.

> When you get to know a person, sometimes you will learn something new. Other times, you will find out that the two of you have something in common.

- Share information about yourself (as appropriate for the classroom), for example, something similar to the following.

  > One thing you might be interested to know about me is that I speak Spanish with my grandmother.

- Guide students to think about questions they could ask to learn this information.

  > What is a question you could ask that might help you learn what languages someone speaks at home?

- Support the conversation as needed. Begin a list on chart paper of interview questions, adding *What languages does your family speak?*

  > A way to get to know each other is by asking questions. What are some other questions you might ask to get to know someone?

- As needed, guide the conversation by sharing information about yourself to help students generate interview questions. Add questions to the chart, keeping the categories general.

Have a Try

Invite students to turn and talk about getting to know each other.

> When you interview someone, you ask questions to get to know the person better. We started a list of some interview questions today. Choose one interview question to ask your partner.

▸ After time for discussion, ask one or two volunteers to share what they learned about a classmate.

Summarize and Apply

Summarize the lesson. Write the principle on the chart.

> Today you learned about getting to know each other. During writing time, choose some interview questions to ask your partner. Try to find out three interesting things about the person and one thing you admire. Write down what you learn and bring your list to share when we meet later.

▸ You may decide to assign partners so that students have an opportunity to interview someone they do not know very well.

> **Get to know your classmates.**
>
> - What languages does your family speak?
> - What do you like to make?
> - Tell about your hobbies.
> - What foods do you eat or cook at home?
> - What do you like to do with your family?
> - What places do you go to after school?
> - What do you like to do with friends?
> - What is one thing that is special about you?
> - Tell me about a family tradition.

Confer

▸ During independent writing, move around the room to confer briefly with students about what they are learning about their classmates. Use the following prompts as needed.
  - *How does getting to know your classmates help our classroom community?*
  - *What is one thing you learned about someone today?*
  - *Let's look at the chart and talk about some interview questions you can ask.*

Share

Following independent writing, gather students in a circle in the meeting area. Ask each student to share what they learned about their partner.

> Share two things you learned about the person you interviewed today.

Umbrella 1: Building Community Through Oral Storytelling

WML 2
MGT.U1.WML2

Writing Minilesson Principle
Tell a story about something from your Me Box.

Building Community Through Oral Storytelling

You Will Need

- Me Boxes for you and for each student or objects for generating story ideas
- paper and pencil for each student (Have a Try)
- chart paper and markers

Academic Language / Important Vocabulary

- stories
- object
- identity
- important
- Me Box

Continuum Connection

- Understand that writers may tell stories from their own lives
- Understand that the writer can look back or think about the memory or experience and share thoughts and feelings about it
- Reveal something important about self or about life
- Look for ideas and topics in personal experiences, shared through talk

GOAL

Get to know classmates through the stories they tell.

RATIONALE

Sharing stories not only prompts new story ideas but also helps students get to know one another. Storytelling can help build the foundation for a strong writing community.

ASSESS LEARNING

- Observe for evidence that students are listening to and learning from each other's stories.
- Notice whether students keep a list of writing ideas.
- Look for evidence that students can use vocabulary such as *stories*, *object*, *identity*, *important*, and *Me Box*.

MINILESSON

To help students generate a list of story ideas, demonstrate thinking about and recording story ideas about an object. Use an object from your Me Box to model the experience. Here is an example.

- Before teaching this lesson, have each student prepare a Me Box filled with meaningful objects (e.g., objects that represent family traditions, special memories, hobbies). Make a Me Box for yourself as well. Alternatively, make sure each student has an object that can be the inspiration for a story.

- Choose an item from your Me Box. Tell a few personal stories about the object you have chosen. This is just an example.

  > In my Me Box there is a bus ticket. When I was younger, I used to take the bus by myself every Saturday to visit my dad. I would count the five stops before I had to change buses. Sometimes, I would have enough time while I waited to talk to Mr. Simms, who had a small shop on the corner. He always made me laugh with his funny stories.

- Write your idea on the chart.

  > How did my story help you get to know me better?
  >
  > There are other stories I could tell about my bus ticket.

- Share one or two more ideas for stories you could tell about the object and add the ideas to the chart. Then engage students in a discussion about the stories you told.

  > Do my stories make you think about any ideas for your own stories?
  >
  > Hearing someone's story can give you some ideas for your own stories.

The Writing Minilessons Book, Grade 3

Have a Try

Invite students to think about story ideas inspired by objects from their Me Boxes.

> Look at the objects in your Me Box. What stories come to mind? Write some ideas for stories. You might have more than one idea for one object.

▸ Invite a few students to share ideas for their stories. Add to the chart.

Summarize and Apply

Summarize the lesson. Have students prepare to tell a story about an object in their Me Boxes.

> How can your classmates get to know you?

▸ Write the principle at the top of the chart.

> Reread your list of ideas. You can add more ideas. Then circle one idea that you can use to tell a story to a partner when we meet later.

▸ Have students save the lists so they can keep adding to them as they think of more story ideas throughout this umbrella.

Tell a story about something from your Me Box.

Object	Story Idea
bus ticket	• talking with Mr. Simms at the bus stop • the time I got off at the wrong stop • meeting my friend Jasper on the bus ride
cornbread package label	• making cornbread with my brother • why cornbread is my favorite food • how I build a cornbread sandwich
photo of a lizard	• the lizard that I named Gus who lived outside my apartment • the funny things Gus does • fantasy story about Gus's family

Confer

▸ During independent writing, move around the room to confer briefly with students about stories they could tell. Use the following prompts as needed.

- *This looks like something that is special to you. What is a story you could tell about it?*
- *Why did you include this object in your Me Box? That can be an idea for a story.*
- *Tell me a story about this object.*

Share

Following independent writing, have students gather in pairs in the meeting area to share stories. If there is time after students share a story, you might want to have them turn to a different partner and retell their stories.

> Tell a short story about one of the ideas on your list to your partner.

WML3
MGT.U1.WML3

Writing Minilesson Principle
Tell a story about your name.

Building Community Through Oral Storytelling

You Will Need

- a familiar book that includes character names, such as *Under the Lemon Moon* by Edith Hope Fine, from Text Set: The Importance of Kindness
- chart paper and markers
- students' writing idea lists started in WML2
- To download the following online resource for this lesson, visit **fp.pub/resources**:
  - chart art (optional)

Academic Language / Important Vocabulary

- stories
- name
- special

Continuum Connection

- Understand that writers may tell stories from their own lives
- Understand that the writer can look back or think about the memory or experience and share thoughts and feelings about it
- Look for ideas and topics in personal experiences, shared through talk
- Make notes about crafting ideas

GOAL

Get to know classmates through the stories they tell.

RATIONALE

Hearing stories read aloud and listening to one another's stories can prompt students to think of their own stories. When they tell stories about part of their identities, such as their names, they share something about who they are and how they are similar to or different from each other. From their stories, they learn what makes each one of them a special human being and supports a safe and respectful classroom community.

ASSESS LEARNING

- Observe for evidence that students are listening to and learning from each other's stories.
- Notice whether students keep a list of writing ideas.
- Look for evidence that students can use vocabulary such as *stories*, *name*, and *special*.

MINILESSON

Demonstrate thinking about how to tell a story about a name by using mentor texts and modeling a story about your own name to support students' experiences of telling stories. Here is an example.

- Reread pages 5–6 in *Under the Lemon Moon*.

  The author chose to use the names Blanca and Rosalinda in this story. Maybe she knew someone with those names, or maybe she liked the names for other reasons. What are your thoughts about the names she chose?

- Support a conversation about the names. If students in the classroom speak both English and Spanish, they might recognize that the name *Blanca* means "white," and the chicken is also white, and that the name *Rosalinda* means "pretty rose," and Rosalinda likes plants.

  The author thought carefully about how to name her characters. When people name their children, they, too, think carefully about names. Some names have a meaning or a story behind them. My grandmother named my uncle after two movie stars she really liked! She named my dad after my grandpa, and I have the same name. I could tell a story about the different things I learned from them and how our names connect us.

- Make a three-column chart and write your name in the left column, where your name comes from in the middle column, and a story idea in the right column.

Have a Try

Invite students to talk to a partner about ideas for stories using their names or someone else's name.

> What about your name? Turn and talk to your partner about an idea for a story about your name. If you don't have a story idea for your name, think of one for another person's name. You could also think about why your name is a good one for you. Maybe your partner's idea will make you think of another story idea.

▸ After time for discussion, ask several volunteers to share their story ideas. Add ideas to the chart.

Summarize and Apply

Summarize the lesson. Have students add to their lists (from WML2) and tell a story to a partner.

> You could tell a story about a name—your name or another name.

▸ Write the principle at the top of the chart.

> Today, add story ideas about your name or about someone else's name to your list. Then circle one story idea. Tell the story to a partner.

▸ Have students save their lists.

Tell a story about your name.		
Mr. Tomás	• same name as my dad and grandpa	• could tell about the things I learned from the others in my family
Yooko	• name means tiger	• could tell about how my family says I act like a tiger sometimes
Leslyn	• made-up name	• could tell about how one parent wanted Lesley and one wanted Lynn
Jasmine	• everyone in the family has a name that begins with J	• could tell about what people say when they hear all the names

My name comes from . . .

I am named after . . .

Confer

▸ During independent writing, move around the room to confer briefly with students about stories they could tell. Use the following prompts as needed.
   • *Think about the people in your family. Do their names make you think of any story ideas?*
   • *What is something that is special about your name? You could write that on your list.*
   • *If you could pick any name to have, what would it be? You could tell about that.*

Share

Following independent writing, gather students in pairs in the meeting area to tell their stories.

> Tell your name story to a different partner.

WML 4
MGT.U1.WML4

Writing Minilesson Principle
Tell a story inspired by a book.

Building Community Through Oral Storytelling

You Will Need

- several familiar books, such as the following from Text Set: The Importance of Kindness:
  - *Last Day Blues* by Julie Danneberg
  - *The Can Man* by Laura E. Williams
- chart paper and markers
- students' writing idea lists started in WML2

Academic Language / Important Vocabulary

- stories
- books
- inspired

Continuum Connection

- Understand that writers may tell stories from their own lives
- Understand that the writer can look back or think about the memory or experience and share thoughts and feelings about it
- Reveal something important about self or about life
- Look for ideas and topics in personal experiences, shared through talk
- Get ideas from books and other writers about how to approach a topic
- Make notes about crafting ideas

GOAL
Get to know classmates through the stories they tell.

RATIONALE
When students tell stories about themselves, they share something about who they are and how they are similar to or different from each other.

ASSESS LEARNING
- Observe for evidence that students are listening to and learning from each other's stories.
- Notice whether students keep a list of writing ideas.
- Look for evidence that students can use vocabulary such as *stories*, *books*, and *inspired*.

MINILESSON

To help students think about the minilesson principle, provide an interactive lesson about using books as inspiration for stories. Here is an example.

- Display a familiar book, such as *Last Day Blues*. Describe how the book gives you an idea for a story.

  > Julie Danneberg wrote *Last Day Blues* about how the students were feeling about the last day of school in Mrs. Hartwell's class. This story gives me an idea for a story I could tell about the last day of school in this classroom. Last year, we heard a strange croaking sound and realized that a frog was hopping around in the classroom. It was very funny and I think I could tell a great story about that.

- On chart paper, start a list of story ideas that are inspired by books and add this idea.

  > Does this book make you think of anything from your own life that might make a good story?

- Support the conversation, revisiting parts of the book as needed to help students generate story ideas.

- Using students' suggestions, add to the list on chart paper.

Have a Try

Invite students to talk to a partner about ideas for stories that are inspired by books.

▸ Show the cover and revisit a few pages from a familiar book, such as *The Can Man*.

> Does *The Can Man* give you any ideas about a story that you could tell? Turn and talk about *The Can Man* and any ideas it gives you for telling a new story.

▸ After time for discussion, ask several volunteers to share their story ideas. Add ideas to the chart.

Summarize and Apply

Summarize the lesson. Have students add to the story ideas list they started in WML2. Add the principle to the chart.

> Today, look back at one or more books you have read. What story ideas do they make you think of? Write those ideas on your list. Then circle one story idea. Tell the story to a partner.

▸ Have students save their lists.

Tell a story inspired by a book.

- A frog hopping around the classroom on the last day of school

- A special card received from grandparents for birthday

- A time someone gave you a surprise gift

- A neighbor who was kind when you hurt your leg

Confer

▸ During independent writing, move around the room to confer briefly with students about stories they could tell. Use the following prompts as needed.

- *What book made you think of this idea?*
- *Let's look at some books we have read together and think about story ideas.*
- *Share the story ideas you have written on your list.*

Share

Following independent writing, gather students in pairs in the meeting area to share their stories inspired by books.

> Tell your story to a different partner.

Umbrella 1: Building Community Through Oral Storytelling

WML 5
MGT.U1.WML5

Writing Minilesson Principle
Tell stories about people and places you don't want to forget.

Building Community Through Oral Storytelling

You Will Need

- several familiar books that include people and a setting, such as the following from Text Set: The Importance of Kindness:
  - *Under the Lemon Moon* by Edith Hope Fine
  - *The Can Man* by Laura E. Williams
- chart paper and markers
- students' writing idea lists started in WML2

Academic Language / Important Vocabulary

- stories
- places
- people

Continuum Connection

- Describe a setting and how it is related to the writer's experiences
- Understand that writers may tell stories from their own lives
- Understand that the writer can look back or think about the memory or experience and share thoughts and feelings about it
- Reveal something important about self or about life
- Generate and expand ideas through talk with peers and teacher
- Look for ideas and topics in personal experiences, shared through talk

GOAL
Get to know classmates through the stories they tell.

RATIONALE
Telling stories about familiar people and places is another way for students to generate story ideas. When one person tells a story, other people get ideas for their own stories. Reminding students that ideas for telling stories can come from their lives helps them understand that what they know has value.

ASSESS LEARNING

- Observe for evidence that students are listening to and learning from each other's stories.
- Notice whether students keep a list of writing ideas.
- Look for evidence that students can use vocabulary such as *stories*, *people*, and *places*.

MINILESSON

To help students think about the minilesson principle, demonstrate thinking about story ideas from books, other people's stories, or students' own stories about people and places. Here is an example.

- Show pages 3–6 of *Under the Lemon Moon*.

    This story is about a girl who lives in the countryside in Mexico. The yard is important to her because it has a special lemon tree.

- Show pages 3–6 of *The Can Man*.

    The author tells a story that takes place in a city and shows the special friendship that Tim and Mr. Peters have.

    What are your thoughts about where these authors probably got their ideas for writing?

- Guide students to notice that the authors probably got their ideas for writing from people and places that they knew or learned about and want to remember.
- Using a personal experience, tell a brief story about a special person and place.
- Write your idea on the chart paper.

Have a Try

Invite students to turn and talk about story ideas about people and places they know.

> Think of someone you know or a place you have been. I told a story about my life, but your story will be about something different that is personal to you. Tell your partner about an idea for a story you could tell about a person or a place.

▸ After time for discussion, invite students to share ideas for their stories. Add ideas to the chart.

Summarize and Apply

Summarize the lesson. Write the principle on the chart. Have students add to the list they started in WML2 and choose a story to tell.

> Today, add to your list several ideas for stories about people you know or places you have been. Then circle one idea. Tell the story to a partner.

Tell stories about people and places you don't want to forget.

* on the farm with Aunt Jenny (feeding the baby goats)

* playing at my cousins' house (the popcorn game)

* racing my mom on the slides down the street from where we live

* weeknights at Tanuk's house (our babysitter) when my parents go to work

---

Confer

▸ During independent writing, move around the room to confer briefly with students about stories they could tell. Use the following prompts as needed.
- Are you ready to tell a story using an idea from your list?
- What made you think of this idea?
- Let's look at your list. What idea would you like to tell a story about?
- What person or place do you not want to forget? You could write that on your list.

Share

Following independent writing, gather students in pairs in the meeting area to share stories about people and places. Model how to thank each student for sharing a story.

> Tell your story to a different partner.

Umbrella 1: Building Community Through Oral Storytelling

Assessment

After you have taught the minilessons in this umbrella, observe students in a variety of classroom activities. Use *The Fountas & Pinnell Literacy Continuum* to notice, teach for, and support students' learning as you observe their attempts at generating story ideas and telling stories.

- What evidence do you have of students' new understandings related to building community through storytelling?
  - Are students interested in getting to know each other?
  - Do students respect and value the diversity of others in the classroom?
  - Are students telling stories about what makes them special?
  - Can they develop stories from their Me Boxes?
  - Do students use ideas, events, places, and people from their own lives to tell stories?
  - Are they using vocabulary such as *community*, *interview*, *special*, *stories*, *objects*, *important*, *Me Box*, *name*, *people*, and *places*?
- In what ways, beyond the scope of this umbrella, are students showing readiness for storytelling?
  - Do they choose a variety of topics for storytelling?
  - Are they using ideas from their own lives when they make books?

Use your observations to determine the next umbrella you will teach. You may also consult Suggested Sequence of Lessons (pp. 605–622) for guidance.

EXTENSIONS FOR BUILDING COMMUNITY THROUGH ORAL STORYTELLING

- In small groups, guide students in making the transition from oral to written storytelling.

- Invite family and community members into the classroom to orally share stories about their lives so that students can experience a wide diversity of storytelling.

- Provide time for students to tell stories from the ideas on their lists. Look for ways that students can make connections to one another through their stories.

- Have students write acrostic name poems: Write the name vertically. For each letter, write a word or phrase that describes the person, or write words that make a phrase or sentence when read consecutively. An acrostic name poem for Ava might be *Awesome, Very smart, Amazing* or *Always Very Athletic*.

- Revisit the charts in this lesson after a writer's notebook is introduced as a way to help students add to their writing ideas. Students can glue their lists of story ideas into their notebooks.

Working Together in the Classroom

Umbrella 2

Interactive Read-Aloud
Kindness

Minilessons in This Umbrella

WML1	Show respect to each other.
WML2	Use an appropriate voice level.
WML3	Find ways to solve problems when you need help.
WML4	Return materials to where they belong.
WML5	Turn and talk to share your thinking.

Before Teaching Umbrella 2 Minilessons

These minilessons have a dual purpose: establishing an orderly, efficient classroom and building a community of writers. Establishing a respectful and organized classroom community at the beginning of the school year creates an environment in which students learn to know and trust one another. If you are using *The Reading Minilessons Book, Grade 3* (Fountas and Pinnell 2019) and have already taught the first umbrellas in the Management and Literary Analysis sections, you may not need to teach every lesson unless students need a reminder.

Note that this umbrella is not focused on rule following; instead, the goal is to create a warm and inviting student-centered classroom in which students take ownership of their space and materials and do their best work. Sharing time each day focuses on both classroom management and on getting to know each other. Use the books listed below from *Fountas & Pinnell Classroom™ Interactive Read-Aloud Collection* or other books related to what it means to be part of a caring community.

Interactive Read-Aloud Collection
The Importance of Kindness

Enemy Pie by Derek Munson

The Can Man by Laura E. Williams

Last Day Blues by Julie Danneberg

Sophie's Masterpiece: A Spider's Tale by Eileen Spinelli

Under the Lemon Moon by Edith Hope Fine

As you read and enjoy these texts together, help students
- think about different ways that people work together, and
- talk about different ways to solve problems.

Section 1: Management

Umbrella 2: Working Together in the Classroom

WML1
MGT.U2.WML1

Writing Minilesson Principle
Show respect to each other.

Working Together in the Classroom

You Will Need

- a familiar book that relates to respect, such as *Enemy Pie* by Derek Munson, from Text Set: The Importance of Kindness
- chart paper and markers

Academic Language / Important Vocabulary

- community
- respect
- kind
- words
- actions

Continuum Connection

- Use conventions of respectful conversation
- Enter a conversation appropriately
- Demonstrate respectful listening behaviors
- Listen and respond to a partner by agreeing, disagreeing, or adding on, and explaining reasons
- Express and reflect on their own feelings and recognize the feelings of others
- Refrain from speaking over others
- Use appropriate conventions in small-group discussion (e.g., "I agree with _____ because . . ."; "I'd like to change the subject . . .")

GOAL

Explore and define what it means to show respect to each other.

RATIONALE

When students learn to show respect to each other, they become conscious of their behavior and ways to improve it. By learning to listen and respond respectfully to communicate their opinions and feelings, they contribute to a positive learning community and learn to show empathy and concern for others.

ASSESS LEARNING

- Observe whether students can agree and disagree respectfully.
- Listen to students interacting with each other and notice if they are respectful.
- Look for evidence that students can use vocabulary such as *community*, *respect*, *kind*, *words*, and *actions*.

MINILESSON

To help students think about the minilesson principle, use a mentor text to engage them in a conversation about respectful words and actions. Here is an example.

- Briefly show and revisit *Enemy Pie*.

    What are your thoughts about how the boys treated each other?

- Guide the conversation to help students recognize that the boys became friends when they treated each other nicely and showed interest in each other.
- Introduce and talk about the concept of respect.

    Respect means that you treat people in a way that shows that you care about them and their feelings. In our classroom community, we can show respect to each other each day. What are some words we can use and some actions we can do to show respect for each other?

- Guide the conversation to help students think of words and actions that are kind and respectful. As they provide suggestions, make two lists on chart paper, placing examples of respectful words in one column and respectful actions in the other.
- If students mention looking at one another, take into consideration that some students may not be comfortable establishing or able to establish eye contact because of cultural conventions or for other reasons. If this is the case in your class, adjust the lesson accordingly.

WML1

MGT.U2.WML1

Have a Try

Invite students to turn and talk about using words and actions in a positive way.

> Look at the chart and think about one way you might show respect through words and actions today. Turn and talk to your partner about some times when you might do that.

▸ After time for discussion, ask a few volunteers to share.

Summarize and Apply

Summarize the lesson. Write the principle on the chart.

> Why should you show respect to your classmates?

> Today you can continue working on a piece of writing you already started or begin something new. As you work, use kind words and actions whenever you can. Showing respect to each other will help make our classroom community a place where you can all work together. Look at the chart to help you remember ideas.

Confer

▸ During independent writing, move around the room to confer briefly with as many individual students as time allows. Sit side by side with them and invite them to talk about showing respect. Use the following prompts as needed.

- How can you use kind words and actions to share what you are thinking?
- When might you say thank you to someone?
- What are some ways you can agree or disagree politely with what someone says?

Share

Following independent writing, gather students in the meeting area to talk about their experiences using or hearing kind words and to share their writing.

> Share a time when you showed respect to someone or when someone showed respect to you.

> How did it make you feel when someone used kind words?

Umbrella 2: Working Together in the Classroom

Section 1: Management

WML 2

MGT.U2.WML2

Writing Minilesson Principle
Use an appropriate voice level.

Working Together in the Classroom

You Will Need

- chart paper and markers
- To download the following online resource for this lesson, visit **fp.pub/resources**:
  - chart art (optional)

Academic Language / Important Vocabulary

- voice level
- appropriate
- silent
- soft
- normal
- loud

Continuum Connection

- Speak at an appropriate volume
- Refrain from speaking over others
- Adjust speaking volume for different contexts

GOAL

Learn to use an appropriate voice level.

RATIONALE

One of the ways students can show respect to one another is to learn to modify their voice level to the situation: loud enough for classmates to hear when speaking to the class and quiet enough when classmates are working. When you teach students appropriate voice levels for different activities, they learn to independently determine which voice level to use and adjust their voices accordingly.

ASSESS LEARNING

- Observe for evidence that students understand why a certain voice level is appropriate for a specific situation.
- Listen as students participate in different activities. Do they adjust their voice levels accordingly?
- Look for evidence that students can use vocabulary such as *voice level*, *appropriate*, *silent*, *soft*, *normal*, and *loud*.

MINILESSON

To help students think about the minilesson principle, engage them in discussing voice levels and in creating an anchor chart. Here is an example.

- Talk about the importance of sometimes using a soft voice and sometimes using a loud voice.

  > When you are on the playground, how does your voice sound?
  >
  > When you are working on some writing, how does your voice sound?
  >
  > Does your voice sound the same when you are on the playground as when you are doing your writing? Why?
  >
  > We can talk about the kind of voice to use by using a number. A zero voice means that you are silent.

- Begin a voice level chart that provides examples to show appropriate voice levels. In the first column, include the numeral *0*, the word *Silent*, and a sketch to show a student who is not speaking.

  > What are times at school when you use a zero voice?

- Add students' examples to the chart.
- Repeat the activity for each voice level. On the chart, indicate that *1* means using a soft voice, *2* means using a normal voice, and *3* means using a loud voice.

The Writing Minilessons Book, Grade 3

Have a Try

Invite students to talk to a partner about using appropriate voice levels.

> With your partner, choose one voice level to talk about. What are other times when you might use that voice level?

- After a brief time for discussion, ask students to share new ideas, and add to the chart. Have them discuss why using an appropriate voice level is important.

Summarize and Apply

Summarize the lesson. Remind students to pay attention to their voice levels as they work.

> Today, you can continue working on a piece of writing you already started or begin something new. As you work, think about the appropriate voice level and practice using that type of voice. Look at the chart to help you remember.

- Keep the voice level chart posted so students can refer to it.

Confer

- During independent writing, move around the room to confer briefly with as many individual students as time allows. Sit side by side with them and invite them to talk about the voice levels they are using. Use the following prompts as needed.
  - Look at the chart. Which voice level are you using?
  - Which voice level will you use during writing time?
  - Why will you use a zero voice during writing time?
  - Which voice level will you use when you work with a partner? Why?

Share

Following independent writing, gather students in the meeting area to talk about the voice levels they have used today and to share their writing.

> What did you do during writing time today? What voice level did you use?

> Share something that you drew or wrote about today. As you share, think about the voice level you will use.

Umbrella 2: Working Together in the Classroom

WML 3
MGT.U2.WML3

Writing Minilesson Principle
Find ways to solve problems when you need help.

Working Together in the Classroom

You Will Need

- a familiar book that shows independent problem solving, such as *The Can Man* by Laura E. Williams, from Text Set: The Importance of Kindness
- chart paper and markers
- To download the following online resource for this lesson, visit **fp.pub/resources**:
  - chart art (optional)

Academic Language / Important Vocabulary

- problem
- solve
- reread
- directions
- help
- questions
- emergency

Continuum Connection

- Write with independent initiative and investment
- Enter a conversation appropriately
- Listen with attention during instruction, and respond with statements and questions
- Listen to, remember, and follow directions with multiple steps

---

GOAL

Find ways to solve problems independently.

RATIONALE

The ability to choose and implement appropriate problem-solving strategies encourages independence in the students and allows time for you to work with small groups or individuals.

ASSESS LEARNING

- Observe for evidence that students are trying to solve problems independently.
- Look for evidence that students can use vocabulary such as *problem*, *solve*, *reread*, *directions*, *help*, *questions*, and *emergency*.

MINILESSON

To help students think about the minilesson principle, engage them in a discussion of how to problem solve independently. Here is an example.

- Show the cover and briefly revisit *The Can Man*.

    What problem did Tim have and how did he solve his problem?

- Briefly support a conversation to help students identify that Tim needed money for a skateboard, so he started collecting cans for recycling. In the end, he gave the money to Mr. Peters for a warm coat and Mr. Peters gave Tim a skateboard for his birthday.

    In the story, Tim had to figure out how to solve a problem. Like Tim, it is important for you to learn to solve some problems on your own. This is especially true when I am working with other students. What are some ways you can try to solve a problem on your own?

- Engage students in a discussion of different problems they might have and solutions they can try. Prompt the conversation as needed. Some suggestions are below.

    - *What if you do not know what materials you need?*
    - *What if you are not sure what to do next?*
    - *What if you finish early?*

- As students provide solutions, record their ideas on chart paper, choosing generalized language. Keep the chart posted and add to it as more problems and solutions arise.

- Briefly discuss that it is okay to interrupt the teacher if there is an emergency.

Have a Try

Invite students to turn and talk about solving problems.

> Why is it important to try to solve problems on your own? Turn and talk about that.

- After time for discussion, ask a few volunteers to share.

Summarize and Apply

Summarize the lesson. Write the principle at the top of the chart.

> Today, you can continue working on something you already started or begin something new. If you have a question when you are working on writing today, look at the chart for ways to solve your problem.

Confer

- During independent writing, move around the room to confer briefly with as many individual students as time allows. Sit side by side with them and invite them to talk about solving problems on their own. Use the following prompts as needed.
  - *If you can't remember the directions, how can you solve that problem?*
  - *What can you do if you do not know how to spell a word?*
  - *Look back at the chart. What is one way you can solve a problem on your own?*

Share

Following independent writing, gather students in the meeting area to talk about problem solving.

> Did anyone solve a problem on your own today? Tell about that.

> Share a way that it helps our classroom community when you try to solve problems on your own.

Find ways to solve problems when you need help.

Problem	Solution
You don't understand what you're supposed to be doing.	Reread the directions. Ask a friend to help you.
You have questions about the writing you're working on.	Reread your writing. Begin another piece of writing.
You don't know where to find something.	Look for a basket with the right label on it.
You have a problem with another student.	Talk politely and calmly to the person about how you feel and try to find a solution together.
You finish your work early.	Review your work and then read, write, or draw silently.

WML 4
MGT.U2.WML4

Writing Minilesson Principle
Return materials to where they belong.

Working Together in the Classroom

You Will Need

- a familiar book that includes an illustration of a classroom with materials, such as *Last Day Blues* by Julie Danneberg, from Text Set: The Importance of Kindness
- two students prepared ahead of time to model taking care of materials
- chart paper and markers
- To download the following online resource for this lesson, visit **fp.pub/resources**:
  - chart art (optional)

Academic Language / Important Vocabulary

- materials
- properly
- return

Continuum Connection

- Listen to, remember, and follow directions with multiple steps

---

GOAL

Learn to take good care of classroom materials by returning them to where they belong.

RATIONALE

Another way to show respect in the classroom is to take good care of shared materials by returning them to their assigned places so that all students can locate them easily. It goes without saying that the materials should be used in such a way as to keep them in good condition.

ASSESS LEARNING

- Observe students as they finish an activity. Do they return the materials to their assigned places?
- Look for evidence that students can use vocabulary such as *materials*, *properly*, and *return*.

MINILESSON

To help students think about the minilesson principle, engage them in a demonstration and conversation about putting away classroom materials. Here is an example.

- Show pages 18–19 in *Last Day Blues*.

  What do you notice about what the students are doing in the classroom?

- Have a brief discussion about how they are taking care of the classroom.

  There are ways that you can take care of our classroom. In our classroom community, we share many materials. Watch closely as _____ and _____ get the materials they need to do their work. We will talk about what they do when they finish working.

- Provide a few minutes for the prepared students to demonstrate getting and returning writing materials. Point out that the materials are labeled to show where they belong.

  What did you notice?

  What are some reasons it's a good idea to return your materials to the places they belong?

- Record responses on chart paper.

  When you are cleaning up, what voice level should you use?

Have a Try

Invite students to turn and talk about the importance of taking care of classroom materials.

> Choose one item on the chart. Turn and talk about why it is important.

- After time for discussion, ask a few volunteers to share.

Summarize and Apply

Summarize the lesson.

> Today, we talked about a way to show respect to your classmates. What did we talk about?

- Write the principle at the top of the chart.

> Today, you can continue working on a piece of writing you have already started or you may begin a new piece of writing. If you use any classroom materials when you work, remember to put them away when you finish and to use a zero voice.

Return materials to where they belong.

- Other students can use the materials.
- You can find the materials when you need them.
- Your work area is not cluttered and messy.
- The classroom is neat and organized for everyone.

Confer

- During independent writing, move around the room to confer briefly with as many individual students as time allows. Sit side by side with them and invite them to talk about using classroom materials. Use the following prompts as needed.
  - *How will you take good care of the materials you use?*
  - *I notice you are using some classroom materials for writing today. What will you do with them when you are finished?*
  - *Where do the _____ belong?*

Share

Following independent writing, gather students in the meeting area to share their writing.

> Who would like to share some writing you worked on today?

> Where did you put your materials when you finished writing?

WML 5
MGT.U2.WML5

Writing Minilesson Principle
Turn and talk to share your thinking.

Working Together in the Classroom

You Will Need

- a student prepared to model turn and talk
- two texts that you have read aloud recently, such as *Sophie's Masterpiece* by Eileen Spinelli and *Under the Lemon Moon* by Edith Hope Fine, from Text Set: The Importance of Kindness
- chart paper and markers
- To download the following online resource for this lesson, visit **fp.pub/resources**:
    - chart art (optional)

Academic Language / Important Vocabulary

- turn and talk
- voice level
- listen
- signal

Continuum Connection

- Engage actively in conversational routines: e.g., turn and talk
- Refrain from speaking over others
- Use conventions of respectful conversation
- Use appropriate conventions in small-group discussion (e.g., "I agree with _____ because..."; "I'd like to change the subject...")
- Listen to and speak to a partner about a given idea, and make connections to the partner's idea

GOAL

Develop guidelines for turn and talk.

RATIONALE

Turn and talk routines allow students to express themselves verbally, to engage in conversation with others, and to share opinions. The routines also offer a chance for students to rehearse their oral language in a safe way before sharing with the class. When students learn and practice procedures for turn and talk, they develop conversational skills that can be applied to speaking in a larger group and in other situations.

ASSESS LEARNING

- Watch and listen to students as they turn and talk and notice if they follow the guidelines.
- Observe whether both students in a pair have a chance to talk.
- Look for evidence that students can use vocabulary such as *turn and talk*, *listen*, *voice level*, and *signal*.

MINILESSON

To help students think about the minilesson principle, choose familiar texts to use in a demonstration of the turn and talk routine. Then engage students in a conversation about what they noticed. Here is an example.

- Ahead of time, decide on a transition signal that you will use each time to indicate that students should end turn and talk and return to the whole group conversation.
- Show the cover of a book you have recently read, such as *Sophie's Masterpiece*.

    Sometimes when you write something or read a book, you turn and talk to a partner about your thinking. Today, _____ is my partner, and we are going to turn and talk about some interesting things that the writer, Eileen Spinelli, has done in *Sophie's Masterpiece*.

    While we turn and talk, watch and listen carefully.

- Briefly model the turn and talk procedure, offering an opinion about the writer's craft. Prompt the student to talk about whether he agrees or disagrees with you and why. Use the transition signal when you finish.

    What did you notice when you watched and listened to the turn and talk?

- As students respond, begin a list on chart paper to create turn and talk guidelines. If students mention looking at each other, take into consideration that some students may not be comfortable establishing or able to establish eye contact because of cultural conventions or for other reasons. Adjust the lesson accordingly.

    When you turn and talk, remember to always give reasons for your thinking.

Have a Try

Invite students to apply what they learned by turning and talking to a partner.

- Show the cover of another book you have recently read with the students, such as *Under the Lemon Moon*.

    Turn and talk to your partner to share your thinking about this story. You can look at the chart to remember the guidelines we made together.

Summarize and Apply

Summarize the lesson.

   Today, you can continue working on a piece of writing you already started or begin something new. Later, you will turn and talk to a partner about your writing.

Turn and Talk

- Turn your body toward your partner.
- Look at your partner.
- Use a 1 voice.
- Take turns telling your thinking.
- Be silent and listen carefully while your partner speaks.
- Say whether you agree or disagree with your partner or add on to what was said.
- Give reasons for your thinking.

Confer

- During independent writing, move around the room to confer briefly with as many individual students as time allows. Sit side by side with them and invite them to talk about how they will share their thinking during turn and talk. Use the following prompts as needed.
    - *Look at the chart. What is one thing you will do when you turn and talk?*
    - *What voice level will you use during turn and talk?*
    - *What will you do when you notice the signal? Why?*

Share

Following independent writing, have students bring their writing to the meeting area so they can engage in turn and talk.

   Turn and talk to your partner about the writing you worked on today.

- After a few minutes, give the signal for students to turn back to you and reflect on their experience of the turn and talk routine.

    What voice level did you use during turn and talk?

    What did you notice when I used the signal?

Umbrella 2: Working Together in the Classroom

Assessment

After you have taught the minilessons in this umbrella, observe students in a variety of classroom activities. Use *The Fountas & Pinnell Literacy Continuum* to notice, teach for, and support students' learning as you observe their attempts at building a classroom community and working together.

- What evidence do you have of students' new understandings related to working together in the classroom?
    - How do students show respect toward one another?
    - How well do students adjust their voice levels to the situation?
    - Do they use a variety of problem-solving strategies?
    - Are classroom materials cared for and returned to where they belong?
    - Do students follow turn and talk procedures?
    - Are they using vocabulary such as *community, respect, actions, voice level, appropriate, problem, solve, reread, directions, materials, properly, return, turn and talk,* and *listen*?
- In what ways, beyond the scope of this umbrella, are students building a classroom community of members who work well together?
    - Are they learning to respect and value one another by listening to each other's stories?
    - Do they understand what to do during independent writing time?

Use your observations to determine the next umbrella you will teach. You may also consult Suggested Sequence of Lessons (pp. 605–622) for guidance.

EXTENSIONS FOR WORKING TOGETHER IN THE CLASSROOM

- Revisit different classroom activities with the whole class, asking volunteers to role-play how responsible classroom community members act.

- Ask students to review voice levels before and after an activity, especially as new activities are introduced.

- Embed problem-solving strategies within classroom activities.

Establishing Independent Writing — Umbrella 3

Minilessons in This Umbrella

- **WML1** Learn the guidelines for independent writing.
- **WML2** Use writing tools to help with your writing.
- **WML3** Choose the paper for your writing projects.
- **WML4** Confer with your teacher or other writers about your writing.

Writer's Notebook

Before Teaching Umbrella 3 Minilessons

We recommend that students have the opportunity for independent writing time every day as part of a writer's workshop in addition to ten minutes per day devoted to writing in the writer's notebook (see WPS.U1.WML2). Learning guidelines for independent writing time will help students build self-confidence by achieving a sense of agency and responsibility for their own work while also allowing time for you to work with individual students or small guided writing groups.

Before teaching the minilessons in this umbrella, it would be helpful to have taught WPS.U1: Introducing the Writer's Notebook. Also, you will want to organize the classroom writing center to facilitate easy access to materials. Materials may include but are not limited to different kinds of paper (including the selection of paper templates in the online resources), pens, pencils, crayons, markers, scissors, tape, glue sticks, and staplers. Students can keep their writer's notebooks and writing folders in a personal box (e.g., a magazine storage box). The writing folders will contain pieces of writing in progress plus resources (e.g., revising checklist, proofreading checklist) fastened inside. Students file finished pieces of writing in a hanging file, where they can be used by you and the students for noticing growth over time and for discussing in conferences with parents and caregivers. Use hanging files in four different colors and store each color in a separate crate to allow students to locate their folders more easily (see pp. 52–56 for more information).

WML1
MGT.U3.WML1

Writing Minilesson Principle
Learn the guidelines for independent writing.

Establishing Independent Writing

You Will Need

- a student prepared to demonstrate the routine for independent writing
- chart paper and markers
- writer's notebooks and writing folders
- To download the following online resource for this lesson, visit **fp.pub/resources**:
  - chart art (optional)

Academic Language / Important Vocabulary

- guidelines
- writing folder
- writer's notebook
- entire

Continuum Connection

- Produce a reasonable quantity of writing within the time available
- Write with independent initiative and investment
- Listen to, remember, and follow directions with multiple steps

---

GOAL

Learn guidelines for what to do during independent writing time.

RATIONALE

Teaching students guidelines for independent writing promotes independence and a sense of responsibility, allows the class to function efficiently, and gives you time to confer with individual students or small groups. Reminding students to use all of the time at their disposal allows them to develop as writers and to build their stamina for and interest in writing.

WRITER'S NOTEBOOK/WRITING FOLDER

Students will work in their writer's notebooks or on a piece of writing in progress from their writing folders.

ASSESS LEARNING

- Notice whether students get ready for independent writing quickly, quietly, and independently and write for the entire time.
- Look for evidence that they can use vocabulary such as *guidelines*, *writing folder*, *writer's notebook*, and *entire*.

MINILESSON

To help students learn guidelines for independent writing, engage them in a short demonstration and discussion. Here is an example.

> Writing time is when you spend time writing on your own. Then we come together so you can share what you wrote. _____ is going to show you what to do during writing time.

- Invite the student to come forward and get started. After one or two minutes, signal that writing time is over.

> What did you notice about how _____ got started? What did he do first?
>
> What could you hear when he went to get his writing folder and materials?
>
> How quickly did he get started?
>
> Did he keep writing until I said that writing time is over?

- On chart paper, make a list of guidelines for independent writing.

> During writing time, you might work on a longer piece of writing that you keep in your writing folder, or you might write in your writer's notebook. What might you do if you think you have finished what you're working on?

- As needed, prompt students to think about actions such as checking the illustrations, rereading the words, adding more words or illustrations, adding more details to the illustrations, thinking about what to write about next, starting a new piece of writing, and exploring ideas in the writer's notebook.

The Writing Minilessons Book, Grade 3

Have a Try

Invite students to talk to a partner about guidelines for independent writing.

> Turn and talk to your partner about what you will remember to do during writing time.

▸ After time for discussion, invite a few pairs to share their responses. Clarify the routine if necessary.

Summarize and Apply

Summarize the learning and remind students to follow the guidelines for independent writing.

> Today you learned what to do during writing time. During independent writing time today and every day, get your writer's notebook or writing folder, start quickly and quietly, and write for the entire writing time. Look at the chart if you need help remembering what to do.

Guidelines for Writing Time

Get started quickly and quietly.

Get your writing folder and materials.

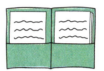

Work on a writing project or write in your writer's notebook.

Write for the entire writing time.

Confer

▸ During independent writing, move around the room to confer briefly with as many individual students as time allows. Sit side by side with them and invite them to talk about what to do during independent writing time. Use prompts such as the following as needed.

- What materials do you need for writing time today?
- What would you like to work on today?
- Do you want to start writing a new book or explore ideas in your writer's notebook?
- There are ten minutes left in independent writing time. What could you work on for the rest of today's writing time?

Share

Following independent writing, gather students in the meeting area to talk about the routine for independent writing.

> What did you work on today during writing time?

> What did you remember to do?

WML2
MGT.U3.WML2

Writing Minilesson Principle
Use writing tools to help with your writing.

Establishing Independent Writing

You Will Need

- for each student and yourself, a personal literacy box containing a writer's notebook and writing folder
- a writing center stocked with various writing materials (paper, pencils, pens, markers, etc.)
- chart paper and markers
- To download the following online resource for this lesson, visit **fp.pub/resources**:
  - chart art (optional)

Academic Language / Important Vocabulary

- writing tools
- writer's notebook
- writing folder

Continuum Connection

- Listen to, remember, and follow directions with multiple steps

---

GOAL

Learn to find, use, and return writing tools during independent writing.

RATIONALE

In addition to writing utensils and paper, students will use two main writing tools during independent writing time: a writer's notebook and a writing folder. When students understand where to find and how to use various writing materials and tools, they will be better prepared to work independently and efficiently during independent writing.

WRITER'S NOTEBOOK/WRITING FOLDER

Students will write in their writer's notebooks or work on a longer piece of writing in their writing folders.

ASSESS LEARNING

- Observe students to make sure they retrieve, use, and put back writing tools appropriately.
- Look for evidence that they can use vocabulary such as *writing tools*, *writer's notebook*, and *writing folder*.

MINILESSON

To help students learn how to find and use writing tools during independent writing, engage them in a short demonstration and discussion. Here is an example.

> Watch as I get ready for writing time.

- Demonstrate retrieving your personal literacy box (with writing folder and writer's notebook) and writing tools such as pens, markers, and a glue stick.

> Let's talk about what you saw me do.

- Briefly engage students in a discussion about what each item can be used for. Explain that you can use different colored markers for revising (green) and editing (red).

> How should I treat the materials from the writing center?
>
> What else did I get to help me with my writing?

- Show students the contents of your personal box and briefly explain what each item is used for.

> I will put the writing projects (longer pieces of writing) I am working on in my writing folder, and I will use my writer's notebook to make notes and lists, collect ideas for writing, and try out some ideas.
>
> What should I do with my writing tools at the end of writing time?

- Demonstrate putting all of the writing tools back where they belong.

The Writing Minilessons Book, Grade 3

Have a Try

Invite students to summarize the learning with a partner.

> What did you learn today about how to use writing tools to help with your writing?

▸ After students turn and talk, invite several pairs to share their responses. Use their responses to summarize the learning on chart paper.

Summarize and Apply

Write the principle at the top of the chart. Read it to students and remind them to use writing tools to help with their writing.

> Today during writing time, get your writing tools and personal box quickly and quietly. Remember to treat your writing tools with care and put them back where they belong at the end of writing time.

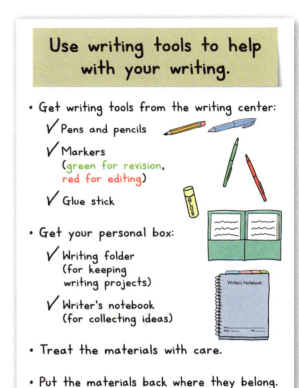

Confer

▸ During independent writing, move around the room to confer briefly with as many individual students as time allows. Sit side by side with them and invite them to talk about using writing tools. Use prompts such as the following as needed.

- What are you going to work on today?
- What writing tools do you need for your writing today?
- Where should you put your writing project at the end of writing time?
- Where should you put your writing tools when you're done with them?

Share

Following independent writing, gather students in the meeting area to discuss how they used writing tools.

> What writing tools did you get at the beginning of writing time?
>
> How did you use them?

WML 3
MGT.U3.WML3

Writing Minilesson Principle
Choose the paper for your writing projects.

Establishing Independent Writing

You Will Need

- students' writing samples that use different types of paper (e.g., a book, a map, a brochure, a glossary)
- examples of paper (attached to chart paper on the left)
- markers
- writing folders
- To download the following online resource for this lesson, visit **fp.pub/resources**:
  - paper templates (optional)

Academic Language / Important Vocabulary

- paper

Continuum Connection

- Use layout of print and illustrations to convey the meaning of a text
- Listen to, remember, and follow directions with multiple steps

GOAL

Learn that writers choose the kind of paper to suit the writing they will do.

RATIONALE

When students begin to think about what kind of paper to use, they understand that writers choose the paper that suits their purpose for writing.

WRITER'S NOTEBOOK/WRITING FOLDER

Students will keep writing projects in their writing folders as they work on them.

ASSESS LEARNING

- Notice whether students choose paper that is appropriate for what they are writing.
- Look for evidence that they can use vocabulary such as *paper*.

MINILESSON

Prior to teaching this lesson, ensure that students are familiar with different kinds of paper (with respect to size, shape, color, thickness, layout, etc.), including paper templates from the online resources, and know where the paper is located. To help students select paper that is appropriate for what they are writing, engage them in talking about how they might use different types of paper. Here is an example.

- Show examples of students' writing on different kinds of paper.

  What do you notice about the paper they used for these writing projects?

- Use the paper samples on the chart along with prompts such as the following to help students think about using different kinds of paper.

  - *What kind of writing project might you do on this folded piece of paper?*
  - *How might you use a blank sheet of white paper for your writing?*
  - *If you wanted to make a book, what type of paper would you choose?*
  - *What type of paper would you use to make a poster (thank you card, letter)?*
  - *Why do you think this writer chose paper that has boxes and lines?*
  - *Why do you think this paper has a dot at the beginning of every other line?*

- Explain that it is sometimes helpful to use draft paper before deciding on a specific type of paper. Show students how to write on the lines that have dots, leaving space in between the lines for revisions and edits.

- As students talk about ways to use each kind of paper, record their answers on the chart.

Have a Try

Invite students to talk to a partner about choosing paper for their writing projects.

> Think about the next writing project you want to start working on. What kind of paper will you use? Why? Turn and talk to your partner about this.

- After students turn and talk, invite a few students to share their responses.

Summarize and Apply

Write the principle at the top of the chart. Summarize the learning and remind students to think about what kind of paper to use when they write.

> What do writers think about when they are choosing a type of paper to use?

> Today during writing time, choose the kind of paper that is best suited to the writing project you're working on. Bring your writing to share when we come back together.

Confer

- During independent writing, move around the room to confer briefly with as many individual students as time allows. Sit side by side with them and invite them to talk about choosing paper for writing. Use prompts such as the following as needed.
  - *What do you want to work on today?*
  - *What kind of paper would work well for that?*
  - *Why did you choose that kind of paper?*

Share

Following independent writing, gather students in the meeting area to talk about their paper choices.

> What kind of paper did you use today?

> Why did you choose that kind of paper?

Umbrella 3: Establishing Independent Writing

WML 4
MGT.U3.WML4

Writing Minilesson Principle
Confer with your teacher or other writers about your writing.

Establishing Independent Writing

You Will Need

- one or two students prepared to demonstrate a writing conference
- chart paper and markers
- writing folders
- To download the following online resources for this lesson, visit **fp.pub/resources**:
  - chart art (optional)
  - What I Have Learned How o Do as a Writer and Illustrator
  - My Writing Goals

Academic Language / Important Vocabulary

- confer
- audience
- feedback

Continuum Connection

- Understand that other writers can be helpful in the process
- Change writing in response to peer or teacher feedback
- Understand the role of the writer, teacher, or peer writer in conference

GOAL

Understand that writers find it helpful to talk about their writing with other people.

RATIONALE

When students read their writing aloud, they can listen for what they are communicating to others. Talking to you or their classmates about their writing gives them an audience that can provide feedback about how they can improve their writing and help them set goals [see MGT.U4: Introducing the Writing Folder].

WRITER'S NOTEBOOK/WRITING FOLDER

Students can keep track of what they have learned how to do as writers and illustrators and their goals in their writing folders.

ASSESS LEARNING

- Notice how students discuss their writing with you and other students.
- Look for evidence that they can use vocabulary such as *confer*, *audience*, and *feedback*.

MINILESSON

To help students understand why and how to talk to you, their classmates, or another audience, plan to talk with one or more students about their writing. Here is an example.

> When you share your writing with an audience, whether it's me or one or more of your classmates, you can hear what they think about your writing. That's called feedback. Often, you will get ideas for making your writing better. _____ will show how to confer, or talk with someone, about your writing.

- Sit with the prepared student in front of the class.

  > Please read your writing aloud, _____.

- Engage the student in a discussion. Model some of the language you might use to provide feedback to the writers in your classroom, such as the following:

  - *I'm wondering how you felt in this part of your story. Could you say more about that?*
  - *I'm interested in knowing more about _____. Is there anything you'd like to add about that to your writing?*
  - *What details could you add to your illustrations to help readers better understand your story?*
  - *Do you have any questions for me? Is there anything you need help with?*
  - *What are you going to work on next?*
  - *I like how you _____.*

The Writing Minilessons Book, Grade 3

Have a Try

Invite students to talk to a partner about what they noticed.

> What did you notice when _____ and I talked about her writing? What did she do? What did I do? Turn and talk to your partner about this.

▸ After students turn and talk, invite several students to share what they noticed. Record responses on chart paper.

Summarize and Apply

Summarize the learning and remind students that talking about their writing helps them grow as writers.

> How can you get help with your writing? Why is that important?

▸ Write the principle at the top of the chart.

> During writing time, I will confer with some of you about your writing just like I did with _____. Some of you might want to talk to a classmate about your writing. Remember to use a level 1 voice. After you confer with me or another writer about your writing, you may want to write in your writing folder what you learned to do or what you want to work on next.

Confer

▸ During independent writing, move around the room to confer briefly with as many individual students as time allows. Sit side by side with them and invite them to talk about their writing. Use prompts such as the following as needed.

- What could you add to help readers understand _____?
- What details could you add to your illustration to help readers understand more?
- What do you want help with today?

Share

Following independent writing, gather students in the meeting area to talk about their writing conferences.

> If you had a writing conference with me or a classmate today, share something that you found helpful as a writer.

Umbrella 3: Establishing Independent Writing

Umbrella 3   Establishing Independent Writing

Assessment

After you have taught the minilessons in this umbrella, observe students as they prepare for, progress through, and conclude independent writing time each day. Use *The Fountas & Pinnell Literacy Continuum* to notice, teach for, and support students' learning as you observe their attempts at reading and writing.

- What evidence do you have of students' new understandings related to the routines for independent writing time?
    - Are students able to sustain working for the whole independent writing time?
    - Do students use writing tools appropriately and put them back where they belong?
    - How are they talking with you and others about their writing?
    - Do they understand and use vocabulary such as *guidelines*, *confer*, *audience*, and *feedback*?
- In what other ways, beyond the scope of this umbrella, are students getting started with independent writing?
    - How are they using their writer's notebooks?
    - Do they keep their writing folders organized?

Use your observations to determine the next umbrella you will teach. You may also consult Suggested Sequence of Lessons (pp. 605–622) for guidance.

EXTENSIONS FOR ESTABLISHING INDEPENDENT WRITING

- Teach students how to use resources in their writing folders, such as a list of writing goals, a list of finished writing pieces, a revising checklist, and a proofreading checklist (see MGT.U4: Introducing the Writing Folder).

- Help students with the organization of their writing folders. Show them where to place their finished pieces of writing. Using hanging file folders in several colors, each color stored separately, will help students find their folders more quickly and efficiently.

- Arrange for students to share their best writing pieces with an audience beyond the classroom, for example, invite family and community members to a young authors' night or arrange with the librarian to make students' writing available in the library. (See WPS.U11: Publishing and Self-Assessing Your Writing.)

Introducing the Writing Folder

Umbrella 4

Minilessons in This Umbrella

- **WML1** Keep a list of your finished writing projects.
- **WML2** Write what you have learned how to do as a writer and illustrator.
- **WML3** Write your goals as a writer.
- **WML4** Use the word list to help with your writing.
- **WML5** Use checklists to help with revising and editing.

Before Teaching Umbrella 4 Minilessons

Before teaching the minilessons in this umbrella, prepare a writing folder for each student. A writing folder is a place for students to keep a record of their writing and reflections, record their writing goals, and refer to important resources for their writing. We recommend using a two-pocket folder with brads in the middle for fastening resources inside.

We suggest placing the following resources (found in online resources or created by you) in each student's writing folder before you introduce them individually:

- Genres and Forms at a Glance
- My Writing Projects
- What I Have Learned How to Do as a Writer and Illustrator
- My Writing Goals
- Commonly Misspelled Words
- Revising Checklist
- Proofreading Checklist

Students should also keep writing projects (e.g., books, poems, and other longer pieces of writing) they are working on in the pockets of their writing folders. When pieces are complete, students should move them to a permanent hanging file in a crate or filing cabinet. The resources in the writing folder can be refreshed as needed or at regular intervals (e.g., every quarter), and the old ones can be stapled together and stored in the same hanging file. Have students keep their writing folders in a personal literacy box along with other resources, such as a writer's notebook and a reader's notebook.

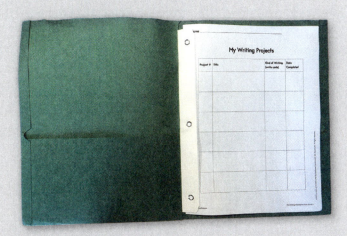

WML1
MGT.U4.WML1

Writing Minilesson Principle
Keep a list of your finished writing projects.

Introducing the Writing Folder

You Will Need

- writing folders
- document camera, or chart paper made to look like the My Writing Projects online resource
- markers
- To download the following online resources for this lesson, visit **fp.pub/resources**:
  - My Writing Projects
  - Genres and Forms at a Glance

Academic Language / Important Vocabulary

- writing folder
- record
- project
- title
- code

Continuum Connection

- Write in a variety of genres across the year
- Produce a reasonable quantity of writing with the time available
- Listen to, remember, and follow directions with multiple steps

GOAL

Learn how to keep track of finished writing to reflect on progress across the year.

RATIONALE

A log of finished writing allows students to communicate to you when they believe a piece of writing is complete so you can plan further instruction. It also allows them and you to reflect on their writing across the year and provides information for you when you discuss students' progress in writing. Seeing a body of work grow builds self-efficacy.

WRITER'S NOTEBOOK/WRITING FOLDER

Have students record their last completed writing project on the My Writing Projects sheet in their writing folders and place it in the hanging file.

ASSESS LEARNING

- Observe students' ability to create and maintain a log of finished writing.
- Notice whether students are appropriately evaluating the completeness of their writing.
- Look for evidence that they can use vocabulary such as *writing folder*, *record*, *project*, *title*, and *code*.

MINILESSON

Students will need their writing folders for this lesson. If you haven't already, fasten a copy of the online resource Genres and Forms at a Glance and My Writing Projects in each student's writing folder. To help students think about the minilesson principle, model filling out the writing log. Below is an example.

- Have students turn to the My Writing Projects sheet in their writing folder.

  What do you think you will write here?

  I wrote a memory story called "My Grandpa Joe." This will be the first project on my list. What number should I write for the project number?

- Add the numeral *1* to the chart. Explain the symbol for number (#).

  What should I write in the next column?

- Fill in the title and continue across the columns.

  The next column is labeled *Kind of Writing (write code)*. This is where you will tell the kind of writing you did. The codes are on the sheet in your folder called Genres and Forms at a Glance. I will write *M* in the column to show I wrote a memory story. I will also put a tally mark next to the words *Memory Story* on the Genres and Forms at a Glance page. This will help me keep track of my writing. What goes in the last column?

- Fill in the date you completed your writing.

136

The Writing Minilessons Book, Grade 3

Have a Try

Invite students to talk to a partner about finished writing projects they could record.

> Think about the last writing project you finished. Use the chart to think about what you will write on your own My Writing Projects page. Turn and talk to your partner about this.

Summarize and Apply

Summarize the learning and remind students to record their finished writing projects on the My Writing Projects sheet in their writing folders.

> Before you start writing today, take a moment to add your last finished writing project to your My Writing Projects sheet in your writing folder. Whenever you finish a new writing project, remember to record it. Bring your writing folder to share when we meet later.

My Writing Projects

Project#	Title	Kind of Writing (write code)	Date Completed
1	My Grandpa Joe	M	10/3

Confer

▸ During independent writing, move around the room to confer briefly with as many individual students as time allows. Sit side by side with them and invite them to talk about recording their writing projects. Use prompts such as the following as needed.

- *What is the last writing project you finished?*
- *Talk through what you will write on your My Writing Projects sheet in your writing folder.*
- *What is the title of that piece of writing?*
- *What kind of writing it is? What is the code for that kind of writing?*

Share

Following independent writing, gather students in the meeting area. Give all students a turn to share what they wrote in their writing logs.

> Who would like to start by sharing what you wrote on your My Writing Projects sheet?

Umbrella 4: Introducing the Writing Folder

WML 2
MGT.U4.WML2

Writing Minilesson Principle
Write what you have learned how to do as a writer and illustrator.

Introducing the Writing Folder

You Will Need

- writer's notebooks and writing folders
- document camera, or chart paper made to look like the What I Have Learned How to Do as a Writer and Illustrator online resource
- markers
- To download the following online resource for this lesson, visit **fp.pub/resources**:
  - What I Have Learned How to Do as a Writer and Illustrator

Academic Language / Important Vocabulary

- writing folder
- reflect
- learn

Continuum Connection

- Self-evaluate writing and talk about what is good about it and what techniques were used
- Show ability in a conference to discuss what is being worked on as a writer
- Be willing to work at the craft of writing, incorporating new learning from instruction
- Compare previous writing to revised writing and notice and talk about the differences
- State what was learned from each piece of writing

GOAL

Reflect on what has been learned as a writer and illustrator throughout the year.

RATIONALE

When students keep a record of what they have learned from their writing, they begin learn to reflect on their writing. This helps them see their progress in writing, giving them more confidence in their writing ability. They learn to view themselves as writers and think about what to work on next. Their reflections give you important information that you can use to inform your teaching.

WRITER'S NOTEBOOK/WRITING FOLDER

Have students begin to fill in the What I Have Learned How to Do as a Writer and Illustrator sheet in their writing folders. They can also continue working on a writing project or write in their writer's notebooks.

ASSESS LEARNING

- Listen carefully to what students say they have learned from their writing. Is there evidence of that learning in their writing?
- Look for evidence that they can use vocabulary such as *writing folder*, *reflect*, and *learn*.

MINILESSON

Students will need their writing folders for this minilesson. If you haven't already, fasten a copy of What I Have Learned How to Do as a Writer and Illustrator in each student's writing folder. Model reflecting on learning as a writer/illustrator and recording it on the form. Below is an example.

- Have students turn to What I Have Learned How to Do as a Writer and Illustrator in their writing folders.

  What do you think you will write about on this sheet in your writing folder?

  Throughout the year, you will regularly stop to think about what you have learned from your writing and illustrating and write it on this sheet in your writing folder. I'm going to write what I learned from writing my memory story. First, I'll put today's date.

- Model how to fill in the resource.

  What are some things you have learned about writing or illustrating?

- Record responses on the chart.

  How can writing down what you have learned from your writing and illustrating help you?

  Writing what you have learned helps you think about the progress you are making as a writer and illustrator and what you want to work on next.

The Writing Minilessons Book, Grade 3

Have a Try

Invite students to talk to a partner about what they learned from their most recent piece of writing.

> What are you learning as a writer or illustrator?
> What did you learn from your last writing project?
> Turn and talk to your partner.

▸ After students turn and talk, invite a few students to share their thinking.

Summarize and Apply

Summarize the learning and remind students to reflect on what they have learned as a writer and illustrator.

> You can use this sheet in your writing folder at any time to reflect on what you have learned as a writer and illustrator. You may write on it after a writing lesson, after discussing your writing with me or another student, or after you have finished a writing project.
>
> During writing time today, reflect on what you have learned as a writer or illustrator and write about it on this sheet in your writing folder. If you have more time, continue writing in your writer's notebook or writing folder. Bring your writing folder to share when we meet later.

What I Have Learned How to Do as a Writer and Illustrator

Date	
10/3	How to use descriptive words and phrases to help readers create pictures in their minds
Date	How to organize information in nonfiction books
Date	How to make characters more believable
Date	How to write interesting beginnings and endings
Date	

Confer

▸ During independent writing, move around the room to confer briefly with as many individual students as time allows. Sit side by side with them and invite them to talk about what they have learned as a writer/illustrator. Use prompts such as the following as needed.

- *What is the last writing project you finished?*
- *What did you learn from that writing project?*
- *Did you try anything new in your writing?*
- *Did you learn anything new from making this illustration?*

Share

Following independent writing, gather students in the meeting area to share their reflections.

> Who would like to share what you have learned how to do as a writer and illustrator?

WML 3
MGT.U4.WML3

Writing Minilesson Principle
Write your goals as a writer.

Introducing the Writing Folder

You Will Need

- writer's notebooks and writing folders
- document camera, or chart paper made to look like the My Writing Goals online resource
- markers
- To download the following online resource for this lesson, visit **fp.pub/resources**:
  - My Writing Goals

Academic Language / Important Vocabulary

- writing folder
- goal

Continuum Connection

- Articulate goals as a writer
- Be willing to work at the craft of writing, incorporating new learning from instruction

GOAL

Make writing goals to stretch and grow as a writer and illustrator.

RATIONALE

When you guide students to identify and record their own writing goals (during a writing conference, for instance), they learn to view themselves as writers and illustrators, and they become more invested in their writing journey.

WRITER'S NOTEBOOK/WRITING FOLDER

Have students begin a list of writing goals on the My Writing Goals sheet in their writing folders. They can also continue working on a writing project or write in their writer's notebooks.

ASSESS LEARNING

- During writing conferences, notice whether students can develop and articulate their goals as writers.
- Look for evidence that students are working toward the goals they set.
- Look for evidence that they can use vocabulary such as *writing folder* and *goal*.

MINILESSON

Students will need their writing folders for this minilesson. If you haven't already, fasten a copy of the My Writing Goals online resource in each student's writing folder. To help students think about the minilesson principle, model identifying, discussing, and writing down writing goals. Below is an example.

- Have students turn to My Writing Goals in their writing folders.

  What do you think you will write on this sheet in your writing folder?

  This is where you will think about and write down your writing goals. Does anyone know what a goal is?

  A goal is something you want to do or accomplish. For example, one of my writing goals this year is to write more poetry. I've been reading and enjoying lots of poems lately, and I would like to get better at writing poetry. Another goal I have is to make my illustrations more interesting by trying different techniques, such as collage. My third goal is to write for at least half an hour every day.

- Model writing your goals on the prepared chart paper or projected resource.

  Does anyone have any goals for your writing or illustrating? Is there any type of writing you would like to do more of or get better at? What are some writing techniques you would like to work on or try for the first time?

- Record students' responses on the chart.

WML 3
MGT.U4.WML3

Have a Try

Invite students to talk to a partner about their writing goals.

> What other writing goals do you have? What could you do this year to help yourself grow as a writer or illustrator? Turn and talk to your partner about your writing goals.

▶ After time for discussion, invite a few students to share their goals. Add any new goals to the chart.

Summarize and Apply

Summarize the learning. Remind students to think about and record their writing goals.

> Why is it a good idea to write down your writing goals?
>
> Writing down your writing goals will help you remember what you want to work on and help you stay focused on your goals. Before you start writing today, write one or two goals on the My Writing Goals sheet in your writing folder. If you have extra time, continue writing in your writer's notebook or writing folder.

Date	My Writing Goals
10/4	Write more poetry
10/4	Try different ways to make my illustrations more interesting
10/4	Write for at least half an hour every day
10/4	Learn how to draw people that look real
10/4	Make my characters more believable
10/4	Write a chapter book
10/4	Do more writing in my writer's notebook

Confer

▶ During independent writing, move around the room to confer briefly with as many individual students as time allows. Sit side by side with them and invite them to talk about their writing goals. Use prompts such as the following as needed.

- *What are your goals as a writer or illustrator?*
- *What type of writing would you most like to work on this year?*
- *Is there anything you would like to try in your writing or illustrating?*
- *What could you do to help yourself grow as a writer?*

Share

Following independent writing, gather students in the meeting area. Give all students a turn to share their writing goals.

> Who would like to start by sharing one of your writing goals?

WML 4
MGT.U4.WML4

Writing Minilesson Principle
Use the word list to help with your writing.

Introducing the Writing Folder

You Will Need

- writer's notebooks and writing folders
- chart paper prepared with misspelled words in a sentence
- markers
- To download the following online resource for this lesson, visit **fp.pub/resources**:
  - Commonly Misspelled Words

Academic Language / Important Vocabulary

- writing folder
- word list
- misspelled

Continuum Connection

- Monitor own spelling by noticing when a word does not "look right" and should be checked
- Use reference tools to check on spelling when editing final draft (dictionary, digital resources)
- Use beginning reference tools: e.g., personal word lists, thesaurus to assist in word choice or checking spelling

GOAL

Use the commonly misspelled words list to help with spelling during writing.

RATIONALE

When you show students how to refer to a list of commonly misspelled words, they will understand how to use resources to help with spelling and correct their own spelling independently.

WRITER'S NOTEBOOK/WRITING FOLDER

Students will try using the online resource Commonly Misspelled Words as they continue working on a longer project in their writing folders or write in their writer's notebooks.

ASSESS LEARNING

- Notice whether students refer to the commonly misspelled words list to help with spelling.
- Look for evidence that they can use vocabulary such as *writing folder*, *word list*, and *misspelled*.

MINILESSON

Students will need their writing folders for this minilesson. If you haven't already, fasten a copy of the online resource Commonly Misspelled Words in each student's writing folder. To help students think about the principle, model referring to the list to help with spelling. Below is an example.

- Direct students to turn to the list of commonly misspelled words in their writing folders.

  What do you notice about this sheet in your writing folder?

  How could this list of words help you as a writer?

  You can use the list to help you with your proofreading and editing.

- Model how to use the list to check and correct the spelling of words in the sentence on the prepared chart paper.

  When you proofread and edit your writing and notice a word that doesn't look right, you can try to find it on the list of commonly misspelled words.

- Then model how students can use the list to find how to spell a word.

  I want to write *Wednesday, February 2*. I'm going to look for *Wednesday* on the list to remind myself how to spell it. There it is! W-e-d-n-e-s-d-a-y. *February* is another challenging word to spell. Can you find *February* on the list? What is the correct spelling of *February*?

- Write the date on the chart paper.

WML4

MGT.U4.WML4

Have a Try

Invite students to talk to a partner about using Commonly Misspelled Words.

> Look through the list of commonly misspelled words. Circle two or three of those words that you might have trouble spelling. Then turn to your partner and show the words you circled.

- After time for discussion, invite several pairs to share their tricky words. Talk with students about ways they might remember how to spell tricky words.

Summarize and Apply

Write the principle at the top of the chart. Read it to students. Summarize the learning and remind students to use the word list to help with writing.

> How can you use the list of commonly misspelled words to help you with your writing?

> Today, try using the list of commonly misspelled words when you work on a writing project in your writing folder or when you write in your writer's notebook. You can also use it when you are editing and proofreading a piece of writing. Bring your writing to share when we meet later.

Use the word list to help with your writing.

Everybody wears   Tuesdays
~~Evrybody wares~~ sneakers on ~~Tusedays.~~

Wednesday, February 2

Confer

- During independent writing, move around the room to confer briefly with as many individual students as time allows. Sit side by side with them and invite them to talk about using the word list. Use prompts such as the following as needed.
  - *What are you writing about today?*
  - *Are there any words you are not sure how to spell?*
  - *Where can you look to find out how to spell that word?*
  - *Let's see if we can find that word on the list of commonly misspelled words.*

Share

Following independent writing, gather students in the meeting area to share their writing.

> Did anyone use the list of commonly misspelled words today?

> How did you use it? How did it help you with your writing?

Umbrella 4: Introducing the Writing Folder

WML 5
MGT.U4.WML5

Writing Minilesson Principle
Use checklists to help with revising and editing.

Introducing the Writing Folder

You Will Need

- two short pieces of writing with clear errors (one unrevised, one revised and ready for proofreading and editing) written on chart paper or projected
- document camera (optional)
- writing folders
- To download the following online resources for this lesson, visit **fp.pub/resources**:
  - Revising Checklist
  - Proofreading Checklist

Academic Language / Important Vocabulary

- writing folder
- revising
- proofreading
- editing
- checklist

Continuum Connection

- Know how to use an editing and proofreading checklist
- Reread a piece asking self, "Have I made clear what I want readers to understand?"
- After reflection and rereading, add substantial pieces of texts (paragraphs, pages) to provide further explanation, clarify points, add interest, or support points

GOAL

Learn how to use checklists to assist with revising and editing writing.

RATIONALE

When you show students how to use revising and editing checklists, they begin to understand the importance of revising and editing their writing and know what to check for. Before teaching this lesson, we recommend teaching several craft and conventions lessons. We also recommend teaching WPS.U8 (revising) and WPS.U9 (editing and proofreading). You may want to break this lesson into two lessons (revising and editing) if you feel it is too much for one lesson.

WRITER'S NOTEBOOK/WRITING FOLDER

Have students use the checklists to help them revise and proofread writing projects from their writing folders.

ASSESS LEARNING

- Notice whether students use checklists to assist with revising and editing their work.
- Look for evidence that they can use vocabulary such as *writing folder*, *revising*, *proofreading*, *editing*, and *checklist*.

MINILESSON

Students will need their writing folders for this lesson. If you haven't already, fasten a copy of the Revising Checklist and the Proofreading Checklist in each student's writing folder. To help students think about the principle, model using the checklists. This can be done over two days, if preferred. Here is an example.

- Have students turn to the Revising Checklist in their writing folders.

  > In your writing folder is a revising checklist that will help you remember what to look for as you revise your writing. Let's try using the checklist.

- Model how to use the checklist by going through some of the questions and thinking aloud about how to revise the first piece of writing.

  > My beginning tells what the piece of writing is about, but I'm not sure if it really will grab my readers and pull them in. I'd like to make my beginning a little more interesting. How could I do that?

- Show another sample piece of writing that has already been revised but not proofread and edited. Have students turn to the Proofreading Checklist.

  > After you revise your writing, proofread it to see if there is anything that still needs to be fixed. The Proofreading Checklist will help you remember what to look for.

- Use the first few questions on the Proofreading Checklist to model how to proofread a piece of writing. Save the punctuation question for Have a Try.

The Writing Minilessons Book, Grade 3

Have a Try

Invite students to talk to a partner about how to correct the second sample piece of writing.

> Let's look at this question: Does each sentence end with the correct punctuation? Look carefully at the punctuation in the piece of writing and then turn and talk to your partner about this question.

> Does each sentence end with the correct punctuation? If not, which sentences need to be corrected, and how?

▸ Using students' input, correct any punctuation errors in the sample piece of writing as needed.

Summarize and Apply

Summarize the learning and remind students to use the revising and proofreading checklists.

> How can the revising and proofreading checklists help you with your writing?

> During writing time today, spend some time revising and proofreading a writing project from your writing folder. Remember to use the revising and proofreading checklists to help you know what to look for.

Confer

▸ During independent writing, move around the room to confer briefly with as many individual students as time allows. Sit side by side with them and invite them to talk about revising and/or proofreading their writing. Use prompts such as the following as needed.

- *Are you ready to start revising your writing? What do you need to look for when you revise your writing?*
- *Let's go through the Revising Checklist together and see how you can use it to improve your writing.*
- *Have you proofread your writing? Did you use the Proofreading Checklist to help?*

Share

Following independent writing, gather students in the meeting area to share how they used the checklists.

> Turn and talk to a partner about how you used the Revising Checklist or Proofreading Checklist today.

Umbrella 4: Introducing the Writing Folder

Umbrella 4: Introducing the Writing Folder

Assessment

After you have taught the minilessons in this umbrella, observe students as they prepare for, progress through, and conclude independent writing time each day. Use *The Fountas & Pinnell Literacy Continuum* to notice, teach for, and support students' learning as you observe their writing.

- What evidence do you have of students' new understandings related to using a writing folder?
  - Do students record each finished writing project on a list?
  - Are they able to reflect and write about what they have learned from their writing and illustrating?
  - Can they identify and record their goals as a writer?
  - Do they use the commonly misspelled word list and the revising and proofreading checklists to help with their writing?
  - Do they understand and use vocabulary such as *record*, *project*, *reflect*, and *goal*?
- In what other ways, beyond the scope of this umbrella, are students expanding their writing experiences?
  - Are they ready to learn new craft moves?

Use your observations to determine the next umbrella you will teach. You may also consult Suggested Sequence of Lessons (pp. 605–622) for guidance.

EXTENSIONS FOR INTRODUCING THE WRITING FOLDER

- Help students revisit their writing goals and discuss and/or write about whether they have achieved them.

- Encourage students to write a longer reflection on a completed writing project. Attach the reflection to the writing project. Keep it handy for conferences with students and parents or caregivers.

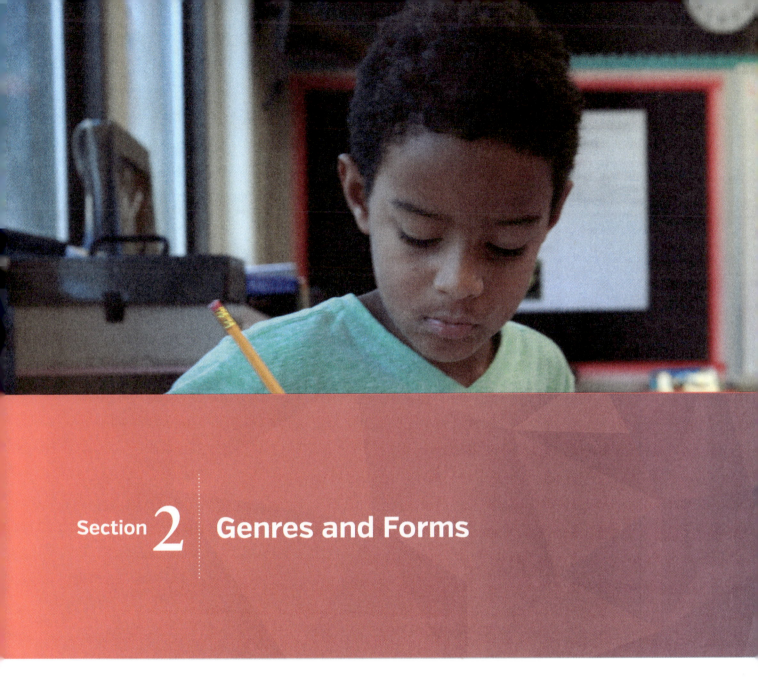

Section 2 | Genres and Forms

Exposure to various genres and forms of writing broadens students' vision for what their writing can be. The minilessons in this section support students by helping them see that they can express themselves in writing in a variety of ways. They write memory stories, informational books, opinion pieces, and poetry, as well as in other forms, such as multimedia presentations and photo essays.

2 Genres and Forms

Functional Writing

UMBRELLA 1	Writing Friendly Letters	**149**
UMBRELLA 2	Writing Procedural Texts	**157**
UMBRELLA 3	Writing to a Prompt: Getting Ready for Test Writing	**165**

Narrative Writing

UMBRELLA 4	Writing Memory Stories	**179**
UMBRELLA 5	Writing Realistic Fiction Stories	**191**

Informational Writing

UMBRELLA 6	Making Informational Books	**203**

Persuasive Writing

UMBRELLA 7	Exploring Opinion Writing	**217**
UMBRELLA 8	Introducing Persuasive Writing Through Powerful Messages	**227**

Poetry

UMBRELLA 9	Making Poetry Anthologies	**235**
UMBRELLA 10	Writing Poetry	**245**
UMBRELLA 11	Writing Different Kinds of Poems	**255**

Other Forms

UMBRELLA 12	Making Picture Books	**265**
UMBRELLA 13	Making Biographical Multimedia Presentations	**275**
UMBRELLA 14	Making Photo Essays	**285**
UMBRELLA 15	Experimenting with Writing in New Ways	**295**

Writing Friendly Letters

Umbrella 1

Minilessons in This Umbrella

- **WML1** Write a letter to someone for a reason.
- **WML2** Write the parts of a letter.
- **WML3** Write the important information in your letter.

Before Teaching Umbrella 1 Minilessons

Functional writing includes letters, lists, directions, and labels. When students have experiences with functional writing, they understand that people write for practical and authentic reasons. Friendly letters are used to give information, to invite, and to give thanks. They may take forms other than traditional letters, such as emails, invitations, cards, or notes.

If you are using *The Reading Minilessons Book, Grade 3* (Fountas and Pinnell 2019) you may choose to teach WAR.U3: Writing Letters About Reading. Use the books listed below from *Fountas & Pinnell Classroom™ Shared Reading Collection*, or choose books from the classroom library that have examples of correspondence.

Shared Reading Collection

Light My Way Home by Shyamala Parthasarathy

Harriett and Violeta: A Long-Distance Friendship by Laura Platas Scott

As you read and enjoy these texts together, help students

- notice details in the letters, and
- observe different reasons that people write letters.

Shared Reading

Writer's Notebook

WML1

GEN.U1.WML1

Writing Minilesson Principle
Write a letter to someone for a reason.

Writing Friendly Letters

You Will Need

- a mentor text that shows friendly letters, such as *Light My Way Home* by Shyamala Parthasarathy, from *Shared Reading Collection*
- examples of friendly letters (invitations, emails, cards, notes)
- chart paper and markers
- writer's notebooks and writing folders
- To download the following online resources for this lesson, visit **fp.pub/resources**:
  - chart art (optional)
  - sample letters (optional)

Academic Language / Important Vocabulary

- friendly letter
- opinion
- invite
- reason
- thanks
- purpose

Continuum Connection

- Understand that written communication can be used for different purposes: e.g., to give information, to invite, to give thanks
- Understand that a friendly letter can be written in various forms: e.g., note, card, letter, invitation, email
- Write notes, cards, invitations and email for a variety of purposes

GOAL

Understand that different types of letters serve different purposes and have different audiences and tones.

RATIONALE

Knowing how to write a letter is a practical life skill. When students understand why people write letters, they begin to think about what they could write in a letter and understand that they can write with purpose and authenticity.

WRITER'S NOTEBOOK/WRITING FOLDER

Have students list ideas for writing a letter in their writer's notebooks and keep the letters they are working on in their writing folders.

ASSESS LEARNING

- Look for evidence of what students understand about friendly letters.
- Look for evidence that students can use vocabulary such as *friendly letter*, *invite*, *thanks*, *opinion*, *reason*, and *purpose*.

MINILESSON

To help students plan and begin writing letters independently, provide examples of different forms of friendly letters (e.g., letters, notes, invitations, cards, emails) and help them think about why people write friendly letters. Here is an example.

- Show and read aloud the examples of friendly letters in *Light My Way Home* on pages 2 and 5.

   What do you notice about these letters? Turn and talk about that.

- After time for discussion, guide students in a conversation about the purpose of the letters. Generalize the purpose of the letters and define *friendly letter*.

   Divya and her grandmother are writing to each other to say hello and share information about their lives. That is their purpose, or reason, for writing the letters. They are examples of friendly letters because they are written in a way that sounds like the letter writers are talking to someone they know.

- Begin two lists on chart paper: one with different examples of friendly letters, and one with different reasons for writing friendly letters. Add this example to the chart.

- Show examples of other types of friendly letters from the online resources or from your own collection (e.g., invitations, emails, cards, notes, messages). Guide the conversation to talk about types of friendly letters and the reasons people write them. Add to the chart.

The Writing Minilessons Book, Grade 3

Have a Try

Invite students to turn and talk about an idea they have for writing a letter.

> Turn and tell your partner the reason you might write a letter.

▸ After time for discussion, ask a few students to share. Add new ideas to the chart.

Summarize and Apply

Summarize the learning. Have students begin writing a letter during independent writing.

> You can write letters for different reasons.

▸ Write the principle on the top of the chart.

> During writing time, choose a purpose, or reason, for writing a friendly letter. Write some ideas in your writer's notebook if you need to, but if you are ready, you can begin writing. Bring your writing to share when we meet later.

Confer

▸ During independent writing, move around the room to confer briefly with as many individual students as time allows. Sit side by side with them and invite them to talk about writing a friendly letter. Use the following prompts as needed.
- *What type of friendly letter are you writing?*
- *What is the reason for your letter?*
- *Let's look at the chart for some ideas.*

Share

Following independent writing, gather students in the meeting area. Ask a few volunteers to share their friendly letters.

> Who would like to share the friendly letter you wrote today?

WML 2
GEN.U1.WML2

Writing Minilesson Principle
Write the parts of a letter.

Writing Friendly Letters

You Will Need

- a mentor text that shows the parts of a friendly letter, such as *Harriett and Violeta: A Long-Distance Friendship* by Laura Platas Scott, from *Shared Reading Collection*
- chart paper prepared with a sample friendly letter (no PS)
- sticky notes
- chart paper and markers
- highlighter or highlighter tape (optional)
- writing folders

Academic Language / Important Vocabulary

- friendly letter
- signature
- greeting
- PS
- closing
- comma

Continuum Connection

- Understand that the sender and the receiver must be clearly shown
- Understand that a friendly letter has parts (date, salutation, closing signature, and sometimes *PS*)
- Write a friendly letter with all parts
- Use underlining for words in titles

GOAL

Understand and write the parts of a letter (date, salutation, closing, signature, PS).

RATIONALE

When students learn how to write friendly letters by looking at examples, they understand that it is important to include each part in a friendly letter.

WRITER'S NOTEBOOK/WRITING FOLDER

Have students keep the letters they are working on in their writing folders.

ASSESS LEARNING

- Observe whether students include all parts of a friendly letter in their letters.
- Look for evidence that students can use vocabulary such as *friendly letter*, *greeting*, *closing*, *signature*, *PS*, and *comma*.

MINILESSON

To help students understand the parts of a friendly letter, have them examine a letter in a mentor text, and talk about a sample friendly letter you have prepared. Below is an example. An alternative would be to do this lesson over a couple of days and write a letter together using shared writing.

- Show page 4 in *Harriett and Violeta*.

  Listen as I read an example of a friendly letter.

- Read all parts of the letter, pointing to each part as you do.

  What do you notice about this letter?

- Guide the conversation to help students notice that the letter is like a conversation, that it is written by Harriett (sender) to Violeta (receiver), and that they know each other personally. Then turn students' attention to the prepared chart paper.

  Look at the parts of this letter. Turn and talk about what you notice.

- After time for conversation, ask volunteers to point to the different parts of the letter. As they do, place a sticky note beside the date, greeting, closing, and signature. Write the name of each part of the letter on the corresponding sticky note. Point out that a PS is sometimes included in a letter when you have a little extra something to say, and add a sticky note where the PS would go.

- You may choose to use a highlighter or highlighter tape to assist students in noticing the parts of the letter as well as the commas after the greeting and the closing.

152

The Writing Minilessons Book, Grade 3

Have a Try

Invite students to turn and talk about writing friendly letters.

> What other information could be included in this letter? Turn and talk about that.

- After time for a brief discussion, ask students to share. Add suggestions as appropriate by using a caret or an asterisk or by attaching a strip of paper (spider leg).
- Add a PS to the letter so students understand the purpose and placement of a postscript.

Summarize and Apply

Summarize the lesson. Remind students to include each part in a friendly letter. Write the principle at the top of the chart.

> During writing time, write a friendly letter or continue working on one in your writing folder. You can share your thoughts about a book, or you can write to a friend or someone in your family who lives in a different place. Bring your writing to share when we meet later.

Confer

- During independent writing, move around the room to confer briefly with as many individual students as time allows. Sit side by side with them and invite them to talk about their friendly letters. Use the following prompts as needed.
  - *Show where you will write the greeting and closing on your letter.*
  - *Whose name will go in the greeting and whose name will go in the signature?*
  - *What words will you use for the closing?*
  - *Point to where you will add commas in your letter.*

Share

Following independent writing, gather students in the meeting area. Ask a few volunteers to share their friendly letters.

> Who would like to share the friendly letter you worked on today?
>
> Show where you placed each part of the friendly letter on the page.

WML 3
GEN.U1.WML3

Writing Minilesson Principle
Write the important information in your letter.

Writing Friendly Letters

You Will Need

- a mentor text that shows examples of friendly letters, such as *Harriett and Violeta: A Long-Distance Friendship* by Laura Platas Scott, from *Shared Reading Collection*
- chart paper prepared with a sample friendly letter
- highlighter or highlighter tape (two colors)
- markers
- writing folders

Academic Language / Important Vocabulary

- friendly letter
- important
- information

Continuum Connection

- Understand that a note or card should include short greetings and relevant information
- Understand how to learn about writing notes, cards, invitations, and friendly letters by noticing the characteristics of examples
- Include the important information in the communication
- Write a friendly letter with all parts

GOAL

Understand that a letter writer includes information in a letter that fits the purpose.

RATIONALE

The information contained in a letter depends on the purpose. Students need to think about the letter's purpose and then decide what information is important to include to meet that purpose.

WRITER'S NOTEBOOK/WRITING FOLDER

Have students keep the letters they are working on in their writing folders.

ASSESS LEARNING

- Look for evidence to determine what students understand about friendly letters.
- Notice whether students include details that support the purpose of their letters.
- Observe whether students can use vocabulary such as *friendly letter*, *important*, and *information*.

MINILESSON

To help students think about the minilesson principle, have them notice the important information that is included in several friendly letters, including one that you have written. Below is an example lesson. An alternative would be to do this lesson over a couple of days and write a letter together using shared writing.

- Show and read a sample friendly letter in a mentor text, such as page 6 in *Harriett and Violeta*.

    What do you notice about the information Harriett included in her letter?

- Guide the conversation to help students notice the important and relevant information that it is included in the letter.

    Harriett included the important information, such as the date, a response to what Violeta had written, and her feelings about her upcoming recital.

- Show the chart paper prepared with a friendly letter.

    What is my purpose in writing this letter?

    What important information fits the purpose of the letter?

    I wrote this letter to thank you, and I gave examples of why I want to thank you.

- Highlight information in the letter that supports the purpose. Also note the date, greeting, closing, signature, and commas.

Have a Try

Invite students to turn and talk about including important information in a friendly letter.

> What important information will you make sure to include in the friendly letter you are writing? Turn and talk to your partner about that.

▸ After time for discussion, ask a few volunteers to share ideas.

Summarize and Apply

Summarize the lesson. Remind students to include important information in the friendly letters they are working on. Write the principle at the top of the chart.

> How do you know what kind of information to write in a letter?

▸ Remind students that the purpose for writing a letter will determine the information they include.

> During writing time, you can work on a friendly letter that you are working on in your writing folder, or you can begin a new letter. You can write about a book or about something from your own life. Think about the important information you want to include in your letter. Bring your letter to share when we meet later.

Confer

▸ During independent writing, move around the room to confer briefly with as many individual students as time allows. Sit side by side with them and invite them to talk about their letters. Use the following prompts as needed.
- What are you writing about in your letter?
- How can I help you with your letter writing?
- What important information will you include in your friendly letter?
- Reread your letter to check the important information.

Share

Following independent writing, gather students in the meeting area to talk about their letters.

> Share your letter with a partner. Tell the important information you included and show the parts of your letter.

Write the important information in your letter.

November 10

Dear Class,

Thank you for being so helpful these past few weeks while I was on crutches. Some of you helped me by opening or closing the classroom door. Some of you carried things for me. All of you showed great kindness, especially on days when my knee really hurt and I had to stay seated.

The most surprising part was receiving the card you all signed. Making and sending a card was such a thoughtful thing to do! I am a lucky teacher to have you as my students.

Your teacher,
Ms. Thornton

PS In the future, I will be sure to watch out for uneven sidewalks so I won't trip and fall again!

Umbrella 1 | Writing Friendly Letters

Assessment

After you have taught the minilessons in this umbrella, observe students in a variety of classroom activities. Use *The Fountas & Pinnell Literacy Continuum* to notice, teach for, and support students' learning as you observe their attempts at writing letters.

▶ What evidence do you have of students' new understandings related to writing friendly letters?
- Do students understand that they can write friendly letters for different reasons?
- Do their friendly letters include the appropriate parts?
- Does the information students include in their letters support their reason for writing?
- Are they using vocabulary such as *friendly letter*, *invite*, *thanks*, *opinion*, *reason*, *purpose*, *greeting*, *closing*, *signature*, *PS*, *comma*, *important*, and *information*?

▶ In what ways, beyond the scope of this umbrella, are students engaged in writing?
- Do they show an interest in more functional writing, such as writing directions in a how-to book?
- Are they interested in writing memory stories?

Use your observations to determine the next umbrella you will teach. You may also consult Suggested Sequence of Lessons (pp. 605–622) for guidance.

EXTENSIONS FOR WRITING FRIENDLY LETTERS

▶ Discuss with students different ways of closing a letter (e.g., *Love*, *Sincerely*, *From*) and when each is appropriate.

▶ Use shared writing to write letters to people in the community (e.g., an invitation to a firefighter for a classroom visit, a thank-you letter to first responders or other medical workers).

▶ Sit side by side at the computer with students as they write an email to a family member.

▶ Assist students with delivering or mailing their letters, Talk about how to address an envelope with the recipient's address and a return address.

▶ Use the teacher and student rubrics available in online resources to evaluate students' friendly letters or to guide them to evaluate their own texts. You might also consider having students co-create rubrics with you.

Writing Procedural Texts

Umbrella 2

Minilessons in This Umbrella

- **WML1** Notice the qualities of good procedural texts.
- **WML2** Choose what you want to teach and how you will teach it.
- **WML3** Write and/or draw the steps or instructions.

Before Teaching Umbrella 2 Minilessons

Across the minilessons in this umbrella, students will study the characteristics and forms of procedural texts and then write their own.

Gather a variety of different types of procedural texts, texts that teach how to make or do something, to use as mentor texts. The following books from *Fountas & Pinnell Classroom™ Interactive Read-Aloud Collection* have examples of procedural texts within them. You will also want to find various other authentic procedural texts, such as recipes, instruction manuals, how-to books, game instructions, and how-to videos or posters. Rubrics for evaluating the students' procedural texts are available in the online resources.

Interactive Read-Aloud Collection

Author/Illustrator Study: Patricia Polacco
Thunder Cake

Genre Study: Expository Nonfiction
Tornadoes! by Gail Gibbons

Genre Study: Realistic Fiction
Dumpling Soup by Jama Kim Rattigan

Hybrid Texts: Fiction and Nonfiction
Yucky Worms by Vivian French

As you read and discuss procedural texts together, help students

- identify what readers can learn from the text,
- notice the characteristics and different types of procedural texts, and
- discuss how the illustrations can support the written directions.

Interactive Read-Aloud
Patricia Polacco

Expository Nonfiction

Realistic Fiction

Hybrid Texts

Writer's Notebook

WML1
GEN.U2.WML1

Writing Minilesson Principle
Notice the qualities of good procedural texts.

Writing Procedural Texts

You Will Need

- a few familiar books with examples of procedural texts, such as the following:
  - *Tornadoes!* by Gail Gibbons, from Text Set: Genre Study: Expository Nonfiction
  - *Dumpling Soup* by Jama Kim Rattigan, from Text Set: Genre Study: Realistic Fiction
  - *Thunder Cake*, from Text Set: Author/Illustrator Study: Patricia Polacco
  - *Yucky Worms* by Vivian French, from Text Set: Hybrid Texts: Fiction and Nonfiction
- various procedural texts, such as recipes, instruction manuals, how-to books, game instructions, and how-to videos or posters
- chart paper and markers
- writer's notebooks

Academic Language / Important Vocabulary

- procedural text
- recipe
- quality
- instructions

Continuum Connection

- Understand that a procedural text helps people know how to do something
- Understand that a procedural text can be written in various forms: e.g., list, directions with steps (how-to)
- Understand how to craft procedural writing from mentor texts

GOAL

Understand that there are different types of procedural texts and notice the qualities of effective ones.

RATIONALE

When you help students identify the forms and qualities of good procedural texts, they will be better prepared and equipped to begin writing their own procedural texts. They will model their own procedural texts on those they have read.

WRITER'S NOTEBOOK/WRITING FOLDER

Have students make notes in their writer's notebooks about the qualities of good procedural texts.

ASSESS LEARNING

- Notice whether students can identify the forms and qualities of good procedural texts.
- Look for evidence that they can use vocabulary such as *procedural text*, *quality*, *recipe*, and *instructions*.

MINILESSON

To help students think about the principle, engage them in studying good procedural texts to identify their qualities. Here is an example.

- Show the cover of *Tornadoes!* Turn to the "What to Do When a Tornado Approaches" feature near the end of the book. Read it aloud.

   What can you learn from this section of the book?

   What do you notice about how the author makes the instructions clear?

- Record the students' noticings on chart paper.

   This part of the book is a procedural text. A procedural text tells readers how to make or do something.

- Turn to the recipe on the inside back cover of *Dumpling Soup*.

   This is also a procedural text. Does anyone know what this is called?

   This is a recipe. What do you notice about how the author teaches you how to make dumpling soup?

   What are the different parts of the recipe?

   How does she make the steps you have to follow clear?

   As far as you know, did the writer include everything you need for the soup?

- Add students' responses to the chart, generalizing them as necessary.

Have a Try

Invite students to talk to a partner about types of procedural texts.

▶ Write the forms of procedural texts just discussed, instructions and recipe, on the chart.

> What other types of writing could tell you how to do or make something? Turn and talk to your partner about this.

▶ After students turn and talk, invite several students to share their thinking. Write their responses on the chart. Point out that any form of procedural text will have at least some of the characteristics students have identified. Save the chart for WML3.

Summarize and Apply

Write the principle at the top of the chart. Summarize the learning and invite students to study procedural texts with a partner or in a small group.

▶ Give each pair or group at least one procedural text.

> Today during writing time, meet with your partner (group) to study the procedural text I gave you. Discuss what you notice about it and write your observations in your writer's notebook. Bring your notes when we come back together.

Notice the qualities of good procedural texts.

Qualities of Procedural Texts
- Sentences are usually short and get right to the point.
- Most sentences start with a verb, or action word.
- The pictures help you understand what to do.
- There is often a list of the materials you will need.
- The steps are written in order.
- The steps are often written in a list and numbered.
- The steps are complete.

Forms of Procedural Texts
- Instructions
- Recipe
- How-to directions
- Instruction manual
- Game instructions
- Poster

Confer

▶ During independent writing, move around the room to confer briefly with students about what they notice. Use prompts such as the following as needed.
  • *What would you call this type of procedural text?*
  • *How does the author make the steps easy to follow?*
  • *What do you notice about the illustrations? Are they helpful? Why or why not?*

Share

Following independent writing, gather students in the meeting area. Ask each pair or group to share what they noticed.

> What qualities did you notice in the procedural text you studied?

WML 2
GEN.U2.WML2

Writing Minilesson Principle
Choose what you want to teach and how you will teach it.

Writing Procedural Texts

You Will Need

- an idea for a procedural text
- chart paper prepared with two columns titled *Topic* and *Form*
- markers
- writer's notebooks

Academic Language / Important Vocabulary

- procedural text
- topic
- form
- purpose
- audience

Continuum Connection

- Understand that a procedural text helps people know how to do something
- Understand that a procedural text can be written in various forms: e.g., list, directions with steps (how-to)

GOAL

Use purpose and audience to help choose the topic and form of a procedural text.

RATIONALE

When you guide students to think about purpose and audience, they have to think about how their readers will experience their writing. This should help them choose the form of procedural text that will be most appropriate for communicating the information effectively.

WRITER'S NOTEBOOK/WRITING FOLDER

Students can reread their writer's notebooks to find ideas for their procedural texts and/or write new ideas to consider.

ASSESS LEARNING

- Observe for evidence that students consider their purpose and audience when choosing what they will teach and how they will teach it.
- Look for evidence that they can use vocabulary such as *procedural text*, *topic*, *form*, *purpose*, and *audience*.

MINILESSON

To help students think about the principle, model how to think about purpose and audience when choosing the topic and form of a procedural text. Here is an example.

> I've been thinking about what I'd like to write a procedural text about. I think I'd like to write a procedural text about making bagels. I'm interested in this topic because my grandfather was a baker, and he taught me how to make bagels. I think lots of other people would like to know how to make them.
>
> My purpose, or reason, for writing is to help people learn how to make bagels. My audience is adults and children who don't know how to make bagels but would like to learn. I will need to make sure my instructions are really clear so people who don't know anything about making bagels can follow them. I could write a recipe, but that might be hard to follow for people who've never made bagels before. I think I will make a how-to video, so I can show my audience exactly what to do.
>
> What did you notice about how I chose what to teach and how to teach it? What kinds of things did I think about?

- Write your chosen topic and form on the prepared chart paper.

The Writing Minilessons Book, Grade 3

WML 2
GEN.U2.WML2

Have a Try

Invite students to talk to a partner about their ideas for procedural texts.

> What could you teach, and how would you teach it? Write a few ideas in your writer's notebook. Then turn and talk to your partner about your ideas.

- Students can use p. 28 in *Writer's Notebook, Intermediate* to record ideas. After students turn and talk, invite a few students to share their ideas. Add their ideas to the chart.

Summarize and Apply

Write the principle at the top of the chart. Summarize the learning and remind students to think about purpose and audience when choosing a topic and form.

> Today during writing time, spend some more time thinking about what you would like to teach and how you would teach it. Remember to think about the best way to teach your audience. You might already have ideas for topics you would like to teach in your writer's notebook. If so, circle one you would like to use. If not, write some ideas in your writer's notebook, and be ready to share when we meet later.

Choose what you want to teach and how you will teach it.

Topic	Form
How to make bagels	Video
How to make a paper airplane	Book
How to brush your teeth	Poster
How to make vegetable soup	Recipe
How to be a superhero	Comic strip

Confer

- During independent writing, move around the room to confer briefly with students about their plans for procedural texts. Use prompts such as the following as needed.
  - *What is something that you know how to do or make that you could teach to others?*
  - *Who are you writing this procedural text for? Who is your audience?*
  - *What do you think is the best way to teach _____? Why?*

Share

Following independent writing, gather students in the meeting area to share their ideas.

> Turn to your partner and talk about what you are going to teach and how you will teach it.

- After partners share, bring the whole group back together to talk about purpose and audience.

WML 3
GEN.U2.WML3

Writing Minilesson Principle
Write and/or draw the steps or instructions.

Writing Procedural Texts

You Will Need

- a familiar procedural text, such as the recipe in *Dumpling Soup* by Jama Kim Rattigan, from Text Set: Genre Study: Realistic Fiction
- the chart from WML1
- an idea for a class procedural text
- chart paper and markers
- writing folders
- To download the following online resource for this lesson, visit **fp.pub/resources**:
  - chart art (optional)

Academic Language / Important Vocabulary

- procedural text
- steps
- instructions
- complete

Continuum Connection

- Write steps of a procedure with appropriate sequence and explicitness
- Use number words or transition words
- Understand that a procedural text often includes a list of what is needed to do a procedure
- Understand that a procedural text often shows one item under another item and may include a number or letter for each item

GOAL

Write and/or draw a procedural text.

RATIONALE

Writing a procedural text requires careful attention to detail. If students skip a step or omit important information, the readers will not be successful. Such attention to detail is not only important in procedural writing but in other types of writing as well.

WRITER'S NOTEBOOK/WRITING FOLDER

Have students keep the drafts of their procedural texts in their writing folders.

ASSESS LEARNING

- Notice whether students write and/or draw the steps or instructions completely and clearly.
- Look for evidence that they can use vocabulary such as *procedural text*, *steps*, *instructions*, and *complete*.

MINILESSON

To help students think about the principle, use shared writing to model writing a procedural text for an activity with which students are familiar. Here is an example.

- Show the recipe on the inside back cover of *Dumpling Soup*.

    What did you notice about how the author wrote the instructions for making dumpling soup? How did she clearly show the ingredients you need and what you need to do?

- Show the chart from WML1 and review the qualities the students noticed.

    Today we're going to write a procedural text together. Let's write about how to make a catapult, since that's something we've done together and we all know how to do. What should we write first?

    What things will readers need to make a catapult?

    What is the first step that readers will need to do?

    How should we show that this is the first step?

- Use shared writing to write the instructions on chart paper.

    How do we know our instructions are complete?

162

The Writing Minilessons Book, Grade 3

Have a Try

Invite students to talk to a partner about the procedure they will write.

> Think about your own procedural text. Turn and talk to your partner about the steps or instructions your readers will need to follow.

Summarize and Apply

Write the principle at the top of the first chart. Summarize the learning and remind students to think about the qualities of good procedural texts when they write their own.

> Today during writing time, start to write your procedural text. You can also add illustrations if you want. If you need help remembering how to write a procedural text, look at the chart we made the other day about the qualities of good procedural texts. Keep your draft in your writing folder.

Confer

- During independent writing, move around the room to confer briefly with students about writing procedural texts. Use prompts such as the following as needed.
    - What will readers need to do (make) _____?
    - What is the first step that readers will need to follow?
    - What is the next step? How can you show which step is second?
    - How will you know your directions are complete?

Share

Following independent writing, gather students in the meeting area to share their writing.

> Who would like to read aloud your procedural text?
>
> Does anyone have any comments or questions for _____?

How to Make a Catapult

You will need:
- 7 jumbo craft sticks (2 of them notched)
- Rubber bands
- Bottle cap
- Double-sided sticky dots
- Small marshmallows or pompoms

Instructions:
1. Stack 5 of the craft sticks.
2. Wrap a rubber band tightly around each end of the stack.
3. Push one notched craft stick under the top craft stick. Flip over the stack.
4. Lay the second notched craft stick across the top of the stack.
5. Fasten the two sticks with a rubber band at the notches.
6. Glue the bottle cap to the end of the top notched craft stick.

Umbrella 2: Writing Procedural Texts

Assessment

After you have taught the minilessons in this umbrella, observe students as they explore writing procedural texts. Use *The Fountas & Pinnell Literacy Continuum* to notice, teach for, and support students' learning as you observe their attempts at reading and writing.

- What evidence do you have of students' new understandings related to writing procedural texts?
  - Can students identify various types and characteristics of procedural texts?
  - Do they consider purpose and audience when they choose what to write and how to write it?
  - Are their procedural texts written clearly, sequentially, and completely?
  - Do students understand and use vocabulary such as *procedural text*, *quality*, *step*, *instruction*, and *complete*?
- In what other ways, beyond the scope of this umbrella, are students exploring genre?
  - Are they ready to begin writing memory stories?
  - Are they showing an interest in writing realistic fiction stories?

Use your observations to determine the next umbrella you will teach. You may also consult Suggested Sequence of Lessons (pp. 605–622) for guidance.

EXTENSIONS FOR WRITING PROCEDURAL TEXTS

- Pull together a small, temporary guided writing group of students who need support in a similar area, for example, writing procedural texts.

- After students engage in social studies and science projects, encourage them to write procedural texts about applicable activities.

- Have students trade procedural texts with a partner and follow the directions in each other's texts. Encourage students to revise their text based on their partner's feedback.

- Teach students how to give an oral presentation, make a multimedia presentation, or make a video to demonstrate how to do something.

- Use the teacher and student rubrics available in online resources to evaluate students' procedural texts or to guide them to evaluate their own texts. You might also consider having students co-create rubrics with you.

Writing to a Prompt: Getting Ready for Test Writing

Umbrella 3

Minilessons in This Umbrella

WML1	Read the directions carefully and make sure you understand what is being asked.
WML2	Start your response with a main idea sentence.
WML3	Write a short response.
WML4	Write a long response.
WML5	Write a response that compares and contrasts two things.
WML6	Write an effective concluding sentence.

Interactive Read-Aloud
Expository Nonfiction

Shared Reading

Writer's Notebook

Before Teaching Umbrella 3 Minilessons

This umbrella provides exploration of and practice in test writing, or writing to a prompt. As you teach the minilessons in this umbrella, provide opportunities for students to write independently in the many genres they have explored, work in their writer's notebooks, and work on independent writing projects.

Before teaching this umbrella, spend time with your teaching team to examine your state's English Language Arts (ELA) tests from prior years, often accessible through a state testing website. Make note of the types of passages, writing prompts, and question or command words used in the prompts. Use this analysis to collect sample prompts or to construct similar prompts as you work through these minilessons.

For mentor texts, use prior years' state tests and the following books from *Fountas & Pinnell Classroom™ Interactive Read-Aloud Collection* and *Shared Reading Collection,* or choose familiar books from the classroom library.

Interactive Read-Aloud Collection
Genre Study: Expository Nonfiction
A Day and Night in the Desert by Caroline Arnold

Shared Reading Collection
The Elephants and the Mice: A Tale from the Panchatantra retold by Shyamala Parthasarathy

A Meerkat Day by Geerhardt Heever

As you read and enjoy these texts together, help students notice
- story elements in realistic fiction or fantasy books,
- themes or main ideas and the details that support them, and
- how two texts can be similar in some ways and different in others.

WML1
GEN.U3.WML1

Writing Minilesson Principle
Read the directions carefully and make sure you understand what is being asked.

Writing to a Prompt: Getting Ready for Test Writing

You Will Need

- in advance, write ELA prompts requiring both short and long responses on strips of paper
- a book to use with the prompts, such as *A Meerkat Day* by Geerhardt Heever, from *Shared Reading Collection*
- chart paper and markers
- tape or glue
- prompts prepared in advance to distribute to each student pair
- writer's notebooks and writing folders

Academic Language / Important Vocabulary

- short response
- passage
- extended response
- prompt
- question words
- key words

Continuum Connection

- Understand that test writing can take various forms: e.g., short constructed response (sometimes called *short answer*), extended constructed response (or *essay*)
- Understand that test writing involves analyzing what is expected of the writer and then planning and writing a response that reflects it
- Understand test writing is a response carefully tailored to meet precise instructions

GOAL

Read and understand an assigned prompt.

RATIONALE

In order to write an effective response to a test prompt, students must learn to read the prompt carefully, noticing key words. Discussing a variety of prompts will help students learn the skills they will need to respond to prompts independently. When you teach this minilesson, use the terminology (e.g., *short answer*, *essay*) that matches your state test.

WRITER'S NOTEBOOK/WRITING FOLDER

If students have extra time, they can write in their writer's notebooks or work on a longer piece of writing in their writing folders.

ASSESS LEARNING

- Observe for evidence that students can identify question words and parts in a prompt.
- Look for evidence that they can use vocabulary such as *short response*, *extended response*, *question words*, *passage*, *prompt*, and *key words*.

MINILESSON

To help students think about the minilesson principle, use ELA prompts you have collected or written to model responding to a prompt. Here is an example.

- Attach a prompt to chart paper.

  I am going to read this question, or prompt, two times. Reading it twice will help me understand what it is asking me to think about and then write about.

- Demonstrate how to think about the prompt in relation to *A Meerkat Day*. Underline *why* and *diagram* as you discuss these words. Add students' noticings about what the prompt is asking.

  Why seems to be a key word in this prompt. The question word why means I need to think about, find, and tell reasons for something. In this case, I need to find and tell reasons why the author used a diagram.

  What do you notice about the amount of space given for my response? This is a short response. The way I know that is by the small amount of space.

- Label the prompt *Short Response* on the chart. Repeat this process with another prompt, choosing one that requires an extended constructed response.

  What are the key words you notice? How much do you think I should write for this response?

- Label the prompt *Extended Response* on the chart.

Have a Try

Invite students to talk to a partner about another prompt.

- Direct students' attention to another prompt on the chart.

    > Read the prompt. Think about the process we just discussed to help you notice what the prompt is asking you to do. What key words would you underline? Turn and talk about that.

- Ask a few students to share. Underline key words on the chart. Repeat as time allows.

Summarize and Apply

Summarize the lesson. Remind students that they are thinking about a new genre of writing, test writing.

> What do you need to think about when you are asked to write to a prompt?

- Write the principle at the top of the chart. Distribute one or more prompts to each pair of students.

    > Today you will be reading other prompts that are part of test writing. Talk to your partner. Remember to read the prompt carefully at least once, underline key words, and make sure you understand what is being asked and whether you need to write a short or long response. Bring your prompt when we meet later.

Read the directions carefully and make sure you understand what is being asked.		
	Prompt	What am I being asked to do?
Short Response	Why did the author include a diagram in the passage?	Find and tell why
	Explain a lesson that can be learned from this folktale.	Tell how or why
	Identify the problem in the story and explain how it is solved.	Find and tell how
Extended Response	Write an essay that describes how the author used text features to teach more about meerkats.	Explain
	What is the theme of _____? Include details that help determine the theme.	Tell and explain
	After reading A Day and Night in the Desert, write a response that compares and contrasts the desert during the day and night.	Tell how things are the same and different

Confer

- During independent writing, move around the room to confer briefly with as many pairs of students as time allows. Sit side by side with them and invite them to talk about test prompts. Use the following prompts as needed.
    - *Remember to read the prompt more than once.*
    - *What do you think are the key words in this prompt? Underline them.*
    - *Do you think this will be a short response or an extended response?*

Share

Following independent writing, gather students in the meeting area to share their work.

> Read your prompt. Share how you and your partner thought about the prompt.

WML 2
GEN.U3.WML2

Writing Minilesson Principle
Start your response with a main idea sentence.

Writing to a Prompt: Getting Ready for Test Writing

You Will Need

- chart paper prepared with the same prompts as in WML1 written on strips of paper (key words underlined) and affixed to chart
- a strip of paper with a main idea sentence frame written in response to the first prompt
- markers and highlighters
- tape or glue
- writer's notebooks and writing folders
- prompts prepared in advance to distribute to each pair of students

Academic Language / Important Vocabulary

- short response
- extended response
- main idea
- passage
- prompt

Continuum Connection

- Write focused responses to questions and to prompts
- Write concisely and to the direction of the question or prompt
- Understand test writing is a response carefully tailored to meet precise instructions

GOAL

Use the words from a prompt to generate a main idea sentence.

RATIONALE

As students begin to understand what a prompt is asking of them, they can start to think about writing a response. Restating the prompt is one way of beginning to write a response, and it can help students to stay focused on the topic of the prompt.

WRITER'S NOTEBOOK/WRITING FOLDER

If students have extra time, they can write in their writer's notebooks or work on a longer piece of writing in their writing folders.

ASSESS LEARNING

- Observe for evidence that students can restate words from the prompt in their responses.
- Look for evidence that they can use vocabulary such as *short response*, *extended response*, *main idea*, *passage*, and *prompt*.

MINILESSON

Students will need their writer's notebooks for the lesson. To help students think about the minilesson principle, remind them to use what they already know about writing engaging and thoughtful beginnings. Use ELA prompts from WML1 to discuss crafting a main idea sentence.

- Read the first prompt on the prepared chart paper aloud.

    We looked at this prompt and talked about what it is asking you to do. Let's think about how to begin writing a response to it. You can give the readers a little bit of information about what they are going to read as one way to begin writing. This is called a main idea sentence.

- Read the first prompt again. Then read aloud the prepared sentence strip with the main idea sentence you wrote. Attach it to the chart. Guide students to notice that the main idea sentence includes words from the prompt.

    What do you notice about what I wrote?

- Guide students to notice how your main idea sentence frame relates to the prompt. Highlight key parts of the prompt. Ask students how they would complete the sentence.

- Repeat this process with several more prompts, asking students to help you write a main idea sentence for each.

    How can I begin my writing? Which key words should I include in my main idea sentence to help my readers know what I am going to write about?

    Do the key words match the prompt?

Have a Try

Invite students to talk to a partner about writing a main idea sentence for another prompt.

- Read the final prompt aloud.

    What do you think the main idea sentence could be? Turn and talk about that. Then write a main idea sentence in your writer's notebook.

- Ask a few students to share what they wrote. Highlight key words in their sentences.

Summarize and Apply

Summarize the lesson. Remind students that they are thinking about writing a beginning sentence for a new genre of writing, test writing. Encourage conversations about noticing what a prompt is asking them to write about and what the main idea sentence could be.

   How should you start your response to a prompt?

- Write the principle at the top of the chart. Distribute one or more prompts to each pair of students.

    Today, talk to your partner and follow the same procedure we went through together. Underline the important words and then think about and write down a main idea sentence in your writer's notebook.

Confer

- During independent writing, move around the room to confer briefly with as many pairs of students as time allows. Sit side by side with them and invite them to talk about test prompts and main idea sentences. Use the following prompts as needed.
    - *What is the prompt asking you to write about?*
    - *What words from this prompt might you use to write your main idea sentence? Underline those.*
    - *What ideas can you start writing about? Jot that down.*

Share

Following independent writing, gather students in the meeting area to share their work.

   Who would like to share the main idea sentence you wrote with your partner?

Start your response with a main idea sentence.

Prompt	Main idea sentence
Why did the author include a diagram in the passage?	The author included a diagram in this passage because _____.
Explain a lesson that can be learned from this folktale.	A lesson can be learned from this folktale.
Identify the problem in the story and explain how it is solved.	The problem in the story is _____, and it is solved by _____.
Write an essay that describes how the author used text features to teach more about meerkats.	The author used text features to teach more about the topic of meerkats.
What is the theme of _____? Include details that help determine the theme.	The theme of _____ is _____.
After reading A Day and Night in the Desert, write a response that compares and contrasts the desert during the day and night.	The book A Day and Night in the Desert compares and contrasts the desert during the day and at night.

Umbrella 3: Writing to a Prompt: Getting Ready for Test Writing

WML 3
GEN.U3.WML3

Writing Minilesson Principle
Write a short response.

Writing to a Prompt: Getting Ready for Test Writing

You Will Need

- a familiar fiction or nonfiction text to provide evidence for the prompt, such as *The Elephants and the Mice* retold by Shyamala Parthasarathy, from *Shared Reading Collection*
- chart paper prepared with the minilesson principle, a prompt (key words underlined), and main idea sentence from WML2 written on strips of paper and attached; leave a small space to cue a short response
- chart paper prepared with the title *Steps for Responding to a Prompt* and steps prewritten on strips of paper ready to attach
- markers, tape or glue
- prompts prepared in advance for each pair of students
- writer's notebooks

Academic Language / Important Vocabulary

- short response
- details
- main idea
- passage
- prompt

Continuum Connection

- Incorporate one's knowledge of craft in shaping responses
- Introduce ideas followed by supportive details and examples

GOAL

Write a short response that includes a main idea sentence, one or two details, and a concluding sentence.

RATIONALE

Continue laying the foundation for careful analysis of reading and test prompts. Students will learn to reread texts or passages to find details that support a main idea. Using shared writing allows students to orally compose a response while you do the writing.

WRITER'S NOTEBOOK/WRITING FOLDER

Students can use their writer's notebooks to practice writing short constructed responses.

ASSESS LEARNING

- Look at students' responses. Do they include a main idea sentence, one or two details, and a concluding sentence?
- Look for evidence that they can use vocabulary such as *short response*, *details*, *main idea*, *passage*, and *prompt*.

MINILESSON

To help students think about the minilesson principle, use ELA prompts and main idea sentences from WML2 to discuss crafting a short response. Refer to a text students have read and enjoyed for evidence to support the lesson.

- Show *The Elephants and the Mice*. Read the prompt on the chart and the main idea sentence.

  > This is a book we have read before and know well. Today we will think about this book as we write to this prompt: *Explain a lesson that can be learned from this folktale.* I have already written the main idea sentence we wrote together yesterday. What do you notice about the amount of space we have to write our response?

  > What main idea sentence could we write? Turn and talk to your partner.

- As students share their ideas, demonstrate rereading the main idea sentence and quickly writing the sentence students suggest.

  > There is only a small space, so we will write a short response. After writing the main idea sentence, we need to write what the lesson is. Then we need to look back in the book and think about why we think that is the lesson. What can we write next? Turn and talk to your partner about that.

- As students share their ideas, demonstrate rereading the sentences on the chart and quickly writing the sentences students suggest for evidence.

- If this section runs long (more than ten minutes), add the concluding sentence (see Have a Try) on a subsequent day.

Have a Try

Remind students of what they already know about writing engaging endings. Then invite students to talk to a partner about writing a concluding sentence for the paragraph developed in the lesson.

> We have talked about ways to end a memory story or an informational text. What might we say to wrap up our thinking about the lesson of this folktale? Turn and talk about that.

▸ After a brief discussion, ask a student to share while you write a concluding sentence onto the chart.

Summarize and Apply

Summarize the lesson. Encourage students to follow the steps for answering a short constructed response prompt.

> What steps did we take to craft a short response to the prompt?

▸ As students respond, quickly add the steps, prewritten on slips of paper, to the chart. Distribute the prepared test prompts.

> Today you will work with a partner to write in your writer's notebook a short response to a prompt that is about a text we have already read together. Talk to your partner and refer to the steps on the chart if you need to.

Confer

▸ During independent writing, move around the room to confer briefly with as many pairs of students as time allows. Sit side by side with them and invite them to talk about responding to test prompts. Use the following prompts as needed.

- *What is the prompt asking you to write about?*
- *Underline words in the prompt you could use to write your main idea sentence.*
- *How much space do you have to write a response to this prompt?*
- *Where did you find the details that support the main idea sentence?*
- *What type of sentence will conclude, or wrap up, your writing?*

Share

Following independent writing, gather students in the meeting area to share their responses.

> Who would like to share the short response you wrote with your partner?

Write a short response.

Prompt: Explain a lesson that can be learned from this folktale.

A lesson can be learned from this folktale. The lesson this folktale taught us is that no matter how small you are you can still be helpful. At the beginning of this folktale the Elephant King didn't think the mice could be helpful. The mice were small but they ended up helping the big Elephant King get out of the net. That is the lesson of this folktale.

Steps for Responding to a Prompt

1. Read the prompt carefully.
2. Find and underline important words and be sure you understand what you are being asked to write about.
3. Write a main idea sentence.
4. Find and write the details that match your idea.
5. Write a concluding sentence.

WML 4
GEN.U3.WML4

Writing Minilesson Principle
Write a long response.

Writing to a Prompt: Getting Ready for Test Writing

You Will Need

- a familiar fiction or nonfiction text to provide evidence for the prompt, such as *A Meerkat Day* by Geerhardt Heever, from *Shared Reading Collection*
- chart paper prepared with the minilesson principle, a prompt (key words underlined), and main idea sentence from WML2 written on strips of paper and attached; a long response written directly on the chart
- *Steps for Responding to a Prompt* chart from WML3
- chart paper
- several colors of markers or highlighters
- prompts prepared in advance for each pair of students
- writer's notebooks

Academic Language / Important Vocabulary

- extended (long) response
- details
- main idea
- passage
- prompt

Continuum Connection

- Elaborate on important points
- Introduce ideas followed by supportive details and examples
- Use examples to make meaning clear

GOAL
Write a long response that includes a main idea sentence, reasons and examples to support the main idea, and a concluding sentence.

RATIONALE
Building upon what students have learned about a short response, this minilesson uses modeled writing of a long response and asks students to compare the two as a way to develop a list of qualities for a long response. This list will be a resource for students as they learn more about the genre of test writing.

WRITER'S NOTEBOOK/WRITING FOLDER
Students can use their writer's notebooks to practice writing extended constructed responses.

ASSESS LEARNING

- When you read students' responses, notice whether they include a main idea sentence, reasons and examples to support the main idea, and a concluding sentence.
- Look for evidence that they can use vocabulary such as *extended (long) response*, *details*, *main idea*, *passage*, and *prompt*.

MINILESSON

To help students think about the minilesson principle, use ELA prompts and main idea sentences from WML2 and a fully crafted long response that you have written in advance. Refer to a text students have read and enjoyed for evidence to support the lesson.

- Show *A Meerkat Day*. Read the prompt on the chart and the main idea sentence.

   This is a book we have read before and know well. We read this prompt the other day and talked about what it is asking you to do. We noticed there was a big space to fill, so we knew we needed to write a long response. Then we thought about and wrote a main idea sentence. I finished writing the long response to this prompt. I am going to read it to you.

   What do you notice is the same or different between a short response and a long response?

- Circle or highlight the components of the response and name the parts. As needed, guide students to notice that there is more than one example and each has a statement that elaborates on the example.

- Display the chart from WML3.

   The steps for writing short and long responses are similar. Both start with a main idea sentence and end with a concluding sentence. The difference is how much information you give in your response.

WML 4
GEN.U3.WML4

Have a Try

Invite students to talk to a partner to compare short and long constructed responses.

> What are some important things to include in a long response to a test prompt? To get started, think about what you already know about writing a short response. Turn and talk about that.

▸ After a brief discussion, ask students to share while you write their suggestions on chart paper. Color code the elements students mention.

Summarize and Apply

Summarize the lesson. Encourage student pairs to refer to the components on the chart when answering the long constructed response prompt you assign them.

> Today you will work with a partner to write a long constructed response to a prompt in your writer's notebook. Talk to your partner and refer to the chart if you need to. Bring your notebook to share when we meet later.

Confer

▸ During independent writing, move around the room to confer briefly with as many pairs of students as time allows. Sit side by side with them and invite them to talk about responding to test prompts. Use the following questions as needed.

- What is the prompt asking you to write about?
- Underline the words in the prompt you could use to write your main idea sentence.
- How do you know this is a long response rather than a short response?
- What transition words can you use to help your paragraph flow together?
- What type of sentence will conclude or wrap up your writing?

Share

Following independent writing, gather students in the meeting area to share their responses.

> Who would like to share the long response you wrote with your partner?

Write a long response.

Prompt: Write an essay that describes how the author used text features to teach more about meerkats.

The author used text features to teach more about the topic of meerkats. One way the author used text features to teach more about meerkats is to have photos with captions. For example, one photo shows a meerkat standing on two feet next to a sitting cat. There is a line that goes across the top of each animal's head. This helps me understand that a meerkat is about the size of a cat. Another way the author used text features to teach more about meerkats is by using drawings. For example, one drawing shows the underground burrows. This helps me understand how the tunnels look and how the underground rooms are connected. The author's use of photos, captions, and drawings helps the reader understand even more about meerkats.

What to Include in a Long Response

Main idea sentence

One example
What it helps you understand

Another example
What it helps you understand

Concluding sentence

Section 2: Genres and Forms

Umbrella 3: Writing to a Prompt: Getting Ready for Test Writing

WML 5
GEN.U3.WML5

Writing Minilesson Principle
Write a response that compares and contrasts two things.

Writing to a Prompt: Getting Ready for Test Writing

You Will Need

- a familiar fiction or nonfiction text to provide evidence for the prompt, such as *A Day and Night in the Desert* by Caroline Arnold, from Text Set: Genre Study: Expository Nonfiction
- chart paper prepared with the principle, a long-answer prompt (key words underlined), and main idea sentence from WML2 written on strips of paper and attached; a compare-and-contrast response written directly on the chart
- charts from WML3 and WML4
- markers or highlighters
- chart paper
- prompts prepared in advance for each pair of students
- writer's notebooks

Academic Language / Important Vocabulary

- compare
- contrast
- main idea
- prompt

Continuum Connection

- Introduce ideas followed by supportive details and examples
- Use examples to make meaning clear
- Understand and use paragraph structure (indented or block) to organize sentences that focus on one idea

GOAL

Write a response that provides reasons and examples for how two things are similar and different.

RATIONALE

You have likely discussed compare and contrast with the students. Now they can apply this learning to write a response to a test prompt. Using modeled writing allows students to use what they have already learned about writing to a prompt to notice what this type of response should include. The chart will be a resource for students as they learn more about the genre of test writing.

WRITER'S NOTEBOOK/WRITING FOLDER

Students can use their writer's notebooks to practice writing responses to prompts.

ASSESS LEARNING

- Read students' responses. Do they include a main idea sentence, reasons and examples for how two things are similar and different, and a concluding sentence?
- Look for evidence that they can use vocabulary such as *compare*, *contrast*, *main idea*, and *prompt*.

MINILESSON

To help students think about the minilesson principle, use ELA prompts and main idea sentences from WML2 with a fully crafted compare-and-contrast response written in advance. Refer to a text students have read and enjoyed for evidence to support the lesson.

- Show *A Day and Night in the Desert*. Read the prompt on the chart and the main idea sentence.

  > This is a book we have read before and know well. We read this prompt the other day and talked about what it is asking you to do. We noticed there was a big space to fill, so we knew we needed to write a long response. Then we thought about and wrote our main idea sentence. I finished writing the long response to this prompt by comparing and contrasting the desert in the day and the night. I am going to read it to you.

  > What did I do to tell how things in the book are the same and different?

- Underline, circle, and highlight the components of the response and name the parts.

  > Notice how I used paragraphs to group my ideas and examples. In this type of response, you might give more than one example of how the two things are the same or different.

The Writing Minilessons Book, Grade 3

WML 5
GEN.U3.WML5

Have a Try

Remind students of what they know about writing short and long responses, referring to the charts from WML3 and WML4 as needed. Then invite students to talk to a partner about writing a compare-and-contrast response.

> What is important to include in a compare-and-contrast response? Turn and talk about that.

▸ After a brief discussion, ask students to share while you write their responses on chart paper.

Summarize and Apply

Summarize the lesson. Encourage students to follow the components on the chart when answering a compare-and-contrast test prompt. Distribute the prepared test prompts and suggest books that students might write about.

> Today you will work with a partner to write in your writer's notebook a response to a test prompt in which you will compare and contrast something from a book we have already read together. Keep in mind what to include in this type of response when you are talking together and writing your response. You can refer to the chart if you need to.

Confer

▸ During independent writing, move around the room to confer briefly with as many pairs of students as time allows. Sit side by side with them and invite them to talk about responding to test prompts. Use the following questions as needed.

- *What is the prompt asking you to compare and contrast?*
- *Underline the words from the prompt you could use to write your main idea sentence.*
- *How are these two ideas similar or the same?*
- *How are these two ideas different from one another?*
- *What will you write first? What will you include next? How will you conclude your writing?*

Share

Following independent writing, gather students in the meeting area to share their writing.

> Who would like to share the response you wrote with your partner?

Chart 1:

Write a response that compares and contrasts two things.

Prompt: After reading *A Day and Night in the Desert*, write a response that compares and contrasts the desert during the day and night.

The book *A Day and Night in the Desert* compares and contrasts the desert during the day and at night. The desert during the day can be similar to the desert at night time. During both times of day animals are looking for food. For example, during the day hummingbirds look for nectar to sip and bighorn sheep are out eating grass. At night peccaries search for roots, fruits, and seeds. Mice come out of their holes to collect seeds. Owls are also out at night looking for food. The desert is different during the day and the night. The temperature in the desert is different. For example, during the day the temperature rises as it gets hotter and hotter. At night the temperature in the desert lowers. Another way the desert is different during the day and the night is that different animals sleep at different times. For example, the hummingbird, the Gila monster, and the lizard are all awake during the day. The owl, the bat, and the coyote are all sleeping during the day and hunting at night. During the day and the night in the desert different animals are looking for food and safe places to hide.

Chart 2: What to Include in a Compare-and-Contrast Response

- Main idea sentence
- How they are the same (compare)
- An example
- How they are different (contrast)
- An example
- How they are different (contrast)
- Another example
- Concluding sentence

Umbrella 3: Writing to a Prompt: Getting Ready for Test Writing

WML 6
GEN.U3.WML6

Writing Minilesson Principle
Write an effective concluding sentence.

Writing to a Prompt: Getting Ready for Test Writing

You Will Need

- charts with prompt and response from WML3, WML4, and WML5
- chart paper prepared with the left-hand column heading and content filled in
- markers
- writer's notebooks

Academic Language / Important Vocabulary

- short response
- extended (long) response
- main idea
- passage
- effective
- concluding sentence (statement)

Continuum Connection

- Write focused responses to questions and to prompts
- Write concisely and to the direction of the question or prompt
- Use a variety of endings to satisfy the reader

GOAL

Write a concluding sentence that summarizes the big idea and leaves the readers satisfied.

RATIONALE

When you teach students how to craft an ending to a test prompt response, they learn to bring all they have learned about test prompt responses together and effectively conclude their writing in a way that is satisfying and stays focused on what the prompt is asking.

WRITER'S NOTEBOOK/WRITING FOLDER

Have students go into their writer's notebooks to revise the concluding sentences of their practice responses.

ASSESS LEARNING

- When you read students' responses, notice whether they include a concluding sentence that summarizes the big idea and leaves the readers satisfied.
- Look for evidence that they can use vocabulary such as *short response*, *extended (long) response*, *main idea*, *passage*, *effective*, and *concluding sentence (statement)*.

MINILESSON

To help students think about the minilesson principle, remind them to use what they know about writing engaging and thoughtful conclusions. Display the prompt and response on the chart from WML3 to discuss crafting an effective concluding sentence.

- Remind students what they already know about crafting effective endings.

    What do you already know about how you might end your writing?

- As students share their ideas, share back generative concepts for writing endings.

    When you write to a prompt, you want to think about how to summarize the big idea in your conclusion while at the same time satisfying your readers. This makes an effective concluding sentence.

    Listen as I reread this prompt and the response we wrote together. Think about what our focus was and notice how we ended our response.

- Display the chart from WML3. Read the prompt and response about the folktale. Guide students to think about how they can write a more engaging conclusion to the paragraph.

    What do you notice about the concluding sentence we wrote at the end of the response? How can we change it to more effectively complete our writing?

- Write their ideas for a revised concluding sentence in the right-hand column of the prepared chart for this lesson.

    Does this concluding sentence keep the focus on what the prompt asked for?

Have a Try

Invite students to repeat this process with a partner using the prompts from WML4 and WML5.

> Remember that an effective concluding sentence answers the prompt and satisfies the reader. Read the prompt and the response carefully. How can you make the concluding sentence even better? Turn and talk about that.

▸ Ask a few students to share their sentences.

Summarize and Apply

Summarize the lesson. Remind students to think about writing a concluding sentence for their responses. Encourage conversations about noticing what the prompt is asking them to write about and how they might revise the conclusion to make it more effective.

> How will you end a response to a prompt?

▸ Write the principle at the top of the chart.

> Today you will reread the responses you have written (short, long, compare and contrast) in your writer's notebook. Talk to your partner about a way of ending your writing that is effective and that matches the prompt. Revise your endings. Be prepared to share your revisions when we come back together.

Write an effective concluding sentence.

Concluding Sentence in First Draft	Effective Concluding Sentence
That is the lesson of this folktale.	From reading this folktale I know that even though I am small I can find ways to make a difference.
The author's use of photos, captions, and drawings helps the reader understand even more about meerkats.	If the author decided to just include words in the book, I would not have learned as much as I did about meerkats.
During the day and the night in the desert different animals are looking for food and safe places to hide.	Different animals do different things at different times, but the desert provides each one with what they need to survive.

Confer

▸ During independent writing, move around the room to confer briefly with as many pairs of students as time allows. Sit side by side with them and invite them to talk about responding to a test prompt. Use the following questions as needed.

- What is the prompt asking you to write about?
- What is the concluding sentence you already wrote?
- What might you add to that as a way to satisfy your readers and at the same time stay focused on the prompt?

Share

Following independent writing, gather students in the meeting area to share their work.

> Who would like to read your response and the new concluding sentence you wrote with your partner?

Umbrella 3 — Writing to a Prompt: Getting Ready for Test Writing

Assessment

After you have taught the minilessons in this umbrella, observe students in a variety of classroom activities. Use *The Fountas & Pinnell Literacy Continuum* to notice, teach for, and support students' learning as you observe their attempts at writing.

- What evidence do you have of students' new understandings related to test writing?
  - Are students able to think and talk about what a prompt is asking them to write?
  - Do their responses start with a main idea sentence, address the prompt, and finish with a concluding sentence?
  - Can they distinguish between a short constructed response prompt and a long constructed response prompt?
  - Do they understand how to write a response that compares and contrasts two things?
  - Are they using vocabulary such as *short constructed response*, *extended constructed response*, *question words*, *passage*, *prompt*, *main idea*, *details*, *compare*, *contrast*, *effective*, and *concluding sentence (statement)*?
- In what ways, beyond the scope of this umbrella, are students showing an understanding of writing to a prompt?
  - Can students apply what they have learned and respond to realistic fiction or personal narrative/personal story prompts?
  - Can they respond to a prompt by rewriting a narrative from a particular point of view?
- Use your observations to determine the next umbrella you will teach. You may also consult Suggested Sequence of Lessons (pp. 605–622) for guidance.

EXTENSIONS FOR WRITING TO A PROMPT: GETTING READY FOR TEST WRITING

- Work with students to reread, revise, and edit their writing. If you have already worked on the umbrellas that discuss this part of the writing process, connect back to that work. Help students understand that they will use everything they have learned about revising and editing on the day of the test because they won't have a chance to go back on another day to revise/edit.

- Use the rubrics from your state to help students understand how they will be assessed. You can also download non-state specific rubrics for writing to a test prompt from the online resources (fp.pub/resources).

- Provide time for students to practice having a limited amount of time to respond to a prompt in writing.

Writing Memory Stories

Umbrella 4

Minilessons in This Umbrella

- **WML1** Notice the qualities of good memory stories.
- **WML2** Choose a small moment or memory that is important to you.
- **WML3** Write details about the most important moments in the story.
- **WML4** Share your thoughts and feelings about the memory or experience.
- **WML5** Tell why the story is important.

Before Teaching Umbrella 4 Minilessons

The purpose of this umbrella is to help students write memory stories about meaningful memories and experiences from their own lives. Guide them to choose a small moment in time that they can write about in detail. You might choose for students to create picture books about their memories or write memory stories. In either case, they can plan their writing by sketching or using planning tools, such as lists and webs, in a writer's notebook.

Prior to teaching these minilessons, it would be helpful to have taught at least some of the minilessons in WPS.U1: Introducing the Writer's Notebook and WPS.U2: Writer's Notebook: Getting Ideas from Your Life. Students can use their webs to help them define small moments to write about. To provide models of memory writing, read aloud a variety of engaging memory stories that reflect diverse cultures and experiences. Use the following texts from *Fountas & Pinnell Classroom™ Interactive Read-Aloud Collection*, or choose books from your classroom library. A rubric for evaluating the students' memory stories is available in online resources.

Interactive Read-Aloud
Memory Stories

Writer's Notebook

Interactive Read-Aloud Collection
Exploring Memory Stories

My Rotten Redheaded Older Brother by Patricia Polacco

Family Pictures by Carmen Lomas Garza

Saturdays and Teacakes by Lester L. Laminack

Grandma's Records by Eric Velasquez

As you read and enjoy these and other memory stories together, help students
- identify the characteristics of memory stories,
- notice the sequence of events,
- discuss the author's word choices,
- notice the use of first person, and
- discuss the significance of each memory.

WML1
GEN.U4.WML1

Writing Minilesson Principle
Notice the qualities of good memory stories.

Writing Memory Stories

You Will Need

- several familiar memory stories, such as *Saturdays and Teacakes* by Lester L. Laminack and others in Text Set: Exploring Memory Stories
- chart paper and markers
- writer's notebooks

Academic Language / Important Vocabulary

- memory story
- quality
- author
- organize

Continuum Connection

- Understand that a memoir is a biographical text in which a writer reflects on a memorable experience, place, time, or person
- Usually write in first person to achieve a strong voice
- Write an engaging beginning and a satisfying ending to a story

GOAL

Study mentor texts to notice the qualities of good memory stories and to learn how to craft them.

RATIONALE

Conducting an inquiry around memory stories and having students name their qualities is an effective way of preparing and equipping students to begin writing their own memory stories. They will model their memory stories on those they have read.

WRITER'S NOTEBOOK/WRITING FOLDER

Students can write about the qualities of good memory stories in their writer's notebooks.

ASSESS LEARNING

- Observe for evidence of what students know about memory stories.
- Look for evidence that they can use vocabulary such as *memory story*, *quality*, *author*, and *organize*.

MINILESSON

To help students think about the minilesson principle, engage them in studying good memory stories and identifying the qualities. Here is an example.

- Show the cover of a memory story, such as *Saturdays and Teacakes*.

  Where did the author, Lester Laminack, get the idea for this book?

- Continue in a similar manner with a few other familiar memory stories.

  All of these stories are memory stories. Why do you think they're called memory stories?

  What have you noticed about memory stories?

- Record students' responses on chart paper, generalizing them as necessary.
- As needed, prompt students' thinking with questions such as the following:
  - *Did the authors write about long periods of time or small moments?*
  - *What do you notice about who told each story?*
  - *In what order did the authors tell their stories?*
  - *What did the authors do to help you picture what is happening in their stories?*
  - *What do you notice about how memory stories end?*

Have a Try

Invite students to talk to a partner about the qualities of memory stories.

> Is there anything else you have noticed about memory stories that we should add to our chart? Turn and talk to your partner about this.

- After time for discussion, invite a few pairs to share their thinking. Add any new ideas to the chart as appropriate.

Summarize and Apply

Write the principle at the top of the chart. Summarize the learning and invite students to further discuss the qualities of memory stories in small groups.

- Assign students to small groups, and give each group at least one familiar memory story to study in detail. Students can exchange books when they finish with them.

> Today during writing time, you will meet with your group to study a memory story. Write the title Good Memory Stories at the top of the next clean page in Section 4 of your writer's notebook. Discuss what you notice. Write your noticings in your writer's notebook. Bring your notes when we come back together.

Notice the qualities of good memory stories.

Memory Stories

- About <u>special memories</u> from the authors' lives
- About a small moment in time
- Usually told from the authors' point of view with words like <u>I, me, and my</u>
- Told in the <u>order that it happened</u>
- Use <u>descriptive words and details</u> to help you picture the characters, setting, and events
- Have authors' personal <u>thoughts and feelings</u> about their memories
- Give a <u>message</u>—something authors want readers to learn from their experiences

Confer

- During independent writing, move around the room to confer briefly with students about what they noticed about memory stories. Use prompts such as the following as needed.
  - *What is this memory story about?*
  - *How did the author make the memory seem real?*
  - *How did the author help you get to know the characters [setting]?*
  - *How did the author feel about the memory? How do you know?*

Share

Following independent writing, gather students in the meeting area to share their notes.

- Invite each group to share the qualities they noticed in the memory story they studied. Add new qualities to the chart.

WML 2
GEN.U4.WML2

Writing Minilesson Principle
Choose a small moment or memory that is important to you.

Writing Memory Stories

You Will Need

- a familiar memory story, such as *My Rotten Redheaded Older Brother* by Patricia Polacco, from Text Set: Exploring Memory Stories
- your writer's notebook with a list of ideas for memory stories
- chart paper and markers
- writer's notebooks

Academic Language / Important Vocabulary

- memory story
- moment
- memory
- important

Continuum Connection

- Understand that writers may tell stories from their own lives
- Select "small moments" or experiences and share thinking and feelings about them
- Select a meaningful topic

GOAL

Understand that writers often focus on a small moment or part of a memory that is meaningful to them in order to make their writing more powerful.

RATIONALE

Authors choose small moments to write about and write in depth about them rather than writing shallowly about expanses of time. When students notice this, they learn to do the same, making the events in their memory stories more focused and meaningful.

WRITER'S NOTEBOOK/WRITING FOLDER

Have students record in their writer's notebooks ideas for small moments or memories that could be developed into a memory story.

ASSESS LEARNING

- Notice whether students are able to write engagingly about a small but significant moment or memory.
- Look for evidence that they can use vocabulary such as *memory story*, *moment*, *memory*, and *important*.

MINILESSON

To help students think about the minilesson principle, use a familiar memory story to help them notice how authors of memory stories choose memories to write about. Then model choosing a topic for a memory story. Here is an example.

- Show the cover of *My Rotten Redheaded Older Brother* and read the title.

  What did Patricia Polacco write about in this book?

  She wrote about her older brother, but she did not write everything she remembers about him. She chose a few particular memories to focus on.

- Read pages 21–25 (when she falls off the carousel).

  Why do you think the author chose to write about this memory?

  That experience helped her realize something important about her brother. She wrote about this memory because it was important and special to her.

  I wrote some ideas for memory stories in my writer's notebook.

- Read aloud your list of ideas for memory stories. Think aloud about how to focus at least one of your ideas.

  One of the ideas I wrote down is "My Grandpa George." The day we helped him move into senior housing was a small but important moment.

  What do you notice about how I chose a memory to write about?

Have a Try

Invite students to talk to a partner about their own ideas for memory stories.

> What could you write a memory story about? Think about small memories or moments from your own life that are important to you. Turn and talk to your partner about your ideas.

▶ After students turn and talk, invite several students to share their ideas. Record them on chart paper.

Summarize and Apply

Help students summarize the learning and invite them to choose a small moment or memory to write about. If you have taught WPS.U2.WML3, refer students to their webs.

> What did you learn today about how authors choose what to write about for a memory story?

▶ Write the principle at the top of the chart.

> Today during writing time, spend some more time thinking about your ideas for memory stories. You might even start writing some details about one of your ideas. Write your ideas in your writer's notebook and bring them to share when we meet later.

Choose a small moment or memory that is important to you.

- Jacob: My first day of kindergarten
- Avery: How I met my best friend
- Gabriel: Making empanadas with my grandmother
- Wyatt: The day my dog got lost
- Genesis: Visiting my baby sister in the hospital

Confer

▶ During independent writing, move around the room to confer briefly with students about their ideas for memory stories. Use prompts such as the following as needed.

- What could you write about for a memory story?
- What special people, places, or events can you remember from when you were younger?
- That's a big idea. What small piece of that, or small moment, could you write about?
- Why is _____ an important memory for you?

Share

Following independent writing, gather students in the meeting area to share their ideas for memory stories. Ask each student to share one idea.

> Who would like to start by sharing your idea for a memory story?

> Share your reasons for choosing to write about that memory.

Umbrella 4: Writing Memory Stories

WML 3
GEN.U4.WML3

Writing Minilesson Principle
Write details about the most important moments in the story.

Writing Memory Stories

You Will Need

- a familiar memory story that is rich with details and descriptive language, such as *Saturdays and Teacakes* by Lester L. Laminack, from Text Set: Exploring Memory Stories
- chart paper and markers
- writer's notebooks and writing folders
- To download the following online resource for this lesson, visit **fp.pub/resources**:
  - chart art (optional)

Academic Language / Important Vocabulary

- memory story
- detail
- moment
- specific
- description

Continuum Connection

- Understand that a factual text may use literary techniques (interesting words and language, descriptions that appeal to the senses, illustrations) to engage and entertain readers as it gives them factual information
- Describe a setting and how it is related to the writer's experience
- Tell details about the most important moments in a story or experience while eliminating unimportant details

GOAL

Understand that authors write the most details about the most important parts of their stories.

RATIONALE

When you help students notice how authors of memory stories use language to construct vivid images of people, places, and events, they become better prepared to use literary techniques and include detailed descriptions in their own memory stories.

WRITER'S NOTEBOOK/WRITING FOLDER

Have students refer to their writer's notebooks for ideas for their memory stories and keep their memory story drafts in their writing folders.

ASSESS LEARNING

- Observe whether students include details about the most important moments in their stories.
- Look for evidence that they can use vocabulary such as *memory story*, *detail*, *moment*, *specific*, and *description*.

MINILESSON

To help students think about the minilesson principle, engage them in noticing the details in a familiar memory story. Here is an example.

- Show the cover of *Saturdays and Teacakes* and read the title. Then read page 1.

  Talk about how the author described his time before leaving the house.

  The author wrote that he got up early and got dressed. These details give a little information, but this is not an important part of the story.

- Read pages 10–13. Pause regularly to draw students' attention to different types of details. Ask questions such as the following:
  - *What is the sound of Mammaw's metal chair?*
  - *What words did the author use to describe the food on Mammaw's table?*

- Coach students to understand that the author wrote in more detail to describe an important moment in the story.

  What do you notice about the amount of detail on these pages compared with the beginning of the book?

  Being at his grandmother's house was important to the author, so he wrote more details in this part of the story. What kinds of details did he write?

- Record students' responses on chart paper, generalizing them as necessary.

Have a Try

Invite students to talk to a partner about their ideas for writing.

> Think about the most important moment in the memory story you're going to write. What details or other important information could you write to help readers understand that moment? Turn and talk to your partner about your ideas.

Summarize and Apply

Summarize the learning and remind students to write details about the most important moments in their stories.

> How can you help your readers understand an important moment in a memory story?

▸ Write the principle at the top of the chart.

> Today during writing time, start writing a memory story. Remember to write details about the most important moments in your story. Look at the chart for types of details you might include and in your writer's notebook for ideas to write about.

Write details about the most important moments in the story.

Details—
- show what the setting is like
- describe what things look, smell, sound, taste, or feel like
- tell what the characters say and do
- are specific

Confer

▸ During independent writing, move around the room to confer briefly with students about their memory stories. Use prompts such as the following as needed.
- *What is this part of your story about?*
- *Is this part very important? Why or why not?*
- *What details could you include to help readers better understand this part of the story?*
- *What did the _____ look (sound, taste, smell, feel) like? How could you write that?*

Share

Following independent writing, gather students in the meeting area to share their writing.

> Who would like to read aloud an important moment in your story?

> What kinds of details did _____ write in the story?

WML 4
GEN.U4.WML4

Writing Minilesson Principle
Share your thoughts and feelings about the memory or experience.

Writing Memory Stories

You Will Need

- a familiar memory story, such as *Saturdays and Teacakes* by Lester L. Laminack, from Text Set: Exploring Memory Stories
- chart paper prepared with a short memory story you have written, showing thoughts and feelings
- markers
- writing folders
- To download the following online resource for this lesson, visit **fp.pub/resources**:
  - chart art (optional)

Academic Language / Important Vocabulary

- memory story
- thoughts
- feelings
- experience

Continuum Connection

- Select "small moments" or experiences and share thinking and feelings about them
- Understand that a writer can look back or think about the memory or experience and share thoughts and feelings about it

GOAL

Understand that authors share their thoughts and feelings about their memories.

RATIONALE

Authors share their thoughts and feelings, both explicitly and implicitly, in their memory stories to engage their readers, who sometimes can relate to how the authors felt. When you help students notice this, they understand that they too can share their thoughts and feelings about a memory. They begin to write with greater depth and meaning.

WRITER'S NOTEBOOK/WRITING FOLDER

Students will continue to work on the memory stories in their writing folders.

ASSESS LEARNING

- Notice whether students share their thoughts and feelings about the memory or experience.
- Look for evidence that they can use vocabulary such as *memory story*, *thoughts*, *feelings*, and *experience*.

MINILESSON

To help students think about the minilesson principle, use a familiar memory story to help them notice how authors reveal their thoughts and feelings about an experience. Here is an example.

- Read page 1 and show the illustration of *Saturday and Teacakes*.

  How did the author feel about Saturdays? How do you know?

  In the illustration, the author has a big grin on his face, and he says, "I couldn't wait for Saturdays."

- Read the second-to-last page of the story.

  How do you think the author felt when he saw Mammaw waving at him?

  What makes you think that?

  He wrote, "She was waving to me. No one else. Just me." That grabs my interest because I would like to feel special just like the author did.

- Read the last page of the book.

  What are the author's feelings about his memories of Saturdays with his grandmother?

  How do you know?

  He says, "Don't worry, Mammaw. I won't ever forget." The time he spent with Mammaw is something that he will always remember.

Have a Try

Invite students to talk to a partner about how you showed emotion in the writing on the prepared chart paper.

> I am working on a memory story about the time my cat got lost. How do you think I felt during this part of the story? How can you tell? Turn and talk to your partner about that.

▸ After students turn and talk, invite a few pairs to share their thinking. Help them identify specific words and phrases that show what you were feeling or thinking and underline them.

Summarize and Apply

Summarize the learning and remind students to share their thoughts and feelings in their memory stories.

> Authors can get you interested in their memory stories by describing their thoughts and feelings because you might have experienced the same feelings.

▸ Write the principle at the top of the chart.

> During writing time, continue writing your memory story. Remember to share your thoughts and feelings. Bring your writing to share when we meet later.

Share your thoughts and feelings about the memory or experience.

We looked everywhere. Fluffy was nowhere to be found. I called out his name at the top of my lungs. My <u>heart was racing</u>. I could <u>feel the tears starting to run down my cheeks</u>. <u>Where could he be? Would I ever see my beloved little fluff ball again?</u>

Confer

▸ During independent writing, move around the room to confer briefly with students about their memory stories. Use prompts such as the following as needed.

- What is this part of your story about?
- How did you feel when that happened?
- What were you thinking about in this part of your story?
- What words can you use to show that?

Share

Following independent writing, gather students in the meeting area to share their writing.

> Who would like to share your writing?
>
> How do you think _____ was feeling in this part of the story? How can you tell?

Umbrella 4: Writing Memory Stories

WML 5
GEN.U4.WML5

Writing Minilesson Principle
Tell why the story is important.

Writing Memory Stories

You Will Need

- a few familiar memory stories that clearly show why the story is important, such as the following from Text Set: Exploring Memory Stories:
  - *Grandma's Records* by Eric Velasquez
  - *My Rotten Redheaded Older Brother* by Patricia Polacco
  - *Saturdays and Teacakes* by Lester L. Laminack
- chart paper and markers
- writing folders

Academic Language / Important Vocabulary

- memory story
- important

Continuum Connection

- Reveal something important about self or about life
- Write in way that shows the significance of the story

GOAL

Write in a way that shows the importance of the story.

RATIONALE

When students notice how authors of memory stories reveal the importance of the story, they learn how to reveal the importance of the memories that they themselves write about. They begin to write richer and more insightful memory stories.

WRITER'S NOTEBOOK/WRITING FOLDER

Students will continue to work on the memory stories in their writing folders.

ASSESS LEARNING

- Notice whether students write in a way that reveals the importance of the story.
- Look for evidence that they can understand and use vocabulary such as *memory story* and *important*.

MINILESSON

To help students think about the minilesson principle, use familiar memory stories to help them notice how authors reveal the importance of the story. Here is an example.

- Show the cover of *Grandma's Records* and read the title. Read pages 6 and 23–24.

  Why do you think the author decided to write about listening to music with his grandma? What did he learn from those experiences?

- Record responses on chart paper.
- Show the cover of *My Rotten Redheaded Older Brother* and read the title. Read page 25.

  What is important about this part of the story?

  The author learned that her brother really cared for her.

- Record responses on the chart.
- Show the cover of *Saturdays and Teacakes* and read the title.

  What made this story important for Lester Laminack to write?

- Record responses on the chart.

  These authors all shared why their memory stories are important to them.

Have a Try

Invite students to talk to a partner about the importance of their own memory stories.

> Think about the memory story you're working on. Turn and talk to your partner about why your story is important to you.

▶ After students turn and talk, invite several students to share their responses.

Summarize and Apply

Write the principle at the top of the chart. Summarize the learning and remind students to tell why their memory stories are important.

> During writing time today, continue working on your memory story. Remember to write in a way that shows why your story is important to you. Bring your writing to share when we meet later.

Tell why the story is important.	
Memory Story	Why the Story Is Important
	The author learned the importance of music. Music can connect you with your past and help you remember special memories.
	The author learned that her annoying big brother actually loved her and cared for her.
	The author loved Mammaw and wanted to remember their time together.

Confer

▶ During independent writing, move around the room to confer briefly with students about their memory stories. Use prompts such as the following as needed.

- What memory are you writing about?
- Why is that memory important to you?
- What did you learn from that experience?
- How can you show your readers why the story is important?

Share

Following independent writing, gather students in the meeting area to share their memory stories.

> Who would like to read your memory story aloud?
>
> Why is _____'s story important? How do you know?

Umbrella 4: Writing Memory Stories

Assessment

After you have taught the minilessons in this umbrella, observe students as they write and talk about writing memory stories. Use *The Fountas & Pinnell Literacy Continuum* to notice, teach for, and support students' learning as you observe their attempts at writing memory stories.

- What evidence do you have of students' new understandings related to writing memory stories?
  - Can students identify the characteristics of good memory stories?
  - Are their stories about an important small moment or memory?
  - Are the most important moments highlighted by more details?
  - Do they share their thoughts and feelings about the memory and reveal why it is important?
  - Do students understand and use vocabulary such as *memory story*, *moment*, *detail*, and *experience*?
- In what other ways, beyond the scope of this umbrella, are students ready to explore genres and forms?
  - Are they showing an interest in writing realistic fiction stories?
  - Are they ready to begin writing poetry?

Use your observations to determine the next umbrella you will teach. You may also consult Suggested Sequence of Lessons (pp. 605–622) for guidance.

EXTENSIONS FOR WRITING MEMORY STORIES

- As you read stories that authors have written about their own lives, engage students in conversations about how the authors told the stories, showed emotion, and revealed important information about themselves.

- Use the rubric available in the online resources to evaluate students' memory stories or to guide them to evaluate their own stories. You might also consider having students co-create a rubric with you.

- Show students how to "skip time" to focus their memory stories on the most important events (see WPS.U8: Revising to Focus and Organize Writing).

- When they start writing memory stories, some students might find that the memory is too big. Pull together a few students in a guided writing group to help them narrow a too-large memory down to a smaller moment so they can write about it in detail.

Writing Realistic Fiction Stories

Umbrella 5

Minilessons in This Umbrella

WML1	Notice the qualities of good realistic fiction stories.
WML2	Think about your own experiences for ideas.
WML3	Use a storyboard to make a plan.
WML4	Make your characters believable.
WML5	Think about what the main character learns.

Before Teaching Umbrella 5 Minilessons

Students stretch their imaginations when they have opportunities to experiment with writing both realistic fiction and fantasy stories. Students love to write fantasy stories, and we should make time and space to listen to and honor those stories to build children's engagement, writing identity, and stamina for writing. However, we recommend spending instructional time in minilessons on teaching realistic fiction because the students will be able to build on their experience of writing other narrative texts, such as memory stories. You can modify some of the lessons from this umbrella to support them in writing fantasy as well as realistic fiction.

We want the process of writing realistic fiction stories to be authentic and individual for each writer, but it is helpful to offer students planning tools for their writing. Some students may find a storyboard helpful in planning their stories (WML3). Any idea on a list or web in students' writer's notebooks can serve as a spark for a story idea. Students should be encouraged to try out elements of their stories in their writer's notebooks.

With students, read and discuss a variety of realistic fiction stories. Use the following texts from *Fountas & Pinnell Classroom™ Interactive Read-Aloud Collection* or any other realistic fiction stories.

Interactive Read-Aloud Collection
Genre Study: Realistic Fiction

Owl Moon by Jane Yolen

SkySisters by Jan Bourdeau Waboose

Tomás and the Library Lady by Pat Mora

Dancing in the Wings by Debbie Allen

Dumpling Soup by Jama Kim Rattigan

As you read and enjoy these texts together, help students
- notice the characteristics of realistic fiction,
- discuss how the author describes the characters, and
- explain what the main character learns.

Interactive Read-Aloud
Realistic Fiction

Writer's Notebook

WML1
GEN.U5.WML1

Writing Minilesson Principle
Notice the qualities of good realistic fiction stories.

Writing Realistic Fiction Stories

You Will Need

- several familiar realistic fiction books, such as those in Text Set: Genre Study: Realistic Fiction
- chart paper and markers
- writer's notebooks

Academic Language / Important Vocabulary

- realistic fiction
- quality
- character
- setting
- problem

Continuum Connection

- Understand that an additional purpose of a fiction text is to explore a theme or teach a lesson
- Understand that a fiction text may involve one or more events in the life of a main character
- Understand that a writer uses various elements of fiction (e.g., setting, plot with problem and solution, characters) in a fiction text
- Understand that writers can learn to craft fiction by using mentor texts as models

GOAL

Study mentor texts to notice the qualities of good realistic fiction stories.

RATIONALE

Writers learn from other writers. By studying realistic fiction, students will be better prepared and equipped to begin writing their own realistic fiction stories. They will model their own stories on those they have read.

WRITER'S NOTEBOOK/WRITING FOLDER

Have students make notes in their writer's notebooks about the qualities of good realistic fiction.

ASSESS LEARNING

- Notice whether students can identify the qualities of good realistic fiction.
- Look for evidence that they can use vocabulary such as *realistic fiction*, *quality*, *character*, *setting*, and *problem*.

MINILESSON

To help students think about the principle, engage them in talking about the qualities of realistic fiction. Here is an example.

- Show the covers of several familiar realistic fiction books, such as *Owl Moon*, *SkySisters*, *Tomás and the Library Lady*, *Dancing in the Wings*, and *Dumpling Soup*.

    > We have read and discussed all these realistic fiction books together. Why do you think they're called realistic fiction?

    > What have you noticed about realistic fiction stories?

- Record students' responses on chart paper, generalizing them as necessary.
- As needed, prompt students' thinking about realistic fiction with questions such as the following.
    - *What have you noticed about the characters?*
    - *What have you noticed about the settings, where the stories take place?*
    - *What kinds of problems do the characters face?*
    - *What have you noticed about how the authors make their stories seem real?*
    - *How do realistic fiction stories often end? Do the characters learn anything?*

The Writing Minilessons Book, Grade 3

Have a Try

Invite students to talk to a partner about the qualities of realistic fiction.

> Is there anything else you have noticed about realistic fiction stories that you think we should add to our chart? Turn and talk to your partner about this.

▸ After time for discussion, invite a few pairs to share their thinking. Add any new ideas to the chart, as appropriate.

Summarize and Apply

Write the principle at the top of the chart. Summarize the learning and invite students to further discuss the qualities of realistic fiction in pairs or small groups.

▸ Have pairs or small groups each study at least one familiar realistic fiction book to notice its qualities.

> During writing time today, meet with your partner (group) to study the realistic fiction book I gave you. Discuss what you notice about the story, and write about your noticings in your writer's notebook. Bring your notes when we meet later.

Confer

▸ During independent writing, move around the room to confer briefly with students about what they notice. Use prompts such as the following as needed.
- *What happens in this realistic fiction story? Could that happen in real life?*
- *How did the author make the main character seem real?*
- *What do you notice about how the author described the setting?*
- *What does the main character learn?*

Share

Following independent writing, gather students in the meeting area. Invite each group to share what they noticed.

> What qualities did you notice about the realistic fiction book you studied?

Notice the qualities of good realistic fiction stories.

- The author imagines the characters and settings, but they seem real.
- The main character usually faces a problem that is like the problems people have in real life.
- The author uses descriptive words and details to help you picture the characters, settings, and events.
- The problem is usually solved by the end of the story.
- The main character often learns an important lesson by the end of the story.

WML 2
GEN.U5.WML2

Writing Minilesson Principle
Think about your own experiences for ideas.

Writing Realistic Fiction Stories

You Will Need

- a familiar realistic fiction book that was inspired by the author's own experiences, such as *Dancing in the Wings* by Debbie Allen, from Text Set: Genre Study: Realistic Fiction
- your writer's notebook with ideas for realistic fiction stories
- chart paper and markers
- writer's notebooks

Academic Language / Important Vocabulary

- realistic fiction
- experience
- problem
- event
- solution

Continuum Connection

- Develop an interesting story with believable characters and a realistic plot
- Write a simple fiction story, either realistic or fantasy

GOAL

Understand that writers use their own experiences as inspiration for fiction writing.

RATIONALE

Students often wonder what to write. Once they become aware that authors of realistic fiction stories often draw from their own experiences, they will have a source of ideas for their own stories. They will write what they know, creating characters, settings, and plots that are more realistic and believable.

WRITER'S NOTEBOOK/WRITING FOLDER

Have students reread their writer's notebooks for ideas.

ASSESS LEARNING

- Notice whether students get ideas for writing from their own experiences.
- Look for evidence that they can use vocabulary such as *realistic fiction*, *experience*, *problem*, *event*, and *solution*.

MINILESSON

Before teaching this minilesson, make sure students have sketched or written some ideas for realistic fiction stories in a writer's notebook. To help students think about the principle, use a familiar realistic fiction book to help them notice that authors of realistic fiction get ideas from their lives. Model coming up with an idea for a realistic fiction story from your writer's notebooks. Here is an example.

- Show the cover of *Dancing in the Wings* and read the title. Read the information about the author on the inside back cover.

    Where did Debbie Allen get the idea to write this book?

    It says that this book is "based on her own experiences as a dancer." This is a fiction book, so what happens in the book is not exactly what happened to the author, but she used her own experiences to get ideas.

- Model how to turn an idea from your writer's notebook into a realistic fiction story.

    One of the childhood memories I wrote about is when I helped a new classmate who spoke only Spanish. Maybe I could write a story about a character that moves from Mexico to the United States and doesn't understand anything her teacher and classmates say at first. She feels sad and lonely, and she misses home. Her problem could be solved when she makes friends with another Spanish speaker.

    What do you notice about how I got my idea for writing realistic fiction story?

Have a Try

Invite students to talk to a partner about their own ideas for realistic fiction writing.

> Reread your writer's notebook to find an experience that you could turn into a story. Then turn and talk to your partner about your idea.

▸ After time for reflection and discussion, invite several students to share their ideas. Record them on chart paper.

Summarize and Apply

Help students summarize the learning and invite them to think further about their own experiences for ideas.

> What can you do to get an idea for a realistic fiction story?

▸ Write the principle at the top of the chart.

> If the idea you talked about with your partner will make a good story, make some notes about the characters and events in your writer's notebook. If not, reread your writer's notebook for more ideas. Bring your ideas to share when we meet later.

Think about your own experiences for ideas.

I could write a realistic fiction story about . . .

- a character who wants to get a dog, but his parents won't allow it because their apartment is too small. (Jace)
- a character whose pet gets lost in the woods. (Lincoln)
- a character who misses her mom when she works late at night. (Mila)
- a character who wants to go on vacation like his friends do, but his family cannot afford to. (Kayden)
- a character who is afraid to try out for the school play. (Clara)

Confer

▸ During independent writing, move around the room to confer briefly with students about their ideas for realistic fiction. Use prompts such as the following as needed.

- *What could you write a realistic fiction story about?*
- *Could you turn one of your own experiences into a story? Which one?*
- *Who will be the main character in your story?*
- *What problem will the main character face? What is the solution to the problem?*

Share

Following independent writing, gather students in the meeting area to share their ideas for realistic fiction stories.

> Who got an idea for a realistic fiction story from one of your own experiences?

> What was the experience? How will you turn it into a realistic fiction story?

WML 3
GEN.U5.WML3

Writing Minilesson Principle
Use a storyboard to make a plan.

Writing Realistic Fiction Stories

You Will Need

- blank storyboard prepared on chart paper
- markers
- writer's notebooks and writing folders

Academic Language / Important Vocabulary

- significant events
- storyboard

Continuum Connection

- Develop a logical plot by creating a story problem and addressing it over multiple events until it is resolved
- Write fiction and nonfiction narratives that are ordered chronologically
- Use sketching to support memory and help in planning
- Understand the difference between drawing and sketching and use them to support planning, revising, and publishing the writing process

GOAL

Use a storyboard to plan a realistic fiction story.

RATIONALE

Using a storyboard to plan a realistic fiction story can help students identify which events are significant and in what order they should be presented before they start writing. When students learn that some writers use tools, such as a storyboard, to help with planning, they begin to try out different tools and learn about which work best for them.

WRITER'S NOTEBOOK/WRITING FOLDER

Students can do their planning in their writer's notebooks before writing a draft on draft paper, which will be kept in their writing folders.

ASSESS LEARNING

- Observe whether students try out using a storyboard to plan their narrative writing.
- Look for evidence that students can use vocabulary such as *significant events* and *storyboard*.

MINILESSON

Before teaching this lesson, be sure that students know what they will write about. To help students think about the minilesson principle, model how to use a storyboard to plan a realistic fiction story. Here is an example.

- Model the process of using a storyboard to plan a realistic fiction story.

    I am thinking about writing a realistic fiction story about a boy who helps at his family's restaurant in the evenings and the interesting thing that happened one time. To help me plan what to write, I am going to use a storyboard.

- Show the prepared blank storyboard.

    A storyboard shows the significant, or main, events in a story and the order in which they happen. Watch how I make my plan. Then we will talk about it.

- Make quick sketches without several events in the storyboard boxes as you think aloud. Add short notes that state what is going to happen in those parts of the story. Support students' understanding of the elements of a story by including the characters, setting, problem, and solution on the storyboard.

    What do you notice?

- Emphasize that these should be quick sketches with just short notes below and that the boxes are in chronological order. Point out that the problem and solution are included on the storyboard because it helps with planning to think about them ahead of time.

Have a Try

Invite students to turn and talk about using a storyboard to plan a realistic fiction story.

> Think about the story you plan to write. Turn and talk about what you might place in the boxes of a storyboard. Remember to include only the significant events.

▸ After time for a brief discussion, ask a few students to share their ideas.

Summarize and Apply

Summarize the learning. Remind students to try using a storyboard for narrative writing. Students can make the storyboard in their writer's notebooks or on plain paper.

> During writing time, try using a storyboard to plan your story. You can make as many boxes as you need to show the important events. Check your writer's notebook for notes that you made about what to write. Use those notes in your storyboard. If you finish the storyboard, you can begin writing. Bring your storyboard when we meet later.

Storyboard

Characters: Enzo (boy), Mateo (young adult cousin), grandma, Enzo's parents

Setting: Mexican tamale restaurant

Problem: Grandma is sick today. Parents must care for her. Who will make the tamales for dinner customers?

Event: Mateo remembers he took a video of Grandma making tamales.

Event: Enzo and Mateo make tamales together. Customers are happy

Confer

▸ During independent writing, move around the room to confer briefly with students about their realistic fiction stories. Use the following prompts as needed.

- *What will you be writing about today?*
- *Let's talk about what significant events will happen in your story.*
- *Tell what will go in each box of your storyboard.*
- *What notes could you write to tell what will happen in this part of the story?*

Share

Following independent writing, gather students in pairs in the meeting area.

> Share your storyboard with your partner.

▸ After partners share, select several students to share their storyboard with the class.

WML 4
GEN.U5.WML4

Writing Minilesson Principle
Make your characters believable.

Writing Realistic Fiction Stories

You Will Need

- a few familiar realistic fiction books, such as the following from Text Set: Genre Study: Realistic Fiction:
    - *Tomás and the Library Lady* by Pat Mora
    - *SkySisters* by Jan Bourdeau Waboose
    - *Dancing in the Wings* by Debbie Allen
- chart paper and markers
- writer's notebooks and writing folders
- To download the following online resource for this lesson, visit **fp.pub/resources**:
    - chart art (optional)

Academic Language / Important Vocabulary

- realistic fiction
- character
- believable

Continuum Connection

- Develop an interesting story with believable characters and a realistic plot
- Show the problem of the story and how one or more characters respond to it
- Describe characters by how they look and what they do
- Show rather than tell how characters feel

GOAL

Describe characters in a way that makes them seem real.

RATIONALE

When students notice how authors of realistic fiction develop and describe characters, they begin to understand how they can create believable characters in their own stories, and they are more likely to write stories with consistent, well-developed characters.

WRITER'S NOTEBOOK/WRITING FOLDERS

Students will work on their drafts from their writing folders. They may find it helpful to sketch their characters in their writer's notebooks before writing about them.

ASSESS LEARNING

- Look at students' writing to see how they are creating believable characters.
- Look for evidence that they can use vocabulary such as *realistic fiction*, *character*, and *believable*.

MINILESSON

To help students think about the principle, use mentor texts to engage them in noticing and talking about how authors make characters seem believable. Here is an example.

- Show the cover of *Tomás and the Library Lady* and read the title.

    Who is the main character in this book?

    Does Tomás seem like a real person? Why or why not?

- Read the first page of the story.

    How does the author make Tomás seem believable, or real?

- Record responses on chart paper, generalizing them as necessary.
- Show the cover of *SkySisters* and read the title. Read the first two pages of the story.

    Do Alex and Allie seem like real people? Why or why not?

    How does the author make them believable?

- Add responses to the chart.
- Show the cover of *Dancing in the Wings* and read the title. Read pages 2–6.

    How does the author make Sassy seem like a real girl?

- Add responses to the chart.

Have a Try

Invite students to talk to a partner about their own main characters.

> Think about the main character in the realistic fiction story you're going to write. What is the character like? How will you make the character seem like a real person? Turn and talk to your partner about your ideas.

Summarize and Apply

Write the principle at the top of the chart. Help students summarize the learning and remind them to make their characters believable.

> How can you make your characters believable?

> During writing time today, start or continue to work on your realistic fiction story. Remember to use what you learned today about making your characters believable. You may find it helpful to sketch your main character in your writer's notebook before writing about the character.

Confer

- During independent writing, move around the room to confer briefly with students about writing realistic fiction stories. Use prompts such as the following as needed.
  - Who is the main character in your story?
  - What is the character like?
  - How can you make the character seem like a real person?
  - Would a real person do that? What would a real person do in that situation?

Share

Following independent writing, gather students in the meeting area to talk about their main character. Give each student a chance to share briefly.

> Tell the name of the main character in your story and a little bit about what the character is like.

WML 5
GEN.U5.WML5

Writing Minilesson Principle
Think about what the main character learns.

Writing Realistic Fiction Stories

You Will Need

- a couple of familiar realistic fiction books in which the main character learns something, such as the following from Text Set: Genre Study: Realistic Fiction:
  - *Dancing in the Wings* by Debbie Allen
  - *Dumpling Soup* by Jama Kim Rattigan
- chart paper and markers
- writing folders

Academic Language / Important Vocabulary

- realistic fiction
- main character

Continuum Connection

- Understand that an additional purpose of a fiction text is to explore a theme or teach a lesson
- Describe characters by how they look and what they do
- Show rather than tell how characters feel

GOAL

Notice how writers often show that a character learns a lesson in a realistic fiction story.

RATIONALE

When you help students notice that main characters in realistic fiction often learn a lesson and understand how authors show that through thoughts, dialogue, or action, they will begin to show personal growth in the characters they create in their own realistic fiction stories. As a result, their characters will be richer and more believable.

WRITER'S NOTEBOOK/WRITING FOLDER

Students will work on their drafts of their realistic fiction stories from their writing folders.

ASSESS LEARNING

- Notice whether students create characters that learn a lesson and convey that change clearly.
- Look for evidence that they can use vocabulary such as *realistic fiction* and *main character*.

MINILESSON

To help students think about the principle, use mentor texts to engage them in noticing and talking about how authors of realistic fiction show that a character learns something. Here is an example.

- Show the cover of *Dancing in the Wings* and read the title.

  In this story, why is the main character, Sassy, afraid to go to a dance audition?

- Read the last two pages of the story.

  What does Sassy learn at the end of the story?

  Sassy learns that being tall and having big feet can't keep her from her dream of being a dancer. How does the author show that she learns this?

- Record responses on chart paper, generalizing as necessary.

- Show the cover of *Dumpling Soup* and read the title.

  How does Marisa feel about the dumplings she made?

- Read the last two pages of the story.

  What does Marisa learn when she and her family eat the dumplings she made?

  How do you know that she learns this?

- Record responses on the chart.

Have a Try

Invite students to talk to a partner about their own characters.

> Think about the main character in the story you're working on. Does your character learn something? If so, what? How will you show this in your writing? Turn and talk to your partner about your ideas.

Summarize and Apply

Write the principle at the top of the chart. Summarize the learning and remind students to think about whether their main character learns something.

> When you write today, continue to work on the draft of your realistic fiction story from your writing folder. Remember to think about whether your main character learns something and, if so, how you can show that. Bring your writing to share when we come back together.

	Think about what the main character learns.	
Book	What the Main Character Learns	How the Author Shows This
Dancing in the Wings	Challenges can't keep her from reaching a goal.	• Through the main character's thoughts
Dumpling Soup	Don't judge a book by its cover.	• Through the main character's thoughts
	Being together with family is the most important thing.	• Through what the other characters say

Confer

▸ During independent writing, move around the room to confer briefly with students about their main characters. Use prompts such as the following as needed.

- *Does your main character learn something?*
- *What does the character learn?*
- *How can you show that the character learns _____?*

Share

Following independent writing, gather students in the meeting area to talk about their writing.

> Who would like to share what the main character learns in your story?
>
> How did you show that the character learns that?

WML 5
GEN.U5.WML5

Section 2: Genres and Forms

Umbrella 5: Writing Realistic Fiction Stories

Umbrella 5: Writing Realistic Fiction Stories

Assessment

After you have taught the minilessons in this umbrella, observe students as they explore writing realistic fiction stories. Use *The Fountas & Pinnell Literacy Continuum* to notice, teach for, and support students' learning as you observe their writing development.

- What evidence do you have of students' new understandings related to writing realistic fiction stories?
  - Can students identify the characteristics of good realistic fiction stories?
  - Are students able to turn a personal experience into a story?
  - Are their characters believable?
  - Do their main characters show evidence of personal growth?
  - Do they understand and use vocabulary such as *realistic fiction*, *quality*, *character*, and *believable*?
- In what other ways, beyond the scope of this umbrella, are students exploring writing fiction?
  - Would they benefit from learning more about describing characters or settings?
  - Are they experimenting with interesting word choices?

Use your observations to determine the next umbrella you will teach. You may also consult Suggested Sequence of Lessons (pp. 605–622) for guidance.

EXTENSIONS FOR WRITING REALISTIC FICTION STORIES

- Pull together a small, temporary guided writing group of students who need support in a similar area of their writing, such as planning and writing a realistic fiction story.

- Use umbrellas in the Craft section, such as CFT.U2: Describing Characters and CFT.U3: Crafting a Setting, to help students explore different aspects of writing fiction in greater depth.

- Use shared writing to help students explore various aspects of writing fiction collaboratively before doing so independently.

- Suggest that students write alternative versions of their favorite stories (for example, by changing the ending, writing a sequel, or placing the main character in a different situation).

- Use the teacher and student rubrics available in online resources to evaluate students' realistic fiction stories or to guide them to evaluate their own texts. You might also consider having students co-create rubrics with you.

Making Informational Books

Umbrella 6

Minilessons in This Umbrella

- **WML1** Notice the qualities of good informational books.
- **WML2** Decide how to organize your book.
- **WML3** Write a strong introduction.
- **WML4** Support your ideas with examples.
- **WML5** Make your nonfiction writing interesting and informative.
- **WML6** Write a strong conclusion.

Before Teaching Umbrella 6 Minilessons

Before you teach this umbrella, students should have already chosen and researched a topic for an informational book. Therefore, we strongly recommend teaching WPS. U4: Writer's Notebook: Becoming an Expert, which takes students through how to choose a topic and find information about it, immediately before this umbrella. Students will use a writer's notebook—*Writer's Notebook, Intermediate* (Fountas and Pinnell 2023) or a plain notebook—to take notes and try out aspects of their writing before working on a final copy, which they will keep in their writing folders. Provide a choice of paper, including appropriate paper templates from the online resources, for students to use to make their books.

Read aloud a variety of engaging informational books. You may use the following books from *Fountas & Pinnell Classroom™ Interactive Read-Aloud Collection* or informational books from your classroom library.

Interactive Read-Aloud Collection
Genre Study: Expository Nonfiction

Hottest, Coldest, Highest, Deepest by Steve Jenkins

Tornadoes! by Gail Gibbons

Knights in Shining Armor by Gail Gibbons

A Day and Night in the Desert by Caroline Arnold

Bats! Strange and Wonderful by Laurence Pringle

Shell, Beak, Tusk: Shared Traits and the Wonders of Adaptation by Bridget Heos

As you read and enjoy these texts together, help students

- identify the qualities of informational books,
- notice how the authors organize information, and
- think about how the authors engage and interest their readers.

Interactive Read-Aloud
Expository Nonfiction

Writer's Notebook

WML1
GEN.U6.WML1

Writing Minilesson Principle
Notice the qualities of good informational books.

Making Informational Books

You Will Need

- several familiar informational books, such as those from Text Set: Genre Study: Expository Nonfiction
- chart paper and markers
- an informational book (or more) for each pair of students
- writer's notebooks

Academic Language / Important Vocabulary

- informational
- quality
- topic

Continuum Connection

- Understand that a writer creates an expository text for readers to learn about a topic
- Understand that the writer may work to get readers interested in a topic
- Understand that a factual text may use literary techniques (interesting language, description, comparison, photos, graphics, drawings with labels) to engage and entertain readers as it gives them factual information
- Understand that a writer can learn how to write an expository text from mentor texts

GOAL

Understand the characteristics and craft of informational texts.

RATIONALE

As students study informational books and name key qualities, they learn what a writer has to do to write a good informational book, and they will be better prepared and equipped to begin writing their own. Students will model their informational books on those they have read.

WRITER'S NOTEBOOK/WRITING FOLDER

Have students take notes about the qualities of informational books in their writer's notebooks.

ASSESS LEARNING

- Observe for evidence of what students know about informational books.
- Look for evidence that they can use vocabulary such as *informational*, *quality*, and *topic*.

MINILESSON

To help students think about the minilesson principle, engage them in an inquiry-based lesson on the qualities of good informational books. Here is an example.

- Show the covers of several familiar informational books. Ask students to identify the topic of each book.

    All of these books are informational books. Why do you think they're called that?

    Informational books give accurate information about a topic. What else have you noticed about informational books? What makes informational books interesting and fun to read?

- Show selected pages to remind students of the features and qualities of informational books. As needed, prompt students' thinking with questions such as the following:
  - *What have you noticed about how nonfiction authors teach you about a topic?*
  - *How do they organize information?*
  - *Besides the words, how else do you get information from an informational book?*
  - *How do the authors help you understand complicated information?*
  - *What features help you find specific information?*
  - *How do you think authors decide what topic to write about?*
- Record students' responses on chart paper, generalizing them as necessary.

The Writing Minilessons Book, Grade 3

Have a Try

Invite students to talk to a partner about the qualities of informational books.

> Turn and talk to your partner about anything else you have noticed about informational books that you think we should add to our chart.

▶ After students turn and talk, invite a few pairs to share their thinking. Add any new ideas to the chart, as appropriate.

Summarize and Apply

Write the principle at the top of the chart. Summarize the learning and invite students to further discuss the qualities of informational books with a partner.

▶ Give each pair of students at least one familiar informational book to examine. Students can exchange books when they finish with them.

> During writing time today, meet with your partner to study an informational book. Write the title *Good Informational Books* at the top of the next empty page in Section 4 of your writer's notebook. Then look at an informational book with your partner. Discuss what you notice. Make a list of what you notice in your writer's notebook. Bring your notes to share when we meet later.

Notice the qualities of good informational books.

- The author gives accurate information about a topic.
- The author organizes information in various ways (categories, sequence, question-and-answer, etc.) to show it clearly.
- The author explains complicated information in a simple way using words the reader can understand.
- Sometimes the author uses pictures, such as photographs, illustrations, diagrams, and maps to give information.
- The author creates tools the reader can use to find information, such as a table of contents, an index, or a glossary.
- The author cares about the topic and shows why the topic is important and interesting.

Confer

▶ During independent writing, move around the room to confer briefly with students about informational books. Use prompts such as the following as needed.

- What is this informational book about?
- How does the author make _____ seem interesting and exciting?
- How does the author organize information about _____?
- What kinds of pictures are in the book? How do the pictures help you better understand the topic?

Share

Following independent writing, gather students in pairs to share what they noticed.

> Turn to a partner different from the one you shared with earlier today. Share the notes that you took about informational books.

WML 2
GEN.U6.WML2

Writing Minilesson Principle
Decide how to organize your book.

Making Informational Books

You Will Need

- a familiar informational book that is organized by category, such as *Shell, Beak, Tusk* by Bridget Heos, from Text Set: Genre Study: Expository Nonfiction
- sample notes about a topic for an informational book (e.g., notes from WPS.U4.WML4)
- chart paper and markers
- writer's notebooks

Academic Language / Important Vocabulary

- informational book
- organize
- topic
- category
- note

Continuum Connection

- Understand that a writer can learn how to write an expository text from mentor texts
- Introduce information in categories and provide interesting supporting details in each category that develops a topic
- Use sketching, webs, lists, and freewriting to think about, plan for, and try out writing

---

GOAL

Organize notes about a topic into categories.

RATIONALE

When you teach students how to organize their notes on a topic into categories, they will produce nonfiction texts that are organized in a logical and cohesive manner.

WRITER'S NOTEBOOK/WRITING FOLDER

Have students reread and reorganize their notes about a topic in their writer's notebooks.

ASSESS LEARNING

- Observe for evidence that students reread their notes and organize them into categories.
- Look for evidence that they can use vocabulary such as *informational book*, *organize*, *topic*, *category*, and *note*.

MINILESSON

Before this minilesson, students should have already chosen and taken notes about a topic for an informational book (see WPS.U4.WML4). To help students think about the principle, use a familiar nonfiction book to engage them in an inquiry-based lesson on organizing information. Then model how to organize information into categories. Here is an example.

- Show the cover of *Shell, Beak, Tusk*. Read the heading for pages 6–7.

  What are these pages about?

- Continue in a similar manner with pages 8–9.

  What do you notice about how the author, Bridget Heos, organized information in this book?

  The author organized information about the topic into groups, or categories. Each part of the book is about a different animal trait, such as spines, or wings. In each part, she grouped facts about that category.

- Show your sample notes (such as the notes from WPS.U4.WML4). Think aloud as you organize your notes into categories.

  First, I'm going to reread my notes. I can see that "Let the cat come to you" and "Say hi to a cat" are both about introducing yourself to a cat. These notes can go in the same category. "Cats 'talk' with their body language" and "Cats purr both when they are happy and scared" are both about how cats communicate. This can also be a category.

  What did you notice about how I organized the information for my book?

- Record students' responses on chart paper.

The Writing Minilessons Book, Grade 3

Have a Try

Invite students to talk to a partner about organizing their books.

- Have students turn to the notes they have written in their writer's notebooks.

    As you look at your notes, think about a way to organize them into categories. What categories could you have in your book? Turn and talk to your partner about your ideas.

Summarize and Apply

Write the principle at the top of the chart. Read it to students. Summarize the learning and invite students to plan the organization of their books (see p. 70 in *Writer's Notebook, Intermediate*).

    What did you learn today about how to organize an informational book?

    During writing time, spend some more time thinking about how to organize the information in your book. Reread your notes in your writer's notebook, put them into categories, and write the name of the category above each group of notes.

Confer

- During independent writing, move around the room to confer briefly with students about organizing their notes. Use prompts such as the following as needed.
    - Let's reread the notes you took about your topic.
    - Are any of your notes about the same idea?
    - Move those two notes so they're together. What could you name this category?
    - What else could go in this category?

Share

Following independent writing, gather students in the meeting area to share how they organized the notes for their informational books. Have students share in triads. Then select several students to share with the class.

    How did you organize the notes about your topic? What categories are you going to have in your book?

Umbrella 6: Making Informational Books

WML3
GEN.U6.WML3

Writing Minilesson Principle
Write a strong introduction.

Making Informational Books

You Will Need

- several familiar nonfiction books with strong introductions that use a variety of techniques, such as the following from Text Set: Genre Study: Expository Nonfiction:
  - *Hottest, Coldest, Highest, Deepest* by Steve Jenkins
  - *Tornadoes!* by Gail Gibbons
  - *Shell, Beak, Tusk* by Bridget Heos
  - *Bats!* by Laurence Pringle
- chart paper and markers
- writer's notebooks and writing folders

Academic Language / Important Vocabulary

- informational book
- introduction

Continuum Connection

- Understand that the writer may work to get readers interested in a topic
- Write a piece that is interesting and enjoyable to read
- Use a variety of beginnings to engage the reader

GOAL

Learn a variety of ways to write an engaging, informative introduction to an informational book.

RATIONALE

When you help students notice how nonfiction authors craft engaging, informative introductions, they will begin to use some of these techniques in their own nonfiction writing. They will write informational books that are interesting and enjoyable to read.

WRITER'S NOTEBOOK/WRITING FOLDER

As students work on nonfiction writing in their writing folders, they may want to try out ideas in their writer's notebooks.

ASSESS LEARNING

- Notice whether students try out a variety of techniques for writing engaging introductions.
- Look for evidence that they can use vocabulary such as *informational book* and *introduction*.

MINILESSON

Use this lesson once students have selected a topic and taken notes. To help students think about the minilesson principle, engage them in an inquiry-based lesson on writing strong introductions. Here is an example.

- Show the cover of *Hottest, Coldest, Highest, Deepest* and read the first page.

  The beginning of an informational book is called the introduction. What do you notice about the introduction to this book? How did the author, Steve Jenkins, get the reader interested in the topic? How did he make the reader want to continue reading his book?

- Begin a list of techniques authors use to write a strong introduction.
- Show the cover of *Tornadoes!* and read the first page.

  What do you notice about the introduction to this book? How did the author, Gail Gibbons, make it interesting?

- Add students' responses to the chart.
- Continue in a similar manner with *Shell, Beak, Tusk* and *Bats!*.

  The authors of these four books used different techniques in their introductions to get readers interested in the topic. Which introduction do you think works best? Why? What did the author do to make you want to keep reading?

- Point out that sometimes writers wait until the main part has been written before they write the introduction and that they may revise it several times before getting it just right.

The Writing Minilessons Book, Grade 3

WML 3
GEN.U6.WML3

Have a Try

Invite students to talk to a partner about their ideas for introductions.

> How might you get readers interested in the topic of your informational book? What techniques might you use in your introduction to grab your reader's attention? Turn and talk to your partner about your ideas.

- After time for discussion, invite a few volunteers to share their ideas.

Summarize and Apply

Help students summarize the learning and invite them to start writing their informational books.

> How do writers make their introductions interesting for their readers?

> During writing time, start writing your informational book. Try a way on the chart to get your readers interested in your topic and make them want to keep reading. You can try out some ideas for an introduction in your writer's notebook and then decide which one will work best.

Ways to Write a Strong Introduction

- Ask questions to make the reader think.
- Tell what the book is about.
- Hint at interesting facts you will write about.
- Use descriptive language to interest readers in the topic.
- Give important information to help readers understand the topic.
- Define important vocabulary.
- Speak directly to the readers (use the word you).
- Use humor.

Confer

- During independent writing, move around the room to confer briefly with students about writing introductions. Use prompts such as the following as needed.
    - *How could you get your readers interested in your topic?*
    - *Do you want to ask your readers a question? What question could you ask to make them think?*
    - *What information do readers need to know before they read the main part of your book?*
    - *Could you use describing words to help readers picture something related to your topic?*

Share

Following independent writing, gather students in the meeting area to share their writing.

> Turn to a partner and read what you have written so far.

WML 4
GEN.U6.WML4

Writing Minilesson Principle
Support your ideas with examples.

Making Informational Books

You Will Need

- a couple of familiar nonfiction books, such as these from Text Set: Genre Study: Expository Nonfiction:
  - *Shell, Beak, Tusk* by Bridget Heos
  - *Bats! Strange and Wonderful* by Laurence Pringle
- chart paper prepared with a vague sentence
- markers
- writer's notebooks and writing folders
- To download the following resource for this lesson, visit **fp.pub/resources**:
  - chart art (optional)

Academic Language / Important Vocabulary

- support
- example
- idea

Continuum Connection

- Introduce ideas followed by supportive details and examples
- Use examples to make meaning clear
- Select information that will support the topic
- Select details that will support a topic or story
- Add words, phrases, or sentences to provide more information to readers

GOAL

Use examples to tell more about a topic.

RATIONALE

Using examples to help explain a topic is a way that a writer can explain a topic more clearly. When you help students notice how nonfiction writers use specific examples in their writing, they learn how to produce nonfiction writing that is detailed and informative.

WRITER'S NOTEBOOK/WRITING FOLDER

As students work on nonfiction writing in their writing folders, they may want to try out ideas in their writer's notebooks.

ASSESS LEARNING

- Notice whether students use specific examples in their own nonfiction texts.
- Look for evidence that students can use vocabulary such as *support*, *example*, and *idea*.

MINILESSON

To help students think about the minilesson principle, engage them in an inquiry-based lesson on how writers support their ideas with examples. Here is an example.

- Show the cover of *Shell, Beak, Tusk* and read the title. Turn to pages 16–17 and read them aloud.

  These pages are about the idea that "a light is for drawing attention." How did the author, Bridget Heos, support, or tell more about, this idea?

  The author gave two examples of animals that use a light to draw attention. What animals did she use as examples?

  She used a firefly and an anglerfish as examples. What did she write about how a firefly uses a light to draw attention?

  What did she write about how an anglerfish uses a light?

- Show the cover of *Bats!* and read the title. Read page 11.

  The author, Laurence Pringle, wrote "All bats in North America are microbats." What example did he give to support this idea? What specific microbat did he write about?

  What details did he give about the little brown bat?

The Writing Minilessons Book, Grade 3

WML 4
GEN.U6.WML4

Have a Try

Invite students to talk to a partner about adding specific examples to a piece of nonfiction writing.

- Display the sample sentence that you prepared on chart paper.

  What examples could I add to my writing to help the reader understand more about this idea? Turn and talk about that.

- After students turn and talk, invite several pairs to share their ideas. Agree on a few sentences and write them on the chart.

Summarize and Apply

Help students summarize the learning. Remind them to think about using examples in their writing.

  What can you do to help your readers understand more about your topic?

- Write the principle at the top of the chart.

  When you write today, work on your informational book. Remember to support your ideas with specific examples and details. You can always use your writer's notebook to try out some ideas before writing them in your draft. Be prepared to share your writing when we meet later.

> **Support your ideas with examples.**
>
> Bats eat many different kinds of food. Many bats eat insects, such as crickets, beetles, and caterpillars. Some bats eat larger animals, such as small birds, mice, frogs, or even other bats. One very unusual bat, the common vampire bat, doesn't catch any prey. Instead, it feasts on the blood of cows and other large mammals!

Confer

- During independent writing, move around the room to confer briefly with students about supporting ideas with examples. Use prompts such as the following if needed.
  - *What examples could you give to support, or tell more about, that idea?*
  - *What might your reader want to know about _____?*
  - *What are some examples of _____?*
  - *What details could you give about _____?*

Share

Following independent writing, have students share their writing with a partner. Listen in to the conversations. Then bring the group together.

  Who would like to share a place in your book where you gave specific examples to support an idea?

Umbrella 6: Making Informational Books

WML 5
GEN.U6.WML5

Writing Minilesson Principle
Make your nonfiction writing interesting and informative.

Making Informational Books

You Will Need

- a few familiar nonfiction books that contain examples of various techniques that make nonfiction writing interesting and informative, such as the following from Text Set: Genre Study: Expository Nonfiction:
  - *A Day and Night in the Desert* by Caroline Arnold
  - *Bats!* by Laurence Pringle
  - *Shell, Beak, Tusk* by Bridget Heos
- chart paper prepared with a vague sentence
- markers
- writer's notebooks and writing folders
- To download the following online resource for this lesson, visit **fp.pub/resources**:
  - chart art (optional)

Academic Language / Important Vocabulary

- nonfiction
- informative
- interesting

Continuum Connection

- Use some vocabulary specific to the topic
- Understand that a factual text may use literary techniques (interesting words and language, descriptions that appeal to the senses, illustrations) to engage and entertain readers as it gives them factual information

GOAL

Learn a variety of techniques to make nonfiction writing interesting and informative.

RATIONALE

When you help students notice how nonfiction authors make their writing interesting and informative, they will begin to use some of these techniques in their own nonfiction writing. They will write informational books that are interesting and enjoyable to read.

WRITER'S NOTEBOOK/WRITING FOLDER

As students work on nonfiction writing in their writing folders, they may want to try out ideas in their writer's notebooks.

ASSESS LEARNING

- Notice whether students try out a variety of techniques for making their nonfiction writing interesting.
- Look for evidence that they can use vocabulary such as *nonfiction*, *interesting*, and *informative*.

MINILESSON

To help students think about the minilesson principle, use familiar nonfiction books to engage them in an inquiry-based lesson on making nonfiction writing interesting and informative. Here is an example.

- Show the cover of *A Day and Night in the Desert*. Then read pages 4–5.

  How did the author, Caroline Arnold, use words to make her writing interesting and informative?

- Begin a list of techniques that authors use to make their writing interesting and informative on chart paper. Add to the list as students notice more techniques.

- Show the cover of *Bats!* Read page 10.

  How did the author, Laurence Pringle, help you learn about the topic?

  What kinds of words did he use?

  How did he teach you what new vocabulary words mean?

  How did he help you understand how small a microbat is?

- Show the cover of *Shell, Beak, Tusk* and read pages 18–19.

  How did the author, Bridget Heos, help you learn about animals?

  What words did she use that are specific to the topic?

  How did she help you understand how strong a macaw's beak is?

Have a Try

Invite students to talk to a partner about making nonfiction writing interesting and informative.

▸ Display the example sentence that you prepared and read it aloud.

> What could I change or add to make my writing more interesting and help readers learn more about this idea? What do you think readers would want to know? What kinds of words could I use to make my writing more interesting? Turn and talk to your partner about your ideas.

▸ After students turn and talk, use shared writing to make your writing more interesting and informative.

Summarize and Apply

Help students summarize the learning and invite them to continue working on their informational books.

> What did you learn today about how to make nonfiction writing interesting and informative?

> When you write today, continue working on your informational book. You can always use your writer's notebook to try out some ideas before writing them on the draft in your writing folder. Be prepared to share your writing when we meet later.

Confer

▸ During independent writing, move around the room to confer briefly with students about writing nonfiction. Use prompts such as the following as needed.

- *What is this page of your book about?*
- *How will you make your writing about _____ interesting?*
- *What vocabulary words related to _____ will readers need to know or learn?*
- *What interesting words and phrases could you use to describe _____?*

Share

Following independent writing, gather students in the meeting area to share their writing.

> Who would like to read aloud a page that you have written?

> How did you make your nonfiction writing interesting and informative?

How to Make Your Writing Interesting and Informative

- Use descriptive language ("scaly body").
- Use alliteration ("whirs its wings").
- Use interesting, specific words and vocabulary related to the topic (venomous).
- Explain what new words mean ("Micro means small").
- Make comparisons (weighs less than a penny).
- Give specific facts (167 pounds per inch).

~~You might notice that your cat sleeps a lot.~~

You might notice that your cat spends much of her day lazily lounging in a sunny corner or catching some Z's on a cozy couch. Don't worry, this is perfectly normal. Wild cats are hunters. They need a lot of sleep to save their energy for catching their prey. As a result, all cats—even house cats—have evolved to need a lot of sleep. Adult cats sleep for as many as twenty hours each day.

WML 6
GEN.U6.WML6

Writing Minilesson Principle
Write a strong conclusion.

Making Informational Books

You Will Need

- a few familiar nonfiction books with strong conclusions, such as the following from Text Set: Genre Study: Expository Nonfiction:
  - *A Day and Night in the Desert* by Caroline Arnold
  - *Bats!* by Laurence Pringle
  - *Knights in Shining Armor* by Gail Gibbons
- chart paper and markers
- writer's notebooks and writing folders

Academic Language / Important Vocabulary

- informational book
- conclusion

Continuum Connection

- Understand that a writer can learn how to write an expository text from mentor texts
- Write a piece that is interesting and enjoyable to read
- Use a variety of endings to engage and satisfy the reader

GOAL

Learn a variety of ways to write a strong conclusion to an informational book.

RATIONALE

When you help students notice how nonfiction authors write strong conclusions, they will begin to use some of these techniques in their own nonfiction writing. They will write informational books that end with strong, satisfying conclusions.

WRITER'S NOTEBOOK/WRITING FOLDER

As students work on nonfiction writing in their writing folders, they may want to try out ideas in their writer's notebooks.

ASSESS LEARNING

- Notice whether students try out a variety of techniques for writing strong conclusions.
- Look for evidence that they can use vocabulary such as *informational book* and *conclusion*.

MINILESSON

To help students think about the minilesson principle, use familiar nonfiction books to engage students in an inquiry-based lesson on writing strong conclusions. Here is an example.

- Show the cover of *A Day and Night in the Desert* and then read page 19.

  The end of an informational book is called the conclusion. What do you notice about how the author, Caroline Arnold, concluded, or ended, her book?

- Begin a list of ways that authors make their conclusions strong.

  The author told you the main idea, or message, that she wanted you to take away from reading this book.

- Show the cover of *Bats!* and read page 31.

  What do you notice about the conclusion to this book? How does the author, Laurence Pringle, make his conclusion interesting and informative?

- Add responses to the chart.

- Show the cover of *Knights in Shining Armor* and read the final two pages of the main text.

  How did the author, Gail Gibbons, make her conclusion interesting?

- Add responses to the chart.

Have a Try

Invite students to talk to a partner about their ideas for conclusions.

> Think about the informational book you are writing. How could you end your book in an interesting way? Turn and talk to your partner about your ideas for your book's conclusion.

▶ After students turn and talk, invite several students to share their ideas.

Summarize and Apply

Help students summarize the learning and invite them to continue working on their informational books.

> What did you learn today about how to write a strong conclusion, or ending, for an informational book?

> When you write today, continue working on your informational book. When you get to the end of your book, try to write a conclusion that is interesting and informative. You may want to sum up the main ideas of the book, tell why the topic is important, or make an interesting connection. Try out some ideas in your writer's notebook so that you can choose the best one.

Ways to Write a Strong Conclusion

- Tell the main idea or message of the book.
- Show why the topic is important.
- Show why you care about the topic.
- Make connections between a historical topic and the present day.

Confer

▶ During independent writing, move around the room to confer briefly with students about writing conclusions. Use prompts such as the following as needed.

- *How could you end your book in an interesting way?*
- *What final thoughts or ideas do you want your reader to take away from your book?*
- *What could you write to show why your topic is important?*

Share

Following independent writing, gather students in the meeting area to share their writing.

> Who has written a conclusion for your informational book?

> Tell about your conclusion.

Umbrella 6: Making Informational Books

Assessment

After you have taught the minilessons in this umbrella, observe students as they explore making books. Use *The Fountas & Pinnell Literacy Continuum* to notice, teach for, and support students' learning as you observe their attempts at writing informational books.

- What evidence do you have of students' new understandings have developed related to making informational books?
  - Can students name qualities of good informational books?
  - Do they plan their informational books and use their plans to write their books?
  - Do they support their ideas with details and examples?
  - Do they use a variety of techniques to make their writing interesting and informative?
  - Do they write strong introductions and conclusions?
  - Do they understand and use vocabulary such as *informational book*, *quality*, *topic*, *organize*, *example*, *introduction*, and *conclusion*?
- In what other ways, beyond the scope of this umbrella, are students ready to explore nonfiction writing?
  - Are they using illustrations and graphics in their nonfiction writing?
  - Are they ready to start using text features in their nonfiction writing?

Use your observations to determine the next umbrella you will teach. You may also consult Suggested Sequence of Lessons (pp. 605–622) for guidance.

EXTENSIONS FOR MAKING INFORMATIONAL BOOKS

- Download rubrics for informational books from the online resources (fp.pub/resources) to help you and your students evaluate how well they are able to apply the concepts in these lessons.

- If you wish to expand on this umbrella, you might also consider teaching CFT.U10: Using Text Features in Nonfiction Writing, CFT.U11: Expanding Nonfiction Writing, and CFT.U14: Illustrating and Using Graphics in Nonfiction Writing.

- Teach students how to organize a book using a question-and-answer text structure instead of categories.

- Invite a nonfiction author to speak to the class about planning and writing a book.

Exploring Opinion Writing

Umbrella 7

Minilessons in This Umbrella

- **WML1** Use your writer's notebook to get ideas for opinion writing.
- **WML2** Write an introduction that clearly states your opinion.
- **WML3** Provide reasons and examples for your opinion.
- **WML4** Write a strong conclusion.

Writer's Notebook

Before Teaching Umbrella 7 Minilessons

For the purposes of this umbrella, the term *opinion writing* refers to a piece of writing in which the writer shares an opinion for a variety of reasons but not necessarily with the goal of changing readers' minds or prompting them to take certain actions. An opinion piece might influence the readers' thinking; however, the main purpose is to inform readers so they can make their own decisions. In opinion writing, the writer gives reasons for an opinion, but these reasons might be more about the writer's beliefs than strictly fact-based or substantiated with rigorous evidence, as they would be in persuasive and argumentative writing, which students will begin to write in grades 4 and 5. Opinion writing lays the foundation for these more complex ways of writing.

In addition to the examples provided in these lessons and in the online resources, you may want to collect other examples of opinion writing from everyday life (e.g., reviews of products, movies, or books; letters to the editor or editorials that are appropriate for the classroom) so that students have a variety of mentor texts.

Students will be more invested in writing about their opinions if they write about topics they care about. In WML1, students will learn to make lists in their writer's notebooks to help them discover these topics. If you have taught WPS.U4.WML1, have students reread their lists from that lesson to get ideas for opinion writing.

As you read and discuss opinion writing together, help students

- notice the characteristics of opinion writing,
- identify the author's opinion,
- explain how the author supports the opinion,
- share their own opinions about the topic, and
- notice transitions the authors use to connect ideas and reasons.

Section 2: Genres and Forms

Umbrella 7: Exploring Opinion Writing 217

WML1
GEN.U7.WML1

Writing Minilesson Principle
Use your writer's notebook to get ideas for opinion writing.

Exploring Opinion Writing

You Will Need

- an example opinion piece (see the online resource)
- chart paper and markers
- writer's notebooks
- To download the following online resource for this lesson, visit **fp.pub/resources**:
  - Opinion Writing

Academic Language / Important Vocabulary

- opinion writing
- opinion
- writer's notebook
- idea

Continuum Connection

- Use a writer's notebook or booklet as a tool for collecting ideas, experimenting, planning, sketching, or drafting

---

GOAL

Gather ideas for opinion writing in a writer's notebook.

RATIONALE

Writers write opinion pieces about topics they care deeply about. By making lists of topics they care about in their writer's notebooks, students will have a repository of ideas they can draw upon whenever they are looking for a topic for opinion writing.

WRITER'S NOTEBOOK/WRITING FOLDER

Have students explore ideas for opinion writing in their writer's notebooks.

ASSESS LEARNING

▸ Notice whether students use their writer's notebooks to gather and explore ideas for opinion writing.

▸ Look for evidence that they can use vocabulary such as *opinion writing*, *opinion*, *writer's notebook*, and *idea*.

MINILESSON

To help students think about the minilesson principle, model how to gather topics for opinion writing in a writer's notebook. This lesson uses "Beauty and the Beast Review" from the online resource Opinion Writing. Here is an example.

▸ Display an example opinion piece on chart paper (or project it), and read it aloud.

> This writing is called opinion writing. What do you notice about opinion writing?

> In opinion writing, you write what you think about something. My opinion is that *Beauty and the Beast* is the best animated movie ever. Some people might disagree with my opinion. That's okay! People are allowed to have their own opinions.

> Today you will write Top Ten lists. If something is on your Top Ten list, you already have an opinion about it.

▸ Have students turn to page 24 of *Writer's Notebook, Intermediate* (or a clean page). If students don't have this tool, they can use a blank notebook.

> Let's start with movies. One of my top ten movies is *Beauty and the Beast*. What are your top ten movies? Start a list of them in your writer's notebook.

▸ Have students turn to page 26 (or a clean page).

> Next, write your opinion about hopes and wishes for yourself, our school, or the world. I think that New Zealand would be a great place to visit, so I will write *Travel to New Zealand* on my list of hopes. What do you hope or wish for? Write a few ideas in your notebook.

Have a Try

Invite students to share their lists with a partner.

> Turn and talk to share what you wrote on your lists with your partner.

▶ After students turn and talk, invite several students to share their ideas with the class. Record them on chart paper.

Summarize and Apply

Summarize the learning and invite students to further explore their ideas for opinion writing in their writer's notebooks.

> What did you learn about opinion writing today?
>
> Where can you collect ideas for opinion writing?

▶ Write the principle at the top of the chart.

> During writing time today, continue to work on your lists in your writer's notebook. Choose one of the ideas from either of your lists and start writing some thoughts about it in your writer's notebook. Bring your ideas to share when we come back together.

Confer

▶ During independent writing, move around the room to confer briefly with individual students about their ideas for opinion writing. Use prompts such as the following as needed.

- What is your favorite (video game, song, part of third grade)? What makes it enjoyable?
- What would make the world (our school) a better place?
- Which of these ideas would you most like to write an opinion piece about?
- Why did you choose this topic for your opinion writing?

Share

Following independent writing, gather students in the meeting area. Invite students to share their ideas for opinion writing.

> What is a topic that you are thinking you want to write an opinion piece about?
>
> What is your opinion about it?

Use your writer's notebook to get ideas for opinion writing.

Top Ten Movies
1. Beauty and the Beast
2. The Wizard of Oz
3. Encanto
4. Toy Story
5. Spider-Man
6. E.T.
7. Up
8. Finding Nemo
9. Moana
10. Inside Out

Hopes for Myself	Hopes for My School	Hopes for My World
• Travel to New Zealand	• Bigger library	• World peace
• Ride a horse	• New playground equipment	• End world hunger
• Visit another planet	• More art and music classes	• No more pandemics
• Become a scientist	• Longer recess	
• Become a famous singer	• Lockers	
• Go scuba diving		

WML2
GEN.U7.WML2

Writing Minilesson Principle
Write an introduction that clearly states your opinion.

Exploring Opinion Writing

You Will Need

- a copy of several opinion pieces for each student (see the online resource for WML1)
- an idea for a shared-writing opinion piece
- chart paper and markers
- writer's notebooks and writing folders

Academic Language / Important Vocabulary

- opinion writing
- introduction

Continuum Connection

- Use a variety of beginnings to engage the reader
- Understand the importance of the lead in a story or nonfiction piece

GOAL

Write an introduction that clearly states an opinion.

RATIONALE

Learning to craft an introduction that introduces the topic and engages the reader is the first step in writing an effective opinion piece.

WRITER'S NOTEBOOK/WRITING FOLDER

Students will try out ideas for an introduction to an opinion piece in their writer's notebooks. If they have extra time, they can work on another writing project in their writing folders.

ASSESS LEARNING

- Observe for evidence that students understand that the introduction to an opinion piece must hook and engage the readers and clearly state the opinion.
- Look for evidence that they can use vocabulary such as *opinion writing* and *introduction*.

MINILESSON

To help students think about the minilesson principle, use mentor texts and shared writing to model how to write a clear and engaging introduction to an opinion piece. Here is an example.

- Distribute a copy of several opinion pieces as mentor texts for each student. Ask them to read (or read aloud to them) the first paragraph of each piece of writing.

    Read the first paragraph of each opinion piece. Then turn and talk to your partner about what you notice in the introductions. Is every introduction written the same way? What is the same? What is different?

- After a brief time, ask volunteers to share their thoughts. Record on chart paper students' responses about how writers introduce their opinion pieces.
- Propose an idea for a class opinion piece.

    Today we're going to write an opinion piece together. A couple of you wrote on your list of hopes for our school that you hope assigned seating in the lunchroom will end. We could write an opinion piece about that topic together.

- Make sure the majority of students agree with that opinion before starting to write.

The Writing Minilessons Book, Grade 3

Have a Try

Invite students to talk to a partner about writing an introduction to an opinion piece.

> How do you want to start an opinion piece about lunchroom seating? What could the introduction say? Turn and talk to your partner about your ideas.

▸ After time for discussion, work with students to write an introduction on chart paper. Save the chart for WML3 so that you and the students can continue writing the opinion piece.

Summarize and Apply

Help students summarize the learning. Have students store the mentor texts for opinion writing in their writing folders and use them for reference when writing their introductions.

> What did you learn today about how to start an opinion piece?

▸ Write the principle at the top of the first chart.

> Today during writing time, reread the lists of ideas for opinion writing that you made in your writer's notebook and choose a topic that you have a strong opinion about. In your writer's notebook, try out some ways to write an introduction to your opinion piece. Bring your notebook to share when we meet later.

Confer

▸ During independent writing, move around the room to confer briefly with students about their introductions. Use prompts such as the following as needed.

- *What are you going to write about in your opinion piece?*
- *Let's look at the lists you made in your writer's notebook. Which of these topics do you have a strong opinion about?*
- *How could you start your opinion piece?*
- *What do you need to remember to include in your introduction?*

Share

Following independent writing, gather students in the meeting area to share their introductions after first sharing with a partner.

> Turn to a partner to share your introduction.

Write an introduction that clearly states your opinion.

- Hook your readers.
  - Ask a question.
  - Begin with a story.
  - Start with a strong emotion.
- State the topic.
- Clearly give your opinion.

Freedom to Sit

Totally not fair! That's what we think about where we have to sit in the lunchroom. This year, we have had assigned seating at lunchtime. The principal decided we should sit in alphabetical order. We think we should be allowed to choose where we sit.

WML 3
GEN.U7.WML03

Writing Minilesson Principle
Provide reasons and examples for your opinion.

Exploring Opinion Writing

You Will Need

- a copy of an opinion piece for each student (see the online resource for WML1)
- the piece of shared writing started in WML2
- markers
- writer's notebooks and writing folders

Academic Language / Important Vocabulary

- opinion writing
- reason
- example
- connecting word

Continuum Connection

- Introduce ideas followed by supportive details and examples
- Use common (simple) connectives and some sophisticated connectives (words that link ideas and clarify meaning) that are used in written texts but do not appear often in everyday oral language: e.g., *although, however, therefore, though, unless, whenever*

GOAL

Understand that writers use reasons and examples to support their opinions.

RATIONALE

When students notice how writers of opinion pieces provide reasons and examples for their opinions, they will be better equipped to write clearly stated reasons and evidence in their own opinion pieces. Learning to use connectives will help students make their opinions clearer to their readers and their writing smoother.

WRITER'S NOTEBOOK/WRITING FOLDER

Students will use their writer's notebooks to try out their ideas for opinion writing.

ASSESS LEARNING

- Notice whether students provide clearly stated reasons and examples for their opinion and use connecting words effectively.
- Look for evidence that they can use vocabulary such as *opinion writing*, *reason*, *example*, and *connecting word*.

MINILESSON

To help students think about the minilesson principle, use a mentor text and shared writing to model how to provide reasons and examples to support an opinion. This lesson uses "What's for Lunch?" from the online resource Opinion Writing, which students may already have in their writing folders. Here is an example.

- Ask students to read (or read aloud to them) "What's for Lunch?" Then invite discussion about the reasons and examples the writer offers.

  > What is this writer's opinion?
  >
  > What did the writer do to support the opinion?
  >
  > The writer gave reasons to explain why the cafeteria should serve better lunches. What are the reasons?

- List the reasons on chart paper in the first column of a two-column chart.

  > Writers often give examples to tell more about their reasons. What examples does the writer of this opinion piece give?

- Write the examples in the second column.
- Point out the connectives (*although, nevertheless, for example, therefore*).

  > Why do you think the writer chose to use these words?

- Guide students to understand the function of each of the words (e.g., *although* connects opposite ideas, *therefore* shows that something will happen as a result of something else) and how they can use such words in their own writing.

Have a Try

Invite students to talk to a partner about providing reasons for an opinion.

- Review the shared writing started in WML2.

    What reasons and examples could we provide to support this opinion?

- Elicit responses from several students, and use shared writing to write several reasons and examples on chart paper. A conclusion will be added in WML4.

Summarize and Apply

Help students summarize the learning and remind them to provide reasons and examples for their opinion when they write opinion pieces.

What did you learn today about writing opinion pieces?

During writing time today, start writing your opinion piece. You have some ideas for the introduction in your writer's notebook. Choose an introduction, write it on draft paper, and then write reasons and examples for your opinion. Remember to help your readers understand your opinion by using connecting words to show how your ideas are related. Bring your writing to share when we come back together.

Confer

- During independent writing, move around the room to confer briefly with students about their opinion writing. Use prompts such as the following as needed.
    - *What reason will you write first? What reason will you write next?*
    - *What example could help support your reason?*
    - *What connecting word could show how those two ideas (sentences) are related?*

Share

Following independent writing, gather students in the meeting area to share their writing.

Who would like to read aloud the reasons and examples you wrote in your opinion piece?

Does anyone have any comments or questions for _____?

Provide reasons and examples for your opinion.

Reasons	Examples
The menu is the same every week.	Sloppy joes, chicken nuggets, macaroni and cheese, hot dogs, pizza
Kids need to eat fresh fruits and vegetables to be healthy.	Only vegetable was tomato sauce
Some people have allergies to the food.	Allergy to foods with milk

Freedom to Sit

Lunchtime should be a chance to relax after a morning of working in class. Sitting with friends will help us relax. Another reason is that we can visit with friends from other classes.

You might have noticed that after lunch there is a lot of talking in class. That's because we don't have a chance to talk with our friends during lunch.

WML 4
GEN.U7.WML4

Writing Minilesson Principle
Write a strong conclusion.

Exploring Opinion Writing

You Will Need

- a copy of several opinion pieces for each student (see the online resource for WML1)
- the piece of shared writing from WML3
- markers
- writer's notebooks and writing folders

Academic Language / Important Vocabulary

- opinion writing
- conclusion

Continuum Connection

- Use a variety of endings to engage and satisfy the reader
- Bring the piece to closure with an ending or final statement

GOAL

Write a conclusion that summarizes the opinion and is interesting to the reader.

RATIONALE

When you help students notice different ways that writers conclude their opinion pieces, they will be better equipped to finish their opinion pieces with a strong conclusion that summarizes the opinion and satisfies the readers.

WRITER'S NOTEBOOK/WRITING FOLDER

Students will finish working on their opinion pieces. If they have extra time, they can work on another writing project in their writing folders.

ASSESS LEARNING

- Notice whether students finish their opinion piece with a strong conclusion.
- Look for evidence that they can use vocabulary such as *opinion writing* and *conclusion*.

MINILESSON

To help students think about the minilesson principle, use mentor texts and shared writing to model how to write a strong conclusion for an opinion piece. Here is an example.

- Distribute a copy of several opinion pieces to each student. Ask them to read (or read aloud to them) the last paragraph of each piece of writing.

    What do you notice about the conclusions in these opinion pieces?

- Record students' responses on chart paper.

    Why is it important to write a strong conclusion?

- Guide students to understand that it's the last thing the readers will read, so it should be memorable.
- Display the piece of shared writing from WML3.

    Today we're going to write a conclusion for our opinion piece about choosing where to sit in the lunchroom. How could we summarize our opinion and conclude our piece in a way that will be interesting to the readers?

- Elicit responses from several students, and use shared writing to write a strong conclusion.

WML 4
GEN.U7.WML4

Have a Try

Invite students to talk to a partner about writing a strong conclusion.

> Think about the opinion piece you're working on now. How might you conclude your writing? Turn and talk to your partner about your ideas.

Summarize and Apply

Help students summarize the learning and remind them to write a strong conclusion.

> What did you learn today about how to finish an opinion piece?

- Write the principle at the top of the first chart.

> Today during writing time, write a strong conclusion for your opinion piece. When you're finished, write in your writer's notebook or work on another writing project in your writing folder. Bring your writing to share when we come back together.

Confer

- During independent writing, move around the room to confer briefly with students about their conclusions. Use prompts such as the following as needed.
  - How could you end your opinion piece?
  - What could you write to summarize your most important reasons?
  - What would be an interesting way to end your writing?

Share

Following independent writing, gather students in pairs in the meeting area to share their writing.

> Share your conclusion with your partner.

- After students share with a partner, invite a few students to share their conclusions with the whole class.

Write a strong conclusion.

A conclusion . . .

- says the opinion again.
- summarizes the most important reasons.
- gives the readers something to think about.

Freedom to Sit

The principal may have had good reasons to make us sit in assigned seats. However, it makes sense for us to be allowed to choose where we sit so that we can relax and talk to our friends. When we return to the classroom, we will be ready to focus on our work.

Umbrella 7 | Exploring Opinion Writing

Assessment

After you have taught the minilessons in this umbrella, observe students as they write and talk about their writing. Use *The Fountas & Pinnell Literacy Continuum* to notice, teach for, and support students' learning as you observe their attempts at opinion writing.

- What evidence do you have of students' new understandings related to opinion writing?
  - Do students write opinion pieces on topics they feel strongly about?
  - Do their opinion pieces include an introduction that clearly states their opinion, reasons and examples that support the opinion, and a strong conclusion?
  - Do students refer to mentor texts to support their writing?
  - Do students understand and use vocabulary such as *opinion*, *introduction*, *reason*, *example*, and *conclusion*?
- In what other ways, beyond the scope of this umbrella, are students ready to share their opinions?
  - Are they ready to use persuasive writing to communicate a message?

Use your observations to determine the next umbrella you will teach. You may also consult Suggested Sequence of Lessons (pp. 605–622) for guidance.

EXTENSIONS FOR EXPLORING OPINION WRITING

- Invite students to write book reviews for books in the class or school library. Bind the reviews together and place them near the library books so that students can use the reviews to select their next book to read.

- Invite students to write opinion pieces about more sophisticated subjects (e.g., current events).

- Teach students how to substantiate their reasoning with factual evidence.

- Introduce students to persuasive writing (a more advanced form of opinion writing in which the writer appeals to the audience for support).

- Use the teacher and student rubrics available in online resources to evaluate students' opinion writing or to guide them to evaluate their own texts. You might also consider having students co-create rubrics with you.

Introducing Persuasive Writing Through Powerful Messages

Umbrella 8

Minilessons in This Umbrella

- **WML1** Find your message.
- **WML2** Find a new way to share your message.
- **WML3** Make your message stand out.

Before Teaching Umbrella 8 Minilessons

Students are exposed to many persuasive messages from a young age. They might not even be aware of all of the messages trying to influence their thoughts or actions that they see, hear, and read every day. The minilessons in this umbrella help students understand effective ways they can find and share messages of their own and are an introduction to persuasive writing.

This umbrella helps students gain confidence as people who have important messages and voices that matter. It also supports them in thinking about the purpose and audience for messages they want to express and the most effective mode for doing that. Written composition is not the only entry point. Students might decide to share their messages in a variety of multimodal ways—an oral presentation, a video, a bumper sticker, a poster, or a button. Encourage them to think about choices for paper and writing utensils, as well as for technologies that can make their messages stand out.

To help students experiment with the concepts taught in these minilessons, you will need to collect in advance several examples of multimodal texts (texts that use more than one mode to express meaning, such as written text combined with a visual or audio element) that communicate a message that is acceptable in your classroom (e.g., T-shirts, magnets, posters, songs, bumper stickers). Along with nontraditional mentor texts, you can use the following texts from *Fountas & Pinnell Classroom™ Interactive Read-Aloud Collection* and *Shared Reading Collection* or choose suitable books that have a message.

Interactive Read-Aloud
Point of View

Shared Reading

Writer's Notebook

Interactive Read-Aloud Collection
Author's Point of View

Oil Spill! by Melvin Berger

Shared Reading Collection

Using Her Voice: A Biography of Mari Copeny by Myra Faye Turner

As you read and enjoy these and other texts together, help students

- notice interesting choices the author or illustrator made,
- identify the author's message, and
- think about how the author communicated the message in a way that stood out.

WML1
GEN.U8.WML1

Writing Minilesson Principle
Find your message.

Introducing Persuasive Writing Through Powerful Messages

You Will Need

- several familiar texts with a strong message, such as the following:
  - *Using Her Voice* by Myra Faye Turner, from *Shared Reading Collection*
  - *Oil Spill!* by Melvin Berger, from Text Set: Author's Point of View
- at least one example of a multimodal text (e.g., T-shirt, magnet, poster, song, bumper sticker) that communicates a message (e.g., "Choose Kindness")
- chart paper and markers
- sticky notes
- writer's notebooks
- To download the following online resources for this lesson, visit **fp.pub/resources**:
  - chart art (optional)

Academic Language / Important Vocabulary

- message
- opinion

Continuum Connection

- Show enthusiasm and energy for the topic
- Reread a writer's notebook to select topics: e.g., select small moments that can be expanded
- Choose topics that are interesting to the writer
- Write with specific readers or audience in mind

GOAL

Choose a message to share with others.

RATIONALE

When you help students notice persuasive messages in writing and all around them, their understanding of writing or communicating to an audience expands. They learn that they can have a message to share with others. This lesson gives students the opportunity to share their opinions about issues or topics they are passionate about and to think about the audience for that message.

WRITER'S NOTEBOOK/WRITING FOLDER

Have students use their writer's notebooks to help them think through important messages they want to share with an audience.

ASSESS LEARNING

- Notice whether students can think of a message to share and then state it in different ways.
- Look for evidence that they can use vocabulary such as *message* and *opinion*.

MINILESSON

To help students think about the minilesson principle, show multimodal texts that communicate student-friendly messages and mentor texts to model ways of communicating a message or an opinion to others. This example lesson is based on using a poster.

- Show and discuss a few items that communicate student-friendly messages.

  What do you think this is?

  Why do you think someone made this poster?

  The author of this poster wants readers to take action to treat others with kindness. The author's message is that choosing to be kind is important. An author's message is the important idea the author wants to share.

- Write the author's message on a sticky note and add to chart paper. Repeat with another poster or other method of communicating a message.

- Share *Using Her Voice* with students to help them understand that some books share opinions or try to persuade the readers to think a certain way.

  What messages or opinions was Mari trying to share with others?

- Add sticky notes with student noticings to the chart.

- Repeat this process with *Oil Spill!*

  What are some other important messages that you might want to share with an audience?

Have a Try

Invite students to talk to a partner about the messages they would like to share.

> Turn and talk to your partner. What are some topics or issues you care a lot about? What is something that you think would make the world a better place? What kind of message can you share to make positive change?

▸ After time for discussion, invite several students to share. Add new ideas on sticky notes to the chart.

Summarize and Apply

Write the principle at the top of the chart. Read it to students. Summarize the learning and remind students to write down different ideas they have for a message.

> What did you learn today about the kinds of messages authors share with others?

> During writing time today, think about the messages you want to share. Take a look in your writer's notebook. Have you jotted down ideas for messages you want to share? Do you have new ideas? List those messages on the next clean page in Section 4 of your writer's notebook. Don't forget to write today's date. Bring your writer's notebook when we come back together.

Confer

▸ During independent writing, move around the room to confer briefly with students about the messages they are considering. Use prompts such as the following as needed.

- *What message would you like to share?*
- *What issue or topic do you care a lot about?*
- *What problems do you see that you could try to change using a positive message? What would your message be?*

Share

Following independent writing, gather students in the meeting area. Ask each student to share one idea for a message.

> What is your message? If you don't have a message yet, you might hear an idea from a classmate.

WML2
GEN.U8.WML2

Writing Minilesson Principle
Find a new way to share your message.

Introducing Persuasive Writing Through Powerful Messages

You Will Need

- a familiar text with a strong message, such as *Using Her Voice* by Myra Faye Turner, from *Shared Reading Collection*
- at least one example of a multimodal text (e.g., T-shirt, magnet, poster, song, bumper sticker) that communicates a message (e.g., "Save the Whales")
- chart paper and markers
- writer's notebooks

Academic Language / Important Vocabulary

- message
- audience

Continuum Connection

- Use engaging titles and language
- Communicate the significance of the topic to an audience
- Write with specific readers or audience in mind
- Understand audience as all readers rather than just the teacher
- Write for a specific purpose: e.g., to inform, entertain, persuade, reflect, instruct, retell, maintain relationships, plan
- Understand writing as a vehicle to communicate something the writer thinks

---

GOAL

Choose a message and share it through a multimodal form of writing.

RATIONALE

Encourage students to think creatively not just about the content of their writing but also the form. Purpose, audience, and form work together to make writing effective. Understanding that there are many ways to convey a message gives students the opportunity to share their opinions about issues or topics they feel passionate about and sets the stage for persuasive writing.

WRITER'S NOTEBOOK/WRITING FOLDER

Students will look in their writer's notebooks for an idea to share. They might also want to use their writer's notebooks to try out some ideas for how to share their messages.

ASSESS LEARNING

- Observe for evidence that students understand the importance of choosing a form appropriate for communicating a message.
- Look for evidence that they can use vocabulary such as *message* and *audience*.

MINILESSON

To help students think about the minilesson principle, use several mentor texts to engage them in talking about multimodal forms of writing that communicate a message. Guide them to think about their audience and the best way to communicate the message to that audience. Here is an example.

- Show and read pages 8–9 from *Using Her Voice*.

  Mari had several powerful messages to share. Let's talk about her audience.

  What is one way she communicated her message?

- After a brief discussion, write ideas on chart paper, placing the audience on the left and the form on the right.
- Repeat this process with pages 14–16.

  Whom might Mari be communicating with here? What is another way she shared her message?

- Show and discuss an item (e.g., a button, a T-shirt) that communicates a student-friendly message.

  What is the author's message? Why do you think the author chose to put that on a button?

Have a Try

Invite students to talk to a partner about the audience for their messages and how they want to share their message.

> You wrote some ideas for messages you might want to share in your writer's notebook. Choose one message. Then think about who should hear your message and how you might share that message. Turn and talk about your ideas.

▸ After students turn and talk, invite several students to share their ideas. Add any new ideas to the chart.

Summarize and Apply

Write the principle at the top of the chart. Summarize the learning and remind students to try different ways of sharing a message.

> What did you learn today about how authors can share their message with others?

> During writing time today, think about the message you would like to share and the audience you want to hear it. Then think about how you want to share your message. You can work in your notebook or make a choice about the kind of paper you would like to use. Bring your work to share when we come back together.

▸ If electronic devices are available, students may wish to use those to share their message via a video or slideshow.

Find a new way to share your message.

Who should hear your message?	How will you share that message?
• Community	• Posters
• Neighbors	• Have a meeting
• People around the country or world	• Large signs
• Students	• Talk to others/give a speech
• Leaders in our world	• Write a book
• Friends	• Write a letter
• Parents	• Bumper sticker
• Teachers	• T-shirt
	• Write a song
	• Magnet
	• Create a video
	• Script for a play

Confer

▸ During independent writing, move around the room to confer briefly with students about the best way to share a message. Use prompts such as the following as needed.

- *What message would you like to share? How would you like to share that message?*
- *Who is your audience?*
- *What is the best way to get your message across to your audience?*

Share

Following independent writing, gather students in the meeting area to share their messages.

> In what form did you decide to share your message? Why?

WML3
GEN.U8.WML3

Writing Minilesson Principle
Make your message stand out.

Introducing Persuasive Writing Through Powerful Messages

You Will Need

- a familiar text with a strong message, such as *Using Her Voice* by Myra Faye Turner, from *Shared Reading Collection*
- at least one example of a multimodal text (e.g., T-shirt, magnet, poster, song, bumper sticker) that communicates a message (e.g., "Choose Kindness")
- chart paper and markers
- writer's notebooks

Academic Language / Important Vocabulary

- message
- share
- audience
- stand out

Continuum Connection

- Tell about a topic in an interesting way
- Communicate the significance of the topic to an audience

GOAL

Understand how word choice, images, and color help readers notice and think about the message.

RATIONALE

Encourage students to think creatively not just about the content of their writing but also the form. Learning to match the form of writing to the purpose and audience results in more effective writing. Understanding that there are many ways to convey a message gives students the opportunity to share their opinions about issues or topics they feel passionate about and sets the stage for persuasive writing.

WRITER'S NOTEBOOK/WRITING FOLDER

Students can use their writer's notebooks to try out some ideas for how to make their messages stand out.

ASSESS LEARNING

- Observe for evidence that students understand what it means to make their messages stand out.
- Look for evidence that they can use vocabulary such as *message*, *share*, *audience*, and *stand out*.

MINILESSON

To help students think about the minilesson principle, use several mentor texts to engage students in an inquiry around how to compose their message in a way that stands out to readers. Here is an example.

- Show one mentor text that communicates a message (e.g., a "Choose Kindness" bumper sticker).

    What do you think this is?

    Why do you think someone made this bumper sticker? Let's talk about the audience for this message.

    The author of this bumper sticker wants everyone to be kind to one another. What did the author do to make the message stand out and get noticed? How did the author make sure that lots of people would see this message?

- List students' ideas on the chart.
- Show pages 8–9 from *Using Her Voice*.

    What do you notice about the signs Mari's community created? How did they make their message stand out?

- Show page 16.

    How do you think Mari prepared to share a speech to the community? What might she say to make her message stand out?

The Writing Minilessons Book, Grade 3

Have a Try

Invite students to talk to a partner about how they would like to make their messages stand out.

> Think about the message you want to share. Who is your audience for the message? How might you make your message stand out to your audience? Turn and talk to your partner about that.

▸ After students turn and talk, invite several students to share their ideas. Add any new ideas to the chart.

Summarize and Apply

Write the principle at the top of the chart. Summarize the learning and remind students to think about how to make their message stand out.

> How can you make your message stand out?

> During writing time today, think about your message and your audience. Then think about how to make that message stand out. You can try out some ideas in your writer's notebook or make a choice about the kind of paper you would like to use. Bring your work to share when we come back together.

▸ If electronic devices are available, students may wish to use those to share their message via a video or slideshow.

Make your message stand out.

- Write one strong sentence or statement.
- Find a way to get your message to as many people as you can.

  Choose Kindness

- Use powerful words.

  Reading Is Incredible

- Choose the color and size of writing—large, clear, bright letters—that make the message stand out.
- Prepare a speech or write a letter.
- Include pictures.
- Tell a story.
- Write a book.
- Ask for help from others.

Confer

▸ During independent writing, move around the room to confer briefly with students about the best way to share a message. Use prompts such as the following as needed.

- *Whom do you want to hear your message?*
- *What is the message you want to share? How did you decide to share that message? What will you do to make that message stand out?*
- *Think about how the size and color of the words can make your message stand out.*
- *Think about words that would be powerful for your audience to hear.*

Share

Following independent writing, gather students in the meeting area to share their messages.

> Hold up what you are working on so we can see how you are making your message stand out.

Umbrella 8: Introducing Persuasive Writing Through Powerful Messages

Assessment

After you have taught the minilessons in this umbrella, observe students as they explore different ways of writing. Use *The Fountas & Pinnell Literacy Continuum* to notice, teach for, and support students' learning as you observe their attempts at writing.

- What evidence do you have of students' new understandings related to sharing a message in a powerful way?
  - Are students able to find a message they are interested in and enthusiastic about?
  - How effective is their choice of words, images, and colors in conveying their messages and making them stand out?
  - Do they understand and use vocabulary such as *opinion*, *message*, *share*, *audience*, and *stand out*?
- In what other ways, beyond the scope of this umbrella, are students beginning to think about persuasive writing?
  - Are they thinking about choosing powerful words while writing?
  - Are they thinking about specific examples when they are writing?
  - How are they using language to create a picture for readers?
  - Are they sharing their writing with an audience?

Use your observations to determine the next umbrella you will teach. You may also consult Suggested Sequence of Lessons (pp. 605–622) for guidance.

EXTENSIONS FOR INTRODUCING PERSUASIVE WRITING THROUGH POWERFUL MESSAGES

- Help students experiment with digital forms of content creation as appropriate (e.g., blog post, slideshow, podcast, video).

- Listen to a student give a persuasive speech or share a powerful message, live or in a video, or play a clip of a speech. Ask students to listen for powerful words. They can also listen for the use of specific or repeated words and consider why the speaker might have used them.

- Provide opportunities for students to create other forms of persuasive or opinion writing (e.g., book reviews, restaurant reviews, movie reviews).

- After students share their messages in one form, provide time for them to share the same message in a different form.

Making Poetry Anthologies

Umbrella 9

Minilessons in This Umbrella

WML1	Make your own poetry anthology.
WML2	Collect poems that show something about you.
WML3	Respond to poems you collect.
WML4	Write a poem in response to a poem.

Before Teaching Umbrella 9 Minilessons

WML1 and WML2 build the foundation for creating a poetry anthology. Provide blank notebooks or prepare blank booklets (approximately thirty stapled pages with a cover) for students to use for their poetry anthologies. In this umbrella, students will not write poems or responses until WML3 and WML4, so spend several days reading, talking about, and collecting poems after teaching WML2.

Creating a poetry anthology is one way to introduce the poetry workshop, an important element of the language and literacy framework. Poetry workshop can take the place of readers' or writers' workshop once every week or one week every month (see pp. 61–64).

Before starting to make their anthologies, students will benefit from hearing about different poets (through poet talks), listening to poetry read aloud, reading and discussing poems with different styles, and writing poetry. Collect as many poetry books as possible, such as those from *Fountas & Pinnell Classroom™ Interactive Read-Aloud Collection* and *Shared Reading Collection* and also from the classroom library.

Interactive Read-Aloud Collection
Genre Study: Poetry

Splish Splash by Joan Bransfield Graham

Flicker Flash by Joan Bransfield Graham

Shared Reading Collection

The Rain Forest Rainbow by Susan B. Katz

Mixed-Up Monsters and Confused Critters by Mike Downs

The Backwards Poem Book by Mike Downs

As you read and enjoy these texts together, help students notice

- how one reads poems, and rhythm, cadence, and repetition in poetry (e.g., alliteration, consonance, assonance, and onomatopoeia),
- the variety of poetic elements (e.g., personification, metaphor, simile), and
- the shape of the words written on the page and some of the forms of poetry (e.g., free verse, lyric, narrative, limerick, cinquain, concrete, list, haiku).

Interactive Read-Aloud Poetry

Shared Reading

WML 1
GEN.U9.WML1

Writing Minilesson Principle
Make your own poetry anthology.

Making Poetry Anthologies

You Will Need

- a variety of books that contain poems, such as the following:
  - *Splish Splash* by Joan Bransfield Graham, from Text Set: Genre Study: Poetry
  - *The Backwards Poem Book* by Mike Downs, from *Shared Reading Collection*
- your own poetry anthology and/or those of former students, including a cover and table of contents
- a blank poetry anthology for each student
- sticky notes
- chart paper and markers, colored pencils, and crayons
- To download the following online resources for this lesson, visit **fp.pub/resources**:
  - chart art (optional)
  - paper templates (optional)

Academic Language / Important Vocabulary

- anthology
- poetry
- poet
- table of contents

Continuum Connection

- Put several stories or poems together
- Add cover spread with title and author information

GOAL

Understand the purpose of a poetry anthology.

RATIONALE

Noticing and naming the characteristics of a poetry anthology helps students construct their own. Having a poetry anthology will encourage them to collect poems they have read or written that are meaningful to them and increase their appreciation for the intense, concise, and skillfully crafted language of poetry.

ASSESS LEARNING

- Notice what students understand about a poetry anthology.
- Look for evidence that they can use vocabulary such as *anthology*, *poetry*, *poet*, and *table of contents*.

MINILESSON

To help students think about the principle, have them notice and discuss the characteristics of a poetry anthology using familiar books of poetry. Here is an example.

- Show the cover of *Splish Splash* and read the title and a few pages.

  What do you notice about the cover of this poetry book?

  What are some other things you notice about this anthology of poems?

- Write the principle at the top of the chart paper. Record students' responses on sticky notes and add them to the chart.

  When a writer puts lots of poems together, it is called a poetry anthology.

- Repeat this process with another poetry book, such as *The Backwards Poem Book*. As needed, direct students' attention to specific elements (e.g., cover, table of contents).

  What do you notice about the cover of this anthology?

  What did the poet place at the beginning of the anthology?

  Poets sometimes have a table of contents to help readers find a certain poem. What else do you notice?

The Writing Minilessons Book, Grade 3

Have a Try

Invite students to talk to a partner about poetry anthologies. Use your poetry anthology or that of a former student as an example.

> You can collect poems you enjoy and poems that you write in your own poetry anthology. Here is an example. Turn and talk to your partner about what to include.

▸ After students turn and talk, invite a few students to share their ideas. Write new ideas on sticky notes and add them to the chart.

Summarize and Apply

Summarize the learning and remind students that they will begin a poetry anthology by creating a decorated cover and table of contents. Add samples of these elements to chart paper as you discuss them. You might want students to use appropriate paper templates for the cover and contents.

> Today you will create the cover for your poetry anthology. What will you need to include on the cover?

> You will also begin a table of contents. Use the first two pages of your anthology as the table of contents. If you finish getting your poetry anthology ready before it is time to clean up, please choose a poetry book to read.

Confer

▸ During independent writing, move around the room to confer briefly with students about their plans for making a poetry anthology. Use the following prompts as needed.
- *What are you going to put on the cover?*
- *How will the table of contents help you as you create this anthology?*
- *What types of poems do you like to read?*

Share

Following independent writing, gather students in a circle in the meeting area so that everyone can share their anthology covers.

> Hold up the cover of your poetry anthology so everyone can see. What do you notice about your classmates' covers?

> As you read poems, look for ones to add to your poetry anthology.

Umbrella 9: Making Poetry Anthologies

WML2
GEN.U9.WML2

Writing Minilesson Principle
Collect poems that show something about you.

Making Poetry Anthologies

You Will Need

- a poem you connect with
- a diverse collection of poetry books and poems in which your students will see themselves, such as "The Caterpillar" from *The Backwards Poem Book* by Mike Downs, from *Shared Reading Collection*
- chart paper, markers, and tape
- principle plus two headings written on strips of paper (see chart)
- students' poetry anthologies
- To download the following online resources for this lesson, visit **fp.pub/resources**:
  - chart art (optional)
  - paper templates (optional)

Academic Language / Important Vocabulary

- anthology
- poetry

Continuum Connection

- Show connections between the setting, characters, and events of a text and the reader's own personal experiences
- Understand poetry as a unique way to communicate about and describe feelings, sensory images, ideas, or stories

GOAL

Choose poems that connect to you in some way.

RATIONALE

Students will gain an affinity for writing in which they can see themselves. When you read poetry with students and help them find and compile poems that are meaningful to them in a poetry anthology, it builds an appreciation for the art of language and the decisions poets make. The anthology becomes a useful reference for each student as a reader and a writer across the year.

ASSESS LEARNING

- Notice whether students can explain why they choose particular poems.
- Look for evidence that they can use vocabulary such as *anthology* and *poetry*.

MINILESSON

Compile in advance a diverse set of poetry books and poems so all of your students see themselves in a poem. To help students think about the principle, model how you connect with a particular poem. Here is an example.

- Read (at least two times) a poem you have selected because you have a connection with it.

    Why do you think I chose this poem?

- Share the connection you feel with the poem. Then read aloud other poems you have selected that you think students will identify with. Display them if possible so that students can join in reading aloud with you. Then discuss the poems, asking questions such as the following as needed.

    - *What does the poet say to you?*
    - *What does the poet make you think about?*
    - *Which words or phrases do you love? Why?*
    - *What picture do you see in your mind when you listen to the poem?*
    - *Where did the poet decide to use rhyme? Are there any sound words or words that begin with the same sound or letter?*
    - *What shape did the poet decide to form with the words of the poem?*

- After discussion, summarize the learning.

    There are so many different poems in the world, just like there are so many different people. You will connect with some poems more than you do others.

WML 2
GEN.U9.WML2

Have a Try

Demonstrate copying a simple poem (or part of a poem). Attach the prepared headings to the chart as you go.

> "The Caterpillar" is a funny poem that reminds me how tricky it can be to teach English. Watch how I copy part of this poem, placing the words exactly as the author did on the page. I will include the poet's name and the book it came from. I might illustrate it a bit, too.
>
> Now I need to write the title of the poem on the table of contents. Since this poem is on the third page, I will write the number *3*.

Summarize and Apply

Add the principle to the top of the chart. Summarize the learning and remind students that they will add to their poetry anthology by finding a poem that shows something about themselves.

> Today, read lots of poems. Take your time to find a poem that you connect with in some way. Be prepared to share the poem you chose and why you chose it. Copy the poem into your poetry anthology exactly as you see it on the page, and illustrate it. Include the author's name and the book title. Then add it to the table of contents page. If you finish early, continue to read more poems.

Confer

- During independent writing, move around the room to confer briefly with students about poems. Use prompts such as the following as needed.
  - *What does the poet make you think about? How does that connect to you and your life?*
  - *What words attracted your attention? How do those words connect to you and your life?*
  - *What do you notice about the way the poet placed the words on the page? Be sure you do exactly that when copying this poem.*

Share

Following independent writing, gather students in the meeting area to share their poems with a partner.

> Turn and talk to your partner. Read aloud the poem you chose and tell why you chose that particular poem.

Umbrella 9: Making Poetry Anthologies

WML3
GEN.U9.WML3

Writing Minilesson Principle
Respond to poems you collect.

Making Poetry Anthologies

You Will Need

- a diverse collection of poetry books and poems in which your students will see themselves, including one written on chart paper, such as "Meg McCoodle and Her Poodle" from *Mixed-Up Monsters and Confused Critters* by Mike Downs, from *Shared Reading Collection*
- sticky notes
- markers, colored pencils, crayons, and glue
- students' poetry anthologies

Academic Language / Important Vocabulary

- anthology
- poetry
- respond

Continuum Connection

- Notice and write about elements of the writer's craft: word choice, use of literary elements
- Create illustrations and writing that work together to express the meaning

---

GOAL

Create art or write words in response to poems you collect.

RATIONALE

Reading and discussing poems helps students develop an appreciation for the artistic language poets use. Each student will respond to an individual poem differently. Encouraging students to respond authentically to poetry through art or written words helps them to show their own understanding of a poet's language.

ASSESS LEARNING

- Observe students as they write and create art in response to the poems they collect.
- Look for evidence that they can use vocabulary such as *anthology*, *poetry*, and *respond*.

MINILESSON

To help students think about the principle, display a poem you have chosen, written on chart paper. Include the poet's name and the title of the book where you found the poem. Here is an example.

- Show the cover of *Mixed-Up Monsters and Confused Critters* by Mike Downs. Turn to the poem "Meg McCoodle and Her Poodle" in the book, and then read it from the chart paper. Invite students to read it with you a second time.

  > What are your thoughts about this poem?

- As students share their responses, write generative questions for their ideas on sticky notes as a way to list prompts for thinking about poems. Review the sticky notes and then place them next to the poem.

  > When you have a conversation about what you are thinking about a poem, you gain a better understanding of the message the poet is sharing.

- Next, demonstrate taking the students' ideas to create a written response to the poem. Write the response on chart paper as you think aloud.

  > Here is one way we could respond to this poem in writing. In your anthology, the poem will be on the left page, and the response will be on the right page.

The Writing Minilessons Book, Grade 3

Have a Try

Using the same poem, invite students to talk in trios about how they might respond to it with art. After they turn and talk, invite a few to share with the group.

> What might you sketch in response to this poem?

▶ Add new generative ideas to the chart and place small sketches around the poem or around the response.

Summarize and Apply

Summarize the learning and remind students that they will add to their poetry anthology in a specific way: by adding a poem and responding to it with writing and art.

> Sometimes you find a poem you connect with in some way, and you can write about it or show it in your art.

▶ Write the principle at the top of the chart.

> Today, take your time to read several more poems to find one that you connect with in some way. Be prepared to share the poem and why you chose that particular poem. Copy it into your poetry anthology exactly as you see it on the page. Then write the title and page number on the table of contents page. Finally, add your response and an illustration.

Confer

▶ During independent writing, move around the room to confer with students about the poems they have chosen. Use prompts such as the generative questions on the chart or the following as needed.
- *What does this poem make you think about?*
- *What does this poem make you feel? How could you write about that? How could you show that through illustrations?*
- *Be sure to copy the poem onto the left page and write your response on the right page.*

Share

Following independent writing, gather students in the meeting area in pairs to share their poems and responses.

> Read the poem you chose to your partner. Talk about why you picked that poem. Read your written response and show the art you created.

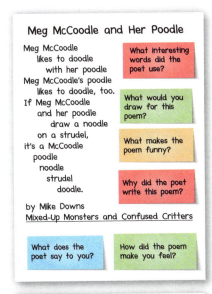

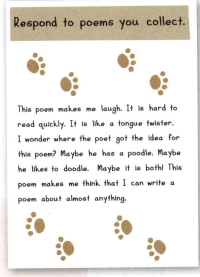

WML 4
GEN.U9.WML4

Writing Minilesson Principle
Write a poem in response to a poem.

Making Poetry Anthologies

You Will Need

- a diverse collection of poetry books and poems, including two chosen in advance, such as the following:
  - an excerpt from *The Rain Forest Rainbow* by Susan B. Katz, from *Shared Reading Collection*
  - "Camera" from *Flicker Flash* by Joan Bransfield Graham, from *Text Set: Genre Study: Poetry*
- chart paper or your poetry anthology prepared with a poem
- markers
- students' poetry anthologies
- To download the following online resource for this lesson, visit **fp.pub/resources**:
  - chart art (optional)

Academic Language / Important Vocabulary

- anthology
- poetry
- poet
- response

Continuum Connection

- Borrow the style or some words or expressions from a writer in writing about a text
- Write a variety of poems
- Write poems that convey feelings or images
- Use poetic language to communicate meaning
- Place words on a page to look like a poem

GOAL
Choose a poem and craft a poem in response.

RATIONALE
Reading and discussing poems helps students develop an appreciation for the artistic language of poets. Each student will respond to an individual poem differently. Encouraging students to respond authentically to poetry by writing their own poems in response provides support for them as they develop their voices as writers.

ASSESS LEARNING

- Observe whether students can articulate their connection to a poem.
- Look for evidence that they can use vocabulary such as *anthology*, *poetry*, *poet*, and *response*.

MINILESSON

To help students think about the principle, demonstrate writing a poem in response to a poem you have chosen in advance. Here is an example.

- Show the chart paper prepared with a poem (or your poetry anthology), such as page 8 of *The Rain Forest Rainbow*.
- Read the poem aloud twice and talk about your connection to it.

  I connect with this poem because I enjoy poems written about animals. The poet used words in Spanish, which adds interest and connects with me because I speak Spanish. I want to write a poem in response to this one. I want it to be similar in some ways to this poem.

- Demonstrate writing your own poem on the chart.

  I notice this poem about a jaguar and the other poems in the book begin with a word to describe an animal, so I will write "Tall is the African giraffe." In the next line the poet describes something that the jaguar does, so I will write about what a giraffe does. The last two lines begin with the Spanish word for the animal and then tell one other thing the animal does. I will add my name because I am the poet.

WML 4
GEN.U9.WML4

Have a Try

Use a different poem, such as "Camera" on page 22 of *Flicker Flash*. Read it aloud and invite students to talk in trios about what they notice.

> Turn and talk to your group. What do you notice about how this poem is written? What does this poem make you think about?

▸ After they turn and talk, invite a few students to share with the class. Then discuss crafting a response.

> What can you try to do that this writer did? How might you place the letters and words on the page? How might you illustrate your poem?

Summarize and Apply

Summarize the learning. Have students add a poem and craft a poem in response in their poetry anthologies.

▸ Write the principle at the top of the chart.

> During writing time today, write a poem in response to a poem. Copy the poem onto the left page of your poetry anthology. Write the poet's name and the book it came from. You can illustrate the poem. Add it to the table of contents.
>
> Then write your own poem in response on the right side of your anthology and illustrate it. Notice what the poet did in the poem, and think about how you can do that in your own poem. Add your own poem to the table of contents, too.

Write a poem in response to a poem.

Fierce is the spotted jaguar.
Narrow eyes squint to spy.
El Jaguar watches the world
perched on branches in the sky.
 by Susan B. Katz
 The Rain Forest Rainbow

Tall is the African giraffe.
Long neck reaches the treetops.
El Jirafa scans the land
while eating its favorite fruit.
 by Ms. Torres

Confer

▸ During independent writing, move around the room to confer briefly with students about their poetry anthology. Use prompts such as the following as needed.

- What does the poet say to you?
- What does the poet make you think about?
- How might you place words on the page for your own poem?
- What do you like about this poem? How might that work in your own poem?

Share

Following independent writing, gather students in the meeting area to share their poems.

> Who would like to share your poem and your response?

Umbrella 9: Making Poetry Anthologies

Assessment

After you have taught the minilessons in this umbrella, observe students as they explore making a poetry anthology. Use *The Fountas & Pinnell Literacy Continuum* to notice, teach for, and support student's learning as you observe their attempts at reading, writing, and responding to poetry.

- What evidence do you have of students' new understandings related to making a poetry anthology?
    - Are students choosing poems they connect with? Can they articulate why?
    - Are they able to craft simple poems engaging the elements they notice in a published poem?
    - Do they understand and use vocabulary such as *anthology*, *poetry*, *poet*, *table of contents*, and *respond*?
- In what other ways, beyond the scope of this umbrella, are students showing an interest in writing poetry?
    - Are they thinking about different types of poems (e.g., haiku, lyrical poems, shape poems)?
    - Are they noticing the world around them as inspiration for ideas?

Use your observations to determine the next umbrella you will teach. You may also consult Suggested Sequence of Lessons (pp. 605–622) for guidance.

EXTENSIONS FOR MAKING POETRY ANTHOLOGIES

- Create a poetry center where students can listen to poetry read aloud.
- Create a bulletin board or chart where students can display/write interesting words or phrases they notice while reading poetry.
- Provide opportunities for students to record themselves speaking original works of poetry.
- Provide opportunities for students to perform poems they have read or written.
- Find autobiographical information about various poets and share this with students. Giving "poet talks" can inspire students in their reading and writing of poetry.
- Have students study what can go on the back cover of a book so that they can make a back cover for their own poetry anthologies. Display students' anthologies face out on a rack in the classroom.

Writing Poetry

Umbrella 10

Minilessons in This Umbrella

- **WML1** Poems look and sound different from other kinds of writing.
- **WML2** Remove words to make your poem more powerful.
- **WML3** Use repeating words or phrases to make your writing interesting.
- **WML4** Use metaphors and similes to describe something.

Before Teaching Umbrella 10 Minilessons

These minilessons help students notice characteristics of poems that they can try out when they write poems on their own. The focus of this umbrella is to help students understand that poems have different characteristics and that poets make decisions about those characteristics when they write. You may want to teach CFT.U7: Making Powerful Word Choices alongside these lessons.

Prior to teaching these minilessons, provide opportunities for reading and talking about poetry, including those with rhyme, repetition, rhythm, and sensory language. Gather student poetry samples or write sample poems yourself or with the class. While Text Set: Genre Study: Poetry does not fall until later in the year if you are following the suggested *Interactive Read-Aloud Collection* sequence, there are individual poems within those texts that can be shared now with students as they begin writing poetry and read in more depth later. Use the books listed below from *Fountas & Pinnell Classroom™ Interactive Read-Aloud Collection* and *Shared Reading Collection*, or choose books from the classroom library that have poems or poetic language.

Interactive Read-Aloud Collection
Genre Study: Poetry

Old Elm Speaks: Tree Poems by Kristine O'Connell George

Splish Splash by Joan Bransfield Graham

Flicker Flash by Joan Bransfield Graham

Shared Reading Collection

The Rain Forest Rainbow by Susan B. Katz

The Backwards Poem Book by Mike Downs

Mixed-Up Monsters and Confused Critters by Mike Downs

As you read and enjoy these texts together, help students
- notice the way the words sound,
- observe the way the words look on the page, and
- notice sensory language.

Interactive Read-Aloud
Poetry

Shared Reading

Writer's Notebook

WML1
GEN.U10.WML1

Writing Minilesson Principle
Poems look and sound different from other kinds of writing.

Writing Poetry

You Will Need

- several mentor texts with poems or poetic language, such as the following:
  - *The Rain Forest Rainbow* by Susan B. Katz and *The Backwards Poem Book* by Mike Downs, from *Shared Reading Collection*
  - *Old Elm Speaks* by Kristine O'Connell George, from Text Set: Genre Study: Poetry
- sticky notes
- chart paper prepared with a poem for this lesson
- chart paper and markers
- writer's notebooks

Academic Language / Important Vocabulary

- poem
- poet
- characteristic

Continuum Connection

- Understand poetry as a unique way to communicate about and describe feelings, sensory images, ideas, or stories
- Understand that poems may look and sound different from one another
- Understand that a writer can create different types of poems: e.g., rhyming poems, unrhyming poems

GOAL

Notice and understand the characteristics of poetry and try writing a poem.

RATIONALE

Helping students recognize some characteristics of poetry will widen their understanding of the decisions they can make when writing a poem (e.g., word choice, rhymes, layout).

WRITER'S NOTEBOOK/WRITING FOLDER

Students will start writing their poems in their writer's notebooks. Finished poems can be copied into students' poetry anthologies.

ASSESS LEARNING

- Observe students' writing behaviors for evidence of trying out in their own poems what they have noticed in other poems.
- Look for evidence that students can use vocabulary such as *poem*, *poet*, and *characteristic*.

MINILESSON

To help students think about the minilesson principle, use mentor texts that will help them notice some characteristics of poetry. If possible, show poems in an enlarged format so they can easily see the layout. Here is an example.

> As I share some poems, think about what you notice about how the poems look and sound.

- Show and read pages from a variety of poetry books. Some suggestions are listed below.
  - *The Rain Forest Rainbow*, page 6
  - *The Backwards Poem Book*, pages 6–8 and 20–23
  - *Old Elm Speaks*, pages 8, 21, 41

- Guide the conversation to help students notice some characteristics of poetry. Encourage them to include characteristics learned through their prior experiences with poetry. Write each characteristic named on a sticky note and place it on chart paper.

> Poets write many different kinds of poems. When you are writing your own poems, you can choose the topic you write about, how the words will sound, and where you will place them on the page.

- Keep the chart posted as students continue writing poems throughout this umbrella.

The Writing Minilessons Book, Grade 3

WML1

GEN.U10.WML1

Have a Try

Invite students to turn and talk about characteristics of poetry.

▸ Display the prepared poem and read it aloud.

> What do you notice about this poem? Does it have any of the characteristics we listed on the chart? Turn and talk about the poem.

▸ After time for discussion, ask a volunteer to choose a sticky note and place it beside the poem. Repeat until all of the sticky notes with relevant characteristics have been placed.

Summarize and Apply

Summarize the learning. Remind students to use some of the characteristics listed on the chart when they write their poems.

> What can you say about poems as compared with other kinds of writing?

▸ Write the principle at the top of the chart.

> During writing time, you will start writing a poem in your writer's notebook. You can choose any topic. Think about how you want your poem to look and sound. Bring your poem to share when we meet later.

Confer

▸ During independent writing, move around the room to confer briefly with students about their poems. Use the following prompts as needed.
  - *What will your poem be about?*
  - *Will your poem rhyme?*
  - *Let's look at the chart and talk about what things you would like to include in your poem.*

Share

Following independent writing, gather students in the meeting area. Ask a few volunteers to share their poems.

> Who would like to share your poem or part of it?

> Let's look at the chart and think about what things _____'s poem includes.

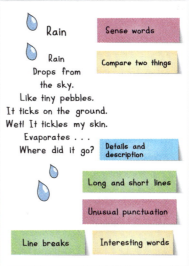

Section 2: Genres and Forms

Umbrella 10: Writing Poetry

247

WML2
GEN.U10.WML2

Writing Minilesson Principle
Remove words to make your poem more powerful.

Writing Poetry

You Will Need

- several mentor texts that have poetry with powerful language, such as the following:
  - *Splish Splash* by Joan Bransfield Graham, from Text Set: Genre Study: Poetry
  - *The Rain Forest Rainbow* by Susan B. Katz, from *Shared Reading Collection*
- chart paper prepared with a poem that has unnecessary words and some vague words
- chart paper and markers
- writer's notebooks

Academic Language / Important Vocabulary

- writing
- poem
- poet
- remove
- powerful

Continuum Connection

- Understand the importance of specific word choice in poetry
- Remove extra words to clarify the meaning and make writing more powerful
- Use language to show instead of tell
- Use language to create sensory images

GOAL

Use only the strongest words when writing poems.

RATIONALE

The power of a poem often lies in its economy of language and carefully chosen words. When students learn that poets think about each and every word they use in a poem and select only the ones that are most important, they learn how to make their own poems more powerful.

WRITER'S NOTEBOOK/WRITING FOLDER

Students will continue working on their poems in their writer's notebooks.

ASSESS LEARNING

- Observe whether students understand that writers select words carefully when they write poems.
- Look at students' poems. Are they using only the words that are necessary?
- Look for evidence that students can use vocabulary such as *writing*, *poem*, *poet*, *remove*, and *powerful*.

MINILESSON

To help students understand that poets are selective with word choice, use mentor and class examples and engage students in shared writing. Here is an example.

> Think about the words the poet uses in this poem.

- Read aloud page 8 in *Splish Splash*.

> What do you notice about the words?

- Guide them to notice that the writer has used just a few words, but they are carefully chosen and powerful.
- Repeat with page 4 in *The Rain Forest Rainbow*.
- Show and read the prepared poem.

> What do you notice about the words in this poem?

- Support a conversation to help students notice that the poem has a lot of words and that the words aren't very strong.

> After poets draft a poem, they read it—probably many times—and think about how it sounds. They listen for words that should be removed or replaced by a more descriptive word. They use only the words that are necessary and the most powerful.

Have a Try

Invite students to turn and talk about removing words from a poem to make the poem more powerful.

> Turn and talk about some ideas you have about words that could be removed or changed to make this poem more powerful.

▸ After time for discussion, use shared writing to write a new version of the poem that uses fewer and more powerful words.

Summarize and Apply

Summarize the learning. Remind students to think about removing or substituting some words in a poem to make it stronger. Write the principle at the top of the chart.

> During writing time, take a look at the poem you are working on in your writer's notebook and think about words you could remove or substitute to make the poem stronger. If you are starting a new poem, think carefully about the words you choose. Bring your poem to share when we meet later.

Remove words to make your poem more powerful.

Butterfly →	Queen Monarch
The butterfly has brightly colored wings.	Brightly colored wings flutter and fly.
The wings move fast and fly all around.	They're symmetrical, orange with black stripes.
They're exactly the same.	Gently she perches on a shimmery green leaf.
The wings are orange with black stripes.	
Softly she lands on a green leaf.	

Confer

▸ During independent writing, move around the room to confer briefly with students about their poems. Use the following prompts as needed.

- *Talk about the poem you are working on.*
- *Let's look at something you have written and think about the words you used.*
- *Are there any words that are not necessary? Cross them out to make your poem stronger.*

Share

Following independent writing, gather students in the meeting area to share their poems.

> Turn to your partner and share the poem you are working on.

▸ After partners share, select several students to share their poems with the whole group.

Umbrella 10: Writing Poetry

WML 3
GEN.U10.WML3

Writing Minilesson Principle
Use repeating words or phrases to make your writing interesting.

Writing Poetry

You Will Need

- mentor texts that have poetry with repeating words or phrases, such as *Mixed-up Monsters and Confused Critters* and *The Backwards Poem Book* by Mike Downs, from *Shared Reading Collection*
- chart paper prepared with a poem that has no repeating words
- chart paper and markers
- writer's notebooks

Academic Language / Important Vocabulary

- writing
- poem
- poet
- repeat
- word
- phrase

Continuum Connection

- Understand the difference between ordinary language and poetic language
- Understand the importance of specific word choice in poetry
- Use range of descriptive words to enhance meaning
- Use engaging titles and language

GOAL

Use repeating words or phrases to make poems more interesting.

RATIONALE

When students learn that poets sometimes repeat words or phrases to make poems more interesting, they begin to think about creative ways they can use language in their own poems.

WRITER'S NOTEBOOK/WRITING FOLDER

Students will continue to work on their poems in their writer's notebooks.

ASSESS LEARNING

- Notice whether students understand that writers sometimes repeat words or phrases in poems.
- Look at students' poems. Do they sometimes repeat words or phrases?
- Look for evidence that students can use vocabulary such as *writing*, *poem*, *poet*, *repeat*, *word*, and *phrase*.

MINILESSON

To help students understand that poems often use repeating words for effect, use mentor texts and class examples to model the process and engage in shared writing. Here is an example.

- Show and read aloud pages 12–13 in *Mixed-Up Monsters and Confused Critters*.

    What do you notice about this poem?

    What is it like to read the poem aloud?

- Guide students to recognize that the word *poodle* (and other words that rhyme with it) are repeated throughout the poem. Help them understand that the author probably repeated these rhyming words to make the poem more fun to read.

- Show and read aloud "The Caterpillar" on pages 20–23 in *The Backwards Poem Book*.

    What do you notice?

- Support students in recognizing that "has no" is used throughout the humorous poem to show that many words, like *caterpillar*, may have no connection to words they contain.

Have a Try

Invite students to turn and talk about using a repeated word or phrase to make a poem more interesting.

▸ Show and read the prepared chart paper.

> Think about how we could revise this poem by repeating a word or words. Turn and talk about that.

▸ After a short time for discussion, use shared writing to write a new poem using the repeated word or words.

Summarize and Apply

Summarize the learning. Remind students to think about repeating a word or phrase in their poems.

> How can you make your poems interesting and maybe fun to read?

▸ Write the principle at the top of the chart.

> During writing time, think about a word or phrase you might repeat in a poem you are working on in your writer's notebook. You can also start a new poem and repeat a word or phrase in it. Bring your poem to share when we meet again.

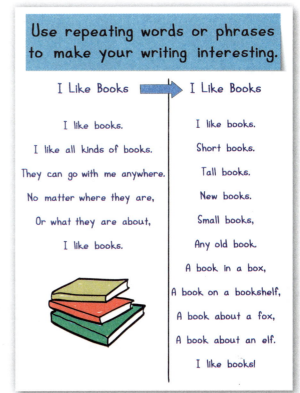

Confer

▸ During independent writing, move around the room to confer briefly with students about their poems. Use the following prompts as needed.

- *Tell me about the poem you are working on.*
- *What word or phrase are you thinking of repeating in your poem?*
- *Share how you used this repeating word.*

Share

Following independent writing, gather students in the meeting area. Ask a few volunteers to share their poetry.

> Who would like to share the poem you are working on?

> What do you notice about _____'s poem?

WML 4
GEN.U10.WML4

Writing Minilesson Principle
Use metaphors and similes to describe something.

Writing Poetry

You Will Need

- several mentor texts with metaphors and similes, such as the following from Text Set: Genre Study: Poetry:
  - *Flicker Flash* by Joan Bransfield Graham
  - *Old Elm Speaks* by Kristine O'Connell George
- chart paper prepared with a poem that has no figurative language
- chart paper and markers
- writer's notebooks

Academic Language / Important Vocabulary

- poem
- simile
- metaphor
- compare
- senses
- describe

Continuum Connection

- Understand the difference between ordinary language and poetic language
- Write poems that convey feelings or images
- Use poetic language to communicate meaning
- Use language to describe how something looks, smells, tastes, feels, or sounds
- Use language to create sensory images

GOAL

Notice and understand how to create sensory images and feelings in poetry.

RATIONALE

Encouraging students to use comparing language to convey sensory images and feelings in a poem expands the possibilities of what they can write about and how to write about it. If metaphors and similes are too much at once, you can teach two separate minilessons, one for metaphors and one for similes. Or, focus on similes if your class is not ready to write metaphors.

WRITER'S NOTEBOOK/WRITING FOLDER

Students will continue working on their poems in their writer's notebooks before copying the final version into their poetry anthologies.

ASSESS LEARNING

- Look at students' poems. Notice if they are trying to incorporate comparative language.
- Look for evidence that students can use vocabulary such as *poem*, *simile*, *metaphor*, *compare*, *senses*, and *describe*.

MINILESSON

Use examples of poems with metaphors and similes to help students recognize that poets use their senses to describe and compare. Here is an example.

- Read and show the poem on page 15 in *Flicker Flash*.

  How does the author describe the moon?

- Guide the conversation to help students notice the senses used to observe the moon (eyes) and the comparative language ("moon like a mirror," a simile).

  When two things are compared using the words *like* or *as*, it is called a simile. Listen as I read another poem. Is there a simile?

- Read and show page 23. Guide the conversation so students notice the senses used (touch) and the comparative language ("incubator is warm as a hen," a simile).

- Read and show page 21 in *Old Elm Speaks*.

  What do you notice?

  In this poem, a tree is compared to a horse, but the words *like* and *as* are not used. When *like* or *as* are not used to compare two things, it is called a metaphor.

- Repeat with page 41. Talk about how a metaphor is used to compare a tree to part of a ship.

Have a Try

Invite students to turn and talk about using their senses and comparative language to make a poem stronger.

- Show and read the prepared poem.

    This poem uses the senses to describe a day at an amusement park, but it could be better with some language that compares what the person is experiencing to something else. Turn and talk about some ways you could change this poem by using similes or metaphors.

- After a short time for discussion, use shared writing to write a new poem.

Summarize and Apply

Summarize the learning. Remind students to use their senses and comparative language in their poems.

    How can you make your poem interesting to read?

- Write the principle at the top of the chart.

    During writing time, work on a poem you have started or begin a new poem in your writer's notebook. Think about what you want your readers to imagine they can see, hear, smell, taste, and/or touch. Think about how you could compare one thing to another. Bring your poem to share when we meet later.

Use metaphors and similes to describe something.

Amusement Park	→	Amusement Park
I see fast rides.		The rollercoaster is a blur of lightning.
I hear people talking.		Voices like hundreds of chattering chipmunks.
I smell food.		Scents as salty as popcorn and as sweet as cotton candy enter my nose.
I taste pizza.		My tongue is a pepperoni factory.
I feel the wind.		The wind is like a lion's hot breath.
		My first day at the amusement park is like a dream.

Confer

- During independent writing, move around the room to confer briefly with students about their poems. Use the following prompts as needed.
    - *What are you writing about? What does it look (sound, smell, feel) like?*
    - *What words can you use to describe that?*
    - *What is something you could compare that to?*

Share

Following independent writing, gather students in the meeting area to share their poems.

    Who would like to share the poem you are working on?

    What do you notice about _____'s poem?

Umbrella 10   Writing Poetry

Assessment

After you have taught the minilessons in this umbrella, observe students in a variety of classroom activities. Use *The Fountas & Pinnell Literacy Continuum* to notice, teach for, and support students' learning as you observe their attempts at writing poetry.

- What evidence do you have of students' new understandings related to writing poetry?
  - Do students recognize that poems look and sound different from other kinds of writing?
  - Do they understand that they can remove words to make a poem stronger?
  - Do they sometimes use repeating words or phrases?
  - Do students' poems have examples of sensory and comparative language?
  - Are they using vocabulary such as *poem, poet, remove, repeat, words, phrases, senses, describe, compare, metaphor,* and *simile*?
- In what ways, beyond the scope of this umbrella, are students showing readiness for writing poetry?
  - Do they show an interest in writing different kinds of poetry?
  - Are they thinking about how to add to poems in order to make them more powerful?

Use your observations to determine the next umbrella you will teach. You may also consult Suggested Sequence of Lessons (pp. 605–622) for guidance.

EXTENSIONS FOR WRITING POETRY

- Place the words from a poem on word cards. Have students move around the words to create new ways of placing the words on a page.

- Go on a walk with students so they can make observations. Have them jot down some notes that they can use to write a poem.

- Provide opportunities to share poetry with students from other classrooms.

- Place a variety of picture and word (noun) cards in a basket to help students think of new topics for making poetry.

- If you are using *The Reading Minilessons Book, Grade 3* (Fountas and Pinnell 2019) you may choose to teach LA.U6: Studying Poetry or LA.U9: Analyzing the Writer's Craft.

Writing Different Kinds of Poems

Umbrella 11

Interactive Read-Aloud
Poetry

Minilessons in This Umbrella

WML1	Write a poem to show a feeling or an image.
WML2	Write a shape (concrete) poem.
WML3	Write a lyrical poem.
WML4	Write a poem for two voices.

Before Teaching Umbrella 11 Minilessons

Prior to teaching these minilessons, provide opportunities for students to listen to, read, and talk about many kinds of poetry, including those with repetition, rhyme, rhythm, and sensory language. Poetry is a form of writing that focuses on word choice and emotions and that helps readers see the world from the poet's perspective. You do not need to teach these lessons consecutively or even at the same time of the year; however, we recommend that you first teach GEN.U10: Writing Poetry so that students have a foundation of the characteristics of poetry and the role figurative language often plays in poems.

Use the books listed below from *Fountas & Pinnell Classroom™ Interactive Read-Aloud Collection* and *Shared Reading Collection,* or choose a variety of poetry books from the classroom library.

Shared Reading

Interactive Read-Aloud Collection

Genre Study: Poetry

Confetti: Poems for Children by Pat Mora

Flicker Flash by Joan Bransfield Graham

Splish Splash by Joan Bransfield Graham

Shared Reading Collection

The Rain Forest Rainbow by Susan B. Katz

Mixed-Up Monsters and Confused Critters by Mike Downs

Made for Mars: The Life of Aaron Yazzie by Susan B. Katz

As you read and enjoy these texts together, help students
- notice the poet's choice of words,
- observe the way the words are placed on the page, and
- notice the way the poems make them feel.

Writer's Notebook

Section 2: Genres and Forms

Umbrella 11: Writing Different Kinds of Poems

WML1
GEN.U11.WML1

Writing Minilesson Principle
Write a poem to show a feeling or an image.

Writing Different Kinds of Poems

You Will Need

- several mentor poems that invoke feelings or images, such as those in *Confetti: Poems for Children* by Pat Mora, from Genre Study: Poetry
- chart paper prepared with the poems you will be using for this lesson
- chart paper and markers
- writer's notebooks
- To download the following online resource for this lesson, visit **fp.pub/resources**:
  - chart art (optional)

Academic Language / Important Vocabulary

- poem
- poet
- feelings

Continuum Connection

- Understand poetry as a unique way to communicate about and describe feelings, sensory images, ideas, or stories
- Understand that poems may look and sound different from one another
- Understand the difference between ordinary language and poetic language
- Write poems that convey feelings or images

GOAL

Understand that poems can express feelings or create a mental image.

RATIONALE

When students learn that poetry can engage the readers' feelings and can create a mental image, they begin to think about word choice and can make choices about what they want their readers to feel when reading their poems.

WRITER'S NOTEBOOK/WRITING FOLDER

Have students reread their writer's notebooks for poem ideas and try out their poems in their writer's notebooks.

ASSESS LEARNING

- Observe whether students are choosing words that engage the readers' feelings or create a mental image.
- Look for evidence that students can use vocabulary such as *poem*, *poet*, and *feelings*.

MINILESSON

Before teaching, read and enjoy poetry with the students in your class. Use mentor texts and model the process of writing a poem that invokes feelings or images. Here is an example.

- Show and read "Abuelita's Lap" on page 21 in *Confetti: Poems for Children*.

  What feelings do you have as you listen to this poem?

  Turn and talk about how the poet, Pat Mora, caused you to have those feelings.

- Show and read "Colors Crackle, Colors Roar" on page 3 in *Confetti: Poems for Children*.

  What picture do you have in your mind as you listen to this poem?

  Writers can choose words and write them in a way that causes the readers to feel something or creates a picture in their minds. Notice what I do as I write a poem like that.

- Choose a topic that students can relate to and model the process of writing a poem that invokes feelings or a mental image. Read the poem when you finish.

  What do you notice about what I did?

- Guide the conversation to talk about the feelings and/or images students have while listening to your poem.

Have a Try

Invite students to turn and talk about writing poems that show feelings or images.

> Turn and talk about some ideas you have for writing a poem that shows feelings or helps readers make a picture in their minds.

▶ After time for a brief discussion, ask a few students to share their ideas.

Summarize and Apply

Write the principle at the top of the chart. Summarize the learning. Have students write a poem in their writer's notebooks that shows feelings or images.

> During writing time, start writing a poem. It can be about anything. Think about the feelings or images you want to show. You might use your senses to create an image—write about what you see, hear, smell, touch, or taste. You can also reread your writer's notebook for ideas. Bring your poem to share when we meet later.

Write a poem to show a feeling or an image.

August

Watching my summer friend go down the street
as her family glides away
One second
Two seconds
Three seconds
TIME, STOP!
Next June
too far away to count.

Confer

▶ During independent writing, move around the room to confer briefly with students. Invite them to talk about their poems. Use the following prompts as needed.

- *What will your poem be about?*
- *What do you think the readers might feel when reading your poem?*
- *What kind of a picture do you have in your mind? How can you let the readers know that?*

Share

Following independent writing, gather students in the meeting area to share their poems.

> Who would like to share the poem you are working on?

Umbrella 11: Writing Different Kinds of Poems

WML 2
GEN.U11.WML2

Writing Minilesson Principle
Write a shape (concrete) poem.

Writing Different Kinds of Poems

You Will Need

- several mentor texts with shape poems, such as *Flicker Flash* and *Splish Splash* by Joan Bransfield Graham from Genre Study: Poetry
- chart paper prepared with the poems you will be using for this lesson or a document camera
- chart paper and markers
- writer's notebooks

Academic Language / Important Vocabulary

- shape poem
- line break
- white space

Continuum Connection

- Understand the way print and space work in poems
- Understand that poems take a variety of visual shapes on a page
- Use line breaks and white space when writing poems
- Place words on a page to look like a poem

GOAL

Think about where to place the words on the page when writing a poem.

RATIONALE

When students learn to notice the shape of a poem, they learn to think about how the layout and white space can be used to add meaning to the poems they write. Use the term that you prefer, either *shape poem* or *concrete poem*.

WRITER'S NOTEBOOK/WRITING FOLDER

Have students reread their writer's notebooks for poem ideas and try out their poems in their writer's notebooks.

ASSESS LEARNING

- Notice whether students use line breaks, spacing, and word placement in their poems.
- Look for evidence that students can use vocabulary such as *shape poem*, *line break*, and *white space*.

MINILESSON

Before teaching, read and enjoy poetry with the students in your class. Use mentor texts and model writing a shape poem to help students think about the way the placement of print and space conveys meaning in poems. Here is an example.

- Show and read "Candle" on page 3 in *Flicker Flash*.

  What do you notice about how this poem looks?

- Engage students in a conversation about the line breaks, white space, and how the shape and placement of the words add meaning to the poem. Prompt the discussion as needed. Here are a few suggestions.

  - *What does the poem look like?*
  - *How does the choice of writing connect to the topic of the poem?*
  - *What do you notice about the line breaks (white space)?*
  - *What words does the writer choose to help you understand the message?*

- Repeat with several more shape poems from *Flicker Flash* and *Splish Splash*.

  I am going to make a shape poem. Notice what I do.

- Choose a topic that is familiar to students and think aloud as you make a shape (concrete) poem.

  What do you notice about how I wrote my poem?

Have a Try

Invite students to turn and talk about writing shape poems.

> A shape poem can be about anything. Turn and talk about an idea you have for writing a shape poem. Tell your partner how you could arrange the words on the page.

▸ After time for discussion, ask a few volunteers to share.

Summarize and Apply

Write the principle at the top of the chart. Summarize the learning. Have students try writing a shape poem in their writer's notebooks.

> During writing time, think about what you could write a shape poem about. Use the idea you talked about with your partner, find an idea in your writer's notebook, or think of a different idea. When you have an idea, start writing your shape poem. Think how you will place the words on the page. Bring your poem to share when we meet later.

Confer

▸ During independent writing, move around the room to confer briefly with students. Invite them to talk about their poems. Use the following prompts as needed.
- *What is your poem about?*
- *Tell how you decided to make a line break after this word.*
- *How does the white space add to the meaning of your poem?*
- *Describe how you arranged the words.*

Share

Following independent writing, gather students in the meeting area to share their poems.

> If you wrote a shape poem, hold it up so that everyone can see it.

▸ Choose several students to read their poems aloud.

Umbrella 11: Writing Different Kinds of Poems

WML3
GEN.U11.WML3

Writing Minilesson Principle
Write a lyrical poem.

Writing Different Kinds of Poems

You Will Need

- several mentor texts with lyrical poems, such as the following from *Shared Reading Collection*:
  - *The Rain Forest Rainbow* by Susan B. Katz
  - *Mixed-Up Monsters and Confused Critters* by Mike Downs
- chart paper and markers
- writer's notebooks

Academic Language / Important Vocabulary

- lyrical poem
- rhythm
- rhyme
- description
- song

Continuum Connection

- Understand that a writer can create different types of poems: e.g., rhyming poems, unrhyming poems
- Understand the importance of specific word choice in poetry
- Understand the difference between ordinary language and poetic language
- Understand that poems may look and sound different from one another

GOAL

Understand that poems can be songlike and have rhythm and sometimes rhyme.

RATIONALE

When students understand that poems can use rhythm in a way that sounds like a song, they are able to try out writing lyrical poetry on their own.

WRITER'S NOTEBOOK/WRITING FOLDER

Have students reread their writer's notebooks for poem ideas and try out their poems in their writer's notebooks.

ASSESS LEARNING

- Observe whether students are using rhythm and sometimes rhyme when they write poetry.
- Look for evidence that students can use vocabulary such as *lyrical poem*, *rhythm*, *rhyme*, *description*, and *song*.

MINILESSON

Before teaching, read and enjoy lots of poetry with the students. Use mentor texts and shared writing to help them think about the minilesson principle. Here is an example.

- Show and read the poems on pages 9–11 in *The Rain Forest Rainbow*. Use rhythm as you read so students can hear the lyrical, songlike quality of the poems.

  What do you notice about how these poems sound?

- Engage students in a conversation about the way the poems sound like songs. The rhythm and rhyme make them seem as if they could be set to music.

- Repeat with another example, such as pages 14–16 in *Mixed-Up Monsters and Confused Critters*.

  These are lyrical poems. Lyrical poems have a steady rhythm, and sometimes they rhyme. They are written in a way that reminds you of a song. They usually express the feelings of the poet or perhaps describe something the poet has observed. Let's think about how to write a lyrical poem.

- Choose a familiar topic and use shared writing to write a song or lyrical poem.

  One thing we have been talking a lot about is the weather, and we noticed how the clouds looked like they were dancing in the sky. That might make a good topic for a lyrical poem. What are some things you noticed about the clouds?

- As students share ideas, model how to begin a song or lyrical poem by choosing descriptive words and then writing them in a rhythmic way. Clapping the beats in a line can help with the rhythm of the words.

Have a Try

Invite students to turn and talk about writing lyrical poems.

> Think about an idea you have for writing a poem that sounds like a song. Tell your partner about your idea and talk about some descriptive words you might include.

▸ After time for a discussion, ask a few students to share ideas.

Summarize and Apply

Write the principle at the top of the chart. Summarize the learning. Have students try writing a lyrical poem in their writer's notebooks.

> During writing time, start to write a lyrical poem. It can be about anything. Think about descriptive words to use and about how you will arrange them so the poem sounds like a song. Bring your poem to share when we meet later.

Confer

▸ During independent writing, move around the room to confer briefly with students. Invite them to talk about their poems. Use the following prompts as needed.
  - Will your poem rhyme?
  - Read this page aloud so you can hear the rhythm.
  - How does this description help your readers make an image?
  - In what ways is this poem like a song?

Share

Following independent writing, gather students in the meeting area to share their poems.

> Share your poem with a partner. When you listen, think of feedback that could help your partner make the poem even better.

Umbrella 11: Writing Different Kinds of Poems

WML 4
GEN.U11.WML4

Writing Minilesson Principle
Write a poem for two voices.

Writing Different Kinds of Poems

You Will Need

- an example of a poem written for two voices, such as *Made for Mars: The Life of Aaron Yazzie* by Susan B. Katz, from *Shared Reading Collection*:
- two students prepared to read several pages of a poem for two voices
- chart paper and markers
- writer's notebooks

Academic Language / Important Vocabulary

- poet
- poem
- two voices
- point of view

Continuum Connection

- Understand the difference between ordinary language and poetic language
- Understand that poems may look and sound different from one another
- Use poetic language to communicate meaning
- Write a variety of poems

GOAL

Notice that a poem can be written in a way that is intended for two speakers.

RATIONALE

When students learn that there are different kinds of poems and that they can choose to write a poem in two voices, they begin to think about and try out writing poetry from multiple perspectives.

WRITER'S NOTEBOOK/WRITING FOLDER

Have students jot down ideas for a poem for two voices and then try writing the poem in their writer's notebooks.

ASSESS LEARNING

- Notice whether students recognize that poetry can be written from multiple perspectives and read by two people.
- Look for evidence that students can use vocabulary such as *poet*, *poem*, *two voices*, and *point of view*.

MINILESSON

Students will need their writer's notebooks for this lesson. To help students think about the minilesson principle, use mentor texts and shared writing to support them as they write a poem for two voices with a partner. Here is an example.

- Show and read the author's note on the title page of *Made for Mars*.

    The poet has shared that she wants two people to read this poem.

- Have the prepared students read a few pages.
- Guide a conversation with the volunteers to talk about how the placement of the print helps the readers know whose turn it is to read, in what order to read the words, and when the words should be read separately and when together.

    When you write a poem for two voices, you can show how two people might notice things in a different way or say things a little differently. Let's think about how a new poem for two voices might look.

- Choose a topic that is relevant to your students.

    In science, we have studied seeds from different fruits. Let's write a poem for two voices by using two fruits. One voice will be from the point of view of a person about to eat a peach and the other will be from the point of view of a person about to eat a cherry. First, we need to think about how to place the words on the page.

- Model writing for a few lines. Then use shared writing to complete the poem.

WML 4
GEN.U11.WML4

Have a Try

Invite students to turn and talk about writing poems for two voices.

▶ Have students sit by the partner they will work with to write a poem for two voices.

> In your writer's notebook, jot down some ideas for topics you might like to write about. Then share them with your partner.

▶ After time for discussion, ask partners to share their ideas. Support the conversation so each pair has an idea for a poem they will write together.

Summarize and Apply

Write the principle at the top of the chart. Summarize the learning. Have students write a poem for two voices in their writer's notebooks.

> During writing time, you and your partner will start writing a poem for two voices. It can be about anything. Think about the topic you want to write about and how you will place the words on the page. Bring your poem to share when we meet later.

Confer

▶ During independent writing, move around the room to confer briefly with students. Invite them to talk about their poems. Use the following prompts as needed.
- *What topic will you write about?*
- *Where will you place the words on the page?*
- *Are there words that both readers will say at the same time? How will you show that?*

Share

Following independent writing, gather students in the meeting area to share their poems.

▶ Select several pairs of students to read their poems for two voices.

> How did you write the poem so that you each knew when to read?

Umbrella 11: Writing Different Kinds of Poems

263

Umbrella 11: Writing Different Kinds of Poems

Assessment

After you have taught the minilessons in this umbrella, observe students in a variety of classroom activities. Use *The Fountas & Pinnell Literacy Continuum* to notice, teach for, and support students' learning as you observe their attempts at writing poetry.

- What evidence do you have of students' new understandings related to poetry?
  - Are students writing poems that show feelings or that create a mental image?
  - Do students use line breaks and white space effectively in their poems?
  - Are students able to incorporate rhythm and sometimes rhyme in poetry?
  - Can students write a poem for two voices?
  - Are they using vocabulary such as *image*, *shape poem*, *line break*, *white space*, *lyrical poem*, *rhythm*, *rhyme*, *description*, and *point of view*?
- In what ways, beyond the scope of this umbrella, are students using what they know about writing poetry?
  - Do they show an interest in trying out different ways to place words on a page when they write in different genres?
  - Are they thinking and talking about topics for poetry?

Use your observations to determine the next umbrella you will teach. You may also consult Suggested Sequence of Lessons (pp. 605–622) for guidance.

EXTENSIONS FOR WRITING DIFFERENT KINDS OF POEMS

- Students might have poems in their writer's notebook that they would like to polish and publish. They could include the finished poems in their poetry anthologies (GEN.U9: Making Poetry Anthologies).

- Repeat the format of these lessons by having students write a five-senses poem or a haiku.

- Have students share their poems in small groups. After they share, bring students back together and create a poem out of favorite lines from everyone's poems.

- In small groups, have students think and talk about choosing titles for their poems that connect to the meaning of the poems.

- Download rubrics from the online resources (fp.pub/resources) to help you and your students evaluate how well they are able to apply the concepts in these lessons..

Making Picture Books

Umbrella 12

Minilessons in This Umbrella

- **WML1** Notice the qualities of picture books you love.
- **WML2** Plan what to put on each page.
- **WML3** Make decisions about what you will say with words and show with pictures.
- **WML4** Choose where to place the pictures and words.

Before Teaching Umbrella 12 Minilessons

Before learning about making picture books, students will benefit from having heard and read lots of fiction and nonfiction picture books. In addition, it will be helpful for them to have experienced at least some of the writer's notebook minilessons in the Writing Process section. When students make their own books, they can use plain paper or any of the paper templates from the online resources that are appropriate.

Before they start making their picture books, it will be important for students to have already read through the ideas in their writer's notebooks and chosen a topic. For mentor texts, consider the following picture books from *Fountas & Pinnell Classroom™ Interactive Read-Aloud Collection*, or choose picture books from the classroom library.

Interactive Read-Aloud Collection
Sharing Our World: Animals
And So They Build by Bert Kitchen

Ape by Martin Jenkins

I Love Guinea Pigs by Dick King-Smith

The Importance of Kindness
Enemy Pie by Derek Munson

Connecting Across Generations: Family
Mooncakes by Loretta Seto

Sitti's Secrets by Naomi Shihab Nye

As you read and enjoy these texts together, help students notice that
- picture books that they love have certain qualities that increase enjoyment,
- there are words and/or pictures on every page,
- the words and the pictures make sense with each other, and
- the words and the pictures are placed in different ways on the page.

Interactive Read-Aloud
Animals

Kindness

Family

Writer's Notebook

WML1
GEN.U12.WML1

Writing Minilesson Principle
Notice the qualities of picture books you love.

Making Picture Books

You Will Need

- several familiar fiction and nonfiction picture books, such as the following:
  - *Enemy Pie* by Derek Munson, from Text Set: The Importance of Kindness
  - *Mooncakes* by Loretta Seto, from Text Set: Connecting Across Generations: Family
  - *And So They Build* by Bert Kitchen and *Ape* by Martin Jenkins, from Text Set: Sharing Our World: Animals
- chart paper and markers
- two familiar picture books for each pair of students
- sticky notes
- writer's notebooks

Academic Language / Important Vocabulary

- topic
- qualities
- characteristics
- author
- pictures
- words

Continuum Connection

- Create illustrations and writing that work together to express the meaning
- Understand that when both writing and drawing are on a page, they are mutually supportive, with each extending the other

266

GOAL

Notice and name characteristics of picture books.

RATIONALE

By noticing the qualities of picture books, students begin to understand the decisions that authors and illustrators make to create their books and make them appealing. Choosing a topic for their own writing helps students learn the power of their own ideas and that drawing and writing can communicate their ideas to others. This supports students in viewing themselves as writers and illustrators.

WRITER'S NOTEBOOK/WRITING FOLDER

Students can record what they notice about picture books in their writer's notebooks.

ASSESS LEARNING

- Observe for evidence of what students understand about picture books.
- Look for evidence that students can use vocabulary such as *topic*, *qualities*, *characteristics*, *author*, *pictures*, and *words*.

MINILESSON

This minilesson is intended as an exploration of picture books. Students will not begin creating picture books today. To help them notice characteristics of picture books, use familiar mentor texts in which both the pictures and the words play important roles. Here is an example.

- Display familiar books, such as *Enemy Pie* and *Mooncakes*, and show the pages to prompt discussion. Guide the conversation to help students notice characteristics of picture books.

  Here is a picture book that we love. What do you notice about this book?

- Write students' noticings on the chart paper. Use one or more of the following prompts to keep the discussion moving:
  - *What do you like about this book? Why?*
  - *What do you notice about the illustrations?*
  - *Where did the illustrator place the illustration on this page?*
  - *What kind of characters did the author create?*

- Repeat this process with a nonfiction picture book, such as *And So They Build*. Use relevant prompts from above and/or one or both of these prompts about nonfiction books to further the discussion.
  - *What did the author write about?*
  - *What makes this book interesting to read?*

The Writing Minilessons Book, Grade 3

Have a Try

Invite students to turn and talk about the qualities of a nonfiction picture book, such as *Ape*.

> Turn and talk about the qualities of this picture book. What do you notice?

▸ After time for discussion, ask a few students to share. Add new ideas to the chart.

Summarize and Apply

Summarize the lesson. Remind students that they can make many types of picture books.

> Writers read lots of books that help them think about what to write. Today, you and a partner will look at two picture books and think about their characteristics. Write what you notice on sticky notes and mark the pages with them. If you are the one who writes the sticky notes, add them to your writer's notebook after you share with the class. If you are not the one who writes the sticky notes, write your notes in your writer's notebook.

Qualities of Picture Books We Love

- Clearly drawn illustrations
- Pictures that add to or match the words
- Pictures of the setting and the characters
- Illustrations placed in a variety of places on the page
- Words placed in a variety of places on the page
- Story has a beginning, a series of events, and an ending
- Dialogue
- Interesting characters that are similar to us
- Parts that are funny, happy, or sad
- Teach us information
- Interesting topic and facts

Confer

▸ During independent writing, move around the room to confer briefly with as many pairs as time allows. Sit side by side with them and invite them to talk about how they can implement what they have noticed in their own picture books. Use the following prompts as needed.

- *What do you notice the author/illustrator did in this book?*
- *What do you notice the illustrator did with the pictures in this book?*
- *What do you notice the writer did with the print in this book?*

Share

Following independent writing, gather students in the meeting area to share their findings.

> Who would like to share what you noticed about picture books today?

> What will you think about as you prepare to make your own picture book?

Umbrella 12: Making Picture Books

WML 2
GEN.U12.WML2

Writing Minilesson Principle
Plan what to put on each page.

Making Picture Books

You Will Need

- familiar fiction and nonfiction picture books, such as the following:
  - *Sitti's Secrets* by Naomi Shihab Nye, from Text Set: Connecting Across Generations: Family
  - *Ape* by Martin Jenkins, from Text Set: Sharing Our World: Animals
- chart paper and markers
- writer's notebooks

Academic Language / Important Vocabulary

- narrative
- page
- plan
- order

Continuum Connection

- Present ideas clearly and in a logical sequence
- Tell one part, idea, event, or group of ideas on each page of a book
- Arrange information in a logical way so that ideas build on one another
- Plan and organize information for the intended readers

GOAL

Make decisions about what text and illustrations to put on each page.

RATIONALE

When students learn that part of making a book is planning what goes on each page, they naturally begin to organize their thoughts and ideas before writing. They also realize that fiction stories have many parts and nonfiction books have many facts, so they must make the decision about what to draw and write on each page.

WRITER'S NOTEBOOK/WRITING FOLDER

Students can sketch the plans for their picture book pages in their writer's notebooks.

ASSESS LEARNING

- Notice whether students' decisions about what goes on each page communicate their ideas effectively.
- Look for evidence that students write about one idea or group of ideas on a page.
- Observe whether students add pictures to support the corresponding text on each page.
- Look for evidence that students can use vocabulary such as *narrative*, *page*, *plan*, and *order*.

MINILESSON

To help students think about the minilesson principle, use mentor texts with pictures to show how authors make logical decisions about which part of a story or piece of information to put on each page. Here is an example.

- Display *Sitti's Secrets*, and briefly review the story.

   Before Naomi Shihab Nye wrote this book, her first decision was to choose what story she wanted to tell.

- Write the heading *Planning a Narrative Book* on chart paper, and under it write the first step.

- Continue discussing the author's thought process as you share the book, adding each step to the chart.

   Narrative writing is story writing. There are many parts to this story. What did the author think about when deciding which part to put first, second, and so on?

   What do you notice about what the author decided to put on each page? What do you notice about the text and the illustrations?

- You may want to point out that sometimes an idea can extend over a few pages. Remind students that if they have a lot to tell about something, they can use or add another page.

The Writing Minilessons Book, Grade 3

Have a Try

Invite students to turn and talk to a partner about the steps they would use to plan the pages of a nonfiction picture book, such as *Ape*.

> What do you think the author thought about as he planned this book? Turn and talk to your partner about that.

- After time for discussion, ask a few volunteers to share. Create a second column on the chart for the steps in planning an informational book. Guide the conversation as needed.

Summarize and Apply

Write the principle at the top of the chart. Summarize the lesson. Remind students to plan what goes on each page of their books.

> Today before you begin writing, plan what will go on each page of your picture book. You can sketch your plans in your writer's notebook. Be prepared to share your topic and your plan for writing when we come back together.

Plan what to put on each page.

Planning a Narrative Book	Planning an Informational Book
Think of a story.	Think of a topic.
Think about the order.	Think about the facts you know.
Put each part of the story on its own page.	Put each type of fact on its own page.
Make sure your pictures match your words.	Make sure your pictures match your words.

Confer

- During independent writing, move around the room to confer briefly with as many individual students as time allows. Sit side by side with them and invite them to talk about making books. Use the following prompts as needed.
  - Tell the story (about the topic) from your notebook that you chose to make a book about.
  - What will you put on the first page? on the next page?
  - What will you draw for this part of the story (to share this information)?
  - What words could go with that drawing?

Share

Following independent writing, gather students in the meeting area to share their writing.

> With a partner, share the book you are working on. Tell how you planned what to write and draw on each page.

Umbrella 12: Making Picture Books

WML3
GEN.U12.WML3

Writing Minilesson Principle
Make decisions about what you will say with words and show with pictures.

Making Picture Books

You Will Need

- familiar fiction and nonfiction picture books, such as the following:
  - *Mooncakes* by Loretta Seto, from Text Set: Connecting Across Generations: Family
  - *I Love Guinea Pigs* by Dick King-Smith, from Text Set: Sharing Our World: Animals
- chart paper and markers
- writer's notebooks and writing folders
- To download the following online resource for this lesson, visit **fp.pub/resources**:
  - chart art (optional)

Academic Language / Important Vocabulary

- illustrations
- decision

Continuum Connection

- Use drawings to add information to, elaborate on, or increase readers' enjoyment and understanding
- Create illustrations and writing that work together to express the meaning
- Understand that when both writing and drawing are on a page, they are mutually supportive, with each extending the other
- Create drawings that are related to the written text and increase readers' understanding and enjoyment

GOAL

Make decisions about how to communicate information and ideas in pictures and words.

RATIONALE

As you teach students how to make decisions about communicating information and ideas in pictures and words, they begin to view themselves as writers and illustrators with the power to make intentional choices in their writing.

WRITER'S NOTEBOOK/WRITING FOLDER

Have students refer to the plans for their picture books in their writer's notebooks and keep the drafts in their writing folders.

ASSESS LEARNING

- Look for evidence that students add pictures and words to the page that are mutually supportive.
- Look for evidence that students can use vocabulary such as *illustrations* and *decision*.

MINILESSON

To help students think about the minilesson principle, use mentor texts to demonstrate deciding what to say in words and what to include in the pictures. Here is an example.

- Show and read aloud pages 7–8 of *Mooncakes*.

  The author wrote about the family's backyard. The illustrator decided to show more about the backyard by adding the teapot, the mooncakes, and the lanterns. Why do you think the author and illustrator made those decisions?

- Guide the conversation to help students recognize that authors and illustrators make decisions about how to share ideas on the page.

  The author's words describe what is happening and how the yard looks. The illustrator's drawings show more details. The words and the pictures work together to help you understand the story.

- Repeat this process with a nonfiction text, such as *I Love Guinea Pigs*. Show and read pages 5–6.

  How do the words and pictures work together to help you understand the information?

  The words say what guinea pigs look like, and the pictures show different types of guinea pigs. What questions might an author and illustrator ask themselves to decide how to write and illustrate a picture book?

- Add generative questions to the prepared chart.

The Writing Minilessons Book, Grade 3

Have a Try

Invite students to turn and talk about a story or informational text they are writing and illustrating.

> Turn and talk about a book you are writing. Your partner can ask you the questions on the chart to help you make decisions about what to write and draw on each page.

Summarize and Apply

Summarize the lesson. Remind students that they can make decisions about what to say with words and show with pictures. Write the principle at the top of the chart.

> Writers and illustrators ask themselves these two questions: "What do I want readers to see in their minds?" and "What do I want readers to see on the page?" Asking these questions makes sure that the words and pictures work together to help readers understand more.

▸ Add the equation to the chart.

> Today during writing time, continue working on your picture book. Be prepared to share your decision making when we meet later.

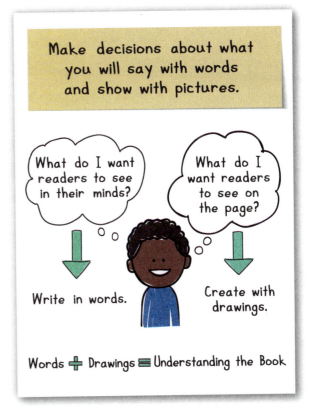

Confer

▸ During independent writing, move around the room to confer briefly with as many individual students as time allows. Sit side by side with them and invite them to talk about making books. Use the following prompts as needed.

- *Talk about what you will write on this page. What do you want to draw?*
- *At this part of the book, what do you want to help readers see in their minds? Say that in words. What do you want readers to see on the page? Draw that.*

Share

Following independent writing, gather students in the meeting area to share their writing.

> Talk about how you decided what to say in the words and what to include in the pictures.

WML 4
GEN.U12.WML4

Writing Minilesson Principle
Choose where to place the pictures and words.

Making Picture Books

You Will Need

- familiar nonfiction and fiction picture books, such as the following:
  - *I Love Guinea Pigs* by Dick King-Smith, from Text Set: Sharing Our World: Animals
  - *Sitti's Secrets* by Naomi Shihab Nye, from Text Set: Connecting Across Generations: Family
- chart paper and markers
- three examples of page layout options prepared in advance on 8" x 11" paper
- tape
- writer's notebooks and writing folders
- To download the following online resources for this lesson, visit **fp.pub/resources**:
  - paper templates (optional)

Academic Language / Important Vocabulary

- author
- illustrator
- illustrations
- decide
- decisions

Continuum Connection

- Arrange print on the page to support the text's meaning and to help the reader notice important information
- Use layout of print and illustrations to convey the meaning of a text

GOAL

Make decisions about where to place the pictures and words on the page in picture books.

RATIONALE

When you teach students how published authors make decisions about where to place pictures and words on the page, the students begin to see themselves as writers and illustrators that can make decisions about their writing. They also learn that intentional placement helps the reader understand and enjoy their book.

WRITER'S NOTEBOOK/WRITING FOLDER

Have students refer to the plans for their picture books in their writer's notebooks and keep the drafts in their writing folders.

ASSESS LEARNING

- Observe whether students make decisions about where to place the pictures and words within their picture books.
- Look for evidence that students can use vocabulary such as *author*, *illustrator*, *illustrations*, *decide*, and *decisions*.

MINILESSON

To help students think about the minilesson principle, use fiction and nonfiction picture books to demonstrate different ways authors decide to place the illustrations and the words. Here is an example.

- Show and read aloud pages 1 and 10 in *I Love Guinea Pigs*.

  What do you notice about the decisions the author and illustrator made about where to put the words and the pictures on these two pages?

- Have students share their ideas. Tape the prepared examples to the chart and label them.

- Repeat this process with a fiction book, such as pages 1–2 in *Sitti's Secret*, taping the example to the chart.

WML 4
GEN.U12.WML4

Have a Try

Invite students to talk to a partner about the book they are writing. Students may find this easier with access to their writing folders.

> What are you planning to draw and write next? Where will you place the illustrations and the words? Turn and talk to your partner about that.

▸ After time for discussion, ask volunteers to share.

Summarize and Apply

Summarize the lesson. Remind students to make decisions about where to place words and pictures on each page in their books.

> What decisions will you need to make about the words and the pictures in your book?

▸ Write the principle at the top of the chart. Show students the different types of paper they can choose: paper templates from online resources, blank paper, and other options you think will support them as writers.

> Today as you write and illustrate, think about the plan you made in your writer's notebook for what you will write and draw on each page of your book. Decide where on the page you will place the words and pictures. Bring your book when we meet later.

Choose where to place the pictures and words.

One large illustration, with writing above and below it.

Several small illustrations, with writing beside them.

One large illustration, with words next to it.

Confer

▸ During independent writing, move around the room to confer briefly with as many individual students as time allows. Sit side by side with them and invite them to talk about making picture books. Use the following prompts as needed.

- *Talk about what you will write and draw on this page. Where will you write the words? Where will you draw the pictures? Why did you make that decision?*

Share

Following independent writing, gather students in the meeting area to share their writing. If you have previewed student writing, identify students who made decisions that differ from those on the chart. Have them share.

> Let's discuss your decisions about where to write the words and place the pictures.

Umbrella 12: Making Picture Books

Assessment

After you have taught the minilessons in this umbrella, observe students as they make books. Use *The Fountas & Pinnell Literacy Continuum* to notice, teach for, and support students' learning as you observe their attempts at writing.

- What evidence do you have of students' new understandings related to making picture books?
  - Are students able to describe and execute some of the characteristics of picture books?
  - After choosing a topic to write about, are students able to plan what will go on each page of their book?
  - Do you see evidence of thoughtful decision making in what students choose to write in the words, what to include in the illustrations, and where to place them on the pages?
  - Do they show evidence of understanding that drawing and writing are mutually supportive and help to extend one another?
  - Are they using vocabulary such as *topic*, *qualities*, *characteristics*, *author*, *pictures*, *words*, *page*, *plan*, *order*, *illustrations*, *illustrator*, *decide*, and *decision*?
- In what ways, beyond the scope of this umbrella, are students showing an interest in making books?
  - Are they thinking about different types of books they would like to make?
  - Are they showing an interest in adding details to illustrations or adding dialogue?

Use your observations to determine the next umbrella you will teach. You may also consult Suggested Sequence of Lessons (pp. 605–622) for guidance.

EXTENSIONS FOR MAKING PICTURE BOOKS

- Gather several books by the same author to show that a writer can write more than one book.
- Gather together a guided writing group of several students who need support with the same aspect of making picture books.
- This umbrella can be extended by teaching about choosing the type of book to make by thinking about purpose and audience (see WPS.U5: Thinking About Purpose, Audience, and Genre/Form).

Making Biographical Multimedia Presentations

Umbrella 13

Minilessons in This Umbrella

- **WML1** Choose and research a subject.
- **WML2** Organize and write the words for your slides.
- **WML3** Add pictures, sound, and video to make your presentation interesting.
- **WML4** Practice and present your presentation.

Before Teaching Umbrella 13 Minilessons

A slide presentation allows for multimodal composition because it can include a combination of words, images, video, and audio. In each lesson, you will use shared writing to work collaboratively with students to create a class biographical multimedia presentation. (Alternatively, display a model multimedia presentation that you have created and guide students to notice the choices you made.) During independent writing time, students will have the opportunity to create their own biographical multimedia presentations about a person they choose. Consider engaging the help of faculty in charge of the technology in your school to assist students in using a slideshow program.

Depending on the technology available in your classroom, you may choose to have students make their presentations directly in slideshow software or on paper or poster board (using one page per slide). You might also have students create rough drafts of their presentations on paper and later convert them to digital presentations.

Before teaching this umbrella, it would be helpful to have taught GEN.U6: Making Informational Books to give students a sense of organization and structure. In addition, read aloud a variety of biographies to provide ideas for presentation subjects. You might use the following texts from *Fountas & Pinnell Classroom™ Interactive Read-Aloud Collection* or biographies from your classroom library.

Interactive Read-Aloud Collection

Genre Study: Biography

Nobody Owns the Sky: The Story of "Brave Bessie" Coleman by Reeve Lindbergh

Odd Boy Out: Young Albert Einstein by Don Brown

Magic Trash: A Story of Tyree Guyton and His Art by J. H. Shapiro

The Tree Lady: The True Story of How One Tree-Loving Woman Changed a City Forever by H. Joseph Hopkins

Wangari Maathai: The Woman Who Planted Millions of Trees by Franck Prévot

As you read and enjoy these and other biographies together, help students

- talk about which people they find most interesting and why, and
- notice how the authors structure and present biographical information.

Interactive Read-Aloud
Biography

Writer's Notebook

WML1
GEN.U13.WML1

Writing Minilesson Principle
Choose and research a subject.

Making Biographical Multimedia Presentations

You Will Need

- several familiar biographies, such as those in Text Set: Genre Study: Biography
- chart paper and markers
- writer's notebooks

Academic Language / Important Vocabulary

- slide presentation
- multimedia
- biography
- research
- subject

Continuum Connection

- Choose topics that one knows about, cares about, or wants to learn about
- Make brief oral reports that demonstrate understanding of a topic
- Locate, evaluate, and analyze content using approved digital resources such as websites, databases, e-books, and apps

GOAL

Choose and research a biographical subject for a multimedia presentation.

RATIONALE

Before students can create a biographical multimedia presentation, they need to learn how to choose and research a subject that interests them. This minilesson will help them understand what kind of information to gather and where to find it.

WRITER'S NOTEBOOK/WRITING FOLDER

Students will take notes on their biographical subjects in their writer's notebooks.

ASSESS LEARNING

- Notice whether students are able to find information about their subjects that will make an interesting slide presentation.
- Look for evidence that they can use vocabulary such as *slide presentation*, *multimedia*, *biography*, *research*, and *subject*.

MINILESSON

To help students think about the minilesson principle, engage them in a discussion around choosing and researching a subject for a biographical slide presentation. Here is an example.

> Today, we're going to start to make a multimedia slide presentation together. A slide presentation is a special kind of presentation that you can make on a computer or on poster board. Each slide has information about the topic. You can use words, pictures, sound, and video to tell about the topic. Slide presentations can be about any topic, but we will make a biographical slide presentation. Like any biography, it is about the life of an important person. First, we will choose a subject for our presentation.

- Display several familiar biographies.

  > Who would be a good subject for a biographical slide presentation? Why?

- Invite students to agree on the subject that will be used.

  > Now that we've chosen a subject, the next step is to gather some information about our subject.

  > We can do some research on Einstein using books and websites. But we need to know what to look for. What kind of information might we include in a biographical slide presentation about Einstein?

- Record the beginning steps of making a slide presentation on the chart, generalizing them as necessary.

The Writing Minilessons Book, Grade 3

WML 1
GEN.U13.WML1

Have a Try

Invite students to talk to a partner about their ideas for a subject.

> We will make a biographical slide presentation together, and you will also make one on your own. Who is a famous person that you are interested in? Turn and talk to your partner about your ideas.

▸ After time for discussion, invite several students to share their ideas.

Summarize and Apply

Summarize the learning. Invite students to choose and start researching a subject.

> What are the first two things you should do to prepare a biographical slide presentation?

▸ Write the principle at the top of the chart.

> Today during writing time, choose a subject for your biographical slide presentation. Make sure to choose a person you find interesting and that you're excited to tell others about. Once you've chosen a subject, you can start to to do some research on your subject in books or on websites. Continue to do research on your person over the next few days. Write your notes in your writer's notebook.

Choose and research a subject.

- Choose an important or famous person.
- Research the person using books and websites.
- Look for information about —
  - Where and when the person was born
  - Childhood
  - Family
  - Why the person is important
  - Challenges the person overcame
  - Accomplishments

Confer

▸ During independent writing, move around the room to confer briefly with as many individual students as time allows. Sit side by side with them and invite them to talk about making a biographical slide presentation. Use prompts such as the following as needed.

- Whom would you like to make a slide presentation about?
- Why did you choose _____ for your slide presentation?
- Where might you be able to find information about _____?

Share

Following independent writing, gather students in the meeting area to talk about their subjects.

> Who is your subject? Why did you choose _____?

> Did you start your research? What have you learned?

Section 2: Genres and Forms

Umbrella 13: Making Biographical Multimedia Presentations

WML 2
GEN.U13.WML2

Writing Minilesson Principle
Organize and write the words for your slides.

Making Biographical Multimedia Presentations

You Will Need

- a subject for a class presentation (see WML1)
- a book about the subject, for example, *Odd Boy Out* by Don Brown, from Text Set: Genre Study: Biography
- a computer with slideshow software or several sheets of paper
- chart paper and markers
- writer's notebooks

Academic Language / Important Vocabulary

- slide presentation
- organize
- information
- subject

Continuum Connection

- Maintain a clear focus on the important or main ideas
- Present ideas and information in a logical sequence
- Have a clear beginning and conclusion
- Vary language according to purpose
- Make brief oral reports that demonstrate understanding of a topic
- Demonstrate understanding of a topic by providing relevant facts and details

GOAL

Plan what to write on each slide. Write ideas clearly with vocabulary appropriate to the subject.

RATIONALE

As students begin to make their slides, they need to think about how best to present the information to the audience. They need to organize the information logically. They also need to consider how they use writing conventions and be aware that on a slide some different conventions are followed. Using fewer words on slides makes it easier for the audience to focus on the meaning, so incomplete sentences and brief bulleted lists are used frequently.

WRITER'S NOTEBOOK/WRITING FOLDER

Students can draw a storyboard in their writer's notebooks to help them plan their slide presentations.

ASSESS LEARNING

- Notice whether students organize information in a logical sequence, focus on the main ideas, use content vocabulary, and follow the conventions for using print on slides.
- Look for evidence that they can use vocabulary such as *slide presentation*, *organize*, *information*, and *subject*.

MINILESSON

To help students think about the minilesson principle, use shared writing to guide them through the process of planning a slide presentation. Here is an example that focuses on Albert Einstein. Use slideshow software for this lesson, or plan the presentation on sheets of paper attached to chart paper.

> We decided to make a biographical slide presentation about Albert Einstein and talked about the kind of information we might include about him. Today we will start to write the words for our slides. First, let's think about how to organize the information. How might you organize information about a famous person? What might go at the beginning (in the middle, at the end)?

- Help students understand that biographical information is usually organized chronologically.

> What should we write about on the first slide of our presentation?
>
> The first slide could be about Einstein's early life–where and when he was born and who his family members were. I'll write *Einstein's Early Life* on the first slide so we'll remember what to write about.

- Use shared writing to plan a few more slides.

> On your slides, write the most important information with as few words as you can so that your audience can read the slides easily. You can add details as you talk about your slides.

Have a Try

Invite students to talk to a partner about what to write on the first slide.

> Now that we've thought about how to organize our presentation, we can begin to write the words for the slides. What do you think we should write on the first slide? Turn and talk to your partner about this.

▸ After students turn and talk, invite several pairs to share their ideas. Use the students' ideas to write the first slide. Help students notice that you are using bullet points and short, incomplete sentences.

Summarize and Apply

Write the principle at the top of a new sheet of chart paper. Summarize the learning, and invite students to start writing their slides.

> What did you learn today about making a slide presentation?

▸ Summarize students' responses on the chart paper.

> During writing time today, start to write the words for your slides. You might draw a storyboard in your writer's notebook and write your plans for the slides in the boxes. Look at the slide and the chart we made together. You can also ask me for help.

Confer

▸ During independent writing, move around the room to confer briefly with as many individual students as time allows. Sit side by side with them and invite them to talk about their slide presentations. Use prompts such as the following as needed.

- How will you organize the information for your slide presentation?
- What will you write about on the first (second, third) slide?
- How can you write the information using just a few words?
- Remember to focus on the main ideas. You can give more details when you talk about your slides.

Share

Following independent writing, gather students in the meeting area to talk about their slides.

> What did you write about on your slides today?

> How is writing a slide presentation different from (similar to) writing a book?

Einstein's Early Life	Einstein at School
• Born in Ulm, Germany, on March 14, 1879 • Parents: Hermann and Pauline Einstein • Younger sister: Maja • Moves to Munich at age of 4	
Einstein's Career	Why Einstein Is Important

Organize and write the words for your slides.

- Organize the information in time order—from the beginning of the person's life to the end.
- Decide what to write about on each slide.
- Use words that are appropriate for your subject.
- Use as few words as possible, but keep the meaning clear.
- Write lists.

Birth Childhood Young Adulthood Career Death

Umbrella 13: Making Biographical Multimedia Presentations

WML 3
GEN.U13.WML3

Writing Minilesson Principle
Add pictures, sound, and video to make your presentation interesting.

Making Biographical Multimedia Presentations

You Will Need

- the shared slide presentation started in WML2, with different kinds of media added (images, audio, and video)
- chart paper and markers
- writer's notebooks

Academic Language / Important Vocabulary

- slide presentation
- multimedia
- sound
- video

Continuum Connection

- Use graphics (e.g., charts, illustrations, or other digital media) as appropriate to communicate meaning or to enhance a presentation
- Use digital tools to create simple documents, multimedia products, presentations, and e-books and to share resources

---

GOAL

Enhance presentations with a variety of media (illustrations, images, or digital media).

RATIONALE

When students add visual and auditory media to a slide presentation, they begin to understand how writers make choices about how best to engage the audience in a multimedia presentation.

WRITER'S NOTEBOOK/WRITING FOLDER

Students will continue to use their writer's notebooks to plan their slide presentations.

ASSESS LEARNING

- Notice whether they choose appropriate media to enhance and/or clarify their written content.
- Look for evidence that students can use vocabulary such as *slide presentation*, *multimedia*, *sound*, and *video*.

MINILESSON

Before this lesson, add a variety of media to the class presentation started in this umbrella. Also, make sure you are familiar with how students can search for visual and auditory media safely, and decide how you will facilitate the process of helping them add it to their presentations. If students are preparing slides on paper or poster board, they could consider adding photos or playing a recording during the presentation. To help students think about the minilesson principle, display the prepared presentation and engage students in a discussion about the media you chose and why. Here is an example.

> You can add pictures, sound, and video, to your slide presentation to make it more interesting and to help people learn more about the topic. Adding video and/or sound to your slides makes it a multimedia presentation. I started to do that for our presentation about Albert Einstein.

▶ Display a slide to which you added an image.

> What did I add to this slide?
>
> Why do you think I added a photograph to this slide?
>
> What do you notice about where I put the photograph on the slide?

▶ Display a slide to which you added audio or video. Play the audio or video.

> What did I add to this slide?
>
> Why do you think I added sound (video) to this slide?
>
> What will the sound (video) help people understand?

Have a Try

Invite students to talk to a partner about their ideas for adding media.

> Think about your own slide presentation. What kinds of pictures, sounds, or videos could you add to your presentation to make it more clear or interesting? Turn and talk to your partner about your ideas.

▸ After time for discussion, invite several students to share their ideas. Record their ideas, generalizing them as necessary, on chart paper.

Summarize and Apply

Write the principle at the top of the chart. Summarize the learning and remind students to think about how they might use pictures, sound, and video to make their presentations more interesting.

> Today during writing time, think about the pictures, sound, and video you could add to your presentation to make it more interesting. Make notes of your ideas in your writer's notebook.

▸ The amount of time necessary for students to add media to their presentations will depend on the technology available in your classroom.

Confer

▸ During independent writing, move around the room to confer briefly with as many individual students as time allows. Sit side by side with them and invite them to talk about their slide presentations. Use prompts such as the following as needed.

- What could you add to this slide to help your audience better understand _____?
- Would a picture, sound, or video work better on this slide? Why?
- What could you search for to find that?
- Where on the slide are you going to put that photograph? Why?

Share

Following independent writing, gather students in the meeting area to talk about their slide presentations.

> What pictures, sound, or video did you add to your slide presentation today?
>
> Why did you decide to add that?

Einstein's Early Life

- Born in Ulm, Germany, on March 14, 1879
- Parents: Hermann and Pauline Einstein
- Younger sister: Maja
- Moves to Munich at age of 4

"I have no special talents. I am just passionately curious."

Add pictures, sound, and video to make your presentation interesting.

Pictures
- The person at different ages
- The person's family
- The person's artwork, inventions, or other creations
- Newspaper article about the person

Sounds
- A quote from the person
- Discussion of the person's work
- Music written by the person

Videos
- An interview with the person
- The person doing something important
- A news clip about the person

Umbrella 13: Making Biographical Multimedia Presentations

WML 4
GEN.U13.WML4

Writing Minilesson Principle
Practice and present your presentation.

Making Biographical Multimedia Presentations

You Will Need

- a completed multimedia presentation (see WML3)
- index cards with prepared notes for the presentation
- chart paper and markers
- blank index cards
- writing folders
- To download the following online resource for this lesson, visit **fp.pub/resources**:
  - chart art (optional)

Academic Language / Important Vocabulary

- slide presentation
- notes
- practice
- present

Continuum Connection

- Have a plan or notes to support the presentation
- Speak about a topic with enthusiasm
- Tell stories and present information in an interesting way
- Show confidence when presenting
- Vary speaking voice for emphasis

GOAL

Prepare notes and present the topic with enthusiasm, confidence, and a strong voice.

RATIONALE

When students prepare notes for and practice their slide presentations, they are better able to communicate their ideas effectively and engage an audience.

WRITER'S NOTEBOOK/WRITING FOLDER

Students can keep printouts of their slides or their index cards in their writing folders.

ASSESS LEARNING

- Notice if students refer to notes, speak with enthusiasm and confidence, and vary their speaking voice for emphasis.
- Look for evidence that they can use vocabulary such as *slide presentation*, *notes*, *practice*, and *present*.

MINILESSON

To help students think about the minilesson principle, model presenting a slide presentation and engage students in a discussion about what they noticed. Here is an example.

- Display the completed slide presentation.

  We worked together to create this biographical slide presentation about Albert Einstein. Before class, I practiced the presentation and now I'm going to present it to you. You will be my audience. Watch what I do.

- Present the presentation, modeling speaking with confidence and enthusiasm, referring to notes, and varying your speaking voice for interest and emphasis.

  What did you notice about how I presented our slide presentation?

- Use questions such as the following, as needed, to prompt students' thinking:
  - *What did you notice about how I spoke?*
  - *How fast or slow (quietly or loudly) did I speak?*
  - *Did I read from the slides?*
  - *How did I remember what to say?*
  - *Did I change my voice when I said certain words? How?*
  - *Where did I look?*

- If students mention looking at the audience, take into consideration that some students may not be comfortable with establishing or able to establish eye contact because of cultural reasons or for other reasons.

WML 4
GEN.U13.WML4

Have a Try

Invite students to talk to a partner about how to present a slide presentation.

> Turn and talk to your partner about two things: How will you prepare to present your slide presentation? What will you remember to do when you are presenting?

- After time for discussion, invite several pairs to share their thinking. Record responses on chart paper.

Summarize and Apply

Write the principle at the top of the chart. Summarize the learning. Help students practice their presentations. They can write their notes on printouts of the slides or on index cards.

> During writing time today, get ready to present your slide presentation. Make notes to help yourself remember what you want to say. Then practice your presentation with a partner or with me. When we meet later, some of you will have the chance to present to the whole class.

Practice and present your presentation.
- Write notes for the main ideas you want to talk about.
- Practice your presentation before presenting.
- Look at your notes to help remember what to say.
- Speak clearly.
- Speak loudly enough for your audience to hear you, but not too loudly.
- Speak at the right speed—not too fast or too slow.
- Change your voice to show that an idea is important.
- Look at your audience.
- Sound excited and interested!

Confer

- During independent writing, move around the room to confer briefly with as many individual students as time allows. Sit side by side with them and invite them to talk about and practice their slide presentations. Use prompts such as the following as needed.
  - *What do you want to say about this slide?*
  - *What can you write to remember what you want to talk about?*
  - *Can you slow down a little bit? I want to make sure I don't miss anything!*

Share

Following independent writing, gather students in the meeting area to start sharing their slide presentations. Set aside a block of time for students to present, or have a few students present each day for several days. Follow the presentations with questions for reflection.

> Does anyone have any questions or comments for _____?

> What did you notice about how _____ gave her presentation?

Umbrella 13: Making Biographical Multimedia Presentations

Umbrella 13: Making Biographical Multimedia Presentations

Assessment

After you have taught the minilessons in this umbrella, observe students as they create and present their slide presentations. Use *The Fountas & Pinnell Literacy Continuum* to notice, teach for, and support students' learning as you observe their written and oral communication skills.

- What evidence do you have of students' new understandings related to making a biographical multimedia presentation?
  - Do students choose and research people they are interested in?
  - Is the information on the slides presented in a logical sequence?
  - Are the ideas written in clear language with vocabulary appropriate to the subject?
  - How effective is students' use of images, video, and sound?
  - Do they practice their presentations and prepare notes?
  - Do they present with enthusiasm, confidence, and a strong voice?
  - Do they understand and use vocabulary such as *slide presentation*, *multimedia*, *biography*, *subject*, *research*, and *present*?
- In what other ways, beyond the scope of this umbrella, are students experimenting with different modes of composition?
  - Are they writing letters and/or poetry?
  - Are they recording scientific observations?

Use your observations to determine the next umbrella you will teach. You may also consult Suggested Sequence of Lessons (pp. 605–622) for guidance.

EXTENSIONS FOR MAKING BIOGRAPHICAL MULTIMEDIA PRESENTATIONS

- Invite guest speakers to present to the class using a multimedia presentation. Afterward, ask students what they noticed about the presentations.

- Regularly include multimedia presentations as part of your lessons in various subjects (e.g., math, science, social studies). Help students notice other ways you can present information in a multimedia presentation (e.g., graphs, maps, tables) and learn how to cite sources.

- Give students regular opportunities to create and present multimedia presentations on a variety of topics besides biographies. Include how to cite their sources.

- Use the teacher and student rubrics available in online resources to evaluate students' biographical multimedia presentations or to guide them to evaluate their own texts. You might also consider having students co-create rubrics with you.

Making Photo Essays

Umbrella 14

Minilessons in This Umbrella

WML1	Notice the qualities of photo essays.
WML2	Choose photos to include and decide how to order and place them on the pages.
WML3	Add text that explains the photos.
WML4	Provide an introduction or conclusion to explain the photo essay.

Before Teaching Umbrella 14 Minilessons

One way to tell a story is through photographs. Photo essays are a mode of storytelling with accompanying information that can be oral or written. Because this is multimodal composition, you may choose to have students create a photo essay that is strictly pictorial with students narrating their essays. Or you may have them write the text alongside the photos, a method that can be seen in the mentor text examples used throughout these minilessons. The technology and devices available will determine how students will obtain photographs (e.g., take and print the photos, find them online, find them in magazines).

Students should be immersed in photo essays before being asked to make their own. Prior to beginning this umbrella, engage them in examining several photo essays. This umbrella aims to guide them through the process of creating a photo essay and learning how to tell a story through pictures by selecting a topic, choosing photos, and adding information. Teach these minilessons several days apart to provide time for students to work on each step in the process. Use the books listed below from *Fountas & Pinnell Classroom™ Interactive Read-Aloud Collection*, or choose photo essays from the classroom library.

Interactive Read-Aloud Collection
Exploring the World: Photo Essays

Mongolia by Jan Reynolds

Down Under by Jan Reynolds

It's Our Garden: From Seeds to Harvest in a School Garden by George Ancona

Meet the Dogs of Bedlam Farm by Jon Katz

As you read and enjoy these texts together, help students
- notice the story that the photographs tell, and
- observe the way that many photo essayists include text alongside the photos.

Interactive Read-Aloud
Photo Essays

Writer's Notebook

WML1
GEN.U14.WML1

Writing Minilesson Principle
Notice the qualities of photo essays.

Making Photo Essays

You Will Need

- photo essays, such as the following from Text Set: Exploring the World: Photo Essays:
  - *Down Under* and *Mongolia* by Jan Reynolds
  - *Meet the Dogs of Bedlam Farm* by Jon Katz
  - *It's Our Garden* by George Ancona
- chart paper and markers
- sticky notes
- writer's notebooks

Academic Language / Important Vocabulary

- photo essay
- topic
- characteristics
- qualities
- tell a story
- give information

Continuum Connection

- Attend to the language and craft of other writers in order to learn more as a writer
- Attend to the nuances of illustrations and how they enhance a text in order to try them out for oneself

GOAL

Understand the characteristics of photo essays and think about topics.

RATIONALE

When students understand that photo essays are another form of storytelling, they have another, more visual, way to express themselves and to tell stories. Because photo essays are mainly visual, with a small amount of writing, they may motivate some less eager writers.

WRITER'S NOTEBOOK/WRITING FOLDER

Have students reread their writer's notebooks to find photo essay ideas or jot new ideas in their writer's notebooks.

ASSESS LEARNING

- Look for evidence that students recognize the characteristics of photo essays.
- Notice whether students are engaged in thinking and talking about photo essay topics.
- Look for evidence that students can use vocabulary such as *photo essay*, *topic*, *characteristics*, *qualities*, *tell a story*, and *give information*.

MINILESSON

To help students notice the characteristics of photo essays, engage them in talking about mentor texts. Here is an example.

- Show the covers of several familiar photo essay texts.

  > Think about these books you know and talk to your partner about what you notice.

- Ask students to share their noticings. If necessary, prompt their thinking by asking these questions.
  - *Is this photo essay telling a story, giving information, or both?*
  - *Do the photos make you feel an emotion?*
  - *How are the photos in each photo essay connected?*

- As students suggest a quality, write it on chart paper.

  > As you have more experiences with photo essays, we can add characteristics that you notice in other photo essays.

Have a Try

Invite students to turn and talk about topic ideas for photo essays.

> Reread your writer's notebook to find an idea that might make a good photo essay. Then turn to your partner and share the idea.

▸ After time for discussion, ask volunteers to share. Using students' suggestions, make a list on chart paper of possible topics. Leave the list posted throughout this umbrella and add to it as new ideas are suggested.

Summarize and Apply

Summarize the learning. Have students gather ideas for photo essays during independent writing.

> You talked about characteristics of photo essays and thought about some topic ideas for making your own.

> During writing time, reread your writer's notebook to find more ideas. Circle or put a sticky note by ideas that might make a good photo essay. You can also jot down some new ideas in your notebook. Bring your notebooks to share when we meet later.

Confer

▸ During independent writing, move around the room to confer briefly with students about their photo essay ideas. Use the following prompts as needed.

- *Would you like to give information, tell a story, or do both?*
- *What are some topics you are interested in for your photo essay?*
- *Let's look back at the list of topics we made as a class. What ideas do you see that you might be interested in?*

Share

Following independent writing, gather students in the meeting area in a circle.

> Let's go around the circle to share photo essay topics. If you haven't chosen a topic yet, just say "pass." You might get an idea from a classmate.

Qualities of Photo Essays

- Photo essays consist mostly of photos.
- The photos are connected in some way.
- The photos might give information, tell a story, or teach how to do something.
- The photos are clear and interesting—you can understand what they are showing.
- The order of the photos makes sense.
- There are words that add information to the photos, but not too many words. The words are placed near the photos they describe.
- The introduction (if there is one) gets you ready to understand the photos.
- The conclusion (if there is one) gives more information about the topic, the author, or how the book was made.

Photo Essay Topic Ideas

- People, places, things
- My city in the morning
- How my family takes care of the garden
- Things my pet does
- A day in the life of the school librarian
- How the cafeteria workers get ready for lunch
- How musical instruments are used at school
- How the art teacher cleans the tools

WML 2
GEN.U14.WML2

Writing Minilesson Principle
Choose photos to include and decide how to order and place them on the pages.

Making Photo Essays

You Will Need

- several mentor texts with photo essays, such as the following from Text Set: Exploring the World: Photo Essays:
  - *It's Our Garden* by George Ancona
  - *Meet the Dogs of Bedlam Farm* by Jon Katz
- chart paper and markers
- writer's notebooks

Academic Language / Important Vocabulary

- photo essay
- choose
- decide
- order
- place

Continuum Connection

- Make decisions about where in a text to place features such as photographs with legends, insets, sidebars, and graphics
- Arrange print on the page to support the text's meaning and to help the reader notice important information
- Use layout of print and illustrations to convey the meaning of a text
- Present ideas clearly and in a logical sequence
- Arrange information in a logical way so that ideas build on one another

GOAL

Make decisions about what photos to include, how to order them, and where to place them on the page.

RATIONALE

When students learn to plan out their photo essays before they begin taking or finding photos, they realize that writers have many decisions to make when creating a photo essay, and they begin to take ownership of each step in the process.

WRITER'S NOTEBOOK/WRITING FOLDER

Students can use their writer's notebooks to plan the layout of their photo essays.

ASSESS LEARNING

- Look for evidence that students can plan what photos to take or find for their photo essays.
- Notice evidence that students can think about how their photos will be placed.
- Look for evidence that students can use vocabulary such as *photo essay*, *choose*, *decide*, *order*, and *place*.

MINILESSON

Before this minilesson, students should have a photo essay topic selected. To help students in planning and organizing photos for their photo essays, use mentor texts and model the process. Here is an example.

- Show the cover and revisit a few pages in *It's Our Garden*.

  What are things the author probably thought about before he wrote this photo essay book?

- Prompt the conversation to help students think about the author's choices, for example:
  - *What was the author's purpose in making this book?*
  - *How do the photos support the author's purpose?*
  - *What do you notice about the order in which the photos are shown?*
  - *What do you notice about how the photos are placed on the pages?*

- Repeat with *Meet the Dogs of Bedlam Farm*.

  What do you need to think about to plan your own photo essay?

- As needed, guide the conversation so students recognize that they need to think about what photos to include and then plan how to order and place them on a page.

Have a Try

Invite students to turn and talk about planning a photo essay.

- Model your thinking in planning a photo essay.

    I am going to make a photo essay about a day in the life of a lunchroom worker. Notice how I drew some boxes so I can plan what to put on each page. Help me start to plan the photos I could include. What happens first?

- Fill in a couple of boxes with a sketch or description of photos. Save the chart for WML3.

Summarize and Apply

Summarize the learning. Have students plan their photo essays during independent writing. Make sure they save their plans for WML3.

   Today you helped me start to plan a photo essay by thinking about what photos to include and in what order they could be placed.

- Write the principle on the top of the chart.

    During writing time, plan the photos you might use for your photo essay. Think about the order you want your photos to go in. You might want to make boxes by drawing them on a piece of paper or in your writer's notebook. Plan one page in each box. You can also make notes about where you want to place photos on the pages. Bring your plan to share when we meet later.

Confer

- During independent writing, move around the room to confer briefly with students about planning their photo essays. Use the following prompts as needed.
    - What are you thinking about the photos you want to include?
    - Let's talk about where you will place the photos on the pages.

Share

Following independent writing, gather students in the meeting area to share their plans.

   Talk about your plan for your photo essay with your partner.

WML 3
GEN.U14.WML3

Writing Minilesson Principle
Add text that explains the photos.

Making Photo Essays

You Will Need

- several mentor texts with photo essays, such as the following from Text Set: Exploring the World: Photo Essays:
  - *Down Under* by Jan Reynolds
  - *Meet the Dogs of Bedlam Farm* by Jon Katz
- prepared photo essay (video, slideshow, or book)
- chart from WML2
- students' photos for their photo essays
- writer's notebooks

Academic Language / Important Vocabulary

- photo essay
- audience
- written
- purpose
- narrated
- explain

Continuum Connection

- Understand that the writer is using language to communicate meaning
- Write with specific readers or audience in mind
- When rehearsing language for an informational piece, use vocabulary specific to the topic
- When rehearsing language for a narrative writing, use action and content words appropriate for the story
- Create illustrations and writing that work together to express the meaning

GOAL

Add written or oral text to go along with each photo.

RATIONALE

Photos tell part of the story, but sometimes words are helpful for more detailed explanation. Words can be added in written form or delivered orally. When students recognize that there are different ways to share the message they want to convey about each photo, the possibilities open up for them to be creative and to personalize their photo essays.

WRITER'S NOTEBOOK/WRITING FOLDER

Students will refer to the plans in their writer's notebooks as they create their photo essays.

ASSESS LEARNING

- Notice whether students are making decisions about how to use written or oral text to explain photos in their photo essays.
- Look for evidence that students can use vocabulary such as *photo essay*, *written*, *narrated*, *audience*, *purpose*, and *explain*.

MINILESSON

Before teaching this lesson, make sure students have taken or found the photos they will use for their photo essays. To model creating text that could accompany a photo essay, revisit your plan on the chart from WML2. To help students decide whether to write or speak the text for their photo essays, provide a discussion of mentor texts. Here is an example.

- Show pages 2–3 in *Down Under*. Read each page, pointing to the corresponding photo as you do.

  What do you notice about the words and the photos?

- Engage students in a conversation about the type of text (written) and the content, ensuring that they recognize that the words complement the photos.

- Show and read pages 4–5 in *Meet the Dogs of Bedlam Farm*.

  What is the purpose of the words the author wrote on this page?

- Display the chart from WML2. Show your photo essay.

  What do you notice about my photo essay?

- Guide the conversation to talk about the type of text (narrated or written) and the content.

  Authors have choices to make about the words in their photo essays and whether to write or narrate the words.

The Writing Minilessons Book, Grade 3

Have a Try

Invite students to turn and talk about the content and form of the text that accompanies photos in a photo essay.

> Think about your topic and the photos you will include in your photo essay. What words will you use to explain the photos? Will you have written descriptions, or will you narrate the information about the photos? Turn and talk about that.

▶ After time for discussion, have students share.

Summarize and Apply

Summarize the learning. Have students plan the words they will use in their photo essays. Add the new principle to the chart.

> During writing time, look at notes in your writer's notebook to decide what to write to explain each photo. You can also decide if your photo essay will have written or narrated words.

▶ Students may choose to write the words to accompany each photo in a book, make a slideshow and narrate the photos, or make a video in which they tell the story of the photos. If students decide to narrate, let them know that they can jot down notes to remember what to say.

Confer

▶ During independent writing, move around the room to confer briefly with students about photo essays. Use the following prompts as needed.
  - *What is the purpose of your photo essay (e.g., storytelling, procedural, informative)?*
  - *What do you want your audience to know about your photos?*
  - *Will the words be written or narrated?*

Share

Following independent writing, gather students in the meeting area. Ask a few volunteers to share their ideas for the words they will use in their photo essays.

> Share your thinking about the words you will use in your photo essay.

WML 4
GEN.U14.WML4

Writing Minilesson Principle
Provide an introduction or conclusion to explain the photo essay.

Making Photo Essays

You Will Need

- several photo essays with introductions and/or conclusions, such as the following from Text Set: Exploring the World: Photo Essays:
  - *Mongolia* by Jan Reynolds
  - *It's Our Garden* by George Ancona
- chart paper and markers
- writer's notebooks

Academic Language / Important Vocabulary

- photo essay
- explain
- introduction
- conclusion

Continuum Connection

- Use a variety of beginnings to engage the reader
- Use a variety of endings to engage and satisfy the reader
- Introduce, develop, and conclude the topic or story
- Understand the importance of the lead in a story or nonfiction piece

GOAL

Understand that a photo essay usually has an introduction and/or conclusion.

RATIONALE

When students recognize that authors often include an introduction and/or conclusion to explain their photo essays, they begin to think about the role an introduction or conclusion can play in their own photo essays.

WRITER'S NOTEBOOK/WRITING FOLDER

Students can work out their ideas for an introduction and/or conclusion in their writer's noteboooks.

ASSESS LEARNING

- Look for evidence to determine students' understandings about introductions and conclusions.
- Look for evidence that students can use vocabulary such as *photo essay*, *explain*, *introduction*, and *conclusion*.

MINILESSON

To help students write an introduction or conclusion for their photo essays, share mentor texts. Here is an example.

- Show and read the introduction in *Mongolia*.

  What are your thoughts about the introduction that the author, Jan Reynolds, included in this photo essay?

- Guide the conversation to help students talk about the type of information that is provided. As they do, begin a list on chart paper of the different things that an introduction can include, using general language.

  Is there anything else you would like to have read in this introduction?

- Add to the chart.
- Show and read the conclusion.

  Why did the author choose to end the photo essay this way?

  What other information could be in a conclusion?

- Begin a new section on the chart for conclusions and add student suggestions.
- Repeat with the introduction in *It's Our Garden*.

  These mentor texts have written words, so the introductions and conclusions are written. If you plan to narrate the words for your photo essay, then your introduction or conclusion will be spoken.

Have a Try

Invite students to turn and talk about using an introduction and/or conclusion in their photo essays.

> Think about if you will write an introduction, a conclusion, or both. Turn and talk to your partner about that.

- After time for a brief discussion, ask several volunteers to share.

Summarize and Apply

Summarize the learning. Have students write or record introductions or conclusions during independent writing.

> Today you learned that in photo essays, writers often include an introduction, a conclusion, or both.

- Write the principle on the top of the chart.

> During writing time, you can begin writing or recording your introduction or conclusion. Use your writer's notebook to work out your ideas. When we meet later, you can share what you are working on.

Provide an introduction or conclusion to explain the photo essay.

Introduction	• Facts about the topic • Why I chose this topic • How I took the photos • How I decided to organize the photos
Conclusion	• Other important facts • Where to learn more • How people can help

---

Confer

- During independent writing, move around the room to confer briefly with students about using an introduction or conclusion in photo essays. Use the following prompts as needed.
  - Will you have an introduction, a conclusion, or both?
  - Tell me about the introduction (conclusion) you are working on.
  - What information might readers need to know before they look at your photo essay? Write that in your introduction.
  - What do you want to leave your readers thinking about in your conclusion?

Share

Following independent writing, gather students in the meeting area. Ask a few volunteers to share their introduction or conclusion.

> Who would like to share the introduction or conclusion to your photo essay?

Umbrella 14: Making Photo Essays

Umbrella 14: Making Photo Essays

Assessment

After you have taught the minilessons in this umbrella, observe students in a variety of classroom activities. Use *The Fountas & Pinnell Literacy Continuum* to notice, teach for, and support students' learning as you observe their attempts at making photo essays.

- ▶ What evidence do you have of students' new understandings related to making photo essays?
  - Are students noticing and talking about the qualities of photo essays?
  - Do they choose appropriate photos and place them in a logical order in their photo essays?
  - How are they deciding whether to write or narrate text to accompany their photos?
  - How helpful are the introduction and/or conclusion to students' photo essays?
  - Are they using vocabulary such as *photo essay, topic, characteristics, qualities, tell a story, give information, choose, order, place, written, narrated, audience, purpose, explain, introduction,* and *conclusion*?
- ▶ In what ways, beyond the scope of this umbrella, are students engaged in trying different forms of writing?
  - Do they show an interest in writing poetry or letters?
  - Are they interested in writing in a variety of genres?

Use your observations to determine the next umbrella you will teach. You may also consult Suggested Sequence of Lessons (pp. 605–622) for guidance.

EXTENSIONS FOR MAKING PHOTO ESSAYS

- ▶ In small groups, discuss the photos in analytical ways (e.g., the perspective of the photographs, how they relate to the purpose of the photo essay, the tone and mood of the photos and words).

- ▶ Pull together a temporary, small guided writing group of students who would benefit from further instruction on the same aspect of making a photo essay.

Experimenting with Writing in New Ways

Umbrella 15

Minilessons in This Umbrella

WML1	Revisit an old topic in a new way.
WML2	Write with a different set of eyes.
WML3	Write a new version of an old tale.

Before Teaching Umbrella 15 Minilessons

The minilessons in this umbrella are designed to help students apply what they have learned about writing to forms of writing that might not be part of the writing curriculum but that they enjoy doing. This umbrella is intended to infuse additional energy into writing and can be broken up and used at different times of the year to inspire new forms of writing.

To help students experiment with the concepts taught in these minilessons, you will need to collect mentor texts for the type of writing students choose and provide them with those mentor texts. It will be helpful to have taught CFT.U1: Reading Like a Writer and Illustrator before teaching this umbrella. This will help students be able to look at mentor texts for ideas. For WML2 and WML3, use the following texts from *Fountas & Pinnell Classroom™ Interactive Read-Aloud Collection*, or choose suitable books that have personification and books that tell traditional tales (e.g., folktales, fables, fairy tales) from your classroom library.

Interactive Read-Aloud Collection

The Importance of Kindness

Sophie's Masterpiece: A Spider's Tale by Eileen Spinelli

Genre Study: Fables

The Tortoise & the Hare by Jerry Pinkney

As you read and enjoy these texts together, help students
- notice interesting choices the author or illustrator made, and
- talk about their own ideas for writing that were inspired by a book.

Interactive Read-Aloud
Kindness

Fables

Writer's Notebook

WML1
GEN.U15.WML1

Writing Minilesson Principle
Revisit an old topic in a new way.

Experimenting with Writing in New Ways

You Will Need

- a few examples of teacher- and/or student-written texts that explore a previous topic in a new genre or form
- chart paper and markers
- writer's notebooks and writing folders

Academic Language / Important Vocabulary

- revisit
- topic

Continuum Connection

- Select the genre for the writing based on the purpose
- Choose topics that are interesting to the writer
- Tell about a topic in an interesting way
- Reread a writer's notebook to select topics: e.g., select small moments that can be expanded
- Write in a variety of genres across the year

GOAL

Write about a previous topic in a different genre or form.

RATIONALE

Some students may choose to write about the same favorite topic in the same way repeatedly. When you show them that they can write about the same topic in different ways, they grow as writers by experimenting with different forms and genres while still indulging their passion and enthusiasm for a particular topic.

WRITER'S NOTEBOOK/WRITING FOLDER

Have students look at finished or nearly finished writing in their writing folders and/or hanging files to find a topic to write about in a different way. Students can jot their notes in their writer's notebooks.

ASSESS LEARNING

- Notice whether students write about the same topic using different genres or forms.
- Look for evidence that they can use vocabulary such as *revisit* and *topic*.

MINILESSON

To help students think about the minilesson principle, display and discuss examples of writing that show how you can write about a topic in more than one way. Help students create a list of different forms and genres of writing. Here is an example.

- Show and discuss two (or more) sample texts you have written about the same topic in different genres or forms.

    > I wrote an informational book about the planet Mars. I loved learning about and writing about this topic, so I thought about different ways I could write about it again. I decided to use what I learned about Mars to write a fictional story about an alien who lives on Mars! Next, I think I might write a how-to comic book about how to survive on Mars.

- Record each form of writing discussed on chart paper.
- If possible, show and discuss an example of a student-written piece of writing that revisits an old topic in a new way.

    > _____ loves trains. He wrote an informational book about trains. He also wrote a memory story about watching freight trains go by with his grandfather. What are some other ways he could write about trains?

- Add each form of writing discussed to the chart in a general way.
- Repeat with other examples, if available.

    > If there's a topic that you love writing about, try writing about it again in a different way.

Have a Try

Invite students to talk to a partner about their own ideas for writing about a topic in a new way.

> Think about a topic that you've enjoyed writing about. How could you write about the same topic using a different genre or form? Turn and talk to your partner about your ideas.

- After time for discussion, invite several students to share their ideas. Add any new genres or forms to the chart.

Summarize and Apply

Write the principle at the top of the chart. Summarize the learning and suggest that students revisit an old topic in a new way.

> During writing time today, look through your writing folder or hanging file to find a topic you particularly enjoyed writing about. Then think about how you can write about that topic in a different way. Make some notes about what you could write in your writer's notebook. Look at our chart to remind yourself of some of the different ways you can write about a topic.

Revisit an old topic in a new way.

- Informational book
- Fiction story
- Procedural text (how-to)
- Comic book
- Memory story
- Recipe
- Letter
- Blog post
- Song
- Poem
- Slide presentation
- Question-and-answer book
- Photo essay
- Picture book

Confer

- During independent writing, move around the room to confer briefly with as many individual students as time allows. Sit side by side with them and invite them to talk about their ideas for writing about a topic in a new way. Use prompts such as the following as needed.
  - What is your favorite topic?
  - How have you written about that topic before?
  - What is another way you could write about that?
  - Could you use that topic in a poem or a how-to book?

Share

Following independent writing, gather students in the meeting area to share their writing.

> Turn and talk to your partner about a topic you want to write about in a new way.

WML2
GEN.U15.WML2

Writing Minilesson Principle
Write with a different set of eyes.

Experimenting with Writing in New Ways

You Will Need

- a familiar book containing examples of personification, such as *Sophie's Masterpiece* by Eileen Spinelli, from Text Set: The Importance of Kindness
- chart paper and markers
- writer's notebooks
- To download the following online resource for this lesson, visit **fp.pub/resources**:
  - chart art (optional)

Academic Language / Important Vocabulary

- point of view
- personification

Continuum Connection

- Tell about a topic in an interesting way
- Take risks as a writer

GOAL

Use personification to write from a different perspective.

RATIONALE

When you teach students how to use personification to write from a different perspective, they begin to think about perspective and point of view in their fiction writing. This can also give students plenty of fresh ideas for their writing and breathe new life into their writing.

WRITER'S NOTEBOOK/WRITING FOLDER

Have students use their writer's notebooks to record ideas for writing with a different set of eyes.

ASSESS LEARNING

- Observe for evidence of what students understand about personification.
- Look at students' writing to see whether they experiment with using personification to write from a different point of view.
- Look for evidence that they can use vocabulary such as *point of view* and *personification*.

MINILESSON

To help students think about the minilesson principle, use shared writing to model using personification to write from a different perspective. Here is an example.

- Show the cover of *Sophie's Masterpiece* and read the title.

  Look at the illustration of Sophie on the cover. Is Sophie like a real spider? How is she different from a real spider?

  In the book's illustrations, Sophie has a person's head and a spider's body. She spins webs like a spider, but she has thoughts and feelings like a person. The author used personification. Personification is when you write about an animal or an object that thinks and acts like a person.

  Let's try writing from the point of view of a spider. Imagine that you are a spider. What would you write about your life as a spider?

- Use shared writing to write, on chart paper, at least a few sentences from the perspective of a spider. Point out the use of the pronoun *I* because the writing is from the point of view of the spider.

- If necessary, guide students' thinking with questions such as the following:
  - *Where might a spider live?*
  - *What would a spider see?*
  - *How could a spider spend its time?*
  - *What might a spider think about?*

Have a Try

Invite students to talk to a partner about their ideas for using personification.

> When you write, you don't always have to write from your own point of view. You can write with a different set of eyes by pretending to be an animal or an object. In your writer's notebook, write some ideas for animals or objects you could pretend to be in your writing. Then turn to your partner and share your ideas.

▸ After students turn and talk, invite several students to share their ideas. Record them on the chart.

Summarize and Apply

Write the principle at the top of the chart. Summarize the learning and encourage students to try writing with a different set of eyes.

> When you write today, try writing with a different set of eyes. Look at the notes you made in your writer's notebook. Choose an animal or object that you would like to pretend to be, and write in your notebook about what that animal or object would think, feel, and experience. Bring your writing to share when we come back together.

Confer

▸ During independent writing, move around the room to confer briefly with as many individual students as time allows. Sit side by side with them and invite them to talk about writing with a different set of eyes. Use prompts such as the following as needed.

- What animal or object would you like to pretend to be?
- How would a _____ spend its time?
- What might a _____ think about?
- How might a _____ feel when _____?

Share

Following independent writing, gather students in the meeting area to share their writing.

> Who wrote with a different set of eyes today?

> What did you pretend to be? Read your writing aloud.

WML 3
GEN.U15.WML3

Writing Minilesson Principle
Write a new version of an old tale.

Experimenting with Writing in New Ways

You Will Need

- a familiar folktale or fable, such as *The Tortoise & the Hare* by Jerry Pinkney, from Text Set: Genre Study: Fables
- a selection of other folktales the students have read or heard
- chart paper and markers
- writer's notebooks

Academic Language / Important Vocabulary

- version
- tale

Continuum Connection

- Write a simple fiction story, either realistic or fantasy
- Understand that writers can learn to craft fiction by using mentor texts as models
- Write in a variety of genres across the year

GOAL

Write a retelling of a familiar old tale (e.g., folktale, fable, fairy tale).

RATIONALE

When you show students how to write a new version of a familiar old tale, they learn that writers get ideas from other authors and mentor texts. Students learn they also can be inspired by others. With this knowledge, they will have a greater range of possible subjects and forms to choose from for their writing and the opportunity to exercise their imaginations.

WRITER'S NOTEBOOK/WRITING FOLDER

Students can use their writer's notebooks to make some planning notes for rewriting a familiar old tale.

ASSESS LEARNING

- Observe students as they read and talk about old tales. Do they talk about their own ideas for writing inspired by the stories?
- Notice whether students write new versions of familiar old tales.
- Look for evidence that they can use vocabulary such as *version* and *tale*.

MINILESSON

To help students think about the minilesson principle, use shared writing to write a new version of a familiar old tale, such as a fable. Here is an example.

- Show the cover of *The Tortoise & the Hare* and read the title.

    What happens in this story?

    What lesson does this story teach?

    This story is an old tale that has been told again and again in lots of different ways. We can write our own version of this story. When you write a new version of an old tale, the basic idea and lesson behind the story stay the same, but many of the details change. You can change who the characters are, when and where the story takes place, and some of the things that the characters say and do.

    What could we change in our version of the Tortoise and the Hare story? Who could the characters be? When and where could our story take place?

- With students' input, use shared writing to write a brief retelling of the story on chart paper. Read aloud the whole story when it is complete.

    What did you notice about how we wrote a new version of an old tale? What did we change? What stayed the same?

WML3
GEN.U15.WML3

Have a Try

Invite students to talk to a partner about their ideas for writing a new version of an old tale.

- Show a selection of familiar old tales.

    > Here are some old tales that we have read together. Think about these tales and other tales you know. Which of these tales could you rewrite? What would you change in your version? Turn and talk to your partner about your ideas.

- After time for discussion, invite several students to share their ideas.

Summarize and Apply

Write the principle at the top of the chart. Summarize the learning and invite students to write a new version of an old tale.

> What did you learn today about how to write a new version of an old tale?

> When you write today, try writing a new version of an old tale. Think about how you can change the characters, settings, and events in the story while keeping the basic idea behind the story the same. You can use your writer's notebook to do some planning before you begin writing. Bring your writing to share when we meet later.

Write a new version of an old tale.

Terry and Harry

"I'm going to try out for the running team!" said Terry.

"You? On the running team?" Harry laughed. "You're such a slow runner!"

Harry always bragged about how fast he could run. Terry was sick of it. He challenged Harry to a three-mile race.

All their friends gathered to watch. Harry sprinted at first. After the first mile, he took a break.

Terry ran at a leisurely pace. He ran past Harry. Harry started to run again, but he was too tired to run fast. And he took more breaks.

Terry never stopped until he reached the finish line. He waited. Finally, Harry collapsed in a heap at the finish line.

"Still think I can't make the team, Harry?"

"I'm sorry I said those things, Terry. Slow and steady really does win the race!"

Confer

- During independent writing, move around the room to confer briefly with as many individual students as time allows. Sit side by side with them and invite them to talk about writing a new version of an old tale. Use prompts such as the following as needed.
  - *What are some old tales that you have read and enjoyed?*
  - *What happens in that story? What lesson does the story teach?*
  - *How could you change the characters in your version of the story?*
  - *Where and when will your version of the story take place?*

Share

Following independent writing, gather students in the meeting area to share their writing.

> Who is writing a new version of an old tale? Talk about what you wrote today.

Umbrella 15: Experimenting with Writing in New Ways

Assessment

After you have taught the minilessons in this umbrella, observe students as they explore different ways of writing. Use *The Fountas & Pinnell Literacy Continuum* to notice, teach for, and support students' learning as you observe their attempts at writing.

- What evidence do you have of students' new understandings related to experimenting with writing in new ways?
  - Have students tried writing about a previous topic in a different genre or form?
  - Have they experimented with using personification to write from a different perspective?
  - Have they tried writing a new version of a familiar folktale?
  - Do students understand and use vocabulary such as *topic*, *version*, and *tale*?
- In what other ways, beyond the scope of this umbrella, are students exploring the writing process?
  - Are they publishing their writing in different ways?
  - Are they sharing their writing with an audience?

Use your observations to determine the next umbrella you will teach. You may also consult Suggested Sequence of Lessons (pp. 605–622) for guidance.

EXTENSIONS FOR EXPERIMENTING WITH WRITING IN NEW WAYS

- Offer students opportunities to write in the same style or genre as a book you have read aloud.

- Help students experiment with digital forms of content creation as appropriate—for example, blog post, multimedia presentation, podcast, or video.

- Read aloud *This Plus That: Life's Little Equations* by Amy Krouse Rosenthal and then challenge students to create their own "word equations."

Section 3 | Craft

THROUGH THE TALK that surrounds interactive read-aloud and shared reading, third graders learn a lot about the craft of writing. The minilessons in this section take this growing knowledge and pull back the curtain on the decisions authors and illustrators make (e.g., choosing powerful words, using dialogue, crafting leads and endings, incorporating text features) to create writing that is interesting and exciting to read.

3 Craft

UMBRELLA 1	Reading Like a Writer and Illustrator	**305**
UMBRELLA 2	Describing Characters	**313**
UMBRELLA 3	Crafting a Setting	**321**
UMBRELLA 4	Adding Dialogue to Writing	**329**
UMBRELLA 5	Crafting a Lead	**337**
UMBRELLA 6	Crafting an Ending	**347**
UMBRELLA 7	Making Powerful Word Choices	**357**
UMBRELLA 8	Making Your Sentences Clear and Interesting	**365**
UMBRELLA 9	Writing with Voice in Fiction and Nonfiction	**373**
UMBRELLA 10	Using Text Features in Nonfiction Writing	**383**
UMBRELLA 11	Expanding Nonfiction Writing	**393**
UMBRELLA 12	Drawing People	**401**
UMBRELLA 13	Adding Meaning Through Illustrations	**411**
UMBRELLA 14	Illustrating and Using Graphics in Nonfiction Writing	**423**
UMBRELLA 15	Exploring Design Features and Text Layout	**435**

Reading Like a Writer and Illustrator

Umbrella 1

Minilessons in This Umbrella

- **WML1** Notice the decisions writers make.
- **WML2** Notice the decisions illustrators make.
- **WML3** Learn from authors through writer talks.

Before Teaching Umbrella 1 Minilessons

The minilessons in this umbrella are designed to help students notice elements of author's craft and illustrator's craft that they can try in their own writing. Consider teaching each lesson over several days, allowing students to immerse themselves in noticing and naming writing and illustrating techniques before they begin to try them on their own. Repeat lessons throughout the year as students get to know different authors and illustrators, tailoring the lessons to the authors and illustrators you are studying.

Read and discuss engaging books with a variety of writing and illustration styles. Use familiar texts so students can focus on craft decisions and begin to think about how these techniques might be useful in their own writing. Consider using the following books from *Fountas & Pinnell Classroom™ Interactive Read-Aloud Collection*, or choose familiar books from your classroom library.

Interactive Read-Aloud Collection

The Importance of Kindness
- *Enemy Pie* by Derek Munson
- *Under the Lemon Moon* by Edith Hope Fine
- *The Can Man* by Laura E. Williams

Connecting Across Generations: Family
- *Sitti's Secrets* by Naomi Shihab Nye
- *Storm in the Night* by Mary Stolz
- *Mooncakes* by Loretta Seto

As you read and enjoy these texts together, help students
- notice and discuss interesting examples of author's and illustrator's craft, and
- discuss how the decisions writers make can help with their own writing.

Interactive Read-Aloud
Kindness

Family

Writer's Notebook

WML1
CFT.U1.WML1

Writing Minilesson Principle
Notice the decisions writers make.

Reading Like a Writer and Illustrator

You Will Need

- several familiar books that exemplify author's craft, such as the following:
  - *Enemy Pie* by Derek Munson and *Under the Lemon Moon* by Edith Hope Fine, from Text Set: The Importance of Kindness
  - *Storm in the Night* by Mary Stolz and *Sitti's Secrets* by Naomi Shihab Nye, from Text Set: Connecting Across Generations: Family
- several books for each pair of students that have recognizable craft moves they could try in their own writing
- chart paper and markers
- sticky notes
- writer's notebooks

Academic Language/Important Vocabulary

- craft move
- technique
- decisions

Continuum Connection

- Attend to the language and craft of other writers in order to learn more as a writer
- Notice what makes writing effective and name the craft or technique
- Be willing to work at the craft of writing, incorporating new learning from instruction

GOAL

Study familiar books and notice crafting decisions writers make.

RATIONALE

Once students become aware of and can name the ways that authors craft their books, they can begin to apply some of the same crafting decisions and techniques to their own writing. This reinforces the practice of learning from other writers.

WRITER'S NOTEBOOK/WRITING FOLDER

Students can use their writer's notebooks to record notes about writer's craft.

ASSESS LEARNING

- Listen to students as they talk about books. Can they identify examples of author's craft?
- Look at student's writing. Are they using techniques they have noticed from other authors?
- Look for evidence that students can use vocabulary such as *craft move*, *technique*, and *decisions*.

MINILESSON

To help students think about the minilesson principle, use mentor texts, samples of your own writing, or students' writing to guide them to notice the authors' craft decisions. Here is an example.

- Show *Enemy Pie* and read the first page.

  > What do you notice about the sentences and the way Derek Munson wrote them?
  >
  > Why do you think he made those decisions?

- Record students' responses on chart paper.
- Think aloud about how you might use a short sentence to draw attention to an idea.

  > I might try this in my own writing about the beginning of a day that was supposed to be good. I could write about all the good things that were happening and then say "It was going to be a great day. But it wasn't." Derek Munson used this craft move to let readers know that something was about to change. Does this technique make you want to read more?

- Discuss other decisions in the same manner with a couple of similarly familiar books, such as *Storm in the Night* (description of sounds, words in italics) and *Sitti's Secrets* (words in another language, sentence alone on a page).

The Writing Minilessons Book, Grade 3

Have a Try

Use a book that has a good example of author's craft.

- Review a few pages of *Under the Lemon Moon*.

    Turn and talk to your partner about something Edith Hope Fine did to make her writing interesting or something she did that helps you understand the story.

- After students turn and talk, invite a few students to share their thinking. Add responses to the chart.

Summarize and Apply

Write the principle at the top of the chart. Summarize the learning. Provide books for each pair of students to look in for decisions the authors made.

    Today, you will work with a partner to look in books to find more examples of authors' decisions. Ask each other these questions: What did the writer do to make the writing interesting? What did the writer do to help you understand more? What might you do that is similar? Mark the author's decisions with sticky notes. If you write the sticky notes, add them to your writer's notebook after sharing with the class. If you did not write the sticky notes, write the notes in your writer's notebook. Bring your books and writer's notebooks when we meet later.

Notice the decisions writers make.		
Author	Writer's Decision	Why?
Derek Munson	Long sentence followed by a short sentence	Draws attention to the words. Creates suspense
	Repetition of a sentence	Shares writer's feelings
Mary Stolz	Description of sounds	Helps the reader imagine the setting. Sets the mood
	Words in italics	Sets the words apart. Shows how to emphasize the words when reading
Naomi Shihab Nye	Words from her native language	Makes the story more authentic by showing details about her culture
	Sentence that stands alone on the page	Makes the sentence extra important
Edith Hope Fine	Sound words	Helps the reader imagine what it sounded like
	Words from her native language	Makes the story more authentic

Confer

- During independent writing, move around the room to confer briefly with pairs of students about writers' decisions that they can try in their own writing. Use prompts such as those below if needed, following each with "Why might the writer have done that?" and/or "How might you try that in your own writing?"
    - What interesting language did the writer use?
    - How did the writer decide to place the words (sentences) on the page?
    - How did the writer decide to begin (end) this book?

Share

Gather students in the meeting area for partners to share their noticings with the whole group. Tell them to listen for ideas they can use in their own writing.

    What did you hear from your classmates that you might try in your writing?

WML2
CFT.U1.WML2

Writing Minilesson Principle
Notice the decisions illustrators make.

Reading Like a Writer and Illustrator

You Will Need

- several familiar books that exemplify illustrator's craft, such as the following:
  - *Storm in the Night* by Mary Stolz and *Mooncakes* by Loretta Seto, from Text Set: Connecting Across Generations: Family
  - *The Can Man* by Laura E. Williams, from Text Set: The Importance of Kindness
- several books for each pair of students that have recognizable craft moves they could try in their own illustrations
- chart paper and markers
- sticky notes
- writer's notebooks

Academic Language/ Important Vocabulary

- decisions
- craft
- illustrations

Continuum Connection

- Attend to the nuances of illustrations and how they enhance a text in order to try them out for oneself
- Understand that when both writing and drawing are on a page, they are mutually supportive, with each extending the other

GOAL

Study illustrations from familiar books and notice the craft decisions that illustrators make.

RATIONALE

Once students become aware of and can name the ways that illustrators craft their illustrations, they can begin to apply some of the same crafting decisions to their own drawings. This reinforces the practice of learning from other illustrators.

WRITER'S NOTEBOOK/WRITING FOLDER

Students can use their writer's notebooks to record notes about illustrator's craft.

ASSESS LEARNING

- Listen to students as they talk about books. Can they identify examples of illustrator's craft?
- Look for evidence that students can use vocabulary such as *decisions*, *craft*, and *illustrations*.

MINILESSON

To help students think about the minilesson principle, use mentor texts to guide them to notice illustrators' craft decisions in books they know. Here is an example.

- Show the cover of *Storm in the Night* and read the title. Show the illustration on pages 1–2.

    Why do you think the illustrator, Pat Cummings, decided to illustrate the boy and his grandfather with a focus on their faces?

- Record students' responses on chart paper. Think aloud about how you might try this in your own writing.

    In my own writing, I can make the characters' faces larger so that my readers can see their expressions and know how they are feeling, just like Pat Cummings did.

- Repeat this process, showing the illustration on pages 13–14.

    What colors do you see? Why do you think Pat Cummings chose these colors? How do the colors help you to understand the story more?

- Add responses to the chart.
- Think aloud about the decisions.

    If I were writing about a picnic in the park, I could use bright colors to let my readers know it is a playful, happy time.

- Continue in a similar manner with the illustrations on pages 23–24 and 25 in *The Can Man*.

WML 2
CFT.U1.WML2

Have a Try

Use a book that has a good example of illustrator's craft, such as *Mooncakes*, to have students think more about reading like an illustrator.

▸ Show the illustrations on pages 11–12 in *Mooncakes*.

> What do you notice about the decision the illustrator made? Turn and talk to your partner.

▸ After students turn and talk, invite a few students to share their thinking. Add responses to the chart.

Summarize and Apply

Write the principle at the top of the chart. Summarize the learning. Provide books for each pair of students to look in for decisions the illustrators made.

> Today, look at books with a partner to find more examples of decisions made by illustrators. Ask each other these questions: What did the illustrator do to make the illustrations more interesting? How did the illustrator use pictures to tell more of the story? What similar thing could you do in your own books? Mark the illustrator's decisions you notice with sticky notes. If you write the sticky notes, add them to your writer's notebook after you share with the class. If you did not write the sticky notes, write the notes on a page in your writer's notebook. Bring your books and writer's notebooks when we meet later.

Notice the decisions illustrators make.

Illustrator	Illustrator's Decision	Why?
Pat Cummings *Storm in the Night*	Focus on faces	Shows that the characters are not afraid even in the storm
	Dark colors	Shows a feeling of calm even though there is a power outage
	Glow from lightning	
Craig Orback *The Can Man*	Different perspective: Reader is looking at the boy looking at Mr. Peters	Shows who the main character is looking at and that the main character is having a change of heart
	Dark gray colors and snow	Shows the reader how cold the day is
Renné Benoit *Mooncakes*	Pictures sitting on top of clouds and painted in a more traditional style	Sets apart the story within the story

Confer

▸ During independent writing, move around the room to confer briefly with pairs of students about illustrators' crafting decisions. Use prompts such as those below if needed, following each with "Why might the illustrator have done that?" and/or "How might you try that in your own books?"

- *What decisions did the illustrator make to give the readers more information or to make the book more interesting?*
- *What do you notice about how the illustrations are placed on the page?*

Share

Gather students in the meeting area for partners to share what they noticed.

> What decisions by the illustrator did you notice in the book you looked at?

Umbrella 1: Reading Like a Writer and Illustrator

WML 3
CFT.U1.WML3

Writing Minilesson Principle
Learn from authors through writer talks.

Reading Like a Writer and Illustrator

You Will Need

- author quotes and writer talks, such as those from Author Advice
- chart paper and markers
- writer's notebooks
- To download the following online resource for this lesson, visit **fp.pub/resources**:
  - Author Advice

Academic Language / Important Vocabulary

- author
- writer talk
- quote

Continuum Connection

- Attend to the language and craft of other writers in order to learn more as a writer

GOAL
Learn about writing from writer talks.

RATIONALE
In writer talks, the speaker offers a glimpse into the writing life and process of authors. When students listen to writer talks, they understand that they can learn about writing not just by reading the authors' works but also from what the authors say about themselves as writers.

WRITER'S NOTEBOOK/WRITING FOLDER
Invite students to write about inspiration they get from authors in their writer's notebooks.

ASSESS LEARNING

- Look for evidence that students reflect on what they learn from writer talks and apply what they learn to their own writing.
- Notice whether they can use vocabulary such as *author*, *writer talk*, and *quote*.

MINILESSON

To help students think about the minilesson principle, present writer talks and engage students in a discussion about them. Have quotes (including samples from the online resource Author Advice) prepared to read on chart paper, a note card, or a device (e.g., phone or tablet). Any quotes that are of interest to you and your students will work. Here is an example.

- Give a short writer talk.

    Lester Laminack is an author whose books I enjoy reading. Mr. Laminack lives in North Carolina and has written several children's books. He said this about writing: "Just pick up a pen and open a notebook and start taking note of what you notice. Let your brain get in the habit of noticing the world." How could this quote from Lester Laminack help you with your own writing?

- Record students' responses on chart paper.
- Give another writer talk.

    Julie Danneberg wrote *First Day Jitters* and other children's books. On her website, she wrote this: "I like to get up VERY early every morning and spend the first part of my day working on my writing. Sometimes I'm just coming up with ideas, sometimes I'm revising and editing an old story, and sometimes I'm drafting a new story." What can you learn from this quote?

- Add responses to the chart.

    A few times a week, I will give a quick writer talk. It might be advice from an author or something about the author's life or writing process. Think about using what you learn from the author in your own writing.

Have a Try

Invite students to talk to a partner about the importance of writer talks.

> How can listening to writer talks like the ones I just gave help you with your own writing? Why is it helpful to hear what other authors have to say about their writing? Turn and talk to your partner about this.

▸ After time for discussion, invite several students to share their thinking.

Summarize and Apply

Summarize the learning. Invite students to use writer talks to help with their own writing.

> What is a way to learn about how to improve your writing?

▸ Write the principle at the top of the chart.

> During writing time today, jot down in your writer's notebook anything you want to remember from the writer talks I gave today. Then, as you write today and every day, keep in mind some of the things we have learned from the authors we know and love. If you ever find helpful advice or something about an author's life that you think would be helpful for all of us to know, share it with the class by giving your own writer talk.

Learn from authors through writer talks.

Quote	What I Think About or Learn from the Quote
"Just pick up a pen and open a notebook and start taking note of what you notice. Let your brain get in the habit of noticing the world." —Lester Laminack	• all the different things I notice and could write about • how writers pay more attention to the world • the importance of always having a notebook with me
"I like to get up VERY early every morning and spend the first part of my day working on my writing. Sometimes I'm just coming up with ideas, sometimes I'm revising and editing an old story, and sometimes I'm drafting a new story." —Julie Danneberg	• what time of day I like to write • how it's a good idea to write in the morning when you have more time and energy • that authors revise and edit their stories, too

Confer

▸ During independent writing, move around the room to confer briefly with students about their writing. Use prompts such as the following as needed.

- *How is your writing going today? Is there anything you need help with?*
- *What have you learned from other writers that could help you with your writing?*
- *Let's see how some of the authors we know would handle this.*

Share

Following independent writing, gather students in the meeting area to share their notes.

> Share with a partner what you worked on today during writing time.

> What advice did you find yourself thinking about today while you were writing?

Umbrella 1 | Reading Like a Writer and Illustrator

Assessment

After you have taught the minilessons in this umbrella, observe students in a variety of classroom activities. Use the behaviors and understandings in *The Fountas & Pinnell Literacy Continuum* to notice, teach for, and support students' learning as you observe their attempts at writing and drawing.

- What evidence do you have of students' new understandings related to reading like a writer and illustrator?
    - Can students notice and talk about the decisions that writers and illustrators make?
    - What craft decisions are they trying in their own writing and illustrations?
    - Do they apply lessons they've learned from writer talks?
    - Do they understand and use vocabulary such as *craft*, *technique*, *decisions*, and *illustrations*?
- In what other ways, beyond the scope of this umbrella, are students ready to expand their writing?
    - Are they beginning to share their writing with others?
    - Are they experimenting with different kinds of leads and endings in their writing?

Use your observations to determine the next umbrella you will teach. You may also consult Suggested Sequence of Lessons (pp. 605–622) for guidance.

EXTENSIONS FOR READING LIKE A WRITER AND ILLUSTRATOR

- Continue adding to the charts created during these minilessons as students notice more examples of crafting decisions that authors and illustrators make. Refer to these charts across the year as you explore similar ideas in different minilessons.

- Apply the first two minilessons in this umbrella to informational texts and any other genres you teach throughout the year.

- Teach WML3 with quotations from illustrators so that students can learn about their illustrating approaches and techniques.

- If you are using *Writer's Notebook, Intermediate*, have students select a quotation from the Section 2 tab to use in a writer talk.

- If you use *The Reading Minilessons Book, Grade 3* (Fountas and Pinnell 2019), teach LA.U2: Studying Authors and Illustrators to complement this umbrella's minilessons.

Describing Characters

Umbrella 2

Minilessons in This Umbrella

- **WML1** Describe how characters look.
- **WML2** Tell what characters do.
- **WML3** Tell what characters think and say.

Before Teaching Umbrella 2 Minilessons

Before teaching, provide opportunities for students to read and discuss books with detailed character descriptions as well as for students to write independently and make their own stories. While the minilessons in this umbrella are best taught when students are writing realistic fiction, they can apply to real people in memory stories or biographies as well.

Make sure students have their writer's notebooks, *Writer's Notebook, Intermediate* (Fountas and Pinnell 2023) or a plain notebook, and their writing folders for the lessons so that they can use them to make notes or sketches about the characters before writing descriptions of them in their drafts. If you are using *The Reading Minilessons Book, Grade 3* (Fountas and Pinnell 2019) you may choose to teach LA.U23: Understanding Characters' Feelings, Motivations, and Intentions and LA.U24: Understanding Character Traits. For mentor texts, choose fiction books with well-developed characters. Use the books listed below from *Fountas & Pinnell Classroom™ Interactive Read-Aloud Collection*, or choose books from the classroom library that have clear descriptions of the characters.

Interactive Read-Aloud Collection
Honoring Traditions

Nadia's Hands by Karen English

Bintou's Braids by Sylviane A. Diouf

Crouching Tiger by Ying Chang Compestine

Crane Boy by Diana Cohn

Genre Study: Realistic Fiction

Dumpling Soup by Jama Kim Rattigan

Dancing in the Wings by Debbie Allen

As you read and enjoy these texts together, help students
- notice how characters are portrayed, and
- talk about what actions, thoughts, and dialogue reveal about characters.

Interactive Read-Aloud
Honoring Traditions

Realistic Fiction

Writer's Notebook

WML1
CFT.U2.WML1

Writing Minilesson Principle
Describe how characters look.

Describing Characters

You Will Need

- several mentor texts with physical descriptions of characters, such as the following from Text Set: Honoring Traditions:
  - *Nadia's Hands* by Karen English
  - *Bintou's Braids* by Sylviane A. Diouf
- chart paper and markers
- writer's notebooks and writing folders

Academic Language / Important Vocabulary

- character
- describe
- descriptive

Continuum Connection

- Describe characters by how they look and what they say
- Understand that writers can learn to craft fiction by using mentor texts as models

GOAL

Understand that authors use descriptive language to tell how their characters look.

RATIONALE

Writers describe how characters look so that readers can visualize them, thereby becoming more fully engaged in the stories. When students recognize this, they think about how to use physical descriptions of the characters in their own writing.

WRITER'S NOTEBOOK/WRITING FOLDER

Students will continue to work on stories from their writing folders. They can use their writer's notebooks to make a character web or sketch or create a list of important phrases or sentences to describe their characters.

ASSESS LEARNING

- Look at students' writing. How well do they describe the characters?
- Look for evidence that students can use vocabulary such as *character*, *describe*, and *descriptive*.

MINILESSON

To help students learn about the minilesson principle, use mentor texts to show how writers describe how a character looks. Here is an example.

- Read the description on page 19 of *Nadia's Hands*.

  How do you know how Nadia's hands look?

- Show the illustration of Nadia's hands on page 20.

  The writer described Nadia's hands because they are important to the story. What words did the author use?

- Write the descriptive words on chart paper.
- Read the first page of text in *Bintou's Braids*.

  What words help you picture Bintou?

- Record the words on the chart.

  These two authors described features of Nadia and Bintou that are important to the stories. Here's a question to ask yourself when you describe the characters in your stories: What is an important feature of the character?

- Write the question on the chart.

  What other questions could you ask yourself?

- Record students' responses on the chart.

Have a Try

Invite students to turn and talk about descriptions of their own characters.

> Turn and talk about a character in the story you are writing. Look at the questions on the chart to think about how to describe how the character looks.

▸ After time for a brief discussion, ask a few students to share their ideas. As needed, guide them to be more specific.

Summarize and Apply

Summarize the learning. Remind students to use descriptive words for the characters they write about. Write the principle at the top of the chart.

> During writing time, check the story you are working on in your writing folder to see if you have described the characters so that your readers can picture them. You might need to add some descriptive details. If you are getting ready to write a new story, you can make some notes or create a sketch in your writer's notebook about how the characters look. Bring your writing to share when we meet later.

Describe how characters look.	
Nadia's hands	amber hands
	deep orange flowers
	swirls and stars
	smooth, shiny ring on her finger
Bintou's hair	short and fuzzy
	plain and silly
	four little tufts

Describing Characters
- What is an important feature of the character?
- Is the character tall or short?
- What is the character wearing?
- What kind of hair does the character have?
- What is the character's face like?
- How does the character walk or move?

Confer

▸ During independent writing, move around the room to confer briefly with students. Invite them to describe their characters. Use the following prompts as needed.

- *How does the character look?*
- *What are some words you can use to describe how the character looks?*
- *What details can you add?*

Share

Following independent writing, gather students in the meeting area. Ask a few volunteers to share their writing.

> Who would like to share how you described a character?

> What questions do you have about the way _____'s character looks?

WML 2
CFT.U2.WML2

Writing Minilesson Principle
Tell what characters do.

Describing Characters

You Will Need

- several mentor texts that describe the actions of characters, such as the following:
  - *Crouching Tiger* by Ying Chang Compestine, from Text Set: Honoring Traditions
  - *Dumpling Soup* by Jama Kim Rattigan, from Text Set: Genre Study: Realistic Fiction
- chart paper and markers
- writer's notebooks and writing folders

Academic Language / Important Vocabulary

- character
- describe
- actions

Continuum Connection

- Describe people by what they do, say, and think and what others say about them
- Show rather than tell how characters feel
- Understand that writers can learn to craft fiction by using mentor texts as models
- Understand how information helps the reader learn about a topic

GOAL

Describe characters through actions.

RATIONALE

Sometimes writers describe a character's behavior or actions to help readers know more about the character. When students realize this, they understand that they have different ways to share information about the characters in their own writing.

WRITER'S NOTEBOOK/WRITING FOLDER

Students will continue to work on their stories from their writing folders. They can use their writer's notebooks to try out descriptions of the characters' actions before adding to their drafts.

ASSESS LEARNING

- Notice whether students understand that a writer includes a character's actions to reveal something about the character.
- Observe whether students sometimes write about what a character does.
- Look for evidence that students can use vocabulary such as *character*, *describe*, and *actions*.

MINILESSON

To help students think about the minilesson principle, engage them in an interactive lesson and use mentor texts to model how writers include the characters' actions to tell about them. Here is an example.

- Show and revisit pages 11, 13, and 15 of *Crouching Tiger*.

  The writer described different things that Vinson does. What does the writer want you to know about Vinson?

- Guide the conversation to help children recognize that the writer shows that Vinson is uncomfortable and embarrassed about his grandpa, who is visiting from a different country. Begin a chart that shows the action and what it reveals about the character.

  As I read more of the story, think about what the writer wants you to understand about Vinson and notice how she lets you know.

- Read pages 33 and 35.

  What do you notice about the writer's decisions?

- Support the conversation and add to chart.
- Repeat with pages 3, 5, 7, and 16 of *Dumpling Soup*.

The Writing Minilessons Book, Grade 3

Have a Try

Invite students to turn and talk about describing a character through actions.

> Think about a character in the story you are writing. What is the character like? Turn to your partner and describe what actions the character could do to show that.

- After time for a brief discussion, ask a few students to share their ideas.

Summarize and Apply

Summarize the learning. Remind students to write about a character's actions.

> How can you show your readers what a character is like?

- Write the principle at the top of the chart.

> During writing time, check the story you are working on to see if you have described a character's actions so that your readers learn about the character. You might need to add some actions. If you need to add some actions, make a few notes in your writer's notebook about what a character might do before you write them into your story. Bring your writing to share when we meet later.

Tell what characters do.

Character	Character's Actions	What the Character Is Like
Vinson	reads, hides in room, puts on headphones to avoid talking to Grandpa	uncomfortable embarrassed
	joins the parade	proud enthusiastic
Marisa	watches closely as dumplings are made	wants to learn
	wakes up early to make dumplings	tries hard is helpful
	concentrates on filling the dumplings	
	gives Grandma a big hug	loves Grandma

Confer

- During independent writing, move around the room to confer briefly with students. Invite them to talk about how they are describing their characters. Use the following prompts as needed.
  - *What is your character like?*
  - *How will you show what this character is like?*
  - *What actions can you add?*

Share

Following independent writing, gather students in the meeting area to share their writing.

> Share what you wrote about a character's actions.

> Who made notes in your writer's notebook about character actions you might include in a book you plan to write? Share what you wrote.

WML 3
CFT.U2.WML3

Writing Minilesson Principle
Tell what characters think and say.

Describing Characters

You Will Need

- several mentor texts that describe the thoughts and words of characters, such as the following:
  - *Crane Boy* by Diana Cohn, from Text Set: Honoring Traditions
  - *Dancing in the Wings* by Debbie Allen, from Text Set: Genre Study: Realistic Fiction
- chart paper and markers
- writer's notebooks and writing folders

Academic Language / Important Vocabulary

- character
- thoughts
- dialogue
- feelings

Continuum Connection

- Describe people by what they do, say, and think and what others say about them
- Describe characters by how they look and what they do
- Show rather than tell how characters feel

GOAL

Describe characters through their thoughts and through dialogue with other characters.

RATIONALE

When students understand that writers reveal something about a character by sharing the character's inner thoughts and feelings and by relaying dialogue, they realize that they can use a character's thoughts and words to convey information in their own writing.

WRITER'S NOTEBOOK/WRITING FOLDER

Students will continue to work on their stories from their writing folders. They can use their writer's notebooks to try out descriptions of their characters' thoughts and feelings before adding to their drafts.

ASSESS LEARNING

- Look at students' writing. Do they sometimes include a character's thoughts and words?
- Look for evidence that students can use vocabulary such as *character*, *thoughts*, *dialogue*, and *feelings*.

MINILESSON

To help students think about the minilesson principle, engage them in an interactive lesson that uses mentor texts to model how writers include characters' thoughts and words to reveal information about them. Here is an example.

> As I read the beginning of *Crane Boy*, I am going to think aloud about what the writer, Diana Cohn, did to help me know more about Kinga.

- Begin reading pages 1–4 and pause when you notice that Kinga's thoughts or dialogue reveal something about him. Begin a chart, thinking aloud as you add several text examples.

  > What do Kinga's thoughts and feelings show about him?

- Repeat with page 10 and guide the conversation as needed. As students provide ideas, add them to the chart.
- Show the cover of *Dancing in the Wings*.

  > As I read *Dancing in the Wings*, put your thumb up when you notice that Sassy's thoughts and words show something about her.

- Begin reading and pause when a volunteer puts up a thumb. Jot down the thought or dialogue. Continue for a few examples.

  > Look at the examples on the chart. Turn and talk about why the writer probably included the information about what Sassy says or thinks.

- After time for a brief discussion, ask volunteers to share. Add to the chart.

Have a Try

Invite students to turn and talk about describing a character through thoughts and spoken words.

> Think about a character in the story you are writing. Turn to your partner and describe what thoughts and spoken words you could include to show something important about the character.

▸ After time for a brief discussion, ask a few students to share their ideas.

Summarize and Apply

Summarize the learning. Remind students to include a character's thoughts and dialogue in their writing.

> How can you show your readers what a character is like?

▸ Write the principle at the top of the chart.

> During writing time, check the story you are working on to see if you can tell what a character thinks or says so that your readers learn about the character. If you can, add that to your writing. Before adding thoughts or dialogue to your story, think through what you want to add by making some notes in your writer's notebook. Bring your writing to share when we meet later.

Tell what characters think and say.

Character	What the Character Thinks or Says	What This Shows
Kinga	• "Look, the cranes!" • "Day after day, I wait for the birds." • "What can I do to help?"	• He is very interested in the cranes. • He cares about the cranes and wants to help them.
Sassy	• "At least I don't have that big forehead lookin' like a street lamp."	• She can be rude.
	• "I couldn't hide the tears I felt welling up in my eyes, so I just grabbed my dance bag and ran to the parking lot."	• She loves dancing.
	• "I'll never get to dance. It's a waste of time to go to that audition."	• She worries that she is too tall.
	• "I made it! I made it! Mama, I made it!"	• She is joyful that she will be able to dance.

Confer

▸ During independent writing, move around the room to confer briefly with students about how they are describing their characters. Use the following prompts as needed.

- *What is your character thinking about?*
- *What will your character say?*
- *What could this character think or say to help your readers learn more?*

Share

Following independent writing, gather students in the meeting area to share their writing.

> Who wrote about a character's thoughts and dialogue today? Share what you wrote.

Umbrella 2 | Describing Characters

Assessment

After you have taught the minilessons in this umbrella, observe students in a variety of classroom activities. Use *The Fountas & Pinnell Literacy Continuum* to notice, teach for, and support students' learning as you observe their attempts at writing.

- What evidence do you have of students' new understandings related to describing characters?
  - Do students use physical descriptions of characters in a way that helps their readers know more about the characters?
  - Are they using actions, thoughts, and dialogue to describe characters?
  - Are they using vocabulary such as *character*, *describe*, *actions*, *thoughts*, *dialogue*, and *feelings*?
- In what ways, beyond the scope of this umbrella, are students showing an interest in writing fiction?
  - Do they show an interest in including detailed illustrations that support the text descriptions?
  - Are they thinking and talking about voice and conventions?

Use your observations to determine the next umbrella you will teach. You may also consult Suggested Sequence of Lessons (pp. 605–622) for guidance.

EXTENSIONS FOR DESCRIBING CHARACTERS

- Extend WML3 by having students think and talk about how writers can show something about the characters by telling what other characters say about them.

- As you read aloud, pause to help students notice how writers use thoughts, actions, and dialogue to help readers learn more about a character. You might want to choose a character from a story and make a character web to model for students how they could use a web to develop characters for their own stories.

- Play a character/physical trait matching game. Have students draw detailed characters and then use the drawings to write detailed physical descriptions on a separate sheet of paper. Students play in small groups to see if they can match the illustrations to the written descriptions.

Crafting a Setting

Umbrella 3

Minilessons in This Umbrella

- **WML1** Use your senses to describe the setting.
- **WML2** Make a sketch to show your thinking about the setting.
- **WML3** Show how the setting is important to the character in a story.

Before Teaching Umbrella 3 Minilessons

Students often focus on the action or the characters when writing and do not necessarily take time to picture and describe the setting. The minilessons in this umbrella help them realize that details or information about time and place add meaning to a story. Guide students to think about how the setting is relevant to the stories they write. Point out that writing about the setting will happen mostly in their fiction writing but might also be relevant in nonfiction writing such as a memory story.

Teach these lessons when students can apply what they are learning about crafting settings directly to their writing. These lessons are intended to complement realistic fiction, but they can be repeated when students are working on memory stories or any kind of narrative writing. You may want to teach GEN.U12: Making Picture Books and CFT.U13: Adding Meaning Through Illustrations. Use the books listed below from *Fountas & Pinnell Classroom™ Interactive Read-Aloud Collection*, or choose books with clearly described settings from the classroom library.

Interactive Read-Aloud Collection

The Importance of Determination

The Paperboy by Dav Pilkey

Soccer Star by Mina Javaherbin

Genre Study: Realistic Fiction

Owl Moon by Jane Yolen

Facing Challenges

First Day in Grapes by L. King Pérez

Goal! by Mina Javaherbin

As you read and enjoy these texts together, help students
- notice the details in the words and drawings that relate to setting, and
- understand how the setting is important to the characters.

Interactive Read-Aloud
Determination

Realistic Fiction

Facing Challenges

Writer's Notebook

WML1
CFT.U3.WML1

Writing Minilesson Principle
Use your senses to describe the setting.

Crafting a Setting

You Will Need

- several mentor texts with a clear setting, such as the following:
  - *The Paperboy* by Dav Pilkey and *Soccer Star* by Mina Javaherbin, from Text Set: The Importance of Determination
  - *Owl Moon* by Jane Yolen, from Text Set: Genre Study: Realistic Fiction
- chart paper and markers
- writer's notebooks
- To download the following online resource for this lesson, visit **fp.pub/resources**:
  - chart art (optional)

Academic Language / Important Vocabulary

- setting
- sensory
- describe
- details
- imagine

Continuum Connection

- Describe the setting with appropriate detail
- Understand that writers can learn to craft fiction by using mentor texts as models
- Use language to create sensory images
- Observe carefully events, people, settings, and other aspects of the world to gather information on a topic

GOAL

Use sensory details to describe the setting.

RATIONALE

Encouraging students to use their senses when they think about how to describe a setting enables them to notice more details, resulting in a richer description.

WRITER'S NOTEBOOK/WRITING FOLDER

Have students use their writer's notebooks to try out using sensory details to describe a setting.

ASSESS LEARNING

- Notice whether students recognize that they can use their senses when they describe a setting.
- Observe whether students sometimes use sensory words to describe the setting.
- Look for evidence that students can use vocabulary such as *setting*, *sensory*, *describe*, *details*, and *imagine*.

MINILESSON

To help students include sensory details to craft their settings, use mentor texts and provide an interactive lesson. Here is an example.

> As I read from *The Paperboy*, listen for words that the writer used to help you picture the setting. Put your thumb up when you notice details that describe where or when the story takes place.

- Begin a three-column chart. Write the book title on the left. Show and read pages 3, 7, and 22, pausing as students put up a thumb when they notice details about the setting. As they do, jot down sensory detail words in the middle column.

> What senses do these words appeal to?

- Record students' responses in the third column.
- Repeat with pages 5–6 of *Owl Moon*.

> These authors used sensory words to show the setting. Sometimes, however, authors show the setting only in pictures.

The Writing Minilessons Book, Grade 3

Have a Try

Invite students to turn and talk about using sensory details to reveal the setting.

▸ Show pages 5–6 of *Soccer Star*.

> On these pages, the author did not describe the setting, so the reader must look at the picture. What sensory words could the writer have used to describe what the two characters might be experiencing? Turn and talk to your partner.

▸ After time for a brief discussion, use students' ideas to fill in the remaining row of the chart.

Summarize and Apply

Summarize the learning. Remind students to include sensory details in their writing to reveal the setting.

> What can you do to write a good description of a setting?

▸ Write the principle at the top of the chart.

> Today, use your senses to write a description of a place in your writer's notebook. You might want to try out a setting for a story you are writing or will write. Bring your writing when we meet later.

Confer

▸ During independent writing, move around the room to confer briefly with students about describing the setting. Use the following prompts as needed.

- *What are some sound (sight, smell, taste, touch) words you might use to show where (when) your story takes place?*
- *How will your readers know where your story is happening?*
- *If you were a character in your story, what would you be noticing with your senses?*

Share

Following independent writing, gather students in triads in the meeting area.

> Share what you wrote with your group.

Umbrella 3: Crafting a Setting

WML 2
CFT.U3.WML2

Writing Minilesson Principle
Make a sketch to show your thinking about the setting.

Crafting a Setting

You Will Need

- a mentor text that shows a setting, such as *First Day in Grapes* by L. King Pérez, from Text Set: Facing Challenges
- chart paper prepared with a sketch of a recent class experience (e.g., class play, field trip) with room left to write a description
- markers
- writer's notebooks

Academic Language / Important Vocabulary

- setting
- sketch
- describe
- details

Continuum Connection

- Use sketching, webs, lists, and freewriting to think about, plan for, and try out writing
- Use sketching to support memory and help in planning
- Use drawings and sketches to represent people, places, things, and ideas in the composing, revising, and publishing process
- Understand the difference between drawing and sketching and use them to support planning, revising, and publishing in the writing process
- Use sketching to create quick representations of images, usually an outline in pencil or pen

GOAL

Use a sketch to prompt details for describing the setting.

RATIONALE

Sketching the setting of a story represents the students' process of thinking and provides a concrete visual to write about. A quick sketch can help remind students of details they might not remember without making a sketch first and can result in more effective writing.

WRITER'S NOTEBOOK/WRITING FOLDER

Students can use the blank (or lined) pages in their writer's notebooks for sketching.

ASSESS LEARNING

- Observe whether students write about the details that are in their sketches.
- Look for evidence that students can use vocabulary such as *setting*, *sketch*, *describe*, and *details*.

MINILESSON

To help students think about the minilesson principle so that they can apply it to stories they are working on, provide an interactive lesson. Here is an example.

- Show and read pages 15–16 in *First Day in Grapes*.

  Chico's teacher has asked him to look at a picture of a house and then write a story about it. Why do you think Chico's teacher did that?

  If I asked you to write a description of the front of our school, would you find it easier to write from your memory or from a sketch? Turn and tell your partner your answer and why you think so.

- After a time for a brief discussion, ask several volunteers to share their thoughts.

  Most of the time, you will find it easier to write a good description of a setting if you think about the setting, picture it in your mind, and then make a sketch of it before you start to write. Making a picture or a sketch can help you think about what to write as you plan how to write about a setting.

WML 2

CFT.U3.WML2

Have a Try

Invite students to turn and talk about making a sketch to show the setting.

▸ Show the sketch you prepared in advance.

> Here is a sketch I made about our class activity. Notice that my sketch doesn't have a lot of detail. What details does the sketch help you remember? Turn and talk about that.

▸ After time for a brief discussion, ask a few students to share their ideas. Then use shared writing to model writing about the setting.

Summarize and Apply

Summarize the learning. Have students use a sketch to help write setting details.

> How does sketching help you when you prepare to write about a setting?

▸ Write the principle at the top of the chart.

> During writing time, think of a setting. It might be the setting of a story you are working on or that you plan to write. Picture it in your mind and make a sketch in your writer's notebook of your setting. Remember that a sketch is a quick drawing to help you with planning. Bring your writer's notebook when we meet.

Confer

▸ During independent writing, move around the room to confer briefly with students about crafting a setting. Use the following prompts as needed.
- *Where does your story take place?*
- *Talk about your sketch.*
- *What details about the setting did your sketch help you think about?*

Share

Following independent writing, gather students in the meeting area to share their sketches with a partner before bringing the whole group back together.

> What information from your sketch will you use in your writing?

Umbrella 3: Crafting a Setting

325

Section 3: Craft

WML 3
CFT.U3.WML3

Writing Minilesson Principle
Show how the setting is important to the character in a story.

Crafting a Setting

You Will Need

- several mentor texts with a clear setting, such as the following:
  - *The Paperboy* by Dav Pilkey from Text Set: The Importance of Determination
  - *Goal!* by Mina Javaherbin, from Text Set: Facing Challenges
- chart paper and markers
- document camera (optional)
- writer's notebooks

Academic Language / Important Vocabulary

- setting
- important

Continuum Connection

- Understand that writers can learn to craft fiction by using mentor texts as models
- Understand that a writer uses various elements of fiction (e.g., setting, plot with problem and solution, characters) in a fiction text

GOAL

Notice and think about how the setting is important to characters in stories.

RATIONALE

When students understand that writers include relevant setting details as a way to help readers know more about characters, they begin to think about what setting information to include in their own writing.

WRITER'S NOTEBOOK/WRITING FOLDER

Have students use their writer's notebooks to try out some ideas for describing a setting that shows something about the character in a story.

ASSESS LEARNING

- Notice whether students recognize that writers choose a setting that is important to the characters in a story.
- Observe for evidence that students include setting details that are relevant to people or characters in the stories they write.
- Look for evidence that students can use vocabulary such as *setting* and *important*.

MINILESSON

To help students think about the minilesson principle, use mentor texts to prompt a discussion about how authors use setting details to reveal information about characters. Here is an example.

- Show and read pages 23–24 in *The Paperboy*.

  What details about the setting does the writer include on these pages of *The Paperboy*?

  How are the time and place important to the boy?

- As students provide ideas, write them on a chart that shows the setting details and how they are important to the character.

- Show pages 29–30 in *Goal!*

  What setting details does the writer share in the words and drawings?

  How are the setting details important to the kids in the story?

- Add to the chart.

  Writers choose what details about time and place to include so readers can learn more about characters. When you write your own stories, you can also choose which setting details to include so your readers can learn more about the characters.

The Writing Minilessons Book, Grade 3

Have a Try

Invite students to turn and talk about how the setting is important to a character in a story.

> Think about a story you are writing or have already written. What are some details of the setting that show how the time and place are important to a character in your story? Turn and talk about that.

- After time for a brief discussion, ask a few students to share their ideas.

Summarize and Apply

Summarize the learning. Remind students to show how setting is important to a character in their writing. Write the principle at the top of the chart.

> During writing time, think about setting details that show how the setting is important to a character in your story. Write some ideas in your writer's notebook. Bring your writer's notebook to share when we meet later.

Show how the setting is important to the character in a story.

Paperboy	cold morning air	The boy gets up very early and on his own. He is responsible and independent.
	sun just coming up	
	in his neighborhood	He lives in a place where he is able to ride his bike alone because there is no traffic.
	warm clothes	

GOAL!	unsafe streets	The kids do not live in a safe area or have a lot of money, but soccer is very important and brings them joy.
	run-down buildings	
	shorts and T-shirts	The weather is warm where they live, so they can play outside.

Confer

- During independent writing, move around the room to confer briefly with students about crafting a setting. Use the following prompts as needed.
  - *What can you include to help your readers know where and when this story takes place?*
  - *What details can you include about the setting that help readers understand more about this character?*
  - *Share some words you might use to show the time and place.*

Share

Following independent writing, gather students in the meeting area to share their writing with a partner. Then select several students to share with the whole group.

> Share the details of the setting you wrote about.

Umbrella 3: Crafting a Setting

Assessment

After you have taught the minilessons in this umbrella, observe students in a variety of classroom activities. Use *The Fountas & Pinnell Literacy Continuum* to notice, teach for, and support students' learning as you observe their attempts at writing.

- What evidence do you have of students' new understandings related to setting?
  - Are students able to use their senses to describe the setting?
  - Do they make a sketch before writing about the setting in a story?
  - Do they show how the setting is important to a character in the story?
  - As part of their planning and rehearsing, do they try out ideas for a setting in their writer's notebooks?
  - Do they use vocabulary such as *setting*, *place*, *time*, *sensory*, *describe*, *details*, and *important*?
- In what ways, beyond the scope of this umbrella, do students show readiness for fiction writing?
  - Do they show an interest in adding illustrations that connect to the text?
  - Are they open to revising their writing in order to improve it?

Use your observations to determine the next umbrella you will teach. You may also consult Suggested Sequence of Lessons (pp. 605–622) for guidance.

EXTENSIONS FOR CRAFTING A SETTING

- When students write memoirs, encourage them to think about how a setting relates to or adds to their experiences.

- Extend these minilessons by introducing similar lessons that focus on drawing details of the setting in the illustrations.

- Encourage students to observe the background illustrations in books to get ideas for when they draw backgrounds to show the setting of their stories. What details do the illustrators show? What colors do the illustrators use? How do the people look in or against the background?

- If you are using *The Reading Minilessons Book, Grade 3* (Fountas and Pinnell 2019), you may choose to teach LA.U21: Thinking About the Setting in Fiction Books.

- If students speak a language other than English at home, suggest that they use some words from it if it helps readers understand the setting.

Adding Dialogue to Writing

Umbrella 4

Minilessons in This Umbrella

- **WML1** Add dialogue to make your writing more interesting.
- **WML2** Make it clear who is speaking when you use dialogue.
- **WML3** Include action with dialogue in your writing.

Before Teaching Umbrella 4 Minilessons

Teach these minilessons when children are working on narrative writing, such as memory stories, pictures books, or realistic fiction, and have experienced a variety of fiction books with dialogue. Use as mentor texts the following books from *Fountas & Pinnell Classroom™ Interactive Read-Aloud Collection*, or use other text examples of dialogue from the classroom library or from class shared writing.

The Importance of Kindness

Enemy Pie by Derek Munson

The Can Man by Laura E. Williams

Last Day Blues by Julie Danneberg

Under the Lemon Moon by Edith Hope Fine

As you read and enjoy these texts together, help students notice
- the way the writers show what the characters say and think,
- how writers let readers know who is talking,
- how dialogue makes stories more interesting, and
- how dialogue is interspersed with action.

Interactive Read-Aloud
Kindness

Writer's Notebook

329

WML1
CFT.U4.WML1

Writing Minilesson Principle
Add dialogue to make your writing more interesting.

Adding Dialogue to Writing

You Will Need

- a few familiar fiction books with dialogue, such as the following from Text Set: The Importance of Kindness:
  - *Last Day Blues* by Julie Danneberg
  - *The Can Man* by Laura E. Williams
  - *Under the Lemon Moon* by Edith Hope Fine
- chart paper and markers
- a short sample text inside speech bubbles and/or thought bubbles
- writer's notebooks and writing folders
- To download the following online resource for this lesson, visit **fp.pub/resources**:
  - chart art (optional)

Academic Language / Important Vocabulary

- dialogue

Continuum Connection

- Use dialogue as appropriate to add to the meaning of the story
- Understand and use quotation marks to indicate simple dialogue to show the exact words someone said
- Add ideas in thought bubbles or dialogue in quotation marks or speech bubbles to provide information, provide narration, or show thoughts and feelings

GOAL

Understand that dialogue adds meaning and interest to a story.

RATIONALE

When you help students notice the different ways that authors use dialogue to make their stories more interesting, they will begin to include meaningful dialogue in their own stories.

WRITER'S NOTEBOOK/WRITING FOLDER

Have students try out some dialogue in their writer's notebooks before adding it to the draft of a story from their writing folders.

ASSESS LEARNING

- Observe whether students use dialogue in ways that make their stories more interesting.
- Look for evidence that they can use vocabulary such as *dialogue*.

MINILESSON

To help students think about the minilesson principle, use mentor texts to engage them in an inquiry-based lesson on how authors use dialogue. Here is an example.

- Show the cover of *Last Day Blues* and read the title. Display and read pages 2–3.

  How did the author show how the children feel about the last day of school?

  She used dialogue, or talking, to show how they feel.

- On chart paper, begin a list of how writers use dialogue.

  How do you know what the characters are saying?

  The author used quotation marks around the words each character says.

- Show the cover of *The Can Man* and read the title. Read the first paragraph of page 4.

  What does Tim's mom tell him about The Can Man?

  Why do you think the author included dialogue, or talking, here? What does the dialogue help you understand?

- Record students' responses on the chart. Help students understand that the dialogue reveals important information about the characters.

- Show the cover of *Under the Lemon Moon* and read the title. Read pages 9–10.

  Why did the author include dialogue on these pages? How does the dialogue help move the story along?

- Record responses on the chart.

The Writing Minilessons Book, Grade 3

Have a Try

Invite students to talk to a partner about using speech and thought bubbles to show dialogue.

- Show the prepared text.

    What do you notice about how I showed what the characters are saying and thinking? Turn and talk to your partner about this.

- After students turn and talk, invite several pairs to share their thinking. Make sure students understand the difference between speech bubbles and thought bubbles.

Summarize and Apply

Summarize the learning and remind students to think about including dialogue when they write fiction.

   What did you learn today about how and why authors add dialogue to their stories?

- Write the principle at the top of the chart.

    If you work on a story from your writing folder during writing time today, think about how you can add dialogue to make your story more interesting. Try out some dialogue in your writer's notebook before adding it to your story. Bring your writing to share when we come back together.

Confer

- During independent writing, move around the room to confer briefly with as many individual students as time allows. Sit side by side with them and invite them to talk about using dialogue. Use prompts such as the following as needed.
    - What might the characters say to each other during this part of the story?
    - How could you use dialogue to show how the character is feeling?
    - Would you like to add a speech bubble to this illustration? What could it say?

Share

Following independent writing, gather students in the meeting area to share their writing.

   Who would like to share how you added dialogue to your writing today?

   Why did you decide to use dialogue in this part of your story?

WML 2
CFT.U4.WML2

Writing Minilesson Principle
Make it clear who is speaking when you use dialogue.

Adding Dialogue to Writing

You Will Need

- familiar fiction books with dialogue, such as the following from Text Set: The Importance of Kindness:
  - *Last Day Blues* by Julie Danneberg
  - *Under the Lemon Moon* by Edith Hope Fine
- highlighter
- chart paper and markers
- writer's notebooks and writing folders

Academic Language / Important Vocabulary

- dialogue
- quotation mark
- comma
- capitalization
- punctuation

Continuum Connection

- Use capital letters correctly in uninterrupted dialogue
- Use dialogue as appropriate to add to the meaning of the story
- Understand and use quotation marks to indicate simple dialogue to show the exact words someone said
- Add ideas in thought bubbles or dialogue in quotation marks or speech bubbles to provide information, provide narration, or show thoughts and feelings

GOAL

Understand how to use punctuation, capitalization, and speaker tags to show who is speaking in a story.

RATIONALE

When you teach students how to correctly write dialogue, readers will be able to follow the story with ease.

WRITER'S NOTEBOOK/WRITING FOLDER

Have students try out some dialogue in their writer's notebooks before adding it to the draft of a story from their writing folders.

ASSESS LEARNING

- Look at students' writing. Do they write dialogue correctly?
- Look for evidence that they can use vocabulary such as *dialogue*, *quotation mark*, *comma*, *capitalization*, and *punctuation*..

MINILESSON

To help students think about the minilesson principle, use mentor texts to engage them in an inquiry-based lesson on how to write and punctuate dialogue. Here is an example.

- Show the cover of *Last Day Blues* and read the title. Read page 2 aloud. Show students the text.

  Who says "I'm going to miss Daisy"?

  How did the author make it clear who is speaking?

- Write the example on chart paper. Ask a student to highlight the speaker tag.
- Show the cover of *Under the Lemon Moon* and read the title. Read page 9 aloud. Show the page.

  What is the last thing Rosalinda says to Esmeralda?

  How do you know who is speaking?

- Write the example on the chart. Ask a student to highlight the speaker tag.

  How is this different from the first example of dialogue we wrote down?

- Help students understand that the speaker tag can come either before or after the dialogue.

  What do you notice about the capitalization and punctuation?

Have a Try

Invite students to talk to a partner about how to use capitalization and punctuation in dialogue.

- Write on chart paper a line of simple dialogue without any punctuation.

    I want to include this line of dialogue in a story I'm writing. What do I need to add? Turn and talk to your partner about this.

- After students turn and talk, invite a few students to share their responses. Have a volunteer come up to add quotation marks and end punctuation.

Summarize and Apply

Summarize the learning and remind students to make clear who is speaking when they use dialogue.

How do authors make clear who is speaking and what is being said when they use dialogue?

- Write the principle at the top of the chart.

    If you are working on a story, think about what your story characters might say. Try out some dialogue in your writer's notebook before you add it to your story. Bring your writing to share when we meet later.

Make it clear who is speaking when you use dialogue.

"I'm going to miss Daisy," said Dan.

Aloud she said, "Gracias."

"Do you want to go home?" asked Maia.

Confer

- During independent writing, move around the room to confer briefly with as many individual students as time allows. Sit side by side with them and invite them to talk about using dialogue. Use prompts such as the following as needed.
    - *What do the characters say to each other in this part of the story?*
    - *How can you make it clear who is saying what?*
    - *Do you want to write the character's name before or after the dialogue?*

Share

Following independent writing, gather students in the meeting area to share their writing.

Did anyone use dialogue in your writing today?

How did you make it clear who is speaking?

WML 3
CFT.U4.WML3

Writing Minilesson Principle
Include action with dialogue in your writing.

Adding Dialogue to Writing

You Will Need

- a couple of familiar fiction books with dialogue, such as the following from Text Set: The Importance of Kindness:
  - *The Can Man* by Laura E. Williams
  - *Enemy Pie* by Derek Munson
- chart paper prepared with excerpts
- two colors of highlighters
- markers
- writer's notebooks and writing folders

Academic Language / Important Vocabulary

- dialogue
- action

Continuum Connection

- Use dialogue as appropriate to add to the meaning of the story
- Add ideas in thought bubbles or dialogue in quotation marks or speech bubbles to provide information, provide narration, or show thoughts and feelings

GOAL

Understand that dialogue is often broken up with narration or action.

RATIONALE

When students notice how writers break up dialogue with narration or action, they begin to see how dialogue can move a story along and can begin to try this approach in their own writing.

WRITER'S NOTEBOOK/WRITING FOLDER

Have students try out some dialogue in their writer's notebooks before adding it to the draft of a story from their writing folders.

ASSESS LEARNING

- Observe for evidence that students try interspersing dialogue with action in meaningful ways.
- Look for evidence that they can use vocabulary such as *dialogue* and *action*.

MINILESSON

To help students think about the minilesson principle, use mentor texts to engage students in an inquiry-based lesson on breaking up dialogue with narration or action. Here is an example.

- Show the cover of *Enemy Pie* and read the title. Read page 6.

  What do you notice about how the author used dialogue on this page? Is the whole page dialogue?

  What else did the author include besides dialogue?

  The author also told what the character is doing, or the action.

- Show the same passage on the prepared chart paper. Highlight the dialogue in blue and the action in yellow.

- Show the cover of *The Can Man* and read the title. Read page 22. Show the excerpt on chart paper. Invite volunteers to highlight the dialogue and action.

Have a Try

Invite students to talk to a partner about why authors break up dialogue with action.

> Why do you think authors include both dialogue and action in their stories? Turn and talk to your partner about this.

▶ After time for discussion, invite several students to share their thinking.

Summarize and Apply

Write the principle at the top of the chart. Summarize the learning and remind students to include action with dialogue in their writing.

> If you are working on a story, think about what your story characters might say and what they might do while they are talking. Try out some dialogue in your writer's notebook before you add it to your story. Bring your story to share when we meet later.

Include action with dialogue in your writing.

"Tell you how? I'll show you how!" he said. He pulled a really old recipe book off the kitchen shelf. Inside, there was a worn-out scrap of paper with faded writing. Dad held it up and squinted at it.

"Enemy Pie," he said, satisfied.

from *Enemy Pie* by Derek Munson

Tim nodded. "I guess so."

The boys looked up as the clatter of The Can Man's cart came toward them. The Can Man stopped at the bottom of the stairs.

"You need help with your bags?"

"Okay," Tim said.

from *The Can Man* by Laura E. William

Confer

▶ During independent writing, move around the room to confer briefly with as many individual students as time allows. Sit side by side with them and invite them to talk about using dialogue. Use prompts such as the following as needed.
- *What is happening in this part of your story?*
- *What are the characters saying?*
- *What is the character doing while speaking?*
- *Would it be better to use action or dialogue to show _____?*

Share

Following independent writing, gather students in the meeting area to share their writing.

> Who would like to read aloud a page from your story where you used both dialogue and action?

Umbrella 4: Adding Dialogue to Writing

Assessment

After you have taught the minilessons in this umbrella, observe students as they write. Use *The Fountas & Pinnell Literacy Continuum* to notice, teach for, and support students' learning as you observe their attempts at reading and writing.

- What evidence do you have of students' new understandings related to adding dialogue to writing?
  - How do they use dialogue to make their writing more interesting?
  - Do they make it clear who is speaking when writing dialogue?
  - Are they able to incorporate a character's actions before and/or after dialogue?
  - As part of their planning and rehearsing, do they try out ideas for dialogue in their writer's notebooks?
  - Do they understand and use vocabulary such as *dialogue* and *action*?
- In what other ways, beyond the scope of this umbrella, are students ready to explore fiction writing?
  - Are they trying to show their own individual voice through their writing?
  - Are they experimenting with different ways of beginning and ending stories?

Use your observations to determine the next umbrella you will teach. You may also consult Suggested Sequence of Lessons (pp. 605–622) for guidance.

EXTENSIONS FOR ADDING DIALOGUE TO WRITING

- Talk about using a speaker tag (e.g., a word such as *shouted*, *whispered*, *cried*, *laughed* plus the character's name) to show how a character says something.

- Teach students how to write split or interrupted dialogue.

- Have students read, discuss, and act out plays and/or write their own plays. Or, you might have students create a readers' theater script.

Crafting a Lead

Umbrella 5

Minilessons in This Umbrella

- **WML1** Start your writing with action.
- **WML2** Start your writing with talking.
- **WML3** Start your writing with a description of the setting.
- **WML4** Start your writing with an interesting fact.

Before Teaching Umbrella 5 Minilessons

Crafting a lead is a revision technique. It's something writers often do toward the end of their writing when they understand what kind of lead would best engage their readers. For these minilessons, students should have one or more pieces of writing in progress or completed so that they can apply what they are learning about leads to specific pieces of writing.

Students can experiment with ways to start their writing in their writer's notebooks. Once they have a few options, they can choose the one that fits their writing the best. The same chart is used throughout the umbrella so that new ideas can be added over time. Use the books listed below from *Fountas & Pinnell Classroom™ Interactive Read-Aloud Collection*, or choose books that demonstrate a variety of leads from the classroom library.

Interactive Read-Aloud Collection
Humorous Texts
The Great Fuzz Frenzy by Janet Stevens and Susan Stevens Crummel
Bedhead by Margie Palatini

The Importance of Determination
The Patchwork Quilt by Valerie Flournoy
Ruby's Wish by Shirin Yim Bridges

Animal Journeys
A Mother's Journey by Sandra Markle
North: The Amazing Story of Arctic Migration by Nick Dowson

Honoring Traditions
Crane Boy by Diana Cohn

As you read and enjoy these texts together, help students
- notice what the writers did to get their readers' attention, and
- observe different ways the stories can begin.

Interactive Read-Aloud
Humorous Texts

Determination

Animal Journeys

Honoring Traditions

Writer's Notebook

WML1
CFT.U5.WML1

Writing Minilesson Principle
Start your writing with action.

Crafting a Lead

You Will Need

- several mentor texts that begin with action, such as the following from Text Set: Humorous Texts:
  - *The Great Fuzz Frenzy* by Janet Stevens and Susan Stevens Crummel
  - *Bedhead* by Margie Palatini
- chart paper and markers
- writer's notebooks and writing folders
- To download the following online resource for this lesson, visit **fp.pub/resources**:
  - chart art (optional)

Academic Language / Important Vocabulary

- beginning
- lead
- action
- sound word

Continuum Connection

- Understand that writers can learn to craft fiction by using mentor texts as models
- Use a variety of beginnings to engage the reader

GOAL

Understand that writers can begin a story with action.

RATIONALE

When students learn that writers make choices about how to begin their writing, they realize that they, too, can make thoughtful decisions about how best to begin their own writing.

WRITER'S NOTEBOOK/WRITING FOLDER

Have students use their writer's notebooks to try out different ways to begin a story in their writing folders.

ASSESS LEARNING

- Observe students' writing to notice whether they sometimes begin books with action.
- Look for evidence that students can use vocabulary such as *beginning*, *lead*, *action*, and *sound word*.

MINILESSON

To help students think about the minilesson principle, use familiar books and an interactive lesson to engage them in noticing that writers sometimes choose to begin their writing with action. Here is an example.

- Revisit the first pages of *The Great Fuzz Frenzy*.

    What do you notice about the way the writers, Janet Stevens and Susan Stevens Crummel, decided to begin this book?

- Guide the conversation to help students recognize that the book begins with action and that sound words are used.

    The story begins with action. The ball is rolling fast and the prairie dogs have to move away quickly. The way that a writer begins a book is sometimes called the lead because it's how the writer leads the reader into the writing.

- Repeat with *Bedhead*.

    When writers begin a story with action, sometimes they include sound effects to get the reader interested in reading on.

- Introduce a story idea and model the process of thinking about some different action leads that could be used for the story.

    Imagine you are almost late for school. If you wanted to write a story about that, you could start with an action, like this: I sprinted down the sidewalk as fast as my legs would take me!

- Title a two-column chart *Writing Strong Leads*. Write the principle in the left column. Write the example in the right column.

WML1

CFT.U5.WML1

Have a Try

Invite students to turn and talk about beginning a story with action.

> Turn and talk about some different ways you might start this story with action. Remember that action can include sound words.

- After time for a brief discussion, ask students to share ideas. Add one more example to the chart.
- Save the chart for WML2.

Summarize and Apply

Summarize the learning. Have students try out some different ways to use action to begin a story.

> During writing time, reread the story you are currently working on. Does it need a stronger lead? If so, title a page in your writer's notebook Leads and write a few ideas for beginning your story with action. Choose one you like best and add it to your story. Or, choose a piece of writing you have finished and try a new lead for it. Bring your ideas and your writing when we meet.

Writing Strong Leads

Start your writing with action.	I sprinted down the sidewalk as fast as my legs would take me!
	"R-r-r-r-r-ing!" I could hear the bell ringing as I raced toward the school door.

Confer

- During independent writing, move around the room to confer briefly with as many individual students as time allows. Sit side by side with them and invite them to talk about crafting how their stories start. Use the following prompts as needed.
  - *How will you start this story?*
  - *What is one way you could use action to begin your story?*
  - *Is there a sound word that you could use to show action?*

Share

Following independent writing, gather students in the meeting area to share their writing in groups of three. Then select a few students to share with the class.

> Read the beginning of your story to your group. Talk about how you decided to write your lead. If you haven't written a lead yet, you might get an idea from one of your classmates.

Umbrella 5: Crafting a Lead

WML2
CFT.U5.WML2

Writing Minilesson Principle
Start your writing with talking.

Crafting a Lead

You Will Need

- a mentor text that begins with talking, such as *The Patchwork Quilt* by Valerie Flournoy, from Text Set: The Importance of Determination
- chart paper and markers
- chart from WML1
- writer's notebooks and writing folders

Academic Language / Important Vocabulary

- beginning
- lead

Continuum Connection

- Understand that writers can learn to craft fiction by using mentor texts as models
- Use a variety of beginnings to engage the reader

GOAL

Understand that writers can begin a story with talking.

RATIONALE

Starting a story with dialogue can pull readers right into the action. When students see how published authors do this, they can try the technique on their own.

WRITER'S NOTEBOOK/WRITING FOLDER

Have students use their writer's notebooks to try out different ways to begin a story in their writing folders.

ASSESS LEARNING

- Observe for evidence that students recognize that writers make choices about how to begin their writing.
- Look at students' writing. Do they try beginning their stories with dialogue?
- Look for evidence that students can use vocabulary such as *beginning* and *lead*.

MINILESSON

To help students think about the minilesson principle, use familiar books and an interactive lesson to engage students in noticing that writers sometimes choose to begin their writing with talking. Here is an example.

- Display the chart from WML1.
- Revisit the first page of *The Patchwork Quilt*.

  What do you notice about the way the writer, Valerie Flournoy, decided to begin this book?

- Guide the conversation to help students recognize that Tanya and Mama are having a conversation in the kitchen. The book begins with talking.

  The writer began this book with talking. Sometimes when books begin with talking, we learn about how the character is feeling, like we do in this story.

- Revisit the story idea used in WML1, this time encouraging students to think about how to begin the story with talking.

  Remember the story we talked about when you imagined that you were almost late for school? If you wanted to start the story a different way, you might begin with talking. You could start with something like this: "Oh, no!" I shouted to my sister. "Run! We are going to be late!"

- On the chart from WML1, write the principle in the left column. Write the example in the right column, leaving room for additional ideas.

WML 2
CFT.U5.WML2

Have a Try

Invite students to turn and talk about beginning a story with talking.

> Turn and talk about some different ways you might start this story with talking.

- After time for a brief discussion, ask students to share ideas. Add one more example to the chart.
- Save the chart for WML3.

Summarize and Apply

Summarize the learning. Have students try out some different ways to use talking to begin a story.

> During writing time, reread the story you are currently working on. Does it need a stronger lead? If so, title a page Leads in your writer's notebook and write a few ideas for beginning your story with talking. Choose the one you like best and add it to the story. Or, choose a piece of writing you have finished and try a new lead for it. Bring your ideas and your writing when we meet.

Writing Strong Leads

Start your writing with action.	I sprinted down the sidewalk as fast as my legs would take me!
	"R-r-r-r-r-r-ing!" I could hear the bell ringing as I raced toward the school door.
Start your writing with talking. ("Oh, no!")	"Oh, no!" I shouted to my sister. "Run! We are going to be late!"
	"Heyyyyyyy, wait for me!"

Confer

- During independent writing, move around the room to confer briefly with as many individual students as time allows. Sit side by side with them and invite them to talk about ways to start their writing. Use the following prompts as needed.
  - *How will you start your writing?*
  - *What is one way you could use talking to begin your story?*
  - *Will your readers learn about how your character is feeling from the dialogue?*

Share

Following independent writing, gather students in the meeting area to share their writing in groups of three.

> Read your lead aloud to your group. Talk about how you decided to write it.

- After time for groups to share, bring the class back together.

> What idea did you hear in your group that you would like to try in your own writing?

Umbrella 5: Crafting a Lead

Section 3: Craft

341

WML 3
CFT.U5.WML3

Writing Minilesson Principle
Start your writing with a description of the setting.

Crafting a Lead

You Will Need

- several mentor texts that begin with a description of the setting, such as the following:
  - *A Mother's Journey* by Sandra Markle, from Text Set: Animal Journeys
  - *Ruby's Wish* by Shirin Yim Bridges, from Text Set: The Importance of Determination
- chart paper and markers
- chart from WML2
- writer's notebooks and writing folders
- To download the following online resource for this lesson, visit **fp.pub/resources**:
  - chart art (optional)

Academic Language / Important Vocabulary

- beginning
- lead
- description
- setting

Continuum Connection

- Use a variety of beginnings to engage the reader

GOAL

Understand that writers can begin a story by describing the setting.

RATIONALE

When students learn that they can begin their writing with a description of where and when something takes place, they understand that they have many decisions to make when they write books.

WRITER'S NOTEBOOK/WRITING FOLDER

Have students use their writer's notebooks to try out different ways to begin the story they are working on in their writing folders.

ASSESS LEARNING

- Look at students' writing. Do they try beginning their stories with a description of the setting?
- Look for evidence that students can use vocabulary such as *beginning*, *lead*, *description*, and *setting*.

MINILESSON

To help students think about the minilesson principle, use familiar books and an interactive lesson to engage students in noticing that writers may choose to begin their writing with a description of the setting. Here is an example.

- Revisit the first page of *A Mother's Journey*.

  What do you notice about the way the writer, Sandra Markle, decided to begin this book?

- Guide the conversation to help students recognize that the book begins with a description of the setting, including the time of day, time of year, and location.

- Repeat with *Ruby's Wish*.

  When writers begin a book with a description of the setting, you can quickly get a picture in your mind of the time and place that the story happens.

- Revisit the story idea used in WML1 and WML2, this time encouraging students to think about how to begin with a description of the setting.

  Think about the story we talked about when you imagined you were almost late for school. If you wanted to start the story a different way, you might begin with a description of the setting. You could start with something like this: Fat raindrops plopped on my head and on the ground as I started to run along the sidewalk to catch the bus.

- On the chart from WML2, write the principle in the left column. Write the example in the right column, leaving room for additional ideas.

The Writing Minilessons Book, Grade 3

Have a Try

Invite students to turn and talk about beginning a story with a description of the setting.

> Turn and talk about some different ways you might start this story with a description of the setting.

- After time for a brief discussion, ask students to share ideas. Add one more example to the chart.
- Save the chart for WML4.

Summarize and Apply

Summarize the learning. Have students try out some different ways to use a description of the setting to begin a story.

> During writing time, reread the story you are currently working on. Does it need a stronger lead? If so, title a page Leads in your writer's notebook and write a few ideas for beginning your story by describing the setting. Choose the one you like best and add it to the story.
>
> Or, choose a piece of writing you have finished and try a new lead for it. Bring your ideas and your writing when we meet.

Writing Strong Leads

Start your writing with action.	I sprinted down the sidewalk as fast as my legs would take me!
	"R-r-r-r-r-r-ing!" I could hear the bell ringing as I raced toward the school door.
Start your writing with talking.	"Oh, no!" I shouted to my sister. "Run! We are going to be late!"
	"Heyyyyyyy, wait for me!"
Start your writing with a description of the setting.	Fat raindrops plopped on my head and on the ground as I started to run along the sidewalk to catch the bus.
	The cold air hit my head as I ran down the sidewalk, having forgotten my hat in the rush out the door.

Confer

- During independent writing, move around the room to confer briefly with as many individual students as time allows. Sit side by side with them and invite them to talk about ways to start their writing. Use the following prompts as needed.
  - *How will you start your writing?*
  - *Talk about how you could begin by describing where your story takes place.*
  - *What time of day (what month, what year) does your story take place?*
  - *The weather seems important to your story. How can you begin with a description of the weather?*

Share

Following independent writing, gather students in the meeting area to share their writing.

> What ideas do you have for beginning a book with a description of the setting?
>
> Who started a writing piece with description? Share the beginning of your story.

WML 4
CFT.U5.WML4

Writing Minilesson Principle
Start your writing with an interesting fact.

Crafting a Lead

You Will Need

- several mentor texts that begin with an interesting fact, such as the following:
  - *North: The Amazing Story of Arctic Migration* by Nick Dowson, from Text Set: Animal Journeys
  - *Crane Boy* by Diana Cohn, from Text Set: Honoring Traditions
- chart paper and markers
- chart from WML3
- writer's notebooks and writing folders
- To download the following online resource for this lesson, visit **fp.pub/resources**:
  - chart art (optional)

Academic Language / Important Vocabulary

- beginning
- lead
- fact

Continuum Connection

- Use a variety of beginnings to engage the reader

GOAL

Understand that writers can begin a story with an interesting fact.

RATIONALE

When students learn that writers use a variety of leads, such as beginning a book with an interesting fact, they start to think about how they can engage their readers with a strong lead.

WRITER'S NOTEBOOK/WRITING FOLDER

Students can use their writer's notebooks to try out different ways to begin a story in their writing folders.

ASSESS LEARNING

- Observe whether students sometimes begin their writing with an interesting fact.
- Look for evidence that students can use vocabulary such as *beginning*, *lead*, and *fact*.

MINILESSON

To help students think about the minilesson principle, use familiar books and an interactive lesson to engage them in noticing that a writer may choose to begin a book with an interesting fact. Here is an example.

- Revisit the first page of *North*.

  > What do you notice about the way the writer, Nick Dowson, decided to begin this book?

- Guide the conversation to help students recognize that the first sentence gives an interesting fact about the Arctic.

  > This information book begins with an interesting fact about the Arctic. Starting a book with an interesting fact is one way to get readers to want to keep reading.

- Repeat with the first paragraph of *Crane Boy*.

- Revisit the story idea used in the previous minilessons, this time encouraging students to think about how to begin the story with an interesting fact.

  > Remember the story we talked about when you imagined that you were almost late for school? If you wanted to use a different lead for this story, you might begin with an interesting fact. You could start with something like this: The average school start time in the US is 8:03 a.m.

- On the chart from WML3, write the principle in the left column. Write the example in the right column, leaving room for additional ideas.

- You may want to point out that interesting facts will most often be used as a way to begin nonfiction books.

The Writing Minilessons Book, Grade 3

Have a Try

Invite students to turn and talk about beginning a story with an interesting fact.

> Turn and talk about some different ways you might start this story with an interesting fact.

- After time for a brief discussion, ask students to share ideas. Add ideas to the chart.

Summarize and Apply

Summarize the learning. Have students try out some different ways to use an interesting fact to begin a story.

> During writing time, reread the story you are currently working on. Does it need a stronger lead? If so, title a page Leads in your writer's notebook and write a few ideas for beginning your story with an interesting fact. Choose the lead you like best and add it to the story. Or, choose a piece of writing you have finished and try a new lead for it. Bring your ideas and your writing when we meet.

Writing Strong Leads

Start your writing with action.	I sprinted down the sidewalk as fast as my legs would take me!
	"R-r-r-r-r-r-ing!" I could hear the bell ringing as I raced toward the school door.
Start your writing with talking. "Oh, no!"	"Oh, no!" I shouted to my sister. "Run! We are going to be late!"
	"Heyyyyyyy, wait for me!"
Start your writing with a description of the setting.	Fat raindrops plopped on my head and on the ground as I started to run along the sidewalk to catch the bus.
	The cold air hit my head as I ran down the sidewalk, having forgotten my hat in the rush out the door.
Start your writing with an interesting fact. FACT!	The average school start time in the US is 8:03 a.m.
	I've already been late to school once this year.

Confer

- During independent writing, move around the room to confer briefly with as many individual students as time allows. Sit side by side with them and invite them to talk about ways to start their writing. Use the following prompts as needed.
  - What are you writing about?
  - How will you start your writing?
  - What is something interesting about your topic you could share with the reader at the beginning?

Share

Following independent writing, gather students in the meeting area. Select students who wrote different kinds of leads to share with the class.

> Tell how you chose to start your writing and read your lead aloud.

Umbrella 5 | Crafting a Lead

Assessment

After you have taught the minilessons in this umbrella, observe students in a variety of classroom activities. Use *The Fountas & Pinnell Literacy Continuum* to notice, teach for, and support students' learning as you observe their attempts at writing.

▶ What evidence do you have of students' new understandings related to writing leads?

- Are students recognizing that writers make decisions about how to begin a book or story?
- Do they start their writing in a way that grabs readers' attention?
- Are they using vocabulary such as *beginning*, *lead*, *action*, and *fact*?

▶ In what ways, beyond the scope of this umbrella, are students showing an interest in making their writing interesting?

- Do they show an interest in trying out different ways to include dialogue in their books?
- Are they thinking and talking about how to end books?

Use your observations to determine the next umbrella you will teach. You may also consult Suggested Sequence of Lessons (pp. 605–622) for guidance.

EXTENSIONS FOR CRAFTING A LEAD

▶ Repeat the minilessons using different types of leads (e.g., a feeling, a flashback, a question).

▶ Extend WML3 by having students notice mentor texts that start with a description of a character and support them in starting their own writing in this way.

▶ As you read aloud, encourage students to notice the way writers choose to begin books. Guide a conversation about the leads that students think work well and why.

Crafting an Ending

Umbrella 6

Minilessons in This Umbrella

- **WML1** End your writing with advice.
- **WML2** End your writing with a feeling.
- **WML3** End your writing with a call to action.
- **WML4** End your writing with a question.

Before Teaching Umbrella 6 Minilessons

This umbrella will expand students' understanding of powerful ways to end their writing. At times, the ending is an afterthought in the rush to finish a piece of writing and so receives less attention. By guiding students to give attention to the beginning, the middle, and the ending, they learn that all parts of their writing deserve careful thought. Emphasize that the way a piece of writing ends is the choice of the writer, and that some endings are better suited for some types of writing than for others. Students may already have a sense of this if they have written a memory story and ended with a reflection about why the story is important to them (see GEN.U4: Writing Memory Stories).

Make sure students have their writer's notebooks, *Writer's Notebook, Intermediate* (Fountas and Pinnell 2023) or a plain notebook, and their writing folders for the lessons so that they can use them to try out a few endings for a piece of writing. Thinking through several endings will allow students to choose the one that works best. If students are not currently engaged in a writing project, they can try new endings for an existing piece of writing. The anchor chart is built across the minilessons in the umbrella. Use the books listed below from *Fountas & Pinnell Classroom™ Interactive Read-Aloud Collection*, or choose other books that end in different ways.

Interactive Read-Aloud Collection

Author's Point of View

Energy Island: How One Community Harnessed the Wind and Changed Their World by Allan Drummond

Oil Spill! by Melvin Berger

What's So Bad About Gasoline? Fossil Fuels and What They Do by Anne Rockwell

The Passage of Time

The Sunsets of Miss Olivia Wiggins by Lester L. Laminack

The Quilt Story by Tony Johnston

Our Seasons by Grace Lin and Ranida T. McKneally

As you read and enjoy these texts together, help students

- notice the different ways authors end their writing, and
- observe which type of ending goes best with which type of writing.

Interactive Read-Aloud
Point of View

Passage of Time

Writer's Notebook

WML1
CFT.U6.WML1

Writing Minilesson Principle
End your writing with advice.

Crafting an Ending

You Will Need

- a piece of writing that ends with advice (by a student or by you)
- chart paper and markers
- writer's notebooks and writing folders

Academic Language / Important Vocabulary

- advice
- ending
- lesson

Continuum Connection

- Understand that the writer may work to get readers interested in a topic
- Understand that a writer can learn how to write an expository text from mentor texts
- Use a variety of endings to engage and satisfy the reader

GOAL

Understand that writers can end their writing with advice.

RATIONALE

The ending is the last thing that readers read and possibly the part they remember the most, so it's important for a writer to craft an ending that is memorable, effective, and appropriate for the writing that precedes it. Writers can help their readers by ending their writing with advice.

WRITER'S NOTEBOOK/WRITING FOLDER

As students continue to work on longer pieces of writing from their writing folders, they can try out a few different endings in their writer's notebooks, choose the one that works best, and add it to the draft.

ASSESS LEARNING

- Notice whether students recognize that writers can end their writing with advice.
- Observe whether students sometimes decide to end their writing with advice.
- Look for evidence that students can use vocabulary such as *advice*, *ending*, and *lesson*.

MINILESSON

To help students think about the minilesson principle, use any piece of writing that ends with advice. This lesson is based on a piece of student writing. Here is an example.

> Liam wrote about things his parents make him do and ended his writing in a certain way. Listen as I read his writing to you. Notice what he did at the end.

- Read the sample piece of writing aloud.

  > What do you notice about the way Liam decided to end his writing?

- Guide the conversation to help students recognize that the writing ends with advice to the readers. Define the word *advice* if it is unfamiliar to students.

  > Why do you think Liam ended his writing with advice?

- Introduce an idea that students in your class will find relevant, similar to the following, and model the process of thinking about some different ways a piece of writing could end with advice.

  > If you want to write about bicycle safety, you might end with some advice for exactly how to be safe when riding a bike. For example, you might end with this: "You should always follow the rules of the road, like stopping at a stop sign."

- Begin a two-column chart that can be used throughout this umbrella entitled *Writing Strong Endings*. Write the principle in the left column. Write the example in the right column, leaving room for additional ideas.

The Writing Minilessons Book, Grade 3

Have a Try

Invite students to turn and talk about ending a piece of writing with advice.

> Turn and talk about a way you could end some writing about bicycle safety with advice for your readers.

▶ After time for a brief discussion, ask a few students to share their ideas. Add to the chart.

Summarize and Apply

Summarize the learning. Have students think about ending a longer piece of writing with advice.

> During writing time, if advice would be a good ending for your writing, try out some ideas in your writer's notebook. Then choose the ending that works best and add it to your draft. Or you can choose an existing piece of writing and try a new ending for that piece. Bring your ideas and writing when we meet.

Confer

▶ During independent writing, move around the room to confer briefly with students. Invite them to talk about how they want to end their writing. Use the following prompts as needed.

- How would you like to end your writing?
- What ideas do you have to end your writing with advice?
- What advice do you want to give your readers?

Share

Following independent writing, gather students in the meeting area to share their ideas.

> What ideas do you have for ending some writing with advice?

> Did anyone try to end your writing with advice? Tell about that.

Umbrella 6: Crafting an Ending

349

WML2
CFT.U6.WML2

Writing Minilesson Principle
End your writing with a feeling.

Crafting an Ending

You Will Need

- several mentor texts whose endings express or evoke feelings, such as the following from Text Set: The Passage of Time:
  - *The Sunsets of Miss Olivia Wiggins* by Lester L. Laminack
  - *The Quilt Story* by Tony Johnston
- the *Writing Strong Endings* chart from WML1
- markers
- writer's notebooks and writing folders

Academic Language / Important Vocabulary

- ending
- feeling

Continuum Connection

- Understand that writers can learn to craft fiction by using mentor texts as models
- Use a variety of endings to engage and satisfy the reader

GOAL

Understand that writers can end their writing with a feeling.

RATIONALE

The ending is the last thing that readers read and possibly the part they remember the most, so it's important for a writer to craft an ending that is memorable, effective, and appropriate for the writing that precedes it. Ending a piece of writing with a feeling is one of the ways that authors decide to end their writing, especially stories.

WRITER'S NOTEBOOK/WRITING FOLDER

As students continue to work on longer pieces of writing from their writing folders, they can try out a few different endings in their writer's notebooks, choose the one that works best, and add it to the draft.

ASSESS LEARNING

- Observe whether students sometimes end their writing with a feeling.
- Look for evidence that students can use vocabulary such as *ending* and *feeling*.

MINILESSON

To help students think about the minilesson principle, use familiar books and an interactive lesson to engage them in noticing that writers may choose to end their writing with a feeling. Here is an example.

- Revisit the last two pages of *The Sunsets of Miss Olivia Wiggins*.

  What do you notice about the way the writer, Lester L. Laminack, decided to end this story?

- Help students recognize that the story ends with a feeling.

  The story ends with a feeling. The writer wanted his readers to feel something after finishing this story. What feeling do you have?

- Repeat with *The Quilt Story*. Point out that a feeling can be an emotion the readers feel or it can be an emotion shared by the writer or by a character.

- Introduce a story idea that students in your class will find relevant, similar to the following example, and model the process of thinking about some ways the story could end with a feeling.

  If you were to write a story about our classmate, Sana, who is going to move away, you might want to end with a feeling. For example, you might end with "I'm sad that Sana is leaving. I will miss my good friend."

- Use the *Writing Strong Endings* chart that you started in WML1. Write the principle in the left column. Write the example in the right column, leaving room for additional ideas.

Have a Try

Invite students to turn and talk about ending a piece of writing with a feeling.

> Turn and talk about a different way you could end a story about Sana with a feeling.

- After time for a brief discussion, ask a few students to share their ideas. Add to the chart.

Summarize and Apply

Summarize the learning. Have students think about ending their writing with a feeling.

> During writing time, if you want to end the story you are working on with a feeling, use your writer's notebook to try out a few ideas. Then choose the ending that works best and add it to your story. Or you can choose an existing piece of writing and try a new ending for it. Bring your ideas and writing when we meet later.

Writing Strong Endings

End your writing with advice.	You should always follow the rules of the road, like stopping at a stop sign.
	It's a very good idea to wear a helmet when you ride your bike.
End your writing with a feeling.	I'm sad Sana is leaving. I will miss my good friend.
	Even though Sana was here only a short time, I feel like I have a lifelong friend.

Confer

- During independent writing, move around the room to confer briefly with students. Invite them to talk about how they want to end their writing. Use the following prompts as needed.
  - *How would you like to end your writing?*
  - *What ideas do you have to end your writing with a feeling?*
  - *What do you want your readers to feel when they finish reading your writing?*

Share

Following independent writing, gather students in the meeting area to share their writing.

> What ideas do you have for ending your writing with a feeling?

> Did anyone try ending your writing with a feeling? Tell about that.

WML 3
CFT.U6.WML3

Writing Minilesson Principle
End your writing with a call to action.

Crafting an Ending

You Will Need

- several mentor texts that end with a call to action, such as the following from Text Set: Author's Point of View:
  - *Energy Island* by Allan Drummond
  - *Oil Spill!* by Melvin Berger
- the *Writing Strong Endings* chart from WML2
- markers
- writer's notebooks and writing folders

Academic Language / Important Vocabulary

- ending
- call to action

Continuum Connection

- Understand that writers can learn how to write an expository text from mentor texts
- Use a variety of endings to engage and satisfy the reader

GOAL

Understand that writers can end their writing with a call to action.

RATIONALE

The ending is the last thing that readers read and possibly the part they remember the most, so it's important for a writer to craft an ending that is memorable, effective, and appropriate for the writing that precedes it. Ending a piece of writing, usually persuasive, with a call to action is how writers try to get their readers to agree with their beliefs or become involved in their causes.

WRITER'S NOTEBOOK/WRITING FOLDER

As students continue to work on longer pieces of writing from their writing folders, they can try out new endings in their writer's notebooks, choose the one that works best, and add it to the draft.

ASSESS LEARNING

- Observe whether students sometimes end their writing with a call to action.
- Look for evidence that students can use vocabulary such as *ending* and *call to action*.

MINILESSON

To help students think about the minilesson principle, use familiar books to engage them in noticing that a writer may choose to end a piece of writing with a call to action. Here is an example.

- Revisit the last two pages of *Energy Island*.

    What do you notice about the way the writer decided to end this book?

    The writer wants readers to work together to save energy.

- Reread the last page, emphasizing "We just need to work together to make the best use of it," and then define *call to action*.

    The words need to show that the writer is asking the readers to do something. A call to action is when someone asks you to do something.

- Repeat with *Oil Spill!*

- Introduce an idea that students will find relevant, and model the process of thinking about some ways the writing could end with a call to action.

    If you were to write about the cleanup project we are doing in our library, you might want to end with a call to action. You might end with "Stop by the library after school to sign up for a cleanup job."

- On the *Writing Strong Endings* chart from WML2, write the principle in the left column. Write the example in the right column, leaving room for additional ideas.

The Writing Minilessons Book, Grade 3

WML 3
CFT.U6.WML3

Have a Try

Invite students to turn and talk about ending their writing with a call to action.

> Turn and talk about a way you could end a piece of writing about the library project with a call to action.

- After time for a brief discussion, ask a few students to share their ideas. Add to the chart.

Summarize and Apply

Summarize the learning. Have students think about ending their writing with a call to action.

> During writing time, if you want to end the story you are working on in your writing folder with a call to action, use your writer's notebook to try out a few ideas. Then choose the ending that works best and add it. Or you can choose an existing piece of writing and try a new ending for it. Bring your ideas and writing when we meet later.

Writing Strong Endings

End your writing with advice.	You should always follow the rules of the road, like stopping at a stop sign.
	It's a very good idea to wear a helmet when you ride your bike.
End your writing with a feeling.	I'm sad Sana is leaving. I will miss my good friend.
	Even though Sana was here only a short time, I feel like I have a lifelong friend.
End your writing with a call to action.	Stop by the library after school to sign up for a cleanup job.
	We need everyone's help to organize the library, so please pitch in. Every little bit counts!

Confer

- During independent writing, move around the room to confer briefly with students. Invite them to talk about how they want to end their writing. Use the following prompts as needed.
  - How would you like to end your writing?
  - What ideas do you have to end your writing with a call to action?
  - What do you want your readers to do when they finish reading your writing?

Share

Following independent writing, gather students in the meeting area to share their ideas for endings.

> How are you thinking of ending your writing?

> Who ended your writing with a call to action? Share how you ended your book.

Umbrella 6: Crafting an Ending

WML 4
CFT.U6.WML4

Writing Minilesson Principle
End your writing with a question.

Crafting an Ending

You Will Need

- several mentor texts that end with a question, such as the following:
  - *What's So Bad About Gasoline?* by Anne Rockwell, from Text Set: Author's Point of View
  - *Our Seasons* by Grace Lin and Ranida T. McKneally, from Text Set: The Passage of Time
- the *Writing Strong Endings* chart from WML3
- markers
- writer's notebooks and writing folders

Academic Language / Important Vocabulary

- ending
- question

Continuum Connection

- Use a variety of endings to engage and satisfy the reader

GOAL

Understand that writers can end their writing with a question.

RATIONALE

The ending is the last thing that readers read and possibly the part they remember the most, so it's important for a writer to craft an ending that is memorable, effective, and appropriate for the writing that precedes it. Ending a piece of writing by asking a question is one way writers get their readers to think about something important.

WRITER'S NOTEBOOK/WRITING FOLDER

As students continue to work on longer pieces of writing from their writing folders, they can try out a few different endings in their writer's notebooks, choose the one that works best, and add it to the draft.

ASSESS LEARNING

- Observe whether students sometimes choose to end their writing with a question.
- Look for evidence that students can use vocabulary such as *ending* and *question*.

MINILESSON

To help students think about the minilesson principle, use familiar books and engage them in an interactive lesson to learn that writers may choose to end their writing with a question. Here is an example.

- Revisit the ending in *What's So Bad About Gasoline?*

    What do you notice about the way the writer, Anne Rockwell, decided to end this book?

    The book ends with a question. The writer is asking you to think about your answer to the question "What ways can you think of to help?"

- Engage students in a conversation about why the writer might have decided to end with a question.
- Repeat with *Our Seasons*.
- Introduce a book idea that students in your class will find relevant, similar to the following example, and model the process of thinking about some ways the book could end with a question.

    If you were to write a book about your favorite family traditions, one way you could end is by asking this question: "What is your favorite family tradition?"

- On the *Writing Strong Endings* chart from WML3, write the principle in the left column. Write the example in the right column, leaving room for additional ideas.

WML 4
CFT.U6.WML4

Have a Try

Invite students to turn and talk about ending their writing with a question.

> Turn and talk about a way you could end a piece of writing about family traditions with a question.

▶ After time for a brief discussion, ask a few students to share their ideas. Add to the chart.

Summarize and Apply

Summarize the learning. Have students think about ending their writing with a question.

> During writing time, if you want to end your writing with a question, use your writer's notebook to try out a few ideas. Then choose the ending that works best and add it. Or you can choose an existing piece of writing and try a new ending for it. Bring your ideas and writing when we meet later.

Writing Strong Endings	
End your writing with advice.	You should always follow the rules of the road, like stopping at a stop sign.
	It's a very good idea to wear a helmet when you ride your bike.
End your writing with a feeling.	I'm sad Sana is leaving. I will miss my good friend.
	Even though Sana was here only a short time, I feel like I have a lifelong friend.
End your writing with a call to action.	Stop by the library after school to sign up for a cleanup job.
	We need everyone's help to organize the library, so please pitch in. Every little bit counts!
End your writing with a question.	What is your favorite family tradition?
	How does your family celebrate holidays?

Confer

▶ During independent writing, move around the room to confer briefly with students. Invite them to talk about how they want to end their writing. Use the following prompts as needed.

- *How would you like to end your writing?*
- *What ideas do you have to end your writing with a question?*
- *What question do you want readers to ask themselves when they finish reading your writing?*

Share

Following independent writing, gather students in a circle in the meeting area to share their ideas for endings.

> Let's go around the circle so that everyone has a turn to tell about how you are ending your writing or plan to end your writing.

> Did you hear an idea from your classmates that you might try sometime?

Umbrella 6 | Crafting an Ending

Assessment

After you have taught the minilessons in this umbrella, observe students in a variety of classroom activities. Use *The Fountas & Pinnell Literacy Continuum* to notice, teach for, and support students' learning as you observe their attempts at writing.

- What evidence do you have of students' new understandings related to ways to craft an ending?
  - Do students understand that writers make decisions about how to end their writing?
  - Do they choose appropriate ways to end their writing?
  - Are they using vocabulary such as *ending*, *advice*, *feeling*, *call to action*, and *question*?
- In what ways, beyond the scope of this umbrella, are students showing an interest in writing?
  - Do they show an interest in writing both fiction and nonfiction?
  - Are they thinking and talking about the ways that writers try to engage their readers?

Use your observations to determine the next umbrella you will teach. You may also consult Suggested Sequence of Lessons (pp. 605–622) for guidance.

EXTENSIONS FOR CRAFTING AN ENDING

- You may want to repeat a lesson by introducing other ways to craft an ending (e.g., with dialogue, an interesting fact or extra information, a surprise ending, a circular ending, or sound effects).

- During interactive read-aloud, pause to have students notice the ways writers choose to end their books and why they may have made those decisions. Ask them to think about other endings the writer could have chosen.

- If you are using *The Reading Minilessons Book, Grade 3* (Fountas and Pinnell 2019), you may choose to teach different ways writers end stories in LA.U9: Analyzing the Writer's Craft (RML6).

Making Powerful Word Choices

Umbrella 7

Minilessons in This Umbrella

- **WML1** Use words to show not tell.
- **WML2** Choose interesting words to describe the way people say something.
- **WML3** Choose interesting words to describe actions.

Before Teaching Umbrella 7 Minilessons

The goal of these minilessons is to make students aware that authors choose words carefully to provide specificity, create variety, and engage their readers. Once students are aware of careful word choice, they will think about it in their own writing.

Use the books listed below from *Fountas & Pinnell Classroom™ Interactive Read-Aloud Collection*, or choose books from the classroom library that have strong and varied word choice.

Interactive Read-Aloud Collection
Genre Study: Realistic Fiction

Tomás and the Library Lady by Pat Mora

Series Study: Dianna Hutts Aston and Sylvia Long

A Seed Is Sleepy

Animal Journeys

A Mother's Journey by Sandra Markle

North: The Amazing Story of Arctic Migration by Nick Dowson

Genre Study: Biography

Magic Trash: A Story of Tyree Guyton and His Art by J. H. Shapiro

Honoring Traditions

Crouching Tiger by Ying Chang Compestine

As you read and enjoy these texts together, help students

- notice the authors' choice of words,
- become aware of how the language makes them feel, and
- notice and talk about the authors' craft.

Interactive Read-Aloud
Realistic Fiction

Dianna Hutts Aston and Sylvia Long

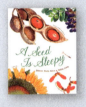

Animal Journeys

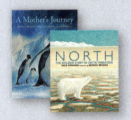

Biography

Honoring Traditions

Writer's Notebook

WML1

CFT.U7.WML1

Writing Minilesson Principle
Use words to show not tell.

Making Powerful Word Choices

You Will Need

- mentor texts with examples of language that shows instead of tells, such as the following:
  - *Tomás and the Library Lady* by Pat Mora, from Text Set: Genre Study: Realistic Fiction
  - *A Seed Is Sleepy* by Dianna Hutts Aston, from Text Set: Series Study: Dianna Hutts Aston and Sylvia Long
  - *A Mother's Journey* by Sandra Markle, from Text Set: Animal Journeys
- chart paper prepared with a passage that describes without telling
- markers and highlighter
- writer's notebooks and writing folders

Academic Language / Important Vocabulary

- describing
- show
- tell

Continuum Connection

- Use language to show instead of tell
- Learn ways of using language and constructing texts from other writers (reading books and hearing them read aloud) and apply understandings to one's own writing
- Use range of descriptive words to enhance meaning

GOAL

Use language to show instead of tell.

RATIONALE

When students understand that writers use language to show instead of tell, they begin to think about finding alternative ways to say things to help readers paint pictures in their minds.

WRITER'S NOTEBOOK/WRITING FOLDER

Students can try using language to show instead of tell in a writing project draft from their writing folders or in their writer's notebooks.

ASSESS LEARNING

- Look for evidence that students understand the concept of using language to show instead of tell.
- Notice whether students use varied and interesting words that show rather than tell.
- Look for evidence that students can use vocabulary such as *describing*, *show*, and *tell*.

MINILESSON

To help students think about the minilesson principle, use mentor text examples to demonstrate what it means to use language that shows instead of tells. Here is an example.

> Make a picture in your mind of what is happening in this story as I read aloud to you.

- Read page 3 in *Tomás and the Library Lady*.

> How do you think Tomás is feeling?
>
> Tomás is hot and thirsty, but the words do not say that. How do you know that it's hot and Tomás is thirsty?

- Support the conversation to help students notice that the writer used words to describe how Tomás is feeling rather than just stating that he is hot and thirsty.

> Pat Mora wanted her readers to know that Tomás is hot and thirsty, so she chose words to show you rather than tell you directly how he is feeling. You can guess that Tomás and his family probably don't have air conditioning in their car.

- Read page 4 aloud.

> What do some of the words on this page tell you about Tomás and his family?
>
> The author used words to show you that Tomás and his family speak Spanish.

WML1
CFT.U7.WML1

Have a Try

Invite students to turn and talk about how writers use words that show not tell.

- Display the prepared chart paper.

    Read the example. What is the writer showing you? What words let you know that? Turn and talk to your partner.

- After time for discussion, ask volunteers to share. Ask a student to highlight words in the passage that show the child's feelings.

    Let's try writing our own example. What could we write to show that there is a fire without saying that there is a fire? Think about what you might hear, see, or smell.

Summarize and Apply

Summarize the learning. Remind students to use language that shows instead of tells when they write. Write the principle at the top of the chart.

    Today we talked about how sometimes writers don't tell you directly what is happening. Instead, they show you what is happening by describing what a character thinks, says, or does. During writing time, reread a draft of a writing project or something you have written in your writer's notebook. Is there a place where you can try using words that show instead of tell?

Use words to show not tell.

"Grampy, I can't wait to tell you!" Sam shouted as he ran up the steps. He burst through the doorway and threw his arms around his grandfather's waist. "Guess what?"

The writer shows that Sam is excited.

First, we heard sirens in the distance. We saw smoke in the air. We heard a crackling noise. The sky had an orange glow.

Confer

- During independent writing, move around the room to confer briefly with as many individual students as time allows. Sit side by side with them and invite them to talk about word choice. Use the following prompts as needed.
    - What is another way you could say this that shows instead of tells?
    - What picture do you want readers to see in their minds when they read this?
    - Let's talk about some words that describe what you want your readers to know.

Share

Following independent writing, gather students in the meeting area to share their writing.

    Did anyone try using words that show instead of tell? Tell about that.

Umbrella 7: Making Powerful Word Choices

WML2
CFT.U7.WML2

Writing Minilesson Principle
Choose interesting words to describe the way people say something.

Making Powerful Word Choices

You Will Need

- a mentor text using alternatives to the word *said* in dialogue, such as *Magic Trash* by J. H. Shapiro from Text Set: Genre Study: Biography
- sticky notes
- chart paper and markers
- writer's notebooks

Academic Language / Important Vocabulary

- interesting
- dialogue
- said

Continuum Connection

- Vary word choice to create interesting description and dialogue
- Show ability to vary the text by choosing alternative words: e.g., *replied* for *said*

GOAL

Understand that writers use words other than *said* to make their writing more descriptive and interesting.

RATIONALE

By choosing a word other than *said* when writing dialogue, writers let their readers know what a character is like and/or how the words should sound when spoken. When students understand this, they learn that they can do the same thing when they write.

WRITER'S NOTEBOOK/WRITING FOLDER

Students can make a list of words to replace *said* in their writer's notebooks.

ASSESS LEARNING

- Look at students' writing to see if they use words other than *said* in dialogue.
- Look for evidence that students can use vocabulary such as *interesting*, *dialogue*, and *said*.

MINILESSON

Students will need their writer's notebooks for this lesson. To help students think about the minilesson principle, use mentor texts and an interactive lesson that focuses on how writers use different words for *said* in order to make writing more interesting. Below is an example.

- Show and read page 5 in *Magic Trash*.

  In a book, when a character speaks, you often see the word *said*. What words do you notice on this page?

- Help students notice that the writer used the words *asked* and *whispered*. Use sticky notes to begin a list of words on chart paper that can replace *said*.

  Writers choose interesting words to help their readers know how the dialogue should be read. As I continue reading, raise your hand if you hear a word the writer used instead of *said*.

- Starting on page 20, read and pause to add words to the list as students identify them, stopping after page 24.

- Write a simple sentence on the chart that uses *said*. Leave room for a sticky note to be placed over the word *said*.

  What word could you use in this sentence instead of *said*? Think about different ways that the speaker might say the sentence.

- Try out several words in the sentence. Have students read the sentence with each new word and comment on how the sentence sounds with each word.

Have a Try

Invite students to turn and talk about words that can replace *said*.

- Write another sentence with *said* on chart paper.

    In your writer's notebook, write three words that you could use instead of *said* in this sentence. Then turn to your partner and share your list.

- After a few moments, ask a few volunteers to share their words. Choose several suggestions to add to the chart.

Summarize and Apply

Summarize the learning. Remind students to notice and use synonyms for *said*.

   When you are reading and notice a word that could be used instead of *said*, write it on a sticky note and add it to the chart.

- Write the principle at the top of the chart.

    During writing time, look at your writing to see if you can use a word other than *said* to describe how a character says something. You can also add words to the list you started in your writer's notebook so that you will have some to choose from when you write dialogue. Bring your writing when we meet later.

Confer

- During independent writing, move around the room to confer briefly with as many individual students as time allows. Sit side by side with them and invite them to talk about what words they could use to show how their characters talk. Use the following prompts as needed.
    - *Is there a different word to describe how the character says this?*
    - *She is talking in an excited voice. What word can you use to show that?*
    - *What kind of voice is he using?*

Share

Following independent writing, gather students in small groups in the meeting area. Make sure each group has at least one student who wrote dialogue.

   Read your dialogue aloud to your classmates.

WML 3
CFT.U7.WML3

Writing Minilesson Principle
Choose interesting words to describe actions.

Making Powerful Word Choices

You Will Need

- mentor texts with examples of interesting verbs, such as the following:
  - *A Seed Is Sleepy* by Dianna Hutts Aston, from Text Set: Series Study: Dianna Hutts Aston and Sylvia Long
  - *North: The Amazing Story of Arctic Migration* by Nick Dowson, from Text Set: Animal Journeys
  - *Crouching Tiger* by Ying Chang Compestine, from Text Set: Honoring Traditions
- chart paper and markers
- sticky notes
- writer's notebooks

Academic Language / Important Vocabulary

- action word
- verb
- interesting
- descriptive

Continuum Connection

- Vary word choice to create interesting description and dialogue
- Learn ways of using language and constructing texts from other writers (reading books and hearing them read aloud) and apply understandings to one's own writing
- Use range of descriptive words to enhance meaning

GOAL

Understand that writers use specific verbs to make their writing more descriptive and interesting.

RATIONALE

By choosing strong verbs, writers help their readers picture what a character is like and/or what the character is doing. When students understand this, they learn that they can do the same thing when they write. Depending on your students, you may decide to use the term *action word* or *verb*, or perhaps use them interchangeably.

WRITER'S NOTEBOOK/WRITING FOLDER

Students can make a list of verbs in their writer's notebooks.

ASSESS LEARNING

- Observe for evidence that students understand why writers use specific verbs.
- Look at students' writing. Do they sometimes use specific verbs to describe an action?
- Look for evidence that students can use vocabulary such as *action word*, *verb*, *interesting*, and *descriptive*.

MINILESSON

To help students think about the minilesson principle, engage them in noticing that writers use different words to show actions. Here is an example.

- Show and read pages 15–16 in *A Seed Is Sleepy*.

  What do you notice about the words the writer chose to show action?

- Define and discuss *action word* and *verb* if needed, as well as the meanings of any unfamiliar verbs. Use sticky notes to begin a list on chart paper of interesting action words.

- Continue using sticky notes to add words that students notice as you show and read page 12 in *North: The Amazing Story of Arctic Migration*. Engage them in a conversation about the importance of word choice. An example is below.

  Think about the words *slides*, *glides*, and *swim*. All of the words are used to show how the whale is moving in the water.

  Why do you think the writer chose these words?

- Support students' thinking by helping them understand that using descriptive action words helps the readers picture what is going on and makes the writing more interesting.

- Repeat with page 15 in *Crouching Tiger*.

Have a Try

Write two simple sentences on chart paper. Invite students to turn and talk about using interesting action words.

> In your writer's notebook, write two words that you could use instead of *walk* in the first sentence and two that you could use instead of *went* in the second sentence. Then turn to your partner and share your words.

- After a few moments, ask a few volunteers to share their words. Choose several suggestions to add to the chart.

Summarize and Apply

Summarize the learning. Remind students to notice and use interesting verbs.

> When you notice an interesting action word, write it on a sticky note and add it to the chart.

- Write the principle at the top of the chart.

> During writing time, look at your writing to see if you can use an action word that better describes what is happening. You can also add words to the list you started in your writer's notebook so that you will have some words to choose from when you write. Bring your writing when we meet later.

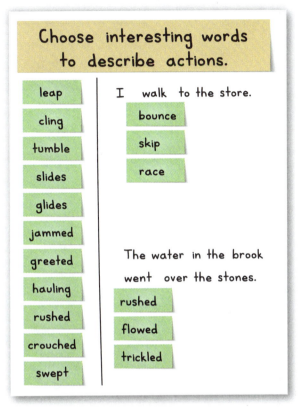

Confer

- During independent writing, move around the room to confer briefly with as many individual students as time allows. Sit side by side with them and invite them to talk about their choice of words. Use the following prompts as needed.
  - *Is there a more interesting way you could describe what this animal is doing?*
  - *What other word could you use to show how the person is moving?*
  - *Let's talk about some words you could use to show this action.*

Share

Following independent writing, gather students in the meeting area to share their writing.

> Who would like to share an interesting word you used to show an action?

> Who added a sticky note to the chart today? Share what word you added.

Umbrella 7: Making Powerful Word Choices

Assessment

After you have taught the minilessons in this umbrella, observe students in a variety of classroom activities. Use *The Fountas & Pinnell Literacy Continuum* to notice, teach for, and support students' learning as you observe their attempts at writing.

- What evidence do you have of students' new understandings related to word choice?
  - Do students use words that show instead of tell?
  - Are they choosing alternatives to the word *said*?
  - Do they choose interesting verbs?
  - Are they using vocabulary such as *describing*, *show*, *tell*, *interesting*, *said*, *action word*, and *verb*?
- In what ways, beyond the scope of this umbrella, are students' reading and writing behaviors showing an understanding of word choice?
  - Are they varying the ways they begin and end their writing?
  - Do they sometimes include figurative language when they write?

Use your observations to determine the next umbrella you will teach. You may also consult Suggested Sequence of Lessons (pp. 605–622) for guidance.

EXTENSIONS FOR MAKING POWERFUL WORD CHOICES

- Encourage students who speak a language other than English to use words from that language to add variety to their writing and to make their writing more authentic, especially when they write about themselves.

- Provide opportunities to talk about overused words and have students work together to come up with alternatives.

- Meet with a small guided writing group of students who would benefit from support in making powerful word choices.

- As opportunities arise, guide students to make powerful word choices through the use of figurative language (e.g., metaphor, simile, or personification).

- Have students make vocabulary webs by placing a commonly used word in the middle of the web (e.g., *move*), and then placing more interesting synonyms for the word around the web.

Making Your Sentences Clear and Interesting

Umbrella 8

Minilessons in This Umbrella

- **WML1** Start your sentences in different ways.
- **WML2** Vary the length of your sentences.
- **WML3** Use connecting words and phrases to help sentences flow.

Before Teaching Umbrella 8 Minilessons

The goals of these minilessons are to help students recognize ways that authors craft their sentences to make them clear and interesting and to help them think about how to apply those techniques in their own writing. Before teaching this umbrella, expose students to books by writers who use varied, clear, and interesting sentences. Also, students should have had many experiences writing stories independently.

Use the books listed below from *Fountas & Pinnell Classroom™ Interactive Read-Aloud Collection* and *Shared Reading Collection,* or choose books that have a good variety of sentence types and lengths from the classroom library. Big books are helpful, but you can also project a page of text or write a sentence from the text on chart paper.

Interactive Read-Aloud Collection

Author's Point of View

Energy Island: How One Community Harnessed the Wind and Changed Their World by Allan Drummond

What's So Bad About Gasoline? Fossil Fuels and What They Do by Anne Rockwell

Animal Journeys

Hachiko: The True Story of a Loyal Dog by Pamela S. Turner

A Mother's Journey by Sandra Markle

The Importance of Determination

Ruby's Wish by Shirin Yim Bridges

Shared Reading Collection

Crows Aren't Creepy by Ashley Storm

The Rain Forest Rainbow by Susan B. Katz

As you read and enjoy these texts together, help students
- observe the way the sentences are written, and
- talk about the way the authors craft sentences.

Interactive Read-Aloud
Point of View

Animal Journeys

Determination

Shared Reading

Writer's Notebook

WML1
CFT.U8.WML1

Writing Minilesson Principle
Start your sentences in different ways.

Making Your Sentences Clear and Interesting

You Will Need

- a mentor text that uses varied sentence beginnings, such as *The Rain Forest Rainbow* by Susan B. Katz, from *Shared Reading Collection*
- chart paper and markers
- writer's notebooks and writing folders

Academic Language / Important Vocabulary

- sentences
- clear
- interesting
- start
- different

Continuum Connection

- Use variety in sentence structure

GOAL

Understand that writers purposely vary how their sentences begin.

RATIONALE

When sentences are well crafted, they have rhythm and flow that make them easy and enjoyable to read. Varying how the sentences begin is one effective craft technique. When students notice that writers pay attention to how their sentences sound, they begin to think about how to do the same in their own writing.

WRITER'S NOTEBOOK/WRITING FOLDER

Students can try out new sentence beginnings in their writer's notebooks and revise sentence beginnings on the draft of a writing project in their writing folders.

ASSESS LEARNING

- Look at students' writing for evidence that they are varying ways to begin their sentences.
- Look for evidence that students can use vocabulary such as *sentences*, *clear*, *interesting*, *start*, and *different*.

MINILESSON

Students will need their writer's notebooks for this lesson. To help them think about the minilesson principle, use mentor texts that have examples of sentences that begin in a variety of ways. Below is an example.

- Show the cover of *The Rain Forest Rainbow*.

    Listen to the sentences that the writer, Susan B. Katz, wrote for *The Rain Forest Rainbow*.

- Begin reading the first few pages of the book, pausing after each page to ask students to identify how the sentences on each page begin.

    What do you notice about the words at the beginning of each sentence?

- As students identify the words, begin a list on chart paper.
- Continue through a few more pages until you have a list of varied sentence beginnings.

    The writer began each sentence in a different way. Why do you think she decided to do this?

    How would the writing sound different if the writer had begun each sentence with "In the rain forest"?

- Engage students in a conversation about how starting sentences in different ways makes their writing more interesting and fun to read.

The Writing Minilessons Book, Grade 3

Have a Try

Invite students to turn and talk about ways to vary how they begin sentences.

▸ On chart paper, write three sentences that all begin the same way. Read them aloud.

> In your writer's notebook, write one or two of the sentences so that they start in a different way. When you finish writing, share your sentences with your partner.

▸ After time for discussion, ask volunteers to share how to vary at least two of the sentence beginnings. Write the new beginnings on the chart as examples.

Summarize and Apply

Summarize the learning. Have students vary the way they begin sentences in their writing pieces.

> What did you learn today about making your sentences clear and interesting?

▸ Write the principle at the top of the chart.

> Before you start writing today, reread the writing project you are working on. Look for places where you have started sentences the same way. You can try out different ways to start at least one of the sentences in your writer's notebook before adding it to the draft. Bring your writing to share when we meet later.

Start your sentences in different ways.

Tropical rain pouring …	El oso perezoso …
Magnificent is …	Scratching mossy …
La mariposa …	Bike riding …
She lands …	Look out for …
Lazy is the …	Freezing cold, I …

The weather yesterday was rainy.

Today, the
~~The~~ weather ~~today~~ is cloudy.

Maybe tomorrow the
~~The~~ weather ~~tomorrow~~ will be sunny.

Confer

▸ During independent writing, move around the room to confer briefly with as many individual students as time allows. Sit side by side with them and invite them to talk about writing clear, interesting sentences. Use the following prompts as needed.

- *What are you writing about today?*
- *Read this sentence. Is there another way you might start it?*
- *Take a look at the sentences on this page. Talk about whether they all begin in the same way or in different ways.*

Share

Following independent writing, gather students in the meeting area to share their writing.

> Who changed how some of your sentences start? Read the original sentence and the sentence after you made the change.

WML2
CFT.U8.WML2

Writing Minilesson Principle
Vary the length of your sentences.

Making Your Sentences Clear and Interesting

You Will Need

- a mentor text that has sentences of varied lengths, such as *Crows Aren't Creepy* by Ashley Storm, from *Shared Reading Collection*
- chart paper prepared with several short sentences all about the same length
- markers
- writing folders

Academic Language / Important Vocabulary

- sentence
- interesting
- vary
- length

Continuum Connection

- Show evidence of using language from story books and informational books that have been read aloud
- Use variety in sentence structure

GOAL

Use sentences of different lengths throughout writing to create a rhythm and flow.

RATIONALE

When sentences are well crafted, they flow smoothly and are easy and enjoyable to read. Varying the length of the sentences is one way to create a smooth flow. When students notice that writers pay attention to how their sentences sound, they begin to think about how to do the same in their own writing.

WRITER'S NOTEBOOK/WRITING FOLDER

Students look at drafts from their writing folders to see where they might vary the lengths of some of their sentences.

ASSESS LEARNING

- Examine students' writing to see whether they are varying the length of sentences throughout a writing piece.
- Look for evidence that students can use vocabulary such as *sentence*, *interesting*, *vary*, and *length*.

MINILESSON

To help students think about the minilesson principle, use mentor texts that have sentences of varying lengths. Here is an example.

- Show and read pages 10–11 of *Crows Aren't Creepy*.

  What do you notice about the sentences the writer, Ashley Storm, wrote?

- Guide students to focus on sentence length and help them notice that some sentences are short and some are long. Write the sentences on chart paper on separate lines so that students can compare sentence lengths.

  The writer used some short sentences and some long sentences. Why do you think she may have decided to do this?

- Engage students in a conversation about how varying sentence length can make writing smooth and easy to read rather than choppy and hard to read. Writing a very short sentence (or sentence fragment) in the middle of longer ones can make that sentence stand out.

The Writing Minilessons Book, Grade 3

Have a Try

Invite students to turn and talk about ways to vary sentence length.

▸ Show the prepared writing. Read the sentences aloud.

> How does my writing sound? Turn and talk about how I could make the sentences sound better. Think about adding more words to a sentence or putting two sentences together.

▸ After time for discussion, ask volunteers to share. Decide on one way to vary each sentence length and write it on the chart.

Summarize and Apply

Summarize the learning. Remind students to vary the length of sentences in their writing.

> We have been talking about how writers include some short sentences and some longer sentences so that the writing is more interesting to read. Varying sentence length makes the writing flow smoothly.

▸ Write the principle at the top of the chart.

> When you write today, think about how you can vary sentence length in the writing project you are working on. Bring your writing to share when we meet later.

Confer

▸ During independent writing, move around the room to confer briefly with as many individual students as time allows. Sit side by side with them and invite them to talk about variety in sentences. Use the following prompts as needed.

- *What are you writing about today?*
- *Read aloud what you have written on this page. How does it sound? Are there any sentences that should be shorter or longer?*
- *These sentences are all about the same length. What ideas do you have for varying the length of some of these sentences?*

Share

Following independent writing, gather students in the meeting area to share their writing.

> Share what you wrote today with a partner. Are there any sentences that could be made longer or shorter?

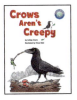

Umbrella 8: Making Your Sentences Clear and Interesting

WML 3
CFT.U8.WML3

Writing Minilesson Principle
Use connecting words and phrases to help sentences flow.

Making Your Sentences Clear and Interesting

You Will Need

- several mentor texts that include a variety of connecting words and phrases, such as the following:
  - *Hachiko* by Pamela S. Turner and *A Mother's Journey* by Sandra Markle, from Text Set: Animal Journeys
  - *Energy Island* by Allan Drummond and *What's So Bad About Gasoline?* by Anne Rockwell, from Text Set: Author's Point of View
  - *Ruby's Wish* by Shirin Yim Bridges, from Text Set: The Importance of Determination
- chart paper and markers
- document camera (optional)
- chart paper prepared with sentences for adding connecting words
- writing folders

Academic Language / Important Vocabulary

- sentence
- connecting
- word
- phrase
- flow

Continuum Connection

- Use a variety of transitions and connections: e.g., words, phrases, sentences, and paragraphs

GOAL
Use a variety of connecting words and phrases.

RATIONALE
When students understand that writers use connecting words and phrases to show how ideas are related and to make their sentences flow, they learn to do this in their own writing.

WRITER'S NOTEBOOK/WRITING FOLDER
Students look at drafts from their writing folders to revise sentences by using connecting words.

ASSESS LEARNING

- Notice whether students are able to identify and use connecting words and phrases.
- Look for evidence that students can use vocabulary such as *sentence*, *connecting*, *word*, *phrase*, and *flow*.

MINILESSON

To help students think about the minilesson principle, use mentor texts that have sentences that use connecting words. Write sentences on chart paper or project the pages so that students can see the words. Here is an example.

- Show and read the second paragraph on page 14 of *Hachiko*.

  What do you notice about the way the writer connected all of these ideas?

- Guide the conversation so students recognize that the words *the next day* and *but* connect the ideas. On chart paper, begin a list of connecting words and phrases that students notice in mentor text examples.

  Look for connecting words as I share pages from a few other books.

- Help students identify the connecting words in several other mentor text examples and add to chart. Repeat until students feel comfortable identifying connecting words. Here are some suggestions:
  - *What's So Bad About Gasoline?* (pp. 23 and 25)
  - *Energy Island* (pp. 22–23)
  - *A Mother's Journey* (pp. 10–11)
  - *Ruby's Wish* (p. 8)

  Why do you think the writers included many connecting words?

- Engage students in a conversation about how connecting words show how ideas are related and help sentences flow smoothly. If you have talked about sentence length, point out that connecting words can combine two short sentences.

The Writing Minilessons Book, Grade 3

Have a Try

Invite students to turn and talk about ways to include transition words and phrases.

- Show the prepared sentences and read them aloud.

    Here are some sentences that don't flow very well. How can you use transition words to connect the ideas and make the sentences sound better? Turn and talk to your partner about that.

- After time for discussion, ask volunteers to share. Write the new sentences on the chart.

Summarize and Apply

Summarize the learning. Have students include some transition words and phrases in their writing.

    How can you make your sentences flow?

- Write the principle at the top of the first chart.

    We have been talking about how writers include connecting words and phrases to make their writing flow. When you write today, think about how you can do this in the piece you are working on. Bring your writing to share when we meet later.

Confer

- During independent writing, move around the room to confer briefly with as many individual students as time allows. Sit side by side with them and invite them to talk about connecting words and phrases. Use the following prompts as needed.
    - *What are you writing about today?*
    - *Read this page. Let's talk about a word you could add to make your writing flow.*
    - *What connecting word or phrase could you add here?*

Share

Following independent writing, gather students in the meeting area. Ask a few volunteers to share their writing.

    Who used a connecting word or phrase in your writing today? Share what you wrote.

Use connecting words and phrases to help sentences flow.

the next day	so
but	on the second day
another kind of	then
instead	because
some of these	whenever
so are	therefore
after that night	however
suddenly	
in fact	

I would like to go with you. I'm busy.

I would like to go with you, <u>but</u> I'm busy.

I would like to go with you. <u>However</u>, I'm busy.

I was going to eat an apple. I ate a pear.

I was going to eat an apple. <u>Instead</u>, I ate a pear.

Umbrella 8: Making Your Sentences Clear and Interesting

Assessment

After you have taught the minilessons in this umbrella, observe students in a variety of classroom activities. Use *The Fountas & Pinnell Literacy Continuum* to notice, teach for, and support students' learning as you observe their attempts at writing.

- What evidence do you have of students' new understandings related to writing sentences?
  - Can students explain why writers start sentences in different ways, vary sentence lengths, and use connecting words?
  - Do they attempt to vary sentences in their own writing?
  - Are they using vocabulary such as *sentences*, *clear*, *interesting*, *start*, *different*, *vary*, *length*, *connecting*, *word*, *phrase*, and *flow*?
- In what ways, beyond the scope of this umbrella, are students' reading and writing behaviors showing an understanding of making writing clear and interesting?
  - Are students looking for ways to show voice in their writing?
  - Do they use varied word choice to make their writing more powerful?

Use your observations to determine the next umbrella you will teach. You may also consult Suggested Sequence of Lessons (pp. 605–622) for guidance.

EXTENSIONS FOR MAKING YOUR SENTENCES CLEAR AND INTERESTING

- Use shared writing to create a song or a chant that uses sentences with varying lengths. Engage in conversation about how the rhythm and beat are affected by sentence length.

- Work with students in small groups to share writing samples and talk about different ways the sentences could be written to make the writing more interesting.

- If you are using *The Reading Minilessons Book, Grade 3* (Fountas and Pinnell 2019) you may choose to teach LA.U9: Analyzing the Writer's Craft.

Writing with Voice in Fiction and Nonfiction

Umbrella 9

Minilessons in This Umbrella

- **WML1** Speak directly to the reader.
- **WML2** Show your voice with different styles of print.
- **WML3** Show your voice with humor.
- **WML4** Read your writing aloud to hear how it sounds.

Before Teaching Umbrella 9 Minilessons

Voice is the authentic connection between talking and writing, so throughout this umbrella, it is important to encourage students to read their writing aloud and listen to how it sounds before reading aloud for voice is covered in depth in WML4. Students can recognize that their personalities can shine through their writing by thinking about how authors do this in mentor texts. Support the link by helping them understand that they can write in a way that is similar to talking but also that writing differs from talking.

Use the books listed below from *Fountas & Pinnell Classroom™ Interactive Read-Aloud Collection* and *Shared Reading Collection*, or choose books with good examples of the writer's voice from the classroom library. To help students see the print clearly, use enlarged texts, project a page of text, or write a sentence from the text on chart paper.

Interactive Read-Aloud Collection
Humorous Texts

Big Bad Bubble by Adam Rubin

Bedhead by Margie Palatini

The Perfect Pet by Margie Palatini

Those Darn Squirrels! by Adam Rubin

The Great Fuzz Frenzy by Janet Stevens and Susan Stevens Crummel

Genre Study: Expository Nonfiction

Hottest, Coldest, Highest, Deepest by Steve Jenkins

Shared Reading Collection

Hummingbird's Nest by Sherry Howard

As you read and enjoy these texts together, help students

- observe the way punctuation and styles of print are used, and
- talk about whether it feels like the writer is speaking directly to the reader.

Interactive Read-Aloud Humorous Texts

Expository Nonfiction

Shared Reading

Writer's Notebook

WML1
CFT.U9.WML1

Writing Minilesson Principle
Speak directly to the reader.

Writing with Voice in Fiction and Nonfiction

You Will Need

- fiction and nonfiction mentor texts with examples of using voice to speak directly to the readers, such as the following:
  - *Big Bad Bubble* by Adam Rubin, from Text Set: Humorous Texts
  - *Hummingbird's Nest* by Sherry Howard, from *Shared Reading Collection*
- chart paper prepared with a writing sample that speaks directly to readers
- highlighter or highlighter tape
- writing folders
- To download the following online resource for this lesson, visit **fp.pub/resources**:
  - chart art (optional)

Academic Language / Important Vocabulary

- voice
- speak
- writing
- directly

Continuum Connection

- Write in an expressive way but also recognize how language in a book would sound
- Write in a way that speaks directly to the reader

GOAL

Write in a way that speaks directly to the reader.

RATIONALE

When students learn that writers can write in a way that speaks directly to readers, they begin to think about how their writing sounds and try to incorporate voice into their writing.

WRITER'S NOTEBOOK/WRITING FOLDER

Make sure students have their writing folders so that they can work on longer pieces of writing during independent writing.

ASSESS LEARNING

- Observe for evidence that students recognize that writers can show voice by speaking directly to their readers and try the technique in their own writing.
- Look for evidence that students can use vocabulary such as *voice*, *speak*, *writing*, and *directly*.

MINILESSON

To help students think about the minilesson principle, use mentor texts that have writing that speaks directly to the reader. Here is an example.

- Show and read page 2 in *Big Bad Bubble*.

  Turn and talk about what you notice about how the writing sounds.

- After time for discussion, ask volunteers to share their thinking. Guide the conversation to help students notice that it sounds like the writer is speaking directly to the reader.

- Show and read page 9.

  When the author writes "Don't listen to Mogo," how do you know whom he is talking to?

- Guide the conversation so students recognize that the writer makes it sound like he is talking to the readers in the same way he might talk to people he knows.

- Show and read page 16.

  What do you notice on this page?

- Repeat with page 6 and page 10 in *Hummingbird's Nest*. Point out that the writer used conversational language like "But, careful!" and "You may see her."

  Your writing voice is what makes your writing sound like you. One way you can show your voice is by writing as if you are talking directly to the reader.

Have a Try

Invite students to turn and talk about using voice in their writing by speaking directly to the reader.

- Read the prepared chart paper.

    In what ways does my writing sound like it speaks directly to you, the readers? Turn and talk to your partner about that.

- After time for discussion, ask volunteers to highlight parts that speak directly to the reader.

Summarize and Apply

Summarize the learning. Have students try speaking directly to the reader as they write.

    What is one way you can show your writing voice?

- Write the principle at the top of the chart.

    During writing time, reread a piece of writing you are working on. Does it need more voice? Would it work to make the writing sound like you are talking directly to your readers? If so, think about how you can do that. Bring your writing to share when we meet later.

Speak directly to the reader.

Have you ever been stung by a bee? Well, I have. It was not a fun experience. Let me tell you what happened. When I was young, my brother and I did not know that if you leave bees alone, they do not bother you. Instead, we bothered them, so guess what? They bothered us back. That day was the first and last time I was ever stung by a bee. Consider this a warning!

Confer

- During independent writing, move around the room to confer briefly with students about their writing voice. Use the following prompts as needed.
    - What are you writing about today?
    - Read this sentence aloud the way you want your readers to read it.
    - How would you say this sentence to a friend? Try writing it that way.
    - How are you using voice in this writing piece?

Share

Following independent writing, gather students in the meeting area to share their writing.

    Share what you wrote today with a partner. When you listen to your partner read, think about whether the writer is speaking directly to you.

Umbrella 9: Writing with Voice in Fiction and Nonfiction

WML 2
CFT.U9.WML2

Writing Minilesson Principle
Show your voice with different styles of print.

Writing with Voice in Fiction and Nonfiction

You Will Need

- several mentor texts with examples of different styles of print, such as the following:
  - *Hottest, Coldest, Highest, Deepest* by Steve Jenkins, from Text Set: Genre Study: Expository Nonfiction
  - *Bedhead* and *The Perfect Pet* by Margie Palatini, from Text Set: Humorous Texts
- chart paper and markers
- writer's notebooks and/or writing folders

Academic Language / Important Vocabulary

- voice
- style
- capitalization
- italics
- bold

Continuum Connection

- Write in an expressive way but also recognize how language in a book would sound
- Write in a way that shows care and commitment to the topic
- Use underlining, italics, and bold print to convey a specific meaning

GOAL

Use different styles of print to convey meaning and support voice.

RATIONALE

When students learn they can use different styles and sizes of print to convey meaning and support voice, they understand that writers have a variety of tools they can use to express themselves, and they might be inspired to use different styles of print in their own writing.

WRITER'S NOTEBOOK/WRITING FOLDER

Make sure students have their writing folders and/or writer's notebooks so that during independent writing they can try using styles of print to show voice in their writing.

ASSESS LEARNING

- Examine students' writing to see whether they are experimenting with styles of print to express voice.
- Look for evidence that students can use vocabulary such as *voice*, *style*, *capitalization*, *italics*, and *bold*.

MINILESSON

To help students think about how writers use different styles of print to show voice, use mentor text examples and provide an interactive lesson. Here is an example.

- Show page 4 of *Hottest, Coldest, Highest, Deepest*.

  What do you notice about the words on the page?

- Support a conversation about how making the words *oldest* and *deepest* bold conveys the idea that these words are important and should be emphasized. Read the page with emphasis on the words in bold. As students talk, begin a two-column chart that shows the styles and text examples.

  The type of print shows voice and helps the readers know how the writer wants the words to be read.

- Repeat with page 2 and page 6 in *Bedhead*. Add examples to the chart.

  Think about a different way print might be used to show a writer's voice.

- Show and read page 15.

  Why do you think the writer decided to use italics (slanted print) on this page?

- Support a discussion about how the writer used italics to show voice. Point out that on a computer, different fonts as well as italics and underlining may be used. In handwritten text, underlining is most commonly used. Add examples to the chart.

The Writing Minilessons Book, Grade 3

WML2

CFT.U9.WML2

Have a Try

Invite students to turn and talk about how a writer uses styles of print to show voice.

▶ Show and read page 12 in *The Perfect Pet*.

> What do you notice about the print on this page? How does Margie Palatini use it to show her voice? Turn and talk about that.

▶ After time for discussion, ask students to share. Write the sentence on the chart. Have students read it aloud, emphasizing *quite*.

Summarize and Apply

Summarize the learning. Have students try using different styles of print to show voice.

> How can you show your voice?

▶ Add the principle to the chart.

> Today during writing time, you might decide to try different styles of print in your writing. If there are words you want your readers to read a certain way or you want a character to speak a certain way, you can make your letters bold, italic, or underlined, or you can put them all in capitals. Bring your writing when we meet later.

Show your voice with different styles of print.

Bold	Lake Baikal, in Russia, is the world's **oldest** and **deepest** lake.
CAPITALIZATION	It was BIG. It was BAD. "Oliver? Oliver? OLIVER!"
Italics (slanted)	And there was now a *bigger* clump of hair way at the back of his head that looked just like a cat's coughed-up fur ball. "A dog is not *quite* perfect, Elizabeth."

Confer

▶ During independent writing, move around the room to confer briefly with students about their writing voice. Use the following prompts as needed.

- *How can you use a different style of print here?*
- *How should this part sound? Is there a way to show that with print?*
- *Can you read this part aloud?*

Share

Following independent writing, gather students in the meeting area. Ask a few volunteers to share their writing.

> Did anyone try using a different style of print in your writing? Show what you wrote.

Umbrella 9: Writing with Voice in Fiction and Nonfiction

WML3
CFT.U9.WML3

Writing Minilesson Principle
Show your voice with humor.

Writing with Voice in Fiction and Nonfiction

You Will Need

- several humorous mentor texts, such as the following, from Text Set: Humorous Texts:
  - *Those Darn Squirrels!* and *Big Bad Bubble* by Adam Rubin
  - *The Great Fuzz Frenzy* by Janet Stevens and Susan Stevens Crummel
- chart paper and markers
- document camera (optional)
- writer's notebooks and/or writing folders

Academic Language / Important Vocabulary

- voice
- humor
- exaggerate

Continuum Connection

- Write in an expressive way but also recognize how language in a book would sound
- Write in a way that shows care and commitment to the topic

GOAL

Use humor in writing to convey voice.

RATIONALE

When students learn to use humor in their writing, their personality and voice shine through and their writing is elevated. Helping students notice how writers use humor (and how they use it appropriately) adds to their enjoyment of both reading and writing.

WRITER'S NOTEBOOK/WRITING FOLDER

Make sure students have their writing folders or writer's notebooks so that during independent writing they can try out using humor in their writing.

ASSESS LEARNING

- Observe whether students sometimes use humor in their writing.
- Look for evidence that students can use vocabulary such as *voice*, *humor*, and *exaggerate*.

MINILESSON

To help students think about the minilesson principle, use humorous mentor text examples and provide an interactive lesson. Here is an example.

- Show (or project) and read page 6 of *Those Darn Squirrels!*

  What are your thoughts about what the writer and illustrator did on this page?

  What choices did they make to try to get readers to laugh?

- Support a conversation about the ways this page shows humor (e.g., dust coming out when Old Man Fookwire sneezes, how unusual it is to hate pie and puppies, the funny way the illustrations are drawn). As students provide suggestions, begin a list on chart paper of the different ways humor has been used, using general terms.

- Repeat with pages 12–13, 18–19, and 30–32. Add to chart.

- Show the cover of *The Great Fuzz Frenzy*.

  Let's take a look at how the authors, one of whom is also the illustrator, used humor in this book.

- Show and read the first few pages of the book, pausing after each to allow time for students to notice the humor.

  What do you notice?

- Add to the chart.

  Humor is one way that voice can be used to show personality in your writing.

Have a Try

Invite students to turn and talk about how a writer uses humor to show voice.

▸ Show and read pages 13–14 in *Big Bad Bubble*.

What do you notice about how voice is shown through humor? Turn and talk about that.

▸ After time for discussion, ask students to share. Add new ideas to the chart.

Summarize and Apply

Summarize the learning. Have students try using humor to show voice.

What is a way to show your voice in your writing?

▸ Add the principle to the top of the chart.

Today during writing time, you might decide to try using humor in your writing. You can look at the chart for ideas. Make sure humor is appropriate for your writing. If you are writing something serious, humor is not a good choice. Bring your writing when we meet later.

Show your voice with humor.

- Funny illustrations
- Unusual behavior
- Mixed-up situation
- Playful words
- Silly language
- Surprise twist
- Exaggeration

Ha ha ha!

Confer

▸ During independent writing, move around the room to confer briefly with students about their writing voice. Use the following prompts as needed.

- How can you use humor here?
- What is something funny this character might say to express her feelings?
- Is there a way to exaggerate this idea to make it funny?

Share

Following independent writing, gather students in the meeting area. Ask a few volunteers to share their writing.

Did anyone try using humor in your writing? Share what you wrote.

WML 4
CFT.U9.WML4

Writing Minilesson Principle
Read your writing aloud to hear how it sounds.

Writing with Voice in Fiction and Nonfiction

You Will Need

- chart paper prepared with a writing sample that uses elements of voice
- marker
- student writing samples (one per student)
- writer's notebooks and/or writing folders

Academic Language / Important Vocabulary

- voice
- writing
- aloud
- sounds

Continuum Connection

- Read writing aloud to help think critically about voice

GOAL

Read one's own writing aloud to hear how it sounds.

RATIONALE

When students read their writing aloud, they learn to hear it in the same way that a reader might hear it. This allows students to use multiple senses in order to have a deeper experience with language. Spoken language has inflection and intonation, so when students read aloud, they think about how to show these attributes in their writing.

WRITER'S NOTEBOOK/WRITING FOLDER

Make sure students have their writing folders or writer's notebooks so that they have access to their writing.

ASSESS LEARNING

- Notice whether students read their own writing aloud to hear how it sounds. Do they also revise to make it sound the way they want it to?
- Look for evidence that students can use vocabulary such as *voice*, *writing*, *aloud*, and *sounds*.

MINILESSON

Students will need their writer's notebooks or writing folders for this lesson. To help students think about the minilesson principle, model reading the prepared writing sample aloud and provide an interactive lesson. Here is an example.

- Display the prepared chart paper.

    Listen as I read this piece of writing.

- Read aloud, using intonation and expressiveness throughout.

    What did you notice?

- Engage students in a conversation about how you read in a way that sounded like you were talking and that your personality came through.

    As I read this writing again, think about what is on the page that helps me know how to read it. Put up your thumb when you notice something.

- As students recognize aspects of the writing that contribute to voice (e.g., words, print style, humor), pause to talk about what they noticed. On chart paper, make a list of their noticings, using general terms.

    Reading your writing aloud helps you hear if your personality comes through.

Have a Try

Invite students to read their writing aloud to a partner.

- Make sure students have their writer's notebooks or writing folders.

    Choose a piece of your writing to read aloud to a partner. Ask your partner to listen to how it sounds. Then talk about what you did to make your voice come through in your writing.

- After time for discussion, ask a few volunteers to share what they noticed as they listened to their own writing and their partner's writing.

Summarize and Apply

Summarize the learning. Have students remember to read their writing aloud to hear how it sounds.

    How does reading your own writing aloud help you become a better writer?

- Add the principle to the chart.

    Today when you are writing, stop every so often to read your writing aloud in a whisper voice to hear how it sounds. Listen to notice if your personality shines through in your writing. You could also ask a classmate to listen to your writing. Bring your writing to share when we meet later.

Read your writing aloud to hear how it sounds.

Clean. Clean. Clean. It is *all* I seem to do! I just wish I didn't act like such a *plecos* fish that is busy cleaning the fish tank all day. I mean, do I look like a fish? It is TOO MUCH, I tell you. Clean. Clean. Clean. I just wish I could relax in the dirt. Embrace it, you know? But each time I try to sit on the couch and chill, I spot a new speck of dust and BAM! Just like that, I'm off to grab the duster. If you have any advice, I will gladly take it because this is <u>exhausting</u>.

repetition	
exaggeration	
bold	
italics	
humor	
capital letters	
underlining	

Confer

- During independent writing, move around the room to confer briefly with students to talk about their writing voice. Use the following prompts as needed.
    - *Read this page aloud. Did your writing sound the way you wanted it to sound?*
    - *What did you notice when you read this aloud to yourself?*
    - *What can you do to make your writing sound the way you want it to sound?*
    - *In what ways does your writing sound similar to (different from) the way you talk?*

Share

Following independent writing, gather students in the meeting area to share their writing.

    Read your writing aloud to a partner.

Umbrella 9: Writing with Voice in Fiction and Nonfiction

Assessment

After you have taught the minilessons in this umbrella, observe students in a variety of classroom activities. Use *The Fountas & Pinnell Literacy Continuum* to notice, teach for, and support students' learning as you observe their attempts at writing.

- What evidence do you have of students' new understandings related to voice?
  - Do students understand that a writer can write in a way that speaks directly to the reader?
  - Do they recognize that writers express voice with creative use of print styles?
  - Are they noticing when a writer uses humor to convey voice?
  - Do they read their own writing aloud to hear how it sounds and revise if necessary?
  - Are they using vocabulary such as *voice*, *speak*, *writing*, *directly*, *style*, *capitalization*, *italics*, *bold*, *humor*, *aloud*, and *sounds*?
- In what ways, beyond the scope of this umbrella, are students' reading and writing behaviors showing an understanding of voice?
  - Are students looking for ways to share their personality through illustrations?
  - Do they try out different uses of punctuation and capitalization?

Use your observations to determine the next umbrella you will teach. You may also consult Suggested Sequence of Lessons (pp. 605–622) for guidance.

EXTENSIONS FOR WRITING WITH VOICE IN FICTION AND NONFICTION

- Encourage students to select different fonts and font sizes on a computer. Encourage creative use of fonts and print styles but also caution against the overuse of styles.
- Notice humor as you read aloud and support a conversation to help students notice the writer's craft.
- Use shared writing to create a class story. Experiment with different punctuation or print styles on one or more sentences from the story. Talk about how changing the punctuation or print style changes how the words would be read.
- As you read aloud both fiction and nonfiction texts, engage in conversations about decisions the author made that show voice.
- If you are using *The Reading Minilessons Book, Grade 3* (Fountas and Pinnell 2019) you may choose to teach the minilesson that focuses on how writers create humor in LA.U9: Analyzing the Writer's Craft.

Using Text Features in Nonfiction Writing

Umbrella 10

Minilessons in This Umbrella

- **WML1** Use headings to tell what a part is about.
- **WML2** Make a table of contents for your book.
- **WML3** Use sidebars to give extra information.
- **WML4** Write captions under pictures.

Before Teaching Umbrella 10 Minilessons

Consider providing a mentor text that students can relate to by writing your own informational book or by using shared writing to write one with the class. We recommend that you teach or revisit GEN.U6: Making Informational Books alongside this umbrella so students can apply the text features taught in this umbrella to their own nonfiction books.

Read and discuss engaging nonfiction books with a variety of text features, including headings, sidebars, tables of contents, and captions. Use the following texts from *Fountas & Pinnell Classroom™ Interactive Read-Aloud Collection* and *Shared Reading Collection*, or choose nonfiction books with text features from the classroom or school library.

Interactive Read-Aloud Collection
Genre Study: Expository Nonfiction

Hottest, Coldest, Highest, Deepest by Steve Jenkins

A Day and Night in the Desert by Caroline Arnold

Bats! Strange and Wonderful by Laurence Pringle

Shared Reading Collection

Tiny but Fierce by Cheri Colburn

As you read and enjoy these texts together, help students

- notice headings and talk about what each page or section is about,
- discuss information provided in sidebars and captions, and
- use the table of contents to find information.

Interactive Read-Aloud
Expository Nonfiction

Shared Reading

Writer's Notebook

WML1
CFT.U10.WML1

Writing Minilesson Principle
Use headings to tell what a part is about.

Using Text Features in Nonfiction Writing

You Will Need

- one familiar nonfiction book that has headings and one that does not, such as the following from Text Set: Genre Study: Expository Nonfiction:
  - *A Day and Night in the Desert* by Caroline Arnold
  - *Bats!* by Laurence Pringle
- document camera (optional)
- sticky notes
- chart paper and markers
- writing folders

Academic Language / Important Vocabulary

- nonfiction
- heading
- page
- author

Continuum Connection

- Use headings, a table of contents, and other features to help the reader find information and understand how facts are related
- Use layout, spacing, and size of print to create titles and headings
- Incorporate book and print features (e.g., labeled pictures, diagrams, table of contents, headings, sidebars, page numbers) into nonfiction writing

GOAL

Write headings that tell the reader what to expect from sections of text.

RATIONALE

When you help students notice headings in nonfiction books, they begin to understand that authors group together related details on a page or in a paragraph or a section. They learn to structure their own nonfiction texts in a similar way and to use headings to help the reader know what to expect. Before or after this lesson, it would be helpful to also teach WPS.U8: Revising to Focus and Organize Writing, particularly WML5: Group similar ideas together in paragraphs.

WRITER'S NOTEBOOK/WRITING FOLDER

Students will work on adding headings to longer pieces of nonfiction writing in their writing folders.

ASSESS LEARNING

- Observe students as they talk about nonfiction books. What do they understand about headings?
- Notice whether students use headings in their own nonfiction texts.
- Look for evidence that they can use vocabulary such as *nonfiction*, *heading*, *page*, and *author*.

MINILESSON

To help students think about the minilesson principle, engage them in an inquiry-based lesson on headings. Then demonstrate how to add headings to a book that does not already have them. Here is an example.

- Point to the heading on page 6 (NOON) of *A Day and Night in the Desert*.

  What do you notice about this word at the top of the page?

  How does it look different from the other words on the page?

  Do you know what this is called? This is a heading. A heading is usually bigger than the other words on the page. It is sometimes in a different color or font. What does the heading tell you?

  The heading tells you what the page or section of the book is about. In this book, most of the headings tell what time of day it is.

- Invite a volunteer to point to and read aloud the heading on page 10.

  What do you think this section of the book is about?

- Display page 20.

  What is this page about?

  How can headings help you when you read or write nonfiction?

- Record students' responses on chart paper.

The Writing Minilessons Book, Grade 3

Have a Try

Invite students to talk to a partner about adding a heading.

▶ Show the cover of *Bats!* and read the title. Read page 11 aloud.

> This book doesn't have headings. What heading could we add to this page to help readers know what it is about?

▶ After time for discussion, invite a few pairs to share their responses. Agree on a heading and add it to the page with a sticky note. Add headings to a few other pages if time allows.

Summarize and Apply

Summarize the learning and remind students to think about using headings when they write nonfiction.

> Why do nonfiction authors use headings?

▶ Write the principle at the top of the chart.

> You can use headings in your own nonfiction writing. If you are working on a nonfiction writing project in your writing folder, look for a place you could add a heading. Add the heading. Bring your writing to share when we come back together.

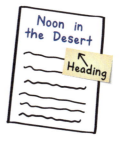

Confer

▶ During independent writing, move around the room to confer briefly with students about adding headings to their nonfiction writing. Use prompts such as the following as needed.

- What is this part of your book about?
- What heading could you add to this page to help readers?
- How can you make the heading look different from the other words on the page?
- What are you going to write about on this page? You can add a heading now to help you organize your ideas before you write.

Share

Following independent writing, gather students in the meeting area to share their headings.

> Who would like to read aloud a heading you wrote?

> What do you think this part of _____'s book is about?

Umbrella 10: Using Text Features in Nonfiction Writing

WML2
CFT.U10.WML2

Writing Minilesson Principle
Make a table of contents for your book.

Using Text Features in Nonfiction Writing

You Will Need

- a familiar nonfiction book that has a table of contents and page numbers, such as *Tiny but Fierce* by Cheri Colburn, from *Shared Reading Collection*
- a sample nonfiction book written by you, the whole class, or an individual child or another familiar book without a table of contents
- chart paper and markers
- writing folders

Academic Language / Important Vocabulary

- page numbers
- table of contents

Continuum Connection

- Use headings, a table of contents, and other features to help the reader find information and understand how facts are related
- Incorporate book and print features (e.g., labeled pictures, diagrams, table of contents, headings, sidebars, page numbers) into nonfiction writing

GOAL

Understand that writers include a table of contents as an organizational tool for the reader.

RATIONALE

When you help students notice and think about tables of contents in nonfiction books, they understand that a table of contents helps readers find information. They learn that they can include a table of contents in their own nonfiction books.

WRITER'S NOTEBOOK/WRITING FOLDER

Students will work on adding a table of contents to informational books in their writing folders.

ASSESS LEARNING

- Observe students as they read and talk about nonfiction books. Are they able to use a table of contents?
- Notice evidence that students know how to make a table of contents.
- Look for evidence that they can use vocabulary such as *page numbers* and *table of contents*.

MINILESSON

To help students think about the minilesson principle, engage them in noticing the characteristics and purpose of a table of contents in a familiar nonfiction book. Then use shared writing to create one. Here is an example.

- Show the cover of *Tiny but Fierce* and read the title. Turn to and display the table of contents.

    This is the table of contents. What information does the table of contents tell you?

    Why do authors sometimes put a table of contents in their books? How does the table of contents help you as a reader?

    What page should I go to if I want to read about a dragonfly's jaws?

- Display a class-written nonfiction text, one written by you or an individual student, or a familiar book without a table of contents.

    Let's make a table of contents for this book.

- If the pages are not numbered, start by adding page numbers. Explain that it is important to be sure the pages are in the correct order and numbered before making a table of contents.

- Write *Table of Contents* at the top of a sheet of chart paper. With students' input, create a table of contents.

The Writing Minilessons Book, Grade 3

Have a Try

Invite students to talk to a partner about how to make a table of contents.

> You can make a table of contents for your own nonfiction books. How will you make one? What will you have to remember to do? Turn and talk to your partner about this.

▶ After students turn and talk, invite several pairs to share their responses. Summarize the learning on a separate sheet of chart paper.

Summarize and Apply

Summarize the learning. Remind students to think about including a table of contents when they write nonfiction books.

> How can you help readers find the information they are looking for in your nonfiction books?

▶ Write the principle at the top of the chart.

> If you are working on a nonfiction book in your writing folder, try making a table of contents for it. Look at the chart we made if you need help remembering what to do. Your book has to be finished before you can add the table of contents. If you make a table of contents today, bring it to share when we meet later.

Confer

▶ During independent writing, move around the room to confer briefly with students about making a table of contents. Use prompts such as the following as needed.
  - *Where should you put the table of contents?*
  - *What will you write in the table of contents?*
  - *What is the first part of your book called? What page does it start on?*

Share

Following independent writing, gather students in the meeting area to share their writing.

> If you made a table of contents today, hold it up.

▶ Select several students to talk about how they made their tables of contents.

Table of Contents

What Bats Look Like............1
Where Bats Live..................3
Types of Bats......................4
What Bats Eat.....................6
Echolocation.......................7
Baby Bats...........................9

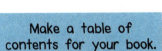

Make a table of contents for your book.

1. Make sure the pages are in the correct order.
2. Number the pages.
3. Write the name of each section of the book and the page number it starts on.

WML3
CFT.U10.WML3

Writing Minilesson Principle
Use sidebars to give extra information.

Using Text Features in Nonfiction Writing

You Will Need

- a familiar nonfiction book that has sidebars, such as *Hottest, Coldest, Highest, Deepest* by Steve Jenkins, from Text Set: Genre Study: Expository Nonfiction
- a sample nonfiction book written by you or the whole class (a shared writing piece) or another familiar book without a sidebar
- chart paper and markers
- writing folders

Academic Language / Important Vocabulary

- sidebar
- nonfiction
- information
- author

Continuum Connection

- Incorporate book and print features (e.g., labeled pictures, diagrams, table of contents, headings, sidebars, page numbers) into nonfiction writing

GOAL

Write sidebars to provide extra information to the reader about the topic.

RATIONALE

When you help students notice and think about sidebars in nonfiction books, they learn that they, too, can use sidebars to give extra information in their own books. They begin to think about what other information readers might need or want to know about the topic.

WRITER'S NOTEBOOK/WRITING FOLDER

Students will work on adding sidebars to informational books in their writing folders.

ASSESS LEARNING

- Listen to students as they talk about nonfiction books. What do they know about sidebars?
- Notice whether students include sidebars in their own nonfiction books.
- Look for evidence that they can use vocabulary such as *sidebar*, *nonfiction*, *information*, and *author*.

MINILESSON

To help students think about the principle, engage them in an inquiry-based lesson on sidebars in a familiar nonfiction book. Then demonstrate how to add a sidebar by creating one for an existing text. Here is an example.

- Show the cover of *Hottest, Coldest, Highest, Deepest* and read the title. Point to the text on pages 12 and 13.

   What do you notice about the words at the top of page 12 compared with the words at the bottom of page 13?

   These words that are off to the side of the page in a smaller font are called a sidebar. Sometimes, sidebars are placed in boxes, but not in this book. What does this sidebar have to do with the other information on these pages?

   The main text on page 12 is about the coldest place on the planet. The sidebar gives extra facts about the temperatures in very cold places, such as the South Pole and Alaska.

   How are sidebars helpful to the reader?

- Guide students to think about using sidebars in their own writing.

   You can use sidebars in your own nonfiction books. What should you think about when you want to make a sidebar?

- Record responses on chart paper.

The Writing Minilessons Book, Grade 3

WML 3
CFT.U10.WML3

Have a Try

Invite students to talk to a partner about what to write in a sidebar.

▶ Display a class-written nonfiction text, a text written by you, or a familiar nonfiction book without sidebars. Read one page aloud.

> Turn and talk to your partner about what a sidebar might be about on this page.

▶ After students turn and talk, invite several pairs to share their ideas. You might demonstrate writing the sidebar on a separate piece of paper and attaching it to the book.

Summarize and Apply

Summarize the learning. Remind students to think about including sidebars when they write nonfiction.

> How do sidebars help your readers?

▶ Write the principle at the top of the chart.

> If you work on an informational book in your writing folder, try adding a sidebar to give extra information. Think about what the reader might like to know in addition to the information in the main text. Bring your book to share when we come back together.

Confer

▶ During independent writing, move around the room to confer briefly with students about adding sidebars to their nonfiction books. Use prompts such as the following as needed.
- *What are you writing about on this page?*
- *What else might readers want to know about that? Do you know any fun facts related to that?*
- *Where on the page would you like to put the sidebar?*
- *How will you make the sidebar look different from the main text?*

Share

Following independent writing, gather students in the meeting area to share their writing.

> Who would like to share a sidebar you added to your book?

> How did you decide what to write in the sidebar?

Umbrella 10: Using Text Features in Nonfiction Writing

WML 4
CFT.U10.WML4

Writing Minilesson Principle
Write captions under pictures.

Using Text Features in Nonfiction Writing

You Will Need

- a familiar nonfiction book that has image captions, such as *Bats!* by Laurence Pringle, from Text Set: Genre Study: Expository Nonfiction
- a sample nonfiction book written by you or the whole class (through shared writing)
- chart paper and markers
- writing folders

Academic Language / Important Vocabulary

- nonfiction
- information
- caption

Continuum Connection

- Incorporate book and print features (e.g., labeled pictures, diagrams, table of contents, headings, sidebars, page numbers) into nonfiction writing

GOAL

Write captions under pictures to provide more information for the reader.

RATIONALE

When students notice and think about captions in nonfiction books, they learn that they can add captions to images to give additional information. They develop the ability to communicate information through different means.

WRITER'S NOTEBOOK/WRITING FOLDER

Students will work on adding captions to the illustrations in informational books in their writing folders.

ASSESS LEARNING

- Look for evidence that students understand the purpose of captions and can distinguish them from other types of text.
- Notice whether students include clear captions in their own nonfiction books.
- Look for evidence that they can use vocabulary such as *nonfiction*, *information*, and *caption*.

MINILESSON

To help students think about the principle, use a mentor text to engage them in a discussion about captions. Then use shared writing to model adding a caption to an image. Here is an example.

- Display pages 18–19 of *Bats!* Point to the two captions and read them aloud.

  These are captions. What do you think a caption is?

  A caption is the group of words near an illustration, often a photograph, that tells more about the illustration. What do these captions tell you?

- Continue in a similar manner with the caption on page 25. Help students understand that captions add additional information beyond what is included in the main text.

- Display a class-written nonfiction text or a sample text written by you. Read one page aloud. Help students compose a caption for the illustration.

  Let's add a caption to our illustration of a bat eating a fish. What could we write to help readers understand this illustration? What might readers want to know about this bat?

- Use students' responses to write a caption.

The Writing Minilessons Book, Grade 3

WML 4
CFT.U10.WML4

Have a Try

Invite students to talk to a partner about captions.

▶ Make sure students have access to a nonfiction book they are working on or have already written.

> Look through your informational book. Take a minute to look for an illustration to which you could add a caption. What might you write? Turn and talk to your partner about your ideas.

▶ After time for discussion, invite a few students to share their ideas.

Summarize and Apply

Write the principle at the top of the chart. Summarize the learning and remind students to think about including captions when they write nonfiction.

> What did you learn today about captions? How are they helpful for readers?

> If you will be working on an informational book in your writing folder during writing time, try adding a caption to at least one of the illustrations. Bring your book to share when we come back together.

Confer

▶ During independent writing, move around the room to confer briefly with students about writing captions. Use prompts such as the following as needed.

- *What does this illustration show?*
- *Where can you write a caption?*
- *What extra information could you give in the caption?*
- *What do you think readers would want to know about this illustration?*

Share

Following independent writing, gather students in the meeting area to share their writing.

> Who would like to share a caption you wrote?

Umbrella 10: Using Text Features in Nonfiction Writing

Umbrella 10: Using Text Features in Nonfiction Writing

Assessment

After you have taught the minilessons in this umbrella, observe students as they write and talk about their writing. Use *The Fountas & Pinnell Literacy Continuum* to notice, teach for, and support students' learning as you observe their attempts at writing.

- What evidence do you have of students' new understandings related to using text features in nonfiction writing?
  - Do students use headings to tell what each part of a book is about?
  - Do they understand how to make a table of contents?
  - Do they use sidebars and captions to give extra information?
  - Do they understand and use vocabulary such as *heading*, *sidebar*, *table of contents*, and *caption*?
- In what other ways, beyond the scope of this umbrella, are students ready to develop their nonfiction writing?
  - Are they ready to learn about how they can expand their nonfiction writing?
  - Are they experimenting with using different types of graphics in nonfiction?

Use your observations to determine the next umbrella you will teach. You may also consult Suggested Sequence of Lessons (pp. 605–622) for guidance.

EXTENSIONS FOR USING TEXT FEATURES IN NONFICTION WRITING

- Teach students how to revise a table of contents if they make substantial changes to a book after making the table of contents.
- Guide students to notice subheadings in books and invite them to use them in their own books.
- Teach students how to make headings, sidebars, a table of contents, and other text features on a computer.
- Guide students to notice features of nonfiction texts, such as glossaries and indexes, and help them make their own.

Expanding Nonfiction Writing

Umbrella 11

Minilessons in This Umbrella

- **WML1** Use description to give the reader a picture.
- **WML2** Tell how two things are the same or different.
- **WML3** Tell about an experience from your life to teach more about a topic.

Before Teaching Umbrella 11 Minilessons

Teach these minilessons when students are writing nonfiction (e.g., informational texts, how-to texts) so that the minilesson concepts are relevant. Before teaching the minilessons in this umbrella, it would be helpful to teach WPS.U7: Adding Information to Your Writing so students understand the mechanics of adding the techniques taught in this umbrella to their in-process writing. It would also be helpful to teach WPS.U8: Revising to Focus and Organize Writing.

Continue to display charts created during other umbrellas related to nonfiction writing for students to refer to and to understand that they will use what they have already learned about nonfiction writing alongside these new techniques. Also, you may consider writing your own nonfiction piece or writing one with the students through shared writing to use as an example in these minilessons.

Read and discuss engaging nonfiction books. Use the following texts from *Fountas & Pinnell Classroom™ Interactive Read-Aloud Collection* and *Shared Reading Collection*, or choose nonfiction books from your classroom library.

Interactive Read-Aloud Collection
Author's Point of View

Energy Island: How One Community Harnessed the Wind and Changed Their World by Allan Drummond

Oil Spill! by Melvin Berger

Series Study: Dianna Hutts Aston and Sylvia Long

An Egg Is Quiet
A Rock Is Lively

Shared Reading Collection

Crows Aren't Creepy by Ashley Storm

As you read and enjoy these texts together, help students
- notice ways in which writers describe information,
- notice descriptive language writers use to help readers picture more about a topic,
- notice how writers compare or contrast things, and
- consider the breadth of ideas that writers share about one topic as a way to understand how much one can write on a topic.

Interactive Read-Aloud
Point of View

Dianna Hutts Aston and Sylvia Long

Shared Reading

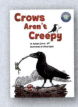

Writer's Notebook

WML1
CFT.U11.WML1

Writing Minilesson Principle
Use description to give the reader a picture.

Expanding Nonfiction Writing

You Will Need

- a familiar nonfiction book, such as *An Egg Is Quiet* by Dianna Hutts Aston, from Text Set: Series Study: Dianna Hutts Aston and Sylvia Long
- writer's notebooks and writing folders
- highlighter
- chart paper prepared with three headings (see first chart)
- chart paper and markers

Academic Language / Important Vocabulary

- description
- describe
- details

Continuum Connection

- Introduce ideas followed by supportive details and examples
- Use memorable words or phrases
- Use a range of descriptive words to enhance meaning
- Tell about a topic in an interesting way
- Select information that will support the topic
- Select details that will support a topic or story
- Add words, phrases, or sentences to provide more information to readers

GOAL

Use descriptive details to create a picture for the reader.

RATIONALE

When you help students notice that writers (of all genres) use descriptive details in their writing to paint a picture that brings a topic to life for the reader, they begin to try this in their own writing.

WRITER'S NOTEBOOK/WRITING FOLDER

Have students sketch in their writer's notebooks what they picture in their minds when they hear descriptive language.

ASSESS LEARNING

- Observe students as they talk about nonfiction books. Do they understand why a writer uses descriptive details?
- Notice whether students add descriptive details to their own writing.
- Look for evidence that students can use vocabulary such as *description*, *describe*, and *details*.

MINILESSON

To help students think about the minilesson principle, engage them in noticing descriptive details in a familiar nonfiction book and sketching what they see in their minds. Make sure students have their writer's notebooks or paper for sketching. Here is an example.

- Show the cover of *An Egg Is Quiet*. Read the title and page 11.

    What do you picture in your mind? Make a quick sketch in your writer's notebook.

- After a brief time, ask several students to share their sketches, talk about how they knew what to draw, and tell what the writer described.

    Tell about your picture. How did the writer help you know what to draw?

- Record students' responses in the columns on the prepared chart paper.
- Repeat this process with page 12 and the first paragraph on page 10.
- Guide students to think about using descriptive details that create a picture in their own writing.

    What are some things you can do as a writer to think about what words to use to give the reader a picture of an idea?

- Add ideas to a new sheet of chart paper.

The Writing Minilessons Book, Grade 3

Have a Try

Invite students to talk to a partner about using descriptive details in their nonfiction writing.

> I want to help my readers picture what it looks like when a polar bear wants to play with another polar bear. I will act that out for you.
>
> What could I write to help the reader picture what it looks like when a polar bear wants to play? Turn and talk about that.

▸ After students turn and talk, invite several pairs to share their ideas. Agree on a few sentences and add them to the bottom of the second chart.

Summarize and Apply

Help students summarize the learning. Remind them that they can use description in their own books to help readers picture a topic.

> What can you do to help your readers picture your topic?

▸ Write the principle at the top of the chart.

> Today as you write, think about what you can do to help your readers picture what you are writing about. Think about how making a quick sketch in your writer's notebook or acting an idea out can help you think of words to describe something in writing. Be prepared to share your writing with a partner.

What You Picture in Your Mind	Details from *An Egg Is Quiet* by Dianna Hutts Aston	What the Writer Described
Holding a big egg in two hands	Big and round Takes two hands to hold one egg	Size of an ostrich egg
A jelly bean next to an egg A tiny egg	The size of a jelly bean One ostrich egg about equal to 2,000 hummingbird eggs	Size of a hummingbird egg
An egg with spots all over A gray egg	Speckled to resemble rocks Gray, the color of mud	How an egg looks Color

Use description to give the reader a picture.

Ways to Write a Good Description
- Make a quick sketch
- Look at a picture in a book
- Act out the ideas.

When a polar bear wants to play with another bear, it stands up on its two back legs. It lets its front legs hang down by its sides and swings its head back and forth, like the pendulum on a clock.

Confer

▸ During independent writing, move around the room to confer briefly with as many individual students as time allows. Sit side by side with them and invite them to talk about expanding their nonfiction writing. Use prompts such as the following as needed.

- *What do you want to help your reader understand about your topic? How could you describe that to help the reader picture it?*
- *Draw a quick sketch of that idea. What words will help your reader picture it?*
- *Act out that idea. What words will help your reader picture it?*

Share

Following independent writing, gather students in the meeting area to share their writing.

> Who would like to share how you helped give the reader a picture?

Umbrella 11: Expanding Nonfiction Writing

WML2
CFT.U11.WML2

Writing Minilesson Principle
Tell how two things are the same or different.

Expanding Nonfiction Writing

You Will Need

- several familiar nonfiction books, such as the following:
  - *Oil Spill!* by Melvin Berger, from Text Set: Author's Point of View
  - *Crows Aren't Creepy* by Ashley Storm, from *Shared Reading Collection*
  - *A Rock Is Lively* by Dianna Hutts Aston, from Text Set: Series Study: Dianna Hutts Aston and Sylvia Long
- excerpt from these books written on pieces of paper
- highlighter
- a sample nonfiction book written by you, the whole class, or an individual student
- chart paper and markers
- writer's notebooks and writing folders

Academic Language / Important Vocabulary

- same
- similar
- different
- topic

Continuum Connection

- Introduce ideas followed by supportive details and examples
- Select information that will support the topic
- Select details that will support a topic or story

GOAL

Compare and contrast one thing with another to provide more information to the reader.

RATIONALE

Comparing and contrasting two things is a very useful way to help readers understand a new concept. When you help students notice how writers (of all genres) use comparison and contrast in their writing as a way to help the reader understand a topic more deeply, they begin to try this in their own writing.

WRITER'S NOTEBOOK/WRITING FOLDER

Students can make notes in their writer's notebooks about how their topics are similar to or different from something else and add that description to a draft from their writing folders.

ASSESS LEARNING

- Notice whether students use comparison and contrast in their own nonfiction books.
- Look for evidence that students can use vocabulary such as *same*, *similar*, *different*, and *topic*.

MINILESSON

Students will need their writer's notebooks for this lesson. To help students think about the minilesson principle, engage them in noticing comparison and contrast in familiar nonfiction books and/or a piece of nonfiction writing by you, a student, or the whole class. Here is an example.

- Show the cover of *Oil Spill!* Read the title and a short excerpt from page 18. Attach the excerpt to the chart.

    What did the author do to teach you more about the topic?

- Add students' responses to the chart.

    The author compared the skimmer to an object you know—a vacuum cleaner—so that you will understand more about how the skimmer removes oil from water.

- Highlight (or have a student highlight) the words in the excerpt that show comparison.

- Repeat this process with other texts, such as page 6 of *Crows Aren't Creepy* and page 5 of *A Rock Is Lively*.

- Use a piece of your own writing to demonstrate how an author might show more by telling how things are different (contrast).

    What did I do in my writing to teach you more about cowbirds?

- Add students' responses to the chart.

WML2

CFT.U11.WML2

Have a Try

Invite students to talk to a partner about how their topics are similar to or different from something else.

- Make sure students have a their writer's notebooks.

  > Think about the nonfiction topic you are writing about now or a topic you have written about in the past. In your writer's notebook, write how that is the same as or different from something else. Then turn and share your notes with your partner.

- After students turn and talk, invite a few students to share their ideas.

Summarize and Apply

Help students summarize the learning. Remind them to think about using comparison and contrast.

> What is another way you can help your readers understand more about your topic?

- Write the principle at the top of the chart.

  > When you write nonfiction, think about ways to describe your topic to your readers. You might think about what is the same or different about your topic and something else. Be prepared to share your writing with your partner.

Tell how two things are the same or different.

Example	Description
For small spills, the experts may call for a skimmer. There are several kinds of skimmers. One type works like a giant vacuum cleaner. It sucks up the oil from the water. —from *Oil Spill!* by Melvin Berger	• The skimmer works like a vacuum.
Well, they're scavengers—they eat dead animals. They're nature's cleanup crew. —from *Crows Aren't Creepy* by Ashley Storm	• A crow is similar to a cleaning crew.
All rocks are made of a mix of ingredients called minerals. Just as a batter of flour, butter, and sugar makes a cookie, a batter of minerals makes a rock. —from *A Rock Is Lively* by Dianna Hutts Aston	• Rocks are made of many things, just like cookie batter.
Unlike most birds, cowbirds do not build their own nests. They lay their eggs in the nests of other birds.	• Cowbirds are different from most birds because they do not build their own nests.

Confer

- During independent writing, move around the room to confer briefly with as many individual students as time allows. Sit side by side with them and invite them to talk about helping their readers understand the topic. Use prompts such as the following if needed.

  - *What is something that is the same as your topic? How are they the same? What could you write to explain that to the reader?*
  - *What is something that is different from your topic? How are they different? What could you write to explain that to the reader?*

Share

Following independent writing, gather students in the meeting area to share their writing.

> Who would like to share how you described how two things are the same or different?

Umbrella 11: Expanding Nonfiction Writing

WML 3
CFT.U11.WML3

Writing Minilesson Principle
Tell about an experience from your life to teach more about a topic.

Expanding Nonfiction Writing

You Will Need

- samples of writing that contain life experiences as a way to teach more (or the samples in the chart)
- sample of your nonfiction writing
- highlighter
- chart paper and markers
- writing folders

Academic Language / Important Vocabulary

- experience
- explain
- topic

Continuum Connection

- Introduce ideas followed by supportive details and examples
- Select information that will support the topic
- Select details that will support a topic or story
- Add words, phrases, or sentences to provide more information to readers

GOAL

Use details from personal experience to explain more about a topic.

RATIONALE

When students notice and think about how authors (of all genres) use details from personal experience to explain more about a topic, they learn another way to engage the reader and can apply this in their own writing.

WRITER'S NOTEBOOK/WRITING FOLDER

Students can apply what they learn about expanding nonfiction writing to a draft from their writing folders.

ASSESS LEARNING

- Notice whether students understand the purpose of using details from their personal experience in nonfiction texts.
- Observe whether students include personal experience to explain more about a topic in their own nonfiction books.
- Look for evidence that students can use vocabulary such as *experience*, *explain*, and *topic*.

MINILESSON

To help students notice how a writer uses information from personal experience to explain more about a topic, use a student's writing, your own writing, or the samples provided. Here is an example.

- Display the writing sample on chart paper.

    This is what Aleena wrote about dogs. This part is about making sure your dog is healthy. Listen as I read it aloud. Notice what Aleena did to provide information about the topic.

- Read the sample. Highlight parts that students point out.

    Aleena's experience helps us learn more about keeping dogs healthy.

- Demonstrate adding information to your own nonfiction writing by telling about an experience from your life that explains your idea. Show what you wrote about polar bears.

    I wrote about polar bears. What part shows how I used my personal experience to help you understand more about polar bears?

- Ask a student to highlight the part that tells your personal experience.

WML 3
CFT.U11.WML3

Have a Try

Invite students to talk to a partner about an experience from their lives to explain a topic they are writing about.

> Think about nonfiction writing that you are working on or have written. What is an experience you have had that would help your readers understand your topic more? Turn and talk about that.

- After time for discussion, invite a few students to share their thinking. Assure students that not everyone has had an experience related to a topic.

Summarize and Apply

Summarize the learning. Remind students to think about including experiences from their lives that explain their ideas.

> What can you do to teach your readers more about a topic?

- Write the principle at the top of the chart.

> During writing time, reread a draft of nonfiction writing from your writing folder. Is there a place where you can add personal experience to one of the pages? Will you use a caret or a spider leg, or will you need another piece of paper? Bring your writing to share when we come back together.

Tell about an experience from your life to teach more about a topic.

Keeping Your Dog Healthy
There are different ways to help keep your dog healthy. One way is playing with your dog. Dogs like to go to the dog park to run around and play with other dogs. *I like to play catch with my dog. I throw the ball in my backyard and she goes to fetch it. She runs back with the ball and wants to keep playing.*

Polar Bears
Polar bears live at the top of the world in the Arctic. There is cold snow and ice there. Even the water where polar bears swim is cold. They have special blubber to help keep them warm. *One time, I saw polar bears at the zoo. Because it was a hot summer day, the polar bears' home had blocks of ice to help them keep cool. There was also a large tank of cold water for swimming just like in the Arctic.*

Confer

- During independent writing, move around the room to confer briefly with as many individual students as time allows. Sit side by side with them and invite them to talk about expanding their nonfiction writing. Use prompts such as the following if needed.
  - *What are you writing about? Do you have a personal experience that would explain more to your readers? Talk about that experience. Add that to your writing.*
  - *What personal experience do you have with your topic? How might that help your readers learn more? Where will you write that?*

Share

Following independent writing, gather students in the meeting area to share their writing with a partner. Listen in to pairs. Choose one example to share with the whole class.

> What did you hear in _____'s writing that helps you understand the idea?

Umbrella 11: Expanding Nonfiction Writing

Assessment

After you have taught the minilessons in this umbrella, observe students as they write and talk about their writing. Use *The Fountas & Pinnell Literacy Continuum* to notice, teach for, and support students' learning as you observe their attempts at writing.

- What evidence do you have of students' new understandings related to nonfiction writing?
  - How clear are students' descriptions?
  - How successfully do they use comparison and contrast to expand their nonfiction writing?
  - Do they tell about a life experience to teach more about a topic?
  - Is there evidence students can use vocabulary such as *examples*, *ideas*, *sentence*, *describe*, *details*, *same*, *different*, *similar*, *topic*, *experience*, and *explain*?
- In what other ways, beyond the scope of this umbrella, are students ready to expand their nonfiction writing?
  - Do they show an awareness of text features, like headings or captions?
  - Have they thought about the illustrations and graphics in their nonfiction books?

Use your observations to determine the next umbrella you will teach. You may also consult Suggested Sequence of Lessons (pp. 605–622) for guidance.

EXTENSIONS FOR EXPANDING NONFICTION WRITING

- Gather a small guided writing group of students who need to strengthen their nonfiction writing.

- Encourage students to think about different text structures they might incorporate as ways to elaborate or expand on their writing (e.g., a question-and-answer section rather than a whole question-and-answer book; a how-to section rather than a how-to book).

- Support students in writing a nonfiction piece with voice, referencing CFT.U9: Writing with Voice in Fiction and Nonfiction.

- Provide time for students to work with a partner as a way to find out where they can expand their nonfiction writing. One student can read parts of the nonfiction writing to a partner. The partner can tell the writer what they are wondering about, allowing the writer to know where to utilize one of the ways to expand their nonfiction writing.

Drawing People

Umbrella 12

Minilessons in This Umbrella

WML1	Use shapes to draw people in different positions.
WML2	Draw people in a setting.
WML3	Use color to capture the way people really look.
WML4	Add details that show how a person feels.

Before Teaching Umbrella 12 Minilessons

Before teaching the minilessons in this umbrella, read and discuss a variety of picture books with different styles of illustrations and provide plenty of opportunities for students to independently draw and color without restrictions. Share a diverse collection of realistic fiction so students have exposure to different ways illustrators draw people in a variety of positions, use perspective when drawing people in different settings, use color to capture how people really look, and use gestures and facial expressions to show characters' feelings. Make sure students can see the illustrations well enough to notice details. Consider using a document camera to project pages of books. Because this umbrella focuses on drawing people, you will want to teach these minilessons as students are working on writing that features people, such as picture books, memory stories, or fiction stories.

For mentor texts, use fiction books that have detailed illustrations of people such as the following books from *Fountas & Pinnell Classroom™ Interactive Read-Aloud Collection* or books from the classroom library.

Interactive Read-Aloud Collection
Connecting Across Generations: Family

Sitti's Secrets by Naomi Shihab Nye

In My Momma's Kitchen by Jerdine Nolen

Mooncakes by Loretta Seto

The Importance of Kindness

The Can Man by Laura E. Williams

Enemy Pie by Derek Munson

As you read and enjoy these texts together, help students study the illustrations to notice

- how the illustrator draws the characters in relation to the background (perspective),
- how the illustrator uses color to show how people really look, and
- the facial expressions and gestures of the characters.

Interactive Read-Aloud
Family

Kindness

Writer's Notebook

WML1
CFT.U12.WML1

Writing Minilesson Principle
Use shapes to draw people in different positions.

Drawing People

You Will Need

- several familiar books with illustrations of people in various positions, such as the following:
  - *Sitti's Secrets* by Naomi Shihab Nye, from Text Set: Connecting Across Generations: Family
  - *The Can Man* by Laura E. Williams, from Text Set: The Importance of Kindness
- chart paper and markers
- writer's notebooks

Academic Language / Important Vocabulary

- shape
- angle
- position
- tilted

Continuum Connection

- Use drawings and sketches to represent people, places, things, and ideas in the composing, revising, and publishing process
- Use sketching to create quick representations of images, usually an outline in pencil or pen

GOAL

Understand that it's helpful to use shapes to draw people in different positions.

RATIONALE

Drawing people in different poses can be challenging. Teaching students to start with basic shapes will help them draw more easily and more representationally. Detailed drawings also may prompt students to include details from their illustrations in their writing.

WRITER'S NOTEBOOK/WRITING FOLDER

Students can practice sketching people in their writer's notebooks before doing their final illustrations.

ASSESS LEARNING

- Watch students draw. Do they draw people in different positions?
- Look for evidence that students can use vocabulary such as *shape*, *angle*, *position*, and *tilted*.

MINILESSON

Students will need their writer's notebook for this lesson. To help students think about the minilesson principle, use several mentor texts to prompt discussion about how illustrators draw people in different positions. Below is an example. Have them sketch alongside you.

- Draw students' attention to pages 3–4 in *Sitti's Secrets*.

  What do you notice about how the illustrator drew Mona on the swings in this illustration? What shapes do you see that make up Mona's body parts?

- Use your finger to trace over the body parts, showing how the body can be broken down into circles, ovals, rectangles, and angles.

  The oval that makes up Mona's body looks tilted to show she is leaning backward on the swing. The two ovals that make up one leg create an angle to show that she is sitting.

- Show *The Can Man* and talk about pages 5–6. Help students to see beyond Mike's clothing and helmet as you use your finger to trace the shapes and angles that make up his body. Quickly sketch the shapes lightly on paper.

  What do you notice about what I have drawn?

  The ovals are drawn lightly because I will erase them after I add Mike's clothes. Watch as I add clothes and a helmet over the shapes.

- Ask students for guidance as to what shapes to draw for the clothing. Finish the drawing by adding facial features, hair, helmet, hands, feet, and a skateboard—but no color. Erase the ovals. Save the chart for WML3.

Have a Try

Invite students to turn and talk about how to draw another position.

▸ Show the second to last illustration in *The Can Man*. Ask a volunteer to sit on a chair imitating Tim sitting on the steps holding the new skateboard.

> Turn and talk about the shapes you see in the drawing of Tim and in your classmate.

▸ Guide the conversation to help students recognize how the illustrator used shapes to draw Tim in a position that looks realistic.

Summarize and Apply

Summarize the lesson. Remind students to draw people in positions that match what they are doing.

> How can you make the illustrations of the characters in your stories more realistic?

▸ Write the principle at the top of the chart.

> When you write today, think about how a person you are writing about would look. Then try drawing that position. You can do your sketches in your writer's notebook. Bring your drawings to share when we meet later.

Use shapes to draw people in different positions.

Confer

▸ During independent writing, move around the room to confer briefly with students. Invite them to talk about drawing people. Use the following prompts as needed.
  - Let's look in some books to see how the people are standing (sitting). How do the legs look? Trace what that oval would look like. Try to make the legs look the same on your paper.
  - Which way should this angle point? Trace over the leg (arm) in the picture. Try drawing the leg (arm) the same as the leg (arm) in the picture.

Share

Following independent writing, gather students in the meeting area to share their drawings from their writer's notebooks.

> Share your sketch with a partner. Have your partner trace the shapes in your writer's notebook.

Umbrella 12: Drawing People

WML 2
CFT.U12.WML2

Writing Minilesson Principle
Draw people in a setting.

Drawing People

You Will Need

- a familiar book that shows detailed settings and perspective, such as *Sitti's Secrets* by Naomi Shihab Nye, from Text Set: Connecting Across Generations: Family
- chart paper and colored markers
- writer's notebooks
- To download the following online resource for this lesson, visit **fp.pub/resources**:
  - chart art (optional)

Academic Language / Important Vocabulary

- background
- close
- setting
- detail

Continuum Connection

- Use drawings and sketches to represent people, places, things, and ideas in the composing, revising, and publishing process
- Add details to drawings to add information or increase interest

GOAL

Learn to use perspective to draw people in a setting.

RATIONALE

When students place people against a background, they have to think about the size and position of the people relative to the background to show what is in the foreground and what is in the background (perspective) to give accurate information to their readers.

WRITER'S NOTEBOOK/WRITING FOLDER

Students can practice sketching people in perspective with the background in their writer's notebooks before doing their final illustrations.

ASSESS LEARNING

- Observe for evidence of what students understand about perspective and the importance of the background.
- Look for evidence that students can use vocabulary such as *background*, *close*, *setting*, and *detail*.

MINILESSON

Use mentor texts with detailed backgrounds to engage students in a discussion about what can be learned from an illustration's background. Help them notice how illustrators use perspective. Here is an example.

- Show pages 3–4 of *Sitti's Secrets*.

  How do you know if Mona is inside or outside?

  What do you know about trees that will help you understand why the illustrator drew the girl this size?

  The tree with the swing and the girl are both at the same distance—close up. And you know that most trees are bigger than people. The trees in the forest are big in real life, but they are far away in the picture because the illustrator drew them smaller than the girl to show they are in the distance.

- Record noticings on chart paper.
- Show pages 9–10 where the men are in the field picking lentils.

  Turn and talk to your partner about the size of the objects—the sky, the lentil plants, the hills of trees—and the people in the illustration. Why did the illustrator choose to draw them those sizes?

- After a brief time for discussion, ask students to share their thinking. Guide the conversation to help them notice that the illustrator thought about whether the objects were close or far away and also thought about the size of objects in real life. Record noticings on the chart.

Have a Try

Invite students to turn and talk about drawing people in a setting.

> • Make sure students have their writer's notebooks.
>
> In your writer's notebook, make a sketch of a person in a setting. Show it to your partner. Ask your partner to tell whether the person is close or far away.
>
> • After discussion, ask volunteers to share.

Summarize and Apply

Summarize the lesson. Remind students to think about the background when they draw to help establish the setting and create accurate perspective. Write the principle at the top of the chart.

> What have you noticed about people and objects in a setting?
>
> When you write and draw today, think about how illustrators draw people in a setting. What do you want to show? Where is the person? What details show that? Is the person (object) close or far away? Bring the illustrations you are working on to share when we meet.

> • Some students may be ready to draw the illustrations for a story they are already writing, while others will want to experiment with drawing people in a setting first.

Draw people in a setting.

	Size of Object or Person	Why is it that size?	In real life it is...
	• big tree	• close	• big
	• girl smaller than the tree but bigger than the forest of trees	• close	• smaller than a tree
	• small forest of trees	• far away	• big but small in the distance
	• small birds	• far away	• small
	• lentil plants bigger than the birds and smaller than the men	• close	• smaller than men
	• men taller than lentils, larger than the birds, and smaller than the sky	• close	• taller/larger than plants

Confer

> • During independent writing, move around the room to confer briefly with students. Invite them to talk about drawing people. Use the following prompts as needed.
>
> • *Talk about this drawing.*
> • *How will you show who is close and who is farther away?*
> • *What can you draw in the background to show where the story takes place?*

Share

Following independent writing, gather students in the meeting area to share their drawings from their writer's notebooks.

> Who would like to share the picture you drew today? Tell about it.

WML 3
CFT.U12.WML3

Writing Minilesson Principle
Use color to capture the way people really look.

Drawing People

You Will Need

- several familiar books with colorful illustrations of people and backgrounds, such as the following:
  - *In My Momma's Kitchen* by Jerdine Nolen, from Text Set: Connecting Across Generations: Family
  - *The Can Man* by Laura E. Williams, from Text Set: The Importance of Kindness
- the black-line sketch from WML1
- crayons or colored pencils of various different colors, including those that can represent different skin tones and hair colors
- writing folders

Academic Language / Important Vocabulary

- diversity
- capture
- illustration
- illustrator

Continuum Connection

- Create drawings that employ careful attention to color or detail

GOAL

Understand that illustrators use color to capture what people look like in real life.

RATIONALE

As students study the way illustrators intentionally use color to make people look realistic, they learn that they can use color in similar ways in their own drawings. Using color thoughtfully becomes important as students create illustrations to go with their own picture books, memory stories, or realistic fiction stories.

WRITER'S NOTEBOOK/WRITING FOLDER

Students will work on illustrations for ongoing writing in their writing folders.

ASSESS LEARNING

- Notice how students use color in their drawings and the consistency of usage across the pages.
- Observe whether students are choosing color to depict their characters in accurate ways.
- Look for evidence that students can use vocabulary such as *diversity*, *capture*, *illustration*, and *illustrator*.

MINILESSON

To help students think about the minilesson principle, use mentor texts to provide an inquiry around color in illustrations. Here is an example.

- Show the illustration on page 19 of *In My Momma's Kitchen*.

  What do you notice about the colors in this illustration? Notice the colors the illustrator used when creating the dad and the daughter.

- Support a conversation about the illustrator's choice of color in skin tone, hair, and clothing.

- Show *The Can Man* and discuss the illustrations on pages 11–12 and 17–18. Guide the conversation to help students notice that the illustrator thought about the color of each individual character's skin, hair, and clothing.

  What do you notice about the colors the illustrator used here? What did the illustrator think about in terms of color for the individual characters? What do you notice about how Tim looks on each page of the book?

  When you choose colors to match the way people and things actually look, your drawings look real. Real people have different skin tones and hair colors, and you can show that in your drawings.

- Point out Tim in several places in the book. Guide students to understand that illustrators draw characters in a consistent way to make them recognizable each time they appear in an illustration.

The Writing Minilessons Book, Grade 3

WML 3
CFT.U12.WML3

Have a Try

Display the black-line sketch from WML1 and the corresponding page in *The Can Man*. Invite partners to talk about colors they would use for the illustration.

> What colors would you add to this sketch we made? Turn and talk to your partner about that.

▸ After time for discussion, invite a few students to share their ideas. Demonstrate adding color while thinking aloud. Compare different shades of colored pencils or crayons to Mike in the illustration.

Summarize and Apply

Summarize the lesson. Remind students to think about using colors that represent how people really look.

> What did you notice about how illustrators use color when illustrating people? What does that mean for you as an illustrator?

▸ Add the principle to the top of the chart.

> Today, you can work on illustrations for the writing you are working on. As you draw pictures, remember to think carefully about what colors to use to capture the real color of people's skin, hair, and clothing. Remember to keep the color of each person consistent across pages.

Confer

▸ During independent writing, move around the room to confer briefly with students. Invite them to talk about drawing people. Show varying shades of colored pencils or crayons to students while talking. Use the following prompts as needed.
- *What did you think about when you made these color choices?*
- *What color(s) could you choose to make this look real?*
- *How will you show the diversity of the characters' skin and hair colors?*

Share

Following independent writing, gather students in the meeting area to share their drawings.

> Talk with a partner about the colors in your picture and how you made those color choices.

Umbrella 12: Drawing People

WML 4
CFT.U12.WML4

Writing Minilesson Principle
Add details that show how a person feels.

Drawing People

You Will Need

- several texts with illustrations that reflect feelings, such as the following:
  - *Enemy Pie* by Derek Munson, from Text Set: The Importance of Kindness
  - *Mooncakes* by Loretta Seto and *Sitti's Secrets* by Naomi Shihab Nye, from Text Set: Connecting Across Generations: Family
- chart prepared in advance with book titles
- markers
- writing folders

Academic Language / Important Vocabulary

- feelings
- characters
- illustration

Continuum Connection

- Create drawings that are related to the written text and increase readers' understanding and enjoyment
- Add details to drawings to add information or increase interest

GOAL

Draw characters' faces and bodies to reflect how the characters are feeling.

RATIONALE

Understanding how illustrators draw the face and/or the body of a character to reflect how the character is feeling helps students gain insight about the story. When they try this technique in their own illustrations, they are able to provide their readers with a stronger understanding of their characters and a deeper understanding of their stories.

WRITER'S NOTEBOOK/WRITING FOLDER

Students will work on illustrations for ongoing writing in their writing folders.

ASSESS LEARNING

- Observe for evidence that students recognize that characters' faces and bodies can reflect how the characters are feeling.
- Notice how students reflect emotion in the characters they draw.
- Look for evidence that students can use vocabulary such as *feelings*, *characters*, and *illustration*.

MINILESSON

To help students think about the minilesson principle, use familiar texts to engage them in noticing how details in characters' faces and bodies reflect feelings. Here is an example.

- Show *Enemy Pie* and read the title. Ask students to look at pages 1–2. Record students' responses on chart paper as they speak.

  What do you notice about the characters wearing the red uniforms?

  What details do you notice the illustrator used to show their facial expressions?

  What do you notice about their bodies?

  What kind of feeling do you get from looking at the members of this team?

- Repeat this process, this time talking about the characters wearing the blue uniforms.
- Continue with pages 7–8 of *Mooncakes*.

  What details do you notice in this illustration that help you know how the family feels?

WML4
CFT.U12.WML4

Have a Try

Invite students to talk to a partner about the feelings shown in another illustration.

- Show pages 7–8 in *Sitti's Secrets* where the girl and the grandmother first meet.

    How do you think the people in this illustration are feeling? What makes you think that?

- After students turn and talk, ask a few to share. Write their responses on the chart.

Summarize and Apply

Summarize the learning and remind students that they can add details to show how a person feels in their own illustrations.

What can you do to show how the people in your writing are feeling?

- Write the principle at the top of the chart.

    Today as you begin to write, reread your story and look at the illustrations. Think about how the people in your story feel. Add details or change the characters' faces or bodies to show those feelings and help your readers understand more. Think about this as you begin new writing, too. Bring your writing to share when we meet later.

Add details that show how a person feels.

Book Title	What does the face or body look like?	What feeling does that show?
Enemy Pie	• Eyes wide open • Big smile • Mouth open • Mouth in an open O • Eyes looking up • Hand on hat	Excitement Surprise
Mooncakes	• Sitting close together • Mom's hand on the child's arm • Mom looking at child • Smiles on their faces	Happiness Love
Sitti's Secrets	• Eyes staring, looking up • Small smile	Wonder Curiosity

Confer

- During independent writing, move around the room to confer briefly with students. Invite them to talk about drawing people. Use prompts such as the following as needed.
    - *Read your story aloud. What is the character feeling in this part? How can you draw the facial expression to help your readers to know that? How can you show that in the way you draw the arms and legs?*
    - *The facial expression of this character looks _____. Your character must feel _____.*

Share

Following independent writing, gather students in the meeting area with their writing. Invite several students to share their illustrations.

What did you think about as you drew the character's face or body?

What ideas did you hear from your classmates that you might try?

Umbrella 12: Drawing People

Umbrella 12 | Drawing People

Assessment

After you have taught the minilessons in this umbrella, observe students as they draw their illustrations. Use *The Fountas & Pinnell Literacy Continuum* to notice, teach for, and support students learning as you observe their attempts at drawing and writing.

▶ What evidence do you have of students' new understandings related to drawing people?

- Are students using shapes to draw people in different positions?
- Do they draw people and objects with accurate perspective and proportionality?
- Are they purposeful when choosing which colors to use to capture what a person really looks like? Are they consistent with their color choices?
- Are students thinking about and drawing facial expressions and body language to show how a character is feeling?
- Are they using vocabulary such as *shape, position, angle, tilted, feelings, characters, close, setting, detail, diversity, illustration, illustrator,* and *background*?

▶ In what ways, beyond the scope of this umbrella, are students showing an interest in drawing?

- Are they expanding what is drawn in the background to help their readers understand more?
- Are they asking to try new writing tools and different styles of paper?

Use your observations to determine the next umbrella you will teach. You may also consult Suggested Sequence of Lessons (pp. 605–622) for guidance.

EXTENSIONS FOR DRAWING PEOPLE

▶ Gather a small group of students who need extra support in drawing people in different positions. Ask a student to model moving in different ways. Invite students to talk about what they notice and then try to draw the student in their writer's notebooks.

▶ Gather a small group of students to review keeping the colors and details of illustrations consistent across pages.

Adding Meaning Through Illustrations

Umbrella 13

Minilessons in This Umbrella

- **WML1** Use illustrations to show more than what the words say.
- **WML2** Use colors to create a feeling.
- **WML3** Draw motion or sound lines to show something moving or making noise.
- **WML4** Draw your picture so the reader knows what is important.
- **WML5** Use light to show the time of day and details to show the season.

Before Teaching Umbrella 13 Minilessons

The minilessons in this umbrella will help students notice techniques illustrators use to support readers in understanding more about a story. Teach these minilessons as students make picture books (see GEN.U12: Making Picture Books) or do any other kind of writing for which illustrations are important. The minilessons can be taught in any order. To further support students when they draw illustrations, teach CFT. U1.WML2, a general inquiry lesson discussing the decisions that illustrators make, and CFT.U12: Drawing People.

Read and discuss enjoyable books with detailed and informative illustrations. Use the following texts from *Fountas & Pinnell Classroom™ Interactive Read-Aloud Collection* and *Shared Reading Collection*, or choose well-illustrated books from the classroom library.

Interactive Read-Aloud Collection

The Importance of Kindness

Under the Lemon Moon by Edith Hope Fine

The Can Man by Laura E. Williams

Last Day Blues by Julie Danneberg

Sophie's Masterpiece: A Spider's Tale by Eileen Spinelli

Connecting Across the Generations: Family

In My Momma's Kitchen by Jerdine Nolen

Mooncakes by Loretta Seto

Sitti's Secrets by Naomi Shihab Nye

Shared Reading Collection

Marissa Margolis, Pet Sitter by Ashley Storm

Cat Belly by Ashley Storm

As you read and enjoy these texts together, help students notice
- what the illustrations show that is not said in the words,
- how illustrators use color,
- the use of motion and sound lines, and
- meaningful details in the illustrations.

Interactive Read-Aloud
Kindness

Family

Shared Reading

Writer's Notebook

WML1
CFT.U13.WML1

Writing Minilesson Principle
Use illustrations to show more than what the words say.

Adding Meaning Through Illustrations

You Will Need

- several texts with detailed illustrations, such as the following:
  - *Last Day Blues* by Julie Danneberg and *Sophie's Masterpiece: A Spider's Tale* by Eileen Spinelli, from Text Set: The Importance of Kindness
  - *Sitti's Secrets* by Naomi Shihab Nye, from Text Set: Connecting Across Generations: Family
- chart paper prepared in advance with book titles and column heads
- markers
- five sticky notes labeled *Who, Feelings, Traits, Word Meaning,* and *Setting*
- writer's notebooks

Academic Language / Important Vocabulary

- details
- illustration
- trait
- setting
- character

Continuum Connection

- Understand that illustrations play different roles in a text: e.g., increase reader's enjoyment, add information, show sequence
- Create drawings that employ careful attention to color or detail
- Create drawings that are related to the written text and increase readers' understanding and enjoyment
- Add details to drawings to add information or increase interest

412

GOAL

Understand that details in an illustration can explain more than what the words say.

RATIONALE

Illustrators often include details in their illustrations that show more information to the reader than what the words say. Helping students understand how these details allow them to enjoy a story more and gain a deeper understanding of it will support them as they begin to try this in their own illustrations.

WRITER'S NOTEBOOK/WRITING FOLDER

Have students sketch in their writer's notebooks as they think through what they will draw in their final illustrations.

ASSESS LEARNING

- Observe for evidence that students recognize that details in drawings give information beyond the words themselves.
- Notice students' use of details in their own illustrations.
- Observe for evidence that students can use vocabulary such as *details, illustration, trait, setting,* and *character*.

MINILESSON

To help students think about the minilesson principle, use familiar texts to engage them in noticing how details in illustrations can show more than what the words say. Here is an example.

- Show the cover of *Last Day Blues* and read the title. Show and read page 2.

  What does the illustration show that is not said in the words?

  What does that detail in the illustration tell you?

- Add responses to the chart paper.

  How might you describe what the illustration shows?

- Add the sticky note labeled *Who* to the chart.
- Repeat this process with the first page of the story and then with page 7.
- Repeat this process with *Sophie's Masterpiece*, showing and reading pages 3–4.

  How do the illustrations give you more information than the words alone?

The Writing Minilessons Book, Grade 3

Have a Try

Invite students to talk with a partner about illustrations that show more than what the words say.

- Read and show the illustrations of Mona's home country on pages 3–6 in *Sitti's Secrets*.

    Turn and talk to your partner. What do you notice in these illustrations? How do they give you more information than the words alone?

- After students turn and talk, ask a few to share. Place noticings and the sticky note labeled *Setting* in the appropriate place on the chart.

Summarize and Apply

Summarize the learning and remind students to include details in their illustrations that show more than what the words say.

   What can you try to do in your illustrations?

- Write the principle at the top of the chart.

    Before you begin to write, reread your writing and look at the illustrations. Think about how your illustrations can help your readers understand more about the characters, setting, or the meanings of words. Do you need to add more detail to an existing illustration? If you are planning to make an illustration today, make a sketch in your writer's notebook before you draw the final illustration. Bring your writing to share when we meet later.

Use illustrations to show more than what the words say.

Book Title	Details	What the Details Tell You	What the Details Describe
Last Day Blues	• Boy looking at a snake in a jar	• Who Daisy is—a snake	Who
	• Kids with their chins in their hands looking up at Mrs. Hartwell	• The kids are going to miss Mrs. Hartwell, too.	Feelings
	• Boy squirting the water fountain at others	• He is mischievous.	Traits
Sophie's Masterpiece	• Checkerboard web • Web with hearts • Web that looks like the sun	• Tells more about wondrous webs	Word Meaning
Sitti's Secrets	• Tall tree • Green grass • Hills with a forest	• Mona's home country	Setting

Confer

- During independent writing, move around the room to confer briefly with students about their illustrations. Use prompts such as the following as needed.
    - *What details might you add to this illustration to tell more about your character?*
    - *What details in your illustrations help your readers understand more about the setting?*

Share

Following independent writing, gather students in the meeting area to share their illustrations with a partner.

   Talk to your partner about the details you added to your illustration.

WML2
CFT.U13.WML2

Writing Minilesson Principle
Use colors to create a feeling.

Adding Meaning Through Illustrations

You Will Need

- several texts with illustrations that convey feelings, such as the following:
  - *Last Day Blues* by Julie Danneberg, from Text Set: The Importance of Kindness
  - *Mooncakes* by Loretta Seto, from Text Set: Connecting Across the Generations: Family
- chart paper prepared with these column heads: *Colors; What feelings do the colors create?*
- colored markers or pencils
- writer's notebooks and writing folders

Academic Language / Important Vocabulary

- feelings
- color scheme
- color
- illustration

Continuum Connection

- Understand that illustrations play different roles in a text: e.g., increase reader's enjoyment, add information, show sequence
- Create drawings that employ careful attention to color or detail
- Create drawings that are related to the written text and increase readers' understanding and enjoyment
- Add details to drawings to add information or increase interest

GOAL

Add colors to drawings to convey a certain tone or feeling in the pictures.

RATIONALE

When students notice that illustrators use color to create a feeling or mood, and that this helps the reader gain deeper understanding of the story, they can begin to try this in their own illustrations to support their readers.

WRITER'S NOTEBOOK/WRITING FOLDER

Have students apply what they learn about using color to the illustrations for stories they are working on in their writing folders.

ASSESS LEARNING

- Observe for evidence of what students understand about the use of color in illustrations.
- Look for evidence that students can use vocabulary such as *feelings*, *color*, *color scheme*, and *illustration*.

MINILESSON

To help students think about the minilesson principle, use familiar texts to engage them in noticing how color can be used in an illustration to create a feeling. Here is an example.

- Show the cover of *Last Day Blues*. Then show pages 4–5 and 26–27.

  What do you notice about the colors the illustrator used here?

  Why do you think the illustrator used those colors? What kind of feeling do you get from the use of those colors?

- Add noticings to the chart.
- Repeat this process with page 14 and pages 22–23.

  When you read, notice the colors in the illustrations. Sometimes they are used to tell you more about how characters are feeling. You can use colors to show a feeling when you illustrate your writing, too.

- Repeat this process with *Mooncakes*, using pages 3–4.
- Next, discuss how the color choices are different in *Last Day Blues* and *Mooncakes*.

  Sometimes illustrators choose a particular color scheme for a book so that a feeling or a tone flows through the whole book. How do the color scheme and the overall feeling of *Last Day Blues* differ from *Mooncakes*?

  What are some other colors you associate with a certain feeling? Have you seen that in a book?

Have a Try

Invite students to talk to a partner about how they might use color to create a feeling.

- Hand each pair or triad of students a colored marker or pencil.

    Look at the marker (pencil) I gave you. What would you draw with it? What feeling would it create? Turn and talk about that.

- After students turn and talk, ask a few to share.

Summarize and Apply

Summarize the learning. Suggest that students think carefully about the colors they use in their illustrations.

   What did you notice about how color can be used in illustrations?

- Write the principle at the top of the chart.

    Today as you begin to write, continue thinking about what you talked about with your partner. Reread the story you are working on in your writing folder. Think about how you or the other people in your story feel. Add some color to the illustrations to create that feeling for your readers. If you are planning to make an illustration today, try it out in your writer's notebook first. Bring your writing to share when we meet later.

Use colors to create a feeling.

Colors	What feelings do the colors create?
Bright colors Red Purple Pink Green	• Fun • Excitement
Brown Gray Light blue	• Sadness
Peach Pink Orange	• Calmness • Happiness

Confer

- During independent writing, move around the room to confer briefly with students about their illustrations. Use prompts such as the following to support students as needed.
    - *What were you feeling in that part? What color might you use to show that?*
    - *What color are you thinking of adding to your illustration? What feeling will that create?*

Share

Following independent writing, gather students in the meeting area to share their writing.

   If you added color to an illustration to create a feeling, hold it up.

   Who would like to tell about your illustration?

Umbrella 13: Adding Meaning Through Illustrations

WML3
CFT.U13.WML3

Writing Minilesson Principle
Draw motion or sound lines to show something moving or making noise.

Adding Meaning Through Illustrations

You Will Need

- several texts with illustrations that use motion and/or sound lines, such as *Marissa Margolis, Pet Sitter* and *Cat Belly* by Ashley Storm, from *Shared Reading Collection*
- chart paper prepared with column heads: *What the Lines Show or Tell You*; *What You Learn*
- labeled sticky notes: *Sound Lines* (two), *Motion Lines*
- markers
- writer's notebooks and writing folders
- To download the following online resource for this lesson, visit **fp.pub/resources**:
  - chart art (optional)

Academic Language / Important Vocabulary

- motion lines
- sound lines

Continuum Connection

- Understand that illustrations play different roles in a text: e.g., increase reader's enjoyment, add information, show sequence
- Create drawings that employ careful attention to color or detail
- Create drawings that are related to the written text and increase readers' understanding and enjoyment
- Add details to drawings to add information or increase interest

GOAL

Add motion or sound lines to show something moving or making noise in a picture.

RATIONALE

When students notice how lines are used in illustrations to indicate motion and sound, they will understand how this technique helps them to enjoy stories more and gain a deeper understanding of the stories. They can then begin to try this in their own illustrations.

WRITER'S NOTEBOOK/WRITING FOLDER

Have students practice using motion and sound lines in their writer's notebooks before applying motion and sound lines to the illustrations for stories they are working on in their writing folders.

ASSESS LEARNING

- Observe whether students recognize that lines can be used to show movement or sound.
- Notice students' use of lines to represent movement or sound in their illustrations.
- Look for evidence that students can use vocabulary such as *motion lines* and *sound lines*.

MINILESSON

Students will need their writer's notebooks for this lesson. To help students think about the minilesson principle, use familiar texts to engage them in noticing how lines can be used in an illustration to indicate motion or sound and how that helps them as a reader. Here is an example.

- Show the cover of *Marissa Margolis, Pet Sitter* and page 5.

  What do you notice about the illustration of the chicken?

  Why do you think the illustrator placed those small lines in the illustration? What do those lines show you?

  How does that help you as a reader?

- Add students' noticings to the chart. Invite a student to add one of the sticky notes labeled *Sound Lines*.

- Repeat this process with page 3 of *Cat Belly*. Ask a student to apply the second sticky note labeled *Sound Lines*.

  Why do you think the illustrator placed the lines around the baby's head?

- Use the same page to repeat this process, noticing the motion lines by the boy throwing a ball. Ask a student to apply the sticky note labeled *Motion Lines*.

The Writing Minilessons Book, Grade 3

WML 3

CFT.U13.WML3

Have a Try

Invite students to turn and talk to a partner about using motion or sound lines in their illustrations.

- Make sure each student has a writer's notebook or piece of paper for sketching.

  Think of something that moves or makes a sound. Quickly sketch it in your writer's notebook. Add motion or sound lines. Then share your sketch with your partner.

- After students turn and talk, ask a few to share their sketches.

Summarize and Apply

Summarize the learning and remind students that they can use sound and motion lines in their own illustrations.

  How can you show something moving or making noise in your illustrations?

- Write the principle at the top of the chart.

  Before you begin to write today, reread the story you are working on in your writing folder. Look for a place to try using motion lines or sound lines to help your readers understand the story better. Think about this as you begin a new piece of writing, too. Bring your writing to share when we meet later.

Draw motion or sound lines to show something moving or making noise.

		What the Lines Show or Tell You	What You Learn
(chicken)	Sound Lines		The chicken is noisy.
(crying baby)	Sound Lines		The boy thinks all the baby will do is cry. The boy is not happy.
(boy throwing)	Motion Lines		The boy wants a dog.

Confer

- During independent writing, move around the room to confer briefly with students about their illustrations. Use prompts such as the following as needed.

  * *Read your story aloud. Who or what is moving in this part of the story? How can you add motion lines to help the reader understand that? What else does that help the reader understand about your story?*

  * *Read your story aloud. What sounds do you hear in this part of the story? How can you add sound lines to help the reader understand that? What else does that help the reader understand about your story?*

Share

Following independent writing, gather students in the meeting area to share their writing.

  How did you use motion or sound lines in your drawings?

Umbrella 13: Adding Meaning Through Illustrations

WML 4
CFT.U13.WML4

Writing Minilesson Principle
Draw your picture so the reader knows what is important.

Adding Meaning Through Illustrations

You Will Need

- several texts with illustrations that draw the reader's attention to what is important, such as the following:
    - *Under the Lemon Moon* by Edith Hope Fine, from Text Set: The Importance of Kindness
    - *Mooncakes* by Loretta Seto and *Sitti's Secrets* by Naomi Shihab Nye, from Text Set: Connecting Across the Generations: Family
- chart paper prepared in advance with column heads (see chart)
- markers
- writer's notebooks and writing folders

Academic Language / Important Vocabulary

- illustration
- illustrator
- details

Continuum Connection

- Understand that illustrations play different roles in a text: e.g., increase reader's enjoyment, add information, show sequence
- Create drawings that employ careful attention to color or detail
- Create drawings that are related to the written text and increase readers' understanding and enjoyment
- Add details to drawings to add information or increase interest

GOAL

Use different techniques to draw the reader's attention to what is important.

RATIONALE

Illustrators make decisions about how to create illustrations that show the reader what is important and express meaning to the reader. When students notice the different techniques illustrators use, they can begin to try them out in their own illustrations.

WRITER'S NOTEBOOK/WRITING FOLDER

Before illustrating their stories, students can practice what they learn about showing what is important in an illustration in their writer's notebooks.

ASSESS LEARNING

- Notice students' use of details to draw the reader's attention to what is important in their illustrations.
- Look for evidence that students can use vocabulary such as *illustration*, *illustrator*, and *details*.

MINILESSON

To help students understand the minilesson principle, use familiar texts to engage them in noticing how an illustrator draws the reader's attention to what is important. Discuss how they can apply these techniques to their own writing and illustrations. Here is an example.

- Show *Under the Lemon Moon*. Then show and read pages 5–6.

    Look closely. What do you notice about how the illustrator drew the lemon tree? What do you think the illustrator wanted you to focus on?

- Record students' noticings in the first of three columns on the chart.

    What does that help you understand about the tree and the story?

    What could you do in your own illustrations to show that something is important?

- Continue to record students' thinking in the next two columns.
- Repeat this process by showing several of the pages in *Mooncakes* of the family sitting close together.

    What do you notice about how the illustrator drew the family? What does that help you understand about the family?

    What could you try in your own illustrations to show how people have strong feelings about each other?

418

The Writing Minilessons Book, Grade 3

Have a Try

Invite the students to talk with a partner about how an illustrator shows what is important.

- Show pages 17–18 in *Sitti's Secrets*.

    What do you notice about this illustration? What do you think the illustrator wants the reader to focus on? Turn and talk about that.

- After students turn and talk, ask a few to share. Add noticings to the chart.

Summarize and Apply

Help students summarize the learning. Remind students to think about how they can use these techniques for their own illustrations.

   What did you learn about drawing illustrations?

- Write the principle at the top of the chart.

    Before you begin to write today, reread your story. Think about what is important at one point in the story and what you want your reader to focus on. How will you draw your picture to help the reader know that? If you are planning to make an illustration today, make a sketch in your writer's notebook before you make the final illustration. Bring your writing to share when we meet later.

Draw your picture so the reader knows what is important.

What details are in the illustration?	What do the details help you understand?	What can you do to try this?
A very large lemon tree spread across two pages.	The lemon tree is not well. The lemons are gone. Rosalinda is sad.	Draw an object or character big/large.
The young girl, her mother, and her father sit together in the big chair. The mother and father touch their cheeks against the little girl's head.	They care very much about each other.	Draw characters sitting close to one another.
Sitti's hair drapes across one page and onto the other as Mona helps to brush it.	Sitti's hair is very long. Sitti trusts Mona. They are close.	Draw part of the illustration across two pages.

Confer

- During independent writing, move around the room to confer briefly with students about their illustrations. Use prompts such as the following as needed.

    • *Talk about the story you are writing. What is important in this part? What do you want the reader to focus on? How will you show that?*

    • *You focus on _____ in your picture. That helps the reader understand that _____ is important.*

Share

Following independent writing, gather students in the meeting area to share their writing with a partner. Then select several students to share their illustrations with the class.

   How did you draw your pictures to help the reader know what is important?

WML 5
CFT.U13.WML5

Writing Minilesson Principle
Use light to show the time of day and details to show the season.

Adding Meaning Through Illustrations

You Will Need

- several texts with illustrations that show the time of day and/or the season, such as the following:
  - *Under the Lemon Moon* by Edith Hope Fine and *The Can Man* by Laura E. Williams, from Text Set: The Importance of Kindness
  - *In My Momma's Kitchen* by Jerdine Nolen, from Text Set: Connecting Across the Generations: Family
- chart paper prepared in advance with book titles and column heads (see chart)
- markers
- writer's notebooks and writing folders
- To download the following online resource for this lesson, visit **fp.pub/resources**:
  - chart art (optional)

Academic Language / Important Vocabulary

- illustration
- illustrator
- details
- season

Continuum Connection

- Understand that illustrations play different roles in a text: e.g., increase reader's enjoyment, add information, show sequence
- Create drawings that employ careful attention to color or detail

GOAL

Draw details in the pictures to reveal the time of day and of the year.

RATIONALE

Illustrators make decisions about how to depict the time of day or the season through their illustrations. Noticing these decisions gives students an understanding of how and why illustrators do this, which provides an opportunity for students to think about what details about time are important to share in their own illustrations.

WRITER'S NOTEBOOK/WRITING FOLDER

Students can practice what they learn about drawing details that show the time of day and the season in their writer's notebooks before they illustrate their stories.

ASSESS LEARNING

- Observe for evidence that students include details about the time of day or the season.
- Look for evidence that students can use vocabulary such as *illustration*, *illustrator*, *details*, and *season*.

MINILESSON

Students will need their writer's notebooks for this lesson. To help students think about the minilesson principle, use familiar texts to engage them in noticing how an illustrator draws the reader's attention to the time of day or the season. Discuss how they can apply these techniques in their own writing and illustrations. Here is an example.

- Show the cover of *Under the Lemon Moon* and read the title. Then show pages 3–4.

  What do you notice about how the illustrator used light in this picture? What does that help you to understand?

- Add responses to the chart paper.
- Repeat this process with pages 5–6.
- Repeat this process with pages 14 and 17 of *In My Momma's Kitchen*. Guide students to think about the details that tell the season.

  What details does the illustrator include in this illustration? What do they help you understand?

- From *The Can Man*, show page 25.

  What details does the illustrator include in these pictures to help you understand the season? Turn and talk about that.

The Writing Minilessons Book, Grade 3

WML 5
CFT.U13.WML5

Have a Try

Invite students to talk to a partner about showing time of day or season in their illustrations.

- Make sure students have a writer's notebook or paper for sketching.

    Make a quick sketch that shows a season. You might sketch something that you do in the season or something that shows how the season looks outdoors. When you finish, ask your partner to identify the season in your sketch.

- After students turn and talk, ask a few to share.

Summarize and Apply

Help students summarize the learning. Remind them to add details that show the time of day or the season.

What did you learn about showing the time of day or time of the year in your illustrations?

- Write the principle at the top of the chart.

    Before you begin to write today, reread your story. Think about how you will draw your picture to show the time of day or the time of year. Think about this as you begin a new piece of writing, too. Bring your writing to share when we meet later.

Use light to show the time of day and details to show the season.

Book title	What details are in the illustration?	What do the details help you understand?
Under the Lemon Moon	Little light in the sky / The moon / Dark mountains	It is nighttime.
	Light in the sky / Green mountains	It is daytime.
In My Momma's Kitchen	Basket of apples / Pumpkin/jack-o-lantern	It is fall.
The Can Man	Winter clothing (heavy jacket, hat) / Trees without leaves / Snow in the air	It is winter.

Confer

- During independent writing, move around the room to confer briefly with students about their illustrations. Use prompts such as the following as needed.
    - *What time of day does this occur? What details will you draw so the reader understands that?*
    - *What time of year does this occur? What details will you draw so the reader understands that?*
    - *You included _____ in your picture. That helps the reader understand that it is _____.*

Share

Following independent writing, gather students in the meeting area. Select several students who added meaning to their illustrations in different ways to share.

Talk about how you added meaning to an illustration.

Umbrella 13: Adding Meaning Through Illustrations

Section 3: Craft

421

Umbrella 13 | Adding Meaning Through Illustrations

Assessment

After you have taught the minilessons in this umbrella, observe students as they draw, write, and talk about their writing. Use the behaviors and understandings in *The Fountas & Pinnell Literacy Continuum* to notice, teach for, and support students' learning as you observe their attempts at drawing and writing.

- What evidence do you have of students' new understandings related to adding meaning through illustrations?
  - Do students add details in the illustrations that show more than what the words say?
  - How effectively do they use colors to convey a certain feeling or mood?
  - Do they use motion or sound lines to show something moving or making noise?
  - Do they draw pictures so the reader focuses on what is important?
  - How do they use light or details to indicate the time of day or the season?
  - Do they notice and use vocabulary such as *feelings, character, illustration, color, color scheme, motion lines, sound lines, setting, illustrator, season,* and *details*?
- In what other ways, beyond the scope of this umbrella, are the students showing an interest in adding meaning through illustrations?
  - Do they use details when they illustrate nonfiction?
  - Are they creating borders that tell more about a book?
  - Are they using speech and thought bubbles?

Use your observations to determine what you will teach next. You may also consult Suggested Sequence of Lessons (pp. 605–622) for guidance.

EXTENSIONS FOR ADDING MEANING THROUGH ILLUSTRATIONS

- Spend time studying poetry books and the illustrations that accompany the poems. Talk about the techniques the illustrators used and how those techniques might help students as they write.

- Provide pairs of students with chapter books from your classroom library that include some illustrations. Have students study these books to think about the techniques the illustrators used to add meaning to the stories. Talk about how those decisions might help students in their writing.

- Gather together a guided writing group of several students who need support in a specific area of writing, such as adding details to their illustrations.

Illustrating and Using Graphics in Nonfiction Writing

Umbrella 14

Minilessons in This Umbrella

- **WML1** Use photographs and detailed illustrations in your nonfiction book.
- **WML2** Draw diagrams to give information.
- **WML3** Use a close-up to show a detail of a bigger picture.
- **WML4** Use maps and legends to give readers information.
- **WML5** Use comparisons to help readers understand size.

Before Teaching Umbrella 14 Minilessons

Read aloud a variety of engaging, illustrated nonfiction books about different topics and give students plenty of opportunities to experiment with creating their own nonfiction texts. For mentor texts, choose nonfiction books that include photographs, diagrams, maps with legends, and different styles of illustration. You might also use a nonfiction shared writing piece that the class composed or some of your own original writing.

Use the following books from *Fountas & Pinnell Classroom™ Interactive Read-Aloud Collection*, or choose other suitable nonfiction books.

Interactive Read-Aloud Collection
Genre Study: Expository Nonfiction

Hottest, Coldest, Highest, Deepest by Steve Jenkins

Tornadoes! by Gail Gibbons

Knights in Shining Armor by Gail Gibbons

A Day and Night in the Desert by Caroline Arnold

Bats! Strange and Wonderful by Laurence Pringle

Shell, Beak, Tusk: Shared Traits and the Wonders of Adaptation by Bridget Heos

As you read and enjoy these texts together, help students
- notice whether each has photographs or illustrations,
- look closely at the pictures and share details that they notice,
- notice and understand maps and diagrams, and
- discuss how the images help them better understand the topics.

Interactive Read-Aloud
Expository Nonfiction

Writer's Notebook

WML1
CFT.U14.WML1

Writing Minilesson Principle
Use photographs and detailed illustrations in your nonfiction book.

Illustrating and Using Graphics in Nonfiction Writing

You Will Need

- one familiar nonfiction book with photographs and one with detailed illustrations, such as the following from Text Set: Genre Study: Expository Nonfiction:
  - *Shell, Beak, Tusk* by Bridget Heos
  - *Bats!* by Laurence Pringle
- a simple nonfiction text without any illustrations
- a collection of photographs (e.g., taken by you, printed from the internet, or cut out from magazines)
- chart paper and markers
- writing folders

Academic Language / Important Vocabulary

- nonfiction
- illustration
- photograph
- detail

Continuum Connection

- Use illustrations (diagrams, graphics, photos, charts) to provide information
- Create drawings that are related to the written text and increase readers' understanding and enjoyment
- Create drawings that employ careful attention to color or detail

---

GOAL

Understand that photographs and illustrations make books interesting and help readers understand more about a topic.

RATIONALE

When students notice the different ways nonfiction authors use photographs and illustrations, they begin to think carefully about how to illustrate their own nonfiction books, and they choose or create meaningful illustrations or photographs.

WRITER'S NOTEBOOK/WRITING FOLDER

Students will continue to work on longer nonfiction writing pieces in their writing folders.

ASSESS LEARNING

- Observe whether students use meaningful illustrations or photographs that enhance the information in their nonfiction writing.
- Look for evidence that they can understand and use vocabulary such as *nonfiction*, *illustration*, *photograph*, and *detail*.

MINILESSON

To help students think about the minilesson principle, use mentor texts to demonstrate the use of photographs and detailed illustrations in nonfiction books. Here is an example.

- Display the cover of *Shell, Beak, Tusk* and read the title. Show several pages.

  What do you notice about the pictures in this book? What kind of pictures do you see?

  This nonfiction book has photographs. Why might a nonfiction author decide to use photographs instead of drawings?

  Photographs let the reader know exactly what something looks like in real life, which is particularly helpful in a book about a science topic. What do the photographs in this book help you understand?

- Show the cover of *Bats!* and read the title. Show pages 16–17.

  What kind of pictures does this book have?

  This book has drawings for the illustrations. How do the illustrations help you learn about bats?

  In drawings, illustrators can show exactly what they want to show you. The illustrator of *Bats!* included a lot of details to help you understand what bats look like. What details do you notice in these illustrations?

Have a Try

Invite students to talk to a partner about adding a photograph or illustration to a nonfiction text.

▶ Show a sample nonfiction text without any illustrations. Read the text aloud.

> I wrote this page about dogs. Do you think I should add a photograph or a drawing? What should it show? Turn and talk to your partner.

▶ After students turn and talk, invite a few students to share their thinking. Demonstrate searching for a photograph or creating a detailed illustration.

Summarize and Apply

Help students summarize the learning and remind them to use photographs or detailed illustrations in their own nonfiction books.

> How are photographs and detailed illustrations helpful for the readers?

▶ Write the principle at the top of the chart.

> If you work on a piece of nonfiction writing today, think about including photographs or detailed illustrations to help readers understand more about the topic. Bring your writing to share when we come back together.

Confer

▶ During independent writing, move around the room to confer briefly with students about using photographs and illustrations in their nonfiction writing. Use prompts such as the following as needed.

- *What is this page about? Would a photograph or drawing help readers better understand that? What should the illustration show?*
- *Let's think about where we could find a photograph for this page.*
- *What details could you include in your illustration to help readers understand _____?*

Share

Following independent writing, gather students in the meeting area to share their writing.

> If you have a photograph or illustration in your nonfiction writing, hold it up for everyone to see.

WML 2
CFT.U14.WML2

Writing Minilesson Principle
Draw diagrams to give information.

Illustrating and Using Graphics in Nonfiction Writing

You Will Need

- familiar nonfiction books with diagrams, such as the following from Text Set: Genre Study: Expository Nonfiction:
  - *Tornadoes!* by Gail Gibbons
  - *Knights in Shining Armor* by Gail Gibbons
- a simple drawing of a familiar animal, such as a bat
- markers
- writing folders
- To download the following online resource for this lesson, visit **fp.pub/resources**:
  - chart art (optional)

Academic Language / Important Vocabulary

- nonfiction
- diagram

Continuum Connection

- Use illustrations and book and print features (e.g., labeled pictures, diagrams, table of contents, headings, sidebars, page numbers) to guide the reader
- Use illustrations (diagrams, graphics, photos, charts) to provide information

GOAL

Learn how to draw diagrams to give information.

RATIONALE

When students study diagrams in nonfiction books and think about why the diagrams were included, they learn that they, too, can create diagrams to give more information about a topic.

WRITER'S NOTEBOOK/WRITING FOLDER

Students will continue to work on their longer pieces of nonfiction writing in their writing folders.

ASSESS LEARNING

- Notice evidence that students understand the purpose of a diagram.
- Observe whether students try creating diagrams for their own nonfiction texts.
- Look for evidence that they can understand and use vocabulary such as *nonfiction* and *diagram*.

MINILESSON

To help students think about the minilesson principle, use mentor texts to demonstrate how diagrams can be used to communicate information. Here is an example.

- Show page 5 of *Tornadoes!* and read the text.

    How is this illustration different from most illustrations?

    What does the illustration help you understand?

    What did the illustrator include to make it easier for you to understand how a tornado forms?

    This is a special kind of illustration called a diagram. The labels and arrows make it easier to understand how tornadoes are formed.

- Show page 15 of *Knights in Shining Armor*.

    This is also a diagram. What does this diagram help you understand?

    How does it help you understand the parts of a knight's armor?

    What have you noticed about diagrams? What would you say a diagram is?

    A diagram is a kind of illustration that shows the parts of something or how something works. A diagram usually has both pictures and words, and it may have lines, arrows, or other shapes. Why do you think nonfiction authors use diagrams?

    A diagram makes it easier to understand a complicated idea. Sometimes words or a simple drawing aren't enough—you need a diagram to explain your idea.

The Writing Minilessons Book, Grade 3

Have a Try

Invite students to talk to a partner about how to make a diagram.

- Show a simple, realistic drawing of an animal, such as a bat.

    > What could we add to this drawing of a bat to turn it into a diagram? What information could we give to readers, and how? Turn and talk to your partner about this.

- After students turn and talk, invite a few pairs to share their thinking. Label the animal's body parts.

Summarize and Apply

Write the principle at the top of the chart. Summarize the learning and remind students that they can include diagrams when they write nonfiction.

> When might you choose to include a diagram in a nonfiction book?

> If you are working on a piece of nonfiction writing today, think about whether you could include a diagram to show the parts of something or how something works. Bring your writing to share when we come back together.

Confer

- During independent writing, move around the room to confer briefly with students about illustrations and graphics for their nonfiction writing. Use prompts such as the following as needed.
    - What are you writing about now? Would a diagram help readers understand more about that?
    - What could the diagram show?
    - What will you write on the diagram?
    - Will your diagram have any arrows? What will the arrows show?

Share

Following independent writing, gather students in the meeting area to share their writing.

> Did anyone make a diagram today?

> What does your diagram show? What will it help readers learn or understand?

WML3
CFT.U14.WML3

Writing Minilesson Principle
Use a close-up to show a detail of a bigger picture.

Illustrating and Using Graphics in Nonfiction Writing

You Will Need

- a familiar nonfiction book with close-up illustrations or photographs, such as *Bats!* by Laurence Pringle from Text Set: Genre Study: Expository Nonfiction
- a simple sketch on chart paper of a small animal, such as a butterfly
- markers
- writing folders
- To download the following online resources for this lesson, visit **fp.pub/resources**:
  - chart art (optional)
  - paper templates (optional)

Academic Language / Important Vocabulary

- nonfiction
- close-up
- detail
- illustration

Continuum Connection

- Use illustrations and book and print features (e.g., labeled pictures, diagrams, table of contents, headings, sidebars, page numbers) to guide the reader
- Use illustrations (diagrams, graphics, photos, charts) to provide information

GOAL

Use close-ups to magnify one part of a bigger picture.

RATIONALE

When students notice close-up illustrations in nonfiction books and think about why they are included, they learn that they, too, can use close-ups to show one part of an illustration in greater detail.

WRITER'S NOTEBOOK/WRITING FOLDER

Students will continue to work on longer pieces of nonfiction writing in their writing folders.

ASSESS LEARNING

- Notice evidence that students understand the purpose of a close-up illustration.
- Observe whether students try creating close-up illustrations for their own nonfiction books.
- Look for evidence that they can understand and use vocabulary such as *nonfiction*, *close-up*, *detail*, and *illustration*.

MINILESSON

To help students think about the minilesson principle, use a mentor text to demonstrate how and why close-ups are used in nonfiction. Here is an example.

- Show the cover of *Bats!* and read the title. Show page 19. Point to the vampire bat feeding in the large illustration and then in the close-up.

   What do you notice about this small illustration?

   The small illustration is called a close-up. Why do you think it's called that?

   A close-up shows one small part of the bigger picture as if you've moved much closer to it. Why might this be helpful to the readers?

   A close-up helps you see one part of the picture in more detail. What details can you see in the close-up that you can't see in the big illustration?

   When might it be helpful to include a close-up in a nonfiction book?

Have a Try

Invite students to talk to a partner about how to create a close-up.

* Show a drawing of a small animal, such as a butterfly, from a distance.

    I drew this illustration for my nonfiction book about butterflies, and I would like to add a close-up. What part of the butterfly might readers want to see in more detail? Turn and talk to your partner.

* After time for discussion, invite a few pairs to share their thinking. Demonstrate drawing a close-up. Ask students what details to include in the close-up.

Summarize and Apply

Help students summarize the learning and remind them that they can use close-ups in their own nonfiction texts.

    Why do writers and illustrators use close-ups?

* Write the principle at the top of the chart.

    If you work on nonfiction writing today, think about whether you could use a close-up to show details from a bigger picture. Bring your writing to share when we come back together.

Confer

* During independent writing, move around the room to confer briefly with students about illustrating nonfiction. Use prompts such as the following as needed.
    * Which part of this illustration might readers want to see in more detail?
    * How could you show that part in more detail? Would you like to add a close-up?
    * What details will you show in the close-up?

Share

Following independent writing, gather students in the meeting area to share their illustrations.

    If you added a close-up to an illustration today, hold it up.

    Tell about your close-up.

WML 4
CFT.U14.WML4

Writing Minilesson Principle
Use maps and legends to give readers information.

Illustrating and Using Graphics in Nonfiction Writing

You Will Need

- familiar nonfiction books with a map and legend, such as the following from Text Set: Genre Study: Expository Nonfiction:
  - *A Day and Night in the Desert* by Caroline Arnold
  - *Hottest, Coldest, Highest, Deepest* by Steve Jenkins
- chart paper prepared with a simple hand-drawn map (with a legend) of your school
- markers
- tracing paper
- writing folders

Academic Language / Important Vocabulary

- nonfiction
- map
- legend
- information

Continuum Connection

- Use illustrations and book and print features (e.g., labeled pictures, diagrams, table of contents, headings, sidebars, page numbers) to guide the reader
- Use illustrations (diagrams, graphics, photos, charts) to provide information

GOAL

Use maps and legends to provide more information for the readers.

RATIONALE

When students study maps in nonfiction books, they learn how to read maps and understand why they are helpful. They also learn that they, too, can use maps and legends to provide more information for the readers.

WRITER'S NOTEBOOK/WRITING FOLDER

Students will continue to work on longer pieces of nonfiction writing in their writing folders.

ASSESS LEARNING

- Observe for evidence that students understand maps and legends and attempt to use them in their nonfiction writing.
- Look for evidence that they can understand and use vocabulary such as *nonfiction*, *map*, *legend*, and *information*.

MINILESSON

To help students think about the minilesson principle, use mentor texts to demonstrate how to use maps and legends. Here is an example.

- Show the cover of *A Day and Night in the Desert* and read the title. Turn to page 21 and point to the map.

  What kind of illustration do you see on this page?

  This page has a map. Tell about maps and what they show.

  What does this map show you?

  It shows where in the world you can find deserts. Who can point to a part of the world where there is a desert?

- Help students understand that the legend gives information about the map.

  In the legend, there is an orange square next to the word *Desert*. The same orange color is used on the map to show where the deserts are located.

- Continue in a similar manner with the map on the last page of *Hottest, Coldest, Highest, Deepest*.

- Show the map you prepared of your school.

  I am writing a booklet about our school for new students. I made this map to help them find their way around. What does my map show?

  Look at the legend. How will it help new students understand the map?

The Writing Minilessons Book, Grade 3

Have a Try

Invite students to talk to a partner about the map of your school.

> Is anything missing from my map of our school? What could we add? Turn and talk to your partner about this.

▸ After time for discussion, invite several pairs to share their ideas. Add at least one more place to the map and legend, perhaps the playground.

Summarize and Apply

Help students summarize the learning and remind them that they can include maps and legends in their own nonfiction texts.

> Why do nonfiction authors use maps and legends?

▸ Write the principle at the top of the chart.

> If you work on a piece of nonfiction writing today, think about whether you could include a map and legend to give your readers more information about the topic. Bring your writing to share when we come back together.

▸ Students can draw their maps if they know enough to do so, or you can assist them in finding a suitable map that they can trace or use.

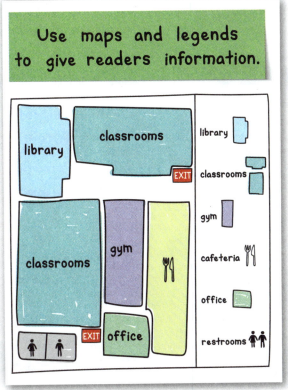

Confer

▸ During independent writing, move around the room to confer briefly with students about using illustrations and graphics in their nonfiction writing. Use prompts such as the following as needed.
  - *What topic are you writing about? Would a map help readers learn more about that?*
  - *What place do you want your map to show? Let's look for a map of that place.*
  - *Where on the page will you put the map?*
  - *Do you want to add a legend to your map? What information will the legend give?*

Share

Following independent writing, gather students in the meeting area to share their writing.

> Did anyone create a map today? Show your map and tell what is on it.

WML 5
CFT.U14.WML5

Writing Minilesson Principle
Use comparisons to help readers understand size.

Illustrating and Using Graphics in Nonfiction Writing

You Will Need

- a familiar nonfiction book that uses graphic comparisons to help readers understand size, such as *Hottest, Coldest, Highest, Deepest* by Steve Jenkins from Text Set: Genre Study: Expository Nonfiction
- document camera (optional)
- a sketch of a large animal or object, such as a Tyrannosaurus rex
- markers
- writing folders
- To download the following online resource for this lesson, visit **fp.pub/resources**:
  - chart art (optional)

Academic Language / Important Vocabulary

- nonfiction
- illustration
- comparison
- size

Continuum Connection

- Use illustrations and book and print features (e.g., labeled pictures, diagrams, table of contents, headings, sidebars, page numbers) to guide the reader
- Use illustrations (diagrams, graphics, photos, charts) to provide information

GOAL

Create graphic comparisons to help readers understand size.

RATIONALE

When you help students notice graphic comparisons in nonfiction books, they think about another way illustrators can convey information in nonfiction books. They learn that they, too, can use comparisons to help readers understand size.

WRITER'S NOTEBOOK/WRITING FOLDER

Students will continue to work on longer pieces of nonfiction writing in their writing folders.

ASSESS LEARNING

- Notice evidence that students understand how to interpret graphic comparisons in nonfiction books.
- Observe whether students try creating graphic comparisons for their own nonfiction texts.
- Look for evidence that they can understand and use vocabulary such as *nonfiction*, *illustration*, *comparison*, and *size*.

MINILESSON

To help students think about the minilesson principle, use a mentor text to demonstrate how illustrators use comparisons to help readers understand size. Here is an example.

- Show page 5 of *Hottest, Coldest, Highest, Deepest*. Point to the graphic that compares the depth of Lake Baikal to the height of the Empire State Building.

  Look closely at this illustration. What did the author-illustrator do to help you understand how deep Lake Baikal is?

  What did he compare Lake Baikal to?

  He made a comparison between the depth of Lake Baikal and the height of the Empire State Building, a very tall skyscraper in New York City. This comparison helps us understand that Lake Baikal is incredibly deep.

- Project or show page 15. Point to the graphic comparing annual precipitation with the height of a man.

  This is another comparison. What is being compared here?

  The author-illustrator compared the height of a person with how much it rains in different places. What does this comparison help you understand?

  This comparison makes it easy to understand how wet it is in Tutunendo, Colombia.

The Writing Minilessons Book, Grade 3

Have a Try

Invite students to talk to a partner about how to use comparisons to help readers understand size.

- Show a sketch of a large animal or object, such as a *Tyrannosaurus rex*.

    I'm writing about dinosaurs. Here is a picture of a *T. rex*. A *T. rex* was about 12 feet tall and 40 feet long. What could I draw next to the *T. rex* to help readers understand how big this is?

- Make sure students understand that the second object in the comparison should be something nearly all readers will be familiar with. Using a student's suggestion, complete the comparison.

Summarize and Apply

Help students summarize the learning and remind them that they can include comparisons when they illustrate nonfiction.

    Why do illustrators use comparisons?

- Write the principle at the top of the chart.

    If you work on a piece of nonfiction writing today, think about whether you could include a comparison to help readers understand the size of something. Bring your writing to share when we come back together.

Confer

- During independent writing, move around the room to confer briefly with students about using comparisons in their nonfiction writing. Use prompts such as the following as needed.
  - How big is a _____?
  - What could you compare a _____ to?
  - How much bigger should the _____ be than the _____?

Share

Following independent writing, gather students in the meeting area to share their writing.

    If you made a comparison to help readers understand size, hold it up.

    What two things did you compare?

Umbrella 14: Illustrating and Using Graphics in Nonfiction Writing

Assessment

After you have taught the minilessons in this umbrella, observe students as they write, draw, and talk about their writing and drawing. Use *The Fountas & Pinnell Literacy Continuum* to notice, teach for, and support students' learning as you observe their writing and drawing.

- What evidence do you have of students' new understandings related to illustrating nonfiction?
    - Do students include photographs and detailed illustrations in their nonfiction texts?
    - Do they include diagrams and maps in their nonfiction texts?
    - Do they use close-ups to show details from a bigger picture?
    - Do they use graphic comparisons to help readers understand size?
    - Do they understand and use vocabulary such as *nonfiction*, *photograph*, *detail*, *diagram*, *map*, and *legend*?
- In what other ways, beyond the scope of this umbrella, are students working on nonfiction writing?
    - Are they attempting to write different kinds of nonfiction texts?
    - Are they trying to add text and organizational features to their nonfiction writing?

Use your observations to determine the next umbrella you will teach. You may also consult Suggested Sequence of Lessons (pp. 605–622) for guidance.

EXTENSIONS FOR ILLUSTRATING AND USING GRAPHICS IN NONFICTION WRITING

- Invite students to bring in photographs from home to use in their nonfiction writing. You might also consider helping students look online for photographs or take their own photographs.
- Encourage students to write captions for the photographs in their nonfiction texts.
- Discuss other types of graphics in nonfiction books (e.g., graphs, charts, and infographics). Invite students to include these types of graphics in their own nonfiction texts.
- Gather together a guided writing group of several students who need support in a specific area of writing, such as deciding what kind of illustrations to add to their nonfiction texts.

Exploring Design Features and Text Layout

Umbrella 15

Minilessons in This Umbrella

- **WML1** Make your illustrations interesting in a variety of ways.
- **WML2** Use scenes to show action and details.
- **WML3** Use the size, color, and placement of words in interesting ways.

Before Teaching Umbrella 15 Minilessons

The minilessons in this umbrella should be taught when they are relevant to the needs of the class rather than sequentially. Provide plenty of time for students to experiment with each technique before introducing another minilesson. In addition to the supplies suggested for each lesson, students will need blank paper. Writers use the blank space to make decisions about orientation (portrait or landscape) and to visualize how and where they will place illustrations and words on the page.

Read and discuss picture books that illustrate a variety of art techniques exemplifying the minilesson principles. Use the following books from *Fountas & Pinnell Classroom™ Interactive Read-Aloud Collection,* or choose books from your classroom library that have interesting features.

Interactive Read-Aloud Collection

The Importance of Kindness
Last Day Blues by Julie Danneberg

Exploring Memory Stories
My Rotten Redheaded Older Brother by Patricia Polacco

Sharing Our World: Animals
Ape by Martin Jenkins
Moon Bear by Brenda Z. Guiberson

Genre Study: Expository Nonfiction
Shell, Beak, Tusk: Shared Traits and the Wonders of Adaptation by Bridget Heos

Humorous Texts
Bedhead by Margie Palatini
The Great Fuzz Frenzy by Janet Stevens and Susan Stevens Crummel

The Importance of Determination
Ruby's Wish by Shirin Yim Bridges
Nothing but Trouble: The Story of Althea Gibson by Sue Stauffacher

As you read and enjoy these texts together, help students notice and talk about techniques and materials illustrators use for their illustrations.

Interactive Read-Aloud
Kindness

Memory Stories

Animals

Expository Nonfiction

Humorous Texts

Determination

Writer's Notebook

WML1
CFT.U15.WML1

Writing Minilesson Principle
Make your illustrations interesting in a variety of ways.

Exploring Design Features and Text Layout

You Will Need

- a variety of books with examples of collage or interesting art techniques, such as the following:
    - *Moon Bear* by Brenda Z. Guiberson, from Text Set: Sharing Our World: Animals
    - *Nothing but Trouble: The Story of Althea Gibson* by Sue Stauffacher, from Text Set: The Importance of Determination
    - *Ruby's Wish* by Shirin Yim Bridges, from Text Set: The Importance of Determination
- chart paper and markers
- writer's notebooks
- To download the following online resource for this lesson, visit **fp.pub/resources**:
    - chart art (optional)

Academic Language/ Important Vocabulary

- materials
- collage
- illustrator
- mix

Continuum Connection

- Understand that when both writing and drawing are on a page, they are mutually supportive, with each extending the other
- Create drawings that are related to the written text and increase readers' understanding and enjoyment

GOAL

Understand that writers and illustrators can use a mix of materials or techniques to create art in books and increase readers' interest.

RATIONALE

By helping students notice that illustrators have different ways of creating their illustrations, you give them a wide choice in designing their own illustrations. This allows students to express their personalities and gives them ownership of their work.

WRITER'S NOTEBOOK/WRITING FOLDER

Students can make a list of art materials in their writer's notebooks.

ASSESS LEARNING

- Observe whether students try combining materials in their illustrations.
- Notice evidence that students understand how to make a collage.
- Look for evidence that students can use vocabulary such as *materials*, *collage*, *illustrator*, and *mix*.

MINILESSON

Students will need their writer's notebooks for this lesson. To help students think about the minilesson principle, use mentor texts to help them notice how authors and illustrators use mixed media to create their illustrations and increase readers' interest. Here is an example.

- Show the cover of *Moon Bear* and read the title. Show several pages.

    What do you notice about the illustrations in this book? How do you think the illustrator made them?

    He made the illustrations using collage. Say it with me, *collage*. You can use collage by tearing or cutting pieces of paper in shapes and gluing them onto a sheet of paper to make a picture.

    How might you try art like this in your own books?

- Show the cover of *Nothing but Trouble: The Story of Althea Gibson*. Show a few pages. Guide students to notice the brush strokes that are visible on some pages and the rainbow that follows Althea through the book.

    What do you notice about the illustrations in this book? How do you think the illustrator made them? What might you use to create art like this?

- Show the cover of *Ruby's Wish* and read the title. Show a few of the pages with decorative borders.

    What do you notice about these pages?

Have a Try

Encourage students to discuss and make a list of materials they might use to create their illustrations.

- Make sure students have their writer's notebooks or paper for making a list.
    - Make a list of materials that you could use to create art in your writer's notebook. Then turn to your partner and share your list.
- After time for conversation, ask students to share. Write their ideas on chart paper.

Summarize and Apply

Summarize the learning and remind students that they can use different art materials to create illustrations.

- What did you learn today about making your books interesting to read?
- Write the principle at the top of the chart.
    - You can use two or more art materials together to make illustrations for your own books. Today during writing time, try doing that.
- During independent writing, provide students with a variety of materials for creating illustrations. Leave these materials out to give students a chance to experiment.

Make your illustrations interesting in a variety of ways.

Watercolors
Torn paper
Glue stick
Colored pencils
Markers
Crayons
Pencils
Things to glue on (string, yarn, googly eyes, cotton balls)
Construction paper

Confer

- During independent writing, move around the room to confer briefly with as many individual students as time allows. Sit side by side with them and invite them to talk about design features and text layout. Use the following prompts as needed.
    - What art materials will you use to create your illustrations?
    - Take this piece of scrap paper. Try mixing watercolors and markers (or two other materials). What do you think about using those to create your illustrations?

Share

Consider asking students to leave their illustrations on top of their desks or hanging them on a clothesline to dry until the next day. Lead students on a walk through the classroom to see one another's illustrations, returning to the meeting area.

What did you learn from your classmates' work that you might try as an illustrator?

WML 2
CFT.U15.WML2

Writing Minilesson Principle
Use scenes to show action and details.

Exploring Design Features and Text Layout

You Will Need

- a variety of books with illustrations that use scenes, such as the following:
  - *Last Day Blues* by Julie Danneberg, from Text Set: The Importance of Kindness
  - *My Rotten Redheaded Older Brother* by Patricia Polacco, from Text Set: Exploring Memory Stories
- chart paper prepared in advance with column heads and excerpts from the books (see chart)
- markers
- writer's notebooks and writing folders

Academic Language/Important Vocabulary

- scenes
- details
- action
- author
- illustrator

Continuum Connection

- Provide important information in illustrations
- Add details to drawings to add information or increase interest
- Create drawings that employ careful attention to color or detail
- Create drawings that are related to the written text and increase readers' understanding and enjoyment

GOAL

Understand that writers and illustrators can use scenes to show action and detail.

RATIONALE

Help students notice how illustrators draw scenes to add small details that show the action the writer is telling about. They can use this technique in their own writing, allowing them to explain what is happening more clearly to the reader.

WRITER'S NOTEBOOK/WRITING FOLDER

Have students try drawing scenes in their writer's notebooks before they illustrate the stories they are working on in their writing folders.

ASSESS LEARNING

- Notice whether students try using scenes in their illustrations.
- Look for evidence that students can use vocabulary such as *scenes*, *details*, *action*, *author*, and *illustrator*.

MINILESSON

To help students think about the minilesson principle, use mentor texts and/or your own writing to discuss how authors/illustrators use scenes to show action and details. Here is an example.

- Show the cover of *Last Day Blues* and read the title. Read and show page 2 and then page 14.
  - What do you notice the illustrator did here?
  - The illustrator drew several pictures instead of one big one. What do the illustrations show?

- Guide students to notice that the illustrations show what is meant by the words in the text. Write responses on chart paper.

- Repeat this process with *My Rotten Redheaded Older Brother*, showing and reading pages 9–10.
  - How do these scenes help you understand the story?

- Write students' thoughts on the chart. Guide students to notice that the illustrations show all the different ways the sister thinks her brother does things better.

The Writing Minilessons Book, Grade 3

Have a Try

Invite partners to talk about how they could use scenes in their books to show details or action.

> Why might an illustrator choose to draw several small scenes instead of one large illustration? Turn and talk to your partner about that.

▶ After students turn and talk, invite a few students to share their ideas.

Summarize and Apply

Help students summarize the learning. Remind them that they can use scenes in their own books.

> What did you discover about authors and illustrators today?

▶ Write the principle at the top of the chart.

> Think about drawing small scenes when you illustrate your own stories. If you plan to draw scenes today, use your writer's notebook to try out how they might look. Bring your illustrations to share when we meet later.

Use scenes to show action and details.

What the Words Say	What the Illustrations Show
Last Day Blues	
"I'm going to miss my friends."	• She will miss acting out stories with friends.
"I'm going to miss Daisy."	• Daisy is a snake.
"She probably doesn't want the year to end."	• The children imagine what Mrs. Hartwell will do.
My Rotten Redheaded Older Brother	
"I guess I would have to face it."	• All the things the brother can do better than she can.

Confer

▶ During independent writing, move around the room to confer briefly with as many individual students as time allows. Sit side by side with them and invite them to talk about design features and text layout. Use the following prompts as needed.

- *What part of your story are you working on? How might you draw scenes to show the reader that action (those details)?*
- *Reread parts of your story and think, "Would using scenes help my reader understand more about the action or details?"*
- *What are you hoping to show in your scenes? How will that help the reader understand the action or details of your story?*

Share

Following independent writing, gather students in the meeting area to share how they used scenes to illustrate their writing.

> Who would like to share where you used scenes to illustrate your story? How did you decide to use scenes for this part of your story?

WML 3
CFT.U15.WML3

Writing Minilesson Principle
Use the size, color, and placement of words in interesting ways.

Exploring Design Features and Text Layout

You Will Need

- a variety of books with interesting placement of words on the page, such as the following:
  - *Ape* by Martin Jenkins, from Text Set: Sharing Our World: Animals
  - *Shell, Beak, Tusk* by Bridget Heos, from Text Set: Genre Study: Expository Nonfiction
  - *Bedhead* by Margie Palatini and *The Great Fuzz Frenzy* by Janet Stevens and Susan Stevens Crummel, from Text Set: Humorous Texts
  - *My Rotten Redheaded Older Brother* by Patricia Polacco, from Text Set: Exploring Memory Stories
- chart paper and markers
- writer's notebooks and writing folders

Academic Language/Important Vocabulary

- place
- author
- placement

Continuum Connection

- Use layout of print and illustrations to convey the meaning of a text
- Use the size of print to convey meaning in printed text
- Understand that when both writing and drawing are on a page, they are mutually supportive, with each extending the other

GOAL

Understand that writers and illustrators make decisions about where and how the words are placed on the page.

RATIONALE

Authors can enhance the meaning of a text by making interesting decisions about the size, the color, and the placement of print on the page. Helping students think about these decisions supports them in understanding more about what they are reading and leads to understanding that they can make similar decisions when writing their own books.

WRITER'S NOTEBOOK/WRITING FOLDER

Have students sketch the layout of a page in their writer's notebook. Work in progress can be stored in their writing folders.

ASSESS LEARNING

- Look for evidence of what students understand about word placement.
- Observe for evidence that students can use vocabulary such as *place*, *placement*, and *author*.

MINILESSON

To help students think about the minilesson principle, use mentor texts to show examples of decisions authors make about size, color, and placement of certain words. Make sure all students can see the pages clearly. Here is an example.

- Show the cover of *Ape* and read the title. Show some pages so that students can observe the print and illustrations.

  What do you notice about the size of the words?

  What does the size of the words show you?

- Write students' responses in two columns on chart paper.
- Repeat this process with *Shell, Beak, Tusk*. Show and read pages 6–7.

  What do you notice about some of the words on these pages?

  What do the colors show you?

- Write students' responses on the chart.
- Repeat this process with *Bedhead*. Show and read pages 2–3.

The Writing Minilessons Book, Grade 3

Have a Try

Invite students to turn and talk about word placement.

> Show the pages of *The Great Fuzz Frenzy* and *My Rotten Redheaded Older Brother* where the authors placed words around the illustrations.
>
>> Turn and talk to your partner about why the authors placed the words the way they did.
>
> After students turn and talk, invite a few students to share.

Summarize and Apply

Help students summarize the learning. Remind them that they can make decisions about the size, color, and placement of words in their own books.

> How can you add meaning to certain words?

> Write the principle at the top of the chart.
>
>> Before you begin to write today, think about how you can place the words on the page to make your writing interesting and to help your readers understand more. Think about the size or color of certain words. Sketch your plan in your writer's notebook. Bring your writing to share when we meet later.

Use the size, color, and placement of words in interesting ways.

What the Words Look Like	What It Shows
Different sizes	• Large words tell the important idea.
Different colors	• What is similar • What is important
UPPERCASE and lowercase letters	• Uppercase letters—loud sound • Lowercase letters—soft sound
Placed around small illustrations	• Who is talking • What is happening in that scene

Confer

> During independent writing, move around the room to confer briefly with as many individual students as time allows. Sit side by side with them and invite them to talk about design features and text layout. Use the following prompts as needed.
>
> * *How will you place the words on the page? How will that help the reader?*
> * *How will you make important words stand out?*
> * *You wrote those words in a different color (made those words larger/smaller, placed them in an interesting way). Talk about your decision to do that.*

Share

Following independent writing, gather students in the meeting area to share their writing.

> Talk about the decisions you made for this page.

Umbrella 15: Exploring Design Features and Text Layout

Assessment

After you have taught the minilessons in this umbrella, observe students as they draw, write, and talk about their drawing and writing. Use *The Fountas & Pinnell Literacy Continuum* to notice, teach for, and support students' learning as you observe their attempts at writing and illustrating.

- What evidence do you have of students' new understandings related to exploring design features and text layout?
  - Are students making illustrations interesting in a variety of ways?
  - Are they using scenes to show action and details?
  - Are they thoughtful about the placement of the illustrations and words?
  - Do they understand and use vocabulary such as *illustration, illustrator, placement, collage, mix, materials,* and *author*?
- In what other ways, beyond the scope of this umbrella, are students ready to expand their bookmaking techniques?
  - Are they creating text features (e.g., table of contents, caption) for their books?
  - Are they revising their writing to make it more focused?

Use your observations to determine the next umbrella you will teach. You may also consult Suggested Sequence of Lessons (pp. 605–622) for guidance.

EXTENSIONS FOR EXPLORING DESIGN FEATURES AND TEXT LAYOUT

- Share other books from your collections that use interesting techniques, such as lift-the-flap and pop-up illustrations. Provide materials for students to try this in their own writing.

- Collaborate with the school art teacher as you explore creating illustrations with your students.

- Explore other ways illustrators use the size and placement of text on the page, for example, different fonts, different font sizes, and strategic placement to provide information. Good examples are these in *Fountas & Pinnell Classroom™ Interactive Read-Aloud Collection: A Seed Is Sleepy* (Series Study: Dianna Hutts Aston and Sylvia Long), *A Day and Night in the Desert* by Caroline Arnold (Genre Study: Expository Nonfiction), and *Flight of the Honey Bee* by Raymond Huber (Hybrid Texts: Fiction and Nonfiction).

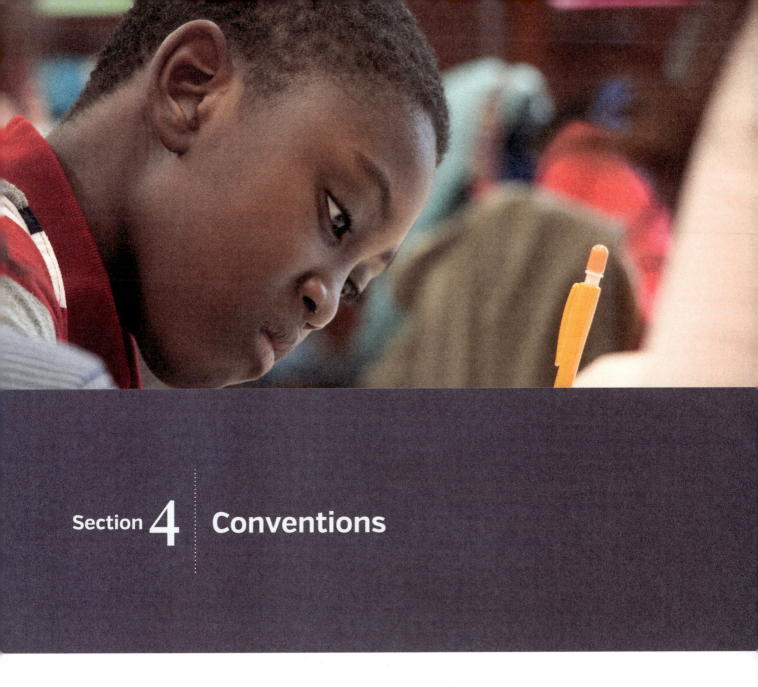

Section 4 | Conventions

A WRITER CAN have great ideas, understand how to organize them, and even make interesting word choices. But the ideas can get lost if the writer doesn't form letters correctly, spell words in recognizable ways, or use conventional grammar and punctuation. For writing to be valued and understood, writers need to understand the conventions of writing. The minilessons in this section are designed to strike a balance between teaching students to write clearly and making them comfortable about taking risks with their writing. Teach these lessons whenever you see that students are ready for them.

4 Conventions

UMBRELLA 1	Writing Words	**445**
UMBRELLA 2	Learning About Punctuation and Capitalization	**453**
UMBRELLA 3	Learning to Paragraph	**467**

Writing Words

Umbrella 1

Minilessons in This Umbrella

WML1 Write your letters clearly and make them the right size within a word.
WML2 Break words into syllables to write them.
WML3 Use what you know about words to write new words.

Writer's Notebook

Before Teaching Umbrella 1 Minilessons

The lessons in this umbrella support students in writing words fluently and as accurately as possible to help them convey their ideas. The goal is to have students write legibly and spell words accurately and efficiently, using known words and syllables, so that they can focus on the message of the writing and their readers can read the words with ease.

Lined paper is recommended, with a top and bottom solid line. As students are practicing writing letters (in manuscript or in cursive) proportionally and forming letters within the space given, they no longer need the support of a dotted middle line. Other paper choices can be provided, including blank unlined paper. You can also fold unlined paper, which gives the writer an idea of how to use space for lines of print without visible lines on the page. The paper templates in the online resources provide some possibilities.

It is not necessary to teach these lessons consecutively, so feel free to teach them whenever students' handwriting indicates a readiness or need for a particular concept. If you need to teach or review how to form each letter, refer to these online resources: Alphabet Linking Chart, Verbal Path for Letter Formation, Verbal Path for Cursive Letter Formation, and A Suggested Order for Cursive Letter Learning.

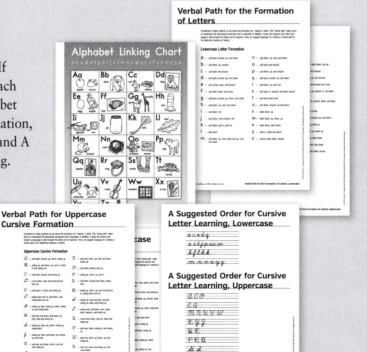

Umbrella 1: Writing Words 445

WML1
CNV.U1.WML1

Writing Minilesson Principle
Write your letters clearly and make them the right size within a word.

Writing Words

You Will Need

- handwriting sentence strips, one with a center dotted line prepared in advance with the word *math*, and two blank without a center dotted line
- chart paper prepared in advance with category headings
- markers
- a writer's notebook or a piece of lined draft paper and pencil for each student
- something for each student to use as support when writing (e.g., clipboard, book)

Academic Language / Important Vocabulary

- space
- clearly
- lowercase (small)
- extend

Continuum Connection

- Write fluently in both manuscript and cursive handwriting with appropriate spacing
- Check and correct letter formation

GOAL

Fluently write letters proportionally within words.

RATIONALE

As students learn to write clearly and proportionally on paper without a center dotted line and become consistent in this practice, they will write legibly and with fluency. Fluent writing allows them to spend more time thinking about what they are writing rather than how.

WRITER'S NOTEBOOK/WRITING FOLDER

Students can practice forming letters in their writer's notebooks.

ASSESS LEARNING

- Observe whether students are writing letters within words clearly and proportionally.
- Notice evidence that students can use vocabulary such as *space*, *clearly*, *lowercase (small)*, and *extend*.

MINILESSON

To help students think about the minilesson principle, model how to write letters clearly and proportionally within the space of lined paper. Here is an example.

- Display the sentence strip with a dotted line and the word *math* on it.

    In the past, you might have used paper that had a dotted line that helped you know how tall to make small letters, like lowercase *m* and *a*, where to cross the *t*, and how high to make the arch in *h*.

- Show one sentence strip without a dotted line as well as some lined paper.

    This is like the paper you will use this year. What do you notice?

    There is less space between the lines, and you have to imagine where the dotted line is. Notice what I do as I write the word *the*.

    The stick of the *t* takes up the entire space. I'll cross it just above the middle. What do I need to remember to write *h*?

- Display the chart with categories of letters. Add the *t* and the *h* to the chart.

    Now I'm going to write the letter *e*. This letter doesn't take up the entire space. What letters take up only half the space? Let's add them to the chart.

- Repeat this process with the word *dog*.

    What will I have to keep in mind when I write this word?

    What other letters have tails that extend below the line?

- Invite responses and add to the chart.

WML1
CNV.U1.WML1

Have a Try

Invite students to write their names on lined paper (such as that in a writer's notebook or draft paper).

> Write your name in the lines. Think about how each of the letters uses the space within the lines. The first letter of your name is capitalized, so it should touch the top and bottom lines.

▸ Invite students to talk about the letters in their names and what they need to remember when writing them. Add other letters from their names to the appropriate section of the chart.

Summarize and Apply

Summarize the lesson. Remind students to write clearly and within the space they are given so others can read it.

> How can you help your readers read what you have written?

▸ Write the principle at the top of the chart.

> Today during writing time, you can work on your writing. Remember to write smoothly and clearly and make each letter the right size. Look at the chart to help you. Bring your writing when we meet together later.

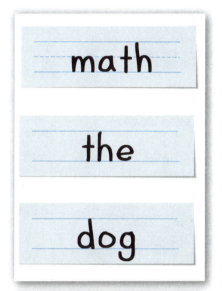

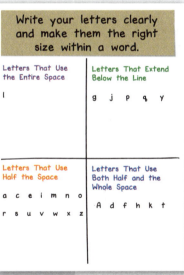

Confer

▸ During independent writing, move around the room to observe whether students are writing clearly and proportionally. Use the following prompts as needed.

- Which letters are easy for you to write on this paper? Which seem to be more challenging?
- How is paying attention to how you form your letters helping you as a writer?

Share

Following independent writing, gather students in the meeting area. Ask a few volunteers to share their writing.

> Are there letters you would like to add to our chart?

> Point to a place where you made your letters the right size.

Umbrella 1: Writing Words

WML 2
CNV.U1.WML2

Writing Minilesson Principle
Break words into syllables to write them.

Writing Words

You Will Need

- a reference list of three- or four-syllable words that have easy-to-hear sounds and syllable breaks
- chart paper and markers
- writer's notebooks

Academic Language / Important Vocabulary

- parts
- word
- syllables
- clap

Continuum Connection

- Use knowledge of syllables and phonogram patterns to generate multisyllable words
- Take apart multisyllables to spell the parts accurately or almost accurately
- Hear, say, clap, and identify syllables in words with three or more syllables: e.g., an/oth/er, bi/cy/cle, fish/er/man, el/e/va/tor, un/u/su/al

GOAL

Clap syllables and listen for the sounds to assist in writing unfamiliar words.

RATIONALE

Breaking a word into syllables helps students isolate the sounds they hear. By attending to all the sounds, they are more likely to represent them in spelling. Clapping syllables helps students write longer, unfamiliar words by focusing on one part at a time.

WRITER'S NOTEBOOK/WRITING FOLDER

Students can practice writing words in their writer's notebooks.

ASSESS LEARNING

- Observe for evidence that students can say and clap syllables in multisyllable words.
- Notice if students use syllables to break apart words when writing.
- Look for evidence that students can use vocabulary such as *parts*, *word*, *syllables*, and *clap*.

MINILESSON

Students will need their writer's notebooks for this lesson. To help students think about the minilesson principle, select words with three or four syllables and easily identifiable syllable breaks. Model clapping the syllables to help isolate and listen to the sounds in each syllable. Here is an example.

- Say the word *hospital* and demonstrate clapping the syllables.

    How many parts, or syllables, do you hear in the word *hos-pi-tal*?

    Hospital has three syllables, so I clapped three times.

    To write the word *hospital*, say the first syllable slowly and write the letters for the sounds you hear. What sounds do you hear?

- Record the letters for the first syllable on the chart. Then have the students clap *hospital* again, stressing the second syllable. Record the letters for the second syllable on the chart. Repeat with the third syllable. Then write the word without the syllable breaks.

    Let's check the word. Clap as I point to each syllable.

    When you write a word you're unsure about, try clapping the syllables. Notice the sounds you hear in each syllable and think about the letters that go with the sounds to help you write the whole word.

- Repeat the process with more words, such as *holiday*, *pretending*, *afternoon*, and/or *hibernate*. Assist in adding letters that are not pronounced (e.g., a silent *e* at the end of a word).

WML 2
CNV.U1.WML2

Have a Try

Invite students to work with a partner to write words with multiple syllables.

* Make sure students have their writer's notebooks.

    Say the parts in the word *supermarket* slowly with your partner as you clap the syllables you hear. Talk to your partner about the number of parts you hear. Talk about the sounds you hear and the letters that stand for those sounds in each part. Write the word in your writer's notebook.

* Invite volunteers to clap the parts of the word and show what they have written. Add the word to the chart. Repeat with another word, such as *alligator*.

Summarize and Apply

Summarize the lesson. Remind students to say the parts of a word slowly when they need to write a new word.

* Write the principle at the top of the chart.

    During writing time, find a word in your writer's notebook you weren't sure how to spell. Give it a try by clapping out the syllables. When you want to write a new word in your writing today, say the parts to help you hear the sounds and write the letters.

Break words into syllables to write them.	
hos / pi / tal	hospital
hol / i / day	holiday
pre / ten / ding	pretending
af / ter / noon	afternoon
hi / ber / nate	hibernate
su / per / mar / ket	supermarket
al / li / ga / tor	alligator

Confer

* During independent writing, move around the room to confer briefly with students. Invite them to talk about writing new words. Use the following prompts as needed.
    * *Listen for the parts. Clap the parts you hear.*
    * *Listen for the sounds you hear in the first (next, last) part and write the letters.*
    * *You can say the part slowly and listen for the sounds you hear (model).*
    * *You can think about the sounds in each part and write the letters.*

Share

Following independent writing, gather students in the meeting area. Invite individual students to share new words they wrote in their writing.

   Who wrote a word with three or more syllables? What did you do?

Umbrella 1: Writing Words

WML 3
CNV.U1.WML3

Writing Minilesson Principle
Use what you know about words to write new words.

Writing Words

You Will Need

- chart paper and markers
- writer's notebooks

Academic Language / Important Vocabulary

- letter
- word
- ending
- beginning
- sounds

Continuum Connection

- Use onsets and rimes in known words to read and write other words with the same parts: e.g., *thr-ow, thr-ee, thr-ow, gr-ow*
- Identify words that have the same letter pattern and use them to solve an unknown word: e.g., *hat/sat, light/night, curious/furious*
- Use known word parts (some are words) to solve unknown larger words: e.g., *in/into, can/canvas*

GOAL

Use knowledge of known words to write unknown words.

RATIONALE

Teaching students to read and write every individual word in a language would be a huge, time-consuming, and impossible task. A more efficient approach is to teach students to use what they know (known words or parts of words, such as a letter or a cluster of letters, word patterns, or smaller words that are part of bigger words) to understand something new. This equips them with tools to solve new words when they read and write.

WRITER'S NOTEBOOK/WRITING FOLDER

Students can practice writing new words in their writer's notebooks.

ASSESS LEARNING

- Notice if students use what they know about words (e.g., a letter or a cluster of letters, word patterns, or smaller words that are part of bigger words) to help write new words.
- Look for evidence that students can use vocabulary such as *letter, word, ending, beginning,* and *sounds*.

MINILESSON

Students will need their writer's notebooks for this lesson. To help students think about the minilesson principle, demonstrate how to use what is known about words to write new words. Here is an example.

- Write the word *tape* on the chart paper.

    This is a word you know well. Say it with me slowly: *tape*.

- Write the word *shape* on the chart directly below *tape*.

    What do you notice about these two words?

- Point under the letters as you guide the students to understand that you used what you knew about the sound of the letters *sh* and the word *tape*.

    How do you think I knew how to write *shape*?

    I used the word *tape* and put the letters *sh* at the beginning instead of *t*.

- Invite students to use *tape* and what they know about other letters to add words to the list. If time permits, repeat this process with the word *grow*.

- Model how to use a known word, such as *for*, to write unfamiliar words.

    You can also use words that you know to write new words. How can you use the word *for* to write the word *form*? What letters should I write?

- Repeat this process with other words that use *for*, such as *force, forever, forty, forget,* and *forest*.

Have a Try

Invite students to use the word *win* to write other words.

> This is the word *win*. In your writer's notebook, write some words you can write using the word *win*.

▶ After a few moments, invite a few volunteers to share their words. Write them on the chart.

Summarize and Apply

Summarize the lesson. Remind students to use what they know about words to write words that are unfamiliar to them.

> What is something you can do to help you write new words?

▶ Write the principle at the top of the chart.

> Whenever you are writing and you want to write a new word, say it and think about how to use a word you already know. Bring your writing to share when we meet later.

Use what you know about words to write new words.

tape	grow	for	win
sh**ape**	sh**ow**	**for**m	**win**d
c**ape**	st**ow**	**for**ce	**win**dy
scr**ape**	bel**ow**	**for**ever	**win**dow
dr**ape**	mead**ow**	**for**ty	**win**ter
esc**ape**	foll**ow**	**for**get	**win**dmill
landsc**ape**		**for**est	tw**in**

Confer

▶ During independent writing, move around the room to confer briefly with students. Invite them to talk about writing new words. Use the following prompts as needed.

- What can you do if you don't know how to write a word?
- Do you know a word that starts like that?
- Do you know a word that ends like that?
- What word do you know that could help you write the word?

Share

Following independent writing, gather students in the meeting area. Invite individual students to share their writing.

> Who would like to share your writing?

> Can you point to a new word you wrote? How did you know what letters to write?

Umbrella 1 | Writing Words

Assessment

After you have taught the minilessons in this umbrella, observe students as they draw, write, and talk about their writing. Use *The Fountas & Pinnell Literacy Continuum* to notice, teach for, and support students' learning as you observe their attempts at writing.

- What evidence do you have that students have learned ways to write words?
  - Are students writing their letters clearly and proportionally within the lines?
  - Do they break apart words into syllables and listen for sounds?
  - Is there evidence that students use what they know about words to write new words?
  - Do they understand and use vocabulary such as *letter*, *word*, *parts*, *syllables*, *ending*, *beginning*, *space*, *clearly*, *extend*, *clap*, and *sounds*?
- In what other ways, beyond the scope of this umbrella, are students developing as writers?
  - Would they benefit from keeping a personal word list and other resources in their writing folders?
  - Are they willing to share their writing with others?

Use your observations to determine the next umbrella you will teach. You may also consult Suggested Sequence of Lessons (pp. 605–622) for guidance.

EXTENSIONS FOR WRITING WORDS

- Support students with using known words to write new words. Encourage them to rearrange magnetic letters to make new words to increase flexibility with this strategy.

- Gather together a guided writing group of several students who need support in a specific area of writing.

Learning About Punctuation and Capitalization

Umbrella 2

Minilessons in This Umbrella

WML1	Notice how authors use capitalization.
WML2	Notice how authors use punctuation.
WML3	Use quotation marks to show what someone said.
WML4	Use commas to separate words in a list.
WML5	Use an apostrophe to show something belongs to someone or to make a contraction.
WML6	Use an ellipsis to show a pause or to build excitement.

Before Teaching Umbrella 2 Minilessons

Conventions and craft are closely related because they work together to convey meaning. Without attention to punctuation and capitalization, ideas can get lost. By teaching conventions through inquiry and with an eye to the writer's craft, students are able to use conventions in ways that deliver meaning to their readers. If you are using *The Reading Minilessons Book, Grade 3* (Fountas and Pinnell 2019), you may want to teach the second minilesson in LA.U9: Analyzing the Writer's Craft, which focuses on how writers use punctuation in interesting ways.

Connecting punctuation and capitalization to a writer's craft will support students' curiosity about and interest in what writers do and encourage them to try out different ways they can use conventions in their own writing to communicate their message. Use the books listed below from *Fountas & Pinnell Classroom™ Interactive Read-Aloud Collection* and *Shared Reading Collection*, or choose books from the classroom library.

Interactive Read-Aloud Collection
The Importance of Kindness
The Can Man by Laura E. Williams

Shared Reading Collection
Light My Way Home by Shyamala Parthasarathy
Cat Belly by Ashley Storm
Nerman's Revenge by Mike Downs
Three Days to Summer by Laura Platas Scott
Hummingbird's Nest by Sherry Howard

As you read and enjoy these texts together, help students
- notice the punctuation and capitalization, and
- notice the impact that punctuation and capitalization have on meaning.

Interactive Read-Aloud
Kindness

Shared Reading

Writer's Notebook

WML1
CNV.U2.WML1

Writing Minilesson Principle
Notice how authors use capitalization.

Learning About Punctuation and Capitalization

You Will Need

- a mentor text that shows a variety of capitalization examples, such as *Light My Way Home* by Shyamala Parthasarathy, from *Shared Reading Collection*
- highlighter or highlighter tape
- chart paper and markers
- baskets of books with a variety of capitalization examples (one set per pair or small group)
- sticky notes
- writer's notebooks and writing folders

Academic Language / Important Vocabulary

- capitalization
- title
- sentence
- uppercase (capital)
- lowercase (small)

Continuum Connection

- Use capitals to start the first, last, and most other words in a title
- Use a capital letter for the first word of a sentence
- Use capital letters appropriately to capitalize days, months, city and state names, and specific places
- Use underlining for words in titles

GOAL
Notice how and why authors use a variety of capitalization.

RATIONALE
When students learn that writers use capitalization to make writing clear and engaging for their readers, they think about how they can use capitalization in their own writing.

WRITER'S NOTEBOOK/WRITING FOLDER
Students can record their observations of capitalization in their writer's notebooks and apply what they have learned when they work on longer pieces of writing in their writing folders.

ASSESS LEARNING
- Notice whether students recognize that punctuation is connected to a writer's craft.
- Observe whether students are using capitalization in their own writing.
- Look for evidence that students can use vocabulary such as *capitalization*, *title*, *sentence*, *uppercase (capital)*, and *lowercase (small)*.

MINILESSON

Before teaching this lesson, make sure students have had multiple experiences using capitalization through authentic writing. Use mentor texts to provide an inquiry-based lesson about how authors use capitalization. Here is an example.

- Show the cover of *Light My Way Home*.

  What do you notice about the letters in the title?

- Engage students in a conversation to help them recognize that the first word and the important words in the title are uppercase.

- Begin a two-column chart and write the title in the left column. Underline the title and point out that you are underlining it because it is a title. Invite a volunteer to highlight the capital letters.

- Show and read pages 2 and 6.

  What do you notice about the letters in the sentences?

- Help students recognize that the first letter in each sentence is capitalized. Write one or two sentences on the chart.

- Point out the names of the cities (Vancouver, Pune) on page 2.

  What do you notice about how the names of the cities are written?

- Write the city names on the chart. Ask a volunteer to highlight the capital letters.

- Have students look at the classroom calendar to notice the capitalization of days and months. Add examples to the chart.

WML1
CNV.U2.WML1

Have a Try

Invite students to turn and talk about capitalization.

> Turn and talk about the reasons that some letters are uppercase and some letters are lowercase in the examples on the chart.

- After time for a brief discussion, ask a few students to share their ideas. Using students' suggestions, add the capitalization rule to the right of each example.

Summarize and Apply

Summarize the learning. Have students notice how capitalization is used in books and make notes to share. Write the principle at the top of the chart.

> Today, you will work with a partner to look in books to see how writers use capital letters. Put sticky notes on pages with examples of capitalization. Each time you find a new reason for a capital letter, write it on a sticky note.

> Label a page in your writer's notebook Ways Writers Use Capital Letters. If you are the one who writes the sticky notes, add them to your writer's notebook after you share with the class. If you are not the one who writes the sticky notes, write the reasons on your writer's notebook page. Bring your books and writer's notebooks when we meet later.

Notice how authors use capitalization.

Light My Way Home	first word and important words in a title
Today was my first day at my new school. It is getting chilly here!	first word in a sentence
Vancouver Pune	place names
Tuesday November	days, months

Confer

- During independent writing, move around the room to confer briefly with pairs of students. Invite them to talk about capitalization. Use the following prompts as needed.
  - *Why do you think the writer made this capitalization choice?*
  - *Which letters will be uppercase and which will be lowercase in your writing?*

Share

Following independent writing, gather students in the meeting area. Ask each pair of students to share one example of capitalization. Add any new ideas to the chart.

> Share how you used uppercase and lowercase letters today.

Umbrella 2: Learning About Punctuation and Capitalization

Section 4: Conventions

WML 2
CNV.U2.WML2

Writing Minilesson Principle
Notice how authors use punctuation.

Learning About Punctuation and Capitalization

You Will Need

- several mentor texts with a variety of punctuation examples, such as the following from *Shared Reading Collection*:
  - *Cat Belly* by Ashley Storm
  - *Three Days to Summer* by Laura Platas Scott
- chart paper and markers
- baskets of books with a variety of punctuation (one set per pair or small group)
- sticky notes
- writer's notebooks and writing folders

Academic Language / Important Vocabulary

- punctuation
- sentence
- period
- question mark
- exclamation point

Continuum Connection

- Consistently use periods, exclamation marks, and questions marks as end marks in a conventional way

---

GOAL

Notice how and why authors use a variety of punctuation.

RATIONALE

When students learn that writers use punctuation to engage their readers and make writing interesting, they think about different ways to use end marks and other punctuation marks in their own writing and are motivated to try out different techniques.

WRITER'S NOTEBOOK/WRITING FOLDER

Students can record their observations of how writers use punctuation in their writer's notebooks and apply what they have learned when they work on longer pieces of writing in their writing folders.

ASSESS LEARNING

- Notice whether students recognize that punctuation is connected to a writer's craft.
- Observe whether students are trying out different ways to use punctuation in their writing.
- Look for evidence that students can use vocabulary such as *punctuation*, *sentence*, *period*, *question mark*, and *exclamation point*.

MINILESSON

Before teaching this lesson, make sure students have had multiple experiences using punctuation through authentic writing. Use mentor texts to provide an inquiry-based lesson about how authors use punctuation. Here is an example.

- Show and read page 7 of *Cat Belly*. Point to each period.

  I notice that there are some periods on this page.

- Begin a two-column chart with the noticed punctuation marks in the left column.

  Why do you think the writer decided to add a period at the end of these sentences?

- Guide the conversation, helping students recognize that a period shows the end of a sentence, or one complete idea. Add a brief description of the purpose of the punctuation mark to the chart.

  What other punctuation do you notice?

- Guide students to recognize that a question mark shows that a question is being asked and an exclamation point shows excitement or surprise. Add to the chart.

- Repeat the activity for apostrophes on page 6.

- Keep the chart posted to use throughout this umbrella as students think more deeply about different punctuation marks.

WML2

CNV.U2.WML2

Have a Try

Invite students to turn and talk about the way a writer uses punctuation to convey meaning.

▸ Show and read page 8 in *Three Days to Summer*.

> Turn and talk about the way the writer, Laura Platas Scott, used punctuation marks on the page.

▸ After time for a brief discussion, ask a few students to share their ideas. Add new ideas to the chart.

Summarize and Apply

Summarize the learning. Have students notice how punctuation is used by writers.

> Today, you will work with a partner to look in books to see how writers use punctuation. Put sticky notes on pages with examples of punctuation. Write the reason for the punctuation on the sticky notes.

> Label a page in your writer's notebook Ways Writers Use Punctuation. If you are the one who writes the sticky notes, add them to your writer's notebook after you share with the class. If you are not the one who writes the sticky notes, write the reasons on your writer's notebook page. Bring your books and writer's notebook when we meet later.

Punctuation Marks

.	complete thoughts
?	asking questions
!	strong emotion / excitement
'	something belongs to someone / two words made into one
,	pause / list
...	something is coming
" "	talking

Confer

▸ During independent writing, move around the room to confer briefly with pairs of students. Invite them to talk about using punctuation. Use the following prompts as needed.

- *What do you notice about the way the writer ended this sentence?*
- *Why do you think the writer made this punctuation choice?*
- *What punctuation marks are you using in the writing you are working on?*

Share

Following independent writing, gather students in the meeting area to share their notes.

> Who would like to share something you noticed about how punctuation is used?

> Share how you used a punctuation mark today.

Umbrella 2: Learning About Punctuation and Capitalization

WML 3
CNV.U2.WML3

Writing Minilesson Principle
Use quotation marks to show what someone said.

Learning About Punctuation and Capitalization

You Will Need

- several mentor texts with examples of quotation marks, such as the following:
  - *The Can Man* by Laura E. Williams, from Text Set: The Importance of Kindness
  - *Nerman's Revenge* by Mike Downs and *Three Days to Summer* by Laura Platas Scott, from *Shared Reading Collection*
- chart paper prepared with unpunctuated dialogue from *Three Days to Summer*
- colored marker
- writer's notebooks and writing folders

Academic Language / Important Vocabulary

- punctuation
- dialogue
- quotation marks
- opening
- closing
- comma

Continuum Connection

- Understand and use quotation marks to indicate simple dialogue to show the exact words someone said
- Use correct punctuation of uninterrupted dialogue

GOAL

Use quotation marks to show dialogue.

RATIONALE

When students learn to punctuate dialogue, their writing becomes clearer to their readers.

WRITER'S NOTEBOOK/WRITING FOLDER

Have students check how they punctuated dialogue in a sample of writing in their writer's notebooks. If they are working on a writing project, they will need their writing folders.

ASSESS LEARNING

- Observe whether students are showing evidence that they know how and why to use quotation marks.
- Look for evidence that students can use vocabulary such as *punctuation*, *dialogue*, *quotation marks*, *opening*, *closing*, and *comma*.

MINILESSON

To help students understand the minilesson principle, engage them in an interactive lesson about why and when writers use quotation marks and how they can use them in their own writing. Here is an example.

- Ahead of time, display the text from page 11 of *The Can Man*.

   What do you notice about the words on this page?

- Guide the conversation so that students recognize that there are multiple people speaking. Introduce the word *dialogue* if it is unfamiliar to students.

   Who can point out the different types of punctuation marks the writer used to let you know when someone is speaking and who is speaking?

- Have volunteers point to each dialogue-related punctuation mark. Support students by naming opening quotation marks, closing quotation marks, and commas. Point out how the writer punctuated the uninterrupted dialogue.

   How do you know when one person stops speaking and another person begins?

   Quotation marks are used to show dialogue and also to show that a writer is writing exactly what someone else said or wrote.

- Repeat with page 24 in *Nerman's Revenge*.

The Writing Minilessons Book, Grade 3

Have a Try

Invite students to turn and talk about adding quotation marks to show dialogue.

- Display the chart paper prepared with unpunctuated dialogue. Read the text aloud.
    - Notice that this dialogue from *Three Days to Summer* is missing punctuation. Turn and talk about where the correct punctuation marks should be placed.
- After time for discussion, have students come up and add quotation marks and the missing commas. Then show the page from the text to compare.

Summarize and Apply

Summarize the learning. Remind students to use quotation marks for dialogue.

> When you write, how do you show that someone is speaking?

- Write the principle at the top of the chart.
    - During writing time, check your writer's notebook to see if you have used dialogue somewhere. Is it punctuated correctly? If not, fix it. If you are working on a piece of writing that has dialogue, think about where to place the quotation marks and commas and add them. Bring your writing to share when we meet.

> Use quotation marks to show what someone said.
>
> "More cows," says my sister.
>
> "More grass," I say, wishing I could run barefoot across nature's soft, wide carpet.

Confer

- During independent writing, move around the room to confer briefly with students. Invite them to talk about dialogue and quotation marks. Use the following prompts as needed.
    - *How will your readers know that someone is speaking?*
    - *Where will the opening (closing) quotation mark be placed?*
    - *Show where you will place the comma before the quotation marks.*

Share

Following independent writing, gather students in the meeting area. Ask a few volunteers to share their writing.

> Who wrote some dialogue today? Read what you wrote and share where you placed the quotation marks and commas.

WML 4
CNV.U2.WML4

Writing Minilesson Principle
Use commas to separate words in a list.

Learning About Punctuation and Capitalization

You Will Need

- several mentor texts with examples of commas in a series, such as the following from *Shared Reading Collection*:
  - *Nerman's Revenge* by Mike Downs
  - *Hummingbird's Nest* by Sherry Howard
  - *Three Days to Summer* by Laura Platas Scott
- highlighter tape
- chart paper and markers
- writer's notebooks and writing folders

Academic Language / Important Vocabulary

- punctuation
- comma
- list

Continuum Connection

- Use commas correctly to separate items in a series

GOAL

Use commas to separate items in a series.

RATIONALE

When students learn that commas are used to separate items in a series, they learn to add commas in order to make their own writing clear to their readers.

WRITER'S NOTEBOOK/WRITING FOLDER

Have students use their writer's notebooks to practice using commas in a series and apply what they have learned when they work on longer pieces of writing in their writing folders.

ASSESS LEARNING

- Observe whether students' writing shows evidence that they are using commas to separate items in a series.
- Look for evidence that students can use vocabulary such as *punctuation*, *comma*, and *list*.

MINILESSON

Students need their writer's notebooks for this lesson. To help students understand the minilesson principle, use examples from a mentor text to illustrate the use of commas in a series and provide an interactive lesson. Here is an example.

- Show page 6 from *Nerman's Revenge* and point to the first sentence in the text box.

  Listen as I read a sentence from *Nerman's Revenge*. What three things does he include in the spell?

  What do you notice about the punctuation?

- Ask a volunteer to come point to the commas and add highlighter tape.
- Repeat with page 12 in *Hummingbird's Nest* and page 4 in *Three Days to Summer*.

  How do commas help you read a list?

- Guide the conversation to help students understand that the commas separate the items in a list.

The Writing Minilessons Book, Grade 3

WML 4
CNV.U2.WML4

Have a Try

Invite students to turn and talk about adding commas to items in a series.

> In your writer's notebook, write a sentence that lists three or more things you did today. When you finish, show your partner your sentence. Talk about where you put the commas.

- After students have shared with their partners, write several of their sentences on chart paper. You may want to have volunteers add or highlight the commas.

Summarize and Apply

Summarize the learning. Remind students to use commas to separate words in a list.

> How can you let your readers know that you are writing a list?

- Write the principle at the top of the chart.

> During writing time, if you write words in a list, remember to add a comma after each item. If your list has just two items, you don't need a comma. Bring your writing when we meet later.

Use commas to separate words in a list.

I did my morning routine, read books, and played basketball.

I ate breakfast, brushed my teeth, and rode the bus.

Confer

- During independent writing, move around the room to confer briefly with students. Invite them to talk about punctuation. Use the following prompts as needed.
  - What punctuation will you use to separate items in your list?
  - In what ways are commas useful for your readers?
  - Read the sentence that has items in a list with commas to separate them.

Share

Following independent writing, gather students in the meeting area. Ask a few volunteers to share their writing.

> Who used commas to separate items in a list? Share the part of your writing that includes the list of items and the commas.

WML 5
CNV.U2.WML5

Writing Minilesson Principle
Use an apostrophe to show something belongs to someone or to make a contraction.

Learning About Punctuation and Capitalization

You Will Need

- several mentor texts with examples of possessives and contractions, such as the following from *Shared Reading Collection*:
  - *Hummingbird's Nest* by Sherry Howard
  - *Three Days to Summer* by Laura Platas Scott
- chart paper and markers
- books from the classroom library with examples of apostrophes and contractions (one to two books per pair of students)
- sticky notes
- writer's notebooks and writing folders

Academic Language / Important Vocabulary

- punctuation
- apostrophe
- possessive
- belongs
- contraction

Continuum Connection

- Use apostrophes correctly in contractions and possessives

GOAL

Use apostrophes to show possessives and contractions.

RATIONALE

For such a small punctuation mark, an apostrophe carries a lot of meaning. It can show possession, or it can represent missing letters in contractions. When students learn that writers use apostrophes to show contractions and possessives, they think about how to use apostrophes in their own writing.

WRITER'S NOTEBOOK/WRITING FOLDER

Students can record examples of how writers use apostrophes in their writer's notebooks and apply what they have learned when they work on writing from their writing folders.

ASSESS LEARNING

- Observe students' writing to see if they are using apostrophes correctly.
- Look for evidence that students can use vocabulary such as *punctuation*, *apostrophe*, *possessive*, *belongs*, and *contraction*.

MINILESSON

Students will need their writer's notebooks for the lesson. To help students understand the minilesson principle, use examples from mentor texts to illustrate how apostrophes are used to show possession and to make contractions. Here is an example.

- Show and read the cover of *Hummingbird's Nest*.

  Whose nest is this?

  How do you know?

- Guide the students to notice the apostrophe that shows possession. Define *possessive* as needed.

  When you want to show that something belongs to someone or something else, use an apostrophe and an s.

- On chart paper, make a two-column chart. Label the left-hand column *Possessive* and add *Hummingbird's Nest*.

- Show and read page 2.

  What do you notice on this page?

- As needed, support students to identify the apostrophe. Define *contraction*. Have a student write the contraction and discuss how the contraction was made. Add to the chart.

- Repeat using *Three Days to Summer* (pages 5 and 8 for possessives; page 2 for contractions). Point out that *it's* can be a contraction for *it is* and also for *it has*.

The Writing Minilessons Book, Grade 3

WML5
CNV.U2.WML5

Have a Try

Invite students to turn and talk about apostrophes.

▸ Provide pairs of students with sticky notes and one or two books that have examples of apostrophes and contractions.

> With your partner, find examples of apostrophes that show possessives and contractions. Mark each page with a sticky note. Talk about why the writer used an apostrophe. Write the words in your writer's notebook under the heading Ways Writers Use Apostrophes.

▸ After time for discussion, ask volunteers to share. Add to the chart.

> Use an apostrophe to show something belongs to someone or to make a contraction.
>
> | Possessive | Contraction |
> |---|---|
> | Hummingbird's Nest | don't = do not |
> | nature's soft, wide carpet | it's = it is or it has |
> | storm's edge | we've = we have |
> | | we're = we are |

Summarize and Apply

Summarize the learning. Remind students to use apostrophes to show possession and form contractions.

> When should you use an apostrophe?

▸ Write the principle at the top of the chart.

> When you write today, remember to use an apostrophe to show possessives and to make contractions. Bring your writing to share when we meet later.

Confer

▸ During independent writing, move around the room to confer briefly with students. Invite them to talk about using apostrophes. Use the following prompts as needed.
- *Show a place in your writing where something belongs to someone or something else.*
- *How will this apostrophe help your readers?*
- *Point to where you will put the apostrophe when you write the contraction.*

Share

Following independent writing, gather students in the meeting area. Ask a few volunteers to share their writing.

> Who used an apostrophe in your writing today? Share the place in your writing with an apostrophe.

Umbrella 2: Learning About Punctuation and Capitalization

WML 6
CNV.U2.WML6

Writing Minilesson Principle
Use an ellipsis to show a pause or to build excitement.

Learning About Punctuation and Capitalization

You Will Need

- a mentor text with examples of ellipses, such as *Nerman's Revenge* by Mike Downs, from *Shared Reading Collection*
- chart paper and markers
- writer's notebooks and writing folders

Academic Language / Important Vocabulary

- punctuation
- ellipsis
- pause
- build suspense
- surprise
- excitement

Continuum Connection

- Understand and use ellipses to show pause or anticipation, often before something surprising

---

GOAL

Use an ellipsis to show a pause or build excitement in a writing piece.

RATIONALE

Learning how to use an ellipsis contributes to voice and adds interest to a student's writing.

WRITER'S NOTEBOOK/WRITING FOLDER

Students can experiment with using an ellipsis in their writer's notebooks and apply what they have learned when they work on longer pieces of writing in their writing folders.

ASSESS LEARNING

- Observe students' writing to see if they sometimes use an ellipsis to indicate a pause or to build excitement.
- Look for evidence that students can use vocabulary such as *punctuation*, *ellipsis*, *pause*, *build suspense*, *surprise*, and *excitement*.

MINILESSON

To help students understand the minilesson principle, use mentor texts to help them notice and talk about ellipses. Here is an example.

- Show page 12 of *Nerman's Revenge*.

    Listen as I read this part of *Nerman's Revenge*.

- Read the sentence with the ellipsis.

    What do you notice?

- Guide the conversation to help students notice the ellipsis and how you paused before you read the word *Disappear*.

    An ellipsis looks like three periods with spaces around each. The writer used an ellipsis here to show that we should pause before reading the next word. When you read the sentence this way, the word *Disappear* is emphasized.

- Show and read the sentence with the ellipsis on page 13. Emphasize the pause at the ellipsis.

    Why do you think the writer placed an ellipsis here?

- Guide the conversation to help students recognize that the writer used the ellipsis to build suspense for what comes next.

    When a writer uses an ellipsis before a page turn, the readers start wondering what is going to happen. It builds suspense.

WML 6
CNV.U2.WML6

Have a Try

Invite students to turn and talk about ellipses.

> Think of what might surprise you or when you might want your readers to pause in a sentence. How might you write that with an ellipsis? Write a sentence in your writer's notebook. Ask your partner to read it aloud.

- After time for discussion, ask volunteers to share ideas. Write the sentences on the chart paper, placing the ellipses where students advise.
- Ask the class to join in as you read the sentences aloud.

Summarize and Apply

Summarize the learning. Have students try using ellipses to build suspense or to indicate a pause.

> What is an ellipsis and when do you use it?

- Write the principle at the top of the chart.

> Today look in your writing for a place you want to build suspense or show a pause. If you find one, use an ellipsis in the sentence. Bring your writing to share when we meet later.

Use an ellipsis to show a pause or to build excitement.

I opened the door and . . . there was Dad with a new puppy!

Suddenly . . . the lights went out!

We're having grilled cheese for lunch . . . again.

I have never been so excited . . . ever!

Confer

- During independent writing, move around the room to confer briefly with students. Invite them to talk about ellipses. Use the following prompts as needed.
  - *Find a place in your writing where something exciting is about to happen.*
  - *How will this ellipsis help your readers?*
  - *Where will you put the ellipsis?*
  - *If you want to try using an ellipsis in this sentence, where might it be placed?*

Share

Following independent writing, gather students in the meeting area. Ask a few volunteers to share their writing.

> Who used an ellipsis in your writing today to make your readers pause? Read the place in your writing with the ellipsis and show how you want your readers to pause.

Umbrella 2: Learning About Punctuation and Capitalization

Section 4: Conventions

Umbrella 2: Learning About Punctuation and Capitalization

Assessment

After you have taught the minilessons in this umbrella, observe students in a variety of classroom activities. Use *The Fountas & Pinnell Literacy Continuum* to notice, teach for, and support students' learning as you observe their attempts at writing.

- What evidence do you have of students' new understandings related to punctuation and capitalization?
    - Are students noticing the ways authors use punctuation and capitalization?
    - Do students capitalize all the words that should be capitalized?
    - Are they using quotation marks in their writing to show that someone is speaking?
    - When students write a list, are the items separated by commas?
    - Are students clear on how to use apostrophes?
    - Are students experimenting with ellipses to show pauses or to build excitement?
    - Are they using vocabulary such as *punctuation, sentence, period, question mark, exclamation point, dialogue, quotation marks, comma, list, apostrophe, contraction,* and *ellipsis*?
- In what ways, beyond the scope of this umbrella, are students showing an understanding of conventions?
    - Do they show an interest in proofreading and editing their work?
    - Are they thinking about craft techniques as they apply to different areas of writing?

Use your observations to determine the next umbrella you will teach. You may also consult Suggested Sequence of Lessons (pp. 605–622) for guidance.

EXTENSIONS FOR LEARNING ABOUT PUNCTUATION AND CAPITALIZATION

- Teach students that the apostrophe goes after the *s* when showing possession with a plural noun (e.g., dogs' bowls).

- Introduce students to using hyphens at the end of a line to break words by syllables.

- Have students work in pairs to reread their writing and notice any places where they might change punctuation in a way that adds to the meaning.

Learning to Paragraph

Umbrella 3

Minilessons in This Umbrella

- **WML1** Make a new paragraph for a new idea.
- **WML2** Use paragraphs to show when a new speaker is talking.
- **WML3** Use good spacing to set off paragraphs.

Before Teaching Umbrella 3 Minilessons

The minilessons in this umbrella will help students organize their writing into paragraphs, including organizing dialogue. The minilessons discuss ways to organize information by topic (without sacrificing craft) so the readers can easily understand and remember what they read.

Begin by discussing how formatting and spacing text into paragraphs helps the readers. Discuss how opening a book and seeing continuous text without breaks might cause a feeling of being overwhelmed and how, conversely, breaking text into paragraphs makes it more accessible.

In the classroom, students are often writing their drafts by hand and skipping a line, so encouraging students to skip a line between paragraphs may not make much sense at this point. When to do that is a decision that you as the teacher will need to make.

Read and discuss enjoyable books with clear use of paragraphs organized by topic and paragraphs used to indicate dialogue. Use the following texts from *Fountas & Pinnell Classroom™ Interactive Read-Aloud Collection*, or choose books from the classroom library that the students will enjoy.

Interactive Read-Aloud Collection

Genre Study: Expository Nonfiction

Bats! Strange and Wonderful by Laurence Pringle

A Day and Night in the Desert by Caroline Arnold

Shell, Beak, Tusk: Shared Traits and the Wonders of Adaptation by Bridget Heos

Genre Study: Realistic Fiction

Sky Sisters by Jan Bourdeau Waboose

Dumpling Soup by Jama Kim Rattigan

As you read and enjoy these texts together, help students

- notice how writers start a new paragraph for a new idea,
- understand that writers use paragraphs to indicate dialogue, and
- notice how paragraphs look.

Interactive Read-Aloud
Expository Nonfiction

Realistic Fiction

Writer's Notebook

WML1
CNV.U3.WML1

Writing Minilesson Principle
Make a new paragraph for a new idea.

Learning to Paragraph

You Will Need

- several familiar texts with clear examples of paragraphs organized by topic, such as the following from Text Set: Genre Study: Expository Nonfiction:
  - *Shell, Beak, Tusk* by Bridget Heos
  - *Bats!* by Laurence Pringle
- chart paper prepared with two column headings (see chart)
- nonfiction writing written by you, the whole class, or an individual student, written on chart paper (or projected)
- document camera (optional)
- markers
- writing folders

Academic Language / Important Vocabulary

- paragraph
- organize
- indent
- space

Continuum Connection

- Understand and use paragraph structure (indented or block) to organize sentences that focus on one idea
- Organize and present information in paragraphs in a way that demonstrates clear understanding of their structure to group ideas

GOAL
Understand that writers use paragraphs to organize their writing.

RATIONALE
When students notice that writers organize their writing into paragraphs, they can begin to do this in their own writing.

WRITER'S NOTEBOOK/WRITING FOLDER
Students will think about how to use paragraphs as they work on longer writing pieces from their writing folders.

ASSESS LEARNING

- Observe for evidence that students recognize they can use paragraphs to organize their writing.
- Observe for evidence that students can use vocabulary such as *paragraph*, *organize*, *indent*, and *space*.

MINILESSON

To help students think about the minilesson principle, use familiar texts to guide them in noticing how writers organize their writing into paragraphs. Here is an example.

- Show *Shell, Beak, Tusk* and read pages 10–11.

  What do you notice about how the author organized her writing on these two pages? Turn and talk with a partner.

- After time for discussion, invite a few students to share.

  Each one of these sections is a paragraph. The writer arranged her sentences into paragraphs to organize her writing.

  What information do these paragraphs tell you?

  This writer put information about the rabbit in one paragraph, and then she started a new paragraph to tell about the bilby. And she used another paragraph to tell about how the rabbit and the bilby are the same and different.

- Record responses in general terms on the prepared chart.

  Why do you think she organized her paragraphs this way?

- Repeat this process with page 7 of *Bats!*

  How do the paragraphs look?

  What do paragraphs help the author do?

- Record responses in general terms on the chart.

The Writing Minilessons Book, Grade 3

WML1
CNV.U3.WML1

Have a Try

Display a piece of writing about a shared experience. Read it aloud and invite students to turn and talk to a partner about how they might organize the writing into paragraphs.

> I wrote about our trip to the aquarium. How might I organize my sentences into paragraphs? When does the topic or idea change? Turn and talk about that.

▸ After time for discussion, decide with the students where to insert paragraph marks.

> When you come to a place where a new paragraph should begin, you can use the paragraph symbol to remind yourself to start a new paragraph.

▸ Save the chart for WML3.

Summarize and Apply

Help students summarize the learning. As students work on a longer writing piece, remind them to start a new paragraph for a new idea.

> What can you do to organize your writing for your readers?

▸ Write the principle at the top of the first chart.

> As you write, think about how your sentences are grouped together. When you start writing about a new topic or idea, start a new paragraph. Remember to put a space between your paragraphs or indent the first sentence.

Make a new paragraph for a new idea.

What do you notice about the paragraphs?	What do paragraphs help the author do?
Tell about one idea	Organize information for the reader
Tell how two things are similar and different	Make it easier for readers to remember what they read
Have space between them	Tell readers new information is coming
The first line is bumped in (indented)	

¶On Monday, our class went to the New England Aquarium. Atlantic harbor seals greeted us outside. We got there just in time to see the aquarium staff feed them a snack of fish and squid. ¶Just inside the front doors is the ray touch tank. This tank has cownose rays that swim gracefully in the shallow water. If you gently put your hand in the tank with your palms flat, they might swim up and let you touch their backs. ¶The penguins were also fun to see. We saw southern rockhopper penguins. Rockhoppers are skilled at climbing the rocky islands where they live. The loud ones were African penguins.

Confer

▸ During independent writing, move around the room to confer briefly with students about how they are using paragraphs in their writing. Use prompts such as the following as needed.

- *Where does your next idea or topic start?*
- *Why did you start a new paragraph here? Do all of these sentences go together?*
- *How do you know you are ready to start a new paragraph?*

Share

Following independent writing, gather students in the meeting area to share their writing.

> Who would like to share where you decided to start a new paragraph to help your readers understand more? Why did you start a paragraph there?

Umbrella 3: Learning to Paragraph

WML2
CNV.U3.WML2

Writing Minilesson Principle
Use paragraphs to show when a new speaker is talking.

Learning to Paragraph

You Will Need

- several familiar texts with clear examples of dialogue in paragraphs, such as the following from Text Set: Genre Study: Realistic Fiction:
  - *Dumpling Soup* by Jama Kim Rattigan
  - *Sky Sisters* by Jan Bourdeau Waboose
- document camera (optional)
- dialogue written by you, the whole class, or an individual student written on chart paper (or projected)
- markers
- writing folders

Academic Language / Important Vocabulary

- dialogue
- speaker
- paragraphs
- indent

Continuum Connection

- Understand and use paragraphs to show speaker change in dialogue

---

GOAL

Understand that writers use paragraphs to show when the speaker changes.

RATIONALE

When students notice that writers start a new paragraph to indicate a change in speaker, they can begin to do this in their own writing.

WRITER'S NOTEBOOK/WRITING FOLDER

Students will think about how to use paragraphs to show dialogue as they work on longer writing pieces from their writing folders.

ASSESS LEARNING

- Observe for evidence that students recognize that writers use paragraphs to indicate a change in speaker.
- Notice students' use of paragraphs in their own writing.
- Observe for evidence that students can use vocabulary such as *dialogue*, *speaker*, *paragraphs*, and *indent*.

MINILESSON

To help students think about the minilesson principle, use familiar texts to guide them in noticing how writers use paragraphs to organize dialogue. Here is an example.

- Show *Dumpling Soup*. Use a document camera, if available, to show and read page 3.

  What do you notice about how the author organized the words the characters say—the dialogue? Turn and talk with a partner.

- After time for discussion, invite a few students to share what they noticed. Record responses on the chart paper in general terms.

  What do the paragraphs help the author do?

- Again, record responses in general terms.
- Repeat this process with a page from *Sky Sisters*.

  Writers use paragraphs to separate dialogue in their writing and to show a different character is talking so that readers can keep track of who is speaking.

WML 2
CNV.U3.WML2

Have a Try

Invite students to turn and talk to a partner about how they might organize writing into paragraphs.

- Display a piece of writing with dialogue and without paragraph breaks. Read it aloud.

    How can you organize this writing into paragraphs? Where does a new speaker start talking? Turn and talk about that.

- After time for discussion, insert (or have a student insert) the paragraph symbol (¶) to show where a new paragraph indicates a new speaker.

Summarize and Apply

Help students summarize the learning. Remind them to start a new paragraph when a new speaker is talking.

What can you do to organize your writing for your readers?

- Write the principle at the top of the first chart.

    As you write, notice where you have talking in your writing. When the speaker changes, start a new paragraph. Remember to put a space between your paragraphs or indent the first sentence. Bring your writing to share when we meet later.

Confer

- During independent writing, move around the room to confer briefly with students about how they are using paragraphs in their writing. Use prompts such as the following as needed.
    - *Reread your writing. Did you use paragraphs to show who is talking in your writing?*
    - *Where does the next speaker start talking?*
    - *Why did you start a new paragraph here?*
    - *Where else are you thinking of grouping your sentences into paragraphs?*
    - *How do you know when to start a new paragraph?*

Share

Following independent writing, gather students in the meeting area to share their writing.

Who would like to share where you decided to start a new paragraph to make it clear who is talking?

Use paragraphs to show when a new speaker is talking.

What do you notice about the paragraphs?	What do paragraphs help the author do?
Each time the speaker changes, the writer starts a new paragraph.	Help readers notice the talking
Sometimes the paragraphs have other sentences in addition to the talking (dialogue).	Tell readers that the speaker is changing
	Show readers who is talking and what the person is doing
The paragraphs are indented.	

¶ "Be back before it gets dark," Mom said. She finished putting my snack and sweatshirt into my backpack.

¶ "Okay, Mom," I replied. "We're going to ride our bikes to John's house to sign his cast. John broke his leg while skateboarding last week. Sam and I are going over to cheer him up."

¶ "I think visiting John is a good idea. Let me give you some cookies for him," Mom said, as she reached into the pantry. "Also, tell John's mom to call me if she needs any help."

Section 4: Conventions

Umbrella 3: Learning to Paragraph

WML 3
CNV.U3.WML3

Writing Minilesson Principle
Use good spacing to set off paragraphs.

Learning to Paragraph

You Will Need

- several familiar texts with clear examples of paragraphs, such as the following:
  - *Bats!* by Laurence Pringle and *A Day and Night in the Desert* by Caroline Arnold, from Text Set: Genre Study: Expository Nonfiction
  - *Sky Sisters* by Jan Bourdeau Waboose, from Text Set: Genre Study: Realistic Fiction
- chart paper and markers
- chart from WML1 (about the aquarium or your own topic)
- document camera (optional)
- writing folders

Academic Language / Important Vocabulary

- paragraphs
- indent
- spacing

Continuum Connection

- Use indentation or spacing to set off paragraphs

GOAL

Understand that writers indent their paragraphs or put spaces between them.

RATIONALE

When you teach students to indent or provide adequate spacing for paragraphs, they can begin to do this in their own writing to make it clearer and more organized for their readers.

WRITER'S NOTEBOOK/WRITING FOLDER

Students will think about how to indent their paragraphs or leave adequate space between them as they work on longer writing pieces from their writing folders.

ASSESS LEARNING

- Observe for evidence that students recognize that writers indent or provide good spacing for paragraphs.
- Notice students' use of indentation or spacing of paragraphs in their own writing.
- Observe for evidence that students can use vocabulary such as *paragraphs*, *indent*, and *spacing*.

MINILESSON

To help students think about the minilesson principle, use familiar texts to guide them in noticing how writers indent or adequately space new paragraphs. (Adjust the lesson accordingly if your school uses block paragraphs.) Here is an example.

- Show *Bats!* Use a document camera, if available, to show page 7.

  What do you notice about how the author started a new paragraph? How does this help you as a reader?

  What do you notice about the spacing between the paragraphs? Turn and talk with a partner.

- After time for discussion, invite a few students to share. Record ideas in general terms on chart paper.

- Repeat this process with page 5 from *Sky Sisters* and page 8 from *A Day and Night in the Desert*.

Have a Try

Demonstrate for students how writers adequately space paragraphs when they write.

▶ Display the writing from WML1.

> Remember we put in paragraph marks to show where to start a new paragraph. Watch as I rewrite the paragraphs. I will indent, or push the first sentence in a bit. When you try this in your writing, put two fingers at the edge of the paper before you write. When you come to the next line, start writing at the edge.

▶ Invite students to point to where each paragraph will begin and then to the next line as you write.

Summarize and Apply

Summarize the learning. Remind students to use good spacing to set off paragraphs in their longer pieces of writing.

> What can you do to organize your writing for your readers?

▶ Write the principle at the top of the first chart.

> As you write, when you want to start a new paragraph, indent by putting two fingers down on the side of the paper. Bring your writing to share when we meet later.

Confer

▶ During independent writing, move around the room to confer briefly with students about how they are using paragraphs in their writing. Use prompts such as the following as needed.
- How does indenting your paragraphs help you organize your writing?
- Why did you start a new paragraph here?
- What can you do to help your readers know this is a new paragraph?
- How do you know when to start a new paragraph?

Share

Following independent writing, gather students in the meeting area to share their writing.

> Who would like to share your writing?

> Show how you indicated a new paragraph. Why did you make a new paragraph there?

Use good spacing to set off paragraphs.

- Writers sometimes put a space between paragraphs.
- Spacing helps readers keep track of who is talking and when the speaker changes.
- Paragraphs are usually indented.

On Monday, our class went to the New England Aquarium. Atlantic harbor seals greeted us outside. We got there just in time to see the aquarium staff feed them a snack of fish and squid.
    Just inside the front doors is the ray touch tank. This tank has cownose rays that swim gracefully in the shallow water. If you gently put your hand in the tank with your palms flat, they might swim up and let you touch their backs.
    The penguins were also fun to see. We saw southern rockhopper penguins. Rockhoppers are skilled at climbing the rocky islands where they live. The loud ones were African penguins.

Umbrella 3: Learning to Paragraph

Assessment

After you have taught the minilessons in this umbrella, observe students as they write and talk about their writing. Use *The Fountas & Pinnell Literacy Continuum* to notice, teach for, and support students' learning as you observe their attempts at writing.

- What evidence do you have of students' new understandings related to organizing paragraphs?
  - Do students start a new paragraph for a new idea?
  - Do they use paragraphs to show when a new speaker is talking?
  - Do they indent or use good spacing to set off paragraphs?
  - Is there evidence students can use vocabulary such as *paragraphs*, *indent*, *spacing*, *dialogue*, *speaker*, and *organize*?
- In what other ways, beyond the scope of this umbrella, are students learning about the conventions of writing?
  - Do they use what they know to write new words?
  - Are they noticing conventions writers use?

Use your observations to determine the next umbrella you will teach. You may also consult Suggested Sequence of Lessons (pp. 605–622) for guidance.

EXTENSIONS FOR LEARNING TO PARAGRAPH

- Create a chart that collects students' noticings about paragraphs as students continue exploring familiar texts.
- Remind students to apply the lessons in this umbrella as they revise their writing.
- Gather a small group of students who need additional support in organizing their writing into paragraphs for guided writing.
- If students type their final draft on a computer, show them how to indent or add space above paragraphs.

Section 5 | Writing Process

WRITERS LEARN TO write by writing. As they write, they engage in some aspect of the writing process. They plan what to write, write a first draft and make changes to improve it, check their work to be sure others can read it, and publish it by sharing it with an audience. Not all aspects of the writing process will happen at one time, and they won't always happen in the same order. Writers tend to move back and forth. But over time, each will experience the full writing process. The lessons in this section will help you guide the students in your class through the writing process.

5 Writing Process

Planning and Rehearsing

UMBRELLA 1	Introducing and Using a Writer's Notebook	**477**
UMBRELLA 2	Writer's Notebook: Getting Ideas from Your Life	**489**
UMBRELLA 3	Writer's Notebook: Getting Inspiration from Writers and Artists	**507**
UMBRELLA 4	Writer's Notebook: Becoming an Expert	**519**
UMBRELLA 5	Thinking About Purpose, Audience, and Genre/Form	**533**
UMBRELLA 6	Observing and Writing Like a Scientist	**541**

Drafting and Revising

UMBRELLA 7	Adding Information to Your Writing	**551**
UMBRELLA 8	Revising to Focus and Organize Writing	**563**

Editing and Proofreading

UMBRELLA 9	Editing and Proofreading Writing	**575**

Publishing

UMBRELLA 10	Adding Book and Print Features	**585**
UMBRELLA 11	Publishing and Self-Assessing Your Writing	**595**

Introducing and Using a Writer's Notebook

Umbrella 1

Minilessons in This Umbrella

- **WML1** Make your writer's notebook your own.
- **WML2** Write in your writer's notebook for at least ten minutes a day.
- **WML3** Collect your thinking in your writer's notebook.
- **WML4** Keep your writer's notebook organized.
- **WML5** Keep building your writer's notebook.

Writer's Notebook

Before Teaching Umbrella 1 Minilessons

A writer's notebook is a very important tool for any writer. It is a place to record seeds of ideas for writing, experiment with quick writes, and reread for ideas for expanded writing. (These expanded writing projects will be done on separate paper and usually kept in a writing folder.) As students build the content in their notebooks, they will realize that they have a rich resource for writing inspiration.

Provide each student with *Writer's Notebook, Intermediate* (Fountas and Pinnell 2023), or guide students to create their own writer's notebooks from composition books or spiral-bound notebooks. (For suggestions on how to organize a writer's notebook if you are creating one, see pages 84–88.) Receiving a new writer's notebook is a time of celebration for young writers. Help students develop a sense of pride in and ownership of their writer's notebooks by delivering it to them in a momentous way and encouraging them to decorate the cover (WML1). Introduce the writer's notebook as you begin teaching the routines of writers' workshop. It will be helpful for you to write in a writer's notebook of your own so that you can provide authentic examples to your students.

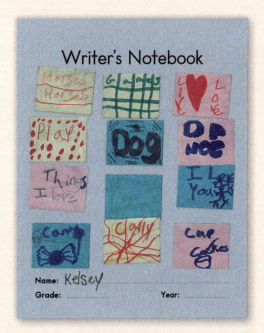

The minilessons in this umbrella do not need to be taught consecutively. WML5 should be taught only after all sections of the writer's notebook have been thoroughly introduced (see WPS.U2: Writer's Notebook: Getting Ideas from Your Life, WPS.U3: Writer's Notebook: Getting Inspiration from Writers and Artists, and WPS.U4: Writer's Notebook: Becoming an Expert).

Section 5: Writing Process

Umbrella 1: Introducing and Using a Writer's Notebook

WML1
WPS.U1.WML1

Writing Minilesson Principle
Make your writer's notebook your own.

Introducing and Using a Writer's Notebook

You Will Need

- a writer's notebook with front cover decorated
- a new writer's notebook for every student
- highlighter
- chart paper and markers
- document camera (optional)
- art materials for decorating the writer's notebook covers (stickers, different kinds of paper, glitter, photos from magazines, markers, etc.)
- To download the following online resource for this lesson, visit **fp.pub/resources**:
  - Writer's Notebook Letter (optional)

Academic Language / Important Vocabulary

- writer's notebook

Continuum Connection

- Use a writer's notebook or booklet as a tool for collecting ideas, experimenting, planning, sketching, or drafting

---

GOAL

Understand that a writer's notebook is a special place to keep ideas about yourself and your world.

RATIONALE

When students learn that a writer's notebook is a place to collect and save ideas for writing that reflects who they are, they begin to understand that what they include in their notebooks (and how they decorate them) is important. The act of keeping a writer's notebook builds a foundation for a lifelong habit of writing.

WRITER'S NOTEBOOK/WRITING FOLDER

Students will start decorating the front and back covers of their writer's notebooks.

ASSESS LEARNING

- Notice evidence of what students understand about a writer's notebook.
- Get to know your students by noticing how they decorate the cover of their writer's notebooks.
- Look for evidence that students use the term *writer's notebook*.

MINILESSON

Demonstrate the delight and possibility of a new writer's notebook as you distribute a new notebook to each student. This lesson is based on the letter at the beginning of *Writer's Notebook, Intermediate*. However, if you are not using it, glue the Writer's Notebook Letter online resource into a blank notebook. Here is an example.

- Display a new writer's notebook. Model the excitement of opening it—the crackling sound of a new binding being opened or a gently turned first page in a spiral notebook.

   > Today is a special day in your writing life—each of you is getting your own writer's notebook! Listen carefully as I open this brand-new notebook.
   >
   > Now I am going to give each of you a writer's notebook. Don't open it yet! We all want to open them at the same time.

- Distribute the notebooks in a fun or ceremonial way.
- When all students have a notebook, indicate they can quietly open them together.
- Use a document camera, if available, to show the letter at the beginning of the writer's notebook. Read it aloud.

   > What are some ideas that stood out to you as you listened to me read the letter?

- Highlight students' responses in the letter if you are projecting it. If not, write their ideas in a column on chart paper. Save room to add ideas for decorating the covers.

WML1
WPS.U1.WML1

Have a Try

Engage students in a conversation about making the front and back covers of their writer's notebook representative of themselves. Add ideas to the chart.

> Look at the cover of my writer's notebook. How did I show what is important to me?
>
> Turn and talk to your partner about ways you might decorate your notebook.

▶ After time for discussion, ask several volunteers to share. Continue to add new ideas to the chart.

Summarize and Apply

Summarize the lesson and write the principle at the top of the chart. Have students decorate their notebooks.

> You learned that writers decorate their writer's notebooks to make them special. During writing time, decorate the cover of your notebook. This can take time, just like writing, so you don't need to finish today. As you work, think about whether there is anything you'd like to bring in from home to decorate your notebook. You'll want to show some things that are important about you. Be prepared to share what you've done so far when we meet later.

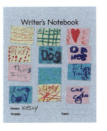

Confer

▶ During independent writing, move around the room to confer briefly with students about making their notebook covers their own. As needed, use the following prompts to help students think of ideas for their notebook covers.

- *How are you going to decorate the cover of your notebook? How does that show what you like or who you are?*
- *Who (what) are the important people (places) in your life?*
- *What is a time in your life you never want to forget?*
- *What is something you know a lot about?*

Share

Following independent writing, gather students in a circle in the meeting area to share their notebook covers. Have students show their covers one at a time.

> What do you notice on your classmates' covers that you might try on your own?

WML2
WPS.U1.WML2

Writing Minilesson Principle
Write in your writer's notebook for at least ten minutes a day.

Introducing and Using a Writer's Notebook

You Will Need
- chart paper and markers
- writer's notebooks

Academic Language / Important Vocabulary
- writer's notebook
- quick write

Continuum Connection
- Produce a reasonable quantity of writing within the time available
- Write routinely over extended timeframes and shorter timeframes from a range of discipline-specific tasks, purposes, and audiences

GOAL
Develop the routine of writing daily in a writer's notebook for a short, predictable timeframe.

RATIONALE
It is important to provide students with many opportunities to do short quick writes every day in addition to independent writing time to help them build writing fluency and stamina, add to their ideas in their writer's notebooks, and expand their ability to write in a variety of ways. Sometimes you may choose to provide a quick prompt for this writing time. Other times students will use ideas from the ways you have shown them how to write in their writer's notebooks. These ten minutes of writing in the writer's notebook can happen outside of writers' workshop at any time of the day.

WRITER'S NOTEBOOK/WRITING FOLDER
Students will do a quick write in their writer's notebooks to help them develop the habit of writing in their writer's notebooks every day.

ASSESS LEARNING
- Observe whether students are able to write for ten minutes at a time.
- Notice evidence that they can use vocabulary such as *writer's notebook* and *quick write*.

MINILESSON

To help students think about the minilesson principle, invite them to write for ten minutes in Section 4, which has plenty of blank pages. Here is an example.

> Jane Yolen is the author of many familiar books. Listen to what she says about writing: "Exercise the writing muscle every day, even if it is only a letter, notes, a title list, a character sketch, a journal entry. Writers are like dancers, like athletes. Without that exercise, the muscles seize up."

> What do you suppose it means to exercise your writing muscle?

> Writers write all the time. Setting aside time to write every day is important for exercising your writing muscle. Each day, you will spend ten minutes writing or sketching in your writer's notebook outside of our normal writing time.

> Let's see what it is like to write for ten minutes. You will do a quick write about a pretend award. The award could be for anything. For example, you could give an award to the person with the loudest laugh, the person most likely to travel to Mars, or the person with the best hat collection. Spend ten minutes writing about this idea in your writer's notebook. First, jot down your ideas for a pretend award. Then, pick one and write about it. You might write about what it would take to win the award, who would win the award, or what the award would look like.

- Set a timer for ten minutes and remind students to write for the entire time.

The Writing Minilessons Book, Grade 3

Have a Try

Invite students to talk to a partner about writing daily in a writer's notebook.

> How did it feel to write in your writer's notebook for ten minutes? Why is it a good idea to write in your writer's notebook for ten minutes every day? How could this help you as a writer? Turn and talk to your partner about this.

▸ After time for discussion, invite several students to share their thinking. Record their responses on chart paper.

Summarize and Apply

Summarize the learning and remind students to write for at least ten minutes a day in their writer's notebooks.

> You learned that writers get better at writing by writing each and every day.

▸ Write the principle at the top of the chart.

> During writing time today, you will do some writing and sketching in your writer's notebook. Think of an idea—any idea—you want to write about. You may continue writing about your pretend award, write about a different pretend award, or write about something else entirely.

Confer

▸ During independent writing, move around the room to confer briefly with students about ideas for writing. Use prompts such as the following as needed.
- *How's your writing work going today?*
- *What are you working on as a writer today?*
- *What else could you write about for ten minutes?*

Share

Following independent writing, gather students in the meeting area to talk about their writing.

> What did you write about in your writer's notebook today?

> What will you like about writing in your writer's notebook every day?

WML 2
WPS.U1.WML2

> Write in your writer's notebook for at least ten minutes a day.

Why write for ten minutes a day?
- To get ideas for writing
- To try out ideas for writing
- To try new types of writing
- To develop the habit of writing
- To become a better writer
- To think about different ideas

Section 5: Writing Process

Umbrella 1: Introducing and Using a Writer's Notebook

WML3
WPS.U1.WML3

Writing Minilesson Principle
Collect your thinking in your writer's notebook.

Introducing and Using a Writer's Notebook

You Will Need

- writer's notebooks
- chart paper and markers

Academic Language / Important Vocabulary

- section
- inspiration
- expert

Continuum Connection

- Use a writer's notebook or booklet as a tool for collecting ideas, experimenting, planning, sketching, or drafting
- Use sketching, webs, lists, and freewriting to think about, plan for, and try out writing
- Have topics and ideas for writing in a list or notebook

GOAL

Learn the organization of the writer's notebook to help with collecting and organizing ideas.

RATIONALE

Students will write many ideas in their notebooks over the course of the year. The sections in the notebook (see pages 84–88 for guidance on creating sections) will help students know where to look when they reread their notebooks to find ideas to expand into longer pieces.

WRITER'S NOTEBOOK/WRITING FOLDER

Students will survey their writer's notebooks to understand how to use them to collect their thinking.

ASSESS LEARNING

- Observe for evidence of beginning understandings of how the writer's notebook is organized and what students will write about in each section.
- Look for evidence that they can use vocabulary such as *section, inspiration,* and *expert.*

MINILESSON

Students will need their writer's notebooks for the minilesson. To help students think about the minilesson principle, provide an inquiry-based lesson to help them survey their writer's notebooks. Below is an example. If you are not using *Writer's Notebook, Intermediate,* you will want to set up the sections in students' notebooks ahead of time.

> Each of you has your own writer's notebook, which you will use this year. Why do you think I've given you a writer's notebook?

> You will use your notebook all year to collect your ideas and thinking about writing. Some of the ideas you collect will be ideas that you will use when you write a story or do some informational writing.

> You have already done some writing in the section you will be writing in the most, but let's explore some of the other sections you will be using this year. Take a couple of minutes to look through your writer's notebook.

- Draw students' attention to the tabs at the top of the writer's notebook.

  > The writer's notebook has four sections. You can use the tabs at the top to find each section. Open your notebook to Section 1, the tab that says Ideas from My Life. What is this section about?

- Use students' responses to write a summary statement in the first column of the chart.

- Continue in a similar manner with the three remaining sections (Inspiration from Artists and Writers, Becoming an Expert, More Writing and Sketching).

The Writing Minilessons Book, Grade 3

Have a Try

Invite students to turn and talk to a partner about the writer's notebook.

> Turn and talk to your partner about what you could write in one of the sections.

▶ After time for discussion, ask a few volunteers to share. Confirm their understanding of a writer's notebook, and clear up any misconceptions that may have arisen.

Summarize and Apply

Write the principle at the top of the chart. Summarize the lesson. Have students write down some ideas in Section 4.

> Why do you think it's a good idea to collect your thinking in a writer's notebook?

▶ Make sure students understand that they will reread their notebooks from time to time to find ideas for longer pieces of writing.

> During writing time, turn to Section 4 in your writer's notebook. Write some ideas on the tabbed page that you can use later in your writing. Once you have collected ideas on your list, you can look there any time you need an idea to write about. If you would like to write about one of the ideas today, turn to the first empty page and start writing. Bring your writer's notebooks to share when we meet later.

Collect your thinking in your writer's notebook.

Ideas from My Life	Inspiration from Writers and Artists	Becoming an Expert	More Writing and Sketching
Collect writing ideas from your everyday life.	Collect ideas from reading someone else's writing or from looking at art.	Collect and organize notes on topics that are interesting to you.	Write or draw about any idea in all types of ways. Try out new writing moves.

Confer

▶ During independent writing, move around the room to confer briefly with students about collecting ideas in their writer's notebooks. Use the following prompts as needed.

- *Did you write some ideas on the list? What made you think of them?*
- *What do you look forward to writing about? Where might you write those ideas in your writer's notebook?*

Share

Following independent writing, gather students in the meeting area to share with a partner an idea for writing. Then bring the class back together.

> What ideas did you hear from your classmates that you might add to your list?

Umbrella 1: Introducing and Using a Writer's Notebook

WML 4
WPS.U1.WML4

Writing Minilesson Principle
Keep your writer's notebook organized.

Introducing and Using a Writer's Notebook

You Will Need

- your own, completed writer's notebook and/or examples from former students or published writers
- writer's notebooks
- chart paper and markers
- document camera (optional)

Academic Language / Important Vocabulary

- guidelines
- organized
- writer's notebook

Continuum Connection

- Use a writer's notebook or booklet as a tool for collecting ideas, experimenting, planning, sketching, or drafting

GOAL

Keep the writer's notebook organized so it can be used efficiently.

RATIONALE

Teach students ways to take care of their writer's notebooks and keep them organized so that they can use them more efficiently. Developing the guidelines for use together helps students take ownership of the guidelines and of the care of their notebooks.

WRITER'S NOTEBOOK/WRITING FOLDER

Students will learn how to take care of their writer's notebooks and keep them organized.

ASSESS LEARNING

- Look at students' notebooks. Are they well cared for and organized?
- Notice evidence that students understand the guidelines for working in a writer's notebook.
- Look for evidence that students can use vocabulary such as *guidelines*, *organized*, and *writer's notebook*.

MINILESSON

To help students understand the minilesson principle, engage them in developing guidelines for using a writer's notebook. Below is an example. Use the guidelines on the inside front cover of *Writer's Notebook, Intermediate*, or have students glue a copy of the guidelines developed in this lesson in their writer's notebooks.

- Each student will need a writer's notebook.

    You have been working to make your writer's notebook show who you are. You will use the notebook across the year, and you will share it with me. So, it will help to have guidelines for working in the notebook.

    Your notebooks are divided into sections. Why do you think there are sections?

    Why is it important to understand the purpose for each section?

- Record responses on chart paper. Continue building guidelines using the questions below as needed. Prompt students to explain why each guideline is important.

    - *What are other ideas for using your writer's notebook so that you can do your best work?*
    - *What might you write whenever you start an entry to help keep your notebook organized?*
    - *What are you thinking about how to use the blank pages within the notebook in an organized way?*
    - *What could you do if you are writing and you want to make a change or you need to correct a mistake?*

Have a Try

Invite students to continue talking to a partner about guidelines and the rationales for them.

> Turn and talk about the guidelines for using your writer's notebook. What other guidelines should we add to our chart? Why are they important?

▸ After time for discussion, ask several volunteers to share. Continue to add to the chart.

Summarize and Apply

Summarize the lesson and remind students to think about keeping their writer's notebooks organized.

> What can you do to make the best use of your writer's notebook?

▸ Write the principle at the top of the chart.

> Today, continue to work on decorating the cover of your writer's notebook to show your unique self. If you finish early, open to Section 4, write today's date on the first empty page, and write whatever comes to mind. You might also think about other guidelines that might help you use your writer's notebook well. Bring your notebook to share when we meet later.

Keep your writer's notebook organized.

How	Why
• Use each section of the notebook correctly.	• It is easier to find what you need.
• Write the date every time you start an entry.	• To know when you worked on that entry.
• Write on the next clean page of the appropriate section.	• You can find your work more easily, and you won't waste any pages.
• Write neatly.	• To help everyone (you, teacher) easily read your work
• Cross out with one line when you make a mistake. ~~mistake~~	• You might change your mind and use the idea later.

Confer

▸ During independent writing, move around the room to confer briefly with students about using a writer's notebook. Use the following prompts as needed.

- What guidelines for keeping your notebook organized will be important for you to keep in mind this year? Why are they important?
- How are you decorating the cover of your notebook? How does that show what is unique about you?

Share

Following independent writing, gather students in pairs in the meeting area to share their notebooks.

> Turn and talk to your partner about what you worked on in your writer's notebook.

> As you looked through your notebook, did you think of other guidelines we can add to our chart?

WML 5
WPS.U1.WML5

Writing Minilesson Principle
Keep building your writer's notebook.

Introducing and Using a Writer's Notebook

You Will Need

- chart paper and markers
- writer's notebooks

Academic Language / Important Vocabulary

- writer's notebook

Continuum Connection

- Write routinely over extended timeframes and shorter timeframes from a range of discipline-specific tasks, purposes, and audiences

GOAL

Continue building a writer's notebook by writing in it in a variety of ways.

RATIONALE

Building a daily habit of writing is important for developing fluent thinkers and writers. This lesson should be taught only after students have been thoroughly introduced to all sections of the writer's notebook. Therefore, we recommend teaching either some or all of the lessons in WPS.U2: Writer's Notebook: Getting Ideas from Your Life, WPS.U3: Writer's Notebook: Getting Inspiration from Writers and Artists, and WPS.U4: Writer's Notebook: Becoming an Expert before teaching this lesson. Students can repeat ideas from these sections with different content to continue building their writer's notebooks.

WRITER'S NOTEBOOK/WRITING FOLDER

Students will look through their writer's notebooks to notice all of the ways they can write in and continue building their notebooks.

ASSESS LEARNING

- Notice whether students use their writer's notebooks in a variety of ways and can decide what to write about independently.
- Look for evidence that they can use vocabulary such as *writer's notebook*.

MINILESSON

Students will need their writer's notebooks for this minilesson. To help students think about the minilesson principle, engage them in an inquiry-based lesson on different ways to write in a writer's notebook. Below is an example.

- Make sure students have their writer's notebooks.

    You have been writing in your writer's notebooks in a lot of different ways. Spend a few minutes looking through the writing you have done in your writer's notebook.

    What are some of the different ways you have written in your writer's notebook?

- Record students' responses on chart paper. If students are using *Writer's Notebook, Intermediate*, refer them to the inside back cover for a list of ways to continue building their writer's notebooks.

WML 5
WPS.U1.WML5

Have a Try

Invite students to talk with a partner about how they would like to write in their writer's notebook.

> What is one way you would like to write in your writer's notebook in the future? It could be something you haven't tried yet or something you would like to do more of. Turn and talk to your partner about this.

▸ After students turn and talk, invite several students to share their thinking.

Summarize and Apply

Write the principle at the top of the chart. Read it to students. Summarize the learning and remind students to keep building their writer's notebooks in a variety of ways.

> Today you thought about different ways you can write in your writer's notebook. Continue to build your writer's notebook by writing in it every day. If you're not sure what to write about, look at the list we made to get ideas. During writing time, keep building your writer's notebook by writing in one of the ways we talked about or in another way. Bring your notebook to share when we come back together.

Keep building your writer's notebook.

- Make a list.
- Make a web.
- Make a map.
- Make a sketch.
- Respond to a poem or song.
- Write from a quote.
- Observe and sketch the world around you.
- Glue in artifacts.
- Collect memorable words and phrases.
- Write about a book you read.
- Write about a piece of art.

Confer

▸ During independent writing, move around the room to confer briefly with students about building their writer's notebooks. Use prompts such as the following as needed.

- *How would you like to write in your writer's notebook today?*
- *Look at the list we made. Are there any ideas on this list that you haven't tried yet? Any that you would like to try again?*
- *Look at the writing you have done in your writer's notebook. Does your writing give you any ideas for new writing?*
- *Would you like to try writing about a book/poem/song?*

Share

Following independent writing, gather students in the meeting area to talk about their writing.

> How did you use your writer's notebook today? What did you write about?

> What is your favorite way to use your writer's notebook? Why?

Umbrella 1: Introducing and Using a Writer's Notebook

Assessment

After you have taught the minilessons in this umbrella, observe students when they use their writer's notebooks. Use *The Fountas & Pinnell Literacy Continuum* to notice, teach for, and support students' learning as you observe their attempts at writing.

- What evidence do you have of students' new understandings related to a writer's notebook?
  - Do students create a cover that demonstrates their uniqueness?
  - Do students understand the purpose and organization of a writer's notebook?
  - Do they write in their writer's notebooks for at least ten minutes a day?
  - Are they using their writer's notebooks in a variety of ways?
  - Do they understand and use the terms *writer's notebook*, *guidelines*, *organized*, and *section*?
- In what ways, beyond the scope of this umbrella, are students using a writer's notebook?
  - Are they expanding ideas they collect, for example, ideas for informational writing, procedural writing, memory stories, or realistic fiction?
  - Do they reread their notebooks to get ideas for writing?

Use your observations to determine the next umbrella you will teach. You may also consult Suggested Sequence of Lessons (pp. 605–622) for guidance.

EXTENSIONS FOR INTRODUCING AND USING A WRITER'S NOTEBOOK

- Support students in using sketches within a writer's notebook to help them generate ideas for writing or as a strategy to revise their writing. For example, they can sketch the setting of a memory as a way to think about what words to use to describe it.

- When students share stories about their activities, weekends, families, etc., with you, remind them to list the ideas in their writer's notebooks.

- When a student shares knowledge of a topic or an experience, encourage the student to add those to Section 3, Becoming an Expert.

- Help students set individual goals for using their writer's notebooks (e.g., write in it for thirty minutes a day, experiment with different ways of using a writer's notebook).

Writer's Notebook: Getting Ideas from Your Life

Umbrella 2

Minilessons in This Umbrella

WML1	Make a heart map to discover what is important in your life.
WML2	Use maps to get ideas.
WML3	Make webs to get ideas from your memories and experiences.
WML4	Think about special places to get ideas.
WML5	Think about people to get ideas.
WML6	Use lists to gather ideas from your life.
WML7	Collect artifacts in your writer's notebook.
WML8	Observe the world around you to get ideas for your writing.

Interactive Read-Aloud
Family

Writer's Notebook

Before Teaching Umbrella 2 Minilessons

Writers gather ideas from their lives in order to generate writing ideas. This umbrella guides students to think about observations and experiences from their own lives and to use their writer's notebooks to gather that information. You are teaching ways to generate and collect ideas. Students will be writing throughout the lessons to gain a deeper understanding of how to use their writer's notebooks. Thus, the minilessons in this umbrella may take longer than typical minilessons. Write alongside them in your own writer's notebook, which will serve as a model and also show them other ways of thinking. In order to model the process at the same time that students are writing in their own notebooks, use a document camera to project your notebook or demonstrate the work on chart paper.

It is recommended that each student have a writer's notebook and that you teach WPS.U1: Introducing and Using a Writer's Notebook prior to this umbrella. If you are using *Writer's Notebook, Intermediate* (Fountas and Pinnell 2023), the writing throughout this umbrella should be done in Section 1, Ideas from My Life. If not, students can create a section in their own notebooks dedicated to ideas from their own lives. Eventually, students will refer to this section and select ideas that they will grow into longer writing projects. Use the books listed below from *Fountas & Pinnell Classroom™ Interactive Read-Aloud Collection*, or choose books from the classroom library.

Interactive Read-Aloud Collection
Connecting Across Generations: Family

Mooncakes by Loretta Seto

Sitti's Secrets by Naomi Shihab Nye

WML1
WPS.U2.WML1

Writing Minilesson Principle
Make a heart map to discover what is important in your life.

Writer's Notebook: Getting Ideas from Your Life

You Will Need

- chart paper prepared with the outline of a large heart map (the first tab in *Writer's Notebook, Intermediate*)
- document camera (optional)
- chart paper and markers
- writer's notebooks

Academic Language / Important Vocabulary

- writer's notebook
- heart map
- matters
- ideas

Continuum Connection

- Use a writer's notebook or booklet as a tool for collecting ideas, experimenting, planning, sketching, or drafting
- Use sketching, webs, lists, and freewriting to think about, plan for, and try out writing
- Have topics and ideas for writing in a list or notebook

GOAL

Use a writer's notebook to record important pieces of one's identity in a heart map to inspire writing ideas.

RATIONALE

Information about what matters to students can inspire their writing. Adding these notions to a heart map (Heard 2016) is a strategy students can use to collect and generate their ideas in a writer's notebook.

WRITER'S NOTEBOOK/WRITING FOLDER

Students will write ideas about themselves on a heart map in their writer's notebooks.

ASSESS LEARNING

- Observe whether students are using a writer's notebook to make and use a heart map.
- Look for evidence that they can use vocabulary such as *writer's notebook*, *heart map*, *matters*, and *ideas*.

MINILESSON

Students will need their writer's notebooks for this minilesson. To help students think about the minilesson principle, model the process of making a heart map and engage students in exploring topics from their lives. Below is an example.

- Display a heart map.

    Writers have different ways of getting ideas for writing in a writer's notebook. One way is to make a heart map. This heart map will be about me. It will show who I am and what is important to me. Watch as I add some things to my heart map.

- Think aloud as you add a few authentic elements about yourself to the heart map. Talk about how the words inspire you to think about writing more and add a quick sketch to one of the words.

    In this section of the heart map I am going to write the word *garden*. My friend has a garden for the Cambodian community. I help her take care of it, so I will add a quick sketch to show something special about the garden. I am going to write the word *cars* over here. I know a lot about fixing cars, so I want to write more about that someday.

    I can refer to the heart map anytime I am looking for ideas for writing. I can also add to this heart map whenever I think of something important about myself that I might want to write about.

Have a Try

Invite students to begin adding to a heart map in their writer's notebooks.

- Have students turn to the first tab in *Writer's Notebook, Intermediate* or draw a heart on paper to glue into their writer's notebooks.

    What are some parts of who you are that you could put on your heart map? Add a few of those ideas to your heart map as I continue working on mine.

- After a few minutes, ask a few volunteers to share their ideas as you make a generalized list on chart paper.

Summarize and Apply

Summarize the learning and remind students to add authentic ideas about themselves to a heart map in their writer's notebooks as inspiration for writing. Write the principle at the top of the chart.

When you write today, add on to what you started on the heart map in your writer's notebook. Or, you can choose one thing you wrote on your heart map and begin writing about it for a few minutes. You will not finish your heart map today because you will add to it throughout the year.

- Students can start to write about something on their heart maps in Section 1 or on the first clean page in Section 4.

Confer

- During independent writing, move around the room to confer briefly with students about their heart maps. Use prompts such as the following as needed.
    - *What is something that is very important to you?*
    - *What is one way that you are unique?*
    - *Show me an idea on your heart map you might like to write about today. What ideas do you have for writing?*

Share

Following independent writing, gather students in the meeting area. Give all students a turn to share something on their heart maps.

Who would like to start by sharing your heart map?

Heart Map

- Cambodia
- mother to Kimberly
- cars
- garden

Make a heart map to discover what is important in your life.

Things to Draw or Write About on a Heart Map
- sports
- interests
- family
- important places
- instruments
- special holidays
- moving to a new city
- becoming a big brother/sister
- coming to the United States
- traveling to visit family

WML 2
WPS.U2.WML2

Writing Minilesson Principle
Use maps to get ideas.

Writer's Notebook: Getting Ideas from Your Life

You Will Need

- a familiar text featuring a special place, such as *Mooncakes* by Loretta Seto, from Text Set: Connecting Across Generations: Family
- chart paper prepared with a simple map of a place that is special to you (p. 2 in *Writer's Notebook, Intermediate*)
- document camera (optional)
- markers
- writer's notebooks

Academic Language / Important Vocabulary

- writer's notebook
- maps
- ideas

Continuum Connection

- Use sketching, webs, lists, and freewriting to think about, plan for, and try out writing
- Generate and expand ideas through talk with peers and teacher
- Look for ideas and topics in personal experiences, shared through talk

---

GOAL
Create maps of special places to generate ideas for writing.

RATIONALE
When students learn to use a writer's notebook to create a memory map of a meaningful place, they learn a way to generate ideas for writing.

WRITER'S NOTEBOOK/WRITING FOLDER
Students will draw a map of a place that has meaning for them in their writer's notebooks.

ASSESS LEARNING

- Observe for evidence that students understand that they can get ideas for writing by drawing and labeling a map of a special place.
- Look for evidence that they can use vocabulary such as *writer's notebook*, *maps*, and *ideas*.

MINILESSON

Students will need their writer's notebooks for this minilesson. To help students think about the minilesson principle, model the process and engage them in thinking about special places in their lives. Below is an example.

- Revisit the first few pages of *Mooncakes*.

    What place is special in *Mooncakes*?

    This book makes me remember things I did with my family when I was young.

- Display your hand-drawn map of a special place. As you think aloud, label the map with stories you remember that happened in a few different places on the map. Here is an example.

    This is a map of my cousin's apartment. I added the hallway to the map because I would smell pancakes cooking as soon as I came up the stairs. I will write *smelling pancakes from the hallway* because I might want to write about that later. Here is the place in the play area where we would build tall block towers. I will write that down because we had hilarious contests with those towers and I want to remember that.

- Have students turn to a clean page in Section 1 of their writer's notebooks (p. 2 in *Writer's Notebook, Intermediate*).

    Draw your own map of a special place and start labeling the map with stories that happened there. I will continue adding ideas to my map, too.

- Provide a few minutes to do this, and then ask volunteers to share.

    Did anyone get an idea from another person's map for something you want to add to your map or an idea for another map you want to make?

The Writing Minilessons Book, Grade 3

Have a Try

Invite students to jot down ideas for stories that relate to an idea on their maps.

> My map inspires in me a lot of ideas for stories that I could write. I am going to choose one story and jot down a few ideas on the next page of my writer's notebook. While I do that, you can do the same thing in your notebook.

▶ Begin modeling the process as students write alongside you on the next page in their writer's notebooks. After a brief time, ask a few volunteers to share.

Summarize and Apply

Summarize the learning. Students can continue working on their maps or make a different one.

> When you write today, add on to what you started on your map. Or, you can make a different map and label it with how the places on the map make you feel. Bring your notebook to share when we meet later.

▶ Remind students that they can use Section 4 of their writer's notebooks if they need more room.

Confer

▶ During independent writing, move around the room to confer briefly with students about their notebook entries. Use prompts such as the following as needed.
  • *Tell why this place is special to you.*
  • *What are some things that happened when you were in this place?*
  • *What other memory maps are you thinking about making?*

Share

Following independent writing, gather students in the meeting area to talk about their notebook entries.

> Who would like to share what you wrote in your writer's notebook today?
>
> What are some writing ideas you thought about when making your map?

WML3
WPS.U2.WML3

Writing Minilesson Principle
Make webs to get ideas from your memories and experiences.

Writer's Notebook: Getting Ideas from Your Life

You Will Need

- two pieces of chart paper, each prepared with a web (see pp. 8–9 in *Writer's Notebook, Intermediate*)
- markers
- document camera (optional)
- writer's notebooks

Academic Language / Important Vocabulary

- writer's notebook
- webs
- memories
- experiences
- details

Continuum Connection

- Use sketching, webs, lists, and freewriting to think about, plan for, and try out writing
- Generate and expand ideas through talk with peers and teacher
- Look for ideas and topics in personal experiences, shared through talk

GOAL

Understand that making a web in a writer's notebook can inspire writing.

RATIONALE

When students first identify things that happened during a time or event they remember and then focus on one of those things, they can more effectively choose and write about small moments when they write memory stories. This lesson shows students another way to generate ideas for writing.

WRITER'S NOTEBOOK/WRITING FOLDER

Students will fill in a web about a memory in their writer's notebooks that will become a source of ideas for their writing.

ASSESS LEARNING

- Observe whether students are creating webs in order to generate writing ideas.
- Look for evidence that they can use vocabulary such as *writer's notebook*, *webs*, *memories*, *experiences*, and *details*.

MINILESSON

Students will need their writer's notebooks for this minilesson. To help students think about the minilesson principle, model the process and engage them in creating a memory web. Below is an example.

- Display the prepared chart paper or project the web on page 8 in *Writer's Notebook, Intermediate*. Fill in the center section with a memory. Then begin filling in the spokes as you think aloud. Here is an example.

  > One of my most vivid childhood memories is going to the county fair for the first time. I think I could write a good memory story about that. To collect my ideas, I'm going to fill in this web with things I remember about the fair.

- After you write a few things you remember, ask students to begin filling in their webs. Have students draw a web on a clean page in their writer's notebooks (p. 8 in *Writer's Notebook, Intermediate*).

  > What is a memory you could write about? Write it in the center of the web. Then write what you remember happening on the spokes as I continue working on my web.

- After a few minutes, ask volunteers to share, encouraging students to get other writing ideas by listening to classmates.

Have a Try

Invite students to begin another web in their writer's notebooks.

- Display the second web (p. 9 in *Writer's Notebook, Intermediate*). Fill in the center and think aloud as you begin to fill in one spoke. Then ask students to begin a second web as you work alongside them.

  > My first web shows several moments of my memory. By filling in a web about one of my moments, I will have some details that will help my writing come alive for my readers when I write my memory story.

  > Go to the next page in your writer's notebook. Choose one thing that happened from the web you just made. Write it in the center. Then add some details in the spaces.

Summarize and Apply

Summarize the learning. Students can continue working on their webs or start writing from them.

> When you write today, add more details to the second web or start writing about the memory on the first empty page in Section 4 of your writer's notebook. Bring your writing to share when we meet later.

Confer

- During independent writing, move around the room to confer briefly with students about their webs. Use prompts such as the following as needed.
  - *Talk about your ideas for your memory web.*
  - *What will you write in the center circle?*
  - *What details will help your readers picture your memory?*

Share

Following independent writing, gather students in the meeting area to share their notebook entries first with a partner and then with the group.

> What are some memories you thought of when you heard your partner's ideas?

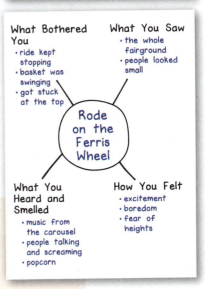

WML 4
WPS.U2.WML4

Writing Minilesson Principle
Think about special places to get ideas.

Writer's Notebook: Getting Ideas from Your Life

You Will Need

- writer's notebooks
- document camera (optional)
- chart paper prepared with a sketch and some writing (e.g., a poem) about a place (pp. 16–17 in *Writer's Notebook, Intermediate*)

Academic Language / Important Vocabulary

- writer's notebook
- places
- ideas

Continuum Connection

- Use a writer's notebook or booklet as a tool for collecting ideas, experimenting, planning, sketching, or drafting
- Use sketching, webs, lists, and freewriting to think about, plan for, and try out writing
- Have topics and ideas for writing in a list or notebook

GOAL

Use a writer's notebook to sketch and think about places to inspire writing.

RATIONALE

When students learn to use a writer's notebook to sketch and write about special places, they learn to think about places as a way of generating ideas for writing.

WRITER'S NOTEBOOK/WRITING FOLDER

Students will use their writer's notebooks to sketch and write about special places that they have been to or would like to visit.

ASSESS LEARNING

- Observe whether students are using a writer's notebook to think about places to generate writing ideas.
- Look for evidence that they can use vocabulary such as *writer's notebook*, *places*, and *ideas*.

MINILESSON

Students will need their writer's notebooks for the minilesson. To help students think about the minilesson principle, model the process of sketching a place and engage them in thinking about special places. Below is an example.

> Writers get ideas for writing from places they have been, places that are important to them, or places they want to visit. You can use your writer's notebook to think about places in order to get ideas for writing.

- Begin sketching a special place in your writer's notebook or on chart paper as students do the same in their notebooks.

   > A place that is special to me is the library in my neighborhood. I go there every weekend to read, check out books, or do some work.

   > What is a place that is special to you? Make a sketch of your special place in your writer's notebook while I make my sketch.

- Have students turn to a clean page in Section 1 of their writer's notebooks (p. 14 in *Writer's Notebook, Intermediate*). Provide time for sketching.

- Then guide students to think about how they could write about the place. Develop a list on chart paper of questions they could ask themselves to decide what to write.

- Give students a few minutes to write about their special places (p. 15 in *Writer's Notebook, Intermediate*). Remind them to refer to the questions on the chart as they think about what to write.

WML 4
WPS.U2.WML4

Have a Try

Invite students to use a special place as inspiration in their writer's notebooks.

▸ Display your prepared sketch of a special place and read the writing you did about it (pp. 16–17 in *Writer's Notebook, Intermediate*).

> What do you notice about what I have done on this page?
>
> Turn and talk to a partner about another place that is special to you, either one you have been to or one you would like to visit, and some things you might include in a poem about the place.

Summarize and Apply

Summarize the learning and remind students to use places as inspiration for writing.

> What can you think about to get ideas for writing?

▸ Write the principle at the top of the chart of questions.

> During writing time, write a poem about a place you have been or a place you would like to visit. Make a sketch to help you think of what to write. Start with whatever is most helpful, either writing or sketching.

Confer

▸ During independent writing, move around the room to confer briefly with students about their notebook entries. Use prompts such as the following as needed.

- What special place will you sketch in your writer's notebook?
- What does this place make you think about?
- What are some special words that describe your place?

Share

Following independent writing, gather students in the meeting area to share their writing.

> Turn and talk to your partner about what you drew and wrote today.

Think about special places to get ideas.

- What does the place look like?
- Why is the place important to you?
- What makes you interested in this place?
- What have you done, or what has happened there?
- How do you feel when you are there?
- What do you hear and see in the place?

Hawaii

Hawaiian palm trees seem to rustle and sway
    on that poster on 3rd Street and Vine.
I imagine visiting there one day
    in a flowered shirt,
        wearing a bright green lei.

WML 5
WPS.U2.WML5

Writing Minilesson Principle
Think about people to get ideas.

Writer's Notebook: Getting Ideas from Your Life

You Will Need

- document camera (optional)
- writer's notebooks
- your writer's notebook or chart paper prepared with the beginning of some writing about a person (pp. 18–19 in *Writer's Notebook, Intermediate*)
- markers

Academic Language / Important Vocabulary

- writer's notebook
- people
- ideas

Continuum Connection

- Use a writer's notebook or booklet as a tool for collecting ideas, experimenting, planning, sketching, or drafting
- Use sketching, webs, lists, and freewriting to think about, plan for, and try out writing
- Have topics and ideas for writing in a list or notebook

GOAL

Use a writer's notebook to sketch and think about people to inspire writing.

RATIONALE

When students learn to use a writer's notebook to sketch and write about people, they learn to think about people as a way of generating ideas for writing.

WRITER'S NOTEBOOK/WRITING FOLDER

Students will use their writer's notebooks to sketch and write about people they know or would like to know.

ASSESS LEARNING

- Observe whether students are using a writer's notebook to think about people to generate writing ideas.
- Look for evidence that they can use vocabulary such as *writer's notebook*, *people*, and *ideas*.

MINILESSON

Students will need their writer's notebooks for this lesson. To help students think about the minilesson principle, model the process and engage them in thinking about a variety of people. Below is an example.

> Writers get ideas for writing from people in their lives—people they know, people they want to know, or even family from long ago. You can use your writer's notebook to sketch and think about people to get ideas for writing.
>
> A person who is special to me is Alyssa. She is special because I love spending time with her doing things like exercising, cooking, and even running errands.
>
> Who is a person in your life who is special to you? Sketch your special person in your notebook at the same time that I sketch mine.

- Have students turn to a clean page in Section 1 of their writer's notebooks (pp. 18–19 in *Writer's Notebook, Intermediate*). Begin sketching a special person in your life as students do the same in their notebooks.
- After some time for sketching, ask several students to share what they sketched.

WML 5
WPS.U2.WML5

Have a Try

Invite students to use writer's notebooks to write about a special person.

▸ Display and read aloud your prepared writing. If you are using *Writer's Notebook, Intermediate*, refer students to page 19.

> I started to write a memory about my special person. That is one of the ways you can write about your person. Decide how you want to write about your person: describe how the person is special, write a memory, write what you would like to know about the person. Then start writing. I will finish my writing while you write.

▸ Allow a few minutes for students to start writing about a person. Make sure everyone has an idea for writing.

Think about people to get ideas.

Alyssa and I love to go on long bike rides. One time, we were riding on a trail that took us away from town. All of a sudden, Alyssa's bike tire hit a pothole. She was thrown from her bike. Luckily, she was wearing a helmet to protect her head. Unfortunately, she broke her leg.

Summarize and Apply

Summarize the learning and remind students that writers can use people as inspiration for writing.

> What are some ways you can use a person to inspire your writing ideas?

▸ Write the principle at the top of the chart.

> During writing time today, add on to what you started in your writer's notebook or choose a different way to write about the person. Bring your writer's notebook to share when we meet later.

Confer

▸ During independent writing, move around the room to confer briefly with students about people in their lives or people they want to know. Use prompts such as the following as needed.
- *What is special about this person?*
- *What would you like to know about this person?*
- *Is there someone in your family from long ago that you might like to sketch?*

Share

Following independent writing, gather students in the meeting area to talk about their writing.

> Who would like to share what you wrote in your writer's notebook today?

Umbrella 2: Writer's Notebook: Getting Ideas from Your Life

Section 5: Writing Process

499

WML 6
WPS.U2.WML6

Writing Minilesson Principle
Use lists to gather ideas from your life.

Writer's Notebook: Getting Ideas from Your Life

You Will Need

- a familiar book with memories, such as *Sitti's Secrets* by Naomi Shihab Nye, from Text Set: Connecting Across Generations: Family
- your writer's notebook (p. 22 in *Writer's Notebook, Intermediate*) or chart paper
- document camera (optional)
- writer's notebooks
- markers

Academic Language / Important Vocabulary

- writer's notebook
- lists
- ideas

Continuum Connection

- Use a writer's notebook or booklet as a tool for collecting ideas, experimenting, planning, sketching, or drafting
- Use sketching, webs, lists, and freewriting to think about, plan for, and try out writing
- Generate and expand ideas through talk with peers and teacher
- Look for ideas and topics in personal experiences, shared through talk

---

GOAL

Use a writer's notebook to make a list of memories in order to inspire writing.

RATIONALE

One way to generate ideas for writing is to make lists. A good starting point for students is for them to make lists of their memories. Encourage students to make many lists in their writer's notebooks so that they can refer to them when they are looking for a writing idea.

WRITER'S NOTEBOOK/WRITING FOLDER

Students will make lists of memories in their writer's notebooks.

ASSESS LEARNING

- Observe whether students are using a writer's notebook to make lists of their memories in order to generate ideas for writing.
- Look for evidence that they can use vocabulary such as *writer's notebook*, *lists*, and *ideas*.

MINILESSON

Students will need their writer's notebooks for this lesson. To help students think about the minilesson principle, model the process and engage students in thinking about their memories. Below is an example.

- Show and revisit a few pages from *Sitti's Secrets*.

    When I read that Mona and her grandma spoke different languages, I remembered that I had to overcome that obstacle with my own grandma. I realized that learning to talk with my grandma is something I could write about. You can create lists in your writer's notebook to collect your memories so that you will have ideas to write about.

- Have students turn to a clean page in Section 1 of their writer's notebooks (p. 22 in *Writer's Notebook, Intermediate*). Project the page from your writer's notebook, or do your writing on chart paper.

- Model making a list of memories. As you do, have students make their own lists in their writer's notebooks.

    Think about memories you have, perhaps times you got hurt or times you experienced something new. I am going to write *Challenges I Have Overcome* on the line as a title for my list. Then I will write *Talk with my grandma* underneath that. Go ahead and start your list while I add to mine. Remember that your list will look different from mine.

- Ask students to share throughout the process so they can add ideas sparked by their classmates' ideas to their lists.

WML 6
WPS.U2.WML6

Have a Try

Invite students to make a new memory list in their writer's notebooks.

> You'll want to have lots of ideas for writing, so let's try a different memory list. I'm going to list times when I was hurt. I'll write the title of the list and then write some details about it. Make another list in your writer's notebook.

- Begin a new list on chart paper and work on your list as students write in their writer's notebooks. After a brief time, invite volunteers to share and add to the list based on the ideas they share.

Summarize and Apply

Summarize the learning and remind students to make memory lists in their writer's notebooks as inspiration for writing.

> During writing time, choose one of your list ideas and do a quick write on the next page in your writer's notebook. Or, begin a new list of ideas. Making lots of memory lists will give you many ideas that you might want to write about, though not all of them will become a writing project. Bring your writing to share when we meet later.

Use Lists to Get Ideas

Challenges I Have Overcome
- Talking with my grandma
- Food poisoning
- Parents getting divorced
- Moving to a new school
- Learning how to read
- Poor eyesight (got glasses)
- Getting a new babysitter

Times When I Was Hurt
- Fell off my bike
- Bit my lip
- Scratched by my cat
- Broke my wrist playing kickball
- Burned my arm baking a cake
- Teddy bear had a pin in it that poked me

Confer

- During independent writing, move around the room to confer briefly with students about their memory lists. Use prompts such as the following as needed.
    - *Talk about your ideas for your memory list.*
    - *What new list would you like to make?*
    - *What do you remember about that memory? Talk about that.*

Share

Following independent writing, gather students in the meeting area to talk about their writing.

> Who would like to share what you wrote in your writer's notebook today?

WML7
WPS.U2.WML7

Writing Minilesson Principle
Collect artifacts in your writer's notebook.

Writer's Notebook: Getting Ideas from Your Life

You Will Need

- artifacts students have collected from home or class activities
- glue or drawing materials
- writer's notebooks
- your writer's notebook (p. 30 in *Writer's Notebook, Intermediate*) or chart paper prepared with an artifact or a sketch of it and the beginning of some writing about the artifact
- document camera (optional)
- chart paper and markers

Academic Language / Important Vocabulary

- writer's notebook
- artifacts
- items
- sparks
- ideas

Continuum Connection

- Take notes or make sketches to help in remembering or generating information
- Participate actively in experiences and recall information that contributes to writing and drawing (using notebooks and artifacts)
- Have topics and ideas for writing in a list or notebook

GOAL

Use a writer's notebook to collect artifacts to inspire writing ideas.

RATIONALE

Objects can inspire ideas for writing. When students use a writer's notebook to collect artifacts, they learn another way to gain inspiration for writing. In addition, you get a glimpse into the lives of your students.

WRITER'S NOTEBOOK/WRITING FOLDER

Students will glue or sketch a personal artifact in their writer's notebooks and then write about it.

ASSESS LEARNING

- Observe whether students are using a writer's notebook to collect artifacts to inspire writing.
- Look for evidence that they can use vocabulary such as *writer's notebook*, *artifacts*, *items*, *sparks*, and *ideas*.

MINILESSON

Students will need their writer's notebooks and artifacts (if they have them) for this lesson. To help students think about the minilesson principle, model the process and engage students in thinking about artifacts for their notebooks. Below is an example.

- Ahead of time, have students bring items from home or gather artifacts from school activities (e.g., photos, stickers, receipts, tickets). If students don't have artifacts with them, they can draw the items.

  > You can use items that remind you of important moments in your life as sparks for your writing. The artifact you have or are thinking of has at least one memory associated with it.

- Show and describe how you could use personal artifacts to spark ideas for writing.

  > This map reminds me of the different exhibits we saw at the science museum. I could write about the lightning show we saw there. This is a strip of photos from my cousin's wedding. It was fun to use a photo booth. I have so many stories I could write about that day and about my cousin.

- Have students turn to a clean left-hand page in Section 1 of their writer's notebooks (page 30 in *Writer's Notebook, Intermediate*).

  > If you have an artifact to glue in, go ahead and do that. If you don't have the artifact, sketch it. Write a label on the page, too.

- Allow a few minutes for students to either glue in or sketch their artifacts.

Have a Try

Invite students to write about an artifact in their writer's notebooks.

▸ Display and read aloud your prepared writing.

> This is the beginning of my writing about a memory that I'm reminded of when I look at my artifact. Choose how you want to write about your artifact—describe it, write a poem, or do something else. Then start writing on the next (right-hand) page. I will finish my writing while you write.

▸ Allow a few minutes for students to start writing about a memory on the page opposite their artifacts. Make sure everyone has an idea for writing.

Summarize and Apply

Summarize the learning and remind students to use artifacts as inspiration for writing. Add the principle to the top of the chart.

> During writing today, you can add on to what you started in your writer's notebook about your artifact. Or, you can write something else about it. You can also choose a different artifact to glue or sketch in your notebook and try writing about that. If you need more pages, go to the first clean page in Section 4. Bring your writing when we meet later.

Use artifacts to get ideas.

My cousin's wedding was so much fun! After we ate, the dancing started. Everyone did the chicken dance! It was funny to watch people flap their arms like a chicken. Two very young cousins of the bride had more fun than anyone doing the dance.

Confer

▸ During independent writing, move around the room to confer briefly with students about their notebook entries. Use prompts such as the following as needed.

- *Talk about this item. What does it make you think about?*
- *What memory does it make you think about? Jot a few words down to help you remember.*
- *What are words you would use to describe this item?*

Share

Following independent writing, gather students in the meeting area to share their writing.

> Share the work you did in your writer's notebook today with a partner.

WML 8
WPS.U2.WML8

Writing Minilesson Principle
Observe the world around you to get ideas for your writing.

Writer's Notebook: Getting Ideas from Your Life

You Will Need

- writer's notebooks
- chart paper and markers

Academic Language / Important Vocabulary

- writer's notebook
- observe
- sketch
- ideas
- senses

Continuum Connection

- Use a writer's notebook or booklet as a tool for collecting ideas, experimenting, planning, sketching, or drafting
- Take notes or make sketches to help in remembering or generating information
- Participate actively in experiences and recall information that contributes to writing and drawing (using notebooks and artifacts)
- Have topics and ideas for writing in a list or notebook

GOAL

Use a writer's notebook to observe and sketch the world to inspire writing.

RATIONALE

Writers get some of their ideas for writing from being keen observers of anything and everything around them. Guiding students to become good observers will help them find ideas for their own writing. Collecting notes and sketches of their observations in their writer's notebooks ensures that students will always have plenty of ideas to write about.

WRITER'S NOTEBOOK/WRITING FOLDER

Students will sketch, record, and write about their observations in their writer's notebooks.

ASSESS LEARNING

- Observe whether students are using a writer's notebook to observe and sketch the world around them to generate writing ideas.
- Look for evidence that they can use vocabulary such as *writer's notebook*, *observe*, *sketch*, *ideas*, and *senses*.

MINILESSON

Students will need their writer's notebooks for the minilesson. To help students think about the minilesson principle, model the process and engage them in noticing the world around them. Below is an example. If possible, plan to take students outdoors or somewhere in the school outside the classroom.

> Writers often get inspired for writing by observing the world around them. Today, we will go outside to do some close observing. When we observe, we use all our senses.

- Have students turn to a clean page in Section 1 of their writer's notebooks (p. 34 in *Writer's Notebook, Intermediate*).

    > Today you will observe and take some notes about what you hear, smell, see, and feel or touch.

- Have students take writer's notebooks and pencils outside the classroom. Model how to take notes about your observations.

    > Everyone, listen. What is something you hear? I hear trash bins being emptied into the trash truck and the truck rumbling along. I will write some notes about that. What do you hear, smell, see, or feel? Write what you observe.

- Give students time to observe and write some notes. Then return to the classroom.

    > What did you write in your writer's notebook?

- Record some of students' observations on chart paper.

WML 8
WPS.U2.WML8

Have a Try

Invite students to share their observations and prepare to write about them.

> I noticed that there were some birds calling back and forth, and several of you noticed that, too. I am going to try writing about that. Turn and talk about which of your observations you will write about in your notebook and what you might write about it.

- Give the students a short time to talk. Then give them a few minutes to begin writing about one of their observations.
- After a short time for writing, do a quick share.

> I started to write a poem for two voices—two bird voices! What did you decide to write?

Summarize and Apply

Summarize the learning and remind students to observe and then sketch something they noticed in their world to get inspiration for writing.

> Use your observations to spark ideas for writing. When you write today, add on to what you started in your writer's notebook. Or, try another idea for writing, possibly with a different observation. You might also want to make a sketch of your observation. If you need more space to write or draw, use the first clean page in Section 4. Bring your notebook to share when we meet later.

Observe Your World to Get Ideas

What do you **hear**?	What do you **smell**?
Trash bins being emptied into the truck	Lunch from the cafeteria—pizza?
Trash truck rumbling	Car exhaust
Birds calling	

What do you **see**?	What do you **feel** (**touch**)?
Squirrel running up a tree	Rough asphalt
People walking their dogs	Cool breeze

Confer

- During independent writing, move around the room to confer briefly with students about their notebook entries. Use prompts such as the following as needed.
  - What details does your sketch show?
  - What does your observation of the object make you think about?
  - How would you like to write about your observations?

Share

Following independent writing, gather students in the meeting area to talk about their writing.

> Who would like to share what you wrote in your writer's notebook today?

Umbrella 2: Writer's Notebook: Getting Ideas from Your Life

Section 5: Writing Process

Umbrella 2: Writer's Notebook: Getting Ideas from Your Life

Assessment

After you have taught the minilessons in this umbrella, observe students as they write in their notebooks and talk about their writing. Use *The Fountas & Pinnell Literacy Continuum* to notice, teach for, and support students' learning as you observe their attempts at collecting ideas from their lives.

▸ What evidence do you have of students' new understandings related to using a writer's notebook?
- Are they making and using heart maps?
- Do they use maps, webs, and lists to get ideas?
- Are they thinking about places and people to generate ideas for writing?
- Are they collecting artifacts in their writer's notebooks?
- Do they make observations and sketches from their own lives?
- Do they understand and use vocabulary such as *writer's notebook*, *heart map*, *matters*, *ideas*, *maps*, *webs*, *memories*, *experiences*, *lists*, *artifacts*, *observe*, and *sketch*?

▸ In what other ways, beyond the scope of this umbrella, are students using a writer's notebook?
- When students are ready to write something new (e.g., a story, a poem, or an informational book), do they reread their writer's notebooks for ideas?

Use your observations to determine the next umbrella you will teach. You may also consult Suggested Sequence of Lessons (pp. 605–622) for guidance.

EXTENSIONS FOR WRITER'S NOTEBOOK: GETTING IDEAS FROM YOUR LIFE

▸ Have students repeat a technique they have learned for collecting ideas (e.g., making a map, web, or list) with a new idea in Section 4 of their writer's notebooks to see whether they can work it into a longer writing project.

▸ Revisit WML6, this time guiding students through making Top Ten lists (see p. 24 in *Writer's Notebook, Intermediate*).

▸ Encourage students to bring in other artifacts to glue or sketch into their writer's notebooks and make a list of questions or wonderings about it.

Writer's Notebook: Getting Inspiration from Writers and Artists

Umbrella 3

Minilessons in This Umbrella

WML1	Collect memorable words and phrases from authors you love.
WML2	Use poems to inspire writing ideas.
WML3	Use books or parts of books to inspire writing ideas.
WML4	Use song lyrics to inspire writing ideas.
WML5	Use art to inspire writing ideas.

Before Teaching Umbrella 3 Minilessons

Many writers get their ideas from other writers and artists, and that is what Section 2 of the writer's notebook, Inspiration from Writers and Artists, guides students to do. There are opportunities for collecting ideas from books, poems, songs, and art. The minilessons in this umbrella are best taught after teaching WPS.U1: Introducing and Using a Writer's Notebook.

Throughout these minilessons students will be getting comfortable using the writer's notebook by writing alongside you. For this reason, these minilessons may take longer than those in typical umbrellas. This umbrella uses *Writer's Notebook, Intermediate* (Fountas and Pinnell 2023). If you are not using this notebook, have students create a section in a plain notebook dedicated to inspirations from other writers and artists (see page 86).

Gather authentic samples of language, poems, books, songs, and art to use as mentor texts. You may also use the books listed below from *Fountas & Pinnell Classroom™ Interactive Read-Aloud Collection* or choose other books from the classroom library that have the potential for inspiring writing ideas.

Interactive Read-Aloud Collection

Connecting Across Generations: Family

  Storm in the Night by Mary Stolz

The Importance of Kindness

  Last Day Blues by Julie Danneberg

  Under the Lemon Moon by Edith Hope Fine

As you read and enjoy these books together, help students notice
- interesting words and phrases, and
- what the story makes them think about.

Interactive Read-Aloud
Family

Kindness

Writer's Notebook

WML1
WPS.U3.WML1

Writing Minilesson Principle
Collect memorable words and phrases from authors you love.

Writer's Notebook: Getting Inspiration from Writers and Artists

You Will Need

- a mentor text with memorable language, such as *Storm in the Night* by Mary Stolz, from Text Set: Connecting Across Generations: Family
- your writer's notebook (the back of the Section 2 tab in *Writer's Notebook, Intermediate*) or chart paper prepared with the chart shown in this lesson, one entry filled in
- document camera (optional)
- writer's notebooks
- markers

Academic Language / Important Vocabulary

- writer's notebook
- memorable
- words
- phrases
- inspire

Continuum Connection

- Continue to learn from other writers by borrowing ways with words, phrases, and sentences
- Have topics and ideas for writing in a list or notebook
- Attend to the language and craft of other writers in order to learn more as a writer

GOAL

Collect memorable words and phrases from authors to inspire writing.

RATIONALE

When students learn how to collect memorable words and phrases from authors they love in their writer's notebook, they also learn to use memorable words and phrases in their own writing.

WRITER'S NOTEBOOK/WRITING FOLDER

Students will collect memorable words, quotes, and phrases in their writer's notebooks to use as inspiration for their writing.

ASSESS LEARNING

- Look for evidence that students collect memorable words and phrases in their writer's notebooks and use them to inspire their own writing.
- Notice evidence that they can use vocabulary such as *writer's notebook*, *memorable*, *words*, *phrases*, and *inspire*.

MINILESSON

Students will need their writer's notebooks for the minilesson. To help students think about the minilesson principle, use your own writer's notebook entry to model how to collect memorable language. Here is an example.

- Display the prepared chart paper or your writer's notebook entry.

    What do you notice about what I've written?

- Support students in recognizing that you have written some of the language you like and the name of the author who wrote it.

    When we read *Storm in the Night*, I noticed some special, or memorable, words and phrases. I wrote them down to remember them.

- Model the process of writing down why you found the words memorable, thinking aloud as you do.

    These words were special to me because they reminded me of the stories my grandpa used to tell me. Also, I love the sound of "carrot-colored flames."

    Turn and talk to your partner about how you think this author's writing could help you with your writing.

- After a short time for discussion, ask students to share what they talked about.

    When you collect memorable words and phrases, you can use them to inspire your own writing.

- Add a few notes in the *Why I Love It* column.

WML1
WPS.U3.WML1

Have a Try

Invite students to write a few memorable words or phrases in their writer's notebooks.

- Read page 9 from *Storm in the Night*.

    What memorable words or phrases caught your attention?

    Turn to the back of the Section 2 tab in your writer's notebook. Write a word or phrase that caught your attention. Add the author's name and a note about why you love that word or phrase.

- After a brief time, ask a few volunteers to share. Add responses to the chart.

Memorable Words/ Quotes/Phrases (include author's name)	Why I Love It
"carrot-colored flames" "a tale of when I was a boy" —Mary Stolz	The words remind me of my grandpa's stories.
"chiming clock" "ping, ping, ping" "siren whined in the distance" —Mary Stolz	The sound words are fun. I can write a story with sound words.

Summarize and Apply

Summarize the learning. Remind students to collect memorable words and phrases to use as resources for their writing.

   During writing time today, add another memorable word or phrase to this section from a book we read together or one you are reading on your own. Or, if you get a writing idea from one of the words or phrases you have written in your notebook, write about it on the next clean page in Section 4. Bring your writer's notebook to share when we meet later.

Confer

- During independent writing, move around the room to confer briefly with students about their notebook entries. Use prompts such as the following as needed.
    - *Why do you love this phrase? Make a note about that.*
    - *How might you use this word in your writing?*
    - *Let's look through the book you are reading and talk about a memorable word or phrase to add to your writer's notebook.*

Share

Following independent writing, gather students in the meeting area to share their notebook entries.

   As I point to you, share one memorable word or phrase from your list. If you hear a word or phrase that you like, add it to your own writer's notebook.

WML 2

WPS.U3.WML2

Writing Minilesson Principle
Use poems to inspire writing ideas.

Writer's Notebook: Getting Inspiration from Writers and Artists

You Will Need

- a copy of a short poem glued onto the first page in Section 2 of your writer's notebook and into each student's writer's notebook (p. 42 in *Writer's Notebook, Intermediate*)
- writer's notebooks
- document camera (optional)
- chart paper and markers

Academic Language / Important Vocabulary

- writer's notebook
- poem
- inspire

Continuum Connection

- Continue to learn from other writers by borrowing ways with words, phrases, and sentences
- Use a writer's notebook or booklet as a tool for collecting ideas, experimenting, planning, sketching, or drafting
- Use sketching, webs, lists, and freewriting to think about, plan for, and try out writing
- Understand that a writer gains ideas from other writers but should credit the other writers and/or put these ideas in one's own words
- Attend to the language and craft of other writers in order to learn more as a writer

GOAL
Collect poems in a writer's notebook to inspire writing ideas.

RATIONALE
Poems provide ideas and examples of memorable language that can inspire ideas for writing. Show students how to collect and respond to poems in their writer's notebooks to spark writing ideas.

WRITER'S NOTEBOOK/WRITING FOLDER
Students will learn to find ideas for writing from poems they collect in their writer's notebooks.

ASSESS LEARNING

- Look for evidence that students collect poems to inspire writing ideas.
- Notice evidence that they can use vocabulary such as *writer's notebook*, *poem*, and *inspire*.

MINILESSON

Students will need their writer's notebooks for the minilesson. To help students think about the minilesson principle, model how to use the writer's notebook pages to get ideas from poems. Below is an example.

- Display the poem. Talk about how you responded to it.

    In your writer's notebook, there is a poem glued into Section 2. There are many ways that you can get ideas for writing from poems, and we are going to try out a few ways today. Watch what I do.

- Draw a speech bubble that points to part of the poem that inspires an idea for writing. In the speech bubble, tell about why you are inspired by that part of the poem.

    You notice that I added a speech bubble that points to a part of the poem that gives me an idea for writing. I like the idea of imagining raindrops in a race. What part of the poem inspires you and why? Turn and talk about that.

- After time for a brief discussion, ask a few students to share.

    Now it is your turn to write in your writer's notebook. Choose a part of the poem that you like or that makes you stop and think. Add a speech bubble to that part and write about what you love or why you are inspired by that part of the poem.

WML2
WPS.U3.WML2

Have a Try

Invite students to notice ways they can use poems for inspiration.

> A speech bubble is just one way to find an idea from a poem to write about. Turn and talk to your partner about other ways that you might use poems to get ideas for writing.

▶ If you are using *Writer's Notebook, Intermediate*, have students browse the pages in Section 2 headed Use Poems to Inspire Writing. After time for partners to talk, ask students to share their ideas. Make a list on chart paper and add the principle to the chart.

Summarize and Apply

Summarize the learning and remind students to use their writer's notebooks to collect poems to get ideas for writing.

> During writing time today, add another speech bubble to the poem, or find a different poem, glue it into your writer's notebook, and respond to it. Bring your writer's notebook to share when we meet later.

Confer

▶ During independent writing, move around the room to confer briefly with students to discuss their responses to poems. Use prompts such as the following as needed.

- How will you use your writer's notebook to write about this poem?
- What does this poem make you think about?
- Why do you love this part of the poem?

Share

Following independent writing, gather students in pairs in the meeting area to talk about using poems for inspiration.

> Turn to your partner and share what you wrote in your writer's notebook today.

Use Poems to Inspire Writing

> How fast are raindrops?

Rain Showers
Pitter patter splat!
Water races to the ground
Forming mini lakes.

Use poems to inspire writing ideas.

- Comment on a poem with a speech bubble.
- Make a list of ideas the poem makes you think about.
- Make a sketch inspired by a poem.
- Write a poem in response to a poem.
- Write about the poem's message.

Section 5: Writing Process

Umbrella 3: Writer's Notebook: Getting Inspiration from Writers and Artists

WML3
WPS.U3.WML3

Writing Minilesson Principle
Use books or parts of books to inspire writing ideas.

Writer's Notebook: Getting Inspiration from Writers and Artists

You Will Need

- two familiar mentor texts, such as the following from Text Set: The Importance of Kindness:
  - *Last Day Blues* by Julie Danneberg
  - *Under the Lemon Moon* by Edith Hope Fine
- writer's notebooks
- document camera (optional)
- chart paper and markers

Academic Language / Important Vocabulary

- writer's notebook
- books
- inspire
- quick write
- opening line

Continuum Connection

- Continue to learn from other writers by borrowing ways with words, phrases, and sentences
- Use sketching, webs, lists, and freewriting to think about, plan for, and try out writing
- Understand that a writer gains ideas from other writers but should credit the other writers and/or put these ideas in one's own words
- Attend to the language and craft of other writers in order to learn more as a writer

---

GOAL

Collect writing ideas from books and list them in a writer's notebook.

RATIONALE

Writers are a source of inspiration for each other. Show students how to collect and respond in their writer's notebooks to a whole book or a line or passage from a book to spark writing ideas. Once you teach them how, they can do it on their own.

WRITER'S NOTEBOOK/WRITING FOLDER

Students will learn to use their writer's notebooks to collect ideas for writing that they get from books.

ASSESS LEARNING

- Look for evidence that students collect ideas for writing inspired by books or parts of books in their writer's notebooks.
- Notice evidence that they can use vocabulary such as *writer's notebook*, *books*, *inspire*, *quick write*, and *opening line*.

MINILESSON

Students will need their writer's notebooks for the minilesson. To help students think about the minilesson principle, model how to use the writer's notebook pages to get ideas from books. Below is an example.

- Before the lesson, read a familiar book or part of a familiar book that lends itself to writing a response, such as *Last Day Blues*.
- Have students open their writer's notebooks to Section 2 (p. 48 in *Writer's Notebook, Intermediate*).

  > Let's do a quick write in response to *Last Day Blues*. Write down anything this book made you think about.

- Write alongside them in your own notebook or on chart paper. After several minutes, read what you wrote and ask a few volunteers to share what they wrote.

  > Turn to Section 4 in your writer's notebook. If you hear something that a classmate shares that inspires an idea for you, write the idea on your ideas list.

Have a Try

Invite students to use an opening line from a book for writing inspiration.

▶ Show (project) an interesting first line from a familiar book, such as *Under the Lemon Moon*.

> Another way to get an idea for writing is to write the first line of a book and then write something about it. Let's try this with the first line in *Under the Lemon Moon*, which says, "Deep in the night, Rosalinda heard noises."

▶ Have students turn to Section 2 in their writer's notebooks and write the opening line and the author's name (p. 50 in *Writer's Notebook, Intermediate*). Then have them write their thoughts about the line or use the line to begin a new story. Write alongside them in your notebook or on chart paper. After a few minutes, ask a few students to share what they wrote.

> **Use books or parts of books to inspire writing ideas.**
> - Write something the story makes you think about.
> - Write about a time you felt the same way as a character in the story.
> - Use an opening line and write a story from that.

Summarize and Apply

Summarize the learning. Remind students that they can use books as inspiration for writing.

> What are some ways you can use books to inspire your writing ideas?

▶ Write the principle at the top of the chart paper and begin a list of ideas.

> When you write today, add on to what you started in your writer's notebook, or choose part of another book you love and try doing one of the things you learned. Bring your notebook to share when we meet later.

Confer

▶ During independent writing, move around the room to confer briefly with students about their notebook entries. Use prompts such as the following as needed.
- *What does this part of the book make you think about?*
- *What part of the book will you use for inspiration?*
- *Is there something you could write about the main character?*

Share

Following independent writing, gather students in the meeting area to share their writing.

> Who would like to share what you wrote in your writer's notebook today?

Umbrella 3: Writer's Notebook: Getting Inspiration from Writers and Artists

WML 4
WPS.U3.WML4

Writing Minilesson Principle
Use song lyrics to inspire writing ideas.

Writer's Notebook: Getting Inspiration from Writers and Artists

You Will Need

- recordings of two songs your students will enjoy
- copies of the lyrics for the two songs glued into your writer's notebook and each student's writer's notebook
- writer's notebooks
- chart paper and markers

Academic Language / Important Vocabulary

- writer's notebook
- song
- lyrics
- inspire
- inspiration

Continuum Connection

- Choose topics that are interesting to the writer
- Use a writer's notebook or booklet as a tool for collecting ideas, experimenting, planning, sketching, or drafting
- Use sketching, webs, lists, and freewriting to think about, plan for, and try out writing
- Understand that a writer gains ideas from other writers but should credit the other writers and/or put these ideas in one's own words
- Have topics and ideas for writing in a list or notebook

GOAL

Understand that writers can use song lyrics to inspire writing ideas.

RATIONALE

Song lyrics can inspire thinking that in turn can be used as the basis of some writing. Show students how to collect and respond in their writer's notebooks to song lyrics to spark writing ideas. Once you teach them how, they can do it on their own.

WRITER'S NOTEBOOK/WRITING FOLDER

Students will learn to use their writer's notebooks to collect ideas for writing that they get from song lyrics.

ASSESS LEARNING

- Look for evidence that students are using their writer's notebooks to collect and reflect on song lyrics to inspire writing ideas.
- Notice evidence that they can use vocabulary such as *writer's notebook*, *song*, *lyrics*, *inspire*, and *inspiration*.

MINILESSON

Students will need their writer's notebooks for the minilesson. To help students think about the minilesson principle, model how to use the writer's notebook pages to get ideas from songs. Glue one song in Section 2 (p. 54 in *Writer's Notebook, Intermediate*) and the other on the next empty page in Section 4. Below is an example.

- Have students turn to the first set of lyrics in Section 2 of their writer's notebooks.

    Turn to Section 2 in your writer's notebook. Follow along with these lyrics as we listen to the song.

- This example uses "Take Me Out to the Ball Game" sung by Harry Caray. Play the recording of the first song as students follow along with the lyrics. Then offer your thoughts.

    I have always loved this song because I love baseball. This song mentions snacks, so it also makes me think about eating popcorn while I watch movies with my family. That is something I might sketch in my writer's notebook.

    What does this song make you think about? Make a sketch about that on the next page in your writer's notebook.

- Make your own sketch while students are making their sketches.
- After a few minutes, ask a few volunteers to share their sketches.

WML 4
WPS.U3.WML4

Have a Try

Invite students to use their writer's notebooks to respond to song lyrics.

▸ Have students turn to the lyrics for the second song in their writer's notebooks as you play the recording.

> What do these song lyrics mean to you? What do they make you think about? This time, write about that in your notebook while I write about it in mine.

▸ After students have had time to get started, ask a few volunteers to share what they are writing about.

Summarize and Apply

Summarize the learning and remind students to use song lyrics as inspiration for writing.

> What are some ways you can use song lyrics to inspire your writing ideas?

▸ Write the principle at the top of the chart paper and then begin a list of ideas.

> When you write today, add on to what you started in your writer's notebook. Or, choose lyrics of another song you love and try doing one of the things you learned. Bring your writer's notebook to share when we meet later.

▸ Revisit the chart at a later time and add to the ideas.

> **Use song lyrics to inspire writing ideas.**
> - Sketch something the song makes you think of.
> - Write what the lyrics mean to you.
> - Write what the lyrics make you think about.

Confer

▸ During independent writing, move around the room to confer briefly with students about their responses to song lyrics. Use prompts such as the following as needed.
  - *What does this song make you think about?*
  - *What part of the song will you use for inspiration?*

Share

Following independent writing, gather students in the meeting area to talk about their notebook entries.

> Turn to your partner and share what you wrote in your writer's notebook.

WML 5
WPS.U3.WML5

Writing Minilesson Principle
Use art to inspire writing ideas.

Writer's Notebook: Getting Inspiration from Writers and Artists

You Will Need

- two examples of art (e.g., student drawings, famous paintings, sculptures)
- writer's notebooks
- document camera (optional)
- chart paper and markers

Academic Language / Important Vocabulary

- writer's notebook
- art
- sketch
- inspire

Continuum Connection

- Use a writer's notebook or booklet as a tool for collecting ideas, experimenting, planning, sketching, or drafting
- Use sketching, webs, lists, and freewriting to think about, plan for, and try out writing
- Have topics and ideas for writing in a list or notebook

GOAL

Understand that writers can use works of art to inspire writing ideas.

RATIONALE

Although art, whether professional or amateur, is a visual medium, it can prompt thoughts that can be used for writing. Teach students how to reflect on and respond to a piece of art in their writer's notebooks. Once you teach them how, they can do it on their own.

WRITER'S NOTEBOOK/WRITING FOLDER

Students will learn to use their writer's notebooks to collect ideas for writing that they get from art.

ASSESS LEARNING

- Look for evidence that students are using their writers' notebooks to reflect on art to inspire writing ideas.
- Notice evidence that they can use vocabulary such as *writer's notebook*, *art*, *sketch*, and *inspire*.

MINILESSON

Students will need their writer's notebooks for the minilesson. To help students think about the minilesson principle, model how to use the writer's notebook pages to get ideas from art. Below is an example based on using students' paintings.

- Show the first art piece you have selected. Prepare students to sketch the main idea of the art. Have students turn to Section 2 in their writer's notebooks (p. 56 in *Writer's Notebook, Intermediate*).

  You can draw and write ideas you get from art in your writer's notebooks.

  Look at this painting. What is it mainly about? Make a sketch to show that.

- After a moment to draw, ask a few volunteers to share their sketches.

  Now turn to the next page in your writer's notebook and write three things that the art makes you think about. I will be doing the same thing in my notebook.

- After students have had some time to get started, pause and ask a few volunteers to share ideas.

Have a Try

Invite students to use their writer's notebooks to respond to art.

▸ Show another piece of art.

> Turn to the next clean page in Section 4 of your writer's notebook. Write the date and then make a quick sketch to remind yourself of the art. Then write about what you would see or do if you were in the painting. Or, write about a story the painting makes you think about.

▸ After students have had time to get started, ask a few volunteers to share what they are writing about.

Summarize and Apply

Summarize the learning and remind students to use art as inspiration for writing.

> What are some ways you can use art to inspire your writing ideas?

▸ Write the principle at the top of the chart paper. Then begin a list of ideas.

> When you write today, you can add on to what you started in your writer's notebook. Or, you can choose a different piece of art and try doing one of the ideas you learned for writing about art.

▸ Revisit the chart at a later time and add to the ideas.

Use art to inspire writing ideas.

- Write three things the art makes you think about.
- Write about what you would see or do if you were in the painting.
- Write a story the art makes you think about.

Confer

▸ During independent writing, move around the room to confer briefly with students about how they might use art to inspire writing. Use prompts such as the following as needed.
- *Tell about what you are writing in your notebook.*
- *What does this sculpture make you think about?*
- *Which magazine photo will you use for inspiration?*

Share

Following independent writing, gather students in the meeting area to talk about their writing.

> Who would like to share what you wrote in your writer's notebook today?

Umbrella 3

Writer's Notebook: Getting Inspiration from Writers and Artists

Assessment

After you have taught the minilessons in this umbrella, observe students as they write and talk about their writing. Use *The Fountas & Pinnell Literacy Continuum* to notice, teach for, and support students' learning as you observe their attempts at writing.

- What evidence do you have of students' new understandings related to using a writer's notebook?
  - Are they collecting memorable words and phrases in their writer's notebook?
  - Do they use poems to inspire writing?
  - Are they using books or parts of books for writing ideas?
  - Do they use song lyrics for writing inspiration?
  - Are they using art to generate writing ideas?
  - Do they understand and use vocabulary such as *writer's notebook, memorable, words, phrases, inspire, poems, inspiration, books, quick write, opening line, song, lyrics, art,* and *sketch*?
- In what other ways, beyond the scope of this umbrella, are students using a writer's notebook?
  - Do they collect ideas and artifacts from their own lives to inspire writing?
  - Do they use a writer's notebook to try out ideas?

Use your observations to determine the next umbrella you will teach. You may also consult Suggested Sequence of Lessons (pp. 605–622) for guidance.

EXTENSIONS FOR WRITER'S NOTEBOOK: GETTING INSPIRATION FROM WRITERS AND ARTISTS

- From time to time while reading aloud, suggest that students listen for memorable words or phrases and write them in their writer's notebooks.

- Make sure students know that any of the writing activities they do in the first three sections of the writer's notebook can be repeated with different ideas in Section 4.

- Revisit WML4 with a song that is popular with your students and have them write a poem or story inspired by the lyrics.

- Do a virtual field trip at a museum and have students use writer's notebooks to make a quick sketch of an art piece they enjoyed so they might write about it later.

Writer's Notebook: Becoming an Expert

Umbrella 4

Minilessons in This Umbrella

- **WML1** Make lists of topics you know, are interested in, and care about.
- **WML2** Use webs to focus a topic.
- **WML3** Make a list of questions and wonderings you have about a topic.
- **WML4** Take notes in your own words about your topic.
- **WML5** Interview or watch an expert on your topic and take notes.
- **WML6** Choose and sketch a few objects to represent the big ideas of your topic.

Writer's Notebook

Before Teaching Umbrella 4 Minilessons

The purpose of the minilessons in this umbrella is to help students use the tools in their writer's notebooks to plan and prepare for nonfiction writing. Teach these lessons as students prepare to make informational books (GEN.U6). Students should already know the topic they will write about. Students who haven't already chosen a topic will find WML1 helpful.

Prepare a writer's notebook for each student. The minilessons in this umbrella refer to Section 3, Becoming an Expert, in *Writer's Notebook, Intermediate* (Fountas and Pinnell 2023). If you are using a plain notebook, prepare a section for the students in which they can make webs, take notes, and list questions to explore and learn about a topic (see p. 86). As some of the lessons in this umbrella are lengthy and involve multiple steps, you may want to break them down and teach them over a few days.

Before teaching this umbrella, you will also want to read and discuss engaging informational books about a variety of topics about which students will be interested in learning more.

As you read and enjoy informational texts together, help students

- talk about what they learn from each text,
- share their questions and wonderings about the topics, and
- discuss their own ideas for writing.

WML1
WPS.U4.WML1

Writing Minilesson Principle
Make lists of topics you know, are interested in, and care about.

Writer's Notebook: Becoming an Expert

You Will Need

- your writer's notebook (the Section 3 tab and p. 59 in *Writer's Notebook, Intermediate*) or two sheets of chart paper prepared with two-column charts:
  - *Topics I Want to Learn More About* and a list of a few topics you are interested in
  - *Use Lists to Get Ideas for Topics You Want to Learn About* and the beginning of a list of interesting facts
- markers
- document camera (optional)
- writer's notebooks

Academic Language / Important Vocabulary

- writer's notebook
- topic
- fascinate

Continuum Connection

- Use a writer's notebook or booklet as a tool for collecting ideas, experimenting, planning, sketching, or drafting
- Use sketching, webs, lists, and freewriting to think about, plan for, and try out writing

GOAL
Make a list of topics of interest to inspire writing ideas for nonfiction writing.

RATIONALE
When students keep a list of topics they want to learn more about, it helps them become better aware of their own interests and what they care about and have a source of ideas for informational writing. They will be more likely to write well about topics they are interested in, will be more engaged in the writing process, and will write with more voice.

WRITER'S NOTEBOOK/WRITING FOLDER
Students will list topics and facts in their writer' notebooks to build a collection of ideas for writing nonfiction.

ASSESS LEARNING
- Notice whether they refer to their lists when choosing a topic for writing.
- Look for evidence that they can use vocabulary such as *writer's notebook*, *topic*, and *fascinate*.

MINILESSON

Students will need their writer's notebooks for the minilesson. To help students think about the minilesson principle, share and discuss your own topics of interest, and then invite students to write down and share their own. Below is an example. This lesson uses Section 3, Becoming an Expert.

- Display the chart paper prepared with the title *Topics I Want to Learn More About* (or project your writer's notebook page).

  You will use your writer's notebook to keep a list of topics you want to know more about. Anytime you come across a topic you would like to learn more about, you can put it on your list.

- Tell students about the topics you wrote on your list.

  I thought about topics I know something about and care about and that I want to learn more about. I care about cats because I have a cat. I would like to learn more about cats. I also know and care about history because I've read a lot of books about it, and it's one of my favorite things to learn about. I'd like to learn more about different periods of history.

- Invite students to start making a list of topics they want to know more about in their writer's notebook.

  Who would like to share some of the topics you wrote on your list?

  Why might it be helpful to you, as a writer, to make a list of topics you want to know more about?

  Making lists of topics you want to know more about can help you get ideas for things to write about.

The Writing Minilessons Book, Grade 3

WML1
WPS.U4.WML1

Have a Try

Invite students to talk in triads about facts they know and care about.

▸ Display the chart paper (or project p. 59 in *Writer's Notebook, Intermediate*) prepared with the title *Use Lists to Get Ideas for Topics You Want to Learn About*.

> I wrote these facts on a list in my writer's notebook because I want to know more about them and might write about them. Talk to two classmates about these facts or another that you know. Write a fact that interests you in your writer's notebook.

▸ After students turn and talk, invite a few students to share.

Summarize and Apply

Summarize the learning and remind students to make lists of topics they want to learn more about.

> Any time you think of a new topic or fact that interests you, add it to your lists. Look at these lists to get ideas for your writing when you are choosing a topic for a nonfiction piece.

> During writing time today, write a few interesting topics and facts that fascinate you in Section 3 of your writer's notebook. You can look at books you have read for interesting facts that make you want to learn more about a topic.

Confer

▸ During independent writing, move around the room to confer briefly with students about topics and facts that interest them. Use prompts such as the following as needed.
- *What are some topics you want to know more about?*
- *What do you like to read books about?*
- *What interesting facts have you learned recently?*
- *What does that make you want to learn more about?*

Share

Following independent writing, gather students in the meeting area to share their lists. Ask students to each share one topic they wrote in their writer's notebooks.

> Is there anything you heard that you would like to add to your own list?

Topics I Want to Learn More About

Cats	Dolphins
History	Knights
Tornadoes	Albert Einstein
Bats	Butterflies

Use Lists to Get Ideas for Topics You Want to Learn About

Facts That Fascinate	This fact makes me want to learn more about . . .
The human heart beats around 100,000 times a day.	How our hearts work
There are more than 1,000 kinds of bats in the world.	Different kinds of bats
An ostrich's eye is bigger than its brain.	Ostriches

WML2
WPS.U4.WML2

Writing Minilesson Principle
Use webs to focus a topic.

Writer's Notebook: Becoming an Expert

You Will Need

- two sheets of chart paper prepared with blank webs
- markers
- an idea for a topic for a nonfiction book
- writer's notebooks

Academic Language / Important Vocabulary

- writer's notebook
- web
- focus
- subtopic
- topic

Continuum Connection

- Use a writer's notebook or booklet as a tool for collecting ideas, experimenting, planning, sketching, or drafting
- Use sketching, webs, lists, and freewriting to think about, plan for, and try out writing

GOAL

Use webs as a tool to explore and narrow down ideas for topics for nonfiction writing.

RATIONALE

A web can be a useful tool for deciding on the focus of a topic for nonfiction writing. Students will begin by using a web to think about the "big ideas" of a topic and then use additional webs to explore each idea in further detail. This will help them decide whether to write about a large topic more generally or a subtopic more deeply.

WRITER'S NOTEBOOK/WRITING FOLDER

Students will make webs in their writer's notebooks to explore and focus a topic in preparation for nonfiction writing.

ASSESS LEARNING

- Notice whether students are able to use a web to focus a topic for writing.
- Look for evidence that they can use vocabulary such as *writer's notebook*, *web*, *focus*, *subtopic*, and *topic*.

MINILESSON

To help students think about the principle, model using webs to decide the focus of a topic idea. Below is an example. If you are using *Writer's Notebook, Intermediate*, the webs are on pages 60 and 61.

- Display the first blank web.

  You can use your writer's notebook to explore topics you're thinking of writing about. One of the topics I put on my list of topics is cats.

- Write *Cats* in the center of the web. Think aloud as you fill in the web.

  I have a cat, so I know about taking care of a pet cat and what a cat's body looks like. I know that there are lots of different kinds of cats, like house cats, lions, tigers, and leopards. I also saw an interesting museum exhibit about cats in Ancient Egypt, so I could write something about that.

  There are a lot of smaller topics, or subtopics, on my web! I could write about all of them, but that's a lot. I could choose to focus on just one subtopic instead. For example, I could write about how to get and own a pet cat.

- Display the second blank web, and write *Taking Care of a Pet Cat* in the center. Model thinking aloud about what to write on the spokes.

  What do I know about getting and owning cats? I could write about how to adopt a pet cat, feed a cat, play with a cat, and clean a cat's litter box. What did you notice about how I used webs to explore my topic, cats?

- Save the webs for WML3.

WML 2
WPS.U4.WML2

Have a Try

Invite students to make a web to explore a topic in their writer's notebooks (p. 60 in *Writer's Notebook, Intermediate*).

> Choose a topic from your list. In your writer's notebook, write the topic in the center of a web. Then write all the things you already know about the topic at the ends of the spokes. Turn and talk to your partner about what you wrote.

Summarize and Apply

Help students summarize the learning and invite them to use webs to help them focus a topic (pp. 61–62 in *Writer's Notebook, Intermediate*).

> Why is it helpful to use webs to explore a topic? How could this help you as a writer?

▸ Write the principle at the top of the chart.

> Today during writing time, look at the web you just made. Choose one of the subtopics on your web and make a new web with that subtopic at the center. Write down all the different things you know about that subtopic. Then do the same thing with another subtopic. Finally, look at all your webs and decide what you would like to write about.

Use webs to focus a topic.

```
            Body parts
             of cats
                |
Getting and    |         Cats in
 owning a ── Cats ── Ancient
  pet cat      |         Egypt
                |
         Different kinds of cats
```

```
            Feeding a cat
                 |
Adopting    Getting      Playing with
 a cat ── and owning ──    a cat
            a Pet
             Cat
                 |
         Cleaning a litter box
```

Confer

▸ During independent writing, move around the room to confer briefly with students about their webs. Use prompts such as the following as needed.

- What topic did you make a web about?
- Which subtopic would you like to explore in greater detail?
- Is there enough or too much information about that subtopic to write about?
- Would you like to write a book about the whole topic or one of the subtopics you explored? Which subtopic? Why?

Share

Following independent writing, gather students in the meeting area to share their webs with a partner.

> Talk with your partner about how using webs helped you decide what to write about. Show each other your web.

Umbrella 4: Writer's Notebook: Becoming an Expert

Section 5: Writing Process

WML3
WPS.U4.WML3

Writing Minilesson Principle
Make a list of questions and wonderings you have about a topic.

Writer's Notebook: Becoming an Expert

You Will Need

- the webs from WML2
- chart paper and markers
- writer's notebooks

Academic Language / Important Vocabulary

- writer's notebook
- question
- wondering
- topic

Continuum Connection

- Use a writer's notebook or booklet as a tool for collecting ideas, experimenting, planning, sketching, or drafting
- Use sketching, webs, lists, and freewriting to think about, plan for, and try out writing

GOAL

Make a list of questions and wonderings about a topic to help define the research focus.

RATIONALE

Making a list of questions and wonderings about a topic helps students identify their specific areas of interest and gaps in their knowledge, which in turn will help them to know what to look for when they do research on the topic.

WRITER'S NOTEBOOK/WRITING FOLDER

Students will explore their topics further by writing questions and wonderings in their writer's notebooks.

ASSESS LEARNING

- Notice whether students make lists of questions and wonderings about a topic.
- Look for evidence that they can use vocabulary such as *writer's notebook*, *question*, *wondering*, and *topic*.

MINILESSON

To help students think about the principle, model making a list of questions and wonderings about a topic. Here is an example.

- Display the webs from WML2.

    I made webs to help me decide the focus of my nonfiction book about cats. I thought about what I already know about this topic, and I decided to write about getting and owning a pet cat. There is a lot I already know about this topic, but there's also a lot that I don't know—and that I need to find out before I write my book. I'm going to think about what questions and wonderings I have about my topic. I wrote on my web *Adopting a cat*. I know that you can adopt a cat from a shelter or a breeder. But I have questions about cat adoption. Is it better to adopt a kitten or an adult cat? How can I choose the cat that is right for me? I'm going to write my questions in my writer's notebook so I'll remember to do research to find the answers.

    What questions do you have about getting and owning a pet cat? What do you wonder about this topic?

- Record each question and wondering discussed on chart paper.

Have a Try

Invite students to start making a list of questions and wonderings in their writer's notebooks (p. 64 in *Writer's Notebook, Intermediate*).

> Turn to Section 3 in your writer's notebook. Look at the webs you made. What do you already know about your topic? What do you want to find out? Write one or two questions you have or things you wonder about your topic. Then turn and talk to share your questions with your partner. Ask your partner if there is another question to add to your list.

▸ After students turn and talk, invite a few students to share their questions and wonderings.

> **Make a list of questions and wonderings you have about a topic.**
> - Is it better to adopt a kitten or an adult cat?
> - How can I choose the cat that is right for me?
> - I wonder if it is better to adopt one or two cats at a time.
> - If I already have a dog, can I get a cat too?
> - What kind of food should I feed my cat?
> - I wonder how to tell if my cat is happy.
> - Should I let my cat go outside?
> - I wonder what it means when my cat swishes her tail.

Summarize and Apply

Write the principle at the top of the chart. Summarize the learning and invite students to add to their list of questions and wonderings.

> Why is it helpful to make a list of questions and wonderings about a topic before you write about the topic?

> Making a list of questions and wonderings will help you know what to look for when you research your topic. When you write today, spend some more time thinking about your topic. What other questions or wonderings do you have? Add them to your list. Bring your list to share when we come back together.

Confer

▸ During independent writing, move around the room to confer briefly with students about their questions and wonderings. Use prompts such as the following as needed.
- *What do you want to learn about _____?*
- *What do you wonder about your topic?*
- *Is there anything you think you know about your topic but that you need to check to make sure it's correct?*

Share

Following independent writing, gather students in the meeting area to share their lists.

> Who would like to share your list of questions and wonderings?

WML 4
WPS.U4.WML4

Writing Minilesson Principle
Take notes in your own words about your topic.

Writer's Notebook: Becoming an Expert

You Will Need

- a topic for a model nonfiction text (e.g., cats)
- a book or website about the topic
- chart paper and markers
- sticky notes
- writer's notebooks

Academic Language / Important Vocabulary

- writer's notebook
- topic
- note

Continuum Connection

- Understand that to write an expository text, the writer needs to become very knowledgeable about a topic
- Use a writer's notebook or booklet as a tool for collecting ideas, experimenting, planning, sketching, or drafting
- Use sketching, webs, lists, and freewriting to think about, plan for, and try out writing

GOAL

Learn to take notes on a topic without copying the author's words.

RATIONALE

When you teach students to conduct research for their nonfiction writing, they begin to understand that nonfiction authors must first learn about a topic before they can write about it. They learn that anyone can become an expert on a topic with the right tools.

WRITER'S NOTEBOOK/WRITING FOLDER

Students will use their writer's notebooks to take notes about their topics.

ASSESS LEARNING

- Notice whether students take notes in their writer's notebooks using their own words.
- Look for evidence that they can use vocabulary such as *writer's notebook*, *topic*, and *note*.

MINILESSON

To help students think about the principle, model gathering information about a topic and taking concise notes in your own words. Here is an example.

> Now that I have my topic and I know what I need to learn about it, I will find out more information by reading and taking notes about what I learn.

- Display a book or website about your topic. Read a short section aloud, and think aloud about the notes you will take.

> This website recommends getting two kittens instead of one. It gives several reasons for this: two kittens can play together, keep each other company, and will learn better behavior. I'd like to remember this information, so I'm going to write it in my writer's notebook. I don't want to write down everything the website says, just the most important ideas. I'm going to write these ideas in my own words on a sticky note, so I can move the sticky notes around when it comes time to organize my notes.

- Model writing the notes on sticky notes and placing them on chart paper or in your writer's notebook (p. 66 in *Writer's Notebook, Intermediate*).
- Continue in a similar manner with at least one more section of text.

> What did you notice about how I took notes about my topic?

> When it's time for me to write about cats, I will have this information to use.

Have a Try

Invite students to talk to a partner about taking notes.

- Read aloud another section of text.

  What information might I want to remember from this section? What could I write in my writer's notebook? Turn and talk to your partner about this.

- After students turn and talk, invite a few pairs to share their thinking. Write the suggested notes on sticky notes and place them on the chart paper.

Summarize and Apply

Write the principle at the top of the chart. Summarize the learning. Students will need access to information about their topics so that they can take notes in their writer's notebooks (p. 66 in *Writer's Notebook, Intermediate*).

  What did you learn today about how and why to take notes?

  During writing time today, look for information about your topic in books or on the internet. Then write short notes on sticky notes and put them in your writer's notebook. Remember to use your own words when you write the notes. Bring your notebook to share when we meet later.

Confer

- During independent writing, move around the room to confer briefly with students about taking notes for their informational books. Use prompts such as the following as needed.
  - Where might you find information about _____?
  - What does that book say about _____?
  - What could you write in your writer's notebook to help you remember that?
  - How could you put that in your own words?

Share

Following independent writing, gather students in the meeting area to share their research in groups of three.

  Take turns talking about the notes you took.

WML 5
WPS.U4.WML5

Writing Minilesson Principle
Interview or watch an expert on your topic and take notes.

Writer's Notebook: Becoming an Expert

You Will Need

- a topic for a model nonfiction text (e.g., cats)
- a short video clip of an expert talking about the topic
- chart paper and markers
- writer's notebooks

Academic Language / Important Vocabulary

- writer's notebook
- expert
- interview
- topic
- notes

Continuum Connection

- Use a writer's notebook or booklet as a tool for collecting ideas, experimenting, planning, sketching, or drafting
- Use sketching, webs, lists, and freewriting to think about, plan for, and try out writing

GOAL

Develop questions to ask an expert about a topic.

RATIONALE

Developing questions before speaking with an expert, watching a video, or listening to a podcast helps students identify gaps in their knowledge and define the focus of their research. They will listen more attentively when they know exactly what information they are seeking.

WRITER'S NOTEBOOK/WRITING FOLDER

Students will write questions they would ask an expert in their writer's notebooks.

ASSESS LEARNING

- Notice whether students can develop productive questions to ask an expert.
- Observe whether the notes they take are useful and in their own words.
- Look for evidence that they can use vocabulary such as *writer's notebook*, *expert*, *interview*, *topic*, and *notes*.

MINILESSON

To help students think about the principle, guide them to develop questions they would want to ask an expert about a topic. Then play a short video clip or podcast about the topic and model taking notes. Here is an example.

> To become an expert on your topic, you might interview an expert. An expert is someone who knows a lot about a particular topic. What does it mean to interview someone?

> When you interview an expert, you ask questions and the expert answers them. If you can't find an expert to interview, you can also watch a video of an expert talking about your topic. I searched online for an expert on pet cats and found someone who has a lot of experience with cats and even made a video about cat behavior. Before we watch it, let's think about questions to ask about cat behavior. One question I have is "Why does my cat meow so much?"

- Write the question on chart paper. Then invite students to pose their own questions on the topic, and add them to the chart.

> Now that you've thought about questions to ask the expert, you are ready to watch the video. As you watch, pay attention and notice if any of your questions are answered. Take notes about what you are learning.

- Play the video. Pause regularly to help students notice when a question has been answered and to model taking notes about the answers.

> What did the expert say about why cats meow? What can you write down to help you remember this information?

The Writing Minilessons Book, Grade 3

Have a Try

Invite students to talk to a partner about interviewing an expert.

> Think of a question about your topic you would want to ask an expert. Turn and talk to your partner about that.

▸ After time for discussion, invite a few students to share their thinking.

Summarize and Apply

Write the principle at the top of the chart. Summarize the learning and invite students to develop questions they would want to ask an expert.

> Why is it important to write down your questions and notes about the expert's answers?

> Today during writing time, turn to Section 3 in your writer's notebook (p. 68 in *Writer's Notebook, Intermediate*). Write some questions you would like to ask an expert about your topic. Bring your questions to share when we come back together.

Interview or watch an expert on your topic and take notes.

1. Why does my cat meow so much?
   - hungry or wants attention
   - don't give in to meows

2. How can I stop my cat from scratching my things?
   - get a scratching post

3. How can I help my cat and dog get along?

4. Why does my cat hide under the bed?
   - scared or stressed

Confer

▸ During independent writing, move around the room to confer briefly with students about questions they would want to ask an expert. Use prompts such as the following as needed.

- *What kind of person would know a lot about _____?*
- *What would you want to ask?*
- *What are you wondering about?*

Share

Following independent writing, gather students in the meeting area to share their questions.

> What questions would you want to ask an expert about your topic?

> How could you find an expert who would be able to answer your questions?

WML 6
WPS.U4.WML6

Writing Minilesson Principle
Choose and sketch a few objects to represent the big ideas of your topic.

Writer's Notebook: Becoming an Expert

You Will Need

- a topic for a model nonfiction text (e.g., cats)
- chart paper and markers
- writer's notebooks
- To download the following online resource for this lesson, visit **fp.pub/resources**:
  - chart art (optional)

Academic Language / Important Vocabulary

- writer's notebook
- topic
- sketch
- object
- represent
- vocabulary

Continuum Connection

- Use some vocabulary specific to the topic
- Use a writer's notebook or booklet as a tool for collecting ideas, experimenting, planning, sketching, or drafting
- Use sketching, webs, lists, and freewriting to think about, plan for, and try out writing

---

GOAL

Choose and sketch a few important objects to focus thinking about a topic for nonfiction writing.

RATIONALE

Choosing and sketching a few important objects related to their topic can help students develop their thinking around their topic and decide what to include in their informational writing. It can also give them ideas for illustrations to include.

WRITER'S NOTEBOOK/WRITING FOLDER

Students will sketch objects and list vocabulary related to their topics in their writer's notebooks.

ASSESS LEARNING

- Notice whether students sketch important objects related to their topics.
- Look for evidence that they can use vocabulary such as *writer's notebook*, *topic*, *sketch*, *object*, *represent*, and *vocabulary*.

MINILESSON

Students will need their writer's notebooks for the lesson (p. 72 in *Writer's Notebook, Intermediate*). To help students think about the principle, model choosing and sketching a few objects related to your topic. Then invite students to begin sketching objects related to their own topics. Below is an example.

> You made webs and wrote questions in your writer's notebook to focus your thinking about your topic. Another way that you can think about your topic is to think about objects or things that are important to your topic. You can ask yourself, "What objects would help someone learn about my topic?" My topic is getting and owning a pet cat, so I started to think about what objects someone would need once they got a pet cat. They would need cat food, bowls for food and water, a litter box and litter, and maybe some cat toys or a scratching post. I'm going to sketch these important things so I remember to write about them in my book.

> Turn to Section 3 in your writer's notebook. As I sketch, think about objects that would help someone learn about your topic. Begin to sketch them in your writer's notebook.

- After students have had time to sketch, invite a few students to share their sketches.

    What did you sketch?

    Why is a _____ important to your topic?

WML 6

WPS.U4.WML6

Have a Try

Invite students to start making a list of topic-related vocabulary.

> If someone is thinking of getting a pet cat, I think they should know important words such as *shelter*, *breed*, *veterinarian*, *litter*, *behavior*, and *groom*. What vocabulary do you want people to know about your topic? Start making a list of these words in your writer's notebook.

- After a few minutes, invite a few students to share the vocabulary words they have written.

Summarize and Apply

Write the principle at the top of the chart. Summarize the learning and invite students to add to their sketches and lists.

> During writing time today, continue sketching important objects that represent your topic and adding important vocabulary words to your list. Later, when it comes time to write, your sketches and lists will help you remember what information you want to include in your writing. Bring your writer's notebook to share when we come back together.

Confer

- During independent writing, move around the room to confer briefly with students about how they are preparing to write an informational book. Use prompts such as the following as needed.
  - *What things or objects do you think of when you think of _____?*
  - *What objects would help someone learn about your topic?*
  - *Why is that object important to your topic?*
  - *What are some words readers should know about your topic?*

Share

Following independent writing, gather students in the meeting area to share their sketches and lists with a partner. Then choose several students to share with the group.

> Tell about the objects you drew and the words you wrote in your writer's notebook.

> Why is that object (word) important to your topic?

Choose and sketch a few objects to represent the big ideas of your topic.

Important Words About My Topic

- shelter
- breed
- veterinarian
- litter
- behavior
- groom

Section 5: Writing Process

Umbrella 4: Writer's Notebook: Becoming an Expert

Assessment

After you have taught the minilessons in this umbrella, observe students as they draw, write, and talk about their writing. Use *The Fountas & Pinnell Literacy Continuum* to notice, teach for, and support students' learning as you observe their preparation for informational writing.

- What evidence do you have of new understandings students have developed related to using the writer's notebook to prepare for and plan nonfiction writing?
    - Do students make lists of topics they are interested in writing about?
    - Do they use webs to decide the focus of an idea for nonfiction writing?
    - Do they make lists of questions and wonderings about topics?
    - Can they take notes about a topic in their own words?
    - Can they develop questions they would want to ask an expert about a topic?
    - Have they tried sketching objects that represent the big ideas of their topic?
    - Do students understand and use vocabulary such as *writer's notebook*, *list*, *topic*, *web*, *focus*, *notes*, and *interview*?
- In what other ways, beyond the scope of this umbrella, are students ready to explore nonfiction writing?
    - Are students interested in making a slide presentation or a photo essay?
    - Would they benefit from learning ways to expand their nonfiction writing?

Use your observations to determine the next umbrella you will teach. You may also consult Suggested Sequence of Lessons (pp. 605–622) for guidance.

EXTENSIONS FOR WRITER'S NOTEBOOK: BECOMING AN EXPERT

- Teach students how to organize information using different text structures (e.g., sequence, question and answer) and choose the text structure(s) most appropriate for their topic.
- Model how to conduct research using books and/or the internet effectively.
- Invite a local expert on a class science or social studies topic to give a presentation to your class. Have students develop questions in advance, and prepare them to take notes.

Thinking About Purpose, Audience, and Genre/Form

Umbrella 5

Minilessons in This Umbrella

WML1 Think about your purpose.
WML2 Think about your audience.
WML3 Think about the kind of writing you want to do.

Before Teaching Umbrella 5 Minilessons

The goal of this umbrella is to make students aware of the relationship between purpose, audience, and genre or form. Purpose and audience are separate ideas, yet they are intertwined because they both influence the type of writing (genre or form) an author chooses to engage in. Prior to beginning this umbrella, students should have an idea of the topic they want to write about so they can think about and make a connection between their purpose, audience, and genre (form). In order to help them make topic decisions, have students reread their writer's notebooks for ideas. As well, it is suggested that you have formally taught several genres. When thinking about audience, encourage students to think beyond the school community (see WML2). These minilessons build on each other, so it is recommended that you teach them in order.

Students should have read a variety of genres and talked about the choices that the writers made. For mentor texts, use the books listed below from *Fountas & Pinnell Classroom™ Interactive Read-Aloud Collection* or books from the classroom library.

Interactive Read-Aloud Collection

Genre Study: Expository Nonfiction

Bats! Strange and Wonderful by Laurence Pringle

Shell, Beak, Tusk: Shared Traits and the Wonders of Adaptation by Bridget Heos

Tornadoes! by Gail Gibbons

Author/Illustrator Study: Janell Cannon

Stellaluna

Crickwing

Author/Illustrator Study: Patricia Polacco

The Bee Tree

As you read and enjoy these texts together, help students

- talk about what purpose the author may have had for writing, and
- talk about who the writer's intended audience might be.

Interactive Read-Aloud
Expository Nonfiction

Janell Cannon

Patricia Polacco

Writer's Notebook

WML1

WPS.U5.WML1

Writing Minilesson Principle
Think about your purpose.

Thinking About Purpose, Audience, and Genre/Form

You Will Need

- two mentor texts that are on the same topic but from two different genres, such as the following:
  - *Bats!* by Laurence Pringle, from Text Set: Genre Study: Expository Nonfiction
  - *Stellaluna* by Janell Cannon, from Text Set: Author/Illustrator Study: Janell Cannon
- chart paper and markers
- writer's notebooks

Academic Language / Important Vocabulary

- reason
- topic
- purpose
- entertain
- give information

Continuum Connection

- Write for a specific purpose: e.g., to inform, entertain, persuade, reflect, instruct, retell, maintain relationships, plan
- Have clear goals and understand how the goals will affect the writing

GOAL

Understand that writers think about why they are writing and how they want their writing to affect their audience.

RATIONALE

When students understand that writers have a purpose for writing, they begin to think about why and what they want to write. They also learn that they have choices in their own writing. Giving students a choice in the topics to write about leads to increased motivation for writing and more authentic writing.

WRITER'S NOTEBOOK/WRITING FOLDER

Students can write their ideas about their purpose for writing in their writer's notebooks.

ASSESS LEARNING

- Observe whether students are talking about different purposes for writing.
- Look for evidence that students can use vocabulary such as *reason*, *topic*, *purpose*, *entertain*, and *give information*.

MINILESSON

To help students think about the minilesson principle, use mentor texts to engage them in a discussion about purposes for writing. Link that discussion to students' own purposes for writing. Here is an example.

- Prior to this lesson, students should have chosen a topic they want to write about.
- Show the covers and revisit a few pages of *Bats!* and *Stellaluna*.

  What is the topic of these two books?

  Why do you suppose Laurence Pringle chose to write *Bats!*?

  What about Janell Cannon—why do you think she wrote *Stellaluna*?

- Engage students in a conversation about the authors' purposes, guiding them to recognize that Laurence Pringle's purpose is to give information and Janell Cannon's purpose is to entertain by telling a story. Ensure that students recognize that the topic is the same (bats), but the purposes are different.

  A purpose is the reason for doing something. Before you write something, think about your purpose for writing.

- Begin a list of purposes for writing on chart paper and write *teach*, *give information*, *tell a story*, and *entertain* on the list.

  Think about some other purposes for writing. Turn and talk about ideas.

- After time for discussion, ask volunteers to share. Add their ideas to the chart.

WML1
WPS.U5.WML1

Have a Try

Invite students to turn and talk about their purposes for writing.

> Think about the different purposes, or reasons, you might write about your topic. Danny, you plan to write about your favorite kind of sandwich. You could describe it or tell a story about it. Or you could give information about how to make it or share how you feel when you eat it.
>
> Share your topic with your partner and talk about your purpose for writing.

▶ After time for discussion, ask students to share their ideas.

Summarize and Apply

Summarize the lesson. Encourage students to think about their purposes for writing.

> Today you talked about some different purposes for writing. In your writer's notebook, write some ideas you have for your purpose for writing about your topic. Look at the chart to help you choose a purpose. Plan to share your ideas when we meet later.

▶ Save the chart for WML3.

Purposes for Writing

- Teach
- Give information
- Tell a story
- Entertain
- Plan something (grocery list, to-do list)
- Invite
- Explain
- Change something
- Have someone feel something
- Express feelings
- Describe something using the senses
- Share ideas
- Organize information

Confer

▶ During independent writing, move around the room to confer briefly with students about a purpose for writing. Use the following prompts as needed.
- *What is your purpose for writing?*
- *Let's talk about your topic and think about some different purposes.*
- *Look back at the chart. Do you see any ideas for a purpose you might choose?*

Share

Following independent writing, gather students in a circle in the meeting area to share their ideas.

> Let's go around the circle so that everyone can share one purpose for writing.

Umbrella 5: Thinking About Purpose, Audience, and Genre/Form

Section 5: Writing Process

WML2
WPS.U5.WML2

Writing Minilesson Principle
Think about your audience.

Thinking About Purpose, Audience, and Genre/Form

You Will Need

- several mentor texts with a clear audience, such as the following:
  - *Shell, Beak, Tusk* by Bridget Heos, from Text Set: Genre Study: Expository Nonfiction
  - *Crickwing* by Janell Cannon, from Text Set: Author/Illustrator Study: Janell Cannon
- chart paper prepared with audience types
- sticky notes
- markers
- writer's notebooks

Academic Language / Important Vocabulary

- audience

Continuum Connection

- Write with specific readers or audience in mind
- Understand that writing is shaped by the writer's purpose and understanding of the audience
- Plan and organize information for the intended readers
- Understand audience as all readers rather than just the teacher

GOAL
Understand that writers think about their intended audience to further define their purpose.

RATIONALE
Once students have decided on a purpose, they need to think who their audience will be and how that affects their writing, such as understanding what the audience needs to know or using simple words for young children. By considering a wider and more authentic audience than just the classroom or family, students realize that their words have an impact and can be powerful and meaningful.

WRITER'S NOTEBOOK/WRITING FOLDER
Students can write their ideas about their intended audience in their writer's notebooks.

ASSESS LEARNING
- Notice whether students understand that they need to adapt their writing to suit their audience.
- Look for evidence that students understand and use vocabulary such as *audience*.

MINILESSON

To help students think about the minilesson principle, use a mentor text and provide an interactive lesson about audience. Here is an example.

> Listen as I read through a few pages of *Shell, Beak, Tusk*.

- Revisit a few pages.

  > Who do you think would like this book, adults or young people? Why?

  > You can tell that Bridget Heos wrote the book for children because she used interesting photos and chose words that children probably can read and understand. Young people are her audience.

- Repeat with *Crickwing*.

  > An audience is the person or group of people you think would like to read something that you write.

- Show and read the prepared audience chart.

  > An audience can be small, like maybe one friend or grandparent. An audience can also be big. An audience can be people you know, like friends or family, and it can also be people you don't know who are outside your smaller community of family and friends. Turn and talk about some people you would like to read your writing.

- After time for discussion, ask a few volunteers to share. Place a few examples on sticky notes and add them to the chart in the corresponding category.

Have a Try

Invite students to turn and talk about a writing audience.

> Think about the different audiences you could write for. Pasqual, you want to write about ice cream. I wonder if you might write for the class about how to make ice cream.

> Turn and talk about who your audience might be and what your audience might want to know.

▶ After time for discussion, ask students to share their ideas.

Summarize and Apply

Summarize the lesson. Encourage students to think about the audience they want to write for.

> Today you talked about who your audience is and what your audience might want to know.

▶ Write the principle at the top of the chart. Add the three questions shown on the chart.

> You have chosen your topic, and you know your purpose. Now think about your audience. During writing time, write down the audience you might like to write for in your writer's notebook near the purposes you wrote. Write what your audience might want to know and what questions they might have about your topic. Bring the ideas you have when we meet later.

▶ Save the chart for WML3.

Think about your audience.

Larger Community
- local newspaper
- first-grade class
- author
- adult expert

Family
- brother
- grandmother

Classmates and Friends
- Audrey
- Owen
- Ahmed

- Who is the audience?
- What would the audience want to know?
- What questions does my audience have?

Confer

▶ During independent writing, move around the room to confer briefly with students about writing for their audience. Use the following prompts as needed.
- Who will be reading this?
- What does your audience know already? What do you think your audience would like to know more about?

Share

Following independent writing, gather students in the meeting area to share their writing ideas.

> Who will be your audience and what might they want to know about? Tell about that.

> Share a question that you think your audience might have.

Umbrella 5: Thinking About Purpose, Audience, and Genre/Form

WML 3
WPS.U5.WML3

Writing Minilesson Principle
Think about the kind of writing you want to do.

Thinking About Purpose, Audience, and Genre/Form

You Will Need

- several mentor texts that have a clear purpose and audience, such as the following:
  - *Tornadoes!* by Gail Gibbons, from Text Set: Genre Study: Expository Nonfiction
  - *The Bee Tree* by Patricia Polacco, from Text Set: Author/Illustrator Study: Patricia Polacco
- chart paper prepared with headings: *Topic, Purpose, Audience, Type of Writing*
- purpose and audience charts from WML1 and WML2
- chart paper and markers
- writer's notebooks and writing folders

Academic Language / Important Vocabulary

- topic
- inform
- purpose
- audience

Continuum Connection

- Tell whether a piece of writing is functional, narrative, informational, or poetic
- Understand how the purpose of the writing influences the selection of genre
- Select the genre for the writing based on the purpose

GOAL

Choose the genre or form of writing based on purpose and audience.

RATIONALE

When students choose the type of writing they want to do by thinking about how it best suits their purpose and audience, they write effectively and with authenticity.

WRITER'S NOTEBOOK/WRITING FOLDER

Students should store their drafts in their writing folders. They may need their writer's notebooks to check for ideas to use in their writing.

ASSESS LEARNING

- Observe whether students recognize that their purpose and audience will help them decide what type of writing they want to do.
- Look for evidence that students can use vocabulary such as *topic, inform, purpose,* and *audience*.

MINILESSON

To help students think about the type of writing they want to do, provide an interactive lesson. Here is an example.

- Show the covers of *Tornadoes!* and *The Bee Tree*.

  > Turn and talk to your partner about the purpose and audience for each of these books.

- Show the prepared chart. Ask volunteers to provide suggestions for the topic, purpose, and audience for *Tornadoes!* Add their ideas to the chart. Repeat for *The Bee Tree*.

  > An informational book gives information. *Tornadoes!* is an informational book. A fiction story entertains. *The Bee Tree* is a fiction story. Both books are written in a way that children can understand and enjoy.

- Add the type of writing for each book to the chart.

  > You might want to write a different kind of book. If you wanted to write something to teach readers how bees make honey, what type of writing would you choose?

- Talk about how an informational book might be a good choice.

  > There are different ways that you can write about the same topic. Choose the way that makes sense for your purpose and audience.

Have a Try

Invite students to turn and talk about purpose, audience, and type of writing.

> Jeannie wants to write about video games. Once she decides her purpose and audience, then she can think about the type of writing. If she wants to invite her family to have a video game night, she could write an invitation.

> Turn and talk about what type of writing would be best for your purpose and audience.

- After time for discussion, ask a few volunteers to share their ideas. Add to the chart.

Summarize and Apply

Summarize the lesson. Remind students to think about what type of writing best fits their purpose and audience. Write the principle at the top of the chart.

> Remember that the type of writing you want to do depends on your topic, purpose, and audience. You have made some notes about purpose and audience in your writer's notebook. Use your notes to choose the type of writing you want to do. You might also have notes about your topic in your writer's notebook. When you are ready, get a piece of draft paper and begin writing. Bring your writing to share when we meet later.

Think about the kind of writing you want to do.

Topic	Purpose	Audience	Type of Writing
Gail Gibbons: tornadoes	Inform	Students	Informational book
Patricia Polacco: bees and honey	Entertain	Students	Fiction story
Jeannie: video games	Invite	Family	Invitation
Danny: favorite sandwich	Describe	Class	Poetry
Pasqual: ice cream	Teach	Students	How-to book
Lili: bats	Change something	Adult expert	Letter

Confer

- During independent writing, move around the room to confer briefly with students about their writing. Use the following prompts and the charts from WML1 and WML2 as needed.
  - *What type of writing is best for your purpose and audience?*
  - *You have chosen a topic. Let's look at the charts and talk about how you might choose the type of writing.*

Share

Following independent writing, gather students in a circle in the meeting area to share their writing.

> Let's go around the circle so that everyone can share the kind of writing you decided to do and why it's best for your purpose and audience.

Umbrella 5: Thinking About Purpose, Audience, and Genre/Form

Umbrella 5: Thinking About Purpose, Audience, and Genre/Form

Assessment

After you have taught the minilessons in this umbrella, observe students as they write and talk about writing. Use *The Fountas & Pinnell Literacy Continuum* to notice, teach for, and support students' learning as you observe their attempts at writing.

- What evidence do you have of students' new understandings related to purpose and audience?
  - Do students' writing behaviors show that they are thinking about purpose and audience?
  - Are they thinking about purpose and audience when they decide what kind of writing they want to do?
  - Are they using vocabulary such as *reason*, *purpose*, *give information*, *audience*, and *inform*?
- In what ways, beyond the scope of this umbrella, are students showing an interest in making choices about their writing?
  - Do they show an interest in choosing their own topics?
  - Are they showing an interest in writing in a variety of genres?

Use your observations to determine the next umbrella you will teach. You may also consult Suggested Sequence of Lessons (pp. 605–622) for guidance.

EXTENSIONS FOR THINKING ABOUT PURPOSE, AUDIENCE, AND GENRE/FORM

- Share other types of writing with students that have different purposes and intended audiences and have them talk about the purpose and audience (e.g., directions, news articles, advertisements).
- Have students add sticky notes to the audience chart as they think of new examples of each audience.
- If you are using *The Reading Minilessons Book, Grade 3* (Fountas and Pinnell 2019), the related umbrella is LA.U8: Thinking About the Author's Purpose.

Observing and Writing Like a Scientist

Umbrella 6

Minilessons in This Umbrella

- **WML1** Write your predictions.
- **WML2** Sketch and take notes about your observations.
- **WML3** Write a procedure.
- **WML4** Explain why you think something happened.

Before Teaching Umbrella 6 Minilessons

This umbrella starts laying the foundation for students to eventually write lab reports or scientific articles. WML3 provides an introduction to writing procedural texts, and the understandings that start here will later be built upon in GEN.U2: Writing Procedural Texts. If preferred, this umbrella can also be taught after GEN.U2.

Before teaching the minilessons in this umbrella, you will need to choose, plan, and gather materials for a science experiment that you will do with the students during WML2. You can use any experiment that is relevant to your class's science curriculum. These minilessons use as an example an experiment in which the students create or you demonstrate making a "tornado in a bottle." Fill a bottle with water to an inch or so from the top. Add a couple of squirts of dish soap and a pinch of glitter, put the cap on the bottle, turn the bottle upside down, and vigorously move the bottle in a circular motion. This will create a swirling funnel of glitter that looks like a tornado. You can find more information about this popular experiment, as well as video demonstrations, by searching online for "tornado in a bottle."

You might also want to read and discuss nonfiction books related to the science topic you have chosen. If you choose an experiment related to tornadoes, you might use the following text from *Fountas & Pinnell Classroom™ Interactive Read-Aloud Reading Collection*.

Interactive Read-Aloud Collection
Genre Study: Expository Nonfiction

Tornadoes! by Gail Gibbons

As you read and enjoy science texts together, help students
- make predictions and inferences,
- notice and discuss details in the illustrations, and
- pose questions and wonderings about the topic.

Interactive Read-Aloud
Expository Nonfiction

Writer's Notebook

WML1
WPS.U6.WML1

Writing Minilesson Principle
Write your predictions.

Observing and Writing Like a Scientist

You Will Need

- a plan and materials for a science experiment (e.g., tornado in a bottle)
- a book related to the science experiment, such as *Tornadoes!* by Gail Gibbons, from Text Set: Genre Study: Expository Nonfiction
- chart paper and markers
- writer's notebooks and writing folders

Academic Language / Important Vocabulary

- science
- experiment
- predict
- prediction

Continuum Connection

- Use vocabulary appropriate for the topic
- Generate and expand ideas through talk with peers and teacher
- Take notes or make sketches to help in remembering or generating information
- Participate actively in experiences and recall information that contributes to writing and drawing (using notebooks and artifacts)

GOAL

Write a prediction related to a science project.

RATIONALE

When you help students write a prediction for a science experiment, they learn that scientists use what they already know about a topic to make a prediction about what will happen. They also learn that scientists use writing for a purpose—to record their predictions in order to have a permanent written record of their scientific process.

WRITER'S NOTEBOOK/WRITING FOLDER

Have students write their predictions in their writer's notebooks. If students have extra time, they can work on an ongoing writing project in their writing folders.

ASSESS LEARNING

- Notice whether students can make and write a prediction for a science experiment.
- Look for evidence that they can use vocabulary such as *science*, *experiment*, *predict*, and *prediction*.

MINILESSON

Introduce the science experiment that you will use for these lessons (see Before Teaching for more information) and help students make predictions. Here is an example.

- Show the cover of *Tornadoes!* and read the title.

    We've been reading and learning about tornadoes. What did you learn about tornadoes from this book?

- Show the materials for the science experiment, explain the procedure, and invite students to use what they know to make predictions.

    We are going to do a science experiment related to tornadoes. To do this experiment, we will use a bottle with a lid, a funnel, a few tablespoons of glitter, and water. First, we will use the funnel to put the glitter into the bottle. Then we will fill the bottle about three quarters full with water and add two drops of dish soap. Next, we will tightly screw the lid back onto the bottle. Then we will turn the bottle upside down and quickly move the bottle in a circular motion, like this [make circular motion with hand], for about fifteen seconds. Finally, we will observe what is happening in the bottle.

    What do you think we will see? Why?

- Record on chart paper the language students use to state their predictions.

Have a Try

Invite students to talk to a partner about making predictions.

> Some of the predictions on the chart predict different things will happen. But, what is the same about the predictions? Turn and talk to your partner about this.

▸ After time for discussion, invite a few pairs to share their thinking. Make sure students understand that they use known information to think about what will happen, and there is always a reason for the prediction.

Summarize and Apply

Write the principle at the top of the chart. Summarize the learning and remind students to record their predictions.

> Why do you think it's important to write down your prediction for a science experiment?

> Write your prediction in your writer's notebook so you will remember it. After the experiment, read your prediction to see if you correctly predicted what would happen. When you finish, continue working on a writing project in your writing folder that you've already started or start a new one.

Write your predictions.

- I think what will happen is that the glitter will go around and around because the bottle will go around and around.

- I predict that the glitter will sink to the bottom of the bottle because it is heavier than the water.

- My prediction is the glitter will go around. The reason I think this is the water will go in a circle after you move the bottle in a circle.

- Because you showed us the tornado book, I think that the glitter will look like a tornado.

Confer

▸ During independent writing, move around the room to confer briefly with as many individual students as time allows. Sit side by side with them and invite them to talk about their predictions. Use prompts such as the following as needed.

- *What do you think we will see in the bottle after we've twirled it around? What will the water and glitter look like?*
- *What makes you think that?*
- *Remember to include a reason for your prediction.*

Share

Following independent writing, gather students in the meeting area to share their predictions.

> Who would like to read aloud your prediction for our science experiment?

WML2
WPS.U6.WML2

Writing Minilesson Principle
Sketch and take notes about your observations.

Observing and Writing Like a Scientist

You Will Need

- materials for a science experiment (e.g., tornado in a bottle: bottle with a cap, water, dish soap, and glitter for you and for small groups)
- chart paper and markers
- writer's notebooks
- To download the following online resource for this lesson, visit **fp.pub/resources**:
  - chart art (optional)

Academic Language / Important Vocabulary

- sketch
- observe
- observation
- label
- scientific

Continuum Connection

- Make scientific observations, use notes and sketches to document them, and talk with others about connections and patterns
- Remember important labels for drawings
- Take notes or make sketches to help in remembering or generating information

GOAL

Use drawing and writing to record important information about the observations.

RATIONALE

When you help students record their scientific observations, they learn to look closely at a subject and observe its different aspects. They begin to understand the importance of keeping a record of their scientific observations.

WRITER'S NOTEBOOK/WRITING FOLDER

Have students add their sketches and notes near their predictions in their writer's notebooks.

ASSESS LEARNING

- Notice whether students sketch and take notes about their observations.
- Look for evidence that they can use vocabulary such as *sketch*, *observe*, *observation*, *label*, and *scientific*.

MINILESSON

Demonstrate the planned science experiment and, at the appropriate point, model using drawing and writing to record scientific observations. Here is an example based on the tornado in a bottle experiment.

- Demonstrate the experiment.

  Look closely at what's happening inside the bottle. What do you see?

- Use students' observations and your own to model writing scientific observations on the chart paper. Read aloud your observations as you write them.

  We've written down our scientific observations. Let's also sketch what we observed to help us better remember what the bottle looked like. What should we draw?

  Labels will help readers understand our sketch and will help us remember what we saw. What could we label?

- Add labels to the sketch. Also add today's date.

544

The Writing Minilessons Book, Grade 3

Have a Try

Invite students to talk to a partner about recording scientific observations.

> I put today's date on our observations. Why is it important to write the date on an observation? Turn and talk to your partner about this.

▸ After students turn and talk, invite several pairs to share their thinking. Students should understand that if the experiment were to be done again at a later date and the two results were compared, it would be important to know when each experiment was done.

Summarize and Apply

Summarize the learning. Remind students to sketch and take notes about their scientific observations.

> How will you remember the results of an experiment?

▸ Write the principle at the top of the chart. Save the chart for WML4.

> Today during writing time, you will do the experiment in a small group and then sketch and write about what you observed in your writer's notebook. Bring your writing to share when we come back together.

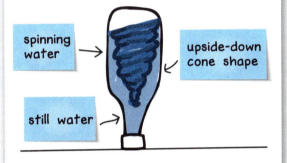

Confer

▸ During independent writing, move around the room to confer briefly with as many individual groups as time allows. Sit side by side with them and invite them to talk about their observations. Use prompts such as the following as needed.
- *What do you notice about how the water is moving?*
- *What shapes do you see?*
- *Does your sketch look like what you saw?*
- *What labels could you add to your sketch?*

Share

Following independent writing, gather students in the meeting area. Ask each group to share their observations.

> How did you record your scientific observations? What did you write and draw?

WML 3
WPS.U6.WML3

Writing Minilesson Principle
Write a procedure.

Observing and Writing Like a Scientist

You Will Need

- chart paper and markers
- writer's notebooks

Academic Language / Important Vocabulary

- science experiment
- procedure
- materials
- steps

Continuum Connection

- Understand that a procedural text often shows one item under another item and may include a number or letter for each item
- Write steps in a procedure with appropriate sequence and explicitness

GOAL

Write the procedure used for a science experiment so that others can replicate it.

RATIONALE

When students learn to write the procedure used for a science experiment, they begin to understand the importance of creating a permanent record of the procedure so others can replicate the experiment and reproduce results to prove scientific hypotheses. They also learn or build on their understanding of the conventions of procedural writing.

WRITER'S NOTEBOOK/WRITING FOLDER

Have students write the procedure for a science experiment in their writer's notebooks.

ASSESS LEARNING

- Notice whether students can accurately recall and write the procedure they followed for a science experiment.
- Look for evidence that they can use vocabulary such as *science experiment*, *procedure*, *materials*, and *steps*.

MINILESSON

This minilesson should be taught shortly after students have seen or conducted a science experiment (see WML2). To help students think about the minilesson principle, use shared writing to begin writing the procedure for the experiment. Below is an example. Students will finish writing the procedure on their own during independent writing.

> If another class wanted to do the experiment that we did, how would they know what to do?
>
> You could write what to do. What is the first thing they would need to know?
>
> They would need to know the materials that are needed. What did we use for the experiment?

- Using students' input, write a materials list on chart paper.

> I wrote a list of the materials. What do you notice about how I wrote the list?
>
> Each material is on its own line.
>
> What else would the other class need to know?
>
> They would need to know what to do. What is the first step? What comes after that?

- Use students' responses to write the first few steps of the procedure. Tell students that they will finish writing the procedure during independent writing.

WML 3
WPS.U6.WML3

Have a Try

Invite students to talk to a partner about how to write a procedure.

> What did you notice about how we wrote the procedure for the science experiment? Turn and talk to your partner about this.

▸ After students turn and talk, invite several pairs to share their thinking. Use their responses to summarize the learning on a separate sheet of chart paper. Write the principle at the top.

Summarize and Apply

Summarize the learning. Invite students to write the procedure for the science experiment they conducted.

> Why is it important for scientists to write the procedure they followed for an experiment?

> If you write the procedure you followed, other people can do the same experiment exactly the same way you did it. If other people do the same experiment and get the same results, then you will know that your results are probably accurate. This can help you prove that your ideas and predictions are correct.

> Today during writing time, write the whole procedure for the science experiment we did in your writer's notebook. Bring your writing to share when we come back together.

Confer

▸ During independent writing, move around the room to confer briefly with as many individual students as time allows. Sit side by side with them and invite them to talk about writing a procedure. Use prompts such as the following as needed.

- *How should you write the list of materials?*
- *What do you need to remember to do when you write the steps?*
- *How can you make the procedure clear to your readers?*

Share

Following independent writing, gather students in the meeting area to share their writing with a partner. Then select several students to share with the whole group.

> How did you make the procedure clear for your readers?

Tornado in a Bottle

Materials
- glass bottle with lid
- funnel
- dish soap
- 2-3 tablespoons of glitter
- water

Procedure
1. Use the funnel to put the glitter into the bottle.
2. Fill the bottle about three quarters (3/4) full with water.
3. Screw the lid back on the bottle tightly.
4.

Write a procedure.

- Write a list of the materials.
- Write exactly what to do.
- Write the steps in order.
- Number the steps.
- Start each step with a verb (action word).

WML 4
WPS.U6.WML4

Writing Minilesson Principle
Explain why you think something happened.

Observing and Writing Like a Scientist

You Will Need

- the chart from WML2
- a book related to the science experiment conducted in WML2, such as *Tornadoes!* by Gail Gibbons, from Text Set: Genre Study: Expository Nonfiction
- chart paper and markers
- writer's notebooks

Academic Language / Important Vocabulary

- science experiment
- results
- explain

Continuum Connection

- Gather information (with teacher assistance) about a topic from books or other print and media resources while preparing to write about it
- Understand that a writer gains ideas from other writers but should credit the other writers and/or put these ideas in one's own words
- Make scientific observations, use notes and sketches to document them, and talk with others about connections and patterns

GOAL

Provide evidence for the results of a science experiment.

RATIONALE

When you guide students to make inferences to explain the results of a science experiment, they begin to understand how scientists make connections between what they already know and what they have observed in order to draw conclusions and advance scientific knowledge.

WRITER'S NOTEBOOK/WRITING FOLDER

Have students write their explanations of the science experiment in their writer's notebooks.

ASSESS LEARNING

- Observe for evidence that students can draw on their prior knowledge to provide a plausible explanation for the results of a science experiment.
- Look for evidence that they can use vocabulary such as *science experiment*, *results*, and *explain*.

MINILESSON

To help students think about the minilesson principle, engage them in a discussion about the results of the science experiment conducted in WML2, and use shared writing to write an explanation for the results. Here is an example.

- Show the chart from WML2.

  What were the results of our science experiment? What happened inside the bottle?

  Scientists do a science experiment and they write notes about their observations. Afterward, they think very carefully about what happened and why it happened. Let's think about why moving the bottle in a circular motion created something that looked like a tornado in the bottle. We can use what we already know about tornadoes to explain why this happened.

- Show the cover of *Tornadoes!* and read pages 4–7.

  Why do you think we were able to create a tornado in the bottle by moving it in a circular motion? Does this book help you understand anything about what happened?

- Engage students in a discussion about their explanations. Encourage them to provide evidence for their thinking.
- Summarize the class's conclusions on chart paper.

The Writing Minilessons Book, Grade 3

WML 4
WPS.U6.WML4

Have a Try

Invite students to talk to a partner about how to explain the results of a science experiment.

> How did we explain the results of our science experiment? What did we think about and do? Turn and talk to your partner about this.

- After time for discussion, invite several pairs to share their thinking.

Summarize and Apply

Write the principle at the top of the chart. Summarize the learning and invite students to write their own explanations for what happened.

> Today during writing time, write a few sentences in your writer's notebook explaining why you think we got these results in our science experiment. Use what you know about tornadoes to explain your thinking. Even if you agree with everything we wrote on the chart, remember to write your own explanation in your own words. Bring your writing to share when we come back together.

Explain why you think something happened.

A tornado happens when two different winds (an updraft and a downdraft) come together and start to spin. As they spin faster and faster, they form a cloud that is shaped like a funnel.

When we moved the bottle rapidly in a circular motion, the water started to spin around in a circle just like the winds of a tornado. This created a funnel shape that looked like a tornado.

Confer

- During independent writing, move around the room to confer briefly with as many individual students as time allows. Sit side by side with them and invite them to talk about their explanations. Use prompts such as the following as needed.
  - What do you know about how tornadoes are formed?
  - How does this help you understand the results of our experiment?
  - What could you write about why the results happened?
  - What reasons or evidence can you give to support your thinking?

Share

Following independent writing, gather students in the meeting area to share their explanations.

> Who would like to read aloud the explanation you wrote for why the results of our experiment happened?

Umbrella 6: Observing and Writing Like a Scientist

Assessment

After you have taught the minilessons in this umbrella, observe students as they write and talk about their writing. Use *The Fountas & Pinnell Literacy Continuum* to notice, teach for, and support students' learning as you observe their attempts at writing.

- What evidence do you have of students' new understandings related to observing and writing like a scientist?
  - Can students write a prediction for a science experiment?
  - Do they write and sketch their scientific observations?
  - Can they accurately recall and write the procedure for a science experiment they have conducted?
  - Can they write an explanation for the results of a science experiment?
  - Do students understand and use vocabulary such as *scientific*, *prediction*, *observation*, and *procedure*?
- In what other ways, beyond the scope of this umbrella, are students ready to write like scientists?
  - Are they ready to write different kinds of texts about scientific topics (e.g., informational books, procedural texts, slide presentations)?

Use your observations to determine the next umbrella you will teach. You may also consult Suggested Sequence of Lessons (pp. 605–622) for guidance.

EXTENSIONS FOR OBSERVING AND WRITING LIKE A SCIENTIST

- Have students take photographs instead of sketching their observations.

- Encourage students to pose questions and wonderings based on their scientific observations. Then help them conduct research or do additional experiments to answer some of their questions and wonderings.

- Teach students how to record and present scientific data and observations in tables, charts, and/or graphs.

- Incorporate writing into science class. Encourage students to write procedural texts about how to do a science experiment or informational books about a science topic.

Adding Information to Your Writing

Umbrella 7

Minilessons in This Umbrella

WML1	Use different tools to add to your writing.
WML2	Add describing words or phrases to help the reader picture the idea.
WML3	Add details to slow down the exciting or important part of the story.
WML4	Add information to support your ideas and help the reader understand your topic.
WML5	Use connecting words to add more information to your writing.

Interactive Read-Aloud
Memory Stories

Patricia Polacco

Expository Nonfiction

Before Teaching Umbrella 7 Minilessons

These minilessons help students expand their thinking about ways to revise their writing. It is not necessary to teach the lessons consecutively. Instead, you might choose to teach them throughout the year. Revision is a high-level concept, and students will need multiple exposures to it. When you do teach the minilessons, make sure students have some writing they can revise so that they can try out their new learning.

These lessons use mentor texts and samples of your own writing to model how to look back at writing to find areas for improvement. Use the following texts from *Fountas & Pinnell Classroom™ Interactive Read-Aloud Collection,* or choose books from the classroom library that your students will enjoy.

Interactive Read-Aloud Collection
Exploring Memory Stories

Saturdays and Teacakes by Lester L. Laminack
The Printer by Myron Uhlberg

Author/Illustrator Study: Patricia Polacco

Some Birthday!
Meteor!

Genre Study: Expository Nonfiction

Bats! Strange and Wonderful by Laurence Pringle

As you read and enjoy these texts together, help students

- think about the author's process to write and revise the book,
- notice interesting details and word choices, and
- discuss what makes the book interesting or exciting.

WML1
WPS.U7.WML1

Writing Minilesson Principle
Use different tools to add to your writing.

Adding Information to Your Writing

You Will Need

- a sample piece of writing you have prepared that demonstrates a variety of tools for adding to writing (e.g., carets, sticky notes, strips of paper, numbered items on a separate page)
- chart paper and markers
- writing folders

Academic Language / Important Vocabulary

- revise
- add
- tool
- caret

Continuum Connection

- Add words, letters, phrases, or sentences using a variety of techniques: e.g., caret, sticky notes, spider's legs, numbered items on a separate page, word-processing
- Use a number to identify a place to add information and an additional paper with numbers to write the information to insert

GOAL

Learn to use a variety of tools for adding information to a piece of writing.

RATIONALE

By teaching students a variety of ways to add to their writing, you make the act of revising more accessible. When students are armed with the tools they need to revise their writing, they will be able to communicate their ideas more effectively.

WRITER'S NOTEBOOK/WRITING FOLDER

Students will revise a longer piece of writing from their writing folders.

ASSESS LEARNING

- Notice whether students effectively use a variety of tools to add to their writing.
- Look for evidence that they can use vocabulary such as *revise*, *add*, *tool*, and *caret*.

MINILESSON

To help students think about the minilesson principle, use a piece of writing that you have prepared before class or a piece of shared writing to demonstrate ways they can add to their writing. Teach the tool(s) that you prefer your class to use. Here is an example.

- Show the sample piece of writing you prepared.

  When you reread your writing and make changes to it, you revise it. Adding information is one way to revise your writing. I'm going to show you some of the different tools I used to add information to my writing.

- Show a page from your writing that demonstrates one tool for adding to writing (e.g., a caret).

  On this page, I added some descriptive words and phrases to make my writing more interesting. What do you notice about how I added them?

  I used carets. A caret looks like an upside-down *V*. Place it right where you want the new word or phrase to go. Then write the word or phrase above the caret.

- Write a description and an example of the tool on chart paper.
- Show a page that demonstrates another tool (e.g., a spider leg).

  How did I add to my writing on this page?

  I added a sentence on a strip of paper. This tool is called a spider leg! Why do you think I used a spider leg instead of a caret to add to my writing here?

- Add the tool to the chart. Continue to teach other tools for adding to writing (e.g., sticky notes, numbered items on a separate page).

WML1
WPS.U7.WML1

Have a Try

Invite students to talk to a partner about how to add information to a page.

> I would like to add a whole new section to my book about _____. Turn and talk to your partner about how I could do that.

- After students turn and talk, invite a few pairs to share their thinking. Discuss how best to add a lot of information.

Summarize and Apply

Summarize the learning and remind students to use different tools to add to their writing.

> How will you choose which tool to use to add to your writing?

- Write the principle at the top of the chart.

> During writing time today, reread a piece of writing from your writing folder. Think about whether there's anything you could add to your writing to improve it. If so, choose the best way to add that information. Bring your writing to share when we meet later.

Use different tools to add to your writing.

Tool	What You Can Add	What It Looks Like
Caret	A word or a few words	turquoise The ˄ sea was shimmering.
Spider leg	A sentence	Atlanta is a city in Georgia.
Sticky note	A few sentences	
Numbers	Put the added information on a separate page.	My grandfather played the ukulele.1 I loved hearing him play. 1. A ukulele is like a small guitar. 2. 3.
New page(s)	A lot more information	

Confer

- During independent writing, move around the room to confer briefly with as many individual students as time allows. Sit side by side with them and invite them to talk about adding to their writing. Use prompts such as the following as needed.
  - What could you add on this page to help readers better understand _____?
  - Is there anything you would like to add to this page? How could you add that?
  - You used a spider leg on this page. Why did you choose that tool?

Share

Following independent writing, gather students in the meeting area to share their writing.

> Turn and talk to your partner about the tool you used to add information to your writing. If you didn't add information to your writing today, what tool might you use in the future?

Umbrella 7: Adding Information to Your Writing

WML 2
WPS.U7.WML2

Writing Minilesson Principle
Add describing words or phrases to help the reader picture the idea.

Adding Information to Your Writing

You Will Need

- a familiar book with examples of descriptive language, such as *Saturdays and Teacakes* by Lester L. Laminack, from Text Set: Exploring Memory Stories
- chart paper prepared with a few basic sentences to which descriptive language could be added (see chart)
- markers
- writing folders

Academic Language / Important Vocabulary

- describing
- word
- phrase
- picture

Continuum Connection

- Add descriptive words (adjectives, adverbs) and phrases to help readers visualize and understand events, actions, processes, or topics
- Add words, phrases, or sentences to make the writing more interesting or exciting for readers

GOAL
Learn to revise writing by adding adjectives, adverbs, or descriptive phrases.

RATIONALE
When students notice the information they gain from the descriptive language that authors use in their writing, they begin to understand the importance of it in their own writing. By teaching students about adding adjectives, adverbs, and descriptive phrases, you give them a specific way to think about revising their writing.

WRITER'S NOTEBOOK/WRITING FOLDER
Students will revise a longer piece of writing from their writing folders.

ASSESS LEARNING

- Observe whether students can identify descriptive language in other authors' writing.
- Notice whether they add descriptive language to their own writing.
- Look for evidence that they can use vocabulary such as *describing*, *word*, *phrase*, and *picture*.

MINILESSON

To help students think about the minilesson principle, use a familiar mentor text to engage them in an inquiry around noticing and using descriptive language. Here is an example.

- Show the cover of *Saturdays and Teacakes* and read the title. Read page 13, pausing frequently to draw students' attention to the author's use of descriptive language. Ask questions such as the following:
  - *What words did the author use to describe the tomatoes Mammaw picks?*
  - *How did the author describe the sounds the mower makes when he pulls the starter rope?*
  - *How did the author help you picture what the grass was like?*
  - *What does the phrase "the mower choked on mouthfuls of wet grass" make you think of?*
- Once students begin to notice descriptive language, guide them to understand how it can be used in their writing.

  Why do you think Lester Laminack used so many interesting words and phrases to describe things? How do these describing words and phrases help you when you are reading?

  Authors use describing words and phrases to help the reader picture what is happening.

554

The Writing Minilessons Book, Grade 3

Have a Try

Invite students to talk to a partner about adding descriptive language.

- Display the prepared chart paper.

  > What words or phrases could you add to these sentences to help you make a picture in your mind? Turn and talk to your partner about your ideas.

- After time for discussion, invite several students to share their ideas. Add descriptive language to the sentences.

Summarize and Apply

Summarize the learning and remind students to add descriptive language to their writing.

> How do describing words and phrases help readers?

- Write the principle at the top of the chart.

  > Today during writing time, reread a piece of writing from your writing folder. Try adding some describing words or phrases. Decide whether and how you will add the words, perhaps with a caret or a spider leg. Bring your writing to share when we come back together.

Confer

- During independent writing, move around the room to confer briefly with as many individual students as time allows. Sit side by side with them and invite them to talk about adding to their writing. Use prompts such as the following as needed.

  - How does _____ look (sound, smell, taste, feel)?
  - What words or phrases could you add to your writing to help readers picture it?
  - What tool could you use to add those words to your writing? Would a caret work?
  - The way you described the _____ as _____ will help readers picture it in their minds.

Share

Following independent writing, gather students in the meeting area to share their writing.

> Who would like to share how you added describing words or phrases to your writing today?

Add describing words or phrases to help the reader picture the idea.

The volcano is spewing lava.
  ^fiery   ^red-hot, molten

The blanket is soft.
              ^as ^as a kitten's fur

The dog crawled into the doghouse.
  ^old, weary   ^sleepily

The spaceship took off.
  ^enormous   ^and zoomed into the starry night sky

WML3
WPS.U7.WML3

Writing Minilesson Principle
Add details to slow down the exciting or important part of the story.

Adding Information to Your Writing

You Will Need

- two familiar fiction books, such as the following from Text Set: Author/Illustrator Study: Patricia Polacco:
  - *Some Birthday!*
  - *Meteor!*
- chart paper and markers
- writing folders

Academic Language / Important Vocabulary

- detail
- exciting
- important
- character
- setting

Continuum Connection

- Tell details about the most important moments in a story or experience while eliminating unimportant details
- Identify the most exciting part of a story
- Add words, phrases, or sentences to make the writing more interesting or exciting for readers

GOAL

Understand that authors add details to slow down the action in their stories to make the moment last.

RATIONALE

When you help students notice how authors use details to slow down the most exciting or important part of a story, they understand that they too can add extra details to their own stories to stretch out an exciting or important moment. Slowing down the most exciting part of the story engages the reader by creating interest or suspense.

WRITER'S NOTEBOOK/WRITING FOLDER

Students will revise a longer piece of writing from their writing folders.

ASSESS LEARNING

- Observe for evidence that students can add details to slow down the most exciting or important part of a story.
- Look for evidence that they can use vocabulary such as *detail*, *exciting*, *important*, *character*, and *setting*.

MINILESSON

To help students think about the minilesson principle, use mentor texts to engage them in an inquiry-based lesson on how authors slow down the most exciting or important part of a story. Here is an example.

- Show the cover of *Some Birthday!* and read the title.
- Read pages 13–19.

  > When Patricia's family gets to the Clay Pit, do they see a monster right away?

  > The author makes you read several pages before you find out what they see in the Clay Pit. Why would an author make you wait so long to find out what happens in a story?

  > How does she make you wait?

- Help students understand that authors slow down and stretch out the action to keep readers engaged by wondering what will happen. Authors do this by including dialogue and/or details about what the characters are thinking, feeling, and doing.
- Continue in a similar manner with pages 2–8 of *Meteor!*
- With students' input, make a list on chart paper of the types of details authors might include to slow down an exciting or important part of a story.

The Writing Minilessons Book, Grade 3

WML 3
WPS.U7.WML3

Have a Try

Invite students to talk to a partner about how to slow down the most exciting or important part of their own story.

▸ Make sure students have their writing folders so they can find a story to look at.

> Reread your story. What is the most exciting or important part? Turn and talk to your partner about what happens in that part of your story.

Summarize and Apply

Summarize the learning and invite students to add more details to slow down the most exciting or important part of their story.

> How can you make your readers want to keep reading your story?

▸ Write the principle at the top of the chart.

> Now that you've identified the most exciting or important part of your story, think about details you could add to slow down and stretch out the moment. Add the details, maybe with a spider leg or a sticky note. Bring your writing to share when we meet later.

Add details to slow down the exciting or important part of the story.

Add details about . . .

- what the characters are thinking or feeling
- what the characters are doing
- what the characters are saying (dialogue)
- what the setting is like (describing words)
- what is going on around the main action

Confer

▸ During independent writing, move around the room to confer briefly with as many individual students as time allows. Sit side by side with them and invite them to talk about adding to their writing. Use prompts such as the following as needed.

- What is the most exciting or important part of your story?
- How could you slow down this part of the story?
- What details could you add about _____ (the setting, a character's thoughts or feelings)?
- What else might be going on while _____ happens? Add that to your writing.

Share

Following independent writing, gather students in the meeting area to share their writing.

> Who would like to share how you slowed down the most exciting or important part of your story?

Umbrella 7: Adding Information to Your Writing

WML 4
WPS.U7.WML4

Writing Minilesson Principle
Add information to support your ideas and help the reader understand your topic.

Adding Information to Your Writing

You Will Need

- a familiar nonfiction book, such as *Bats! Strange and Wonderful* by Laurence Pringle, from Text Set: Genre Study: Expository Nonfiction
- a short, simple piece of informational writing that is intentionally vague
- chart paper and markers
- writing folders

Academic Language / Important Vocabulary

- information
- support
- idea
- topic

Continuum Connection

- Add words, phrases, or sentences to provide more information to readers
- Add words, phrases, or sentences to clarify meaning for readers
- After reflection and rereading, add substantial pieces of text (paragraphs, pages) to provide further explanation, clarify points, add interest, or support points

GOAL

Add examples or evidence to support ideas and help the reader understand the topic.

RATIONALE

When you model how to make your informational writing clearer by adding details and examples to support your ideas, students learn how to revise their own informational writing and communicate information more effectively.

WRITER'S NOTEBOOK/WRITING FOLDER

Students will revise a longer piece of writing from their writing folders.

ASSESS LEARNING

- Observe whether students reread their informational writing to identify parts that need supporting evidence or examples.
- Notice whether students show a willingness to add information to their writing.
- Look for evidence that they can use vocabulary such as *information*, *support*, *idea*, and *topic*.

MINILESSON

To help students think about the minilesson principle, use a mentor text to engage them in an inquiry-based lesson on adding examples and evidence to informational writing. Here is an example.

- Show the cover of *Bats! Strange and Wonderful* and read the title. Read the first paragraph of page 5.

    What information does the author give to support, or tell more about, the idea that bats are mammals?

    The author says that bats nurse milk from their mothers, like human babies and mouse babies, which helps you understand how bats are like other mammals. What makes bats a "special group of mammals"?

    The author supports the idea that bats are a special group of mammals by explaining that they are the only mammals that fly.

- Read the first two paragraphs of page 7.

    What information does the author give to explain why some bats are known as "megabats"?

    He explains that megabats are large–up to four pounds–and have mega-wings and mega-eyes.

    The author says that megabats can see very well. What extra information does the author give about this? How does being able to see well help megabats?

    The author gives lots of details and examples to support, or tell more about, the big ideas in his book.

The Writing Minilessons Book, Grade 3

WML 4
WPS.U7.WML4

Have a Try

Invite students to talk to a partner about adding information to an informational text.

▸ Display the prepared piece of informational writing and read it aloud.

> Is anything unclear, or is there anything more you think readers would want to know? Turn and talk to your partner about this.

▸ After time for discussion, invite several pairs to share their thinking. Using their suggestions, demonstrate adding additional information using the tools that students have been learning to use (see WML1).

Summarize and Apply

Summarize the learning. Remind students to think about what information they could add to their informational writing.

> How do nonfiction authors support their ideas and help readers understand the topic?

▸ Write the principle at the top of the chart.

> Today during writing time, reread a piece of writing from your writing folder. Think about whether you could add some additional information to support your ideas and help the reader better understand your topic. Bring your writing to share when we come back together.

Add information to support your ideas and help the reader understand your topic.

Microbats

Some bats are known as microbats. "Micro" means small. The world's smallest microbat lives in Thailand.[1] Most microbats have a special way of catching insects in the dark.[2] They can catch hundreds of insects in an hour.

1. It is called a bumblebee bat because its body is about the size of a bumblebee!
2. It is called echolocation. As these bats fly, they make high-pitched noises and listen for the echoes. Using the echoes, they can locate insects and other objects in the pitch-black night.

Confer

▸ During independent writing, move around the room to confer briefly with as many individual students as time allows. Sit side by side with them and invite them to talk about adding to their writing. Use prompts such as the following as needed.

- What could you add to help readers understand this idea?
- What else might readers need or want to know about _____? How could you add that to your writing?

Share

Following independent writing, gather students in the meeting area to share their writing.

> Did anyone add information to your writing to support your ideas? What did you add? Would you like to read aloud your writing?

WML 5
WPS.U7.WML5

Writing Minilesson Principle
Use connecting words to add more information to your writing.

Adding Information to Your Writing

You Will Need

- a familiar book with numerous examples of connecting words, such as *The Printer* by Myron Uhlberg, from Text Set: Exploring Memory Stories
- chart paper and markers
- a brief sample of writing that contains examples of connecting words
- highlighter
- writing folders
- To download the following online resource for this lesson, visit **fp.pub/resources**:
  - chart art (optional)

Academic Language / Important Vocabulary

- connecting words
- revise
- information

Continuum Connection

- Use common (simple) connectives and some sophisticated connectives (words that link ideas and clarify meaning) that are used in written texts but do not appear often in everyday oral language: e.g., although, however, therefore, though, unless, whenever

GOAL

Understand that writers use connecting words (e.g., *although*, *however*, *therefore*, *though*, *unless*, *whenever*) to add information to improve their writing.

RATIONALE

When you help students notice how authors use connecting words to connect ideas, they learn to use connecting words in their own writing. Connecting words make writing clearer by linking ideas, and they add variety in sentence structures.

WRITER'S NOTEBOOK/WRITING FOLDER

Students will revise a longer piece of writing from their writing folders.

ASSESS LEARNING

- Notice whether students can identify connecting words in mentor texts.
- Observe whether students correctly use a variety of connecting words in their own writing.
- Look for evidence that they can understand and use vocabulary such as *connecting words*, *revise*, and *information*.

MINILESSON

To help students think about the minilesson principle, use a mentor text to engage them in noticing and understanding connecting words. Here is an example.

- Show the cover of *The Printer* and read the title. Display page 2 and read it aloud.

   What does the word *after* help you understand here?

   The word *after* is a connecting word. A connecting word connects two things, events, or ideas. The word *after* connects two actions: reading the paper and folding it into a hat. It tells when the father folded the hat—*after* he read the paper.

- Display page 3 and read the first paragraph aloud.

   The word *though* is another connecting word. What does the word *though* help you understand in this sentence?

   The word *though* is used to connect two ideas when there is something surprising, different, or unexpected about the second idea. The author's father could not *hear* the sounds the printing presses made, but he could *feel* the sounds through the soles of his feet.

- Continue in a similar manner with a couple of other examples of connecting words in the book (e.g., *and*, *because*, *but*, *even*). Record each connecting word on chart paper and discuss its function in the sentence.

The Writing Minilessons Book, Grade 3

Have a Try

Invite students to talk to a partner about connecting words.

- Display a sample piece of writing that contains several connecting words.

  > Look at what I wrote about why I think dogs make the best pets. What connecting words did I use? Why did I use them? Turn and talk about this with your partner.

- After time for discussion, invite volunteers to highlight the connecting words. Discuss how they work in the sentences.

Summarize and Apply

Summarize the learning and remind students to use connecting words when they add information to their writing.

> Why do authors use connecting words?

- Write the principle at the top of the chart.

  > During writing time, reread a piece of writing from your writing folder. Think about information you would like to add. If you add information, you might need to use connecting words like *though*, *however*, *because*, and *unless*. Bring your writing to share when we come back together.

Confer

- During independent writing, move around the room to confer briefly with as many individual students as time allows. Sit side by side with them and invite them to talk about adding to their writing. Use prompts such as the following as needed.
  - What information could you add to this page?
  - How does _____ relate to _____? What word would show how they connect?
  - Would you like to add something about why _____ happened? What connecting word could you use to connect what happened with the reason it happened?

Share

Following independent writing, gather students in the meeting area to share their writing.

> Who would like to share how you added information to your writing?

Use connecting words to add more information to your writing.

- after
- though
- and
- because
- but
- even

- however
- unless
- although
- whenever
- therefore

Why Dogs Make the Best Pets

Cats are nice. **However**, I prefer dogs. It is fun to walk a dog. I walk my dog three times a day, **unless** it is raining. **Although** having a dog can be a lot of work, it is worth it. My dog cheers me up **whenever** I am sad. He always wants to play with me. **Therefore**, I think that dogs make the best pets!

WML 5
WPS.U7.WML5

Section 5: Writing Process

Umbrella 7: Adding Information to Your Writing

561

Umbrella 7: Adding Information to Your Writing

Assessment

After you have taught the minilessons in this umbrella, observe students as they write and talk about their writing. Use *The Fountas & Pinnell Literacy Continuum* to notice, teach for, and support students' learning as you observe their writing skills.

- What evidence do you have of students' new understandings related to adding to writing?
  - Do students understand that they can (and show a willingness to) revise their writing to make it better?
  - Are they using tools (e.g., caret, spider leg, numbered items on a separate page) to add to their writing?
  - Do they understand what it means to slow down the most exciting or important part of a story?
  - Do they use describing and connecting words to make their writing clearer and more interesting?
  - Are they using vocabulary such as *detail*, *revise*, *connecting word*, and *information*?
- In what other ways, beyond the scope of this umbrella, are students exploring the writing process?
  - Are they ready to revise their writing in other ways?
  - Are they showing an interest in writing informational texts?

Use your observations to determine the next umbrella you will teach. You may also consult Suggested Sequence of Lessons (pp. 605–622) for guidance.

EXTENSIONS FOR ADDING INFORMATION TO YOUR WRITING

- Pull together a small group of students who would benefit from guided instruction on adding to their writing.
- Revisit WML5 to teach additional connecting words.
- Teach students how to add to their writing when typing it on a computer.
- Suggest that students read their writing to a friend and then ask whether there is something that could be better explained by adding information.

Revising to Focus and Organize Writing

Umbrella 8

Minilessons in This Umbrella

- **WML1** Take out information that does not add to the important ideas or message.
- **WML2** Organize your writing to make sure the order makes sense.
- **WML3** Change words to make your writing more specific.
- **WML4** Skip time to focus your story.
- **WML5** Group similar ideas together in paragraphs.

Before Teaching Umbrella 8 Minilessons

It is not necessary to teach these minilessons consecutively. Instead, you might choose to teach them throughout the year as needed. Revision is a high-level concept, and students will need multiple exposures to these lessons. These lessons are most effective when students are working on longer pieces of writing and can apply what they learn about revising. You might want to have students refer to the Revising Checklist in their writing folders (see MGT.U4: Introducing the Writing Folder).

Students should know how to create paragraphs and write more complex nonfiction texts before you teach WML5. Also give them plenty of opportunities to read texts that are organized with similar ideas grouped together in paragraphs. To model the minilesson principles, use the following familiar texts from *Fountas & Pinnell Classroom™ Interactive Read-Aloud Collection*, or choose suitable books from your classroom library.

Interactive Read-Aloud Collection
Exploring Memory Stories

My Rotten Redheaded Older Brother by Patricia Polacco

Saturdays and Teacakes by Lester L. Laminack

Genre Study: Expository Nonfiction

Knights in Shining Armor by Gail Gibbons

Genre Study: Realistic Fiction

Dumpling Soup by Jama Kim Rattigan

As you read and enjoy these texts together, help students notice that
- all the text on a page is relevant and connected to the most important ideas,
- authors often use specific and interesting word choices,
- the writing is organized in an order that makes sense, and
- information about the same idea is grouped together in paragraphs.

Interactive Read-Aloud
Memory Stories

Expository Nonfiction

Realistic Fiction

Writer's Notebook

WML1
WPS.U8.WML1

Writing Minilesson Principle
Take out information that does not add to the important ideas or message.

Revising to Focus and Organize Writing

You Will Need

- a familiar book with a clear message, such as *My Rotten Redheaded Older Brother* by Patricia Polacco, from Text Set: Exploring Memory Stories
- chart paper prepared with a sample piece of writing that contains some irrelevant or unimportant information
- markers
- writing folders

Academic Language / Important Vocabulary

- information
- idea
- message

Continuum Connection

- Delete words or sentences that do not make sense or do not fit the topic or message
- Delete pages when information is not needed
- Take out unnecessary words, phrases, or sentences that are repetitive or do not add to the meaning

GOAL
Identify the important ideas and messages and take out information that does not add to them.

RATIONALE
Some students may think that the more they write the better their writing will be. However, including information that is not relevant weakens the writing. Once students learn this, they will begin to reread their own writing and remove extraneous information.

WRITER'S NOTEBOOK/WRITING FOLDER
Have students revise a piece of writing in their writing folders to take out unnecessary information.

ASSESS LEARNING
- Notice whether students can reread their own writing, identify the most important ideas, and take out information that does not add to the important ideas.
- Look for evidence that they can use vocabulary such as *information*, *idea*, and *message*.

MINILESSON

To help students think about the minilesson principle, use a mentor text to help them notice that all the information on a page adds to the important ideas or message. Then model revising a brief text to take out unimportant information. Here is an example.

- Show the cover of *My Rotten Redheaded Older Brother* and read the title.

  What did the author learn about her older brother in this memory story?

  This story is about how the author learned that her brother was not so bad after all. This is the important idea or message of the story.

- Read pages 4–6 of the story.

  What are these pages about?

  All the information here adds to the most important idea or message.

- Show the sample text that you prepared.

  I am working on a memory story about my grandmother. I'm going to reread my writing to see how I can make it better.

- Read the text aloud.

  What is the most important idea or message on this page?

  The most important idea is "My grandma Patty was very special to me." All the other information should add to, or tell more about, this idea. Is there a sentence that does not tell more about my important idea?

  I will cross out that sentence.

WML1
WPS.U8.WML1

Have a Try

Invite students to talk to a partner about taking out information.

> Is there anything else in my writing that doesn't add to the most important idea? Turn and talk to your partner about that.

▸ After time for discussion, invite several pairs to share their thinking. Using students' input, cross out any irrelevant or unimportant information.

Summarize and Apply

Summarize the learning and remind students to take out information that does not add to the important ideas or message.

> How can you make your writing better?
>
> What should you do if you find information that does not add to the important ideas or message?

▸ Write the principle at the top of the chart.

> During writing time today, reread a writing project from your writing folder. It could be one that you already started or one that you recently finished. Take out any information that does not add to the important ideas or message. Bring your writing to share when we meet later.

Take out information that does not add to the important ideas or message.

Grandma Patty

My grandma Patty was very special to me. Every Sunday, I would go to her house. We usually spent the whole morning in her garden, planting beans, carrots, and other vegetables. ~~Beans are my favorite vegetable.~~ Grandma let me eat all the cherries I wanted from her cherry trees.

In the afternoon, we would sell the cherries and other vegetables at a little stand. As we sat there, we would talk and talk. She listened to everything that was on my mind. She never interrupted me. ~~Grandpa Joe interrupted her a lot.~~ She was the best listener I ever met.

Confer

▸ During independent writing, move around the room to confer briefly with students about revising their writing. Use prompts such as the following as needed.

- What is your story about? What is the most important idea?
- What do you want readers to understand from reading your story?
- Does _____ add to this idea?
- Remember that all the information in your writing should add to the most important ideas or message.

Share

Following independent writing, gather students in the meeting area to talk about their writing.

> Raise your hand if you took out information from your writing today.
>
> How did you decide what to take out?

Umbrella 8: Revising to Focus and Organize Writing

WML2
WPS.U8.WML2

Writing Minilesson Principle
Organize your writing to make sure the order makes sense.

Revising to Focus and Organize Writing

You Will Need

- a familiar book with a clear chronological sequence, such as *Dumpling Soup* by Jama Kim Rattigan, from Text Set: Genre Study: Realistic Fiction
- chart paper prepared with a simple text that has some sentences out of order
- markers
- writing folders

Academic Language / Important Vocabulary

- organize
- order

Continuum Connection

- Rearrange and revise writing to better express meaning or make the text more logical: e.g., reorder drawings, reorder pages, cut and paste
- Reorder the information in a text to make the meaning clearer by cutting apart, cutting and pasting, laying out pages, using word-processing

GOAL
Understand that writers revise their writing so that the order makes sense.

RATIONALE
When you teach students to reread their writing to make sure the order makes sense, they begin to think about the structure of their writing and they learn to communicate their ideas more effectively.

WRITER'S NOTEBOOK/WRITING FOLDER
Have students reread a piece of writing in their writing folders to make sure the order is correct.

ASSESS LEARNING

- Look for evidence that students reread their own writing to determine if the order makes sense and that they are willing to revise their writing.
- Look for evidence that they can use vocabulary such as *organize* and *order*.

MINILESSON

To help students think about the minilesson principle, use a mentor text to engage them in a discussion about how the order of events should make sense. Here is an example.

- Show the cover of *Dumpling Soup* and read the title. Show several pages of the book and help students summarize the major events of the story in order.

    Does the order of events that happen in the story make sense? Why or why not?

    The author organized the events in the same order that they happened and in a way that makes sense when you read the story.

- Show the recipe on the inside back cover of the book.

    In this recipe, the author told what steps you have to follow to make Jama's dumpling soup. How did the author organize the steps?

    Does the order make sense?

    The author organized the steps in the order you have to follow them. First you do step 1, then you do step 2, then you do step 3, and so on. This order makes sense!

Have a Try

Invite students to talk to a partner about how to change the order of writing.

▶ Display the prepared chart paper.

> What do you notice about the order of my writing? Is there anything I should change? Turn and talk to your partner about that.

▶ After students turn and talk, invite a few pairs to share their thinking. Demonstrate reorganizing your writing.

Summarize and Apply

Summarize the learning and remind students to reread their writing to make sure the order makes sense.

> Why might you need to reorganize your writing?

▶ Write the principle at the top of the chart.

> During writing time today, reread a piece of writing in your writing folder that you're working on or one you've already finished. Make sure the order of your writing makes sense. If it doesn't, mark your writing to show where the part that is out of order should go. Bring your writing to share when we meet later.

Organize your writing to make sure the order makes sense.

Yesterday, we went on a field trip to the natural history museum. We spent the morning exploring the museum's dinosaur exhibit. Then we ate lunch on the grass outside the museum. We saw a giant T-rex skeleton! After lunch, we saw an exhibit about Ancient Egypt. We saw lots of human mummies . . . and even a cat mummy! We took a long bus ride to the museum. We then took the bus back to school. It was such a fun and interesting day!

Confer

▶ During independent writing, move around the room to confer briefly with students about revising their writing. Use prompts such as the following as needed.

- Read this part of your writing aloud. Is there anything that needs to be revised?
- Does _____ happen before or after _____?
- Where should you move that sentence to?
- How can you move it?

Share

Following independent writing, gather students in the meeting area to share their writing.

> Raise your hand if you changed the order of your writing today.
>
> How did you change it?

Umbrella 8: Revising to Focus and Organize Writing

WML3
WPS.U8.WML3

Writing Minilesson Principle
Change words to make your writing more specific.

Revising to Focus and Organize Writing

You Will Need

- a familiar book with specific and powerful word choices, such as *Saturdays and Teacakes* by Lester L. Laminack, from Text Set: Exploring Memory Stories
- chart paper prepared with a shared writing piece that contains examples of generic language
- writer's notebooks and/or writing folders
- markers

Academic Language / Important Vocabulary

- specific

Continuum Connection

- Change words to make the writing more interesting
- Identify vague parts and provide specificity

GOAL

Replace vague words with more specific and powerful words to make writing more interesting and accurate.

RATIONALE

When you help students notice the specific and powerful word choices used by published authors, they will be more likely to think carefully about the words they use in their own writing. They will reread their writing and identify and replace generic language.

WRITER'S NOTEBOOK/WRITING FOLDER

Have students reread their writing in their writer's notebooks or writing folders to find less-specific words that they could replace with words that are more specific or descriptive.

ASSESS LEARNING

- Look for evidence that students reread their writing, evaluate their word choices, and change words to make their writing more specific.
- Look for evidence that they can use vocabulary such as *specific*.

MINILESSON

To help students think about the minilesson principle, use a mentor text to engage them in an inquiry-based lesson around word choices. Then revise a piece of shared writing together. Here is an example.

- Show the cover of *Saturdays and Teacakes* and read the title. Then read the third paragraph on page 16.

    How did the author eat his sandwich? How did Mammaw eat hers?

    The author says that he "gobbled" his sandwich and that Mammaw "nibbled" at hers. He could've just written that they both ate their sandwiches. Why is it better to use words like *gobbled* and *nibbled* than words like *ate*?

    Gobbled and *nibbled* are more specific, or exact. They help you make a picture in your mind of exactly how the two people ate their sandwiches.

- Read the fifth paragraph on page 16.

    What kind of birdcalls did they listen to?

    The author names the specific kind of birds they heard—blue jays—instead of writing that they listened to birdcalls. Why do you think the author made that decision?

    When you choose words that are specific and interesting, readers can make a clear picture in their mind of whatever you're writing about.

WML 3
WPS.U8.WML3

Have a Try

Invite students to talk to a partner about how to revise the shared writing piece.

- Display the piece of shared writing you selected and read it aloud.

    > What words would you change to make this writing more specific? Sometimes you might replace two or three words with just one word that is more interesting. Turn and talk to your partner about how to revise this writing.

- After time for discussion, invite students to share their ideas. Make the changes using carets, sticky notes, or spider legs.

Summarize and Apply

Help students summarize the learning and remind them to reread their writing and think about their word choices.

> What is one way you can revise your writing to make it more interesting?

- Write the principle at the top of the chart.

    > During writing time today, look at a writing project from your writing folder or some writing in your writer's notebook. Are there any words you could change to make your writing more specific? Bring your writing to share when we meet later.

Chart: Change words to make your writing more specific.

Today, we ~~looked at~~ observed the weather from our classroom window. In the morning, the sky looked dark and ~~sad~~ gloomy. It was ~~raining lightly~~ drizzling.

We even heard some ~~loud~~ booming thunder. Then, the clouds started to ~~go away~~ clear, and the sun ~~slowly showed up~~ emerged. We saw a ~~pretty~~ dazzling rainbow!

Confer

- During independent writing, move around the room to confer briefly with students about revising their writing. Use prompts such as the following as needed.

    - *Can you think of a word that would be more helpful to your readers than _____? How else could you describe _____?*
    - *What is another word that means _____?*
    - *What kind of animals did you see? What kind of food did you eat?*

Share

Following independent writing, gather students in the meeting area to share their writing.

> Who would like to share a place where you made your writing more specific?

Umbrella 8: Revising to Focus and Organize Writing

WML 4
WPS.U8.WML4

Writing Minilesson Principle
Skip time to focus your story.

Revising to Focus and Organize Writing

You Will Need

- a familiar book with clear examples of skipping time, such as *Dumpling Soup* by Jama Kim Rattigan, from Text Set: Genre Study: Realistic Fiction
- chart paper prepared with a piece of narrative writing that contains extraneous detail and does not skip time
- chart paper and markers
- writing folders

Academic Language / Important Vocabulary

- focus
- story
- skip

Continuum Connection

- Delete words, phrases, or sentences from a text (crossing out or using word-processing) to make the meaning clearer
- Take out unnecessary words, phrases, or sentences that are repetitive or do not add to the meaning
- Identify the most exciting part of a story

GOAL

Focus writing by using transitional words to skip time and remove unimportant details.

RATIONALE

When beginning narrative writing, students may write about everything that happens in a day, including many unimportant details. When you help them notice that authors often "skip time" and include only important details, they will begin to do the same in their own writing.

WRITER'S NOTEBOOK/WRITING FOLDER

Have students reread stories in their writing folders to find places they could revise to focus the writing.

ASSESS LEARNING

- Observe whether students focus their stories by using transitional words to skip time and removing unimportant details.
- Look for evidence that they can use vocabulary such as *focus*, *story*, and *skip*.

MINILESSON

To help students think about the minilesson principle, use a familiar narrative book to discuss how the author skipped time to focus the story. Then revise a piece of writing together. Here is an example.

- Show the cover of *Dumpling Soup* and read the title. Read page 18.

    How can you tell that some time passed between when the children played the shoe-store game and when they heard Hiram and the older cousins running?

    Why do you think the writer chose not to tell you everything that happened between those two events?

    The author started a new section of writing and began the new section with "When it is almost midnight" to let us know that she skipped time—perhaps several hours—and only wrote what we need to know. When you write your own stories, you don't have to describe everything that happens. You can skip minutes, hours, days, weeks, months, or even years so you can focus on the important events.

- Show the piece of writing that you prepared. Read it aloud.

    I wrote this piece of writing about going to Ohio for my sister's wedding. What could I take out to focus my story on the important things about the wedding?

- Help students identify extraneous details, cross them out, and add transition words as needed.

WML 4
WPS.U8.WML4

Have a Try

Invite students to talk to a partner about transitional words.

> When you skip time in your writing, make it clear that you're skipping time by telling when the next important thing happened. Use words like *the next morning*. What are some other words or phrases you could use to show you are skipping time? Turn and talk to your partner about this.

▶ After time for discussion, invite several pairs to share their thinking. Make a list of transitional words on chart paper.

Summarize and Apply

Summarize the learning. Remind students that they can skip time to focus their stories.

> Why do authors sometimes skip time in their stories?

▶ Write the principle at the top of the chart.

> During writing time today, reread a story that you've already written. Look for places where you can skip time to focus your story on the most important events.

Confer

▶ During independent writing, move around the room to confer briefly with students about revising their stories. Use prompts such as the following as needed.
  - *Let's read your story together to see if there are any places where you could skip time.*
  - *Is _____ an important event? Do your readers need to know about this?*
  - *When does _____ happen?*
  - *What words could you add to show that you are skipping time?*

Share

Following independent writing, gather students in the meeting area to share their writing.

> Would anyone like to read aloud a place in your story where you skipped time?
>
> Why did you decide to skip time there?

Skip time to focus your story.

My Sister's Wedding

Last weekend, my family went to Ohio for my sister's wedding. We flew to Ohio on Friday evening. It was my children's first time on an airplane! On Saturday, we watched my sister get married outside in a beautiful garden. My daughter was the flower girl. She loved dressing up in a fancy dress. ~~Then we drove back to our hotel to take a nap. We were all very tired. Then~~ *That evening,* we went to the wedding reception. We had a delicious dinner, ate lots of cake, and danced for hours. It was so much fun! ~~Then we went back to our hotel and went to sleep.~~

~~We woke up early the next morning. Then we showered, got dressed, and had breakfast. Then we~~ *The next morning,* visited my uncle's art studio. My children enjoyed seeing the canvases and paints. After that, it was time to fly back home. We had a great time in Ohio!

Words for Skipping Time
- The next morning
- Later
- When it is almost midnight
- That evening
- At five o'clock
- Later that day
- One week later

Umbrella 8: Revising to Focus and Organize Writing

WML 5
WPS.U8.WML5

Writing Minilesson Principle
Group similar ideas together in paragraphs.

Revising to Focus and Organize Writing

You Will Need

- a familiar nonfiction book with multiple paragraphs per page, such as *Knights in Shining Armor* by Gail Gibbons, from Text Set: Genre Study: Expository Nonfiction
- chart paper prepared with a short nonfiction text that is missing paragraph breaks and has at least one fact out of order
- markers
- writing folders

Academic Language / Important Vocabulary

- group
- similar
- idea
- paragraph

Continuum Connection

- Arrange information in a logical way so that ideas build on one another
- Rearrange and revise writing to better express meaning or make the text more logical: e.g., reorder drawings, reorder pages, cut and paste
- Reorder the information in a text to make the meaning clearer by cutting apart, cutting and pasting, laying out pages, using word-processing

GOAL

Organize writing so that similar ideas are grouped together in paragraphs.

RATIONALE

When you teach students to reread their writing to make sure similar ideas are grouped together in paragraphs, they begin to think about the structure of their writing. They learn to communicate their ideas more effectively.

WRITER'S NOTEBOOK/WRITING FOLDER

Have students reread a draft from their writing folders to check paragraphing and revise it.

ASSESS LEARNING

- Look for evidence that students reread their own writing to make sure similar ideas are grouped together in paragraphs.
- Notice whether students are willing to reorganize their writing and add paragraph breaks as needed.
- Look for evidence that they can use vocabulary such as *group*, *similar*, *idea*, and *paragraph*.

MINILESSON

To help students think about the minilesson principle, use a mentor text to engage students in an inquiry-based lesson around how authors group similar ideas in paragraphs. Then revise a teacher-written piece of writing together. Here is an example.

- Show the cover of *Knights in Shining Armor* and read the title. Display and read aloud the first paragraph on page 16.

  What is this paragraph about?

- Read the second paragraph.

  What is this paragraph about?

  All the facts in the first paragraph are about knights' horses, and all the facts in the second paragraph are about battles between knights. The author groups similar ideas together in paragraphs.

- Display the nonfiction text you prepared. Read it aloud.

  I want to group similar ideas together in paragraphs in my own writing. Right now, there's only one paragraph. How could I split it into two paragraphs?

- Help students identify the place in your writing where you transition to a new subtopic, and demonstrate adding a paragraph symbol (¶) to indicate where the second paragraph should begin. Make sure students understand the reason for having two paragraphs.

Have a Try

Invite students to talk to a partner about how to revise your writing.

> Let's read my writing again to make sure it's organized in a way that makes sense. Are there any facts that are in the wrong place? Turn and talk to your partner about this.

- After students turn and talk, invite a few pairs to share their thinking. If necessary, help students identify the idea that is out of place. Then show how to move it.

Summarize and Apply

Write the principle at the top of the chart. Summarize the learning. Remind students to reread their writing to make sure similar ideas are grouped together in paragraphs.

> During writing time today, reread a draft from your writing folder. Make sure that similar ideas are grouped together in paragraphs. If you need to start a new paragraph, use the paragraph symbol like I did on the chart. If you find an idea that is out of place, one way to move it is by circling it and drawing an arrow pointing to where it should go.

Group similar ideas together in paragraphs.

Mount Everest

¶ Mount Everest is the highest mountain in the world. Standing more than 29,000 feet tall, it is located on the border of Nepal and Tibet. ~~Many brave mountaineers have attempted to reach its peak, but not all have been successful.~~ It is part of a mountain range known as the Himalayas.

¶ Mount Everest is one of the most challenging mountains to climb. ^ Edmund Hillary and Tenzing Norgay were the first to reach the top of Mount Everest. Since their trailblazing climb in 1953, many others have followed in their footsteps.

Confer

- During independent writing, move around the room to confer briefly with students about organizing their writing. Use prompts such as the following as needed.
  - Is all the information about the same idea? Could this big paragraph be split up into more than one paragraph?
  - Where should the second paragraph begin? Where do you start telling about a new idea?
  - How can you show that a new paragraph should begin here?
  - Does this idea fit better in the first paragraph or the second paragraph? Why?

Share

Following independent writing, gather students in the meeting area to share their writing.

> Who would like to share how you grouped similar ideas together in paragraphs?
>
> How did you know where to start a new paragraph?

Umbrella 8: Revising to Focus and Organize Writing

Assessment

After you have taught the minilessons in this umbrella, observe students as they write and talk about their writing. Use *The Fountas & Pinnell Literacy Continuum* to notice, teach for, and support students' learning as you observe their attempts at writing.

- What evidence do you have of students' new understandings related to revising writing?
  - Do students show a willingness to revise their writing?
  - Are they able to evaluate information that does not add to the important ideas and remove it?
  - Do they replace vague words with more specific and interesting words?
  - How successful are students at skipping time in their narrative writing?
  - Do they understand how to reorder writing?
  - Do they group similar ideas together in paragraphs?
  - Do they understand and use vocabulary such as *information*, *idea*, *specific*, *organize*, and *paragraph*?
- In what other ways, beyond the scope of this umbrella, are students exploring the writing process?
  - Are they experimenting with writing different genres and subgenres?
  - Are they including various types of illustrations and graphics in their nonfiction writing?

Use your observations to determine the next umbrella you will teach. You may also consult Suggested Sequence of Lessons (pp. 605–622) for guidance.

EXTENSIONS FOR REVISING TO FOCUS AND ORGANIZE WRITING

- Gather together a guided writing group of several students who need support in a specific aspect of writing, such as reorganizing parts that are out of order.

- Teach CNV.U3.WML2 to show children how to use paragraphing to indicate a change of speaker in dialogue.

- Teach CFT.U7: Making Powerful Word Choices to give students additional guidance and practice in choosing specific, interesting words.

- Show students how to revise their writing on a computer, using tools such as cut and paste.

Editing and Proofreading Writing

Umbrella 9

Minilessons in This Umbrella

WML1	Make sure your writing makes sense.
WML2	Make sure you made your letters easy to read.
WML3	Make sure you wrote the words you know correctly.
WML4	Check your punctuation and capitalization.

Shared Reading

Writer's Notebook

Before Teaching Umbrella 9 Minilessons

The goal of this umbrella is to help students understand how to proofread and edit their own writing. Teach these minilessons when students have some writing in progress in their writing folders to which they can apply what they are learning. A basic checklist for proofreading will be built as a chart across the minilessons to show how to mark corrections in a draft, for example, using a caret to insert a missing word. It will be a useful anchor chart to hang in the classroom. A more detailed Proofreading Checklist can be found in the online resources (see MGT.U4: Introducing the Writing Folder). Decide whether you will have the students use the Proofreading Checklist throughout the minilessons or after all the minilessons have been presented. Students should keep the checklist in their writing folders.

Before teaching these lessons, make sure students have had many experiences writing and rereading their writing. It will also be helpful to have taught CNV.U1–CNV.U3. Throughout this umbrella, use writing samples written by students or by you. Make sure the samples are large enough for everyone to see—either project them or write them on chart paper. Use the book suggested below from *Fountas & Pinnell Classroom™ Shared Reading Collection,* or choose other big books from the classroom library to serve as models of edited text.

Shared Reading Collection

From Buds to Bananas by Betty Riggs

As you read and enjoy this text together, help students notice

- how letters are easy to read,
- spaces between words,
- punctuation and capitalization, and
- print that makes sense.

WML1
WPS.U9.WML1

Writing Minilesson Principle
Make sure your writing makes sense.

Editing and Proofreading Writing

You Will Need

- a big book that has clear and simple writing, such as *From Buds to Bananas* by Betty Riggs, from *Shared Reading Collection*
- a writing sample with some parts that do not make sense (written on chart paper, provided to each student, or projected with a document camera)
- chart paper and markers
- document camera (optional)
- writing folders
- To download the following online resource for this lesson, visit **fp.pub/resources**:
  - Proofreading Checklist
  - Proofreading Sample 1

Academic Language / Important Vocabulary

- make sense
- edit
- proofread

Continuum Connection

- Edit for capitalization, punctuation, and sentence sense
- Delete text to better express meaning and make more logical
- Add word, phrases, or sentences to clarify meaning for readers
- Know how to use an editing and proofreading checklist

GOAL

Proofread and edit writing to make sure sentences make sense.

RATIONALE

Writing is a form of communication from writers to their audience. For writing to be effective, it needs to make sense and be understood by the audience.

WRITER'S NOTEBOOK/WRITING FOLDER

Students will proofread and edit a piece of writing they are working on in their writing folders. If students will use the Proofreading Checklist in this lesson, make sure that a copy is fastened inside each student's writing folder.

ASSESS LEARNING

- Look for evidence that students understand that readers need to be able to understand what they are reading.
- Observe whether students proofread and edit their writing to make sure it makes sense.
- Look for evidence that students can use vocabulary such as *make sense*, *edit*, and *proofread*.

MINILESSON

To help students proofread and edit their work, provide an example of a mentor text with clear writing. Model how writing can be corrected when it does not make sense. Here is an example.

- Show the cover of *From Buds to Bananas* and then read page 2.

  Think about what the writer has written here. Does it make sense?

- Guide the conversation so students notice that it is clear and easy to understand.

  The writer, Betty Riggs, proofread her book, or reread it to make sure that readers could understand her writing. If something did not make sense, she edited, or made changes to correct, her work.

- Show the prepared writing sample.

  When you do your own writing, check to be sure your readers will understand it. One thing to check for is whether your writing makes sense. Let's look at this writing. Is there any part that doesn't make sense?

- Read the writing. Ask students to raise a hand when something doesn't make sense. Show them how to use one line to cross out (not erase) extra words and a caret to add in missing words. Reread the writing and discuss whether it makes sense after the corrections.

Have a Try

Invite students to turn and talk about checking writing for sense.

> Continue proofreading the writing. Are there more errors that should be edited? Turn and talk to your partner about that.

- After time for discussion, ask a few volunteers to share what they noticed.

Summarize and Apply

Summarize the lesson. Have students proofread and edit a longer piece of writing from their writing folders for sense.

- Begin a proofreading and editing checklist on chart paper. Write the principle on the left. This will be the first item on the checklist. On the right, add several examples that students noticed from the sample writing. Keep the checklist posted and continue adding to it throughout this umbrella. Save the checklist for WML2.

> During writing time today, share the writing you are working on with a different partner. If you talk about any parts that do not make sense, cross out extra words and add in words so that it makes sense. Bring your writing when we meet later.

Confer

- During independent writing, move around the room to confer briefly with as many individual students as time allows. Sit side by side with them and invite them to talk about proofreading and editing. You might wish to have them use the Proofreading Checklist. Use the following prompts as needed.
  - *Reread this part. Does it make sense?*
  - *Let's talk about words that could be added so that this makes sense.*
  - *Show me an extra word that should be crossed out.*

Share

Following independent writing, gather students in the meeting area to share their writing.

> Turn and talk to your partner about how you edited your writing.

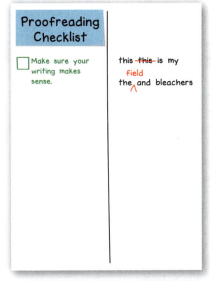

Umbrella 9: Editing and Proofreading Writing

WML2
WPS.U9.WML2

Writing Minilesson Principle
Make sure you made your letters easy to read.

Editing and Proofreading Writing

You Will Need

- a writing sample with some incorrect letter formation, proportion, and orientation (written on chart paper, provided to each student, or projected with a document camera)
- sentence strip or chart paper with handwriting lines
- markers
- document camera (optional)
- proofreading checklist chart from WML1
- writing folders
- To download the following online resource for this lesson, visit **fp.pub/resources**:
  - Proofreading Checklist
  - Proofreading Sample 2

Academic Language / Important Vocabulary

- letters
- handwriting
- sink

Continuum Connection

- Write fluently in both manuscript and cursive handwriting with appropriate spacing
- Check and correct letter formation
- Know how to use an editing and proofreading checklist

GOAL

Reread writing to check or correct letter formation, proportion, and orientation so the readers can understand the message.

RATIONALE

When students check their writing to be sure their letters are easy to read, paying attention to letter size and orientation, they are better able to get their message across to their readers, and they learn to write in an efficient and proportional manner. They also gain independence and confidence over their own writing.

WRITER'S NOTEBOOK/WRITING FOLDER

Students will proofread and edit a piece of writing they are working on in their writing folders. If students will use the Proofreading Checklist in this lesson, make sure that a copy is fastened inside each student's writing folder.

ASSESS LEARNING

- Observe whether students edit and proofread their work to check for letter formation, proportion, and orientation.
- Look for evidence that students can use vocabulary such as *letters*, *handwriting*, and *sink*.

MINILESSON

To help students learn to proofread and edit their work, model how writing can be corrected when letters are not written with proper formation, proportionality, and orientation. Here is an example.

> What do you know about making sure handwriting is easy to read?

- Show the prepared writing sample.

> What do you notice about how the letters are written?

- Guide the conversation to talk about whether the letters are written so they are easy to read and go from left to right. Have a conversation about whether letters are tall, small, or sink below the line.

> Are there some letters that could be fixed so they are easier to read?

- Help students notice any letters that need correction for formation, proportionality, or orientation. As they do, rewrite the letters correctly on the handwriting lines. Have students guide you through the formation using the verbal path or ask volunteers to come up and write the letters.

> When you proofread your writing, check to make sure that your letters are clear and easy to read. If you notice a letter that you can write better, cross out the word instead of erasing and rewrite it above.

WML2
WPS.U9.WML2

Have a Try

Invite students to turn and talk about editing and proofreading writing.

> Look at the writing. Are there more letters that should be fixed? Turn and talk to your partner about how they should be fixed.

▶ Ask volunteers to share what they noticed. Model how to cross out each word that has a letter that could be made better and write the word clearly above.

Summarize and Apply

Summarize the lesson. Have students check a longer piece of writing from their writing folders to make sure the letters are formed properly.

▶ Add the principle to the proofreading checklist you began in WML1, along with an example. Read the checklist.

> During writing time, read your writing to make sure that you have written each letter the best that you can. If you find a letter that you need to fix, cross the word out neatly and write it above. Bring your writing to share when we meet later.

▶ Save the checklist for WML3.

Confer

▶ During independent writing, move around the room to confer briefly with as many individual students as time allows. Sit side by side with them and invite them to talk about proofreading and editing their writing. You might wish to have them use the Proofreading Checklist. Use the following prompts as needed.

- *Do you see any letters that you need to fix so your readers can read the words easily?*
- *Where can you look to know how to make a letter?*
- *Show how you can write this letter in a different way so it is easier to read.*
- *Show how you used the Proofreading Checklist.*

Share

Following independent writing, gather students in the meeting area. Ask a few volunteers to share their writing.

> Who would like to share how you edited your writing?

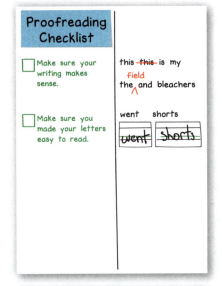

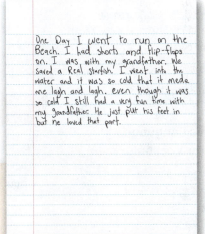

WML 3
WPS.U9.WML3

Writing Minilesson Principle
Make sure you wrote the words you know correctly.

Editing and Proofreading Writing

You Will Need

- a big book, such as *From Buds to Bananas* by Betty Riggs, from *Shared Reading Collection*
- a writing sample with spelling errors (written on chart paper, provided to each student, or projected with a document camera)
- document camera (optional)
- chart from WML2
- writing folders
- To download the following online resource for this lesson, visit **fp.pub/resources**:
  - Proofreading Checklist
  - Proofreading Sample 3

Academic Language / Important Vocabulary

- edit
- spelling
- proofread

Continuum Connection

- Monitor own spelling by noticing when a word does not "look right" and should be checked
- Understand that a writer uses what is known to spell words
- Understand that the more accurate the spelling and the clearer the space between words, the easier it is for the reader to read it
- Edit for spelling errors by circling words that do not look right and spelling them another way
- Edit for the conventional spelling of known words

GOAL

Reread writing to check or correct spelling so the readers can understand the message.

RATIONALE

When students learn to edit and proofread by checking for misspelled words, they understand that it is the writer's responsibility to spell the words they know correctly. Allow students to use temporary, approximated spellings while they are writing so that they can concentrate on the content of their writing by using the most appropriate words, not just words they know how to spell.

WRITER'S NOTEBOOK/WRITING FOLDER

Students will proofread and edit a piece of writing they are working on in their writing folders. If students will use the Proofreading Checklist in this lesson, make sure that a copy is fastened inside each student's writing folder.

ASSESS LEARNING

- Look for evidence that students understand the importance of correct spelling.
- Observe whether students edit and proofread their work to check for correct spelling.
- Look for evidence that students can use vocabulary such as *edit*, *proofread*, and *spelling*.

MINILESSON

To help students learn how to edit and proofread their work, display mentor texts with proper spellings of words students know. Model how writing can be corrected when words they know are spelled incorrectly. Here is an example.

▸ Show and read page 4 in *From Buds to Bananas*.

What is a word you know on this page?

▸ Guide the conversation to help students notice familiar words that are spelled correctly.

You know the words see and green. Notice that they are spelled here the same way you would spell them. That's how you know what those words are. You also know the words yellow and eat. They are spelled the same way each time they are written.

▸ Show the prepared writing sample.

Are there any words you know that might not be spelled correctly?

▸ Guide the conversation to help students notice misspelled familiar words or words that are important to the story (e.g., *fries*, *because*, *There*). Model how to circle the words that don't look right and encourage them to try writing them correctly. Have them check spelling in places they know (e.g., dictionary, digital resource, word list).

The Writing Minilessons Book, Grade 3

WML 3
WPS.U9.WML3

Have a Try

Invite students to turn and talk about how to correct misspelled words.

> Look at the writing. Turn and tell your partner about a word you know that should be fixed and how you would fix it.

▸ After time for a brief discussion, ask a few volunteers to share how they can fix any words that are misspelled. Make the corrections.

Summarize and Apply

Summarize the lesson. Have students proofread and edit a longer piece of writing from their writing folders for spelling.

▸ Add the principle to the proofreading checklist from WML2, along with an example. Read the checklist.

> Today you learned to proofread by checking to make sure the words you know are spelled correctly. When you do your own writing, it's important to spell the words you know correctly so that your readers will understand what you wrote. During writing time, check your spelling by rereading your writing. Bring your writing to share when we meet later.

▸ Save the checklist for WML4.

Confer

▸ During independent writing, move around the room to confer briefly with as many individual students as time allows. Sit side by side with them and invite them to talk about proofreading and editing their writing. You might wish to have them use the Proofreading Checklist. Use the following prompts as needed.

- *Read this sentence to make sure the words you know are spelled correctly.*
- *What do you notice about this sentence?*
- *How can you fix the spelling of this word?*
- *Show how you used the Proofreading Checklist.*

Share

Following independent writing, gather students in the meeting area to share their writing.

> Who would like to share how you edited your writing?

WML 4
WPS.U9.WML4

Writing Minilesson Principle
Check your punctuation and capitalization.

Editing and Proofreading Writing

You Will Need

- two writing samples with some missing punctuation marks and capitalization errors (each written on chart paper, provided to each student, or projected with a document camera)
- document camera (optional)
- highlighter or sticky notes
- writing folders
- To download the following online resource for this lesson, visit **fp.pub/resources**:
  - Proofreading Checklist
  - Proofreading Sample 4

Academic Language / Important Vocabulary

- read aloud
- edit
- proofread
- punctuation
- capitalization

Continuum Connection

- Read one's writing aloud and think where punctuation would go
- Edit for capitalization, punctuation, and sentence sense

GOAL

Use reading aloud as a tool for editing punctuation and capitalization.

RATIONALE

When students learn that reading aloud one's own writing is helpful in making punctuation and capitalization decisions, they take ownership of their own writing and learn to think about conventions.

WRITER'S NOTEBOOK/WRITING FOLDER

Students will proofread and edit a piece of writing they are working on in their writing folders. If students will use the Proofreading Checklist in this lesson, make sure that a copy is fastened inside each student's writing folder.

ASSESS LEARNING

- Notice whether students are reading aloud their own writing to check for punctuation and capitalization.
- Look for evidence that students can use vocabulary such as *read aloud*, *edit*, *proofread*, *punctuation*, and *capitalization*.

MINILESSON

To help students think about the minilesson principle, model the process and provide an interactive lesson. Here is an example.

> Notice what I do as I reread this piece of writing.

- Slowly reread the writing and think aloud about where the missing punctuation should go, highlighting or placing a sticky note in each location.

  > "I made a cake for my mom's birthday." I know that when I am talking about myself, the *I* is always capitalized.
  >
  > Whose birthday is it? How do I show that?
  >
  > I will highlight those spots to remind myself to write a capital *I* and to add an apostrophe when I make a final copy of my story.

- Read the next sentence ("I put yellow sprinkles") aloud.

  > I think something is missing here. What do you think?

- Highlight where a period should go.

  > How does reading this writing aloud help me think about where to place the punctuation marks and capital letters?
  >
  > My voice dropped after *sprinkles*. That helped me realize that a period was missing.

WML 4
WPS.U9.WML4

Have a Try

Invite students to turn and talk about reading aloud a piece of writing to think about where to place punctuation marks and capital letters.

> With your partner, slowly read the rest of the writing on the chart aloud. Talk about where the punctuation marks and capital letters should be placed.

▸ After time for discussion, ask volunteers to share ideas.

Summarize and Apply

Summarize the learning. Have students read aloud a longer piece of writing from their writing folders as a way to check punctuation and capitalization.

▸ Add the principle to the proofreading checklist you began in WML1, along with an example. Read the checklist.

> During writing time, choose a piece of writing you are working on in your writing folder. Read it aloud to yourself quietly and notice places where you need to fix punctuation and capitalization. Bring your writing to share when we meet.

Confer

▸ During independent writing, move around the room to confer briefly with as many individual students as time allows. Sit side by side with them and invite them to read aloud their writing to help with proofreading and editing. Use the following prompts as needed.

- *Read this page aloud. Are there any places where you need to add punctuation?*
- *That sounds like a question. What punctuation mark could you add at the end?*
- *Do you notice any places where you should write a capital letter?*

Share

Following independent writing, gather students in the meeting area to share their writing.

> Who would like to share how you edited your writing?

Umbrella 9: Editing and Proofreading Writing

Umbrella 9: Editing and Proofreading Writing

Assessment

After you have taught the minilessons in this umbrella, observe students in a variety of classroom activities. Use *The Fountas & Pinnell Literacy Continuum* to notice, teach for, and support students' learning as you observe their attempts at writing.

- What evidence do you have of students' new understandings related to editing and proofreading?
  - Do students understand that they should reread their writing to check that it makes sense?
  - Are students looking at their letters to make sure they are easy to read?
  - Are they writing the words they know correctly?
  - Do they check for correct punctuation and capitalization?
  - Are you noticing evidence that they are using an editing and proofreading checklist?
  - Are they using vocabulary such as *make sense*, *letters*, *handwriting*, *edit*, *proofread*, *spelling*, *punctuation*, and *capitalization*?
- In what ways, beyond the scope of this umbrella, are students showing an interest in the writing process?
  - Are they revising and organizing their writing?
  - Are they adding to and deleting from their writing?

Use your observations to determine the next umbrella you will teach. You may also consult Suggested Sequence of Lessons (pp. 605–622) for guidance.

EXTENSIONS FOR EDITING AND PROOFREADING WRITING

- If students are typing their work, discuss the automatic grammar and spell checks. Point out that although the computer indications can be helpful, they are not always correct.

- Meet with students in small groups for guided instruction on proofreading and editing their writing.

- From time to time while reading mentor texts, ask students to point out the clear writing and correct spelling, punctuation, and capitalization. Talk about how the writer needed to proofread and edit before publishing the book.

Adding Book and Print Features

Umbrella 10

Minilessons in This Umbrella

WML1 Choose a title for your book.
WML2 Make an author page.
WML3 Dedicate your book to someone and thank people who helped you.
WML4 Make endpapers for your book.

Before Teaching Umbrella 10 Minilessons

When students are writing books, use the minilessons in this umbrella to introduce them to the idea of getting their books ready to share with an audience by adding book and print features. You do not need to teach the minilessons one right after another. Teach them when you observe that the students are ready.

Before teaching these minilessons, read and discuss engaging books from a variety of genres, especially books that have features such as an author page or dedication. For these minilessons, use the following books from *Fountas & Pinnell Classroom™ Interactive Read-Aloud Collection*, or choose books with a variety of book and print features from the classroom library.

Interactive Read-Aloud Collection

Exploring Memory Stories
Saturdays and Teacakes by Lester L. Laminack
Grandma's Records by Eric Velasquez

Sharing Our World: Animals
And So They Build by Bert Kitchen

The Importance of Kindness
Sophie's Masterpiece: A Spider's Tale by Eileen Spinelli

Connecting Across Generations: Family
Sitti's Secrets by Naomi Shihab Nye

The Passage of Time
The Quilt Story by Tony Johnston
Our Seasons by Grace Lin and Ranida T. McKneally

Author's Point of View
Meadowlands: A Wetlands Survival Story by Thomas F. Yezerski
What's So Bad About Gasoline? Fossil Fuels and What They Do by Anne Rockwell

Series Study: Dianna Hutts Aston and Sylvia Long
A Seed Is Sleepy

As you read and enjoy these texts together, help students
- use the title to predict what the book will be about,
- notice and talk about author pages and dedications, and
- share what they notice about cover illustrations and endpapers.

Interactive Read-Aloud
Memory Stories

Animals

Kindness

Family

Passage of Time

Point of View

Dianna Hutts Aston and Sylvia Long

Writer's Notebook

Section 5: Writing Process

WML1
WPS.U10.WML1

Writing Minilesson Principle
Choose a title for your book.

Adding Book and Print Features

You Will Need

- a few familiar books, such as the following:
  - *Saturdays and Teacakes* by Lester L. Laminack, from Text Set: Exploring Memory Stories
  - *And So They Build* by Bert Kitchen, from Text Set: Sharing Our World: Animals
- chart paper prepared with a book cover (no title)
- markers
- writer's notebooks
- To download the following online resource for this lesson, visit **fp.pub/resources**:
  - chart art (optional)

Academic Language / Important Vocabulary

- cover
- title

Continuum Connection

- Use engaging titles and language
- Select an appropriate title for a poem, story, or informational book
- Generate multiple titles for the piece and select the one that best fits the content of an informational piece or the plot or characterization in narrative

GOAL

Write a title for your book.

RATIONALE

The title is often what entices readers to pick up a book, so a writer must choose a title that gives a hint about the book's content as well as catches the readers' attention. As students study familiar books, talk about how and why authors title their books. They can then think about interesting and fitting titles for their own books.

WRITER'S NOTEBOOK/WRITING FOLDER

Students can try out titles in their writer's notebooks to use for the books they are writing.

ASSESS LEARNING

- Observe for evidence that students understand the purpose of and thought behind book titles and add fitting titles to their own writing.
- Look for evidence that students can use vocabulary such as *cover* and *title*.

MINILESSON

To help students think about the minilesson principle, use several familiar books to start a discussion about book titles. Here is an example.

- Display the covers of several familiar books.

  How do you know the name of this book?

  The name of the book is the title. The title and the illustration on the front cover help you understand what the book is about.

  What do you notice about where the title is written on the cover?

  The title is usually written near the top of the cover, but sometimes it's at the bottom or in the middle. When you're the author, you decide where to put it.

- Display the cover of *Saturdays and Teacakes*.

  Lester Laminack chose the title *Saturdays and Teacakes* for his book. I wonder what else he considered for a title—perhaps *Riding My Bike to Mammaw's* or *How I Spent My Saturdays*. Why do you think he chose *Saturdays and Teacakes*? What makes that title interesting?

- Display the cover of *And So They Build*.

  How do you think the author, Bert Kitchen, decided on a title for this book?

  What do you notice about how the title *And So They Build* looks? Do authors use full sentences as titles?

Have a Try

Have students help you write a title for the cover on the prepared chart.

> Let's choose a title for this book. The author wrote about learning to read and write in a Cambodian language called Khmer by going to a special school with her sister in addition to the school she went to every day. She mentioned her friends. She described learning to dance. What might be a good title for this book? Turn and talk to your partner about this.

▸ After time for discussion, invite several students to share their ideas. Record all reasonable suggestions on chart paper. Then discuss which title would be the most fitting and why. Discuss where on the cover to put the title. Write the title.

Summarize and Apply

Write the principle at the top of the chart. Summarize the learning. Remind students to write a title on the front cover of their books.

> During writing time, try out some titles for your book in your writer's notebook. Choose the one that best fits your book and write it on the front cover. Think about a title that hooks your readers and makes them want to read more. Bring your book to share when we meet later.

Confer

▸ During independent writing, move around the room to confer briefly with as many individual students as time allows. Sit side by side with them and invite them to talk about choosing a title for their books. Use the following prompts as needed.

- *What is your book about?*
- *What are your ideas for a title? Which title do you think is the best? Why?*
- *What title might make your readers want to read more?*
- *Where on the cover will you write the title?*

Share

Following independent writing, gather students in the meeting area to share their book covers.

> If you made a cover, hold it up so everyone can see.

WML2
WPS.U10.WML2

Writing Minilesson Principle
Make an author page.

Adding Book and Print Features

You Will Need

- a few familiar books with an author page, such as the following:
  - *Sophie's Masterpiece* by Eileen Spinelli, from Text Set: The Importance of Kindness
  - *Grandma's Records* by Eric Velasquez, from Text Set: Exploring Memory Stories
  - *Sitti's Secrets* by Naomi Shihab Nye, from Text Set: Connecting Across Generations: Family
- chart paper and markers
- writing folders
- To download the following online resources for this lesson, visit **fp.pub/resources**:
  - chart art (optional)
  - paper templates (optional)

Academic Language / Important Vocabulary

- author
- author page

Continuum Connection

- In anticipation of an audience, add book and print features during the publishing process: e.g., illustrations and other graphics, cover spread, title, dedication, table of contents, about the author piece

---

GOAL

Write an author page to share information about yourself.

RATIONALE

Helping students study author pages and supporting them in writing their own author pages helps them view themselves as writers. It encourages students to take pride in and celebrate their writing.

WRITER'S NOTEBOOK/WRITING FOLDER

Students will write an author page for the book they are working on in their writing folders.

ASSESS LEARNING

- Look for evidence that students understand the purpose of an author page.
- Notice if students write author pages in their own books.
- Look for evidence that students can use vocabulary such as *author* and *author page*.

MINILESSON

To help students think about the minilesson principle, study author pages in several familiar texts. Engage students in a discussion about the information that authors share about themselves on an author page. Here is an example.

- Read aloud the author information on the back cover of *Sophie's Masterpiece*.

  What does this part of the book tell you about?

  What do you learn about the author, Eileen Spinelli, from this part of the book?

  What do you learn about what inspired her to write this book?

- Continue in a similar manner with *Grandma's Records* and *Sitti's Secrets*. Guide students to understand that Naomi Shihab Nye's experience visiting her grandmother in Jerusalem was meaningful to her and inspired her to write *Sitti's Secrets*.

  The information about the author is called the author page.

  What information do authors tell on their author pages?

- Record students' responses in general terms on chart paper.

  Where in a book might you find the author page?

  The author page may be in the front or back of the book, or on the back cover or back flap. When you write your own books, you can decide where to put the author page.

Have a Try

Invite students to talk to a partner about what they would write on their own author page.

> Turn and talk to your partner about what you might write about yourself on the author page in a book you've written.

- After time for discussion, invite several students to share their thinking.

Summarize and Apply

Summarize the learning. Remind students that they can write an author page in their own books. When students make their author pages, they can use plain paper or the author page from the paper templates in the online resources.

> Why might an author decide to write an author page?

- Write the principle at the top of the chart.

> During writing time today, think some more about what you would like your readers to know about you. Write an author page about yourself. Bring your book to share when we come back together.

Make an author page.
- Where the author lives and with whom
- How the author got the idea for the book
- Where the author went to school
- What inspired the author to write about the topic
- Why the book is meaningful to the author
- A photo or illustration of the author
- Other books the author has written
- The author's website
- Awards the author has won
- The author's other jobs

Confer

- During independent writing, move around the room to confer briefly with as many individual students as time allows. Sit side by side with them and invite them to talk about their author pages. Use prompts such as the following as needed.
  - What would you like your readers to know about you?
  - What could you write to share why you wrote the book?
  - What other books have you written?
  - Where would you like to put the author page?

Share

Following independent writing, gather students in the meeting area to share their author pages with a partner and then with the group.

> What did you learn about _____ from the author page?

> What did you hear other students include on an author page that you might try in your own books?

Umbrella 10: Adding Book and Print Features

WML 3
WPS.U10.WML3

Writing Minilesson Principle
Dedicate your book to someone and thank people who helped you.

Adding Book and Print Features

You Will Need

- a few familiar books with a dedication, such as the following:
  - *The Quilt Story* by Tony Johnston and *Our Seasons* by Grace Lin and Ranida T. McKneally, from Text Set: The Passage of Time
  - *Meadowlands* by Thomas F. Yezerski and *What's So Bad About Gasoline?* by Anne Rockwell, from Text Set: Author's Point of View
- chart paper and markers
- writing folders
- To download the following online resource for this lesson, visit **fp.pub/resources**:
  - paper templates (optional)

Academic Language / Important Vocabulary

- author
- dedicate
- dedication

Continuum Connection

- In anticipation of an audience, add book and print features to the text during the publishing process: e.g., illustrations and other graphics, cover spread, title, dedication, table of contents, about the author piece

---

GOAL

Write a dedication to someone or something that is important to you.

RATIONALE

When students study dedications and think about the reasons authors choose to dedicate a book to someone, they understand that authors are real people who care about and are influenced by others. They also begin to think of themselves as authors.

WRITER'S NOTEBOOK/WRITING FOLDER

Students will write a dedication for the book they are working on in their writing folders.

ASSESS LEARNING

- Look for evidence that students understand the purpose of a dedication and try writing one.
- Look for evidence that students can use vocabulary such as *author*, *dedicate*, and *dedication*.

MINILESSON

To help students think about the minilesson principle, use mentor texts to engage them in a discussion about dedications. Here is an example.

- Read aloud the author's dedication in *The Quilt Story*.

  Does anyone know what this part of the book is called?

  This is the dedication. What do you think a dedication is?

  In a dedication, the author dedicates the book to a person or a group of people. Dedicating a book to someone is a way of showing appreciation.

  Why does the author, Tony Johnston, dedicate this book to Ann Doherty Johnston?

  It sounds like Ann taught Tony how to quilt—or at least to have fun trying! Maybe Ann gave her the idea for the book. They have the same last name, so I wonder if they are related.

- Read the dedication in *Our Seasons*.

  To whom do the authors dedicate this book?

  Who do you think Robert and Luke are? Why do you think the authors chose to dedicate the book to each of them?

- Continue with *Meadowlands* and *What's So Bad About Gasoline?*

  To whom do authors dedicate their books?

- Generalize students' responses and record them on chart paper.

  What do you notice about where authors put dedications?

The Writing Minilessons Book, Grade 3

Have a Try

Invite students to talk to a partner about their own dedications.

> Think about the book you're working on or the last book you wrote. Is there someone to whom you would like to dedicate your book? Why? Turn and talk to your partner about your dedication.

▸ After students turn and talk, invite several students to share their thinking. Add new ideas to the chart.

Summarize and Apply

Summarize the learning. Remind students that they can dedicate their books to someone and/or thank people who helped them. When students make their dedication pages, they can use plain paper or the dedication page from the paper templates in the online resources.

▸ Write the principle at the top of the chart.

> Why do authors write dedications?
>
> During writing time today, think about whether you would like to write a dedication. Decide where you would like to place the dedication in your book. Bring your book to share when we come back together.

Dedicate your book to someone and thank people who helped you.

- Someone who gave you the idea for the book
- Someone who has taught you something
- Someone you respect, love, or care about
- Someone who has helped you with something
- Someone who might be interested in the topic of the book

Dedication

This book is dedicated to my parents, who gave me a love for reading and writing.

Confer

▸ During independent writing, move around the room to confer briefly with as many individual students as time allows. Sit side by side with them and invite them to talk about writing a dedication. Use prompts such as the following as needed.

- *Did someone give you the idea to write this book?*
- *Would you like to dedicate it to someone special in your family?*
- *What could you write about why you are dedicating your book to that person?*
- *Where in your book would you like to put the dedication?*

Share

Following independent writing, gather students in the meeting area to share their dedications.

> Would you like to read aloud your dedication? Share why you decided to dedicate your book to _____.

WML 4
WPS.U10.WML4

Writing Minilesson Principle
Make endpapers for your book.

Adding Book and Print Features

You Will Need

- a few familiar books with interesting endpapers, such as the following:
  - *A Seed Is Sleepy* by Dianna Hutts Aston, from Text Set: Series Study: Dianna Hutts Aston and Sylvia Long
  - *What's So Bad About Gasoline?* by Anne Rockwell, from Text Set: Author's Point of View
  - *The Quilt Story* by Tony Johnston, from Text Set: The Passage of Time
- chart paper and markers
- writing folders
- To download the following online resource for this lesson, visit **fp.pub/resources**:
  - chart art (optional)

Academic Language / Important Vocabulary

- endpapers
- illustrator
- author

Continuum Connection

- In anticipation of an audience, add book and print features during the publishing process: e.g., illustrations and other graphics, cover spread, title, dedication, table of contents, about the author piece

GOAL

Make endpapers that are related to the meaning of the text and increase readers' understanding and enjoyment.

RATIONALE

When students think about how endpapers relate to a book's meaning, they gain an appreciation for the thought and care that went into creating every aspect of the book. They understand that they, too, can put the same thought and care into creating their own books by adding endpapers.

WRITER'S NOTEBOOK/WRITING FOLDER

Students can make endpapers for the book they are working on in their writing folders.

ASSESS LEARNING

- Look for evidence that students understand that endpapers can add to the meaning of a text and increase the readers' enjoyment.
- Notice if students add endpapers to their own books.
- Observe for evidence that students can use vocabulary such as *endpapers*, *illustrator*, and *author*.

MINILESSON

To help students think about the minilesson principle, study the endpapers in familiar texts. Engage students in a discussion about endpapers. Here is an example.

- Show the cover of *A Seed Is Sleepy*. Open to the endpapers, helping students to notice they are at the beginning and end of the book.

  What do you notice about the beginning and final pages in this book?

  There are no words on these pages, but there is an illustration. Talk about this illustration and why it is important.

  The illustration shows seeds that look like they are blowing in the wind. These pages tell or remind you that you are learning about seeds in this book. Though these are called endpapers, they can appear before and after the main part of the book.

- Show the endpapers in *What's So Bad About Gasoline?*

  What do you notice about these endpapers?

  The endpapers show vehicles and the puffs of smoke they create.

- Continue in this manner with a fiction story, *The Quilt Story*.

  Why might authors and illustrators sometimes add endpapers to their books?

- Record responses on chart paper.

The Writing Minilessons Book, Grade 3

Have a Try

Invite students to talk to a partner about their own books.

> Think about the book you're working on or another book you've written recently. What might you put on the endpapers of your book? Turn and talk to your partner about your ideas.

▸ After students turn and talk, invite several students to share their ideas.

Summarize and Apply

Write the principle at the top of the chart. Summarize the learning. Remind students that they can make endpapers for their books.

> During writing time, make endpapers for your book that will help readers understand the topic or make your book more fun to read. You can make the endpapers on paper and then glue them into your book, or you can make them right in your book. If they are in the front of your book, one side is the inside of the front cover and the other side is the front of your first page. If they are at the end of your book, one side is the back of your last page and the other side is the inside of your back cover. Bring your book to share when we come back together.

Make endpapers for your book.
- Remind readers of what they learned
- Give more information
- Make the book more fun to read
- Hook readers' attention

Confer

▸ During independent writing, move around the room to confer briefly with as many individual students as time allows. Sit side by side with them and invite them to talk about making endpapers. Use prompts such as the following as needed.

- *What might you draw that would help readers understand more about the topic?*
- *What might you draw that would make your book even more fun to read?*
- *Why did you decide to put _____ on your book's endpapers?*

Share

Following independent writing, gather students in the meeting area to show their endpapers to each other. Select several students to talk about them.

> Talk about your decision to draw _____ on the endpapers.

Umbrella 10: Adding Book and Print Features

Assessment

After you have taught the minilessons in this umbrella, observe students as they draw, write, and talk about their writing. Use *The Fountas & Pinnell Literacy Continuum* to notice, teach for, and support students' learning as you observe their bookmaking skills.

- What evidence do you have of students' new understandings related to adding book and print features for an audience?
  - Do students add a title to the front cover of their books?
  - Can they write an author page about themselves?
  - Have they experimented with writing a dedication for a book?
  - Have they experimented with making endpapers for a book?
  - Do they understand and use vocabulary such as *author*, *author page*, *cover*, *title*, *dedicate*, *dedication*, and *endpapers*?
- In what other ways, beyond the scope of this umbrella, are students exploring the writing process?
  - Are they sharing their writing with others?
  - Are they incorporating what they know about illustration to enhance the meaning of their writing?
  - Are they publishing their writing in different ways?

Use your observations to determine the next umbrella you will teach. You may also consult Suggested Sequence of Lessons (pp. 605–622) for guidance.

EXTENSIONS FOR ADDING BOOK AND PRINT FEATURES

- To help students know which words to capitalize in their titles, consider teaching CNV.U2.WML1.
- Help students study back covers to learn the kind of information usually included. Then have them make a back cover for their own books.
- Teach students how to make a copyright page and an acknowledgment page.
- Students might revisit finished pieces in their hanging files to add a dedication, author page, or endpapers.

Publishing and Self-Assessing Your Writing

Umbrella 11

Minilessons in This Umbrella

- **WML1** Choose a piece you want to publish.
- **WML2** Publish your writing.
- **WML3** Use a self-assessment rubric.
- **WML4** Select a piece of writing that shows your growth as a writer.

Before Teaching Umbrella 11 Minilessons

We recommend teaching at least some of the minilessons in WPS.U10: Adding Book and Print Features before teaching WML2. It would also be helpful for you to prepare some sample writing projects to use for demonstrating this umbrella's principles. Teach the first two minilessons when students have completed several writing pieces and are ready to choose one for a more formal publishing treatment. Teach the last two minilessons when students have a body of work that they can use to assess and reflect on how they are progressing as writers.

The purpose of the minilessons in this umbrella is to prepare students to choose pieces they are proud of to publish, share, and reflect upon. How you define "publishing" writing for third graders is up to you and your students. In some cases, students might enjoy publishing their work by typing and printing it, while in other cases they may rewrite their final draft in their best handwriting. Some teachers may prefer to help their students prepare a perfectly edited final product, while others may choose to have their students handle their own editing and proofreading. Of course, not every piece of writing will be published.

Students will need their writing folders to access longer pieces of writing for publishing and self-assessing. They will also need access to their finished writing, kept in hanging files (see p. 54), from which they will choose a piece that shows how they have grown as writers.

Writer's Notebook

WML1
WPS.U11.WML1

Writing Minilesson Principle
Choose a piece you want to publish.

Publishing and Self-Assessing Your Writing

You Will Need

- a draft version of a piece of writing that you have prepared as an example
- a published children's book
- chart paper and markers
- writing folders

Academic Language / Important Vocabulary

- publish
- audience

Continuum Connection

- Understand publishing as the sharing of a piece of writing with a purpose and an audience in mind
- Select a poem, story, or informational book to publish in a variety of appropriate ways: e.g., typed/printed, framed and mounted or otherwise displayed

GOAL

Select a piece to publish for an audience.

RATIONALE

Before students can "publish" their work for an audience, they must first choose which piece to publish. This lesson helps them think about the criteria they can use to evaluate their work. When students think carefully about choosing pieces, they are more likely to select work that they are truly proud of and confident about sharing.

WRITER'S NOTEBOOK/WRITING FOLDER

Students will select a draft from their writing folders to get ready to share (publish).

ASSESS LEARNING

- Listen to students' reasons for choosing pieces to publish.
- Look for evidence that they can use vocabulary such as *publish* and *audience*.

MINILESSON

To help students think about the principle, discuss what it means to publish a piece of writing. Then share why you have chosen to publish a particular piece and help students generate a list of criteria for choosing a piece to publish. Here is an example.

- Show the draft and the published book, side by side.

    How are these two pieces of writing different?

    This is a draft, and this is a published book. What does it mean to publish a piece of writing?

    When you publish a piece of writing, you finish it and get it ready so other people can read it. A published piece of writing shows the author's best work.

    Authors don't publish every piece of writing they write. Sometimes, an author may decide that a piece of writing is finished but choose not to share it with an audience. Authors think very carefully about which pieces of writing to publish.

- Display the draft again.

    Here is a draft of mine, and I've decided that I would like to publish it because I worked very hard on it and I'm proud of it. I think it shows my best work. It's about an important topic that I care a lot about and that I think other people should learn about, too.

    What do you notice about why I chose this book to publish?

- Record students' responses on chart paper.

WML1
WPS.U11.WML1

Have a Try

Invite students to talk to a partner about a piece of writing they would like to publish.

> Think about the pieces of writing you have worked on lately. Which one would you like to publish, or get ready for an audience to read? Why? Turn and talk to your partner about this.

▸ After students turn and talk, invite several students to share their reasons for choosing a particular piece of writing to publish. Add any new reasons to the chart, generalizing them as necessary.

Summarize and Apply

Summarize the learning. Invite students to choose a piece of writing to publish.

> Today you learned how to choose a piece of writing to publish, or get it ready for an audience to read. During writing time, look in your writing folder and think about which piece of writing you would like to publish. Be ready to share your reasons for choosing it when we come back together.

Reasons to Publish a Piece of Writing

- You worked very hard on it.
- You are proud of your work.
- It shows your best work.
- You care a lot about the topic.
- You want other people to learn about the topic.
- You think other people will enjoy reading it.
- You are excited about this piece of writing.
- You love what you wrote.

Confer

▸ During independent writing, move around the room to confer briefly with as many individual students as time allows. Sit side by side with them and invite them to talk about publishing a piece of writing. Use prompts such as the following as needed.

- *Which piece of writing would you like to publish?*
- *What have you written that you are proud of?*
- *Why do you want to publish this piece of writing?*
- *Does this piece of writing show your best work?*

Share

Following independent writing, gather students in the meeting area to talk about their writing.

> Turn to your partner and share how you chose a draft to publish.

Umbrella 11: Publishing and Self-Assessing Your Writing

WML 2
WPS.U11.WML2

Writing Minilesson Principle
Publish your writing.

Publishing and Self-Assessing Your Writing

You Will Need

- examples of writing (yours or a student's) that have been published in different ways (as a picture book, with cover, framed and mounted, etc.)
- chart paper and markers
- writing folders

Academic Language / Important Vocabulary

- publish
- type
- cover
- title page
- author page

Continuum Connection

- Use reference tools to check on spelling when editing final draft (dictionary, digital resources)
- Understand that the teacher will be final spelling editor for the published piece after the student has used everything known
- Add cover spread with title and author information
- In anticipation of an audience, add book and print features during the publishing process: e.g., illustrations and other graphics, cover, spread, title, dedication, table of contents, about the author piece
- Attend to layout of text in final publication

GOAL

Determine the form for publishing writing and preparing writing for publication.

RATIONALE

When you teach students different ways to make their writing accessible to others, they begin to understand that bookmaking is a process that involves several steps beyond writing the words and drawing the illustrations. They also begin to conceptualize the idea of writing not just for themselves but also for an audience.

WRITER'S NOTEBOOK/WRITING FOLDER

Students will work on getting a draft from their writing folders ready to share (publish).

ASSESS LEARNING

- Notice whether students experiment with different ways of publishing their writing (e.g., adding a cover and title page, framing or mounting a poem).
- Look for evidence that they can use vocabulary such as *publish*, *type*, *cover*, *title page*, and *author page*.

MINILESSON

To help students think about the minilesson principle, engage them in a discussion about how to prepare their writing for publication. Here is an example.

- Show students a piece of published writing by you or a student, and discuss how it was prepared for publication.

    I decided to publish this piece of writing as a nonfiction picture book. I did several things to get my writing ready to be published. First, I proofread and edited my writing very carefully to make sure there weren't any spelling or punctuation mistakes. Then I typed my writing on a computer to make it look nice and be easy to read. I added a title page and an author page. Finally, I put a cardboard cover on my book so it won't tear easily. What did I write on the cover?

    What do you notice about how I published my writing?

- Display and discuss a few other pieces of writing that have been published in different ways (e.g., a framed and mounted poem, a spiral-bound book, typed on a computer).

    I rewrote my poem in my best handwriting. Then I put it on a piece of construction paper to make it look nice. Finally, I put it in a frame. What are some other ways you could publish a piece of writing?

- On chart paper, record different ways of publishing a piece of writing.

Have a Try

Invite students to talk to a partner about how they would like to publish their writing.

> Yesterday, you chose a special piece of your writing that you would like to publish. How would you like to publish it? What will you do to get it ready to be published? Turn and talk to your partner about your ideas.

▶ After students turn and talk, invite a few students to share their thinking. Add responses to the chart.

Summarize and Apply

Write the principle at the top of the chart. Summarize the learning and invite students to start preparing their writing for publication.

> Today we talked about different ways to publish your writing and how to prepare it to be published. During writing time today, decide how you want to publish your writing and start getting it ready to be published.

Confer

▶ During independent writing, move around the room to confer briefly with as many individual students as time allows. Sit side by side with them and invite them to talk about publishing their writing. Use prompts such as the following as needed.

- *How would you like to publish your writing?*
- *How did you check your spelling?*
- *Would you like to type your writing or write it in your best handwriting?*
- *Is there anything you would like to add to your writing, like a cover or title page?*

Share

Following independent writing, gather students in the meeting area to talk about publishing their writing.

> How did you get your writing ready to be published today?

> Has anyone finished publishing your writing? Would you like to share it with the class?

WML 3
WPS.U11.WML3

Writing Minilesson Principle
Use a self-assessment rubric.

Publishing and Self-Assessing Your Writing

You Will Need

- a sample memory story you have prepared
- a copy of the rubric for you and for each student
- markers
- writing folders
- To download the following online resource for this lesson, visit **fp.pub/resources**:
  - Rubric for Memory Stories (Student)

Academic Language / Important Vocabulary

- assess
- self-assessment
- rubric

Continuum Connection

- Self-evaluate writing and talk about what is good about it and what techniques were used
- Talk about oneself as a writer
- Notice what makes writing effective and name the craft or technique

GOAL

Use a self-assessment tool to reflect on areas of strength and determine goals for writing.

RATIONALE

When you teach students how to use a self-assessment rubric, they are able to independently evaluate their own work, reflect on areas of strength, and identify areas for future development.

WRITER'S NOTEBOOK/WRITING FOLDER

When students are ready to evaluate a finished piece of writing from their writing folders, provide the appropriate rubric.

ASSESS LEARNING

- Notice whether students think carefully about their work and are able to identify areas of strength and areas for future development.
- Look for evidence that they can use vocabulary such as *assess*, *self-assessment*, and *rubric*.

MINILESSON

To help students think about the minilesson principle, model using a self-assessment rubric to evaluate your writing. For the lesson, project a copy of the rubric or provide a copy to each student. (Students will need their own rubrics for Summarize and Apply.) Here is an example.

- Show the Rubric for Memory Stories (Student).

    This is a rubric. Does anyone know what a rubric is?

    A rubric is a tool that you can use to assess your writing. When you assess your writing, you reread it and you think about what you did well and what you need to work on. This rubric is for assessing memory stories. What do you notice about the rubric?

- Read the memory story. Then model how to use the rubric.

    The first section is called Genre Understandings. It is about how well you understand the type of writing and show the qualities of the genre in your own writing. The first row in this section asks if I wrote about a special moment or memory. There are three choices. I think I stayed focused on a special moment or memory and wrote why the memory is important to me. I will circle the third column in the first row.

    Next to Word Choice, the rubric asks if I used interesting words and phrases to help readers imagine what things looked, sounded, smelled, tasted, and felt like. I think I could have done that more, so I will circle the second column.

- Continue as needed to make sure students understand how to use the rubric.

The Writing Minilessons Book, Grade 3

Have a Try

Invite students to talk to a partner about how to use a self-assessment rubric.

> What did you notice about how I assessed my memory story using the rubric? What did I do? What did I think about? Turn and talk to your partner about this.

▸ After students turn and talk, invite several pairs to share their thinking. Record their responses on chart paper.

Summarize and Apply

Summarize the learning. Students may need assistance using the rubric if this is their first time using one.

> Why do you think it's important to assess your own writing? How can this help you grow as a writer?

> Today during writing time, use this self-assessment rubric to evaluate the last memory story you wrote. I will help you if you need help.

How to Use a Rubric

- Reread your writing.
- Read across the first row of the rubric.
- Think about which description fits your writing.
- Circle it.
- Repeat for each row.
- At the end, think about what you could do better next time.

Confer

▸ During independent writing, move around the room to confer briefly with as many individual students as time allows. Sit side by side with them and invite them to talk about assessing their writing. Use prompts such as the following as needed.

- *Read the first row of the rubric. What does it ask you to notice?*
- *Do you think you stayed focused on a special moment or memory? What makes you think that?*
- *What time words did you use in your memory story?*
- *Can you hear your voice in your writing? Where? Can you find some examples?*
- *Where did you use quotation marks in your story? Did you use them correctly?*

Share

Following independent writing, gather students in the meeting area to talk about self-assessing their writing.

> How did you use a self-assessment rubric today?

> How did the rubric help you think about your writing?

WML 4
WPS.U11.WML4

Writing Minilesson Principle
Select a piece of writing that shows your growth as a writer.

Publishing and Self-Assessing Your Writing

You Will Need

- a sample piece of your writing
- chart paper prepared with a reflection on the writing
- chart paper and markers
- writing folders

Academic Language / Important Vocabulary

- growth
- writer
- reflect

Continuum Connection

- Notice what makes writing effective and name the craft or technique
- Select best pieces of writing from own collection and give reasons for the selections
- Talk about oneself as a writer

GOAL

Select a piece of writing and reflect on how the piece shows growth.

RATIONALE

In addition to reflecting on their work regularly throughout the writing process, it is also helpful for students to select a piece of writing specifically for looking at their growth as a writer a few times a year (e.g., quarterly). This allows them to see and reflect on the "big picture" of their writing progress.

WRITER'S NOTEBOOK/WRITING FOLDER

Students will select a piece of writing from their writing folders or their hanging files, reflect on how it shows their growth as a writer, and note what they have learned.

ASSESS LEARNING

- Notice whether students are able to select a piece of writing that shows their growth as a writer and explain why they selected it.
- Look for evidence that they can use vocabulary such as *growth*, *writer*, and *reflect*.

MINILESSON

A few times a year, have students write a longer reflection about a piece of writing that shows their growth as writers and illustrators. More frequently, you will have students write short reflections on the writing folder resource What I Have Learned to Do as a Writer and Illustrator (see MGT.U4: Introducing the Writing Folder). This example lesson shows how you might do the former.

- Read aloud and show the sample piece of writing you prepared. Then explain why you chose to reflect on this piece of writing.

    > I chose this poem to think about and reflect on because I think it shows some of my best work. This poem shows my growth as a writer because I never used to write poems. But I worked hard on this one, and I'm very proud of it. I used a lot of interesting describing words, and I shared some very personal thoughts and feelings. This poem shows that I am no longer afraid to take risks in my writing.

- Show and read the prepared reflection.

    > In this kind of reflection, you will write about what you have learned to do as a writer and illustrator. What will you need to think about to choose a piece of writing?

- Remind students of what they have learned to do as writers and illustrators, such as make a table of contents, draw people, use paragraphing, choose powerful words, and so forth. Record responses on a clean sheet of chart paper.

Have a Try

Invite students to talk to a partner about a piece of writing that shows their growth as a writer.

> Think about the writing projects that you have worked on lately. Can you think of a piece of writing that shows your growth as a writer? How does it show growth? Turn and talk to your partner about this.

- After students turn and talk, invite a few volunteers to share their reflections.

Summarize and Apply

Write the principle at the top of the chart. Summarize the learning and invite students to reflect on their writing progress.

> Today during writing time, spend some time looking through the writing you have done lately and reflecting on your growth as a writer. Choose a piece of writing that shows your growth as a writer, and write at least a few sentences explaining how it shows growth. Bring your reflection and your writing to share when we meet later.

Confer

- During independent writing, move around the room to confer briefly with as many individual students as time allows. Sit side by side with them and invite them to talk about their growth as a writer. Use prompts such as the following as needed.
  - Which piece of writing shows something you've learned how to do as a writer or illustrator?
  - Why did you choose this piece of writing?
  - How does this piece of writing show something you did that you didn't know how to do before?
  - What makes you proud of this piece of writing?

Share

Following independent writing, gather students in the meeting area to share their reflections.

> Talk about why you chose that piece of writing. How does it show what you have learned how to do as a writer and illustrator?

> I thought that I didn't know how to write poems, and I was afraid to try. But I started writing poems this year, and I'm very proud of this one.
>
> I think I used a lot of interesting describing words in this poem, and I shared some very personal thoughts and feelings. This poem shows that I am no longer afraid to take risks in my writing.

Select a piece of writing that shows your growth as a writer.

You tried a new type of writing.

You chose interesting words.

You worked very hard on the writing.

The illustrations have lots of details.

You tried something new in your writing (for example, made a table of contents, used paragraphs).

You like the way you started the writing.

The ending is satisfying.

Umbrella 11: Publishing and Self-Assessing Your Writing

Assessment

After you have taught the minilessons in this umbrella, observe students as they draw, write, and talk about their writing. Use *The Fountas & Pinnell Literacy Continuum* to notice, teach for, and support students' writing development.

- What evidence do you have of students' new understandings related to publishing and self-assessing writing?
  - How are students explaining their choices of what to publish?
  - How do they prepare and publish their writing?
  - Do they use self-assessment rubrics to reflect on their work?
  - Are they able to notice and name their growth as a writer?
  - Do students understand and use vocabulary such as *publish*, *self-assessment*, *rubric*, and *growth*?
- In what other ways, beyond the scope of this umbrella, are students exploring the writing process?
  - Are they revising, editing, and proofreading their writing?
  - Are they adding book and print features to their books?

Use your observations to determine the next umbrella you will teach. You may also consult Suggested Sequence of Lessons (pp. 605–622) for guidance.

EXTENSIONS FOR PUBLISHING AND SELF-ASSESSING YOUR WRITING

- Help students identify and talk about different text features in published books (e.g., title page, table of contents, glossary). Invite them to add the same features to their own books (see WPS.U10: Adding Book and Print Features).

- Dedicate a section of the classroom library or area of the school (e.g., hallway or lobby) to displaying and celebrating students' published writing projects.

- Teach students how to publish a collection of several of their stories or poems.

- When students write a longer reflection on a separate piece of paper, attach it to the piece of writing and place in their hanging folders. You may find it helpful to have two or three writing pieces with reflections available for when you hold conferences with parents and caregivers. For more frequent, shorter reflections, use the writing folder online resource What I Have Learned How to Do as a Writer and Illustrator (see MGT.U4.WML2).

- Teach children to make cover spreads, both front and back covers, for their books. Have them study the content on the front and back of published books to learn possibilities for their own books.

Appendix:
Suggested Sequence of Lessons

The Suggested Sequence of Lessons is also available on the Fountas & Pinnell Online Resources site (**fp.pub/resources**).

Suggested Sequence of Lessons

This sequence shows when you might teach the writing minilessons across the year. It also aligns the lessons with the texts from *Fountas & Pinnell Classroom™ Shared Reading Collection* and *Interactive Read-Aloud Collection*, as well as the reading minilesson umbrellas from *The Reading Minilessons Book, Grade 3*. (Note that the order of Shared Reading books here differs slightly from the order in the *Shared Reading Collection*.) You do not need these other resources to teach the writing minilessons this book, but this comprehensive sequence helps you see how all these pieces can fit together and think about how you might organize reading and writing across the year. Note that the number of days suggested in the writing minilessons column refers to approximately how long it will take to teach the lessons rather than how long your students might spend applying new ideas or experimenting with new kinds of writing.

Suggested Sequence of Lessons

Months	Texts from *Fountas & Pinnell Classroom™ Shared Reading Collection*	Text Sets from *Fountas & Pinnell Classroom™ Interactive Read-Aloud Collection*	Reading Minilessons (RML) Umbrellas	Writing Minilessons (WML) Umbrellas	Teaching Suggestions for Extending Learning
Months 1 & 2	Cat Belly Marissa Margolis, Pet Sitter	The Importance of Kindness Connecting Across Generations: Family	MGT.U1: Working Together in the Classroom	**MGT.U1: Building Community Through Oral Storytelling (5 days)**	We recommend teaching this umbrella first because it serves several purposes. It allows children to orally rehearse stories, build community through listening to one another's stories, and get ideas for writing. It is helpful to provide time between the lessons in this umbrella for students to tell their stories. For example, instead of teaching a minilesson, provide a time each day for a few students to share their stories, or have students tell their stories in pairs or small groups. You could also have them tell stories to one another as they work on the lessons in MGT.U2. Alternating between lessons in MGT.U1 and MGT.U2 is a nice way to build community while establishing important routines.

Key
MGT: Management   GEN: Genres and Forms   CFT: Craft   CNV: Conventions
WPS: Writing Process

Suggested Sequence of Lessons (cont.)

Months	Texts from *Fountas & Pinnell Classroom™ Shared Reading Collection*	Text Sets from *Fountas & Pinnell Classroom™ Interactive Read-Aloud Collection*	Reading Minilessons (RML) Umbrellas	Writing Minilessons (WML) Umbrellas	Teaching Suggestions for Extending Learning
Months 1 & 2 (cont.)	The Rain Forest Rainbow Trapped in Tar Bats Aren't Bad Snakes Aren't Slimy Crows Aren't Creepy	Sharing Our World: Animals	MGT U2: Exploring the Classroom Library MGT U3: Getting Started with Independent Reading LA.U1: Thinking and Talking About Books	MGT.U2: Working Together in the Classroom (5 days)	If you are using *The Reading Minilessons Book, Grade 3*, you do not need to teach the lessons that repeat in MGT.U2. Both the RML and WML books establish the same basic routines. You may choose to teach these lessons while students are engaged in storytelling (MGT.U1) so they can apply many of these behaviors as they engage in conversation and community building with peers. They can also write some of the stories they have told while they work on practicing these important routines.
				WPS.U1: Introducing and Using a Writer's Notebook, WML1–WML4 (4 days)	We recommend introducing a writer's notebook as soon as you can in the school year so that students can write in them daily for ten minutes outside of writers' workshop. Teach most of this umbrella at one time, or interweave these lessons with the first two MGT umbrellas.
				WPS.U2: Writer's Notebook: Getting Ideas from Your Life, WML1–WML2 (2 days)	The minilessons in WPS.U2 can be taught over time to help students learn how to gather ideas in their notebooks and to develop the routine of writing in their notebooks daily for ten minutes.
				GEN.U12: Making Picture Books (4 days)	Inviting students to make picture books is an exciting way to kick off writing projects during writer's workshop. Students can look through the ideas they gathered in their writer's notebooks through the first two lessons in WPS.U2 to select topics for their books.
				MGT.U3: Establishing Independent Writing (4 days)	As students begin to work on making books, you can take time to establish the guidelines for independent writing. One idea is to alternate between the lessons in GEN.U12 and MGT.U3 so students learn how to use the routines and tools of independent writing while working on their first writing project.

Suggested Sequence of Lessons (cont.)

Months	Texts from *Fountas & Pinnell Classroom™ Shared Reading Collection*	Text Sets from *Fountas & Pinnell Classroom™ Interactive Read-Aloud Collection*	Reading Minilessons (RML) Umbrellas	Writing Minilessons (WML) Umbrellas	Teaching Suggestions for Extending Learning
Months 1 & 2 (cont.)	Three Days to Summer	Exploring Memory Stories	WAR.U1: Introducing a Reader's Notebook	CFT.U12: Drawing People (4 days)	Students can practice sketching people in their writer's notebooks, or they can apply these minilessons directly to illustrations in the picture books they are making. Repeat this umbrella whenever students need support in making their drawings of people look realistic.
				CFT.U13: Adding Meaning Through Illustrations (5 days)	Students can apply the lessons in this umbrella as they engage in making picture books.
				CFT.U1: Reading Like a Writer and Illustrator (3 days)	The lessons in this umbrella can be applied to any of students' writing and illustrating. We recommend teaching these lessons early in the year to help students develop a mindset for looking at mentor texts and noticing the craft moves of authors and illustrators.
		Author/Illustrator Study: Patricia Polacco	LA.U2: Studying Authors and Illustrators (RML1–RML2)	WPS.U10: Adding Book and Print Features, WML1–WML2 (2 days)	You can teach the lessons in WPS.U10 all at once or spread them out over time. We recommend teaching the first two lessons at the beginning of the year and the last two when students have more experience with making books. They can apply these lessons to the picture books they have made or to any type of writing in which they are currently engaged.
				WPS.U11: Publishing and Self-Assessing Your Writing, WML1–WML2 (2 days)	Teach the first two minilessons in this umbrella whenever you are interested in having your students publish a piece of writing. We recommend teaching the last two minilessons after students have a significant number of writing pieces to self-assess.
			LA.U5: Understanding Fiction and Nonfiction Genres (RML1–RML2)	MGT.U4: Introducing the Writing Folder, WML1–WML3 (3 days)	The first three minilessons in this umbrella support students in listing their writing projects, reflecting on their learning, and establishing writing goals. Teach the last two lessons when students have more experience revising and editing their writing.

Suggested Sequence of Lessons (cont.)

Months	Texts from *Fountas & Pinnell Classroom™ Shared Reading Collection*	Text Sets from *Fountas & Pinnell Classroom™ Interactive Read-Aloud Collection*	Reading Minilessons (RML) Umbrellas	Writing Minilessons (WML) Umbrellas	Teaching Suggestions for Extending Learning
Months 1 & 2 (cont.)			LA.U3: Giving a Book Talk	WPS.U2: Writer's Notebook: Getting Ideas from Your Life, WML3–WML6 (4 days)	These four minilessons in WPS.U2 expose writers to different ways of generating ideas from their memories. These lessons also teach students generative ways to build their notebooks over time.
			WAR.U2: Using a Reader's Notebook	GEN.U4: Writing Memory Stories (5 days)	Encourage students to revisit stories they have told (MGT.U1) and to reread their writer's notebooks for ideas for their memory stories. Offer the option of turning a memory story into a picture book or a multimedia presentation.
			LA.U23: Understanding Characters' Feelings, Motivations, and Intentions	CFT.U4: Adding Dialogue to Writing (3 days)	Invite children to add dialogue to the memory stories they are writing. You may also want to teach CNV.U2.WML3, which addresses how to punctuate dialogue, alongside this umbrella. Alternatively, you can revisit the use of quotation marks when you teach the entire CNV.U2 umbrella later in the year.
			LA.U4: Getting Started with Book Clubs	WPS.U7: Adding Information to Your Writing, WML1–WML3 (3 days)	We recommend teaching the minilessons in this umbrella over time. Repeat them whenever your students need support with revision. You might invite them to apply these lessons to their memory stories, though they can apply them to any writing they are working on.
				WPS.U8: Revising to Focus and Organize Writing, WML1 (1 day)	We recommend teaching the first minilesson in this umbrella early in the year so students think about the message or big idea of their writing from the very beginning.
				WPS.U11: Publishing and Self-Assessing Your Writing, WML3 (1–3 days)	Through this lesson, students learn to use a rubric to self-assess their writing. Invite them to apply the rubric to one of the memory stories they have written. Revisit WML1 and WML2 as needed.
Months 3 & 4	Harriett and Violeta: A Long-Distance Friendship Light My Way Home		WAR.U3: Writing Letters About Reading	GEN.U1: Writing Friendly Letters (3 days)	Students learn how to write friendly letters for a variety of purposes. One purpose might be to write about their reading to you or to other readers in the class. If you are using *The Reading Minilessons Book, Grade 3*, WAR.U3 helps establish a process of using letters to write about reading.

Suggested Sequence of Lessons (cont.)

Months	Texts from *Fountas & Pinnell Classroom™ Shared Reading Collection*	Text Sets from *Fountas & Pinnell Classroom™ Interactive Read-Aloud Collection*	Reading Minilessons (RML) Umbrellas	Writing Minilessons (WML) Umbrellas	Teaching Suggestions for Extending Learning
Months 3 & 4 (cont.)				WPS.U3: Writer's Notebook: Getting Inspiration from Writers and Artists, WML1–WML2 (2 days)	Teach the minilessons in this umbrella all at once or over time. The first two minilessons establish for students the idea that they can use the work of other writers and artists to inspire ideas and build their writer's notebooks.
				GEN.U9: Making Poetry Anthologies, WML1–WML2 (2 days)	Building on WPS.U3.WML2, invite students to make poetry anthologies in which they can collect poems, respond to poems in pictures and words, and write their own poems. Teach this umbrella across several weeks to give students time and experience with poetry in between lessons. Consider hosting a poetry workshop one day a week or one week a month to teach poetry-focused minilessons and to integrate poetry throughout the year.
			SAS.U1: Monitoring, Searching, and Self-Correcting	CNV.U1: Writing Words (3 days)	Repeat the lessons in this umbrella as needed across the year. Use any enlarged text for these lessons. If you have the *Shared Reading Collection*, read *From Buds to Bananas* now and again later in the year as part of a series.
				MGT.U4: Introducing the Writing Folder, WML4 (1 day)	In WML4, students are introduced to a list of commonly misspelled words to help them with their spelling. We recommend keeping the list in the writing folder for easy reference.
				WPS.U4: Writer's Notebook: Becoming an Expert (6 days)	WPS.U4 will help students learn how to explore and narrow topics for nonfiction writing, how to take notes, and how to develop questions and wonderings about a topic in preparation for writing informational texts.
	Far Above Earth: A Day on the Space Station			GEN.U9: Making Poetry Anthologies, WML3 (1 day)	Continue to help students build their poetry anthologies. Provide watercolors, colored pencils, and other art materials for students to respond creatively to the poems with both words and illustrations. We recommend teaching this lesson (and other poetry lessons) during a weekly or monthly poetry workshop.

Suggested Sequence of Lessons (cont.)

Months	Texts from *Fountas & Pinnell Classroom™ Shared Reading Collection*	Text Sets from *Fountas & Pinnell Classroom™ Interactive Read-Aloud Collection*	Reading Minilessons (RML) Umbrellas	Writing Minilessons (WML) Umbrellas	Teaching Suggestions for Extending Learning
Months 3 & 4 (cont.)	Exploring Underground Mixed-Up Monsters and Confused Critters The Backwards Poem Book	Genre Study: Expository Nonfiction	LA.U11: Studying Informational Books	GEN.U6: Making Informational Books (6 days)	Students can use the work they have done in their writer's notebooks (WPS.U4) to make informational books about topics they are interested in and have researched.
				GEN.U10: Writing Poetry, WML1 (1 day)	Students can take a break from nonfiction writing to work on poetry during poetry workshops and resume their work on nonfiction writing afterward. If you have the *Interactive Read-Aloud Collection*, use mentor texts from the text set Genre Study: Poetry. If you use these books early in the year, revisit them as part of the genre study later in the year, though you could do a genre study at this point. If you conduct one now, it will serve as a foundation for students' further study. If you wait until later in the year, students will bring all of the rich poetry experiences they have had across the year to the genre study.
			LA.U14: Thinking About the Topic in Nonfiction Books		
			WAR.U5: Writing About Nonfiction Books in a Reader's Notebook (RML1–RML3)	CFT.U10: Using Text Features in Nonfiction Writing (4 days)	Invite students to apply these minilessons to the informational books they are writing.
				GEN.U11: Writing Different Kinds of Poems, WML1 (1 day)	The minilessons in all of the umbrellas dedicated to poetry can be taught over time. Students can take a break from other writing projects and devote workshop time to poetry one day a week or one week a month.
				CFT.U14: Illustrating and Using Graphics in Nonfiction Writing (5 days)	Students can apply these minilessons to any nonfiction pieces they are working on. For example, they might apply them to the informational books they are writing.

Suggested Sequence of Lessons (cont.)

Months	Texts from *Fountas & Pinnell Classroom™ Shared Reading Collection*	Text Sets from *Fountas & Pinnell Classroom™ Interactive Read-Aloud Collection*	Reading Minilessons (RML) Umbrellas	Writing Minilessons (WML) Umbrellas	Teaching Suggestions for Extending Learning
Months 3 & 4 (cont.)		Author/Illustrator Study: Janell Cannon	LA.U2: Studying Authors and Illustrators (RML1–RML2)	WPS.U7: Adding Information to Your Writing, WML4 (1 day)	Teach or revisit this lesson whenever students need to add more information to support their ideas.
				GEN.U10: Writing Poetry, WML2 (1 day)	Invite students to apply this lesson to the poetry they are writing during poetry workshop.
	Nerman's Revenge	Humorous Texts		CNV.U2: Learning About Punctuation and Capitalization, WML1–WML2 (2 days)	You may decide to spend more than two days on this inquiry study of punctuation and capitalization, particularly if students are excited and engaged in the study. They can apply these lessons to any writing (e.g., informational books or material in their writer's notebooks).
				Revisit WPS.U11: Publishing and Self-Assessing Your Writing, WML1–WML2 (1–2 days)	Invite students to select one of their informational books to publish. Revisit the lessons in WPS.U11 as needed.
	Baseball for Bedros	Genre Study: Realistic Fiction		GEN.U11: Writing Different Kinds of Poems, WML2 (1 day)	Introduce students to different types of poetry throughout the year so they can make choices about the kind of poem they want to write.
				WPS.U2: Writer's Notebook: Getting Ideas from Your Life, WML7–WML8 (2 days)	Continue to help students build their notebooks with daily quick writes like the ones in WPS.U2. These two minilessons focus on students getting ideas from treasured artifacts (e.g., photos, tickets) and by closely observing the world around them.
		Honoring Traditions	LA.U22: Understanding Plot	WPS.U1: Introducing and Using a Writer's Notebook, WML5 (1 day)	Repeat the last minilesson in WPS.U1 whenever your students need encouragement for building their writer's notebooks. This lesson teaches them to look at the ways they have gathered ideas in their writer's notebooks through the lessons in WPS.U2, WPS.U3, and WPS.U4 and to try using those ways on their own.
			LA.U21: Thinking About the Setting in Fiction Books		
Months 5 & 6	Callaloo Soup	Facing Challenges	LA.U17: Studying Realistic Fiction	GEN.U9: Making Poetry Anthologies, WML4 (1 day)	Invite students to respond to poems in their poetry anthologies by writing their own poems. Poetry anthologies deepen students' work with poetry and can be used during poetry workshop.

Appendix: Suggested Sequence of Lessons

Suggested Sequence of Lessons (cont.)

Months	Texts from *Fountas & Pinnell Classroom™ Shared Reading Collection*	Text Sets from *Fountas & Pinnell Classroom™ Interactive Read-Aloud Collection*	Reading Minilessons (RML) Umbrellas	Writing Minilessons (WML) Umbrellas	Teaching Suggestions for Extending Learning
Months 5 & 6 (cont.)	Tiny but Fierce	The Importance of Determination	SAS.U2: Solving Words	GEN.U5: Writing Realistic Fiction Stories (5 days)	If you are using *The Reading Minilessons Book, Grade 3*, we recommend teaching LA.U17 before students write their own realistic fiction stories. After students have had the opportunity to write realistic fiction, you might invite them to try writing fantasy stories.
				GEN.U10: Writing Poetry, WML3 (1 day)	Invite students to apply this lesson to poems they are writing. They can also apply many of the craft techniques they learn in poetry to other types of writing.
			LA.U24: Understanding Character Traits	CFT.U2: Describing Characters (3 days)	Students can apply the lessons in CFT.U2 to their realistic fiction stories. Encourage them to use their writer's notebooks to try out ideas for developing characters in words and illustrations.
			WAR.U4: Writing About Fiction Books in a Reader's Notebook (RML5)	CFT.U3: Crafting a Setting (3 days)	Students can use their writer's notebooks to experiment with crafting a setting. You can also invite them to apply these lessons to their realistic fiction stories. Revisit this umbrella as needed, especially when many of your students are engaged in narrative writing (e.g., fiction, memory stories, biographies).
			LA.U25: Thinking About Character Change	GEN.U10: Writing Poetry, WML4 (1 day)	Students explore metaphors and similes during poetry workshop. Invite students to apply this minilesson not only to the poems they write but to any type of writing.
				WPS.U8: Revising to Focus and Organize Writing, WML2 and WML4 (2 days)	These two minilessons in WPS.U8 are best applied to narrative writing. Invite students to apply them to writing they have in their writer's notebooks or to one of the realistic fiction stories they are writing.
			WAR.U4: Writing About Fiction Books in a Reader's Notebook (RML6)	CNV.U2: Learning About Punctuation and Capitalization, WML3–WML6 (4 days)	Students can apply these lessons to the writing in their writer's notebooks or to a writing project. They can always revisit writing they have drafted previously to apply these lessons. You might choose to teach WML3 when you teach how to punctuate dialogue or wait until you are working on paragraphing.

Suggested Sequence of Lessons (cont.)

Months	Texts from *Fountas & Pinnell Classroom™ Shared Reading Collection*	Text Sets from *Fountas & Pinnell Classroom™ Interactive Read-Aloud Collection*	Reading Minilessons (RML) Umbrellas	Writing Minilessons (WML) Umbrellas	Teaching Suggestions for Extending Learning
Months 5 & 6 (cont.)	Hummingbird's Nest A Meerkat Day Wolf Pack Saving Cranes	Animal Journeys	LA.U26: Studying Illustrators in Fiction Books WAR.U4: Writing About Fiction Books in a Reader's Notebook (RML1–RML3)	WPS.U11: Publishing and Self-Assessing Your Writing, WML4 (1 day)	Invite students to reflect on the writing they have done so far this year and choose one or two pieces that show their growth in writing.
				WPS.U3: Writer's Notebook: Getting Inspiration from Writers and Artists, WML3–WML5 (3 days)	These lessons will help reinvigorate students' daily writing in their writer's notebooks. Revisit any of these lessons using different examples until students begin to independently collect inspirational passages, sketch interesting artwork, and record song lyrics to inspire their writing.
				GEN.U15: Experimenting with Writing in New Ways, WML1 (1 day)	In the first lesson in GEN.U15, students learn they can revisit topics of interest in new ways. Invite them to try writing in different genres and forms about favorite topics. Teach the lessons in this umbrella over time to inspire creativity in students and to continue to inspire new ways of writing throughout the school year.
				WPS.U5: Thinking About Purpose, Audience, and Genre/Form (3 days)	It is important to give students plenty of opportunities to select their own genres for writing based on their purpose and audience. If you are using *The Reading Minilessons Book, Grade 3*, students will revisit the idea of purpose and audience from a reading perspective later in the year in LA.U8. Learning to make these choices as writers early in the year will help students think more critically about them later as readers. Encourage students to write different pieces over the next couple of weeks, using ideas they have collected in their writer's notebooks.
				CFT.U5: Crafting a Lead (4 days)	Students can use their writer's notebooks to experiment with different types of leads. Encourage them to apply these lessons to writing they are working on or have written previously.
				CFT.U9: Writing with Voice in Fiction and Nonfiction (4 days)	Encourage students to show their individuality by writing with voice in both fiction and nonfiction texts. Revisit these minilessons throughout the year as your students learn more about crafting with voice.

Appendix: Suggested Sequence of Lessons

Suggested Sequence of Lessons (cont.)

Months	Texts from *Fountas & Pinnell Classroom™ Shared Reading Collection*	Text Sets from *Fountas & Pinnell Classroom™ Interactive Read-Aloud Collection*	Reading Minilessons (RML) Umbrellas	Writing Minilessons (WML) Umbrellas	Teaching Suggestions for Extending Learning
Months 5 & 6 (cont.)	Renaissance Man Using Her Voice Made for Mars	Genre Study: Biography	LA.U12: Studying Biography . WAR.U5: Writing About Nonfiction Books in a Reader's Notebook (RML4)	CNV.U3: Learning to Paragraph (3 days)	Teach the lessons in this umbrella whenever you think your students are ready to learn about paragraphing. Revisit across the year as needed.
				CFT.U7: Making Powerful Word Choices (3 days)	Students can apply these lessons to writing they have done in their writer's notebooks or to one of their writing projects.
				WPS.U8: Revising to Focus and Organize Writing, WML3 (1 day)	This lesson can be taught at any time, but it would be particularly powerful after students have studied how and why authors make specific word choices.
				WPS.U9: Editing and Proofreading Writing (4 days)	Teach this umbrella all at once or teach these lessons over time as you see evidence that students need them. The mentor text used in this umbrella comes a little later on in the Shared Reading sequence, but we recommend using it now and revisiting it again later. You can also use any other big book or enlarged text instead.
				MGT.U4: Introducing the Writing Folder, WML5 (1 day)	Introduce the revising and proofreading checklists available in the online resources. Have students keep a copy of each resource in their writing folders for easy reference.
				GEN.U13: Making Biographical Multimedia Presentations (4 days)	This umbrella introduces students to a new form of composition—multimedia presentations. Here, we offer students the opportunity to show some of what they have learned about biographies by creating multimedia presentations and also to establish a foundation for writing biographies in later grades. Multimedia presentations can be made for any content area.

Suggested Sequence of Lessons (cont.)

Months	Texts from *Fountas & Pinnell Classroom™ Shared Reading Collection*	Text Sets from *Fountas & Pinnell Classroom™ Interactive Read-Aloud Collection*	Reading Minilessons (RML) Umbrellas	Writing Minilessons (WML) Umbrellas	Teaching Suggestions for Extending Learning
Months 5 & 6 (cont.)		Series Study: Dianna Hutts Aston and Sylvia Long	LA.U2: Studying Authors and Illustrators (RML1–RML2) LA.U9: Analyzing the Writer's Craft (RML1–RML4)	Revisit **CFT.U1: Reading Like a Writer and Illustrator**, WML1 (1 day)	Revisit CFT.U1 or any other umbrellas in the craft section that you think would benefit your students. If you are using *The Reading Minilessons Book, Grade 3*, LA.U9 presents craft moves from a reader's perspective. By revisiting CFT.U1 or other craft lessons, you will help students deepen their understanding of craft and how to apply craft moves to their own writing.
Months 7 & 8	From Flower to Honey From Beans to Chocolate From Buds to Bananas	The Passage of Time Author's Point of View	SAS.U3: Maintaining Fluency LA.U16: Using Text Features to Gain Information LA.U13: Noticing How Authors Choose to Organize Nonfiction LA.U15: Learning Information from Illustrations/Graphics	**WPS.U6: Observing and Writing Like a Scientist** (4 days)	Building on the work they have done in informational writing, WPS.U6 gives students the opportunity to think and write scientifically. This umbrella also provides a foundation for writing procedural texts.
				Revisit **WPS.U4: Writer's Notebook: Becoming an Expert** as needed. (1–4 days)	Revisit any of the minilessons in WPS.U4 that you think would be helpful in guiding students to gather ideas for procedural writing.
				GEN.U2: Writing Procedural Texts (3 days)	Encourage students to look through their writer's notebooks for ideas for writing procedural texts. You could also invite them to include a short procedural text as part of an informational piece. Students get excited to share their knowledge in different types of procedural texts (e.g., game instructions, recipes, how-to videos).
				Revisit **CFT.U10: Using Text Features in Nonfiction Writing** and **CFT.U14: Illustrating and Using Graphics in Nonfiction Writing** (1–6 days)	You may want to revisit certain minilessons in CFT.U10 and CFT.U14 to help expand your students' procedural writing. If you are using *The Reading Minilessons Book Grade 3*, LA.U15 and LA.U16 will also support this work and help students think more deeply about these craft moves.
				Revisit **WPS.U11: Publishing and Self-Assessing Your Writing** (1–4 days)	Revisit the lessons in WPS.U11 to help students periodically publish their writing and self-assess their work using rubrics.

Appendix: Suggested Sequence of Lessons

Suggested Sequence of Lessons (cont.)

Months	Texts from *Fountas & Pinnell Classroom™ Shared Reading Collection*	Text Sets from *Fountas & Pinnell Classroom™ Interactive Read-Aloud Collection*	Reading Minilessons (RML) Umbrellas	Writing Minilessons (WML) Umbrellas	Teaching Suggestions for Extending Learning
Months 7 & 8 (cont.)			WAR.U5: Writing About Nonfiction Books in a Reader's Notebook (RML5–RML6)	GEN.U7: Exploring Opinion Writing (4 days)	If you use *The Reading Minilessons Book, Grade 3*, your students have likely had many opportunities to write their opinions about their reading. GEN.U7 builds on students' understandings of opinion writing and expands them. These lessons provide a strong foundation for test-writing since many state tests ask students to state and defend their opinions.
				CFT.U8: Making Your Sentences Clear and Interesting (3 days)	Invite your students to try these minilessons in their writer's notebooks or when revising the opinion pieces they are writing. Revisit these lessons as needed.
				GEN.U3: Writing to a Prompt: Getting Ready for Test Writing (6 days)	Teach only the lessons from this umbrella that are appropriate for your students and that correspond to your state tests. As with any minilessons, customize them to meet the needs of your classroom, district, and state.
			LA.U7: Thinking About the Author's Message	GEN.U8: Introducing Persuasive Writing Through Powerful Messages (3 days)	This umbrella builds on opinion writing and shifts to persuasive writing in which the goal is to convince others. The minilessons in this umbrella allow students to be playful with their persuasive messages by choosing multimodal forms to communicate their messages (e.g., posters, T-shirts, hats, videos).
			LA.U8: Thinking About the Author's Purpose	Revisit WPS.U4: Writer's Notebook: Becoming an Expert, WPS.U5: Thinking About Purpose, Audience, and Genre/Form, or GEN.U6: Making Informational Books (1–6 days)	Invite students to write in the genres and forms that fit their purpose and audience. You may also have them revisit making informational books.

618   The Writing Minilessons Book, Grade 3

Suggested Sequence of Lessons (cont.)

Months	Texts from *Fountas & Pinnell Classroom™ Shared Reading Collection*	Text Sets from *Fountas & Pinnell Classroom™ Interactive Read-Aloud Collection*	Reading Minilessons (RML) Umbrellas	Writing Minilessons (WML) Umbrellas	Teaching Suggestions for Extending Learning
Months 7 & 8 (cont.)			SAS.U4: Summarizing	CFT.U11: Expanding Nonfiction Writing (3 days)	You can teach this umbrella whenever you feel your students would benefit from learning more about crafting nonfiction writing. We recommend teaching it later in the year after they have read and written lots of informational texts. If students are not currently working on nonfiction, ask them to apply these lessons to writing in their writer's notebooks. Sometimes trying out a craft technique can spark new writing as well as refresh old writing.
			WAR.U4: Writing About Fiction Books in a Reader's Notebook (RML4)	CFT.U6: Crafting an Ending (4 days)	Encourage students to apply these lessons to both fiction and nonfiction writing.
				WPS.U8: Revising to Focus and Organize Writing, WML5 (1 day)	Students can apply this minilesson to most types of writing. If they are not currently working on a piece that involves multiple paragraphs, invite them to revisit writing they have done previously (e.g., informational books or opinion writing).
			WAR.U5: Writing About Nonfiction Books in a Reader's Notebook (RML7)		
	The Elephants and the Mice	Genre Study: Fables	LA.U18: Studying Fables	Revisit WPS.U11: Publishing and Self-Assessing Your Writing (1–4 days)	Invite students to periodically publish their work and to self-assess it using rubrics. Revisit the lessons in WPS.U11 that you think would help your students do this work.
		Genre Study: Folktales		GEN.U15: Experimenting with Writing in New Ways, WML2 (1 day)	Use the second lesson in GEN.U15 to introduce students to the idea of personification—writing from the viewpoint of an animal or inanimate object. It is a fun way to inspire new writing in your classroom and reinvigorate use of the writer's notebook. Provide a few days for students to experiment with this type of writing in their writer's notebooks before teaching the last lesson in the umbrella.
	Momotarō: A Folktale from Japan				
		Exploring Pourquoi Tales			

Appendix: Suggested Sequence of Lessons

Suggested Sequence of Lessons (cont.)

Months	Texts from *Fountas & Pinnell Classroom™ Shared Reading Collection*	Text Sets from *Fountas & Pinnell Classroom™ Interactive Read-Aloud Collection*	Reading Minilessons (RML) Umbrellas	Writing Minilessons (WML) Umbrellas	Teaching Suggestions for Extending Learning
Months 9 & 10		Fractured Fairy Tales	LA.U19: Studying Folktales	**GEN.U15: Experimenting with Writing in New Ways, WML3 (1 day)**	The last minilesson in GEN.U15 engages students in learning how to write a new version of an old tale. Provide time for students to experiment with this form of fiction writing. Encourage them to write multiple stories using traditional literature (e.g., fables, folktales, pourquoi tales, fairy tales) for inspiration.
				Revisit **GEN.U12: Making Picture Books (1–4 days)**	Encourage students to look through their writer's notebooks for ideas for making more picture books. You could also invite them to turn one of the tales they have written into a picture book.
			WAR.U4: Writing About Fiction Books in a Reader's Notebook (RML7)	**CFT.U15: Exploring Design Features and Text Layout (3 days)**	Encourage students to turn some of their writing into picture books and use CFT.U15 to help them think about different ways to make the text interesting. You can teach these lessons all at once or over time when students seem ready to explore design and layout.
			LA.U10: Noticing Text Resources	**WPS.U10: Adding Book and Print Features, WML3–WML4 (2 days)**	In the last two lessons of WPS.U10, students learn how to add a dedication and endpapers to a book. Students who aren't currently working on a book can revisit one they have already made to try adding these features.
			LA.U20: Understanding Fantasy	Revisit **WPS.U5: Thinking About Purpose, Audience, and Genre/Forms (3 days)**	Students can use all of their experiences with writing in a variety of genres over the course of the year to choose a genre that fits their purpose and audience. If you are using *The Reading Minilessons, Grade 3*, and following the sequence, you may want to invite them to write their own fantasy books after studying fantasy in LA.U20. Revisit any craft, conventions, or writing process lessons that would benefit your students based on the types of writing they are doing.
		Genre Study: Poetry		Revisit **WPS.U3: Writer's Notebook: Getting Inspiration from Writers and Artists (1–5 days)**	Revisit lessons from the writer's notebook to reinvigorate writing in your classroom. These lessons will help students gather ideas they can use as they embark on writing more poetry.

Suggested Sequence of Lessons (cont.)

Months	Texts from *Fountas & Pinnell Classroom™ Shared Reading Collection*	Text Sets from *Fountas & Pinnell Classroom™ Interactive Read-Aloud Collection*	Reading Minilessons (RML) Umbrellas	Writing Minilessons (WML) Umbrellas	Teaching Suggestions for Extending Learning
Months 9 & 10 (cont.)			LA.U6: Studying Poetry	**GEN.U11: Writing Different Kinds of Poems, WML3–WML4 (2 days)**	If you are using *The Reading Minilessons Book, Grade 3*, and following the sequence, LA.U6: Studying Poetry is where students can bring together their understandings of poetry from across the year in an inquiry-based study. Invite them to write all different types of poetry. WML3 specifically introduces them to lyrical poems, which may be a new form of poetry for many. Use the inspiration they get from recording song lyrics in their writer's notebooks (WPS.U3) to help them create their own lyrical poems. Allow them time to work on lyrical poems before introducing poems for two voices in WML4.
			LA.U9: Analyzing the Writer's Craft (RML5–RML8)	Revisit **GEN.10: Writing Poetry (1–4 days)**	Revisit any of the poetry minilessons you have taught previously to help students refine and grow their understanding of how to write meaningful and well-crafted poetry.
		Exploring the World: Photo Essays		Revisit **WPS.U2: Writer's Notebook: Getting Ideas from Your Life (1–8 days)**	Revisit minilessons in WPS.U2 for students to continue to build their writer's notebooks and to prepare them to continue writing during the summer by noticing topics in their daily lives. WML8 might be particularly useful in preparing students for writing photo essays.
		Hybrid Texts: Fiction and Nonfiction	LA.U5: Understanding Fiction and Nonfiction Genres (RML3)	**GEN.U14: Making Photo Essays (4 days)**	Invite your students to make their own photo essays, particularly if you are using the *Interactive Read-Aloud Collection*, which contains a text set on photo essays. If you are not using this collection, you can gather your own examples of photo essays. Photo essays are a wonderful way for students to make important decisions about how pictures and words will work together. Students can make photo essays by printing out photos or creating digital photo essays.

Appendix: Suggested Sequence of Lessons

Suggested Sequence of Lessons (cont.)

Months	Texts from *Fountas & Pinnell Classroom™ Shared Reading Collection*	Text Sets from *Fountas & Pinnell Classroom™ Interactive Read-Aloud Collection*	Reading Minilessons (RML) Umbrellas	Writing Minilessons (WML) Umbrellas	Teaching Suggestions for Extending Learning
Months 9 & 10 (cont.)				Revisit **WPS.U7: Adding Information to Your Writing** and **WPS.U8: Revising to Focus and Organize Writing (1–5 days)**	Choose any of the revision lessons as needed to help students continue to make changes to their writing.
				Revisit **CFT.U11: Expanding Nonfiction Writing (1–3 days)**	Revisit any of the lessons in CFT.U11 that you think will help your students expand the writing in their photo essays or in whatever they are working on.
				Revisit **WPS.U9: Editing and Proofreading Writing (1–4 days)**	It is helpful at the end of the year to remind students to proofread their writing to make it the best it can be.
		Illustrator Study: Jerry Pinkney	LA.U2: Studying Authors and Illustrators (RML1, RML3)	Revisit **CFT.U1: Reading Like a Writer and Illustrator, WML1–WML2 (2 days)**	Revisit CFT.U1, perhaps using texts by illustrator Jerry Pinkney. After the work they have done all year, students will be able notice more about the decisions authors and illustrators make when they craft a book. Invite them to try out any of their noticings in their writer's notebooks or on writing projects they are engaged in.
				Revisit **WPS.U11: Publishing and Self-Assessing Your Writing (1–4 days)**	Have your students publish, self-assess, and celebrate their writing. A special way to end the year is with a writing celebration in which students can share how they have grown as writers.

Glossary

all-about book A nonfiction book that tells about only one subject or topic.

alliteration The repetition of identical or similar initial consonant sounds in consecutive or nearby words or syllables.

alphabet book A book that helps children develop the concept and sequence of the alphabet by pairing alphabet letters with pictures of people, animals, or objects with labels related to the letters.

alphabet linking chart A chart containing upper- and lowercase letters of the alphabet paired with pictures representing words beginning with each letter (*a, apple,* for example).

assessment A means for gathering information or data that reveals what learners control, partially control, or do not yet control consistently.

assonance The repetition of identical or similar vowel sounds in stressed syllables in words that usually end with different consonant sounds. Compare with *consonance* and *rhyme*.

audience The readers of a text. Often a writer crafts a text with a particular audience in mind.

behaviors Actions that are observable as children read or write.

biography A biographical text in which the story (or part of the story) of a real person's life is written and narrated by another person. Biography is usually told in chronological sequence but may be in another order.

bold / boldface Type that is heavier and darker than usual, often used for emphasis.

book and print features The physical attributes of a text (for example, font, layout, and length). Also, elements of a book (for example, acknowledgments, author page, dedication, and endpapers). See also *text features*.

character An individual, usually a person or animal, in a text.

chronological sequence An underlying structural pattern used especially in nonfiction texts to describe a series of events in the order they happened in time.

compare and contrast An underlying structural pattern used especially in nonfiction texts to compare two ideas, events, or phenomena by showing how they are alike and how they are different.

compose Think about the message and how to say it.

concrete poetry Poems with words (and sometimes punctuation) arranged to present a concrete picture of the idea the poem is conveying. See also *shape poem*.

connective A word or phrase that clarifies relationships and ideas in language. Simple connectives appear often in both oral and written language (e.g., *and, but, because*). Sophisticated connectives are used in written texts but do not appear often in everyday oral language (e.g., *although, however, yet*).

consonance The repetition of the final consonant sounds in words with different vowels. Compare with *assonance* and *rhyme*.

construct Write the message that has been composed together; includes sharing the pen.

conventions In writing, formal usage that has become customary in written language. Grammar, usage, capitalization, punctuation, spelling, handwriting, and text layout are categories of writing conventions.

craft In writing, how an individual piece of writing is shaped. Elements of craft are organization, idea development, language use, word choice, and voice. Compare with *style* and *voice*.

cursive A form of handwriting in which letters are connected.

dialogue Spoken words, usually set off with quotation marks in text.

directions (how-to) Part of a procedural nonfiction text that shows the steps involved in performing a task. A set of directions may include diagrams or drawings with labels. See also *procedural text*.

draft An early version of a writer's composition.

drafting and revising The process of getting ideas down on paper and shaping them to convey the writer's message.

drawing In writing, creating a rough image (i.e, a drawing) of a person, place, thing, or idea to capture, work with, and render the writer's ideas.

editing and proofreading The process of polishing the final draft of a written composition to prepare it for publication.

elements of fiction Important elements of fiction include narrator, characters, plot, setting, theme, and style.

elements of poetry Important elements of poetry include figurative language, imagery, personification, rhythm, rhyme, repetition, alliteration, assonance, consonance, onomatopoeia, and aspects of layout.

English learners People whose native language is not English and who are acquiring English as an additional language.

family, friends, and school story A contemporary realistic text focused on the everyday experiences of children of a variety of ages, including relationships with family and friends and experiences at school.

fiction Invented, imaginative prose or poetry that tells a story. Fiction texts can be organized into the categories realism and fantasy. Along with nonfiction, fiction is one of two basic genres of literature.

figurative language An element of a writer's style, figurative language changes or goes beyond literal meaning. Two common types of figurative language are metaphor (a direct comparison) and simile (a comparison that uses *like* or *as*).

font In printed text, the collection of type (letters) in a particular style.

form A kind of text that is characterized by particular elements. Mystery, for example, is a form of writing within the realistic fiction genre. Another term for form is *subgenre*.

free verse A form of poetry with irregular meter. Free verse may include rhyme, alliteration, and other poetic sound devices.

friendly letter In writing, a functional nonfiction text usually addressed to friends or family that may take the form of notes, letters, invitations, or email.

functional text A nonfiction text intended to accomplish a practical task, for example, labels, lists, letters, and directions with steps (how-to).

genre A category of written text that is characterized by a particular style, form, or content.

grammar Complex rules by which people can generate an unlimited number of phrases, sentences, and longer texts in that language. *Conventional grammar* refers to the accepted grammatical conventions in a society.

graphic feature In fiction texts, graphic features are usually illustrations. In nonfiction texts, graphic features include photographs, paintings and drawings, charts, diagrams, tables and graphs, maps, and timelines.

guided writing Instructional support for a small, temporary group of writers who have similar needs.

haiku An ancient Japanese form of non-rhyming poetry that creates a mental picture and makes a concise emotional statement.

high-frequency words Words that occur often in spoken and written language (for example, *because*).

how-to See *directions (how-to)* and *procedural text*.

illustration Graphic representation of important content (for example, art, photos, maps, graphs, charts) in a fiction or nonfiction text.

independent writing A text written by children independently with teacher support as needed. Also, a time during writers' workshop for children to write on their own.

informational text A nonfiction text in which a purpose is to inform or give facts about a topic. Informational texts include the following genres: biography, autobiography, memoir, and narrative nonfiction, as well as expository texts, procedural texts, and persuasive texts.

innovate on a text Change the ending, the series of events, the characters, or the setting of a familiar text.

interactive read-aloud An instructional context in which students are actively listening and responding to an oral reading of a text.

interactive writing A teaching context in which the teacher and students cooperatively plan, compose, and write a group text; both teacher and students act as scribes (in turn).

italic (italics) A styling of type that is characterized by slanted letters.

label A written word or phrase that names the content of an illustration.

layout The way the print and illustrations are arranged on a page.

learning zone The level at which it is most productive to aim one's teaching for each student (the zone of proximal development).

lowercase letter A small letterform that is usually different from its corresponding capital or uppercase form.

main idea The central underlying idea, concept, or message that the author conveys in a nonfiction text. See also *message*.

memory story A story about something experienced personally.

mentor texts Books or other texts that serve as examples of excellent writing. Mentor texts are read and reread to provide models for literature discussion and student writing.

message An important idea that an author conveys in a fiction or nonfiction text. See also *main idea*.

metaphor A type of figurative language that describes one thing by comparing it to something else without using the words *like* or *as*. Compare with *simile*.

modeled writing An instructional technique in which a teacher demonstrates the process of composing a particular genre, making the process explicit for students.

nonfiction Prose or poetry that provides factual information. According to their structures, nonfiction texts can be organized into the categories of narrative and nonnarrative. Along with fiction, nonfiction is one of the two basic genres of literature.

onomatopoeia The representation of sound with words.

opinion writing A type of writing whose purpose is to express a belief. Compare with *persuasive writing*.

organization The arrangement of ideas in a text according to a logical structure, either narrative or nonnarrative. Another term for organization is *text structure*.

organizational tools and sources of information A design feature of nonfiction texts. Organizational tools and sources of information help a reader process and understand nonfiction texts. Examples include tables of contents, headings, indexes, glossaries, appendices, author bios, and references.

personification A figure of speech in which an animal is spoken of or portrayed as if it were a person, or in which a lifeless thing or idea is spoken of or portrayed as a living thing. Personification is one type of figurative language.

persuasive writing A nonfiction text intended to convince the reader of the validity of a set of ideas—usually a particular point of view. Compare with *opinion writing*.

photo essay A form of nonfiction text in which meaning is carried by a series of photographs with no text or very spare text.

picture book An illustrated fiction or nonfiction text in which pictures work with the text to tell a story or provide information.

planning and rehearsing The process of collecting, working with, and selecting ideas for a written composition.

plot The events, action, conflict, and resolution of a story presented in a certain order in a fiction text. A simple plot progresses chronologically from start to end, whereas more complex plots may shift back and forth in time.

poetry Compact, metrical writing characterized by imagination and artistry and imbued with intense meaning. Along with prose, poetry is one of two broad categories into which all literature can be divided.

principle A generalization that is predictable. It is the key idea that children will learn and be invited to apply.

print feature In nonfiction texts, features that include the color, size, style, and font of type, as well as various aspects of layout.

procedural text A nonfiction text that explains how to do something. Procedural texts are almost always organized in temporal sequence and take the form of directions (or how-to texts) or descriptions of a process. See also *directions (how-to)*.

prompt A question, direction, or statement designed to encourage the child to say more about a topic.

proportionality In handwriting, the idea that letters of a similar size (e.g., *a* and *e*) should be the same size as one another.

publishing The process of making the final draft of a written composition public.

punctuation Marks used in written text to clarify meaning and separate structural units. The comma and the period are common punctuation marks.

purpose A writer's overall intention in creating a text, or a reader's overall intention in reading a text. To tell a story is one example of a writer's purpose, and to be entertained is one example of a reader's purpose.

question and answer A structural pattern used especially in nonfiction texts to organize information in a series of questions with responses. Question-and-answer texts may be based on a verbal or written interview or on frequently arising or logical questions about a topic.

quick write Informal writing in which students write their immediate thoughts and feelings usually in response to a prompt or something they have read.

repetition Repeated words or phrases that help create rhythm and emphasis in poetry or prose.

rhyme The repetition of vowel and consonant sounds in the stressed and unstressed syllables of words in verse, especially at the ends of lines.

rhythm The regular or ordered repetition of stressed and unstressed syllables in poetry, other writing, or speech.

sequence See *chronological sequence* and *temporal sequence*.

setting The place and time in which a fiction text or biographical text takes place.

shape poem Poetry with words (and sometimes punctuation) arranged in interesting ways that may be tied to the poem's meaning. See also *concrete poetry*.

shared reading An instructional context in which the teacher involves a group of students in the reading of a particular big book to introduce aspects of literacy (such as print conventions), develop reading strategies (such as decoding or predicting), and teach vocabulary.

shared writing An instructional context in which the teacher involves a group of students in the composing of a coherent text together. The teacher writes while scaffolding children's language and ideas.

sidebar Information that is additional to the main text, placed alongside the text and sometimes set off from the main text in a box.

simile A type of figurative language that makes a comparison of two different things using the words *like* or *as*. Compare with *metaphor*.

slide presentation A series of slides or pages often prepared on a computer and presented on a screen. Slides contain minimal print and (if on a computer) possible audio or video that can be played to enhance the presentation.

small moment Part of a memory that a writer focuses on. For example, rather than writing about a whole event, the writer writes in detail about one thing that happened during the event.

speech bubble A shape, often rounded, containing the words a character says in a cartoon or other text. Another term for *speech bubble* is *speech balloon*.

split dialogue Written dialogue in which a "*said* phrase" divides the speaker's words (e.g., "Come on," said Mom. "Let's go home.").

story A series of events in narrative form, either fiction or nonfiction.

story map A representation of the sequence of events from a text using drawings or writing.

style The way a writer chooses and arranges words to create a meaningful text. Aspects of style include sentence length, word choice, and the use of figurative language and symbolism. Compare with *craft* and *voice*.

subtopic A subject or idea that is part of a larger, more general topic.

syllable A minimal unit of sequential speech sounds composed of a vowel sound or a consonant-vowel combination. A syllable always contains a vowel or vowel-like speech sound (e.g., *pen/ny*).

temporal sequence An underlying structural pattern used especially in nonfiction texts to describe the sequence in which something always or usually occurs, such as the steps in a process or a life cycle. See also *procedural text*.

test writing A type of functional writing in which students are prompted to write a short constructed response (sometimes called *short answer*) or an extended constructed response (or *essay*).

text features Parts of a text designed to help the reader access or better understand it (for example, tables of contents, headings, sidebars, captions). See also *book and print features*.

text structure The overall architecture or organization of a piece of writing. Another term for text structure is *organization*.

thought bubble A shape, often rounded, containing the words (or sometimes an image that suggests one or more words) a character thinks in a cartoon or other text. Another term for *thought bubble* is *thought balloon*.

tools In writing, resources that support the writing process (writer's notebook, writing folder, pens, pencils). Also, a physical means of revising or editing a piece of writing, such as a caret, a spider leg, or a numbered list.

topic The subject of a piece of writing.

uppercase letter A large letterform that is usually different from its corresponding lowercase form. Another term for *uppercase letter* is *capital letter*.

verbal path Language prompts paired with motor movements to help children learn to form letters correctly.

viewing self as writer Having attitudes and using practices that support a student in becoming a lifelong writer.

voice In writing, the unique way a writer "sounds" as a result of word choice, point of view, and arrangement of words and sentences. Compare with *craft* and *style*.

wordless picture book A form in which a story is told exclusively with pictures.

writer's notebook A notebook of bound pages in which students gather ideas for writing and experiment with writing. A writer's notebook is a record of children's writing across the year. It may have several different sections to serve a variety of purposes.

writers' workshop A classroom structure that begins with a whole-group minilesson; continues with independent writing, individual conferences, and small-group instruction; and ends with a whole-group share.

writing Children engaging in the writing process and producing pieces of their own writing in many genres.

writing about reading Children responding to reading a text by writing and sometimes drawing.

writing folder A two-pocket folder with brads in the middle. Writing that is in progress is stored in the pockets. Resources, such as checklists and spelling lists, are fastened in the middle. When a piece of writing is finished, it is removed from the folder and placed in a hanging file.

writing process Key phases of creating a piece of writing: planning and rehearsing, drafting and revising, editing and proofreading, and publishing.

Credits

Cover image from *Almost Gone* by Steve Jenkins. Copyright © 2006. Used by permission of HarperCollins Publishers.

Cover image from *And So They Build* by Bert Kitchen. Copyright © 1993. Reproduced by permission of the publisher, Candlewick Press, Somerville, MA, on behalf of Walker Books, London.

Cover image from *Ape* by Martin Jenkins, illustrated by Vicky White. Copyright © 2007. Illustrations copyright © 2007. Reproduced by permission of the publisher, Candlewick Press, Somerville, MA, on behalf of Walker Books, London.

Cover image from *Bats! Strange and Wonderful* by Laurence Pringle, illustrated by Meryl Henderson. Copyright © 2000 by Laurence Pringle and Meryl Henderson. Published by Boyds Mills Press. Used by permission.

Cover image from *Bedhead* by Margie Palatini, illustrated by Jack E. Davis. Text copyright © 2000. Illustrations copyright © 2000. Reprinted with the permissions of Simon & Schuster Books for Young Readers, an imprint of Simon & Schuster Children's Publishing Division. All rights reserved.

Cover image from *Big Bad Bubble* by Adam Rubin, illustrated by Daniel Salmieri. Text copyright © 2014. Illustrations © 2014. Reprinted by permission of Houghton Mifflin Harcourt Publishing.

Cover image from *Bintou's Braids* by Sylviane A. Diouf, illustrated by Shane Evans © 2001. Used with permission of Chronicle Books LLC, San Francisco. Visit ChronicleBooks.com.

Cover image from *The Can Man* by Laura E. Williams, illustrated by Craig Orback. Copyright © 2010. Permission arranged with Lee & Low Books, Inc., New York, NY 10016.

Cover image from *Confetti: Poems for Children* by Pat Mora, illustrated by Enrique O. Sanchez. Copyright © 1996. Permission arranged with Lee & Low Books, Inc., New York, NY 10016.

Cover image from *Crane Boy* by Diana Cohn. Copyright © 2015. Cover illustration by Youme Nguyen Ly, copyright © 2015. Used by permission of Cinco Puntos Press, www.cincopuntos.com.

Cover image from *Crickwing* by Janell Cannon. Copyright © 2005 by Houghton Mifflin Harcourt Publishing Company. Reprinted by permission of Houghton Mifflin Harcourt Publishing.

Cover image from *Crouching Tiger* by Ying Chang Compestine, illustrated by Yan Nascimbene. Text copyright © 2011. Illustrations copyright © 2011. Reproduced by permission of the publisher, Candlewick Press, Somerville, MA.

Cover image from *A Day and Night in the Desert* by Caroline Arnold. Copyright © 2015. All rights reserved. Reprinted by permission of Capstone.

Cover image from *Down Under: Vanishing Cultures* by Jan Reynolds. Copyright © 1992. Permission arranged with Lee & Low Books, Inc., New York, NY 10016.

Cover image from *Dumpling Soup* by Jama Kim Rattigan and Lillian Hsu-Flanders. Copyright © 1993. Reprinted by permission of Little Brown Books for Young Readers, an imprint of Hachette Book Group, Inc.

Cover image from *An Egg Is Quiet* by Dianna Hutts Aston, illustrated by Sylvia Long. Copyright © 2006. Used with permission of Chronicle Books LLC, San Francisco. Visit ChronicleBooks.com.

Cover image from *Enemy Pie* by Derek Munson, illustrated by Tara Calahan King. Copyright © 2000. Used with permission of Chronicle Books LLC, San Francisco. Visit ChronicleBooks.com.

Cover image from *Energy Island: How One Community Harnessed the Wind and Changed Their World* by Allan Drummond. Copyright © 2011. Reprinted by permission of Farrar and Straus Giroux Books for Young Readers. All rights reserved.

Cover image from *Family Pictures* by Carmen Lomas Garza. Copyright © 2005. Permission arranged with Lee & Low Books, Inc., New York, NY 10016.

Cover image from *First Day in Grapes* by L. King Perez, illustrated by Robert Casilla. Copyright © 2002 Permission arranged with Lee & Low Books, Inc., New York, NY 10016.

Cover image from *Flicker Flash* by Joan B. Graham. Copyright © 2003 by Houghton Mifflin Harcourt Publishing Company. Reprinted by permission of Houghton Mifflin Harcourt Publishing.

Cover image from *Goal!* by Mina Javaherbin, illustrated by A. G. Ford. Text copyright © 2010. Illustrations copyright © 2010. Reproduced by permission of the publisher, Candlewick Press, Somerville, MA.

Cover image from *Grandma's Records* by Eric Velasquez. Copyright © 2001 Eric Velasquez. Used by permission of Bloomsbury Publishing, Inc.

Cover image from *The Great Fuzz Frenzy* by Janet Stevens and Susan Stevens Crummel. Text copyright © 2005. Illustrations © 2005. Reprinted by permission of Houghton Mifflin Harcourt Publishing.

Cover image from *Hachiko: The True Story of a Loyal Dog* by Pamela S. Turner. Copyright © 2009 by Houghton Mifflin Harcourt Publishing Company. Reprinted by permission of Houghton Mifflin Harcourt Publishing.

Cover image from *Hottest, Coldest, Highest, Deepest* by Steve Jenkins. Copyright © 2004 by Houghton Mifflin Harcourt Publishing Company. Reprinted by permission of Houghton Mifflin Harcourt Publishing.

Cover image from *I Love Guinea Pigs* by Dick King-Smith. Text copyright © 1994 by Foxbusters Ltd. Illustrations copyright © 1994 by Anita Jeram. Reproduced by permission of the publisher, Candlewick Press, Somerville, MA, on behalf of Walker Books, London.

Cover image from *In My Momma's Kitchen* by Jerdine Nolen, illustrated by Colin Bootman. Cover art © 1999. Text copyright © 1999. Used by permission of HarperCollins Publishers.

Cover image from *It's Our Garden* by George Ancona. Text and photographs copyright © 2013. Illustrations copyright © 2013 by the students of Acequia Madre Elementary School. Reproduced by permission of the publisher, Candlewick Press, Somerville, MA.

Cover image from *Knights in Shining Armor* by Gail Gibbons, copyright © 1995. Reprinted by permission of Little Brown Books for Young Readers, an imprint of Hachette Book Group, Inc.

Cover image from *Last Day Blues* by Julie Danneberg, illustrated by Judy Love. Copyright © 2006. Used by permission of Charlesbridge Publishing, Inc. www.charlesbridge.com.

Cover image from *Magic Trash* by J. H. Shapiro, illustrated by Vanessa Brantley-Newton. Copyright © 2011. Used by permission of Charlesbridge Publishing, Inc. www.charlesbridge.com.

Cover image from *Meadowlands: A Wetland's Survival Story* by Thomas F. Yezerski. Illustration copyright © 2011. Reprinted by permission of Farrar, Straus and Giroux Books for Young Readers. All rights reserved.

Cover image from *Meet the Dogs of Bedlam Farm* by Jon Katz. Illustration © 2011. Reprinted by permission of Henry Holt Books for Young Readers. All rights reserved.

Cover image from *Mongolia: Vanishing Cultures* by Jan Reynolds. Copyright © 1994. Permission arranged with Lee & Low Books, Inc., New York, NY 10016.

Cover image from *Moon Bear* by Brenda Z. Guiberson, illustrated by Ed Young. Copyright © 2010. Illustration © 2010. Reprinted by permission of Henry Holt Books for Young Readers. All rights reserved.

Cover image from *Mooncakes* by Loretta Seto, illustrated by Renné Benoit. Copyright © 2013. Reprinted by permission of Orca Book Publishers Ltd.

Cover image from *A Mother's Journey* by Sandra Markle, illustrated by Alan Marks. Copyright © 2005. Used by permission of Charlesbridge Publishing, Inc. www.charlesbridge.com.

Cover image from *My Rotten Redheaded Older Brother* by Patricia Polacco. Copyright © 1994. Reprinted with the permissions of Paula Wiseman Books, an imprint of Simon & Schuster Children's Publishing Division. All rights reserved.

Cover image from *Nadia's Hands* by Karen English, illustrated by Jonathan Weiner. Copyright © 1999 by Karen English and Jonathan Weiner. Published by Boyds Mills Press. Used by permission.

Cover image from *Nobody Owns the Sky* by Reeve Lindbergh, illustrated by Pamela Paparone. Text copyright © 1996. Illustrations copyright © 1996. Reproduced by permission of the publisher, Candlewick Press, Somerville, MA.

Cover image from *North: The Amazing Story of Arctic Migration* by Nick Dowson, illustrated by Patrick Benson. Text copyright © 2011. Illustrations copyright © 2011. Reproduced by permission of the publisher, Candlewick Press, Somerville, MA, on behalf of Walker Books, London.

Cover image from *Odd Boy Out: Young Albert Einstein* by Don Brown. Copyright © 2008 by Houghton Mifflin Harcourt Publishing Company. Reprinted by permission of Houghton Mifflin Harcourt Publishing.

Cover image from *Oil Spill!* by Melvin Berger, illustrated by Paul Mirocha. Cover art copyright © 1994. Text copyright © 1994. Used by permission of HarperCollins Publishers.

Cover image from *Old Elm Speaks* by Kristine O'Connell George. Copyright © 2007 by Houghton Mifflin Harcourt Publishing Company. Reprinted by permission of Houghton Mifflin Harcourt Publishing.

Cover image from *Our Seasons* by Grace Lin and Ranida T. McKneally, illustrated by Grace Lin. Copyright © 2006. Used by permission of Charlesbridge Publishing, Inc. www.charlesbridge.com.

Cover image from *The Paperboy* by Dav Pilkey, Scholastic, Inc./Scholastic Press. Copyright © 1996. Used by permission.

Cover image from *The Perfect Pet* by Margie Palatini. Cover art © 2003 by Bruce Whatley. Text copyright © 2003. Used by permission of HarperCollins Publishers.

Cover image from *The Printer* by Myron Uhlberg, illustrated by Henri Sorensen. Text copyright © 2003, illustrations copyright © 2003. Published by arrangement with Peachtree Publishers.

Cover image from *A Rock Is Lively* by Dianna Hutts Aston, illustrated by Sylvia Long. Copyright ©2012. Used with permission of Chronicle Books LLC, San Francisco. Visit ChronicleBooks.com.

Cover image from *Ruby's Wish* by Shirin Yim Bridges, illustrated by Sophie Blackall. Copyright © 2002. Used with permission of Chronicle Books LLC, San Francisco. Visit ChronicleBooks.com.

Cover image from *Saturdays and Teacakes* by Lester Laminack, illustrated by Chris Soentpiet. Text copyright © 2004, illustrations copyright © 2004. Published by arrangement with Peachtree Publishers.

Cover image from *A Seed Is Sleepy* by Dianna Hutts Aston, illustrated by Sylvia Long. Copyright © 2014. Used with permission of Chronicle Books LLC, San Francisco. Visit ChronicleBooks.com.

Cover image from *Shell, Beak, Tusk: Shared Traits and the Wonders of Adaptation* by Bridget Heos. Copyright © 2017 by Houghton Mifflin Harcourt Publishing Company. Reprinted by permission of Houghton Mifflin Harcourt Publishing.

Cover image from *Sitti's Secrets* by Naomi Shihab Nye, illustrated by Nancy Carpenter. Text copyright © 1994. Illustrations copyright © 1994. Reprinted with the permissions of Simon & Schuster Books for Young Readers, an imprint of Simon & Schuster Children's Publishing Division. All rights reserved.

Cover image from *Sky Sisters* by Jan Bourdeau Waboose, illustrated by Brian Deines. Cover image © 2000. Used by permission of Kids Can Press, Toronto.

Cover image from *Soccer Star* by Mina Javaherbin, illustrated by Renato Alarcão. Text copyright © 2014. Illustrations copyright © 2014. Reproduced by permission of the publisher, Candlewick Press, Somerville, MA.

Cover image from *Some Birthday!* by Patricia Polacco. Copyright © 1994. Reprinted with the permissions of Paula Wiseman Books, an imprint of Simon & Schuster Children's Publishing Division. All rights reserved.

Cover image from *Sophie's Masterpiece* by Eileen Spinelli, illustrated by Jane Dyer. Text copyright © 2002. Illustrations copyright © 2002. Reprinted with the permissions of Simon & Schuster Books for Young Readers, an imprint of Simon & Schuster Children's Publishing Division. All rights reserved.

Cover image from *Splish Splash* by Joan B. Graham. Copyright © 2003 by Houghton Mifflin Harcourt Publishing Company. Reprinted by permission of Houghton Mifflin Harcourt Publishing.

Cover image from *Stellaluna* by Janell Cannon. Copyright © 1993 by Houghton Mifflin Harcourt Publishing Company. Reprinted by permission of Houghton Mifflin Harcourt Publishing.

Cover image from *Storm in the Night* by Mary Stolz, illustrated by Pat Cummings. Cover art © 1988. Text copyright © 1988. Used by permission of HarperCollins Publishers.

Cover image from *The Sunsets of Miss Olivia Wiggins* by Lester Laminack, illustrated by Constance Bergum. Text copyright © 1998, illustrations copyright © 1998. Published by arrangement with Peachtree Publishers.

Cover image from *Those Darn Squirrels* by Adam Rubin, illustrated by Daniel Salmieri. Text copyright © 2008. Illustrations © 2008. Reprinted by permission of Houghton Mifflin Harcourt Publishing.

Cover image from *Tornadoes!* by Gail Gibbons. Copyright © 2009. Reprinted by permission of Holiday House.

Cover image from *The Tortoise and the Hare* by Jerry Pinkney. Copyright © 2013 by Jerry Pinkney. Published by Little Brown Books for Young Readers. All rights reserved. Used with permission of Sheldon Fogelman Agency, Inc.

Cover image from *The Tree Lady* by H. Joseph Hopkins, illustrated by Jill McElmurry. Text copyright © 2013. Illustrations copyright © 2013. Reprinted with the permissions of Beach Lane Books, an imprint of Simon & Schuster Children's Publishing Division. All rights reserved.

Cover image from *Under the Lemon Moon* by Edith Hope Fine, illustrated by René King Moreno. Copyright © 1999. Permission arranged with Lee & Low Books, Inc., New York, NY 10016.

Cover image from *Wangari Maathai: The Woman Who Planted Millions of Trees* by Franck Prevot, illustrated by Aurelia Fronty. Copyright © 2015. Reprinted by permission of Charlesbridge Publishing. www.charlesbridge.com.

Cover image from *What's So Bad About Gasoline?* by Anne Rockwell, illustrated by Paul Meisel. Cover art copyright © 2009 by Paul Meisel. Text copyright © 2009 by Anne Rockwell. Used by permission of HarperCollins Publishers.

Cover image from *Yucky Worms* by Vivian French, illustrated by Jessica Ahlberg. Text copyright © 2009. Illustrations copyright © 2009. Reproduced by permission of the publisher, Candlewick Press, Somerville, MA, on behalf of Walker Books, London.

Works Cited

Fletcher, Ralph. 2003. *A Writer's Notebook: Unlocking the Writer Within You*. New York: HarperCollins.

———. 2017. *Joy Write: Cultivating High-Impact, Low-Stakes Writing*. Portsmouth, NH: Heinemann.

Fountas, Irene C., and Gay Su Pinnell. 2012. *Genre Study: Teaching with Fiction and Nonfiction Books*. Portsmouth, NH: Heinemann.

———. 2017, 2022. *The Fountas & Pinnell Literacy Continuum: A Tool for Assessment, Planning, and Teaching*. Portsmouth, NH: Heinemann.

———. 2017. *Guided Reading: Responsive Teaching Across the Grades*, 2nd ed. Portsmouth, NH: Heinemann.

———. 2018. *The Literacy Quick Guide: A Reference Tool for Responsive Literacy Teaching*. Portsmouth, NH: Heinemann.

———. 2019. *Fountas & Pinnell Classroom™ Interactive Read-Aloud Collection*. Portsmouth, NH: Heinemann.

———. 2019. *Fountas & Pinnell Classroom™ System Guide, Grade 3*. Portsmouth, NH: Heinemann.

———. 2019. *Phonics, Spelling, and Word Study System, for Grade 3*. Portsmouth, NH: Heinemann.

———. 2019. *The Reading Minilessons Book, Grade 3*. Portsmouth, NH: Heinemann.

———. 2022. *Fountas & Pinnell Classroom™ Shared Reading Collection*. Portsmouth, NH: Heinemann.

Glover, Matt. 2009. *Engaging Young Writers, Preschool–Grade 1*. Portsmouth, NH: Heinemann.

Heard, Georgia. 1999. *Awakening the Heart: Exploring Poetry in Elementary and Middle School*. Portsmouth, NH: Heinemann.

———. 2016. *Heart Maps: Helping Students Create and Craft Authentic Writing*. Portsmouth, NH: Heinemann.

Heard, Georgia, and Jennifer McDonough. 2009. *A Place for Wonder: Reading and Writing Nonfiction in the Primary Grades*. Portsmouth, NH: Stenhouse.

VanDerwater, Amy. 2018. *Poems Are Teachers: How Studying Poetry Stengthens Writing in All Genres*. Portsmouth, NH: Heinemann.

Vygotsky, Lev. 1979. *Mind in Society: The Development of Higher Psychological Processes*. Cambridge, MA: Harvard University Press.